C0-AYN-964

PERSONALITY VARIABLES IN SOCIAL BEHAVIOR

PERSONALITY VARIABLES IN SOCIAL BEHAVIOR

EDITED BY

THOMAS BLASS
University of Maryland Baltimore County

LAWRENCE ERLBAUM ASSOCIATES, PUBLISHERS
1977 Hillsdale, New Jersey

DISTRIBUTED BY THE HALSTED PRESS DIVISION OF

JOHN WILEY & SONS
New York Toronto London Sydney

Lawrence Erlbaum Associates, Inc., Publishers
62 Maria Drive
Hillsdale, New Jersey 07642

Distributed solely by Halsted Press Division
John Wiley & Sons, Inc., New York

Library of Congress Cataloging in Publication Data

Main entry under title:

Personality variables in social behavior.

Includes bibliographical references and indexes.
1. Personality and situation. 2. Social psychology.
I. Blass, Thomas. [DNLM: 1. Personality. 2. Social behavior. BF 698 P469]
BF698.9.S55P47 301.11'3 77-3538
ISBN 0-470-99133-X

Printed in the United States of America

Contents

Preface

In the fall semester of 1974, I offered a seminar in social psychology dealing with the relationship between personality and social behavior. Although a cognitively-oriented social psychologist, I have also had a continuing interest in personality differences and a conviction that, by taking personality variables into account – especially as they interact with situational variables – we may be able to make more precise statements about social behavior. This interest and conviction originated during my graduate school days in the late 1960s when, in my dissertation research, I predicted and found tolerance for cognitive imbalance to be an interactive effect of a personality dimension I developed, and a characteristic of the situation. In line with this approach, one of my goals in that seminar was to show how specific personality constructs can be valuable in the prediction of social behavior, when the behavior to be predicted has a conceptual link to the personality variable. I was thinking of the number of important theory-based personality variables developed within the last two or three decades – such as authoritarianism, locus of control, and approval motivation – which have relevance for various domains of social behavior.

Early in 1974, as I planned the seminar and compiled a reading list for it, I realized that with notable exceptions, e.g., locus of control, there was a lack of up-to-date theoretical statements and reviews on the most important and widely used personality constructs in psychology today. It then became apparent to me that there was a need for a book that would bring together authoritative presentations on these personality variables, not only to provide a solid introduction to them, but also to disseminate information about current theoretical and research developments. The volume then would serve as a useful sourcebook both for the relative newcomer to the topic (such as the upper-level undergraduate) and for the graduate student, teacher, or researcher in personality and social psychology who has some prior familiarity with earlier developments.

This volume is meant to fill that need. All the chapters, except my own, are devoted to specific individual difference variables and are by authorities whom I invited to write on their topics. To maximize the usefulness of the book to the researcher, I have asked authors, where feasible and relevant, to include the personality scales dealt with in their chapters. Thus, in addition to the theoretical presentations and literature reviews which comprise the heart of the book, the reader will also find the following personality scales reproduced in this volume:

The California F Scale
Byrne's Balanced F Scale
Levenson's Multidimensional Locus of Control Scale
The Nowicki-Strickland Locus of Control Scale for Children
Rokeach's Dogmatism Scale
The Marlowe-Crowne Social Desirability Scale
Crandall, Crandall, and Katkovsky's Children's Social Desirability Scale

In addition to the chapters dealing with specific personality variables, there is an introductory chapter in which I discuss a number of issues I feel need to be considered when assessing the relative value of personality variables and situational factors in accounting for social behavior. My intent in that chapter, in addition to providing a context for the chapters that follow, is to argue for the increased recognition by social psychologists of the importance of looking at social behavior as a function of *both* personality and situation.

My acknowledgments to Stanley Feldstein and Jonathan Finkelstein for reading and commenting on my chapter. Thanks also to my wife, Anne, whose extra efforts and forbearance made it possible for me to be oblivious to everything going on in the house while I was working on this book, and for her help, as well as that of Helen Feldman, with some of the details necessary to get a manuscript into final form.

THOMAS BLASS

1

On Personality Variables, Situations, and Social Behavior

Thomas Blass

University of Maryland Baltimore County

Since its beginnings as a scientific discipline, psychology has embraced two contrasting approaches to the study of behavior. These distinct orientations have had a variety of overlapping designations, such as: experimental versus correlational (Cronbach, 1957); mind-in-general versus mind-in-particular (Allport, 1937); situational versus dispositional. Whatever its specific label, the dichotomy is one between a search for general principles of behavior that would account for most people's behaviors most of the time versus an attempt to provide a systematic account of differences among individuals, and perhaps even of personal uniqueness (mind-in-particular). It is, also, a methodological distinction between observing responses to experimentally created differences in the environment and the study of relationships between observed or measured characteristics of individuals and their other characteristics or behaviors. The situational versus dispositional dichotomy involves, additionally, assumptions about the primary causes of behavior: the characteristics of the situation the person finds himself in or the personal characteristics he brings into the situation. According to the situational view, changes in a person's behavior over time as well as differences among individuals are seen as resulting from environmental or situational influences. The second approach, the dispositional one, has been guided by the belief that, while it is true that there may be general principles of behavior that apply to most people, it is no less true that people differ among each other in a variety of ways. In order to properly account for the diversity of behavior, according to this view, it is necessary to provide some systematic framework for understanding individual differences. For the most part, this has involved the development of constructs encompassing some relatively stable predispositional attributes of the individual such as his abilities, personality traits, beliefs, attitudes, or motives, and the construction of measures of these attributes. These contrasting approaches to the study of behavior were already present in the earliest days of psychological research. Even in the pioneering experimental psychology laboratories of Wilhelm Wundt in the late 1800s, there were researchers interested in studying the variation they found among their subjects (Tyler, 1963, p. 26).

Contemporary social psychology has tended to favor the situational approach over the dispositional one. Even a brief glance at the journals in the field will reveal that in most cases the major variables under focus have been operationally defined by systematically varying some characteristics of the immediate environment (such as the experimenter's behavior, instructions, or the physical setting) and then randomly assigning subjects to conditions which represent some specific combinations of these experimental manipulations. Less frequently do we find in the literature a personality variable, or any other kind of "chronic" dimension, playing a focal role in testing hypotheses about the antecedents of social behavior. There are two major reasons for the preferential treatment given to situational manipulations in social psychological research: historical and practical.

Contemporary experimentally oriented social psychology is a product of two important theoretical traditions. It has been primarily influenced by Gestalt psychology (especially the Lewinian version of it) and, secondarily, by behaviorism. The imprint of the former can be seen in the recognition given by most social psychologists to the importance of cognitive organizing principles in accounting for the individual's behavior in relation to his social environment, while the impact of the latter is evidenced in the meticulousness with which social psychologists try to operationalize concepts. We can also recognize a related contribution of behaviorism in the following quote from Berger and Lambert's (1968) discussion of contemporary S–R theory:

> Although all psychologists accept order when it is found, S–R theorists tend to pursue analysis until the conditions controlling the behavior under analysis have been either experimentally elucidated or at least theoretically *postulated* according to the most probably relevant hypothesis or data at hand [p. 95].

Both Kurt Lewin's approach and behaviorism place considerable importance on situational determinants of behavior – but for somewhat different reasons. For the behaviorist, his simultaneous aversion to mentalistic concepts and his stress on physically observable events made environmental events the logical candidates as the primary determinants of behavior, both as cues for the elicitation of behavior and as reinforcers for their maintenance. For Lewin, maximal explanation for a person's current behavior was to be attained not by turning to past occurrences in his life history, but through a precise specification of what is "real" for him at this particular time, i.e., his psychological life space (Lewin, 1935, 1936). The life space, according to Lewin, is comprised of both the person and the environment. Thus, "every psychological event depends upon the state of the person and at the same time on the environment, although their relative importance is different in different cases" (Lewin, 1936, p. 12). Lewin (1935) saw his task as providing "a workable representation of a concrete psychological situation according to its individual characteristics and its associated functional properties, and of the concrete structure of the psychological person and its internal dynamic facts [p. 41]." Although, as these quotes indicate. Lewin viewed behavior as being dependent on *both* the characteristics of the person and the environment – $B = f(P\ E)$ (Lewin, 1936, p. 12) – with notable exceptions (Altman & Taylor, 1973; Hornstein, 1972; Rokeach, 1960) social psychologists have generally not built on Lewin's conceptualizations about the person, but have limited themselves to the environmental component of his equation. Noteworthy in this regard, is that Heider's (1959, pp. 108–119) discussion of Lewin's concept of the life space focuses almost completely on the environmental component, with only a passing mention of the way the person is represented in the life space.

On the practical side, the preference for situational manipulations over correlational variables in social psychological research is no doubt due to the greater potential for payoff inherent in the former as far as causal inferences are concerned. It is almost an axiom of psychological research that the experimental method, because of its feature of random assignment of subjects to treatments, is the most powerful technique available to the researcher, since it allows him to specify the nature of the causal link between the variables he is studying. Although recent advances in statistical procedures, such as the cross-lagged correlation technique and time series analyses[1], added to such earlier techniques as partial correlations, have made it increasingly possible to extract causal statements from nonmanipulated variables, it nonetheless still remains true that the experimental method provides the most direct and unambiguous information about the causal relationship between variables (but see Bowers, 1973; Rubin, 1974). At the same time the secondary status of correlational variables in terms of causal inference has led investigators to overlook their value in other areas, such as in the prediction of behavior. Yet, in principle, correlational relationships contain as much predictive information as do experimentally derived causal relationships. Let us suppose, for example, that you have generally found that whenever your pet's fur was unusually thick a cold winter followed. If your dog is especially shaggy this year, it would be a good idea to stock up on extra logs and longjohns in spite of the fact that the animal's extra coat obviously does not

[1] An interesting recent social psychological application of the cross-lagged correlation technique can be found in a study on the relationship between group cohesiveness and performance in a field study of isolated groups (Bakeman & Helmreich, 1975). A recent use of time series analysis can be seen in a study on the effects of the Kennedy assassination and of the murder of eight nurses on the nationwide incidence of violent crime (Berkowitz & Macaulay, 1971).

cause the cold. More seriously, though, the point is that a predictive link, even in the absence of specification of causality, can provide important information (Blass, 1976, Chapter 8).

Intuitively, we are aware of this, since in our everyday perceptions of people we rely on both causal and predictive inferences. Specifically, I am referring to two major organizing principles in person perception, the attribution process and the balance tendency (Heider, 1958), which rely on causal inference and predictive inference, respectively. The attribution process refers to the perceiver's tendency to trace observable behaviors to their underlying *causes* in the relatively stable features of the person or the environment. The tendency toward balance in person perception, on the other hand, need only involve assumptions about *co-occurrence* or *covariation* in the perceived person's characteristics. More specifically, the balance principle refers to our tendency for simplicity, harmony, and homogeneity in our perceptions of others. One consequence of this is "that if several parts, or traits, or aspects, of a person are considered, the tendency exists to see them all as positive, or all as negative" (Heider, 1958, p. 183). This tendency to form unitary impressions of others has also been referred to as the halo effect (Bruner & Tagiuri, 1954). Whatever the name one uses, the defining mechanism is one of assumed co-occurrence of certain traits or characteristics in the other person. Knowing the existence of one attribute in the other person, we *predict* that he possesses others. There is in most cases no assumption of a causal link between attributes. It would be unnecessary, since knowledge about the co-occurrence of certain traits in the other person should be sufficient to allow the perceiver to predict the other's behavior without his having to know whether or not they are causally related. Thus, for example, to the extent that perceivers assume that certain personal characteristics co-occur with beauty (Dermer & Thiel, 1975; Dion, Berscheid, & Walster, 1972), they probably do so without any additional assumptions about a causal link between beauty and personality characteristics.

Thus, one reason social psychologists have tended to favor situational manipulations over personality variables in testing hypotheses about social behavior is because the latter, as one class of correlational variables, do not permit as unambiguous inferences about causality as do the former. This is in spite of the fact that personality variables should be potentially as useful as situational variables as *predictors* of behavior. As Helmreich (1975) aptly put it: "Classic, laboratory social psychology has generally ignored individual differences, choosing to consider subjects as equivalent black boxes or as two-legged (generally white) rats from the same strain [p. 551]." Yet, over the years there have been researchers both within the field, as well as in the neighboring disciplines of personality, motivation, and clinical psychology who have been developing personality constructs to provide systematic accounts of behavioral variation among individuals. A primary purpose of this book is to provide concrete evidence for the usefulness of taking individual differences into account in making more precise predictions about social behavior, by presenting in the subsequent chapters several of these important personality variables which have relevance for social behavior.

No attempt to account for the relative neglect of personality variables by social psychologists would be complete without mentioning the impact of criticisms which have been leveled periodically at the concept of transsituational personality dispositions or traits (e.g., Bem, 1972; Guthrie, 1944; Mischel, 1968, 1969; Wallace, 1966). Guthrie (1944), for example, stated: "The search for universal traits, or traits that attach to all of an individual's behavior, is mistaken in its conception and bound to fail [p. 63]." My intent in this introductory chapter is to provide a context for the chapters that follow by presenting salient issues that enter into a consideration of the relative roles of personality and situational factors in accounting for social behavior. While I will take up some of the issues involved in the "trait versus situation" controversy and hopefully provide some new perspectives on it, is not my primary purpose to wade deeply into the fray. Articulate presentations of predispositional viewpoints of personality have been given by a number of writers (e.g., Alker, 1972; Allport, 1937, 1961, 1966; Averill, 1973; MacKinnon, 1944[2]; Wachtel, 1973). In particular, Bowers' (1973) insightful criticism of "situationism" has provided some important logical and philosophical arguments to offset the impact which behavioristic views of personality functioning have apparently had on current thinking about personality.

The position taken here is that individuality – both in others and in ourselves – has a phenomenal reality for us in our everyday social interactions. To overlook such a salient aspect of our cognitions about our social environment is to give an incomplete picture of the potential determinants of social behavior. While there are problems in "capturing" or measuring this individuality, these problems are logically not different from the kind of difficulties one normally encounters in attempting to operationalize some abstract conceptual variable (Aronson & Carlsmith, 1968) by means of a concrete situational manipulation. A broader perspective, one that looks to both the person *and* the situation as potential sources of behavioral variation, is necessary if we hope to have a more complete understanding of the determinants of social behavior.

This chapter, then, will attempt to provide an assessment of the relative value of situational factors and individual difference variables, in particular personality

[2] John W. Atkinson (personal communication, July 7, 1975) has remarked on the "staleness" of contemporary discussions in personality. Indeed, MacKinnon's (1944) chapter, which he brought to my attention, contains a presentation of theoretical approaches to the study of personality that has a remarkably contemporary ring to it.

constructs, in understanding social behavior by examining their characteristics in terms of the following issues and topics:

1. the epistemological status of personality descriptions and definition of the situation;
2. personality measures and operational definitions;
3. transsituational consistency;
4. the Person X Situation interaction.

EPISTEMOLOGICAL STATUS OF PERSONALITY DESCRIPTIONS AND DEFINITION OF THE SITUATION

The data of everyday experience has provided valuable heuristic tools with which to build more systematic analyses of many psychological phenomena. This is no less the case with the concept of personality. The reason why many theorists have taken the notion of personality as a unified structure seriously is because in the "naive psychology" of our everyday interpersonal relations, to use Fritz Heider's (1958) term, *we* do. Individuality and distinctiveness are the salient features of persons we interact with. What we remember most about people are not the ways they are similar to everyone else, but their characteristics and styles of behavior that make them different from everyone else. While all of us have in common a basic set of anatomical and physiological features, some of us walk more slowly, think more clearly, get angry more quickly, are more generous, less condescending, and more likely to be spellbound by the wail of a blues harmonica, than others. Part and parcel of our phenomenal experience of the other's distinctiveness is the sense of unity and coherence in the other's characteristics that is communicated to us. We do not think of most people as stimulus bound, reactive, disjointed, or inconsistent in their patterns of traits and behaviors. If we did, we would have to reacquaint ourselves with our friends every time we met them. While there are potential hazards in overestimating the unity of personality (Ichheiser, 1949, 1970, pp. 49–51, nonetheless it is the qualities of continuity and consistency in others that create the necessary stability and predictability in our interpersonal relations. Asch (1952) has described the perception of unity in others as follows: "Although he possesses many tendencies, capacities, and interests, we form a view of *one* person, a view that embraces his entire being or as much of it as is accessible to us [p. 206]."

But how *do* the other person's inner characteristics become accessible to us? Several writers have suggested that our phenomenal experience of personal qualities in others can provide information about the actual nature of these qualities. Kohler (1947/1959) felt that the psychological states of others are accessible to us through immediate experience as are other perceptual phenomena. He argued that "as a matter of principle facts of inner life and perceptual facts may have certain traits in common. . . . Behavior . . . tends to be seen as organized in forms which copy the organization of corresponding inner developments [pp. 135, 137]." The examples Kohler uses to develop his argument about the structural similarity between observed behaviors and inner states, such as hesitation and uncertainty, indicate that the "inner developments" he was addressing directly were relatively transient states, and it is not clear whether or not he would have extended his argument to cover more stable personality dispositions (see also Allport, 1937, pp. 534–536). Other, more contemporary, phenomenologically oriented investigators in the area of person perception, even if they may acknowledge the reality of personality traits, have generally limited themselves to the study of *perceived* personality characteristics in attempts to develop systematic conceptualizations of the principles by which perceivers form and organize their impressions of others, perhaps agreeing with Heider (1958) that "the study of common-sense psychology may be of value because of the truths it contains [p. 5]."

According to Allport (1937), understanding the other's personality involves both intuition and inference.

> Our understanding of personality comes . . . partly from without, but partly also from within. The first cues come from the structuration of the outer field; where these prove insufficient (as they usually do) then memory, imagination, and abstract conceptualization come to aid the process. We obtain what organization we can from the outer field and supply the remainder from within [p. 548].

Bowers (1973) has provided a conceptualization of the process of knowing the other person which, although couched in Piagetian terms, is quite compatible with Allport's view. According to Piaget's genetic epistemology (Bowers, 1973), "reality emerges out of a balanced relationship between the knower and the known, between assimilation and accommodation [p. 333]." Bowers argues that if the process of acquiring knowledge involved only assimilation there would indeed be the danger, as some writers have claimed, that the characteristics attributed to the person perceived would be primarily a reflection of the perceiver's categories of cognitive organization. It is the process of accommodation that prevents "our conceptual spectacles" from serving as our "perceptual blinders." "It is the accommodative aspects of adaptation that puts us in touch with the 'out-thereness' of things. And it is accommodation that makes us sensitive to the various particularities of individuals and situations [p. 328]."

In a more recent presentation, Allport (1966) proposed an approach he calls *heuristic realism*, as an "epistemological position for research in personality." He described heuristic realism, as applied to the study of personality, as a position that

> holds that the person who confronts us possesses inside his skin generalized action tendencies (or traits) and that it is our job scientifically to discover what they are. Any form of realism assumes the existence of an external structure ("out there") regardless of our shortcomings in comprehending it. Since traits, like all intervening variables, are never directly observed, but only inferred, we must expect difficulties and errors in the process of discovering their nature [p. 3].

To a great extent, whether or not, or to what degree, one agrees with this or a similar "trait" view is not an empirical issue, but rather is derivable from one's more general theoretical position regarding the primary determinants of behavior as well as one's position about the acceptability of inferred variables as explanatory concepts. Regarding the latter, Wylie (1974) has noted:

> The theoretical constructs or inferred variables of the personality theorist fulfil the same role as the theoretical constructs in other psychological theory. That is these constructs are introduced to help explain behavior variations which occur under constant external stimulation, and similarities of behavior which occur under varying external stimulating conditions [p. 18].

Thus, personality characteristics have the epistemological status of other inferred intervening structures or processes which have been of value in psychology, such as "intelligence," "cognitive dissonance," and so on.

Inherent in the preference of social psychologists for situational manipulations over personality variables as independent variables is the implicit assumption of an epistemological distinction between the two. Situational variables, since they are usually operationalized by means of some physically observable variations in the experimental setting or experimenter's behavior, are viewed as having an objective existence that is lacking in inferred states such as personality characteristics. Closer examination, however, reveals that this distinction between situational variables and personality variables is overdrawn. While it is true that situational variables have greater veridicality by virtue of their having been created by the experimenter, the nature of their impact or their *meaning* for the subject is ultimately an inference. The use of self-report measures as manipulation checks does not completely alter the inferential nature of the effects of the experimental manipulation since no rating scale can tap all the possible meanings the situation has for the subject. Besides, by the experimenter's relying on response-based information as a check on his manipulations, his situational manipulation is no longer a truly *independent* variable and he is in a sense dealing with correlational data. While most social psychologists, even among those that are behaviorally oriented (Berkowitz, 1963; Mischel, 1973b), agree on the necessity for defining stimulus inputs cognitively – that is, the subject's interpretation and understanding of the situation is crucial – the epistemological and methodological implications of this point are not usually recognized (but see Bowers, 1973).

PERSONALITY MEASURES AND OPERATIONAL DEFINITIONS

The failure of many personality measures to predict behavior reliably has been a major problem in the systematic study of individual differences. Although the poor performance of many measures is indisputable, the reasons for this phenomenon are open to question. For some theorists (e.g., Bem, 1972; Mischel, 1968, 1969)[3] the failure of personality variables as predictors has been considered as evidence against the existence of durable transsituational personality characteristics. Yet there are several equally plausible alternative explanations. Let us consider some:

1. The ease with which a paper-and-pencil measure of personality can be administered in contrast to the amount of effort that goes into experimental manipulations has often resulted in the use of the former in a scatter-gun manner. That is, personality variables have often been used to attempt to predict behaviors which have no conceptual link to the personality variable measured. No one would expect a laboratory-created independent variable to be applicable to all behavioral domains, yet personality variables have often been pressed into service when there was only the most tenuous theoretical link to the behavior to be predicted. Even one of the staunchest defenders of the trait concept, Gordon Allport (1937), recognized the fact that "traits are often aroused in one type of situation and not in another [p. 331]." Thus, at least some of the failure of personality variables as predictors of behavior is attributable to their relative indiscriminate use. A similar point has been made by Blass (1974), regarding the relationship of personality variables to differential tolerance for cognitive imbal-

[3] It should be noted that both these authors have in their more recent writings (Bem & Allen, 1974; Mischel, 1973a,b) moved away from the strongly situationist viewpoints expressed in these earlier writings. Thus, Mischel (1969), after presenting some findings from a longitudinal study on delay of gratification in children, concluded:

> Some significant prediction of length of voluntary delay of gratification can certainly be made from individual differences data; but the most powerful predictions by far come from knowledge of the cognitive and incentive conditions that prevail in the particular situation of interest. These results are not at all atypical. . . . I am more and more convinced . . . hopefully by data as well as on theoretical grounds, that the observed inconsistency so regularly found in studies of noncognitive personality dimensions often reflects the state of nature and not merely the noise of measurement [p. 1014].

Recently, however, Mischel (1973b) has stated that "it would be wasteful to create pseudo-controversies that pit person against situation in order to see which is more important. The answer must always depend on the particular situations and persons sampled" [pp. 255–256].

Similarly, in 1972 Bem stated:

> we implicitly adopt Mischel's position that inconsistency is the norm and that it is the phenomenon of consistency which must be explained (or constructed) [p. 21]. . . . There was nothing silly about the initial assumption of personologists that everything was glued together until proved otherwise. But since it has now proved otherwise, it seems only fair to give a sporting chance to the counterassumption that nothing is glued together until proved otherwise [p. 25].

More recently, however, Bem (Bem & Allen, 1974) has argued that, in addition to attending seriously to situations as recently advocated by several writers, "personality assessment must also begin to attend seriously to persons [p. 518]."

ance, and by Strickland (Chapter 6 in this volume) in reference to use of the locus of control construct without an awareness of its theoretical underpinnings. Thus, in seeking to understand why a personality variable is a poor predictor, it is necessary to broaden the scope of one's search to include not only the personality characteristic or its measure, but also the behavior to be predicted. As Borgatta (1968) said regarding people's reactions to the poor performance of personality inventories in prediction: "People usually raise the question of what is the matter with the personality inventory rather than examining whether or not they have established an appropriate prediction task [p. 514]." Although his point was directed at personality inventories, it is applicable to personality measures in general.

2. A personality variable may not reliably predict behavior because the construct it is meant to be a measure of may not in fact be a stable individual difference characteristic. To accept the possibility that there are stable personality dispositions that distinguish individuals does not mean that every personality characterization that is available in the language or that every personality construct proposed by an investigator actually corresponds to a stable personality trait. Furthermore, even with personality characteristics which may describe fairly stable dispositions, there may be problems of measurement if the characterization is not relevant to all individuals. This is illustrated in an early study by Conrad described in Allport (1937) in which three teachers were required to rate preschool children on 231 traits, "thus being forced to make the assumption that all children did possess exactly these self-same qualities in some degree [p. 301]." Degree of agreement among teachers ranged from +.14 to +.78, with the median being +.48. The teachers were also asked to "star" their ratings of the characteristics they felt to be of "central or dominating importance in the child's personality." On this task there was much greater degree of agreement among the teachers' judgments with their ratings on these starred traits correlating from +.93 to +.96.

3. When an experimenter fails to obtain a predicted effect of his independent variable on the dependent variable, one possible reason may be that his manipulation did not provide an adequate operationalization of his independent variable. Analogously, one reason why a particular personality measure does not adequately predict behavior may be because it is not a valid measure of the personality construct it is meant to measure. The point is that in an experiment, failure to confirm a hypothesis is not automatically regarded as a disconfirmation of the hypothesis since the fault may lie in the operationalization of concepts. In the same vein, failure of a personality measure to predict need not necessarily imply that the conceptualization of the personality construct is incorrect, but rather that the measure may be poor.

In noting the parallel between measurement problems with personality variables and the problem of operational definitions with experimentally manipulated variables, it is important to note a problem inherent only in the latter:

specifying the nature of the similarities and differences among situations. In order for an experimenter to be able to generalize his findings beyond his laboratory, he needs to be able to state the degree of similarity between the situation confronting the subjects in the laboratory and other situations. Without an adequate way of categorizing or scaling the attributes of situations, the failure of replication attempts to reproduce an effect remains a puzzle (see, for example, Storms & Nisbett, 1970; and then, Kellogg & Baron, 1975). The need for a systematic description or measurement of situational inputs has been stressed by social and personality psychologists (e.g., Cherry & Byrne, Chapter 3 this volume; Gergen & Marlowe, 1970; Milgram, 1965; Mischel, 1969). For example, Milgram (1965) stated: "Ultimately, social psychology would like to have a compelling *theory of situations* which will, first, present a language in terms of which situations can be defined; proceed to a typology of situations; and then point to the manner in which definable properties of situations are transformed into psychological forces in the individual [p. 74]." Attempts at solving the problem of systematic description of situations have mainly come from investigators interested in studying the environmental context of naturally occurring behaviors, exemplified in the ecological psychology approach of Roger Barker (1960) and colleagues. Although much of the work in the area has focused on relatively molar units, such as the various kinds of school environments, recent reviews (Ekehammar, 1974; Frederiksen, 1972; Moos, 1974) contain also some potentially useful approaches for categorizing the smaller types of situational units that experimental social psychologists are primarily interested in.

TRANSSITUATIONAL CONSISTENCY

The assumption that the person's behavior is characterized by transsituational consistency or congruency has been a central one for dispositional views of human functioning. In fact, the observation of consistency in the pattern of a person's behavior across different situations is the primary basis for inferring the existence of a personality trait (Allport, 1937, p. 330). At the same time, the concept of consistency has been very bothersome for the empirically oriented personologist since the actual evidence for transsituational consistency has been rather weak.

Historically, the heaviest blow against the concept of transsituational personality traits has come from a large-scale study of deception involving close to eleven thousand school children, conducted by Hartshorne and May (1928) as part of their Character Education Inquiry. Since their work invariably comes up in discussions of behavioral specificity and consistency, discussing it in some detail would be worthwhile. In that study children were given a battery of tests and put into a variety of situations designed to provide opportunities for dishonest behavior. The settings were classrooms, athletic contests, parties, and the home; and the kinds of deception tapped were cheating, stealing, and lying. Hartshorne and May found that the children were fairly consistent in the level of deception among the various tests within a particular category, ranging from r = .440 for level of cheating on speed tests to an r = .836 for the various measures of lying (Hartshorne & May, 1928, p. 382, Table 71). However, their level of consistency across the various kinds of testing situations was low. For example, the average correlation between cheating at puzzles and lying was .208, and between stealing and lying was .132. Although all the correlations (with the exception of one r of −.003) were positive, the highest was only .312 (p. 383, Table 72). On the basis of these findings, Hartshorne and May concluded that "honesty appears to be a congeries of specialized acts which are closely tied up with particular features of the situation in which deception is a possibility and is apparently not greatly dependent on any general ideal or trait of honesty [p. 15]." Also: "Most children will deceive in certain situations and not in others. Lying, cheating, and stealing as measured by the test situations used in these studies are only very loosely related [p. 411]."

Although some writers have agreed with Hartshorne and May's conclusions and consider their study as providing powerful evidence against the view of personality traits as relatively global transsituational dispositions, others have disagreed with them. Allport (1961) presents the following arguments, among others. Firstly, the fact that there were low correlations among various measures of deception or dishonesty is not evidence that children lack traits, but that dishonesty, as measured in the study, may not itself be a trait. The particular behaviors studied may, in fact, be consistent with other behaviors not studied by the investigators and, therefore, they may be part of as yet undiscovered traits or dispositions. Taking as an example the low correlation between lying and stealing mentioned earlier, Allport suggests the following kinds of possibilities:

> A child who has the habit of stealing pennies may do so because he is saving up to buy a tool kit; or because he is revengeful in an anti-social way; or because he feels socially inferior and wishes to buy candy to curry favor from his playmates. A child who lies may do so because he is fearful of punishment; because he does not wish to hurt the teacher's feelings. [Another child] may lie because he has a chronic hunger for praise and approval [p. 316].

In a similar vein, Asch (1946) stated that the failure of Hartshorne and May to consider the psychological content of the children's behaviors "introduces a serious doubt concerning [their] conclusions [p. 288]."

A final point about Hartshorne and May's work. It is interesting to note that, although Hartshorne and May saw behavioral specificity in the dimensions of character they studied and their work is often cited by critics of the trait concept as supporting evidence, one of the participants in the Character Education Inquiry, Maller, apparently did not view the evidence in this manner. For Maller (1944), the fact that all the correlations among the four groups of character tests used in the Character Education Inquiry, measuring honesty, cooperation, inhibition, and persistence, were positive, provided evidence for a general trait which he called *factor C* and defined as "the readiness to forego an immediate gain for the sake of a remote but greater gain [p. 179]" (see also Allport, 1961, and MacKinnon, 1944).

No matter how one views Hartshorne and May's findings, however, the fact is that today, almost half a century later, the issue of consistency it highlighted is still unresolved. Empirically the evidence for transsituational consistency "has not been inspiring," to use Block's (1968) phrase, who goes on to suggest some explanations for what he considers is only an apparent inconsistency. On the other hand, the evidence for what might be called cross-personal consistency, that is, the ability for a particular kind of situation to evoke a consistent pattern of responding, is not much more inspiring. If the reader disagrees with the latter point, I suggest considering the number of experimental paradigms in social psychology using situational manipulations which have failed to yield consistent, replicable effects. Although such an appraisal should lead to a more modest view regarding the accomplishments of a situational approach, it should not deter us from attempting to refine our methods so that more precise and consistent results can be obtained from situational variables. One approach to refining situational predictions is the recognition of the possibility that a particular variation in the situational input may have different effects on individuals with different personality, or other stable, characteristics. Analogously, the weak empirical evidence for consistency of personality should not hamper efforts at refining concepts and measures of personality to make them more meaningful and useful in the prediction of behavior. An important step in accomplishing this goal is a conceptualization of personality dispositions that recognizes that only a limited number of situations may arouse a particular disposition, and that a behavior must be logically linked to the personality disposition in order for a measure of that disposition to be a predictor of that behavior.[4]

THE PERSON X SITUATION INTERACTION

An experimental approach suggested by these considerations, as well as those in earlier portions of this chapter regarding the relative strengths and weaknesses of personality and situational approaches, is one which looks at behavior jointly as a function of personality and situational variables. Several writers have argued in favor of this interactional or moderator variable approach (e.g., Alker, 1972;

[4] Another approach, which shows promise in increasing the predictive power of personality variables, is to consider the possibility that behavioral consistency may itself be an individual difference characteristic. Empirical support for this possibility comes recently from a number of interesting studies (Bem & Allen, 1974; Campus, 1974; Snyder & Monson, 1975) although in 1937 Allport had already referred to attempts "to determine whether consistency (or its opposite, variability) is itself a consistent attribute of personality [p. 356]."

Bem, 1972; Bowers, 1973; Ekehammar, 1974; Endler, 1973) although others have expressed their reservations (e.g., Argyle, 1975; Carlson, 1975; Wallach & Leggett, 1972; Zedeck, 1971). My own view is that studies which allow the assessment of the interactive effects of the characteristics of the individual and of the situation can only serve to increase the precision of our predictions about social behavior.

This view has guided my work on the development of the personality construct of objectivity–subjectivity. Thus, in an attitude-change study (Blass, 1969) I predicted and found attitude change in response to cognitive imbalance to be an interactive effect of a personality variable – objectivity-subjectivity as measured by the Blass Objectivity Subjectivity Scale (BOSS) – and a situational variable, the relevance of the source to the communication. More recently (Blass, 1974), among students in an introductory psychology course I found the positive relationship between a student's test grade and evaluations of the teacher and the course to be moderated by the student's degree of objectivity–subjectivity. Thus, although for the group as a whole there were significant positive correlations between grade received on a midterm exam and course evaluations on six out of nine evaluation items, a more precise account emerged when students' degree of objectivity–subjectivity was taken into account. The group of subjects was dichotomized on the basis of their scores on the BOSS into an objective group (high BOSS scorers) and a subjective group (low BOSS scorers) and correlations between grades and evaluations were computed separately for the two groups. Among the subjective individuals the six correlations were still significant (and, in fact, numerically higher than those for the group as a whole), but among the more objective persons only two of the grade-evaluation correlations were significant.

An increasing recognition by social psychologists of the necessity of taking individual differences, in addition to situational factors, into account would also be in line with the dictum of the father of experimental social psychology, Kurt Lewin (1935): "*The dynamics of environmental influences* can be investigated *only simultaneously with the determination of individual differences* and with *general psychological laws* [p. 73]." In this regard, it is encouraging to note that there is recent evidence that social psychologists are increasingly designing studies which allow the determination of the interaction between individual difference and situational variables (Sarason, Smith, & Diener, 1975).

THE CONTENTS OF THIS BOOK

The chapters that follow provide concrete evidence for the importance of taking individual differences into account in understanding social behavior. Each of the chapters (with the exception of the one on sex differences) deals with a personality construct whose durability and ability to generate research attest to its usefulness. It is to a brief preview of each of the chapters that we will now turn.

Motivation for Achievement

Achievement motivation has been one of the most durable constructs in psychology. In his chapter, Atkinson provides a personal account of its evolution, beginning with the development of a thematic apperception measure of need for achievement in the 1940s, through the formulation of a theory of achievement motivation and the work it led to in the 1950s and 1960s, to its current status within a more general theory of action.

Aside from its intrinsic interest, the work described here exemplifies the value of an explicitly formulated theory for guiding research and for providing an explanatory framework to encompass a wide array of behavioral phenomena. The need for achievement is distinguishable from the other personality constructs dealt with in this book, in several ways. While a person's position on the other dimensions (with the exception of psychological differentiation) is determined by his responses to items on a self-report scale, the primary measure of need for achievement is a TAT–like projective test. Although some criticisms have been leveled at this measure on psychometric grounds, Atkinson reaffirms its validity and reliability and in the process raises some questions about some generally unquestioned assumptions of traditional psychometric theory.

Another noteworthy feature of work on the need for achievement construct is that from its very beginnings it took seriously Kurt Lewin's dictum, mentioned above, about behavior being viewed as a function of the person and the situation. First, it can be seen as early as Atkinson's (1953) dissertation in which he found the Zeigarnik effect (the tendency to recall more incompleted than completed tasks) to be an interactive effect of personality – i.e., the subject's need for achievement level – and the situation – i.e., the kind of task orientation provided for the subject by means of the instructions. Secondly, and more generally, the theory of achievement motivation sees the achieving tendency as comprised of both a relatively stable or "chronic" individual-difference characteristic and also a more transient or "acute" state evoked by the situation. Formally, this is indicated by the equation $T_s = M_S \times P_s \times I_s$, in which T_s (the tendency to achieve success) is seen to be a function of the relatively stable disposition, M_S (the motive to achieve success), and two attributes of the immediate situation, P_s and I_s (which stand for the strength of expectancy about success at the task and the incentive value of success, respectively).

Authoritarianism

The search for the Authoritarian Personality grew out of an attempt to understand and prevent the recurrence of the horrors of the Nazi era during which millions of Jews were killed by the Germans in a systematic program of genocide. In order to accomplish this goal, a group of researchers, with the support of the American Jewish Committee, began a series of investigations at the end of the Second World War to determine the personality characteristics associated with anti-Semitic and antidemocratic tendencies. Their investigations culminated in the publication of *The Authoritarian Personality* (Adorno, Frenkel-Brunswik, Levinson, & Sanford, 1950), which presented the results of their efforts.

In their chapter, Cherry and Byrne discuss some of the issues of measurement that concerned early work on authoritarianism, as well as studies on the parental antecedents of authoritarianism. The main thrust of their chapter is, however, on the necessity of conceptualizing authoritarian behavior as a function of both personality and situation. As Cherry and Byrne note, the authors of *The Authoritarian Personality* did consider situational factors as well as intrapsychic influences. However, they were referring to situations in a more global sense – the socioeconomic and political conditions at a given time – and not to the characteristics of the more immediate environment which experimental social psychologists usually focus on. Cherry and Byrne point up the value of an interactive approach to authoritarianism by applying it to illustrative studies from three conceptually relevant behavioral domains: conformity and obedience to authority, aggression and punitiveness, and reactions to erotica.

Psychological Differentiation

A major contribution of Gestalt psychologists has been to demonstrate the operation of certain organizing principles in perception. They showed that, in order to account for the close correspondence between what is "out there" and our perception of it, it is necessary to postulate that the organism imposes some structure of its own on the stimulus input. This active structuring process is assumed to follow certain principles, such as similarity and proximity. Although recognizing the importance of going beyond the stimulus, and of the necessity of taking into account the contribution of the perceiver, Gestalt psychologists were primarily interested in formulating general principles of perception. Thus, they did not systematically explore the possibility that there might be individual differences in reliance on certain perceptual principles. The work of Witkin and his colleagues on the personality dimension of psychological differentiation or field dependence–independence represents a systematic attempt at looking at individual differences in perceptual styles and the implications these differences have for various areas of personality functioning. In his chapter, Karp traces the theoretical development of the construct, describes the various measures of psychological differentiation that have been used, and then reviews the literature on the relationship between field dependence and various domains of social behavior.

Introversion/Extraversion

The distinction of introversion/extraversion is among the oldest descriptions of personality. As Wilson points out in his chapter, by the late nineteenth century its everyday meaning was similar to current common usage – an innerdirectedness versus an outerdirectedness – although a similar distinction can be traced to ancient times. The person most responsible for transforming these terms into a scientifically rigorous personality construct is Hans Eysenck. It is mainly to Eysenck's theory and the research that evolved from it that the chapter by Wilson is devoted, although a more recent formulation of Gray is also presented.

Among the measured personality variables considered in this book, introversion/extraversion is clearly the most nativistic. Hereditary factors are assumed to account for a sizable portion of the variance among people on this characteristic. The focus on the biological basis of introversion/extraversion has manifested itself in two ways in research on this personality variable: (1) in the use of twin studies to determine the relative magnitude of the contributions of genetic and environmental factors in introversion; and (2) in the specification of explicit neurophysiological models to account for behavioral differences between introverts and extraverts.

Internal–External Control of Reinforcement

Unquestionably, the most widely used personality variable in contemporary research in personality and social psychology is Rotter's construct of internal–external control of reinforcement (I–E), or locus of control. In her chapter, Strickland provides a historical perspective on the development of the construct within a social learning framework, discusses the major issues confronting research with I–E, and provides an extensive review of the literature on I–E, especially as it relates to social behavior. Strickland stresses the importance of maintaining cognizance of the theoretical roots of the I–E construct within social learning theory. Within that theoretical model, I–E is seen as only one of the possible determinants of behavior, the others being the nature of the situation in terms of its potential for providing reinforcements, and the importance for the individual of receiving reinforcements in that particular situation. The possibility of losing sight of the underpinnings of the I–E construct within a theoretical model stressing the Person × Situation interaction is enhanced by the fact that I–E, having been included in so many studies, sometimes predicts behavior even when there is no apparent theoretical reason to expect it to do so.

How does one know in which situations I–E – or for that matter, any other personality construct – will serve as a predictor of behavior? To a great extent, the domains of relevance of the construct can be derived deductively from the theory the personality construct is embedded in. As research progresses with a personality variable, the accumulated empirical evidence should, in turn, result in a more refined and precisely differentiated conception of the domains of relevance of the measure. Strickland's chapter reviews the predictive ability of I–E within a number of important domains of social behavior and thereby provides substantive material with which the process of refinement can progress.

Dogmatism

Among the various criticisms that were leveled at *The Authoritarian Personality* soon after its publication was that the measure of authoritarianism, the California F scale, was not a pure measure of authoritarianism, but rather that it was confounded with a politically conservative ideology. Arguing that authoritarianism can characterize the belief systems of adherents of left-wing, as well as right-wing, ideology, Rokeach developed the Dogmatism scale (or D scale) as an ideology-free measure of authoritarianism. Rokeach's early work on dogmatism. as well as his theory on the nature of belief systems within which the construct of dogmatism is embedded, was described in his book, *The Open and Closed Mind* (1960). In his chapter, Vacchiano[5] reviews the current status of dogmatism research with a primary focus on social behavior. His chapter serves to update his earlier review (Vacchiano, Strauss, & Hochman, 1969) and to pinpoint the assumptions of dogmatism theory which have continued to receive empirical support and those which have not.

Approval Motivation

Psychologists have long been aware that individuals, when placed in a situation in which they may be evaluated (such as when taking a personality test or participating in an experiment), will tend to present themselves in as favorable a light as possible. The possibility that there may be individual differences in this tendency to respond in a socially desirable manner led Edwards (1957) and then Crowne and Marlowe (1960) to create scales to measure this tendency. As Strickland points out in her chapter, Crowne and Marlowe (1964) later formulated a motivational construct – the need for approval – in order to understand these differential tendencies to respond in a socially desirable manner. Strickland's chapter presents the theoretical background of the construct, reviews the major areas of research on approval motivation, and presents some of the problems and issues that confront the researcher in this area. Among other things, Strickland demonstrates the value of the need for approval dimension in moderating the effects of situational variables. Thus, for example, she shows that, in studies using the Asch-type conformity paradigm which have incorporated the Marlowe–Crowne Social Desirability Scale, need for approval was a significant predictor of degree of conformity.

[5] It is with sadness that I note the death of Ralph B. Vacchiano on August 15, 1976.

Sex Differences

The focus of the final chapter of the book is on an individual difference variable – sex – which differs from the personality variables presented in several ways. As Deaux points out, unlike the usual personality variable, "sex is (1) descriptive rather than conceptual; (2) dichotomous rather than continuous; and (3) readily identifiable to most observers." Perhaps because of its pervasiveness and distinctive status as an individual difference variable, social psychologists have generally tended to ignore sex as a variable or generalize from one sex to the other, in spite of continuing evidence for the existence of sex differences in social behavior. In her chapter, Deaux presents a two-dimensional conceptual framework to account systematically for observed sex differences in social behavior which takes into account the importance of both person and situation. Males and females are seen, firstly, as differing in the self-presentation strategies they adopt, with different situations having either a facilitating or inhibiting effect on the emergence of one or another mode of self-presentation. Secondly, they are seen as differing in terms of task familiarity, with some tasks having generally male associations while others are typically more familiar for females. Deaux demonstrates the value of her conceptual scheme by using it as an organizing framework for the findings on sex differences in many areas of social behavior, and by bringing it to bear on some general issues in sex differences research and on the importance of considering both personality and situational influences on social behavior.

CONCLUSIONS

Contemporary social psychology has tended to favor experimental manipulations over measures of personality dispositions to test hypotheses about the determinants of social behavior. That the use of experimentally manipulated variables allows the investigator to draw causal inferences from his results makes that preference an understandable one. Yet, in making experimental manipulations the research strategy of choice, social psychologists have overlooked the potential value of personality variables as predictors of behavior. No doubt the behavioral tendency to overlook the predictive value of personality variables has also been maintained by earlier contentions (e.g., Mischel, 1968, pp. 82–83, 1969) that situational factors are more powerful predictors of behavior than individual difference variables. It is now generally agreed that the question of the relative predictive power of persons or situations is a pseudoissue, and that persons and situations each account for smaller proportions of the variance than the Person X Situation interaction (Argyle & Little, 1972; Bowers, 1973; Endler, 1973; Mischel, 1973b). Thus, in Bowers' (1973) survey of 11 articles published since 1959, which permitted the determination of the percentage of variance accounted for by persons, situations, and the Person X Situation interaction, the average percentage of variance due to situations was 10.17%; to persons, 12.71%; and to the Person X Situation interaction, 20.77%.

The "amount of variance" question is further complicated by the fact that a somewhat different picture emerges when we consider studies that have examined the effects of *measured* individual difference variables rather than individuals, per se (as had the studies reviewed by Bowers), in relation to situational effects. Sarason, Smith, and Diener (1975) examined 102 studies involving 138 analyses of variance which appeared in the 1972 issues of the *Journal of Personality and Social Psychology* and the *Journal of Personality* and in the 1971 and 1972 issues of the *Journal of Consulting and Clinical Psychology.* They found that the average percentage of variance accounted for by either personality or situational variables alone was relatively small (8.7 and 10.3%, respectively), but that the average percentage of variance due to Personality X Situation interactions was even smaller – only 4.6%. Although this is much smaller than the 20.77% average for Person X Situation interactions reported by Bowers, as well as the averages reported by other similar analyses, Sarason *et al.* did not find it surprising, for the following reasons. Firstly, their low percentage-of-variance figure represents an average derived from studies which varied widely in terms of the theoretical relevance of the individual difference variable used, to the situational variable or to the behavior being studied. One could reasonably expect a higher proportion of the variance to be accounted for by the Person X Situation interaction the more theoretically relevant the personality variable is. Second, a basic difference between the studies summarized by Bowers and by Sarason *et al.* is that the former computed Person X Situation interactions (i.e., in which individuals constitute one of the variables in the design), whereas the figures in Sarason *et al.* (1975) are based on measured Personality X Situation interactions. One would expect the Person X Situation interactions to account for higher proportions of the variance than measured Personality X Situation interactions because the former are "composite [s] of all possible Personality X Situation interactions for the particular situations of interest" [Sarason *et al.*, 1975, p. 204].

A portion of Sarason *et al.*'s (1975) discussion of their findings is worth quoting for its general relevance for research in personality and social psychology:

> Our survey reveals surprisingly low percentages of variance accounted for by all classes of variables investigated: situational, personality, demographic, and interactions among these variables. If our somewhat negative evaluations of this result is reasonable, then many of the theoretical disputes that permeate the personality literature are explicable in terms of the narrow margin by which results are regarded as psychologically meaningful. Attainment of the .05 level of statistical significance may not provide a sufficiently firm base upon which to erect crisp psychological interpretations and powerful theories.

From another perspective, however, by what standard is accounting for, say, only 10% of the variance a poor or disappointing performance? It appears that most current studies are directed toward the investigation of relatively subtle psychological phenomena, so that we might expect the present results. If an independent variable is truly powerful (i.e., accounts for a massive proportion of the variance), it is generally also too obvious to be of "theoretical" interest. In any event, no matter how one views the results of the present survey with regard to the potency of individual variables, the state of affairs for situational variables alone is only slightly more favorable [p. 203].

Clearly then, the amount of variance accounted for is not the primary consideration. What is crucial is that we provide as precise an account of social behavior that is feasible given our state of knowledge. Thus, the possibility that a particular behavior may be a function of both personality and situational factors should be a *heuristically* useful assumption whatever one's theoretical persuasion. The recent surge of interest in and increasing advocacy of interactionism cited earlier is encouraging and suggests that more and more investigators are taking Lewin's[6] dictum seriously. By increasing our understanding of some of the most important and durable personality constructs, the chapters of this book, it is hoped, will provide meaningful input toward increased consideration of the person, as well as the environment, as important determinants of social behavior.

REFERENCES

Adorno, T. W., Frenkel-Brunswik, E., Levinson, D. T., & Sanford, R. N. *The authoritarian personality.* New York: Harper & Row, 1950.

Alker, H. A. Is personality situationally specific or intrapsychically consistent? *Journal of Personality,* 1972, *40,* 1–16.

Allport, G. W. *Personality: A psychological interpretation.* New York: Holt, 1937.

Allport, G. W. *Pattern and growth in personality.* New York: Holt, Rinehart & Winston, 1961.

Allport, G. W. Traits revisited. *American Psychologist,* 1966, *21,* 1–10.

Altman, I., & Taylor, D. *Social penetration: The development of interpersonal relationships.* New York: Holt, Rinehart & Winston, 1973.

Argyle, M. *Predictive and generative rules models of P × S interaction.* Paper presented at the Symposium on Interactional Psychology, Stockholm, June 1975.

Argyle, M. Predictive and generative rules models of P × S interaction. Paper presented at *Theory of Social Behaviour,* 1972, *2,* 1–35.

Aronson, E., & Carlsmith, J. M. Experimentation in social psychology. In G. Lindzey & E. Aronson (Eds.), *The handbook of social psychology* (Vol. 2). Reading, Mass.: Addison-Wesley, 1968.

[6] While Kurt Lewin's interactionist position is the most well known and has probably been the most influential, Ekehammar's (1974) useful historical survey shows that other important psychologists have also espoused interactionist viewpoints. Many of these were themselves undoubtedly influenced by Lewin.

Asch, S. E. Forming impressions of personality. *Journal of Abnormal and Social Psychology,* 1946, *41,* 258–290.

Asch, S. E. *Social psychology.* Englewood Cliffs, N.J.: Prentice-Hall, 1952.

Atkinson, J. W. The achievement motive and the recall of interrupted and completed tasks. *Journal of Experimental Psychology,* 1953, *46,* 381–390.

Averill, J. R. The dis-position of psychological dispositions. *Journal of Experimental Research in Personality,* 1973, *6,* 275–282.

Bakeman, R., & Helmreich, R. Cohesiveness and performance: Covariation and causality in an undersea environment. *Journal of Experimental Social Psychology,* 1975, *11,* 478–489.

Barker, R. G. Ecology and motivation. In M. R. Jones (Ed.), *Nebraska Symposium on Motivation* (Vol. 8). Lincoln: University of Nebraska Press, 1960.

Bem, D. J. Constructing cross-situational consistencies in behavior: Some thoughts on Alker's critique of Mischel. *Journal of Personality,* 1972, *40,* 17–26.

Bem, D. J., & Allen, A. On predicting some of the people some of the time: The search for cross-situational consistencies in behavior. *Psychological Review,* 1974, *81,* 506–520.

Berger, S. M., & Lambert, W. W. Stimulus–response theory in contemporary social psychology. In G. Lindzey & E. Aronson (Eds.), *The handbook of social psychology* (Vol. 1). Reading, Mass.: Addison-Wesley, 1968.

Berkowitz, L. Social psychological theorizing. In M. H. Marx (Ed.), *Theories in contemporary psychology.* New York: Macmillan, 1963.

Berkowitz, L., & Macaulay, J. The contagion of criminal violence. *Sociometry,* 1971, *34,* 238–260.

Blass, T. Personality and situational factors in tolerance for imbalance. Doctoral dissertation, Yeshiva University, 1969 (University Microfilms, No. 69–15, 207).

Blass, T. Measurement of objectivity–subjectivity: Effects of tolerance for imbalance and grades on evaluations of teachers. *Psychological Reports,* 1974, *34,* 1199–1213.

Blass, T. (Ed.), *Contemporary social psychology: Representative readings.* Itasca, Illinois: F. E. Peacock, 1976.

Block, J. Some reasons for the apparent inconsistency of personality. *Psychological Bulletin,* 1968, *70,* 210–212.

Borgatta, E. F. Traits and persons. In E. F. Borgatta & W. W. Lambert (Eds.), *Handbook of personality theory and research.* Chicago: Rand McNally, 1968.

Bowers, K. S. Situationism in psychology: An analysis and a critique. *Psychological Review,* 1973, *80,* 307–336.

Bruner, J. S., & Tagiuri, R. The perception of people. In G. Lindzey (Ed.), *Handbook of social psychology* (Vol. 1). Reading, Mass.: Addison-Wesley, 1954.

Campus, N. Transituational consistency as a dimension of personality. *Journal of Personality and Social Psychology,* 1974, *29,* 593–600.

Carlson, R. Personality. *Annual Review of Psychology,* 1975, *26,* 393–414.

Cronbach, L. J. The two disciplines of scientific psychology. *American Psychologist,* 1957, *12,* 671–684.

Crowne, D. P., & Marlowe, D. A new scale of social desirability independent of psychopathology, *Journal of Consulting Psychology,* 1960, *24,* 349–354.

Crowne, D. P., & Marlowe, D. *The approval motive: Studies in evaluative dependence.* New York: Wiley, 1964.

Dermer, M., & Thiel, D. L. When beauty may fail. *Journal of Personality and Social Psychology,* 1975, *31,* 1168–1176.

Dion, K., Berscheid, E., & Walster, E. What is beautiful is good. *Journal of Personality and Social Psychology,* 1972, *24,* 285–290.

Edwards, A. L. *The social desirability variable in personality assessment and research.* New York: Holt, 1957.

Ekehammar, B. Interactionism in personality from a historical perspective. *Psychological Bulletin,* 1974, *81,* 1026–1048.

Endler, N. S. The person versus the situation – A pseudo issue? A response to Alker. *Journal of Personality,* 1973, *41,* 287–303.

Frederiksen, N. Toward a taxonomy of situations. *American Psychologist,* 1972, *27,* 114–123.

Gergen, K. J., & Marlowe, D. Personality and social behavior. In K. J. Gergen & D. Marlowe (Eds.), *Personality and social behavior.* Reading, Mass.: Addison-Wesley, 1970.

Guthrie, E. R. Personality in terms of associative learning. In J. McV. Hunt (Ed.), *Personality and the behavior disorders* (Vol. 1). New York: Ronald Press, 1944.

Hartshorne, H., & May, M. A. *Studies in the nature of character. I: Studies in deceit.* New York: The Macmillan Company, 1928.

Heider, F. *The psychology of interpersonal relations.* New York: Wiley, 1958.

Heider, F. On Lewin's methods and theory. *Psychological Issues,* 1959, *1*(3), 108–119.

Helmreich, R. Applied social psychology: The unfulfilled promise. *Personality and Social Psychology Bulletin,* 1975, *1,* 548–560.

Hornstein, H. A. Promotive tension: The basis of prosocial behavior from a Lewinian perspective. *Journal of Social Issues,* 1972, *28*(3), 191–218.

Ichheiser, G. Misunderstandings in human relations: A study in false social perception. *American Journal of Sociology,* 1949, *55* (2, Pt. 2), 1–70.

Ichheiser, G. *Appearances and realities.* San Francisco: Jossey-Bass, 1970.

Kellogg, R., & Baron, R. S. Attribution theory, insomnia, and the reverse placebo effect: A reversal of Storms and Nisbett's findings. *Journal of Personality and Social Psychology,* 1975, *32,* 231–236.

Kohler, W. *Gestalt psychology.* New York: Mentor, 1959. (Originally published by Liveright Publishing Corporation, 1947.)

Lewin, K. *A dynamic theory of personality.* New York: McGraw-Hill, 1935.

Lewin, K. *Principles of topological psychology.* New York: McGraw-Hill, 1936.

MacKinnon, D. W. The structure of personality. In J. McV. Hunt (Ed.), *Personality and the behavior disorders* (Vol. 1). New York: Ronald Press, 1944.

Maller, J. B. Personality tests. In J. McV. Hunt (Ed.), *Personality and the behavior disorders* (Vol. 1). New York: Ronald Press, 1944.

Milgram, S. Some conditions of obedience and disobedience to authority. *Human Relations,* 1965, *18,* 57–76.

Mischel, W. *Personality and assessment.* New York: Wiley, 1968.

Mischel, W. Continuity and change in personality. *American Psychologist,* 1969, *24,* 1012–1018.

Mischel, W. On the empirical dilemmas of psychodynamic approaches. *Journal of Abnormal Psychology,* 1973, *82,* 335–344. (a)

Mischel, W. Toward a cognitive social learning reconceptualization of personality. *Psychological Review,* 1973, *80,* 252–283. (b)

Moos, R. H. Systems for the assessment and classification of human environments: An overview. In R. H. Moos & P. M. Insel (Eds.), *Issues in social ecology: Human milieus.* Palo Alto: National Press Books, 1974.

Rokeach, M. *The open and closed mind.* New York: Basic Books, 1960.

Rubin, D. B. Estimating causal effects of treatments in randomized and nonrandomized studies. *Journal of Educational Psychology,* 1974, *66,* 688–701.

Sarason, I. G., Smith, R. E., & Diener, E. Personality research: Components of variance attributable to the person and the situation. *Journal of Personality and Social Psychology,* 1975, *32,* 199–204.

Snyder, M., & Monson, T. C. Persons, situations, and the control of social behavior. *Journal of Personality and Social Psychology,* 1975, *32,* 637–644.

Storms, M. D., & Nisbett, R. E. Insomnia and the attribution process. *Journal of Personality and Social Psychology,* 1970, *16,* 319–328.

Tyler, L. E. *Tests and measurements.* Englewood Cliffs, N.J.: Prentice-Hall, 1963.

Vacchiano, R. B., Strauss, P. S., & Hochman, L. The open and closed mind: A review of dogmatism. *Psychological Bulletin,* 1969, *71,* 261–273.

Wachtel, P. L. Psychodynamics, behavior therapy, and the implacable experimenter: An inquiry into the consistency of personality. *Journal of Abnormal Psychology,* 1973, *82,* 324–334.

Wallace, J. An abilities conception of personality: Some implications for personality measurement. *American Psychologist,* 1966, *21,* 132–138.

Wallach, M. A., & Leggett, M. I. Testing the hypothesis that a person will be consistent: Stylistic consistency versus situational specificity in size of children's drawings. *Journal of Personality,* 1972, *40,* 309–330.

Wylie, R. C. *The self-concept (Vol. 1, Rev. ed.).* Lincoln: University of Nebraska Press, 1974.

Zedeck, S. Problems with the use of "moderator" variables. *Psychological Bulletin,* 1971, *76,* 295–310.

2
Motivation for Achievement

John W. Atkinson
The University of Michigan

Achievement motivation has been referred to as the need for achievement (and abbreviated *n* Achievement) since the beginning of its systematic study (McClelland, Clark, Roby, & Atkinson, 1949). It is an important determinant of aspiration, effort, and persistence when an individual expects that performance will be evaluated in relation to some standard of excellence. Such behavior is generally called achievement oriented.

This encyclopedia definition would adequately introduce a substantive review of the behavioral effects of individual differences in achievement motivation, per se. But such a limited review might miss completely the broader coherent conceptions of *motivation for achievement* and of the dynamics of action that have evolved as fundamentally important products of research that originally and continually has had individual differences in *n* Achievement as its central focus.

The goal of basic science in study of personality, as elsewhere, is the development and refinement of a conceptual scheme (Conant, 1951). We seek to formulate theory that is vulnerable to empirical test and amenable to refinement and correction. Such a conceptual scheme becomes a way of thinking about the subject that is immediately more enlightening and ultimately more practically useful than traditional wisdom.

William James (1890) once introduced an essay that would be tilted towards emphasis of a general conception (which is my aim) rather than simply be an exhaustive survey of relevant facts, with a quip: "having the goose which lays the golden eggs, the description of each egg already laid is a minor matter [p. 449]."

The point nicely captures the relation of theory to fact in science. But there are two additional reasons for my selective emphasis of the theory that has evolved relating personality–motivation–action. First, that has been the central aim of our 25-year research program at Michigan, the one with which I am most familiar. Second, the literature on achievement motivation has become so vast and includes so many substantive contributions, many ultimately reported in books by the major contributors, that none of us, I think, has yet had the time to comprehend all of it. To minimize the deficiency in scope of coverage, I shall at least try to provide a useful reader's guide along the way. But I shall certainly not miss this opportunity to stress that theory evolved in disciplined experimental–conceptual analysis of achievement motivation has brought the study of how individual differences in motivation influence behavior from the horse and buggy era of psychology into the era of computer simulation. We are now guided in our studies by an immensely talented theoretically-minded collaborator to consider study of problems that were too complex to be thinkable a decade ago (Seltzer, 1973; Seltzer & Sawusch, 1974). We now know, for example, that it is logically (theoretically) possible for a thematic apperceptive measure of the strength of a motive to have construct validity without the diagnostic test having internal consistency reliability (Atkinson, Bongort, & Price, 1977). Since this contradicts something you have already been taught as one of the fundamental tenets of traditional psychometrics, it is essential that you become aware of the theoretical advance concerning motivation and action and its potential implications for the logic of personality measurement.

Why study the need to achieve at all? It is one of the significant phenomena in human history. Social scientists concerned with the rise and fall of civilizations, their economic development, and comparisons among contemporary societies in basic values that account for obvious differences in the standard and quality of life continually emphasize effects attributable to the relative importance of achievement. Lipset (1963, 1968), for example, compares the four Anglo-American societies and calls attention to the obviously greater achievement-orientation of Americans than British, Canadians, or Australians. The Horatio Alger myth was a vital part of the cultural heritage of young Americans between the Civil War and World War I (Huber, 1971). In the middle of this period, around 1890, concern over achievement expressed in the books used to teach children how to read in America peaked, according to deCharms and Moeller (1962). It has declined ever since. What does this imply for our society? Striving to excel, to get ahead, to win in competition with some standard or others, whatever it is called, is generally conceded to be a mainspring of the upward social mobility that has characterized the relatively open American society (Crockett & Schulman, 1973; Duncan, Featherman, & Duncan, 1972; Lipset & Bendix, 1959; McClelland, Baldwin, Bronfenbrenner, & Strodtbeck, 1958; Rosen, Crockett, & Nunn, 1969).

This is the broad social and historical context, dealt with most explicitly and definitively by McClelland (1961) in *The Achieving Society* and updated in McClelland (1971b). It establishes the relevance of efforts to measure and study the development and behavioral effects of achievement motivation. The effort has confronted virtually every important conceptual issue arising in the psychology of personality, motivation, and action. How are individual differences in personality to be conceived within a set of systematic principles that explain human action (Sears, 1951)? How are the two traditionally isolated disciplines of scientific psychology, the correlational approach of those primarily concerned with individual differences, and the experimental approach of those primarily concerned with basic psychological processes, to be unified (Cronbach, 1957)? What form should the specification of the interaction of personality and immediate situation take as we are guided by Kurt Lewin's (1943, 1946) succinct identification of the problem of motivation for psychology, $B = f(P, E)$, especially when our aim is to provide a generally useful conception of the individual, personality–motivation–action, for social science?

These were urgent questions immediately after World War II when my generation of psychologists faced the task of trying to make a *science* of human motivation. On the one hand were the conjectures based on years of clinical observations from Freud to Henry Murray. This provided a fund of insightful hypotheses. On the other hand were systematic extrapolations to human socialization and motivation of principles developed in experimental studies of animals lacking, unfortunately, the empirical evidence concerning human behavior needed to justify their validity.

The most sophisticated guesses about the nature of human personality then combined insights of Freud and subsequent psychoanalysis concerning the primary importance of early childhood in formation of personality and the prevalence of unconsciously motivated behavior. Equally persuasive was evidence and argument from cultural anthropology (Benedict, 1934; Linton, 1945; Mead, 1935) that the content and emphasis of early life experience differed substantially from one society to the next (and by analogy among social groups and families within the same society). As a result, *the basic personality structure* (Kardiner, 1945) might be expected to differ. Later in life, assuming continuity of experience and relative stability in these acquired attributes, there should be important differences in the *national character* of different societies (see Inkeles & Levinson, 1969) and in the *modal personality* of social groups within a society. Also, of course, we would expect individual differences within what a sociologist treats as a relatively homogeneous demographic group, that is, persons alike in the occupational level of the head of the household, the level of education achieved by parents, the family income, the household neighborhood, etc. (Kluckhohn & Murray, 1948). In broad strokes, these are some underlying premises expressed in the 25-year program of research on achievement motivation.

A most persuasive argument that there should be a limited number of common (nomothetic) social motives is one advanced in McClelland's (1951, pp. 341–352) early text on personality. He identified a common set of problems that must be faced early in life in all societies, with possibilities of intermittent reward and punishment for how they are solved that would account for early, stable emotional (affective) conditioning, the formation of relatively general motives, before the full development of language provides a capacity for more refined discriminative learning.

The empirical work on achievement motivation (under that rubric) began in 1947 in McClelland and Atkinson's (1948) search for a valid method of measuring human motivation. As it proceeded, having found an adequate one in thematic apperception (Atkinson & McClelland, 1948; McClelland *et al.*, 1949), the continued analysis of achievement-oriented behavior has literally forced a redefinition of the problem of motivation as traditionally conceived and a reconstruction of the conceptual framework within which to consider the problem of individual differences in motivation and effects on action (Atkinson & Birch, 1970, 1974). As we review key steps in the study of one aspect of personality (achievement-related motivation), the reader should be alert to more general implications. There is a spelling out of the sheer number of separate components to be taken into account in reference to any one kind of motivation. There is a concrete illustration of how what might appear to be inconsistency in observable behavior can be deduced from explicit theory about how stable differences in personality interact with variable features of the immediate environment. There is the clarification of what it means, in observable behavioral terms, to conceive the basic personality of an individual as (in part) a set of relatively general and stable motives which differ in strength, as conjectured earlier particularly by Murray (1938), McClelland (1951), and Maslow (1954). These more generally applicable conceptual advances, the new ways of thinking about motivational aspects of personality and how they influence the dynamics of action, may be of greater significance for the future science of personality–motivation–action than the accumulation of factual knowledge about effects of individual or cultural differences in achievement motivation which has been the substantive focus of study.

EXPERIMENTAL VALIDATION OF THEMATIC APPERCEPTIVE MEASUREMENT OF MOTIVATION

Henry Murray (1938) had argued convincingly that an individual is better understood if one knows about the general effects he is striving to bring about, the strength and pattern of needs or motives, than merely about transsituational consistencies in observable behavior called traits (Allport, 1937). Morgan and Murray (1935) had developed and employed a projective test, the thematic apperceptive method, to allow an individual to express motivation in the content of imaginative stories which could then be coded and interpreted clinically (Murray, 1937, 1938, 1943). Was there any hard evidence that motivation was expressed imaginatively? Very little then. Murray (1933) had discovered that fear, in children, influenced their estimates of the maliciousness of faces cut from magazines. Soon after, Sanford (1936) discovered that abstinence from food had an influence on perceptual–imaginal processes. These suggestive explorations provided the seed for systematic study of the effects of experimentally induced motivation on imaginative processes beginning with hunger (Atkinson & McClelland, 1948; McClelland & Atkinson, 1948).

Hunger was chosen to study the validity of content analysis of imaginative behavior as a possible method of measuring motivation – other than self-descriptively, which has never really worked (McClelland, 1958a, 1971a) – because hunger is one of the very few kinds of motivation that had already been sufficiently studied in lower animals to have an established and generally accepted method by which its strength could be controlled. And a unique opportunity presented itself for systematic control of hunger (time since last meal) among candidates for submarine training without their knowing it was happening. When assembled, some of the sailors hadn't eaten for 16 hours, others had eaten their normal breakfast 4 hours earlier, and a third group, tested early in the afternoon, had eaten lunch an hour earlier. They all wrote 4-min stories in response to each of a set of pictures. The results of this foundation experiment were positive. Certain kinds of imaginative responses related to food–deprivation and/or pursuit of food and eating increased in frequency in the stories as the degree of hunger increased. These imaginative responses could be identified with high coding reliability by independent coders, and the total frequency of these diagnostic symptoms of hunger could, conceivably, be used as an index of individual differences in strength of hunger or need for food. But rather than pursuing that possibility in the context of behavior related to eating, and now with confidence that content analysis of spontaneously produced imaginative stories did hold the promise of being a valid way of measuring different human motives, interest turned to that kind of motivation which, when gratified, produces the feeling of accomplishment or success. "There are many names for this learned drive," Sears (1942) had stated when psychologists were just beginning to learn how to induce "ego involvement" in human subjects by varying instructions given to them concerning experimental tasks to be performed and by controlling whether or not the subject succeeded or failed at some test of skill. Sears (1942) listed terms frequently used in reference to this important kind of human motivation – "pride, craving for superiority, ego-impulse, self-esteem, self-approval, self-assertion; but these terms represent different emphases or different terminological systems, not fundamentally different concepts. Common to all is the notion that the feeling of success depends on the gratification of this drive, and failure results from its frustration [p. 236]."

Borrowing from Murray's suggested list of basic psychogenic needs, David McClelland and his early coworkers tagged this type of motivation "the need for achievement" in their first demonstration that experimental (or situational) control of its strength produced systematic changes in the content of imaginative stories, comparable to those produced by hunger, which could be reliably identified and counted (McClelland, Clark, Roby, Atkinson, 1949). Later they introduced a more neutral synonym, one that would not carry the implication of deprivation, *The Achievement Motive,* as the title of the recently reissued progress report of the first five years of research using this new experimentally validated method of measuring achievement motivation (McClelland, Atkinson, Clark, & Lowell, 1953/1976). By realistically varying experimental conditions immediately preceding the writing of imaginative stories in response to pictures by male college students, McClelland, Clark, Roby, and Atkinson (1949) and McClelland, Atkinson, Clark, and Lowell (1953/1976) were able to identify and to describe, in a coding manual, 11 diagnostic symptoms of the motive to achieve in imaginative behavior. These categories of response had occurred significantly more often following experimental induction of achievement motivation.

In general, achievement imagery takes the form of thoughts about performing some task well, of sometimes being blocked, of trying various means of achieving, and of experiencing joy or sadness contingent upon the outcome of the effort. Together, the sum total of these different kinds of imaginative response in the set of stories written by a particular person constitute that person's *n* Achievement score, presumably an indicator of the strength of achievement motivation in the person at the time (McClelland, Atkinson, Clark, & Lowell, 1953/1976, Chapter 4). The fact that the average *n* Achievement score is higher following experimental induction of achievement motivation than under neutral or relaxed control conditions, in predominantly white male samples from age 10 through college age, was soon replicated at least a dozen times and probably many more since unnoted here (e.g., see Angelina (Brazil), 1955; French, 1955; Haber & Alpert, 1958; Hayashi & Habu (Japan), 1962; Lowell, 1952; McClelland *et al.*, 1949; Ricciuti & Clark, 1954; Veroff, Wilcox, & Atkinson, 1953; Winterbottom, 1958). By 1958, when a variety of different studies of motivation conducted in the first decade of research were collated in *Motives in Fantasy, Action, and Society* (Atkinson, 1958a), there could no longer be much ground for doubt about the validity of thematic apperception as a generally useful method of assessing human motives. For, by then, the effects of arousal of need for affiliation (Atkinson, Heyns, & Veroff, 1954; Shipley & Veroff, 1952), need for power (Veroff, 1957), sexual motivation (Clark, 1952; Mussen & Scodel, 1955), aggressive motivation (Feshbach, 1955), and fear (Walker & Atkinson, 1958) had all been added to the earlier studies of hunger and *n* Achievement to solidify the empirical foundation and generality of the claim that motivation influences the content of thematic apperception. Recent critics of the validity of the thematic apperceptive measure of achievement motive (e.g., Entwistle, 1972;

Klinger, 1966) have avoided addressing the more general conclusion that could be confidently stated as early as 1958 (Atkinson, 1958a):

> . . . disciplined content analysis of thematic apperceptive stories can be considered a generally valid method to be exploited in the investigation of any kind of motivating condition. While not by any means exhausting the list of springs of human action, hunger, achievement, affiliation, power, sex, fear, and aggression represent as comprehensive a list of kinds of motivation studied *by the same method* as can be found anywhere in psychological literature [p. 45].

In recent years, this same method has become the primary tool for studying the conflict produced by "fear of success" (Horner, 1968, 1970, 1974a), perhaps the major complication in the achievement motivation of many women.

A simple summary of the degree of objectivity (coding reliability) achieved by investigators who have taken time to learn the skill with training materials provided by Smith and Feld (1958) can be reported. In 48 published studies representing the mainstream of work collated by Feld and Smith (1958) and later included in Atkinson and Feather (1966) and Atkinson and Raynor (1974), the median scoring reliability for *n* Achievement score was .89 and the upper limit of the lowest quartile was .85. That probably ought to be established as the minimum standard for publication of research. Among 38 Michigan graduate students (1971–1974), who routinely learned the skill as part of their training in social motivation, the median scoring reliability for *n* Achievement was .87, and again the lowest quartile, .85. The scorings of novice coders were compared with that of a consensus of 5 experts on the 5-story protocols of 22 subjects. The median agreement in scoring achievement imagery, the basic scoring decision, was 86% among these students.

This skill is the sine qua non of successful research. When one can code imaginative thought in a way that yields scores correlating .90 or better with the consensus of experts, the concept of achievement motive as defined in the published scoring manual by McClelland *et al.* (1953/1976) and in Atkinson (1958) has been learned, and there is 81% or more common variance in the distributions of scores by experts and novice representing individual differences in strength of motivation. If one's coding reliability (checked against that of another expert) is only .75, there is only 56% in common variance. The subjects who wrote the stories are now being ordered quite differently according to inferred strength of motivation. With scoring reliability that low, one is only about 70% (56/81) as skillful or technically competent as one could be and *should* be to use the technique at all.

It is well known that the most frequent cause of airplane accidents is not some deficiency in the theory of aerodynamics, or inadequacy of the equipment, but pilot error. I think the same can be said, but rarely is, of psychological research.

The most frequent cause of meaningless or negative results in empirical research is not deficiency in theory, or methodology, but lack of experimental skill and judgment in the investigator. In published research on achievement motivation, the level of scientific competence brought to an inquiry can often be inferred from the coding reliability reported and the description of how it was obtained.

We shall hold until the end a definitive reply to the rather constant skepticism concerning the validity of TAT *n* Achievement on grounds of its low internal consistency (or split-half) reliability (e.g., Entwistle, 1972), for it involves reference to computer simulation of thematic apperceptive expression of motivation guided by the theory of motivation developed through continued use of it for 25 years in the face of that skepticism. Here, let it suffice to say that in 1950, when two equivalent three-picture forms were constructed as the first order of business and were administered to a group of college men on one occasion (in a Latin Square design so as to separate the effects of pictures and serial location), the product moment correlation of the two sets of *n* Achievement scores was a respectable .64 ($N = 32$) and the percentage agreement in categorizing subjects as high or low relative to the median score on each form was 78.1% (Atkinson, 1950).[1] When these same two forms were administered one week apart to a different group of male college students by Lowell (reported in McClelland *et al.*, 1953/1976, Chapter 7), the product moment correlation dropped dramatically to .22 ($N = 40$) but the extent of high–low agreement between forms was essentially the same, 72.5%. A little simple arithmetic suggested that 5.6% of 40 subjects (2.24 persons) had changed their position relative to the median score over that interval of time. It seemed then, and still does, that a number of the assumptions that are unquestioned in traditional psychometrics (e.g., the subject is unchanged by a first test; independence of error variances; homoscedasticity) and in the use of parametric statistics (that there is a unit of measurement in the index employed) are unwarranted with TAT *n* Achievement. So conventional practice in research has usually settled for high–low discrimination among subjects at the median score with the presumption that the crude but experimentally validated measuring instrument would correctly discern the relative strength of motive correctly in about 75% of the

[1] The coefficient alpha, α, was not introduced until a year later by Cronbach (1951) as the mean of all possible split-half coefficients and recommended as a best estimate of internal consistency reliability. It was recently recalculated for scores obtained using all 8 pictures initially included in the original study, and listed in its appendix, and also for the 6 pictures represented in the equivalent form after two lacking validity were eliminated. The values of α were .57 and .64, respectively, and not .37 as estimated by Entwistle (1972) from inspection of cell means in the published table of the Latin Square. The α of .64 is exactly equivalent to the actual split-half reliability of the two equivalent forms.

cases. That, it has turned out, is more than sufficiently adequate measurement of individual differences in *n* Achievement to have allowed substantial theoretical advance. Another early and thorough restudy of both split-half and retest reliability by Haber and Alpert (1958) sustained this original conclusion about the adequacy of the tool in skillful hands.

Right from the outset, there was a second kind of evidence to indicate the validity of TAT *n* Achievement as a measure of motivation. McClelland and Liberman (1949) found that individual differences in *n* Achievement were related to perceptual recognition of achievement-related words. Lowell (1952) found that college men who scored high in *n* Achievement showed higher level of performance on both verbal and arithmetic tasks, even when independently measured differences in aptitude were taken into account. And soon there was comparable evidence from studies using the experimentally validated measures of *n* Affiliation and *n* Power. Atkinson, Heyns, and Veroff (1954) found that those scoring high in TAT *n* Affiliation were more often described as *approval seeking* by fraternity brothers who had a good observational basis for the judgement. Those high in *n* Affiliation also more frequently contacted relatives by telephone and correspondence (Lansing & Heyns, 1959) than those scoring low. Atkinson and Walker (1956) found that college men high in *n* Affiliation showed greater perceptual sensitivity to faces than those scoring low, when a tachistoscope flashed four objects (only one a human face) on a screen so rapidly that no one could identify any of the objects and subjects merely had to indicate which figure "stood out the most" or was "most clear" to them. Veroff (1957) found that college males scoring high in *n* Power expressed it sufficiently in their classroom behavior to be more often rated by their instructor as argumentive and more frequently trying to convince others than those scoring low in *n* Power. Elizabeth French (1956), among the first to classify subjects simultaneously as high or low on two motives, *n* Achievement and *n* Affiliation, found motivational selectivity in choice of a work partner. Those high in *n* Achievement but low in *n* Affiliation preferred a successful stranger to an unsuccessful friend, the latter being preferred by those low in *n* Achievement but high in *n* Affiliation.

This is a small illustrative sample of the kind of empirical evidence, much of it collated in *The Achievement Motive* (McClelland, Atkinson, Clark, & Lowell, 1953/1976), *Motives in Fantasy, Action, and Society* (Atkinson, 1958), and *The Anatomy of Achievement Motivation* (Heckhausen, 1967), that established confidence that thematic apperceptive measures of *n* Achievement, *n* Affiliation, and *n* Power were valid indicators not only of situationally induced motivation but of individual differences in personality, that is, individual differences in strength of achievement motive, or affiliative motive, or power motive, etc., that are also expressed in perceptual and instrumental behavior.

PRELIMINARY EVIDENCE OF INTERACTION OF PERSONALITY AND SITUATIONAL DETERMINANTS OF MOTIVATION

What else was learned from some of the earliest studies of effects of individual differences in *n* Achievement (e.g., Atkinson, 1953; Moulton, Raphelson, Kristofferson, & Atkinson, 1958; Raphelson, 1957)? The results showed two things: that the motivational state must involve an interaction of personality disposition and immediate situational factors, and that in an achievement situation, motivational tendencies having exactly opposite behavioral implications were apparently being aroused.

The interaction of personality and situation was most clearly seen when the classic Zeigarnik experiment concerned with the effect of interruption on recall was conducted under three experimental conditions: when subjects were *relaxed* because the importance of the tasks was explicitly minimized by instructions; when subjects were *task oriented,* being instructed how to perform the tasks with no further embellishments; when subjects were explicitly *achievement oriented* by instructions that emphasized the importance of the "tests" to be given and encouraged everyone to do his best. As shown in Figure 1, those classified high in *n* Achievement increased significantly in recall of interrupted tasks (then interpreted as evidence of how strongly motivated they were to complete them) as the instructions and other situational cues increased the likelihood that subjects would perceive completion as an achievement, a personal success, and interruption as a failure. Those classified low in *n* Achievement displayed a diametrically opposite trend, recalling fewer incompleted tasks as the perception of that event as failure became more explicit. Moulton *et al.* (1958) reported comparable trends across treatments in a study of perceptual sensitivity to words connoting failure. We soon began to appreciate that the behavioral effects of individual differences in anxiety, being studied by Mandler and Sarason (1952) at Yale, and by Taylor and Spence (1952) at Iowa, were exactly opposite to those of differential achievement motivation across treatments. Those scoring high in anxiety, measured by self-descriptive tests, behaved like those scoring low in *n* Achievement measured by content analysis of imaginative behavior, and vice versa. This initial evidence of interaction of personality and situation in behavioral expression of achievement motivation (see Figure 1) has been repeatedly confirmed in a quarter of a century of experimental study of personality, for example, in studies of the effects of differential anxiety (Spielberger, 1966) as well, and most recently in evidence of how instructions which control the attribution process interact with individual differences in achievement motivation (Weiner, 1974b).

Alfred Raphelson (1957) brought the diagnostic tests of *n* Achievement and of Test Anxiety and Manifest Anxiety together for the first time. His major interest was skin conductance, an indicator of anxiety, in an achievement-oriented test situation when subjects were confronted with a stressful perceptual–motor task.

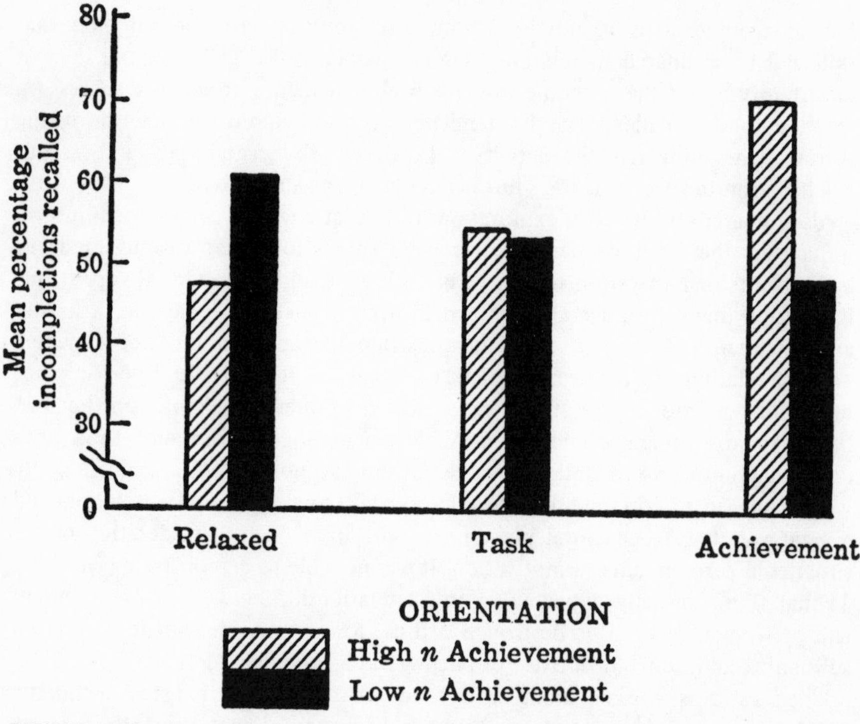

FIGURE 1 Mean percentage of interrupted tasks recalled by college males with high and low *n* Achievement scores following performance under three different experimental conditions. (From Atkinson, 1950).

The pattern of results for those scoring high in *n* Achievement corresponded to the pattern for those scoring low in anxiety. The pattern for those scoring low in *n* Achievement corresponded to that of those scoring high in anxiety. When those scoring both low in *n* Achievement and high in Test Anxiety (called "anxious") were compared with those scoring both high in *n* Achievement and low in Test Anxiety (called "nonanxious"), the difference was most clearcut.

We soon rejected the idea that *n* Achievement and Test Anxiety were simply measures of the same variable. We had evidence of diametrically opposite behavioral trends across experimental treatments of those scoring high and low in *n* Achievement and mirror image trends in the literature on anxiety. In addition, many studies following Raphelson's and using diagnostic measures of both motives (as became standard practice at Michigan) failed to produce any consistent correlation between *n* Achievement and Test Anxiety when both were diagnosed under neutral conditions (Atkinson & Feather, 1966, p. 341). This implied two variables which apparently influence achievement-related behavior, and its emotional concomitants, in diametrically opposite ways. Whenever an individual undertakes an activity assuming responsibility for the outcome, that skill will be evaluated in relation to some standard of excellence, and there is uncertainty about the outcome, there is both a tendency to achieve success (in reaction to the challenge) and a tendency to avoid failure (in reaction to the threat). One motivates the activity. The other produces anxiety and, as our results began to suggest, is the source of resistance to the activity.

Also apparent in the early explorations of how strength of achievement motive influenced the level of performance were suggestions that various kinds or components of motivation for the same task were additive and that very strong motivation might produce a decrement in performance. For example, Atkinson and Reitman (1956) wanted to demonstrate that one should not expect a positive relationship between strength of achievement motive and performance under all conditions. The study was designed to quell the skepticism that had begun to arise when studies of *n* Achievement and performance took on a now-you-see-it-now-you-don't character in the psychological literature as many workers began to correlate TAT *n* Achievement scores with grades in school and a great variety of behavioral phenomena with little or no consideration of the situational determinants of motivation. It was possible to demonstrate (see Table 1) that the "normally expected" positive relationship between *n* Achievement and performance could be destroyed if those low in *n* Achievement were given substantial additional incentives for putting out a good deal of effort.

When subjects worked alone in a room on complex, three-step arithmetic problems presented as a test of ability (achievement orientation), there was a significant positive relationship between performance and *n* Achievement. It, presumably, was the major source of the strength of the tendency to perform the task. But in a so-called multi-incentive condition, the same achievement-orienting instructions were used but subjects worked in a coactive, competitive group setting with two roving proctors who deliberately looked into the eyes of

TABLE 1
Arithmetic Performance (14 min) as a Function of Achievement Motive and Experimental Condition[a]

	Achievement-orientation (alone)				Multiincentive (coacting group)			
Achievement motive	*N*		Attempted	Correct	*N*		Attempted	Correct
High	21	*M*	78.1	71.6	24	*M*	67.1	60.3
Low	30	*M*	60.3	55.5	21	*M*	69.1	60.1
Difference (H–L)			17.8	16.1			−2.0	.2
			$p<.01$	.01			n.s.	n.s.

[a]From Atkinson and Reitman (1956). Copyright 1956 by the American Psychological Association. Reproduced by permission.

anyone who did not work (trying to act like agents of social approval/disapproval). In addition, a substantial monetary prize was offered for the best performance. In conceiving the experiment, it was presumed that those highly motivated to achieve might be working near their upper limit of performance when alone and could therefore not improve much even with additional incentives. On the other hand, those low in *n* Achievement would have, it was presumed, the additive tendency to work for social approval and to work for the monetary prize. Thus it was expected and found that there would be less difference in level of performance attributable to the difference in *n* Achievement in the multi-incentive condition. McKeachie (1961) found a similar result comparing level of performance under different classroom atmospheres.

This demonstration that the expected positive relationship could be experimentally destroyed, that it was not a transsituational phenomenon but dependent upon the incentive character of the situation, was clear enough. In addition, there was the suggestion of the possibility of an overmotivation-produced decrement among those high in *n* Achievement, a point to which we shall later return. Other experiments of this kind, documenting the interaction of personality and situation, were accomplished by French (1955), and Atkinson and Raphelson (1956), and by McKeachie (1961) in the college classroom.

A THEORY OF ACHIEVEMENT MOTIVATION

Initial Formulation for a Simple Task (1957–1966)

By the late 1950s, it had become apparent that developments in the mathematical theory of decision making provided a very precise and coherent statement of the kind of cognitive theory of motivation worked out earlier, but less formally by Edward Tolman (1951), Kurt Lewin (1938), and Cartwright and Festinger (1943), and then being employed by Julian Rotter (1954) in the context of social learning and by us to interpret the joint effect of personality and the immediate situation on achievement motivation (Atkinson, 1954; Feather, 1959). All conceived an individual's actions to be determined by expectations concerning different kinds of rewarding or punishing consequences of various alternative activities and the importance or value to the individual of these expected consequences. W. Edwards (1954) reviewed the history of decision theory, concluding with a formulation that emphasized the subjective nature of the expectancy, or feeling of certainty, that an activity would produce a certain consequence (as distinct from objective evidence of its likelihood) and the subjective nature of the attractiveness or repulsiveness of various consequences, the subjective value as distinct from objective evidence of value. This model of decision among alternatives stated that individuals act so as to maximize the *subjectively expected utility* (SEU) where for each alternative activity available to them in some setting,

$$\mathrm{SEU} = P_1 U_1 + P_2 U_2 + \cdots + P_n U_n,$$

where there are n possible consequences of that course of action, the first consequence has utility (U_1), or valence (V_{a_1}) to use the equivalent Lewinian term for the attractiveness of an event, and subjective probability P_1, that is, a strength of expectancy, or degree of certainty, represented as a probability from 0 to 1.00. This formulation clearly captured the generally accepted premise of Tolman and Lewin that the environment which has an impact on how one behaves is the *psychological environment,* the immediate situation as it is perceived and experienced subjectively by the individual in terms of available actions and degree of certainty of various consequences that are anticipated, expected, or imagined likely to happen, given the past experience of the individual in similar circumstances.

Guided by this conception, one can think of the overall strength of an inclination or tendency to undertake a particular task or activity (corresponding to SEU) to be the sum of various component motivational tendencies such as tendency to achieve success (e.g., corresponding to $P_1 U_1$), plus tendency to gain approval (e.g., corresponding to $P_2 U_2$), and so on. Presumably, experimental manipulations of the nature of the situation at the time of task performance (e.g., working alone versus in a proctored competitive group) and of the content of instructions, explicitly designed to relax or to achievement orient a subject, could be conceived as influencing the subject's cognitive expectations of consequences (e.g., successful achievement, approval, money, etc.). The measurement of individual differences in strength of motives to achieve, to affiliate, etc. on the other hand, could be conceived as tapping differences in the subjective value, utility, or valence (all equivalent terms) of achievement, affiliation, and other kinds of consequence among different individuals (Atkinson, 1958b, c). Winterbottom (1953, 1958), in finding a relationship between *n* Achievement and early parental emphasis on rewarding independent accomplishment, also had discovered that, according to teachers' reports, ten-year-olds high in *n* Achievement got greater pleasure out of success than those scoring low.

The final clue needed to formulate a simple theory of achievement motivation came, unexpectedly, from a study mainly designed to see how the level of performance of college women on two very different kinds of tasks (simply drawing *X*s inside of circles and solving complicated arithmetic problems) would be influenced by experimental variation in the value of a monetary incentive offered ($1.25 or $2.50) and in the actual probability of winning one (Atkinson, 1958c). Each subject was told the number of other persons with whom she was competing and the number of monetary prizes that would be awarded contingent on the comparative level of performance. For example, some subjects were instructed that they were one of a randomly selected group of 4 and that $2.50

would be awarded to the 3 highest scorers in the group, others that they were one of 20 and the highest scorer would win $1.25, etc.

The result (see Figure 2) indicated that both the monetary incentive and the strength of expectancy (or probability) of winning had a significant effect on the level of performance. There was no surprise in finding evidence of greater effort to win $2.50 than $1.25. But what did it mean to find that effort as expressed in the level of performance peaked when the probability of winning was 1/2 or .50?

At just about the same time, McClelland's (1955) interest in the calculated risk taking he found associated with successful entrepreneurial activity and which he suspected to be a symptom of achievement motivation led him to study the

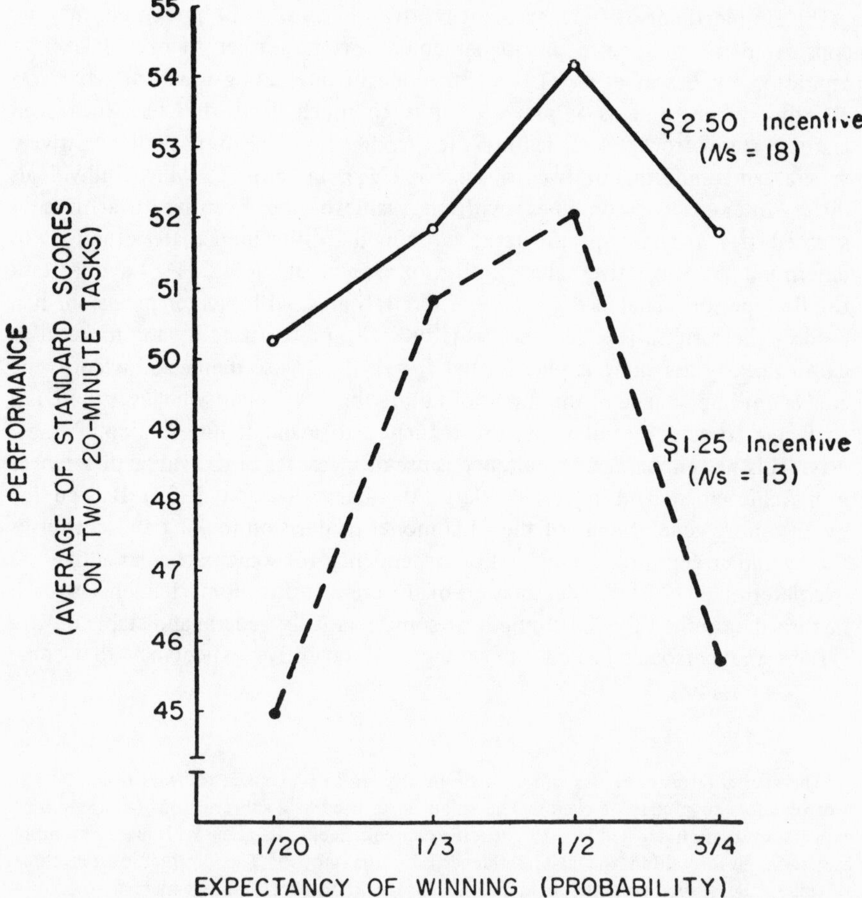

FIGURE 2 Motivation directly expressed in level of performance of college women as a function of monetary incentive and expectancy of winning (probability). (From Atkinson, 1958c. Copyright 1958 by Litton Educational Publishing, Inc. Reprinted by permission of D. Van Nostrand Company.)

risk-taking behavior of children in a simple ring-toss game (McClelland, 1958b). He found that children designated highly motivated to achieve preferred shooting from intermediate distances rather than from very close to the peg or very far back. At that point, everything fell into place if it were assumed that the college women who worked hardest when probability of winning was 1/2 or .50 were motivated not only by the value of the monetary incentive as such, but also to win, to achieve, to succeed in the competitive task and that the incentive value of success (i.e., of achievement per se) was greater the lower the chance of winning. The general idea, that attractiveness of success is greater the more difficult a task, had been proposed much earlier by Lewin, Dembo, Festinger, and Sears (1944).

The simple theory of achievement motivation, now to be presented, may be considered a much more precise statement of the earlier theory of level of aspiration by Lewin *et al.* (1944). Its value in integrating much of what was already known, and as a heuristic guide to much more that has since been learned, stems from several features. It specifies how the strength of a relatively general and enduring motive to achieve (M_S), in terms of which individuals differ, interacts (or combines) with the value of the incentive to achieve or succeed (I_s) in some specific task, as defined by the immediate situation, to determine the subjective value, utility, or valence of success (V_{a_s}) at that task for that person. That is $V_{a_s} = M_S \times I_s$.[2] It states, with greater precision than before, the assumption that success is typically more attractive the more difficult a task by assuming explicitly that $I_s = 1 - P_s$. It also then acknowledges the equivalent importance of the threat of failure that is inherent whenever there is a challenge to achieve and treats the tendency to avoid failure in a comparable way. This has encouraged simultaneous use of measures of individual differences in *n* Achievement and in Test Anxiety (Mandler & Sarason, 1952). It is guided by the more general logic of the SEU model of decision making and conceives the overall strength of the inclination or tendency for some particular activity as overdetermined, i.e., as a summation of different motivational tendencies, each in turn determined by the strength of some relatively general and stable motive (M) in the personality, and the strength of cognitive expectancy that some

[2] The capital letter used as a subscript on motive, in this case M_S, is meant to imply that motive refers to a class of events. The small letter used as a subscript on the strength of expectancy that an act will lead to a specific consequence, in this case P_s, is meant to imply a specific event within the class influenced by the motive. The product of the three variables, the strength of the tendency to engage in the act that is expected to have a specific consequence, also has a small letter, in this case T_s, to imply, again, a specific action and outcome. As distinct from *drive* in S–R behavior theory, which is completely nonspecific in its influence, motive is conceived as a relatively nonspecific influence, one that has a selective or directional effect favoring a particular class of behavioral events.

activity will produce an instance of that kind of consequence (P), and the incentive value (I) of the specific consequence (situation).

Perhaps, for some students of personality, the simple theory of achievement motivation represents a first exposure to the coherence and deductive potentiality of a mathematic model of motivation. After comprehending what the theory stated algebraically implies, one should attempt to say the same thing with words to appreciate both the parsimony and specificity achieved by mathematical models of empirical phenomena in science. This one provides a succinct and coherent way of thinking about achievement motivation.[3]

The Tendency to Achieve Success

It was assumed that the strength of the tendency to achieve success (T_s), which is expressed in the interest, effort, and involvement of an individual in some particular task, is a multiplicative function of three variables: motive to achieve success (M_S), conceived as a relatively general and stable disposition of personality; and two variables which represent the effect of the immediate environment – the strength of expectancy (or subjective probability) that performance of the task will be successful (P_s), and the relative attractiveness of success at that particular activity, which we call the incentive value of success (I_s). In other words,

$$T_s = M_S \times P_s \times I_s,$$

following the order of the more general terms in the programmatic equation,

$$B = f(P,E);\text{ or } T_s = P_s \times (M_S \times I_s) = P_s \times V_{a_s} \text{ or } P_s \times U_s$$

to show more directly the correspondence with the earlier Lewinian and SEU models of decision making. Given the further assumption that the attractiveness of success is greater the more difficult the task, $I_s = 1 - P_s$ (where $1 - P_s$ is also equivalent to probability of failure (P_f) since $P_s + P_f = 1.00$), one may describe the implications graphically as in Figures 3 and 4.

Figure 3 shows the inverse relationship between P_s and I_s in a simple ring-toss game where the average estimated P_s by one group of subjects decreases as distance from the peg increases and the average estimate of a recommended monetary prize for success at each distance (symbolic of the achievement) by an

[3] One must distinguish the use of a mathematical model as a way of thinking precisely and coherently about the complexities of some phenomenon from the problem of exact measurement and use of statistics in research design. One may be way ahead in the former while lagging far behind, as is so generally true in psychology, in the latter. One may seldom achieve the same precision in testing a hypothesis empirically (measurement) that one can achieve in the conception from which that hypothesis is deduced. The aim of basic science is to enhance the conception in a way that allows its validity to be subject to at least a weak empirical test.

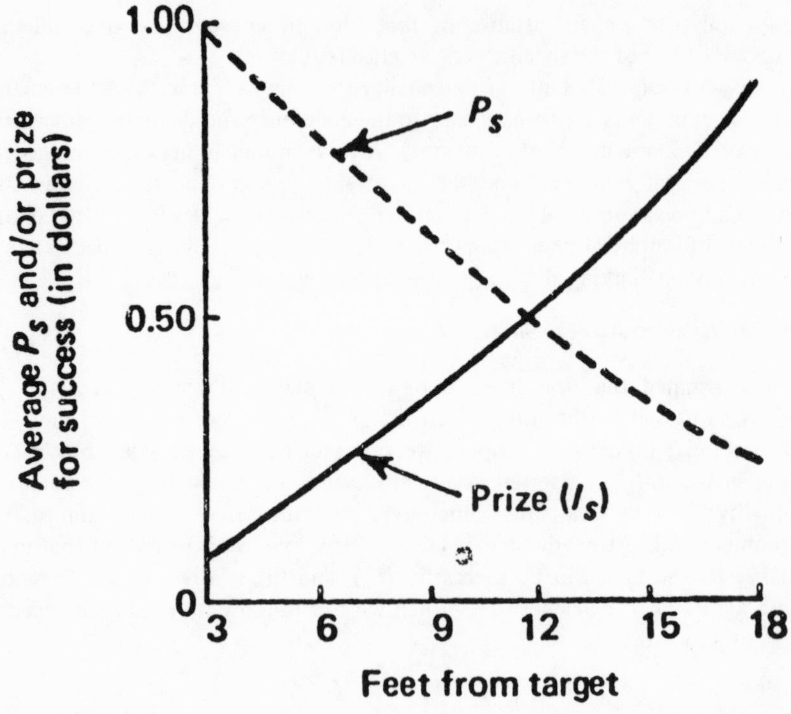

FIGURE 3 Estimated probability of success (P_S) and prize recommended for success (I_S) by two different groups of college men ($N = 10$) for a ring-toss game. (From Litwin, 1958.)

independent group of subjects increases (Litwin, 1958, 1966). The same pattern has been repeatedly shown in the recent research relating attribution theory to achievement motivation (Weiner, 1974a, p. 36, 1974b, p. 63).

Figure 4 shows (a) that the strength of motivation to achieve at simple activities which differ in difficulty will typically be strongest where $P_s = .50$, a moderately difficult task, and weakest where the task is very easy ($P_s = .90$) or very difficult ($P_s = .10$); and (b) that holding the difficulty of the task constant, strength of motivation to achieve is stronger, the stronger the motive to achieve (M_S) in the individual. This summarizes the results of a number of studies which have shown stronger preference for intermediate risk or moderate difficulty among persons scoring high in *n* Achievement (Atkinson & Feather, 1966; Hamilton, 1974; Heckhausen, 1968). And it provides a foundation for the general hypothesis of stronger motivation when *n* Achievement is strong but suggests that differences in strength of motivation (that is, T_s) attributable to personality (M_S) may be very small, even negligible, when tasks are either very easy or very difficult. This suggests that if our measures of individual differences are relatively crude, rather

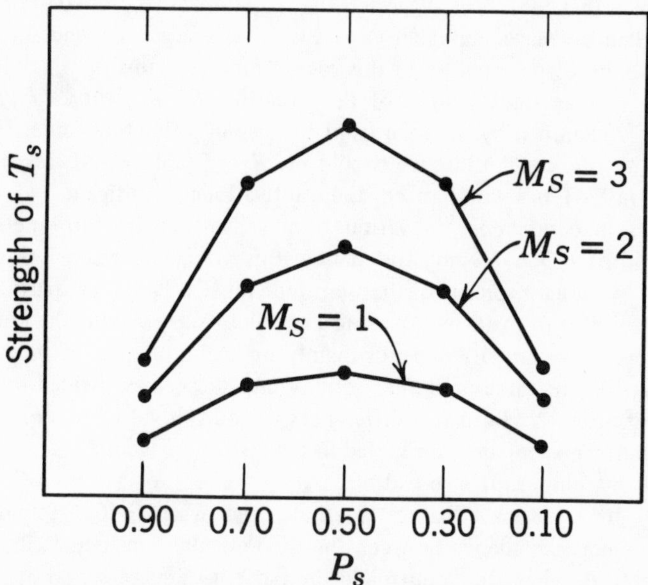

FIGURE 4 Graphic representation assuming that $T_S = M_S \times P_S \times I_S$ and that $I_S = 1–P_S$, when M_S = 1, 2, and 3. (From Atkinson & Feather, 1966, p. 329.)

than highly precise and reliable, one should then expect to find observed differences in level of performance positively related to individual differences in TAT *n* Achievement, for example, only when the theoretically expected difference in strength of motivation is very substantial, viz., where P_s is near .50 for all individuals and the difference between persons in M_S is also quite substantial. Many empirical studies undertaken both before and since this scheme was first published (Atkinson, 1957, 1964, Chapter 9, 1965; Atkinson & Feather, 1966) have failed to consider the degree of difficulty of the task or even the probable range of differences in strength of motive (M_S) represented in the particular population studied. Still another sound reason for not always expecting a positive relationship between *n* Achievement and performance will be spelled out in the next section.

Is subjective probability of success the same for all individuals confronting the same task? Is P_s merely a function of distance from the peg in a ring-toss game or from the cup in a golf putting contest no matter who are the players? Obviously not. For most duffer golfers, $P_s = .50$ about 3 to 5 feet from the cup. For a professional golfer, P_s at that distance is probably .95 or better. The professional's moderately difficult putt, where $P_s = .50$, is probably a 10 or 12 footer.

Generalize that idea. It is suggested that P_s (subjective probability of success) like V_{a_s} (subjective value, valence, or utility of success) depends in part upon some attribute of personality, in this case *ability,* in terms of which individuals differ, as well as some feature of the situation, *the difficulty of the task* as defined, for example, by distance from the peg in a ring-toss game. Thus, to be complete in our conception, we should say $P_s = f$ (ability and task difficulty). Moulton (1974) has emphasized the motivational significance of individual differences in *competence* in various domains of activity (arithmetic, sports, music). Morris (1966) demonstrated how this affects vocational choice. More precisely, we might presume that an individual's P_s for a particular task, throwing a ringer from 10 feet, passing a calculus exam, making the honor roll at college, and so on, usually depends mainly upon the number of times a person has engaged in the same or similar activity and succeeded, divided by the sheer number of attempts. Both real differences in ability (and effects of motivation on prior performance) are represented in the history of success.

Guided by this simple equation, P_s = Number of successes/Number of attempts, Jones, Rock, Shaver, Goethals, and Ward (1968) found a rather remarkable correspondence between the theoretically expected P_s and the average reported P_s when they controlled the pattern of successes so that each of 2 groups of subjects would end with 50% success. One group did particularly well early in the series of trials and the other group did well later. Weiner (1970, 1972, 1974a) has emphasized the determinative role of an individual's causal attributional processes in the case of both V_{a_s} and P_s in the new effort to transcend simple frequency of association and to achieve a more comprehensive cognitive theory of motivation.

The Tendency to Avoid Failure

It is assumed that the strength of tendency to avoid failure (T_f) is a multiplicative function of the strength of motive to avoid failure (M_F), the subjective probability of failure (P_f, where $P_f = 1{-}P_s$), and the incentive value of failure (I_f). Failure hurts. The incentive value is negative, and the hurt (shame, embarrassment, discouragement) is greater the easier the task at which one fails. So, $I_f = -P_s$. Weiner and Kukla (1970) find that the degree to which success and failure are perceived as attributable to internal factors (ability and effort) rather than to external factors, when plotted in relation to information about percentage of others who succeed at a task, corresponds almost exactly to the assumed magnitude of I_s and I_f in relation to P_s and may be considered the reason that pride in success (I_s) and shame in failure (I_f) vary, as they do, in relation to P_s.

The implications of this conception of the determinants of tendency to avoid failure are shown graphically in Figure 5. There are two important things to note. First, since the incentive value of failure is negative, so also is the strength of tendency to avoid failure negative. The expectancy that an act may produce a negative, painful consequence should *always* produce a tendency *not* to perform

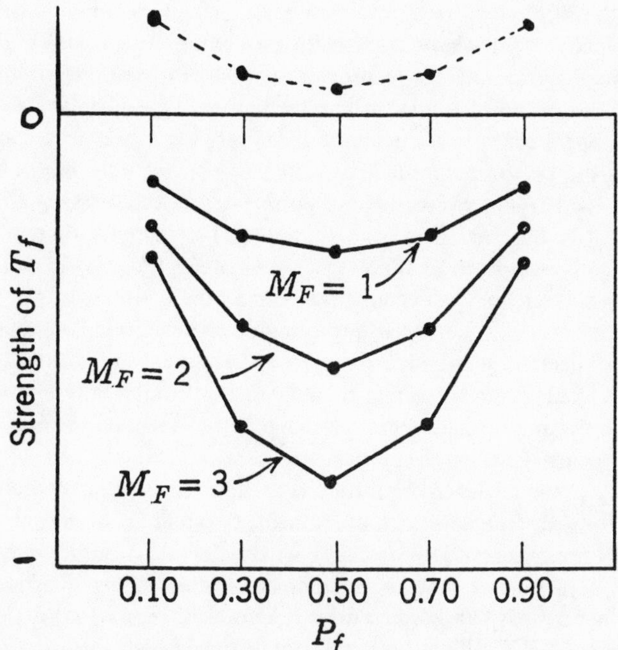

FIGURE 5 Graphic representation of assuming that $T_f = M_F \times P_f \times I_f$, that $P_s + P_f = 1.00$, and that $I_f = -P_s$, when $M_F = 1, 2,$ and 3. The value of T_f is always negative implying *resistance* that must be overcome by addition of some extrinsic tendency (if not a stronger T_s). Here it is assumed that $T_s = 0$ and that a constant T_{ext} for all levels of difficulty overcomes resistance for the activities as shown in the hatched curve.

the act, an inhibitory tendency. Later, in *The Dynamics of Action* (Atkinson & Birch, 1970), we refer to this as a *negaction* tendency. The tendency to avoid failure opposes, resists, dampens, subtracts from the strength of tendency to achieve success (when added to it algebraically) to produce a weaker resultant tendency to achieve ($T_{Res} = T_s - T_f$). This is why the strength of T_f is graphically portrayed as resistance to achievement-oriented activity, as having negative strength, in Figure 5.

Secondly, we see that resistance to achievement-oriented activity, the tendency to avoid failure that is accompanied by anxiety or dread of failing, is also greatest where $P_s = .50$ and weakest when the task is either very easy ($P_s = .90$, so $P_f = .10$) or very difficult ($P_s = .10$, so $P_f = .90$).

Given only a motive to avoid failure (a disposition to be anxious about failure), there is no impetus to action. One merely resists undertaking any activity when evaluation of performance by the self (or others) poses the threat of failure. The resistance is weakest when the probability of success is very high and failure very unlikely, and when the probability of success is very low. In the latter case, the task is so difficult that failure is virtually assured and the cause for embarrassment or self-blame is virtually eliminated. This means that if there were no motive to achieve (M_S) to provide positive motivation to overcome the resistance, it should require some other kind of positive incentive (social approval for cooperation, or a monetary incentive, etc.) and a corresponding motive within the person to produce a sufficiently strong *extrinsic tendency* to undertake the activity to overcome the resistance. In this case, where T_{Res} = $(T_s - T_f)$ is negative because there is no T_s, the total strength of the tendency for an activity (T_a) is composed as follows: $T_a = (T_s - T_f) + T_{ext}$, where T_{ext} (any so-called extrinsic tendency) depends upon some of the effects of one or more such incentives as money or social approval for merely trying, cooperating or doing what is expected by one's reference group in a social situation.

In Figure 5, to illustrate the effect of resistance attributable to a tendency to avoid failure on normal achievement-related activity, we have assumed that the person expects sufficient social approval for merely trying any one of the tasks (a constant T_{ext} for all levels of difficulty), that resistance is overcome even where it is strongest. But note, the strength of T_a (an inclination to do the task for some extrinsic "reason") is strongest where the task is either very easy or very difficult. This means that given a choice, the person in question should prefer either a very easy task (set a very low level of aspiration) or, paradoxically, prefer a very difficult task (set an unrealistically high level of aspiration). To the extent that the person can be cajoled into performing a task in the face of resistance attributable to threat of failure, the level of performance should be most dampened (lowest) where the task is one of moderate difficulty.

The Relative Strength of Motives to Achieve Success and to Avoid Failure

It should be apparent, comparing Figures 4 and 5, that if M_S and M_F are equally strong (both equal 1 or both equal 2), then $T_{Res} = T_s - T_f = 0$, and what happens should depend entirely upon the nature and strength of extrinsic incentives in the situation for so-called achievement-related activities.

When $M_S > M_F$ (for example, if $M_S = 3$ and $M_F = 1$), then the resultant tendency (T_{Res}) is positive and its strength, in relation to P_s, corresponds exactly to the curve for $M_S = 2$ in Figure 4. This can be shown by stating the theory of achievement motivation in its simplest algebraic form:

$$T_a = T_{Res} + T_{ext} \quad (1)$$

$$T_a = (T_s - T_f) + T_{ext} \quad (2)$$

$$T_a = (M_S \cdot P_s \cdot I_s) + (M_F \cdot P_f \cdot I_f) + T_{ext} \quad (3)$$

But since

$$I_s = 1 - P_s, P_f = 1 - P_s, \text{ and } I_f = -P_s,$$

$$T_a = (M_S \cdot P_s \cdot 1 - P_s) - (M_F \cdot 1 - P_s \cdot P_s) + T_{ext} \quad (4)$$

$$T_a = (M_S - M_F)(P_s \cdot 1 - P_s) + T_{ext} \quad (5)$$

If we give M_S and M_F the values of 3 and 1 in (5), and ignore T_{ext}, we recover the positive bell-shaped curve for $M_S = 2$ in Figure 4.

When $M_F > M_S$ (for example, $M_S = 1$ and $M_F = 2$), the resultant tendency to achieve (T_{Res}) is negative and its strength, in relation to P_s, corresponds exactly to the curve for $M_f = 1$ in Figure 5. Again, one may make the appropriate assignment of values in Eq. (5), and ignore T_{ext}, to see this.

What assumption should be made about the strength of T_{ext}? This is a question that requires considerably more research attention than it has been given. In the absence of contrary knowledge, and for simplicity in deductive use of this theory, it has typically been assumed that T_{ext} is constant across tasks which differ in difficulty and that, *on the average,* T_{ext} is not different among a group of persons in whom $M_S > M_F$ and a group in whom $M_F > M_S$. But both are questionable assumptions.

Heckhausen (1968) and Hamilton (1974) have correctly noted that the most preferred task by those relatively high in *n* Achievement typically has a P_s somewhat lower than .50 and suggest this implies the need for some change in the assumed relation between I_s and P_s to accommodate the fact. Perhaps they are correct, but it seems that since more social approval typically accompanies merely trying a very difficult task than an easy one (irrespective of outcome), more refined experimentation is needed concerning the trend line of T_{ext} in relation to P_s which, for simplicitly and in the absence of much evidence, we have treated as constant across tasks. When a really substantial effort has been made to achieve the "ideal case" of achievement motivation, one in which $T_{ext} = 0$, a number of times, and should the peak of preference continue to fall somewhat below .50, then some assumption of the theory must give way to a more useful one that will accommodate other related facts as well.[4]

In empirical research with male college students, TAT *n* Achievement provides the measure of M_S and the Mandler–Sarason Test Anxiety Questionnaire (Mandler & Cowen, 1958; Mandler & Sarason, 1952) or Alpert–Haber (1960) Debilitating Anxiety Scale have provided the most consistently useful measures of M_F. In Germany, Heckhausen (1963, 1967) has obtained measures of both hope of success and fear of failure from thematic apperception. Typically, subjects are classified high or low relative to the median score of the sample studied, and results are presented for subgroups who differ in resultant achieve-

[4] Both of these suggestions are probably premature. The new and more comprehensive conception of the dynamics of action, presented later in the chapter, is just beginning to be applied to the details of evidence concerning achievement-oriented activity as this is written. Revelle and Michaels (1976) have argued that preference for tasks having P_S lower than .50 can be attributed to the differential effects of success and failure on persisting motivational tendencies in a series of trials. And Blankenship (1976) has done computer simulations of risk preference based on dynamics of action which show that some degree of substitution among different activities can also have this effect. We are beginning to learn that the whole theory of motivation must be explicitly stated and taken into account in reference to any behavioral phenomenon.

TABLE 2

Effect of Individual Differences in *n* Achievement and Test Anxiety on Risk-Taking Preference, Persistence in an Examination, and Performance on Examination (Subjects are classified in terms of each motive separately and simultaneously in terms of both motives.)[a]

	Above combined group median (%)					
	N	Prefer intermediate risk (%)	*N*	Persistence on exam (%)	*N*	Performance on exam (%)
n Achievement						
High	(23)	61	(25)	60	(25)	64
Low	(22)	36	(19)	32	(19)	32
		$p<.04$		$p<.03$		$p<.02$
Test anxiety						
High	(23)	35	(22)	32	(22)	41
Low	(22)	64	(22)	64	(22)	59
		$p<.04$		$p<.06$		$p<.06$
n Achievement-Test Anxiety						
High–Low	(13)	77	(15)	73	(15)	67
High–High	(10)	40	(10)	40	(10)	60
Low–Low	(9)	44	(7)	43	(7)	43
Low–High	(13)	31	(12)	25	(12)	25
		$p<.025$		$p<.01$		$p<.025$

Note. Tests of significance are one-tailed Mann–Whitney U-Tests of predicted differences between extreme groups. One subject missed the final examination.

[a]After Atkinson and Litwin (1960).

ment motivation as shown in Table 2. Here we see how each personality measure, separately, and simultaneous classification of subjects on both are related to three different measures of achievement-oriented behavior obtained, by good fortune, from the same sample of subjects under very lifelike conditions (Atkinson & Litwin, 1960). This study was designed to replicate the first explicit test of the hypothesis that subjects high in *n* Achievement would show greater preference for moderately difficult tasks (Atkinson, Bastian, Earl, & Litwin, 1960). The ring-toss preferences in Table 2 were obtained during one of the earliest sessions of an undergraduate laboratory course in 1957 (before there was any mention of achievement motivation or even much about thematic apperception in popular introductory texts). The student subjects were naive in a way that today's college sophomores may no longer be about this subject. Subjects were identified only by code numbers as they sought to show how good they were, given five shots at the peg, with everyone else standing around hooting or cheering. Then, several months later, while these same students were taking the final exam in the course, it occurred to the investigators, on the spur of the moment, that they could obtain real-life measures of achievement-oriented performance level (on the exam) and persistence (time spent working on it) *if* they could catch each student out in the hallway, beyond the sight of others, and ask him to identify himself by code number on the final exam on which they also recorded the exact time he left. Here, quite spontaneously under lifelike conditions, we were able to obtain three theoretically-relevant behavioral measures from the same subjects. It is virtually impossible to replicate the natural conditions of this kind of study by calling a number of students in from the subject pool of an introductory course some evening for a three-hour test period in an effort to obtain a variety of supposedly related measures in one artificial setting (see, e.g., Weinstein, 1969).

This study, every result of which has been replicated in some one or more other studies (e.g., French & Thomas, 1958), included a serious effort to compare the construct validity and predictive validity of a measure of *n* Achievement obtained by the experimentally validated method of imaginative content analysis applied to French's (1958) adaptation of TAT with a very carefully constructed *self-descriptive* test purporting to measure Murray's psychogenic needs, the Edwards Personal Preference Schedule (Edwards, 1954). The self-descriptive *n* Achievement scores obtained from PPS were uncorrelated with imaginative *n* Achievement and Test Anxiety. And not one of the theoretically deduced relationships was obtained using the self-descriptive scale as if it provided a measure of the theoretical M_S. The pattern of results was inconsistent and, in fact, those scoring high in PPS *n* Achievement actually displayed significantly less preference for moderate difficulty than those scoring low.

This lack of correspondence of results using traditional self-descriptive tests purporting to measure positive motives and results using the experimentally validated methods for content analysis of operant imaginative behavior is perhaps the best substantiated fact in the 25 years of research on achievement motivation (see, e.g., Atkinson, 1960; McClelland, 1958a, 1971a; McClelland *et al., 1953*/1976). The number of such shorter, apparently more economical, objective tests referred to as measures of achievement motivation is legion. And none, to date, can make a very confident claim to construct validity.[5] Our own efforts to construct a self-descriptive test, guided by knowledge of the behavioral correlates of TAT *n* Achievement and the theory derived in its use, have also failed (Atkinson, 1969b; Atkinson & O'Connor, 1966) after initially promising results. Since there are no trademarks in the psychological literature, one may do the equivalent of bottling dishwater and labeling it Coca Cola. This has happened often in the psychological literature on "*n* Achievement."

The motivational determinants of self-descriptive behavior is a topic deserving intensive study in its own right, particularly since certain self-descriptive tests of anxiety *have* proven to be unusually heuristic and *can* make confident claim to construct validity when used to indicate strength of M_F as here conceived.

The nature of the interaction of personality and situation specified in the theory of achievement motivation emphasizes the likelihood of diametrically opposite trends in the pattern of behavior from one situation to the next depending upon whether the *psychological environment of a particular individual* presents mainly a challenge to achieve or mainly a threat of failure. Consider the motivational impact of moving from a task that is subjectively very easy (P_s = .90) to one of the intermediate difficulty (P_s = .50). If $M_S > M_F$ within the person, this should produce a heightening of interest and level of performance. If $M_F > M_S$ within the person, this should produce an intensification of anxiety and greater resistance. It should be expressed in a decrement in the level of performance. This is the sort of thing that should happen, for example, when students are moved from the traditional classroom which is heterogeneous in ability to ability-grouped classes. The most able and least able among the students are persons for whom P_s is usually very high and very low, respectively, in the traditional classroom when everyone faces the same competitive task. The level of difficulty is usually set so as to be appropriate for the average student.

O'Connor, Atkinson, and Horner (1966) expected and found both significantly enhanced performance and heightened interest among both boys and girls in the sixth grade who were high in *n* Achievement and low in Test Anxiety when they were moved into ability-grouped classes. The results for those low in *n* Achievement and high in Anxiety were only partially as expected. The dampening of interest, relative to that exhibited in a traditional heterogeneous control class, was obvious. But there was no evidence of a decrement in academic performance. It was slightly better in the ability-grouped than traditional (control) class, but the difference was not significant. In effect, the

[5]Objective tests developed by Mehrabian (1968, 1969) and Hermans (1970) may be promising candidates at this writing, but the evidence is still much too thin to claim their construct validity as equivalent to that of TAT *n* Achievement.

"anxious" students held their own but apparently with greater personal cost as indicated in the attitudinal response, and perhaps, though we do not know this, by greater time devoted to preparation outside of class.

A similar change in subjective probability of success is produced by the person's own behavior when he succeeds or fails in some activity. Consider the situation in which a person first chooses among tasks that differ in difficulty exhibiting, as has so often been shown (Atkinson & Feather, 1966; Hamilton, 1974; Heckhausen, 1968), the differential preference for moderately difficult tasks. If the person in whom $M_S > M_F$ succeeds when P_s is initially .50, the P_s is higher on a subsequent occasion in that situation for the same and similar tasks. He should act in a way that is described as raising his level of aspiration as a consequence of the change in motivation mediated by the change in cognitive expectancy of success (see Figure 6). If he fails when P_s is initially .50, then this and similar tasks seem subjectively more difficult on a later occasion. Here the change in motivation for a future trial contingent upon a decrease in P_s implies the behavioral phenomenon of a lowering of aspiration. To raise aspiration following success and to lower it following failure had often been called the "typical" (most frequently observed) pattern in the early studies of aspiration (Lewin *et al.*, 1944). We think this is probably because most of the subjects, then undifferentiated with respect to strength of *n* Achievement and Test Anxiety, were ones in whom $M_S > M_F$. (Recall that only about 20% of persons in the college-age range actually attended college in the United States in the 1930s and 1940s as compared to more than twice that percentage in the 1960s, and only about a quarter as many attended college in European countries during each period. This selectivity in who attends college should have some influence on the modal personality of the sample of college sophomores in a psychological experiment.)

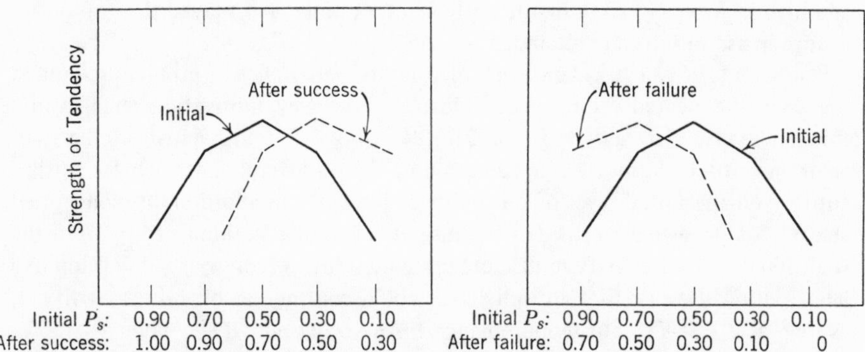

FIGURE 6 Change in strength of *resultant* tendency following success and failure at a task. Since $I_S = 1 - P_S$, and $I_f = -P_S$, there is a change in motivation for a subsequent task. The curves have positive value when $M_S > M_F$ and represent resistance when $M_F > M_S$. (Based on Atkinson and Feather, 1966, p. 338.)

If, on the other hand, the subject is one in whom $M_F > M_S$, the very anxious person who is most resistant to moderately difficult tasks, the initial choice of task will be either an easy one or a very difficult one. The most probable outcome in each case (success at the easy task and failure at the very difficult task) produces a change in P_s that has the effect of weakening subsequent anxiety and the tendency to avoid failure. (Consider Figure 6 now as representing the resultant resistance when $M_F > M_S$.) There is no dynamic for a change in aspiration. But consider what should happen if the "anxious" person fails even when P_s = .90 or succeeds even though P_s = .10. Now the easy task will subsequently appear more like a moderately difficult one as P_s drops from .90 towards .50. And the very difficult task (P_s = .10) now begins to appear like a more realistic risk as P_s increases towards .50. In both cases, the strength of tendency to avoid failure and resistance at the initial task is substantially increased and, if the subsequent choice of level of difficulty depends upon the relative strength of the total tendency for each activity ($T_a = (T_s - T_f) + T_{ext}$), and T_{ext} is constant across tasks, we should expect, paradoxically, a substantial raising of the level of aspiration after failing at an easy task and a substantial lowering of it after succeeding at a very difficult task. The other extreme on the continuum of difficulty then provides the least unattractive alternative since the tendency to avoid failure is now weakest there. These apparently irrational trends, noted in the early literature (Lewin *et al.*, 1944), are the defensive behavioral reactions now deduced from the several assumptions of the theory (Vitz, 1957).

Moulton (1965) ingeniously arranged experimental procedures that enabled him to control success and failure after subjects had indicated their initial choices (the predicted ones) and found that 30 out of 31 high school boys who were high in *n* Achievement and low in Anxiety displayed the "typical" shift in aspiration after success and failure. Among 31 classified low in *n* Achievement and high in Anxiety, 10 (a significantly greater number) displayed the "atypical" change in aspiration as predicted.

Feather's (1961, 1962) landmark of study of persistence in problem solving in the face of repeated failures both illustrates the way motivation changes in a fundamentally different way for subjects who differ in relative strength of achievement-related motives and shows how the behavioral consequences depend entirely on the initial level of difficulty of the task. In addition, his conceptual analysis of persistence provided the insight we needed to break away from the traditional view of activity in discrete episodic terms, which we shall develop in a later section. He saw that an individual would continue at his initial activity *A*, as long as $T_A > T_B$, but would change to the other activity *B*, when $T_A < T_B$. His analysis focused attention on the problem of a change in activity (Atkinson, 1964, Chapter 10; Atkinson & Cartwright, 1964).

Feather confronted male college students, individually, with several booklets each consisting of a set of puzzles. Presumably, these were a new set of items for a perceptual reasoning test for which he was then obtaining norms. The task required a person to connect all of a scattered series of dots without lifting the pencil and without retracing. When one wanted to make a new start, he merely tore off the sheet he had been working on and tried again on the next sheet. The subject, given the impression that he would have to do each of the several puzzle items, was asked by the experimenter to begin on either one described as rather easy, which he was told about 70% of college students had solved, or one described as very difficult which he was told only about 5% could solve. The subject was completely unaware that the puzzles were, in fact, insoluble. He was told that he might take as many 40-sec trials as he wanted on each item, that the several booklets of puzzles differed in difficulty, and that should he feel that he was not getting anywhere with the item, he could move on to the next one anytime.

Feather deduced what should happen when P_s was initially .70 and .05. For those in whom $M_S > M_F$ repeated failure should lower P_s producing an initial strengthening of resultant tendency to achieve until P_s fell below .50. Then continued failure should produce successively weaker motivation to continue until finally the total strength of tendency for the first task, T_A, would become weaker than that for some other task, T_B, and the person would change from one to the other. But this should take a substantially larger number of trials and more time among those in whom $M_S > M_F$ when the task was initially perceived as easy ($P_s = .70$) than as very difficult ($P_s = .05$).

For those in whom $M_F > M_S$, repeated failure at the easy task ($P_s = .70$) should immediately increase the strength of tendency to avoid failure and resistance to continuing it as P_s drops towards .50. They should quit after very few trials. But when initially told the task was difficult ($P_s = .05$), each failure which lowered the subsequent P_s even more would, paradoxically, reduce the strength of tendency to avoid failure and the resistance to continuation. The "very anxious" subjects might be expected to continue failing, where failing was expected, almost indefinitely.

This result (see Table 3), perhaps more clearly than any other in the literature on achievement motivation, dramatizes the interaction of personality and situation and the variations in phenotypic behaviors that can be derived from assumptions about consistent differences in personality when the latter are embedded in an explicitly stated theory which specifies the nature of the interaction of personality and immediate environment in the determination of motivation.

Looking at Table 3, one might imagine the perplexity of a traditional experimentalist who, ignoring differences in personality in his random samples assigned to the two treatments, would find and report no difference. And one might imagine the equally perplexed correlationist whose traditional mental-test mentality so minimizes systematic consideration of environmental influences that the differences between a situation in which $P_s = .70$ and $P_s = .05$ would most likely

TABLE 3
Persistence Among College Men (N = 34) in the Face of Continued Failure as a Function of Personality and Initial Difficulty of Task[a]

		Above median in persistence (%)	
n Achievement	Test anxiety	Task seen initially as easy (P_s = .70)	Task seen initially as difficult (P_s = .05)
High	Low	75	22
Low	High	33	75

[a]From Feather (1961). Copyright 1961 by the American Psychological Association. Reproduced by permission.

be unspecified, unnoticed, ignored, or glossed over. With these particular measures of personality, he would merely conclude that there was no consistency since the correlation of personality test with persistence was sometimes positive and sometimes negative. The literature in personality is clogged with results and discussions expressing a specious sophistication that are anchored in one or the other of these simplistic and anachronistic approaches, the so-called isolated disciplines of psychology (Cronbach, 1957).

As in the more complete review of the evidence relevant to this early theoretical formulation (Atkinson & Feather, 1966), we have here tended to emphasize the process of motivation rather than the individual personality. But here, as there, we can illustrate how easily one may shift from a process orientation to a personality orientation by considering the image this theory and accumulated evidence from a number of separate studies then projected of an *Achievement-Oriented Personality* as distinct from a *Failure-Threatened Personality.* From the continuum of quantitative differences in relative strength of M_S and M_F let us consider extreme cases. (Atkinson & Feather, 1966.):

> *The Achievement-Oriented Personality.* The achievement-oriented person is generally attracted to activities which require the successful exercise of skill. He is not particularly interested in gambling, where the outcome depends upon chance. Among activities that pit his skill against some standard or the skill of others he is more challenged by the task of intermediate difficulty, the 50–50 risk, than easier and safer ventures or much more difficult speculative ones. If he is successful, he will raise his sights; if he is unsuccessful, he will lower them accordingly. He is realistic. Although less interested in easy or very difficult tasks, he is more likely than others to undertake even these when they are the only available opportunities. He does this because he likes the challenge and the sense of having done something well a good deal more than others do, and probably a good deal more than he likes other potentially gratifying activities. Whatever the level of the challenge to achieve, he will strive more persistently than others when confronted with an opportunity to quit and undertake some different kind of activity instead. But within the context of his effort to achieve, he does not waste time in pursuit of the impossible

nor rest content with continual mastery of old familiar tasks when there are new, realistic possibilities of accomplishment open to him. In contrast to those who are not really much involved in the effort to achieve, he will not stick doggedly at a highly improbable venture when there is a more moderate risk available to him. Although he does not exhaust himself in the pursuit of illusory goals, he does believe that substantially greater prizes (whatever form they may take) should be awarded to persons who perform very difficult feats rather than easier ones. This is an expression of his pride in accomplishment and the extent to which he, more than others, sensitively appraises differences in merit. When he approaches a task in which there is considerable ambiguity about the possibility of success, he will be more confident than others. Why? This is probably because his realistic approach to challenges in the past, his enthusiasm, and persistence have made him more successful than others. He extrapolates this higher "batting average" (i.e., more frequent success) to the new venture when little concrete information about his chances is available. Consequently, many tasks which appear very difficult to others are likely to be viewed as realistic or calculated risks by the achievement-oriented personality. He is so often surrounded by ambiguous possibilities that he can construct for himself a world of interesting challenges. This he does in imagination, providing the most generally useful measure of the strength of his motive to achieve.

The Failure-Threatened Personality. In contrast, we have the individual in whom the motive to avoid failure greatly exceeds the motive to achieve. He is dominated by the threat of failure, and so resists activities in which his competence might be evaluated against a standard or the competence of others. Were he not surrounded by social constraints (i.e., spurred by a need to be approved for doing what is generally expected by his peers) he would never voluntarily undertake an activity requiring skill when there is any uncertainty about the outcome. When forced into achievement-oriented activities, he is most threatened by what the other fellow considers the greatest challenge. Constrained, but given a choice, he will defend himself by undertaking activities in which success is virtually assured or activities which offer so little real chance of success that the appearance of trying to do a very difficult thing (which society usually applauds) more than compensates for repeated and minimally embarrassing failures. Given an opportunity to quit an activity that entails evaluation of his performance for some other kind of activity, he is quick to take it. Often constrained by social pressures and minimally involved, not really achievement-oriented at all, he will display what might be taken for dogged determination in the pursuit of the highly improbable goal. But he will be quickly frightened away by failure at some activity that seemed to him to guarantee success at the outset. The dogged persistence is really rigid, apathetic compliance, as is his tolerance for continual routine success at tasks offering virtually no possibility of failure. This fellow's general resistance to achievement-oriented activity opposes any and all sources of positive motivation to undertake the customary competitive activities of life. Thus he suffers a chronic decrement in achievement tests. His long history of relative failure means he will view his chances in new ventures more pessimistically than others unless there is specific information to contradict a simple generalization from past experience. Most startling, perhaps, are the erratic changes in his level of aspiration, which take place when the least likely outcome occurs. Should this fellow fail at a task he undertook as a reasonably safe venture, he might respond with a startling increase in his level of aspiration instead of persistence at the initial activity. Should he begin to succeed at a task initially conceived as very difficult, he might then exhibit a dramatic decrease in his level of aspiration, a retreat to the safest of

> ventures. These apparently irrational moves – like his inability to move away from continual failure when the probability of success is remote – are to be understood as aspects of a defensive strategy, the avoidance of an intermediate degree of risk, the peak of competitive activity, where his anxiety reaches an intolerable level.
>
> The level of anxiety is symptomatic of the degree of resistance to an activity. When it is strong, we know that the individual has been constrained to overcome great resistance. When it is weak, the resistance to that activity must be weak. Because the level of experienced anxiety is symptomatic of the strength of resistance (i.e., the tendency to avoid failure), we are able to assess the strength of this man's motive to avoid failure from self-report questionnaires concerning the great amount of anxiety he has experienced in the nonvoluntary achievement tests endured in schooling. In the strange pattern of defensive behavior expressed by the person who is dominated by dread of failure, we confront pathology in the domain of achievement-oriented activity [pp. 368–370].

Future Orientation and a More General Theory of Achievement Motivation (1969–)

Still within the general context of the SEU model of decision making, Joel O. Raynor (1969, 1974a) has provided a cognitive elaboration of the theory of achievement motivation of the sort anticipated in earlier work by Lewin (1938), Peak (1955), Thomas and Zander (1959), and Vroom (1964). Raynor calls attention to the fact that the theory of achievement motivation, as initially stated, takes into account only the *immediate* consequences of a specific task or activity, for example, success, failure, and such immediate extrinsic incentives as social approval, money, etc. This suits the typical laboratory experiment which has little or no further significance for a person (except, perhaps, when a task is presented as something akin to an intelligence test). Certainly a ring-toss game is a classic example of a task having immediate but no more distant future consequences for a person. What happens when, as in many real-life situations (like taking a college course), an individual perceives success at the immediate task as also instrumental to future opportunities, as a step in a longer path leading on to one or more future consequences, and not merely as an isolated task. Raynor's analysis of this problem gives us a more general theory of achievement motivation in terms of which the earlier statement (Atkinson, 1957; Atkinson & Feather, 1966) and its various implications are recovered as instances of the simplest case.

Perceiving that some future opportunity, and the consequences of it, are contingent upon *success* in the present activity should intensify the characteristic achievement-related motivation of a person and also extrinsic motivation. Let us see, in very simple terms, why.

The strength of tendency to achieve success in an immediate activity will now depend upon at least two components, the strength of the tendency to succeed in reaching a more distant (d) expected goal in addition to the strength of tendency to succeed in the immediate task (i). Thus

$$T_s = T_{s_i} + T_{s_d}.$$

That means

$$T_s = (M_S \cdot P_{s_i} \cdot I_{s_i}) + (M_S \cdot P_{s_d} \cdot I_{s_d}).$$

Simplified, this becomes

$$T_s = M_S\,(P_{s_i} \cdot I_{s_i} + P_{s_d} \cdot I_{s_d}).$$

The quantity $(P_{s_d} \cdot I_{s_d})$ represents the motivational impact of the expected future goal of present activity. It comes in as a multiplier of the strength of M_S, and so intensifies the strength of motivation, that is, T_s.

The same should apply to the strength of tendency to avoid failure and behavioral resistance to the present activity. It, too, should be a summation of separate components, one referring to immediate failure (i) and the other to failing to achieve a more distant goal(s) (d). Thus

$$T_f = T_{f_i} + T_{f_d} = (M_F \cdot P_{f_i} \cdot I_{f_i}) + (M_F \cdot P_{f_d} \cdot I_{f_d}).$$

Simplified, this becomes

$$T_f = M_F\,(P_{f_i} \cdot I_{f_i} + P_{f_d} \cdot I_{f_d}).$$

Here again, the strength of the tendency is greater when the immediate task has more distant future implications than when it does not.

Continuing to employ the assumptions of the initial theory viz., $I_s = 1 - P_s, P_f = 1 - P_s, I_f = -P_s$, one can simplify the general expression for the resultant tendency to achieve when both an immediate and a single distant consequence are taken into account:

$$T_{Res} = (M_S - M_F)\,(P_{s_i} \cdot 1 - P_{s_i} + P_{s_d} \cdot 1 - P_{s_d}).$$

The characteristic motivation of a person is accentuated or intensified by future orientation (viz., by $(P_{s_d} \cdot 1 - P_{s_d})$ in this simplified presentation).

A comparable consideration of an extrinsic motivational tendency, $T_{ext} = T_{ext_i} + T_{ext_d}$, suggests a similar intensification of extrinsic motivation for an immediate activity that is perceived by the person as instrumental to attainment of a future extrinsic incentive. Simplified,

$$T_{ext} = M_{ext}\,(P_{ext_i} \cdot I_{ext_i} + P_{ext_d} \cdot I_{ext_d}).$$

Now, having the basic ideas out in simple form, let us follow Raynor's statement of the more general theory of achievement motivation, one that accommodates both the isolated tasks of the laboratory and single step projects (games, crafts, etc.) and more important activities of life like the pursuit of a career in which there may be a number of future consequences. Here we shall paraphrase Raynor's (1974a) argument[6]:

> A particular activity is considered the immediate next step in a path. A path may consist of a series of steps, each representing an activity and its expected consequences. Any achievement-related step may also have expected outcomes of extrinsic rewards (positive incentives) or threats (negative incentives). A consequence of any step in a path is a "goal" when it has positive incentive value. An individual's knowledge of what activities will lead on to what subsequent opportunities and goals determines the length of the path as it exists for that individual confronting the immediate task. The tendency to achieve success in immediate activity (T_s) is determined by the summation of component tendencies to achieve, each referring to a particular step in the anticipated path, and each a multiplicative function of motive (*M*), subjective probability of successfully achieving the goal of that step (*P*), and its incentive value (*I*). So:
>
> $$T_{\mathrm{s}} = T_{\mathrm{s}_1} + T_{\mathrm{s}_2} + \cdots T_{\mathrm{s}_n} + \cdots T_{\mathrm{s}_N}, \tag{6}$$
>
> where the subscripts 1, 2, . . . , *n*, . . ., *N* represent the anticipated order of steps (activities and outcomes) in a path, from the first (1) to the last (*N*), and *n* represents a general term for any particular position in this anticipated sequence. In a similar manner, the tendency to avoid failure (i.e., not to engage in achievement-related activity) is assumed to be additively determined by component inhibitory tendencies that refer to future steps in the anticipated path:
>
> $$T_{\mathrm{f}} = T_{\mathrm{f}_1} + T_{\mathrm{f}_2} + \cdots + T_{\mathrm{f}_n} + \cdots + T_{\mathrm{f}_N}. \tag{7}$$
>
> The strength of the resultant achievement-oriented tendency for the immediate activity is obtained by the summation of the tendencies to achieve success and to avoid failure. It is written symbolically as $(T_{\mathrm{s}} - T_{\mathrm{f}})$ where T_{s} and T_{f} are determined as described above [pp. 127–128].

By *contingent path* we mean that an individual believes success is necessary to guarantee the opportunity to continue to strive for some number of future successes while failure means future failure, as well, by guaranteeing the loss of an opportunity to continue. If an individual believes that the outcome of an immediate activity does not influence the opportunity to strive for some future success, we have a *noncontingent path.* Since there is no associative link between present and subsequent activity in this case, there is no intensification of present motivation attributable to future orientation.

The subjective probability that the immediate activity (1) will lead to some future success (e.g., $P_{1\mathrm{s}_2}$) can be represented by the product of subjective probability of success in the immediate task or first step ($P_{1\mathrm{s}_1}$) and the subjective probability of future success given the opportunity to strive for it

[6] The notation has been changed so that it is consistent throughout this chapter. The equations have been renumbered so as to be cumulative in this chapter. Thus, Raynor's (1) is here numbered (6).

(P_{2s_2}). The combined difficulty of the immediate task and the succeeding task determines how difficult it appears, at the outset, to attain that future success. Thus, if one feels confident of success generally, and both P_{1s_1} and P_{2s_2} can be represented as .90, their product would be .81. The person is more confident of reaching the immediate goal (P_{1s_1} = .90) than of reaching the future goal (P_{1s_2} = .81).

More generally, it is assumed that the strength of expectancy that an immediate activity will result in some future success (P_{1s_n}) is the product of subjective probabilities of success in each step of the path to that future goal:

$$P_{1s_n} = P_{1s_1} \times P_{2s_2} \times P_{3s_3} \times \cdots \times P_{ns_n}. \tag{8}$$

It continues to be assumed that incentive values of success and failure are related to subjective probability of success as stated earlier. So

$$I_{s_n} = 1 - P_{1s_n} \text{ and } I_{f_n} = -(P_{1s_n}).$$

Now, as we shall see, this more general theory has implications for the level of performance in a particular immediate activity that differ only in degree with those of the earlier statement. There should be an intensification of the characteristic motivation of the person as already shown. But other behavioral implications of the two statements may differ as the contingent path, in which the immediate task is perceived as but a step, increases in length.

In a simple task, with no future implications for a person, those in whom $M_S > M_F$ are most strongly motivated for activities in which P_s = .50 (see again Figure 4). But now consider Figure 7. To simplify the discussion, let us assume: (1) that our subject approaches a choice between three activities *X, Y*, and *Z;* (2) that all three are perceived as contingent paths to future goals; and (3) that he assumes P_s for each separate step will be .90 (easy) along contingent path *X*, .50 (moderately difficult) along contingent path *Y*, and .10 (very difficult) along contingent path *Z*. Which immediate task and/or path will be chosen?

We can consider the strength of resultant achievement motivation plotted in Figure 7 as positive for a person in whom $M_S > M_F$ and as negative (resistance) for a person in whom $M_F > M_S$. The strength of resultant achievement motivation ($T_s - T_f$) contributed to the immediate activity by each anticipated step in a path is shown graphically for paths *X, Y*, and *Z*. The height of the curve at each step represents the contribution of that step to the strength of motivation for the immediate activity. Thus, considering only the immediate activity (Step 1), the resultant tendency is stronger for *Y*, where P_s = .50, than for *X* or *Z* where P_s = .90 and .10 respectively. The sum of all these components of motivation (actually the total area under each of the curves) determines the overall strength of motivation for the first step or immediate activity.

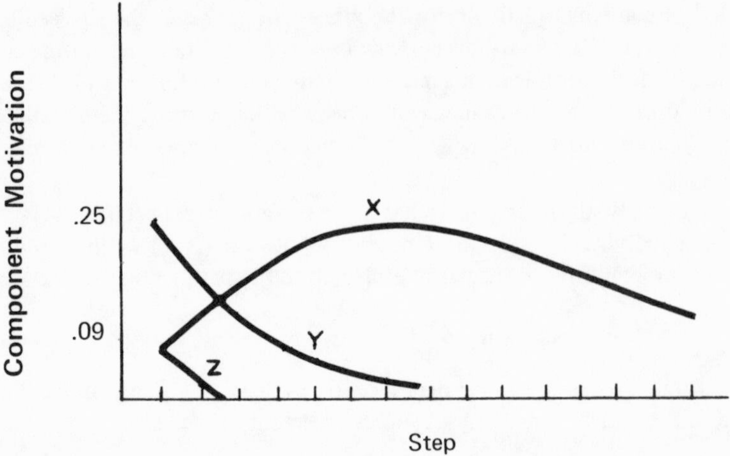

FIGURE 7 Strength of components of resultant tendency to achieve (a positive magnitude when $M_S > M_F$ and a negative magnitude when $M_F > M_S$) attributable to each step in a series when each step appears easy (*X*), moderately difficult (*Y*), or very difficult (*Z*) to the person. (Based on Raynor, 1974a.)

Several things are obvious:

1. When there is future orientation, resultant achievement motivation will be strongest with $M_S > M_F$, and resistance greatest with $M_F > M_S$, where $P_s = .90$ for the immediate task (and succeeding steps) and weakest where $P_s = .10$.
2. The strength of both positive and negative achievement motivation aroused by the immediate task itself (when $P_s = .90$) is relatively small (height of curve for first step only) in relation to the overall strength of motivation attributable to the subsequent activities anticipated as parts of the path (total area under the curve).
3. If we assume that the strongest component of positive tendency that is aroused in a contingent path defines the content of the person's "phenomenal goal" (the goal consciously in mind) as one confronts the immediate activity, it is a moderately distant future success where P_{1s_n} from the starting point seems near .50 for the person in whom $M_S > M_F$ in Path *X*.

In both paths *Y* and *Z* that goal is success at the immediate task. One can grasp this by using Equation 8 and assuming (as for Path *X*) that $P_{ns_n} = .90$ for each step. The future goal for which P_{1s_n} would appear near .50 *at the outset* is the outcome of the seventh step in Path *X*. That is $.9 \times .9 \times .9 \times .9 \times .9 \times .9 \times .9 =$ .486.

Now let us change our set concerning Figure 7. Suppose that there are very substantial individual differences in competence (Moulton, 1974). Over a period of years, this will produce substantial differences in the confidence of three persons, X, Y, and Z, all of whom may nevertheless be characterized by $M_S > M_F$. Now we may consider Figure 7 as showing how future orientation would influence the strength of motivation when these three different people confront the very same task. For Individual X (the most able), P_s is chronically .90 for each step in life. Individual Y faces every step as a 50–50 risk. And Individual Z (who chronically expects to fail) has a P_s that is normally about .10. Who among them will be most strongly motivated for the immediate task? Obviously, it will be the most able person (X), who will also be future oriented in goal orientation. This person is most concerned to attain the future goal that seems, at the outset, to be a 50–50 risk as reported by Mahone (1960) concerning vocational aspirations of college men in whom $M_S > M_F$ and replicated by Atkinson and O'Connor (1963) among high-school boys who were high in intelligence (very able). The more anxious students tended most frequently to set unrealistically high vocational aspirations.

The moderately able person (Y) will be less strongly motivated and the least able (Z), weakly motivated. And both will be mainly concerned about success at the immediate task. Where Y and Z might say they "hope to pass the exam in a college course," X might be expected to say, "I'm hoping to become a lawyer" when asked to explain what they are trying to accomplish in their present activity. Given the same differences in competence among persons in whom $M_F > M_S$, the resistance is paradoxically greatest for the most able person and/or simplest task.

In reference to McClelland's (1961) emphasis of calculated risk taking in business enterpreneurs, Raynor (1974a) points out that "it is the future challenge which offers the moderate risk" and that those who are achievement-oriented should be less speculative in everyday (immediate) risky decisions than the earlier discussion had suggested. They do, after all, face "the necessity of guaranteeing 'staying in the ballgame' long enough to achieve future career success [pp. 146–147]."

Let us consider some new illustrative evidence. Table 4 shows the effect of future orientation in an experiment by Raynor and Rubin (1971) in which college men were presented with several tests. In one condition, subjects were told that the opportunity to take the next test in the series was contingent on how well they did on the previous test. In another condition there was no contingency. They simply were told that they would have an opportunity to take each of four tests regardless of their performance on any of them. The trends of the performance level for subjects high in n Achievement and low in Test Anxiety versus subjects low in n Achievement and high in Test Anxiety concretize the intensification of positive motivation and of resistance in a contingent path.

A similar result was obtained by Raynor (1970) in one study of academic achievement in an introductory course. Students were simply asked how important getting a good grade was for having their career plans work out and then

TABLE 4
Mean Number of Problems Attempted as a Function of Motive Groups and Experimental Conditions[a]

Motive group	Condition			
	Noncontingent		Contingent	
n Ach. TA	*N*	*M*	*N*	*M*
High–Low	8	15.63	7	18.43
High–High	6	11.67	6	14.17
Low–Low	10	14.40	6	12.67
Low–High	7	14.14	8	8.38

[a]From Raynor and Rubin (1971). Copyright 1971 by the American Psychological Association. Reprinted by permission.

subdivided, in the analysis of results, according to the perceived instrumentality of the course grade. Those high in *n* Achievement and low in Test Anxiety achieved higher grades when they perceived the course as instrumental to future goals than when they did not. Those low in *n* Achievement and high in Test Anxiety, on the other hand, performed worse with future orientation than without it!

Other results obtained by Raynor, Atkinson, and Brown (1974) from college men who came a half-hour early for a final exam in a course show similar trends in their introspective reports describing their thoughts and feelings just before the exam in common everyday language. The measure of *n* Achievement and Test Anxiety had been obtained at the beginning of the term. Here, the picture we get of the covert effects of future orientation on the motivational state complements the overt behavioral evidence.

Sometimes, Raynor (1974b) points out, the effect of future orientation is mainly attributable to the intensification of the various components of extrinsic motivation such as potential income, social approval, prestige, etc., the motives for which may be equally strong among subjects otherwise differentiated only according to measures of resultant achievement motivation. In this case, the motivational effect of future orientation will be additive and equivalent for subjects who differ in achievement-related motives.

A striking illustration of this possibility comes from a follow-up study of a representative sample of high-school sophomores who had individual differences in achievement-related motivation measured in 1966. The question of interest is what percentage of them were still involved in some form of post-high school educational training in 1970, four years later. The result, shown in Table 5 from a secondary analysis by O'Malley (Atkinson, Lens, & O'Malley, 1976) is based on data collected by Bachman, Kahn, Mednick, Davidson, and Johnston (1967) in the project on youth in transition at Survey Research Center.

TABLE 5
Percentage of a Representative Sample of Male Sophomores in Public High Schools in the United States in 1966 Who Went on to Some Form of Post-High School Education[a]

	Perceived instrumentality of education			
n Achievement-Test Anxiety	*N*	Low (%)	*N*	High (%)
High–Low	77	40.3	285	58.6
High–High[b]	133	34.0	307	55.0
Low–Low[b]	100	48.9	318	56.3
Low–High	144	27.1	370	45.1

[a]From Atkinson, Lens, and O'Malley (1976), based on secondary analysis of data by Bachman *et al.* (1967).

[b]There is no a priori basis for ordering these two groups according to the inferred strength of Resultant Achievement Motivation and so the convention of earlier work is followed (Atkinson & Feather, 1966; Atkinson & Raynor, 1974).

Raynor's (1974a,b) theoretical analysis furthermore recovers, in contemporary terms, such concepts as *psychological distance* from a goal and *instrumental value* as distinct from *intrinsic value,* and it provides a framework needed to consider the joint effects on motivation of both the length of a path and the subjective probability of success. Raynor (1974b) provides an insightful analysis of motivation and career striving emphasizing that *"the anticipation that eventual success in . . . a contingent career path involves movement to higher levels of knowledge, skill, or proficiency with its concommitant larger extrinsic rewards provides . . . the greatest single source of motivational impetus for career striving* [p. 372]."

In now having the conceptual tools needed to analyze what happens to motivation in the early, middle, and late stages of a career, Raynor can identify certain personality types. His "compulsive career striver" is a future- and success-oriented person whose extrinsic motives are also very strong. The excessive time and energy expended early in career-related activity may go beyond what can be sustained over an extended period of time. Susceptible to performance decrements attributable to overmotivation (discussed in the next section), this individual "pulled by the future" may become a candidate for the exhaustion of physical and emotional reserves called a "nervous breakdown." In contrast, he identifies "uptight career striving" with a personality in which $M_F > M_S$ is coupled with strong extrinsic motives and future orientation. Intensified resistance and chronic anxiety is the cost of the career. This person would prefer to give up pursuit of success in a contingent career path and probably does, eventually, if a less anxiety-provoking means of satisfying the extrinsic motives can be found.

Perhaps the reader can see the implications of a future-oriented career path that is *open.* Each success leads to the anticipation of one or more additional distant future possibilities. The length of the path does not decrease as new possibilities for future achievement become apparent. And the "phenomenal goal," the 50–50 risk, continues to be in the *psychological* future. In contrast, in a *closed* path, one having a definite terminal point from the outset, continued success should produce decreasing motivation to achieve as the number of steps to the ultimate goal decreases. But if, as Raynor (1974b) has proposed, extrinsic rewards (money, power, prestige, security, public acclaim, approval of family and friends) are dispensed by society in greater amounts *after* an individual has acquired the skill and experience to contribute to the social welfare, then extrinsic motivation should become the more potent source of career-sustaining motivation later in life.

This suggests (to this writer) a plausible explanation of a well-known fact concerning the relationship of age and achievement. Figure 8 includes a curve based on Lehman's (1953) study of when the single most creative or best work of an individual is accomplished. The peak period is generally between ages 30 and 39, yet sheer productivity (as distinct from *distinguished achievement*) does not decline with age. This could be attributable to a change in the quality, if not the strength of career motivation, from an early dominance of motivation to achieve (concern with excellence) to a later, compensatory increase in various sources of extrinsic motivation. Anticipation of the reality of retirement, old age, ill health, and death itself must at some point project ahead a closed door on what had heretofore been an open-ended achievement-oriented path in a creative career. If not that, then certainly there is at least a decline in the P_s that characterizes each step in a long open path as the creative scientist, for example, finds himself years away from his doctoral training and faces the fact of the relative obsolescence of his background (see again Figure 7).

Also presented in Figure 8 are some results obtained in a national survey study of *n* Achievement, *n* Affiliation, and *n* Power accomplished in the late 1950s (Veroff, Atkinson, Feld, & Gurin, 1960) and soon to be repeated. The correspondence between an age trend for *n* Achievement derived for this essay from Veroff's national sample of males and the curve for actual achievement from Lehman (1953) is only one of the many interesting results of this study reported further in Veroff (1961), Veroff and Feld (1970), Veroff, Feld, and Crockett (1966), Veroff, Feld, and Gurin (1962).

Rich in its deducible implications, this more general theory of achievement motivation, emphasizing the motivational significance of the cognitive structure of an individual concerning paths to future goals, and the contingencies that define further opportunities, provides a much better conceptual bridge than before between the study of personality and sociological analysis of achievement, (education and occupational attainment) as in Crockett's (1962, 1964) demonstration of the relationship of *n* Achievement and social mobility (see,

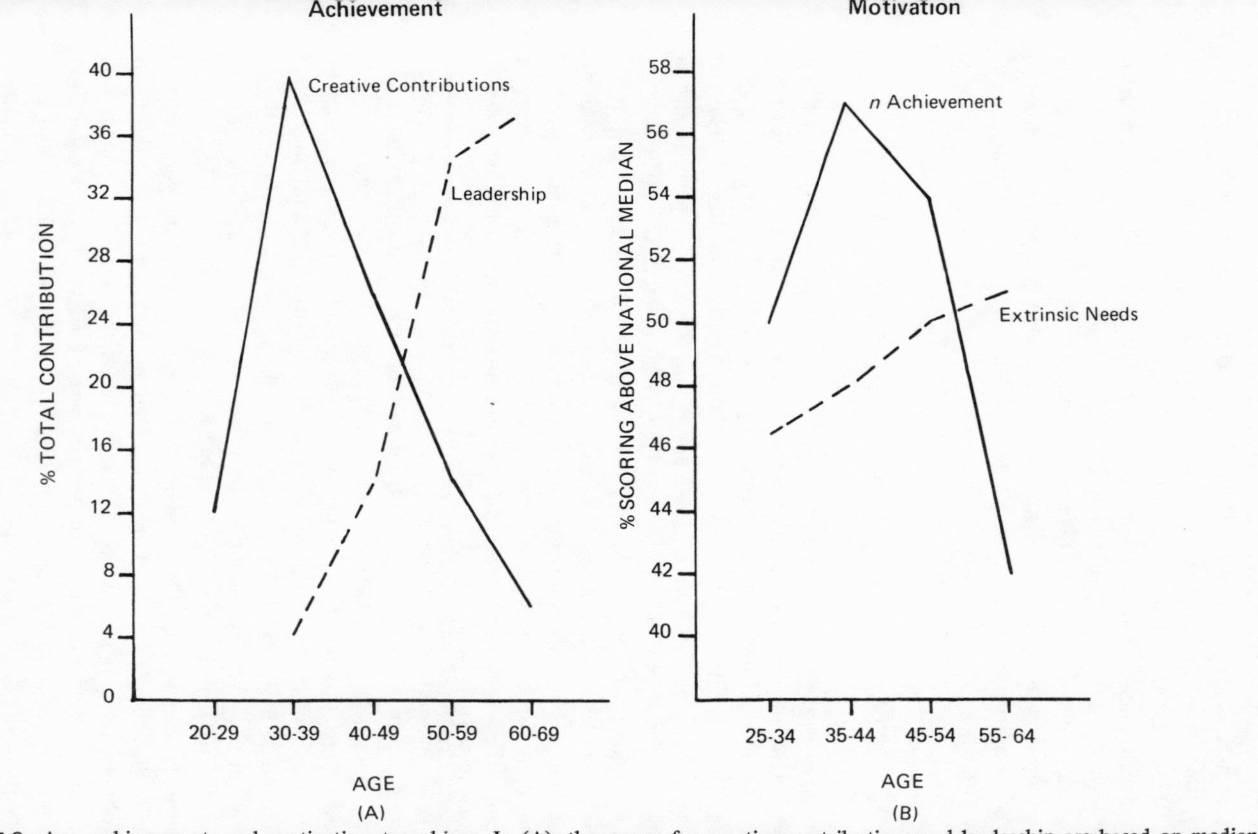

FIGURE 8 Age, achievement, and motivation to achieve. In (A), the curves for creative contributions and leadership are based on medians of fairly recent work in 15 fields of creative endeavor and in 10 fields of governmental, judicial, and military leadership respectively (Lehman, 1953, pp. 250–251. Copyright 1953 by the American Philosophical Society. Published by permission of Princeton Unversity Press). In (B), the curves for TAT *n* Achievement and extrinsic needs (the average of *n* Power and *n* Affiliation) are based on results from a representative sample of males in the United States in 1957. (From Veroff, Atkinson, Feld, & Gurin, 1960. Copyright 1960 by the American Psychological Association. Published by permission.)

e.g., also Crockett & Schulman, 1973; Duncan *et al.*, 1972; Lipset & Bendix, 1959; Rosen *et al.*, 1969; Sewell, 1971; Sewell, Hauser, & Featherman, 1976) and the long term entrepreneurial activities that have interested McClelland (1961, 1971b) and McClelland and Winter (1969).

Other developments that also serve to link personality with achievement in society have to do with clarification of the dual role of motivation in the determination of behavior: its effect on the efficiency of performance, and its effect on the way an individual distributes time among competing activities as conceived within the new dynamics of action. It is to these developments that we now turn.

MOTIVATION AND EFFICIENCY OF PERFORMANCE

A collation of studies of the effect of individual differences in *n* Achievement on the level of various types of intellective performance (Atkinson, 1974b) finds support for a hypothesis long advocated by others (e.g., Broadhurst, 1959; Eysenck, 1966; McClelland, 1951; Vroom, 1964; Yerkes & Dodson, 1908). The relationship between strength of motivation and the level of performance is nonmonotonic and generally to be described by an inverted U-shaped curve as shown in Figure 9(a). The idea is a very old one (Yerkes & Dodson, 1908). It has taken this long to achieve sufficient confidence in a conception of the determinants of strength of human motivation on other grounds and to attain equivalent confidence in the availability and use of valid techniques for assessment of individual differences in motives and experimental manipulation of relevant incentives to feel reasonably confident about the treatment of this question.

For years we were misled by the simple, and for the most part, implicit hypothesis that as the strength of motivation expressed in an activity increased so also would the level of performance increase, at least until some physical limit was reached. At this point, a person presumably could not run any faster or solve any more arithmetic problems per minute even if offered a million dollars as an additional incentive. The analysis which follows provides another reply to the frequent criticism of now-you-see-it-now-you-don't in reference to the "generally expected" positive relationship between strength of an individual's motivation to achieve (i.e., the resultant tendency to achieve) and performance.

Table 6 describes a paradigm for experimental analysis of how strength of motivation (+ to ++++) influences efficiency of performance. It presumes that the total strength of motivation for performance of a task (T_a) is a summation of component motivational tendencies ($T_a = T_s - T_f + T_{app}$) and that each component tendency depends upon interaction of personality (strength of motives) and the nature of the immediate environment (expectation or not of attaining a relevant incentive).

TABLE 6
A Paradigm for Experimental Analysis of the Effects of Strength of Motivation (+ to ++++) on Efficiency of Performance[a,b]

Personality (motives)		Environment (incentives)			
Resultant *n* Achievement (*n* Achievement-Test Anxiety)	*n* Affiliation	Achievement related only		Achievement related and social approval	
High	High	(A)	++	(E)	++++
High	Low	(B)	++	(F)	+++
Low	High	(C)	+	(G)	+++
Low	Low	(D)	+	(H)	++

[a]From Atkinson (1974b).

[b]It is assumed that strength of motivation for the task, $T_a = (T_s - T_f) + T_{app}$ and that motives (*P*) and incentives (*E*) combine multiplicatively in determination of component tendencies. For simplicity, High = 2 and Low = 1 in reference to strength of motives; and presence of a relevant incentive = 1 and its absence = 0. The number of +s indicates strength of T_a for each subgroup in the table.

You may recall that an early study showed that college students scoring high in TAT *n* Affiliation (or social acceptance) were described by people who knew them well as approval seeking (Atkinson *et al.*, 1954). So the measure called *n* Affiliation has been used with confidence that it taps the degree to which one will be motivated in performance by an incentive for social approval such as that provided by an audience.

To simplify the motivational implications of the eight-celled table, assume that high = 2 and low = 1, in reference to strength of motives, and that the presence of the relevant incentive is indicated by 1 and its absence by 0 in the columns representing experimental control of the immediate work situation. The number of + signs in each of the eight cells represents the sum of the products of personality (motive) and environment (incentive) that is deduced from the expression, $T_a = T_s - T_f + T_{app}$.

Combined use of diagnostic tests of personality and experimental manipulation of the work environment yields at least four distinguishable levels of intensity of motivation for performance of the task. If, to get into the problem, one assumed that groups of subjects who differ in motives do not also differ in average level of ability, one could combine various subgroups to form a four-point continuum of intensity of motivation for performance of a task. In order of increasing strength, we have (*C, D*), (*A, B, H*), (*F, G*) and (*E*). There is no way of confidently ordering the subgroups within a particular set for example, (*A, B,* and *H*), according to strength of motivation, but we can assume, with confidence, that *A, B,* and *H* should all be more strongly motivated than *C* or *D,* and so on.

Entin (1968) followed this plan explicitly for a sample of junior high-school boys given a rather simple and a more complex arithmetic task. Half received private feedback, being told that their scores would be posted on the bulletin board by a code number which each subject alone knew. This was considered analogous to working alone in a room (*A, B, C, D*). The other half received public feedback. Their scores were to be identified, they knew, by name, a situation analogous to having an audience as in groups *E, F, G, H.* His results, for level of performance of both simple and complex tasks, interspersed during performance, describe the inverted U-shaped curve peaking for subgroups *A, B,* and *H.*

With this much as background, let us focus on a particular question: How should individual differences in need for achievement (or any other single determinant of the strength of motivation) be related to level of performance *as a function of the overall level of motivation for performance in a given situation?* In Figure 9a we find an alternative to the earlier misleading idea that the relationship should always or even normally be positive. When the final strength of tendency is in the low to moderate range (1–3), as is likely when a person is achievement oriented and working alone in a room (as shown earlier in Table 1), or knowing the feedback will be private, then the relationship between *n*

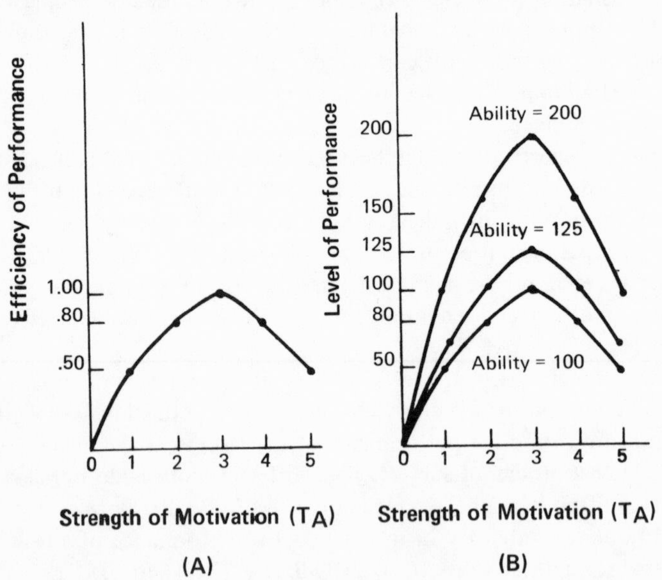

FIGURE 9 (A) The effect of strength of motivation on efficiency of performance; and (B) The effect of strength of motivation on level of performance when level of performance = ability × coefficient of efficiency. (From Atkinson, 1974a.)

Achievement (1–3) and performance level should be positive. But when other factors in the personality that influence motivation or other situational incentives serve to heighten motivation for everyone so that the final strength of tendency now falls in the middle range (2–4) for everyone, the linear correlation between *n* Achievement (2–4) and performance level will be zero. Suppose that the systematic effect of still other strongly aroused motives attributable to a number of different incentives, or the number and strength of distant future consequences viewed as contingent upon good performance should produce a very intense average level of final strength of motivation for the task (range 3–5). We now expect that the person who scores highest in *n* Achievement will perform least well. The correlation between *n* Achievement (3–5) and performance should now be negative.

Paralleling hypotheses that the linear relationship between *n* Achievement and level of performance can be positive, zero, or negative *depending* upon the conditions, but exactly opposite in direction, are hypotheses concerning the effects of individual differences in Test Anxiety on performance, *if* our supposition is correct that expectation of failure always produces a tendency that opposes, resists, dampens, *subtracts from* the strength of positive motivation. Under the special circumstances that produce excessive positive motivation, (range 3–5), the dampening effect of the tendency to avoid failure should, paradoxically, enhance performance. Specifically, this means that a person with very strong motives to achieve and for social approval, who would be "overmotivated" when performing for both incentives in a situation (like working on a test with an audience), should perform better if he is also high in anxiety (the dampener) than if he is low in anxiety.

Some results obtained by Smith (1961, 1966) illustrate the enhancing effect of resistance when motivation is too strong (see Table 7). Subjects worked at complex arithmetic problems for 14 min in a *relaxed* condition that minimized their importance; in an *extrinsic* condition where the only incentive to work fast was to finish quickly so as not to miss the evening meal; alone under *achievement orientation;* in a *multi-incentive* coactive, competitive group situation with achievement orientation and proctors as potential agents of approval/disapproval and also the offer of a monetary prize. The two latter conditions are essentially the same as those represented earlier in Table 1. The conditions are arranged in order according to an a priori appraisal of the incentives offered and according to ratings that subjects made immediately afterward concerning how hard they had worked at the task.

If one looks at the levels of performance of the subgroups most positively motivated (high *n* Achievement–low Test Anxiety) and those most likely to be more strongly motivated to avoid failure (low *n* Achievement–high Test Anxiety), one sees the hint of enhancement of efficiency by resistance when, without it, one might suffer a decrement in performance attributable to overmotivation.

TABLE 7
Mean Correct Arithmetic Performance (14 Min) According to Strength of Achievement-Related Motives under Various Conditions[a]

Mean posttest rating by *S*s: how hard they had worked	Relaxed (3.41)	Extrinsic (3.97)	Achievement (4.00)	Multi-incentive (4.39)
n Achievement				
High[b]	52.07	56.47	70.69	58.39
Low	51.43	55.93	64.93	76.94
Difference	.63	.54	6.36	−18.55
Test anxiety				
High[c]	48.33	56.00	58.92	70.31
Low	55.42	56.38	75.71	64.74
Difference	−7.10	−.38	−16.79	5.57
n Achievement-Test Anxiety				
High–Low[d]	53.0	51.7	78.8	55.3
High–High	55.1	60.6	66.0	58.7
Low–Low	56.4	60.0	71.3	71.5
Low–High	34.8	49.8	55.8	85.3

Note. Differences attributable to *n* Achievement here are smaller than when one picture of questionable validity is eliminated from the set of six (Smith, 1961, Table 15). This picture is removed for the joint classification based on Smith, 1961, Table 58. Generally the differences are somewhat smaller but the pattern is unchanged with quantitative ability controlled statistically (Smith, 1961).

[a]From Smith (1961, 1966) and Atkinson (1974b).

[b]N_s = 14 to 18 in each subgroup.

[c]N_s = 13 to 19 in each subgroup.

[d]N_s = 4 to 10 in each subgroup.

More recent evidence of inefficiency attributable to excessive positive motivation is shown in a similar study by Horner (1974b). Here each male subject worked alone under achievement orientation, or in direct competition with a female, or with a male. In the interpersonal competitive conditions, subjects were told that it would be announced which of them had done the best.

In Table 8, the three situations are ordered in terms of absence versus presence of an additional incentive for performance (social approval) according to earlier evidence (from Atkinson & Reitman, 1956) that the persons whose performance increases the most from working alone to working with an incentive for approval are those classified low in *n* Achievement and high in *n* Affiliation (those concerned about positive affective reactions from others). This trend, which justifies the ordering of the two competitive conditions, is outlined in Table 8. One also finds theoretical justification in Table 6. There it is shown that a substantial increase in motivation is expected between subgroups *C* and *G* within

TABLE 8

Mean Anagrams Performance of Men Working Alone and in Competition According to Resultant Achievement Motivation and Affiliative Motivation[a]

	Alone		Competition with: Female		Male	
	N	*M*	*N*	*M*	*N*	*M*
High Resultant *n* Achievement (*n* Achievement–Test Anxiety)						
High *n* Affiliation	(10)	46.5	(7)	53.9	(7)	48.4
Low *n* Affiliation	(8)	48.4	(6)	53.4	(5)	53.7
Low Resultant *n* Achievement (*n* Achievement–Test Anxiety)						
High *n* Affiliation	(6)	41.8	(7)	53.6	(6)	56.1
Low *n* Affiliation	(6)	40.8	(10)	47.7	(10)	46.7
Resultant *n* Achievement (*n* Achievement–Test Anxiety)						
High	(18)	47.4	(13)	53.7	(12)	50.3
Low	(12)	41.3	(17)	49.4	(16)	50.2
Difference		+6.1		+4.3		+.1
		$p < .025$		n.s.		n.s.

Note: Raw scores on 10-min anagrams task were normalized to yield a mean of 50 and an *SD* of 10.

[a]From Horner (1968).

the low to moderate range of motivation, so it should be directly expressed in an increased level of performance.

At the bottom of Table 8 where subjects are classified only in terms of Resultant *n* Achievement, we see again a positive relationship only when the influence of extrinsic incentives is minimized. The details of results when subjects are classified in terms of both Resultant *n* Achievement and *n* Affiliation are intriguing. Note first that the verbal performance scores are standardized with a mean of 50 and standard deviation of 10. So the improvement in performance level among those classified low in Resultant *n* Achievement and high in *n* Affiliation across conditions is on the order of magnitude of 1.5 times the standard deviation. Those also low in *n* Affiliation should increase some, but not as much, as those high in *n* Affiliation when an incentive for approval is introduced. They do. In the *Alone* condition, where there is no incentive for approval in the immediate environment, there should be no evidence of differential arousal of *n* Affiliation. There is none.

Now consider those who are high in Resultant *n* Achievement. Moving across conditions one expects a greater increase in motivation among those who are also high rather than low in *n* Affiliation. But we note that the performance level in competition with a female is the same, 53.9 and 53.4 for both subgroups. Is this evidence contrary to the hypothesis? No. Not if the greater expected increase in motivation of those high in *n* Affiliation has put them beyond the optimal level of motivation (corresponding to Level 4 in Figure 9a) and the weaker expected increase of those low in *n* Affiliation has produced less than that optimal level (corresponding to Level 2 in Figure 9a). With that supposition, which is completely consistent with the notion that the subgroup having a stronger motive should increase more in motivation, the one further result for those high in Resultant *n* Achievement and high in *n* Affiliation must come out a certain way. If they are already beyond the optimal level of motivation in competition with a female, they *must* perform even less adequately in competition with a male where the strength of motivation should be still more intense. And they do perform less adequately. Their performance drops from 53.9 to 48.4. The final result, the level of 53.7 of subjects high in Resultant *n* Achievement but low in *n* Affiliation, can be interpreted as the result of an increase in motivation from the weak side of optimal motivation to the strong side of optimal motivation (from 2 to 4 in Figure 9a). The pieces of the puzzle do seem to fall into place given the guiding hypothesis.

One can see a curvilinear relationship between strength of motivation and efficiency of performance in two places. First, it is evident across situations among the subgroup of subjects who are most disposed to be very highly motivated when there are incentives both to achieve and for social approval (high Resultant *n* Achievement–high *n* Affiliation). Second, it is evident across personality types ordered according to their potential to be highly motivated in the condition providing the strongest incentives for performance (competition with a male). Apparently, under the conditions of this experiment, and for performances of a verbal anagrams task, the level of motivation attained by those low in Resultant *n* Achievement (which implies high Test Anxiety) and high in *n* Affiliation comes closest to being the optimal level. The level of performance of the most highly motivated subgroup is about .8 of a standard deviation lower. And the level of performance of the least motivated subgroups is about 1.5 of a standard deviation lower.

Can one possibly decide, looking at Table 8, which subgroup has the highest verbal *ability?* What would one conclude had the intellective task employed been the kind that is traditionally called a test of intelligence? The subjects were assigned randomly to conditions before the diagnostic tests of personality were even scored. (That is why the *N*s are not exactly equivalent.)

A more comprehensive treatment of these questions, based on review and reinterpretation of compatible results in seven studies (Atkinson & O'Connor, 1966; Atkinson & Reitman, 1956; Entin, 1968, 1974; Horner, 1968, 1974b; Reitman, 1957, 1960; Sales, 1970; Smith, 1961, 1966) considers possible causes of inefficiency attributable to overmotivation in execution of an activity and concludes with the proposal that Level of Performance = Ability × Efficiency. This implies that the level of intellective performance is an expression of the true level of an intellective ability only when one is optimally motivated taking the test and therefore 100% efficient. One may speak of a Coefficient of Efficiency = Level of Performance/Ability, whatever the explanation of inefficiency in the execution of an activity. Its relationship to strength of motivation may be considered as shown in Figure 9a.

The simplistic assumption that observed differences in the level of intellective performance merely reflect differences in ability is challenged in Figure 9b. It has long been tacitly and erroneously assumed, without adequate justification, that the level of motivation is optimal for everyone taking some test of ability, or a constant among individuals, or only negligibly different among all individuals at the time of test performance or, perhaps, that individual and/or situational differences in strength of motivation, though substantial, have little effect on intellective performance.

If the present conception of motivation and efficiency of performance is essentially correct, the implication for mental testing is spelled out programmatically in Figure 9b. A person of relatively high ability whose motivation at the time of a test is substantially dampened by the dread of failure, or one whose motivation is excessively high by virtue of a combination of strong positive motives enhanced, perhaps, by an articulated sense of the critical importance of the test for attainment of future life goals may perform very inefficiently and score lower than a person of more modest ability who happens to be optimally (only moderately) motivated when taking the critical test.

Only systematic research of the kind described here but using the so-called tests of intelligence and academic aptitude now employed in current practice will determine, definitively, whether the psychology of motivation has finally brought a new idea to the mental test movement.

So much for a review of how motivational differences in personality are expressed in the efficiency of executing an activity. Even more fundamentally important is the new insight achieved concerning such questions as *when* will that activity be initiated, *how long* will it continue, *when* will it cease, *when* will it be resumed, *how frequently* will it occur, *what proportion of time* will be devoted to it instead of other competing activities. We now turn to a reconstruction of the general theory of motivation, which provides coherent answers to these questions with a single principle and which is one product of changing the focus in the study of motivation to analysis of a simple change in activity (Atkinson & Birch, 1970, 1974), following Feather's (1961, 1962) confrontation with that problem in the study of persistence.

THE DYNAMICS OF ACTION APPLIED TO ACHIEVEMENT-RELATED ACTION

An understanding of how the relative strength of different motives within an individual (*n* Achievement, *n* Affiliation, *n* Power, etc.) may have a controlling influence on the way the individual distributes time among different activities is one of the most illuminating products of the new dynamics of action (Atkinson & Birch, 1970; Birch, 1972). This reconstruction of the theory of motivation provides an explicit, coherent theoretical justification for the popular supposition that the basic personality is essentially a configuration or hierarchy of different psychogenic needs or motives (Maslow, 1954; McClelland, 1951; Murray, 1937).

How can the essentials of a completely new conceptual framework for motivation and action be stated simply and clearly? Traditional theories of motivation, both cognitive (e.g., Cartwright & Festinger, 1943; Edwards, 1954; Lewin, 1938; Tolman, 1955) and within S–R behavior theory (e.g., Hull, 1943; Miller, 1959; Spence, 1956), are stimulus bound. This means that the individual is implicitly viewed as at rest, not doing anything, and unmotivated *to do* anything, until exposed to the stimulus situation of critical interest. The theory of achievement motivation is also like that. It treats the person as if the individual were dead until confronted with the stimulus situation, e.g., a ring-toss game, at which time, as a result of some kind of sudden interaction of personality and environment there occurs – *instantaneously* – a set of competing motivational tendencies of certain magnitudes that control behavior. Life is not like that (Atkinson, 1964, Chapter 10; Atkinson & Cartwright, 1964).

The new dynamics of action exposes the simplistic character of this conventional *episodic* view of behavior, where every new action begins like an event at a track meet with a stimulus situation analogous to the starter's gun. This S–O–R *paradigm* of traditional psychological theory, to use Kuhn's (1962) term, is founded in the Cartesian concept of reflex (1637/1935) that served the new science of physiology so well in the nineteenth century and was a great help to psychology during the first half of this century.

Now, however, we begin with a new premise: that an individual is already active in two senses of the word before being exposed to the traditional stimulus situation that in the past was supposed to get things started. The individual is already doing something when a scientific observer initially takes notice. Second, the individual is also already actively motivated to do many other different things before exposure to the stimulus situation of traditional interest. This was one of Freud's great insights: that wishes, inclinations, or tendencies, once aroused – whenever – persist until expressed in behavior, directly or substitutively, long past the point of direct exposure to their initial instigating stimulus.

This means, in effect, that we break out of the traditional mode of thought that has always considered behavioral episodes as isolated events and begin viewing the behavioral life of an individual as a continual stream characterized by change from one activity to another even in a constant environment. The focus of interest shifts from concern with the initiation, instrumental phase, and consummatory phase of particular isolated activities to the continuity of behavior and the juncture between different activities, a change from one to another.

To explain a simple change in activity coherently becomes the fundamental problem for a science of motivation. And to be able to do it gives one the conceptual tools needed to account for a series or sequences of changes, a much longer temporal unit of behavior, and the various measurable aspects of the stream of operant behavior, for example, relative frequency of various activities, operant level, proportion of time spent in an activity, and others (Birch, 1972).

In *The Dynamics of Action* (Atkinson & Birch, 1970, 1974), we conceived the impact of the immediate environment (or stimulus situation) on behavior to be the various instigating and inhibitory forces it produces. These influence the arousal of an individual's tendencies to engage or not to engage in certain activities. If a certain kind of activity has been intrinsically satisfying or rewarded in this kind of situation, there will be an *instigating force* (F) for that activity. This will cause a more or less rapid increase in the strength of an inclination to engage in that activity, an *action tendency* (T), depending on the magnitude of the force. If a certain kind of activity has been frustrated or punished in the past, there will be an *inhibitory force* (I) and a more or less rapid growth in the strength of a disinclination to act or *negaction tendency* (N). This is a tendency *not* to do it. The duration of exposure to these forces (t for time) will determine how strong the action or negaction tendency becomes. The latter, the tendency not to do something, will produce *resistance* to the activity. It opposes, blocks, dampens, the action tendency. That is, it subtracts from the action tendency to determine the *resultant action tendency* ($\overline{T} = T - N$). The resultant action tendency competes with resultant action tendencies for other incompatible activities. The strongest of them is expressed in behavior.

The expression of an action tendency in behavior is what reduces it. Engaging in an activity produces a *consummatory force* (C) which depends in part on the *consummatory value* (c) of the particular *kind* of activity and in part on the *intensity* of the activity as determined by the strength of tendency then being expressed in the activity ($C = c\overline{T}$). Similarly, resistance to an action tendency, produced by the opposition of a negaction tendency, constitutes an analogous *force of resistance* (R) which reduces, in a comparable way, the strength of the negaction tendency.

This, very briefly, introduces our conception of the causal factors involved in the continuous rise and decline in strength of tendencies illustrated in Figure 10. These changes in motivation in turn account for the changes from one activity to another (*x*, *y*, *z*, etc.) that characterize the normal stream of an individual's behavior, even in a constant environment. The figure is the result of one of our earliest computer simulations of what should be expected to happen if an individual were exposed to instigating forces of different magnitudes for three incompatible activities in the same environment (Seltzer, 1973).

A single and fairly simple principle of change in activity can be derived. It yields hypotheses about how the magnitude of instigating and inhibitory forces will influence the initiation of an activity (latency of response), choice, the

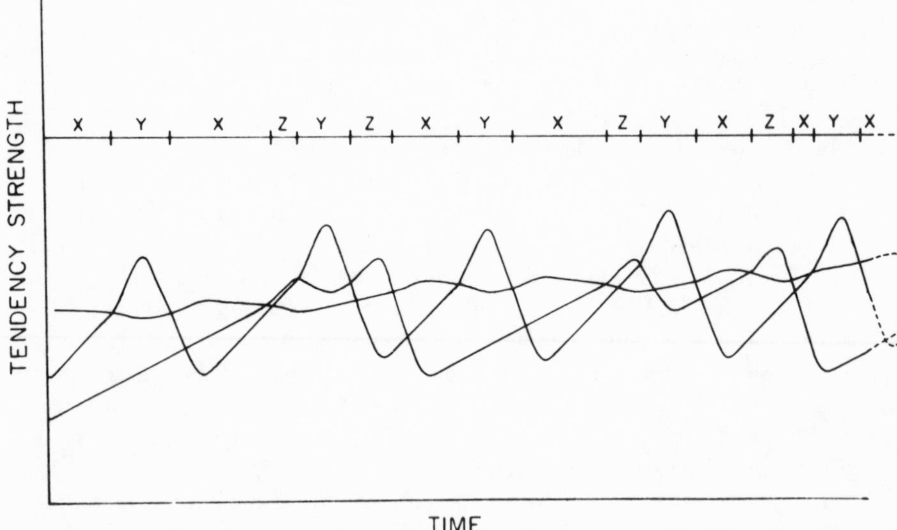

FIGURE 10 An example of a stream of activity (*x*, *y*, *z*) and its underlying tendency structure. (From Seltzer, 1973.)

TABLE 9
Analogous Concepts in the Treatment of Instigation of Action and Resistance to Action[a]

Instigation of action	Resistance to action
Instigating force, F	Inhibitory force, I
Action tendency, T	Negaction tendency, N
Action	Resistance
Consummatory force, C	Force of resistance, R

[a]From Atkinson and Birch (1970).

duration or persistence of a particular activity, the proportion of total time spent in a given activity, relative frequency of activities, and, derivately, the operant level or rate of an activity in a constant environment.

The basic concepts, presented in Table 9, should not seem totally unfamiliar. In the framework of the new dynamics of action, *the theory of achievement motivation is now to be considered a theory about the determinants of instigating forces to achieve success* (F_s) *and inhibitory forces to avoid failure* (I_f) *in various activities and not, as heretofore assumed, of the final strength of tendencies to achieve success and to avoid failure in a particular situation.* A distinction is made between the arousability (or rate of arousal) of a tendency, the magnitude of force (F), and the level of arousal or strength of that tendency (T) at a particular time. A similar distinction has been made by Whalen (1966) in analysis of sexual motivation.

To understand the new concepts, consider the various ways in which an observed change of activity, from A to B, might come about after a certain period of time (t) in a constant environment. In Figure 11, we assume that initially (i) $T_{A_i} > T_{B_i}$, but when the change finally (f) occurs, $T_{B_f} > T_{A_f}$.[7] The change in activity implies a change in the strength of one or both of the action tendencies. For example, think of an individual studying (achievement) who finally puts down a book and begins to talk to a nearby friend (affiliation). Or think of a student engaged in a friendly conversation (affiliation) who stops, at a certain point, and begins to study (achievement). In both simplified examples we are pitting the strength of tendency for affiliation against the strength of tendency to achieve.

What causes the change(s) in motivation implied by the observed change in activity? We begin very conservatively, eschewing the idea that action tendencies

[7]Now we shall begin to use capital letters A, B, C, etc., to designate particular activities and as the subscript to indicate strength of tendency for that activity (T_A, T_B, T_C, etc.). to be consistent with notation used by Atkinson and Birch (1970).

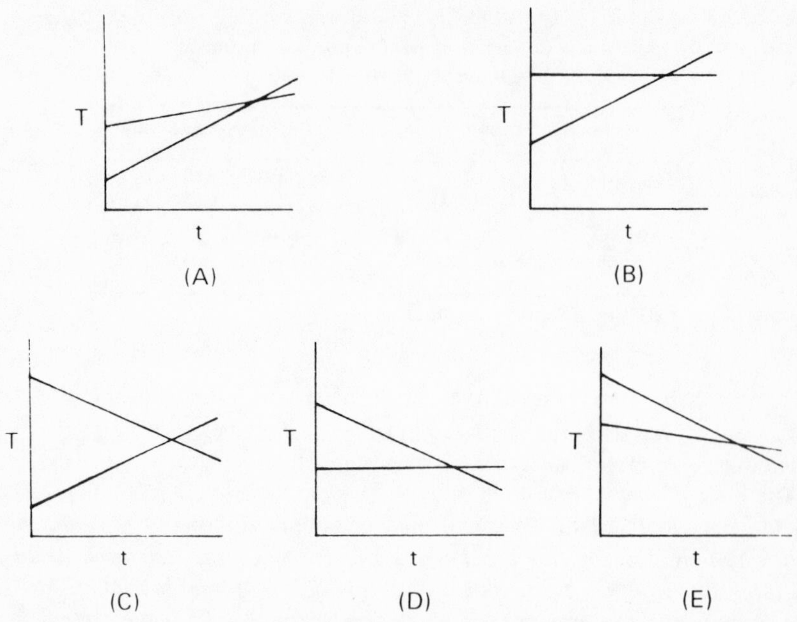

FIGURE 11 Various ways in which a change in relative strength of T_A and T_B can come about during an interval of time (t). (From Atkinson & Birch, 1970, 1974.)

change in strength spontaneously by mere random oscillation from moment to moment (an assumption in traditional theory). Freud argued that the wish persists until it is expressed. We sharpen that language somewhat. A behavioral tendency, once aroused, will persist in its present state until acted upon by some psychological force that either increases or decreases its strength.

This first assumption explains why all of the tendencies in the graphs of Figure 11 have some initial (or inertial) strength above zero at the beginning of the interval of observation. (The person is active – already doing something (activity A) and already actively motivated to do activity B, and certainly many other activities, should we care to complicate both the graphs and discussion.)

The cause of the change in the strength of a tendency must be something that occurs during the time interval. We suppose that the source of the *instigating force* (F), which functions to increase the strength of a particular inclination to act (T), is most often some discriminable feature of the immediate environment – a stimulus – to which the individual is exposed. And we suppose that the consummatory force (C), which reduces the strength of a particular tendency, is usually attributable to expression of that tendency in the activity itself, the other thing happening during the time interval. The change in strength of a particular tendency during the interval of time should then depend upon the relative strengths of instigating and consummatory forces. That is,

$$\frac{T_{\mathrm{f}} - T_{\mathrm{i}}}{t} = F - C. \tag{9}$$

Clearly if $F > C$, the tendency (T) will become stronger. If $C > F$, T will become weaker. And if $F = C$, the strength of T will remain constant.

Now consider what is different about the dominant tendency, T_A, which is initially being expressed in activity A, and T_B, a subordinate tendency which is not? Since activity B is not occurring, there is no consummatory force (C_B). But since there is an F_B, the strength of T_B is going to increase. The amount of increase, $T_f - T_i$, can be attributed to the exposure of the person to F_B throughout the time interval (t). That is, $T_{B_{\mathrm{f}}} - T_{B_{\mathrm{i}}} = F_B \cdot t$. Suppose F_B had been twice as strong? Then it would have produced an equivalent increase in strength of T_B in half the time. By strength or magnitude of F we refer to the arousability of a tendency as shown by the upward slope of the curves representing the strength of T_B in the graphs (see Figure 11) which describe the rate of change in the strength of that tendency.

We can say it another way: $T_{B_{\mathrm{f}}} = T_{B_{\mathrm{i}}} + F_B \cdot t$. Look at any one of the graphs. At the outset, $T_{B_{\mathrm{i}}}$ has a certain strength above zero to which is added the increase in strength attributable to exposure to the magnitude of F_B times the duration of exposure to it, t.

The conditions are different for T_A. Since activity A is occurring, T_A is being expressed in behavior, and so there is the consummatory force (C_A) of activity A in addition to F_A attributable to some feature of the immediate environment. We have assumed (see above) that the magnitude of C_A depends upon the consummatory value (c_A) of the particular *kind of activity* that is occurring (eating a cherry pie versus eating a piece of celery serve as examples of different kinds of eating activities) and the *intensity of the activity,* which here depends on the magnitude of T_A being expressed in behavior. So $C_A = c_A \cdot T_A$. We thus can determine when the strength of T_A will become relatively stable or constant, whether it is increasing because $F_A > C_A$ at the outset, or decreasing because $C_A > F_A$ at the outset. It will become stable when $F_A = C_A$, that is when $F_A = c_A \cdot T_A$, that is when $F_A / c_A = T_A$. The strength of T_A will become relatively constant when it begins to reach a level defined by the ratio of the instigating force for the activity (F_A) and the consummatory value of that activity (c_A). In general, then, T_A will tend to be strong when F_A (the numerator) is strong and weak when F_A is weak.[8]

[8] This means that our now viewing the theory of achievement motivation as a theory about the determinants of instigating forces to achieve success (F_s), and inhibitory forces to avoid failure (I_f), as previously stated, does not change earlier conclusions dramatically. If

Now we can derive a basic principle of a change in activity, one which will tell us *when* the change from A to B will occur. When we observe activity A initially in progress, it implies that $T_{A_i} > T_{B_i}$. When we observe that activity A ceases and activity B is is initiated, it implies that $T_{B_f} > T_{A_f}$ (or that $T_{B_f} = T_{A_f}$ plus a very small and negligible amount which we shall ignore). If we now substitute the determinants of T_{B_f} for T_{B_f}, we can say activity B is initiated *when* $T_{B_i} + F_B \cdot t = T_{A_f}$. And the principle of change in activity emerges when we solve that equation for *when*, the time, t:

$$t = \frac{T_{A_f} - T_{B_i}}{F_B}. \tag{10}$$

If activity A has been going on for a while and T_A has become relatively stable, we may restate the principle to identify the motivational functions of both F_A and F_B, features of the immediate environment, by substituting F_A/c_A for T_{A_f}:

$$t = \frac{F_A/c_A - T_{B_i}}{F_B}. \tag{11}$$

In reference to our first example of a change from achievement-related to affiliative activity, consider the effect of a very strong motive to achieve (M_S). If this strong M_S is sustaining the activity in progress by having an influence on F_A, it will be more difficult to interrupt studying than if M_S is weak. The time to change to affiliative activity will be long.

In reference to our second example, suppose the strong M_S is now influencing F_B. This should promote a greater willingness to initiate activity B (begin studying) promptly than would a weak motive. Thus, other things equal, the person strong in achievement motive should be more willing than others to initiate achievement activities when engaged in or confronted with other alternatives. And since the strength of the tendency expressed in an ongoing activity will approach a higher level when F_A is strong, the person strongly motivated to achieve should express a stronger tendency in behavior and be more persistent in achievement-related activity once he gets started.

Of course, the time to change from achievement to affiliative activity, and vice versa, will depend on the relative strength of the two motives within the person. This will influence the relative strength of F_A and F_B in these examples. Suppose M_S is weak and M_{aff} is strong in both examples we have just considered?

$F_s = M_S \cdot P_s \cdot I_s$, as now assumed for the simplest case, the new deduction that the strength of T_s will become stable in a given situation at a level proportionate to the magnitude of F_s is not a great departure from the earlier idea that, in a given situation, $T_s = M_S \cdot P_s \cdot I_s$, a notion which we now discard.

One, perhaps, can now begin to see how the principle of a change in activity provides a theoretical foundation for expecting to find correlations among different behavioral symptoms of individual differences in strength of motives. Probably most important, this principle constitutes a specification of how an individual with several motives that differ in strength will distribute time among different kinds of activity when it is applied to a continuous stream of behavior (see Figure 10). Only when the achievement motive is very strong relative to the affiliative motive, within a person, will the person be very slow to leave an achievement activity for an affiliative activity and very prompt to go the other way. And only when the achievement motive is very weak relative to the affiliative motive within the person will he be quick to leave an achievement-oriented activity for affiliation and very slow to resume it. In between these imagined extreme types, we have the quantitative continuum of individual differences in strength of motives and of the relative strengths of different motives within the person. We only need to expand our conception to include a larger number of general motives in the basic personality structure (*n* Power, *n* Autonomy, *n* Sex, *n* Eat, etc.), to consider each as an important determinant of an instigating force for a different kind of activity, and to include further consideration of the more specific and situationally defined determinants of each force (competence in particular kinds of activities, (P_s), future orientation (or not), etc.) to see that the principle of a change in activity provides a very specific answer to the question of how various determinants of instigating force, differing in degree of generality–specificity, but all critical dimensions of personality, should be expressed in behavior.

Resistance

How does the inhibitory force to avoid failure, or any other inhibitory force attributable to expectancy of a negative or punishing consequence, influence a change in activity? The essentials can be simply presented in reference to Figure 12.

In Figure 12 we picture what happens when there are both instigating and inhibitory forces for the same activity B to achieve (F_s) and to avoid failure (I_f).

A hatched line shows the arousal and linear growth of the action tendency, T_B, that is attributable to exposure to the F_B of the immediate environment. Simultaneously, below, another hatched line shows the trend of growth in the tendency *not* to engage in activity *B*, the negaction action tendency (N_B) that is attributable to the I_B of the immediate environment.

As soon as N_B is aroused, it begins to oppose or resist T_B to determine the strength of the resultant action tendency ($\bar{T}_B = T_B - N_B$). This process of blocking the expression of T_B, resistance, produces a force of resistance (R), analogous to the consummatory force (C) that occurs when an action tendency is expressed in action. The negaction tendency increases in strength as long as $I_B > R_B$. But as N_B becomes stronger, it is expressed in greater resistance, so R_B,

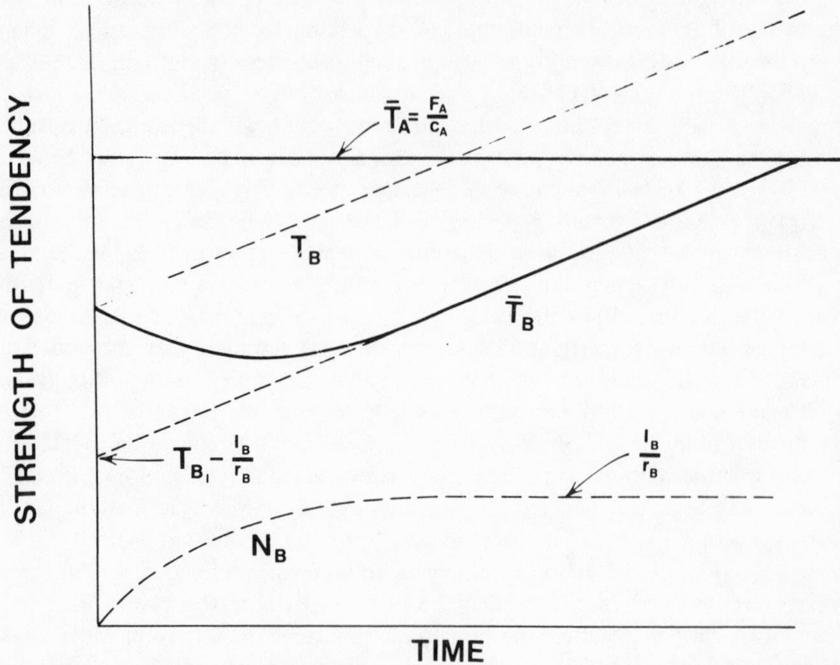

FIGURE 12 The effect of resistance to an alternative activity on time to initiate that activity. See text for discussion. (From Atkinson & Birch, 1970, 1974.)

the force of resistance, also becomes stronger. As it does, the initial difference in strength of I_B (which functions to increase N_B) and R_B (which functions to reduce N_B) diminishes. So N_B grows less rapidly. In time, $R_B = I_B$, so N_B approaches its maximum strength and becomes relatively stable as shown in Figure 12.[9]

The effect of N_B, in opposition to T_B, is shown in the trend of $\bar{T}_B$, the resultant action tendency in Figure 12. The effect of the resistance produced by N_B, and attributable to an inhibitory force is always a temporary suppression of the action tendency. It delays the initiation of activity B for a period of time. This amount of time is sufficient for T_B to continue to grow strong enough eventually to compensate for the maximum strength of N_B. That, too, is shown in the figure.

[9] In the treatment of resistance, there is a parameter r (analogous to c in treatment of consummation) which represents the extent to which a negaction tendency (N) is reduced per unit of time in resistance to an action tendency (T). As a result, N becomes stable at a level defined by I/r as noted in Figure 12.

In brief, the trend of the curve describing the strength of the resultant action tendency, $\overline{T}_B$, is determined at every point by subtraction of the strength of N_B from T_B. In the case of achievement-oriented behavior, the resultant tendency to achieve success $\overline{T}_s = T_s - N_f$, would be temporarily suppressed and the initiation of achievement-oriented action delayed or less likely to occur at all if the inhibitory force is so strong that some other kind of activity X, also instigated in that situation, becomes dominant before $\overline{T}_s$, weakened by resistance, can do so. Often we call such an activity an avoidance activity when it removes the person from the situation posing the threat of a punishment that is the source of resistance to action.

The principle of a change in activity is easily rephrased to include the effect of the resistance. It can be seen in Figure 12 that a negaction tendency has an effect equivalent to having a greater initial *gap* between T_{A_i}, the dominant tendency, and T_{B_i}, which motivates the new alternative activity. That is shown in the graph of Figure 12 and also in the algebraic statement when the principle of change of activity is modified to include the effect of the resistance that is attributable to, and proportionate to the strength of inhibitory force:

$$t = \frac{(F_A/c_A - T_{B_i}) + N_{B_f}}{F_B} = \frac{(F_A/c_A - T_{B_i}) + I_B/r_B}{F_B}. \tag{12}$$

In Figure 13, we have superimposed the resultant action tendencies from Figure 12 where there is and is not resistance, to show comparatively what

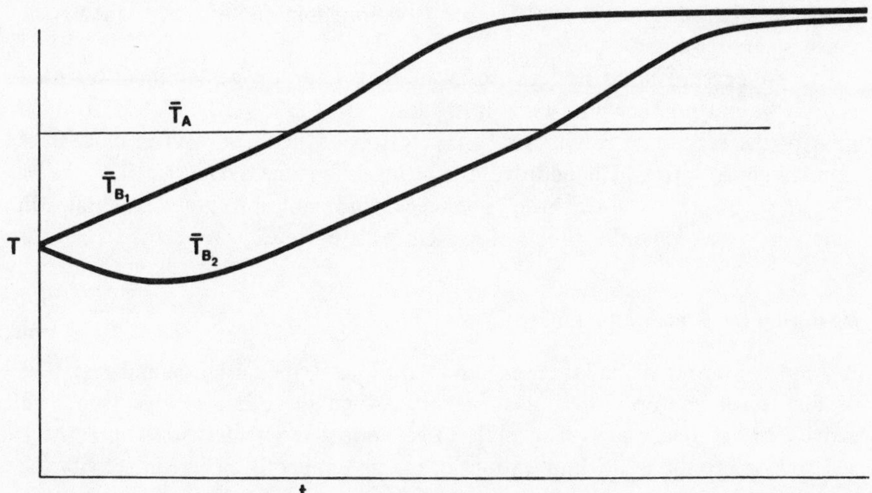

FIGURE 13 The effect of resistance on initiation of an activity ($\overline{T}_{B_1} = T_B$, and $\overline{T}_{B_2} = T_B - N_B$) and the level of resultant tendency, $\overline{T}_B$, expressed in the activity. (From Atkinson & Birch, 1974.)

should be expected concerning initiation and level of motivation for continuous performance of an achievement-related activity, perhaps an important test in a college course, when M_S is identical in two individuals but only one of them has any M_F. This means that F_s is equal for the two individuals but only one of them is exposed to I_f.

The positively motivated person will initiate the achievement-oriented activity sooner and become more completely involved in it sooner than his more anxious peer. After a period of time, however, the strength of motivation expressed in the task, $\overline{T}_s$, will become more nearly equal for the two individuals. How long this takes depends upon the magnitude of I_f. But by then, most of the detrimental effects on performance attributable to the tendency to avoid failure should have occurred – early rather than late in a test period. Here we assume (for simplicity) that the maximum level of $\overline{T}$ for both persons is in the low to moderate range and not complicated further by the inefficiency attributable to overmotivation should $\overline{T}$ be beyond the optimal level for the task.

One important difference between the new dynamics of achievement-oriented action, here pictured, and the old static model of achievement motivation deserves comment. Previously it seemed essential always to assume the presence of some extrinsic motivational tendency to overcome an initially negative resultant achievement motivation (i.e., whenever $M_F > M_S$). Now it is evident that the effect of resistance is a temporal delay, a temporary suppression of achievement-oriented action, but that the initiation of an achievement-oriented activity should occur sooner or later without any necessary help of an extrinsic incentive *if* the individual stays in the situation long enough even when resistance is very strong.

The presence of additional extrinsic incentives for the achievement-oriented activity would produce additional instigating forces ($F_{approval}$, $F_{\$}$, etc.) which refer to the very same activity as F_s. The effect of the three positive tendencies simultaneously aroused is additive as previously assumed. That is, $T_B = T_{B,s} + T_{B,app} + T_{B,\$}$, etc. The extrinsic tendencies, while not absolutely essential, still function to overcome the effects of resistance as previously supposed.

Measuring the Stream of Activity

A simple assumption that there is a short time lag in the initiation and cessation of the consummatory force of an activity, when there is a change from one activity to another, makes it possible to generate a series of changes in activity and to begin studying the implications of the principle of a change in activity for a succession of changes, a much longer temporal unit of behavior in a constant environment than previously considered. Birch (1972) has specified the theoretical foundation of such measures as frequency of an activity, time spent in an activity, and the derivative measure of rate or operant level of an activity, among others. A computer program for the dynamics of action originated by Seltzer

(1973) and refined and extended by Seltzer and Sawusch (1974) and Bongort (1975) spells out the behavioral implications of differences in personality (M_S and M_F) using the theory of achievement motivation as a specification of the instigating and inhibitory forces as illustrated for a ring-toss game (see Table 10).

In addition to recovering what is already known, computer simulation has enabled us to check the applicability to a situation involving many competing alternative activities of Birch's mathematical expressions for the simple two alternative case (Atkinson & Birch, 1970; Birch, 1968, 1972). Thus we find, as shown in Figure 14, that the percentage of time spent in a particular kind of activity (achievement, affiliative, power, eating, etc.) in a particular (constant) environment depends upon the asymptotic strength of a particular kind of tendency ($T_A = F_A/c_A$) relative to the sum of asymptotic strengths of all the alternatives in that setting:

$$\text{Time in activity } A\ (\%) = \frac{F_A/c_A}{F_A/c_A + F_B/c_B + \cdots + F_N/c_N}. \tag{12}$$

Treating motive to achieve (M_S) as a determinant of F_s and other relatively general social motives (affiliation, power, autonomy, etc.) as determinants of instigating forces for different kinds of activity, it is clear that we now have *a specification of how basic personality conceived as a hierarchy of general motives will be expressed in behavior.* It will be reflected in an individual's distribution of time among various activities. It is perhaps unnecessary to spell out that the same principle which applies to initiation of an activity (latency), choice among alternatives, persistence in an activity, and proportion of time spent in an activity, can also account for the more popular and derivative measure, the operant level or rate of an activity. And in doing so, it provides a theoretical foundation for the expectation of intercorrelations among the various behavioral measures of the relative strength, within a person, of personality variables called motives.

It can be seen in Figure 14 that we deduce a positive monotonic relationship between strength of instigating force (and therefore more generally of motive) and percentage of time spent in related activity. For simplicity, in the next section, we shall treat this relationship as linear.

The single most important result of our simulations of motivational determinants of behavior have come from application of the theory derived through persistent use of thematic apperceptive measurement of motives, in the face of rather constant and substantial criticism concerning their alleged lack of psychometric respectability, to the measuring instrument itself. The stream of imaginative behavior instigated by a particular TAT picture is 4 min long in a constant, picture-defined environment. Then, immediately, a new picture is shown and another 4-min stream of imaginative behavior ensues, and so on for a set of 4 or more pictures. No particular difficulty is faced confronting a number of hypothetical individuals who differ in strength of achievement motive (and motives

TABLE 10

Computer Simulation of Effects of Individual Differences in Achievement Motivation on Risk Preference under Free Operant Conditions, such as Shooting from Different Distances in a Ring-Toss Game[a]

Task	P_s	50 time units		150 time units	
		Time spent	Activity initiated[b]	Time spent	Activity initiated[b]
When M_S = 500 and M_F = 100					
A	.93	0.1	0	12.6	3
B	.70	8.8	1	39.0	5
C	.50	23.6	3	49.7	6
D	.33	17.5	2	33.9	4
E	.10	0.0	0	15.6	2
When M_S = 100 and M_F = 500					
A	.93	20.9	1	37.1	4
B	.70	7.8	1	30.8	4
C	.50	0.0	0	22.2	3
D	.33	1.0	1	24.8	3
E	.10	20.2	2	35.6	4

NOTE.–It is here assumed that there is neither displacement nor substitution among alternatives; that $F = F_S + F_{ext}$ and that $F_{ext} = 45$ for each alternative; that c for each activity is .1; that r for each activity is .05; that T_i and N_i for each activity are 0; that selective attention for each alternative is 1.00; that the parameters for initial and cessation lags are 10 and for each curve are .40.

[a]Simulation run and contributed by Mio Kawamura Reynolds. Table from Atkinson and Birch (1974).

[b]The actual frequency of shots taken, and hence the operant level, may correspond more closely to the time spent in the activity than to the number of separate initiations of the activity.

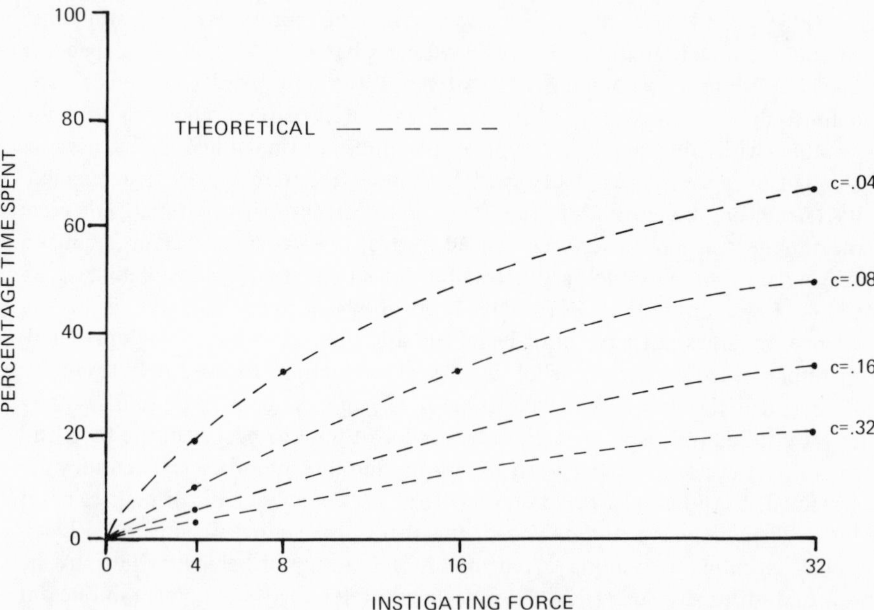

FIGURE 14 Correspondence of simulated (•) and theoretical percentage of time spent in activity A assuming percentage of time doing A equals ratio of F_A/c_A to $F_A/c_A + F_B/c_B + \cdots F_N/c_N$ in that environment. (From Atkinson, Bongort, & Price, 1977.)

for other kinds of activity) with a series of 4 or more environments (i.e., pictures) that differ in their incentive properties. The uninterrupted stream of behavior on Story 1 and Story 2, etc, each one looking like Figure 10, provides separate measures of time spent in imaginative achievement-related activity and a total time score for the set of simulated stories. These measures represent the theoretically deduced time that a particular motivational tendency is dominant during the time interval (100 units) of a particular story. We now can answer, without hesitation or qualification, a persistent criticism of thematic apperception based on its very modest internal consistency reliability. We have found that construct validity of the total score (time spent) *does not* require internal consistency reliability.

In our very first effort along this line (conducted by Margaret Moffett, April 1974), the internal consistency of a hypothetical 5-story TAT test, as indicated by Cronbach's α based on simulated time spent in imaginative achievement activity in each story was .08, yet 87% of 30 hypothetical subjects were correctly placed into High, Mid, and Low thirds of the distribution according to the strength of achievement motive specified in the computer input. Other simulations of a 5-story TAT have yielded $\alpha = .18$ with 80% of 30 subjects correctly placed on the basis of total score and $\alpha = .07$ with 90% of 30 subjects correctly placed according to relative strength of motive. We have still other computer simulation studies in which α ranges between .27 and .90, depending upon variations in parameters of the theory. The only point to be made here, definitively, is that a very substantial degree of construct validity is logically possible with thematic apperceptive measures of individual differences in strength of motives (personality) with absolutely no internal consistency reliability (Atkinson, Bongort, & Price, 1977). Some critics of thematic apperceptive measurement of motivation have tended to treat the whole research program as a 25-year sham because their estimates of internal consistency is a very modest .35 to .40 (e.g., Entwistle, 1972). The lesson to be learned from this is that in science one does not have prior belief in basic premises – as in religions – and, therefore, predetermined belief in logical deductions from those premises. Rather, it is the other way around. One works up to some premise (a theory) by creative induction from empirical observations using the best available tools and then down again, deductively, to empirically testable hypotheses. When they are sustained, confidence in the premise (theory) is enhanced but, of course, never final. When they are not sustained, the theory is repaired or discarded. Traditional psychometrics is not a religion. It is a theory of behavior that must be repaired, discarded, or at least now declared irrelevant to the domain of operant imaginative behavior, the domain of measurement of motivation.

Potentially productive young scientists may have been warned away from what has turned out to be the most heuristic method of studying human motivation by mistaken myths of measurement, dogmatically repeated, year in and out in standard textbooks. The use of the controversial TAT method has contributed to development of theory that can be usefully applied to the content of long temporal units of behavior in either a constant or changing environment. And, in relation to the limited studies of the stream of behavior represented in operant conditioning, and by some social psychological ecologists, the content analysis of operant imaginative behavior now appears to be a most promising and still virtually untapped resource for future study of personality and for social psychology more generally.

MOTIVATION AND ACHIEVEMENT

Seeing that motivation influences behavior in two ways, efficiency of performance and time spent in an activity, helped us to distinguish two often confused meanings of the term achievement. On some occasions, one means to refer to the quality or level of performance on a particular occasion (e.g., a test in a course, a particular surgical operation, a particular baseball game). On other occasions, one means to refer to cumulative achievement over a span of time (e.g., the overall academic record in college, upward social mobility, a productive career). The point of the distinction is made in Figure 15. It should suggest analogies if

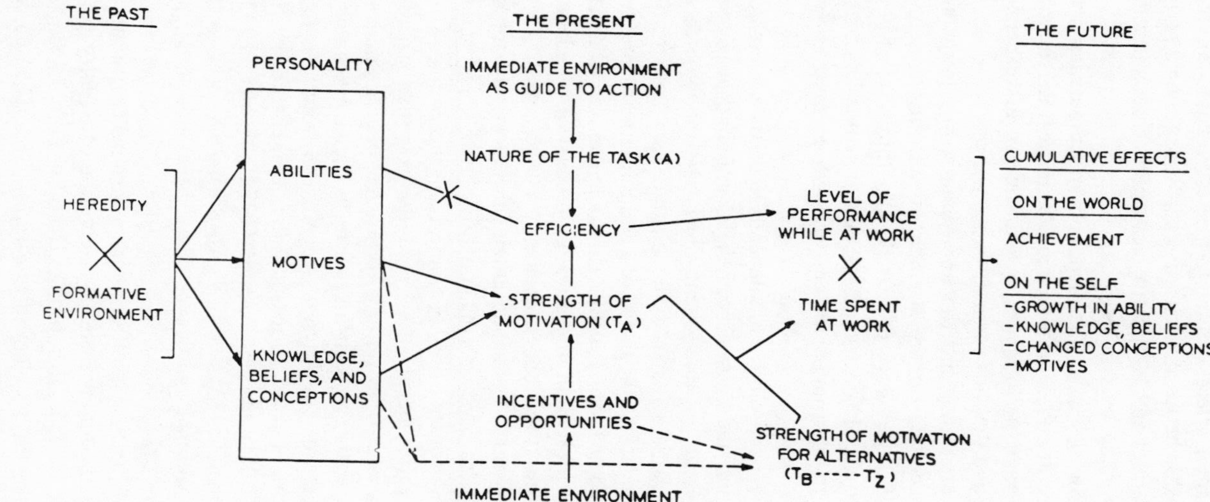

FIGURE 15 The dual role of motivation as a determinant of cumulative achievement. Level of performance while at work is attributed to ability, the nature of the task, and the effect of strength of motivation (T_A) on efficiency of performance. Time spent at work depends upon the strength of motivation for the critical task (T_A) relative to number and strength of motivation for other activities ($T_B \ldots T_Z$). Cumulative effects on the self are also shown. (From Atkinson, 1974a, as elaborated in Atkinson, Lens, and O'Malley, 1976.)

one uses it as a guide and thinks in terms of effects of affiliative or power motivation (Veroff & Veroff, 1972; Winter, 1973), instead of motivation to achieve, as in this chapter. Here, with our interest focused on the specific question of the relationship between intellective performance on a particular test (e.g., of academic aptitude) and cumulative academic achievement, we have a general conception that guides current research.

Working backwards in the causal sequence from cumulative achievement (overall academic record at college as a concrete example), we suppose it to be the product of the level of performance (when engaged in academic achievement-oriented activity) and the time spent in that activity.

The interaction of personality and the immediate environment, as we have come to conceive it, accounts for the strength of motivation for the relevant activity (T_A) which influences both efficiency, and thus level of performance while at work, and also the time spent in relevant activity when its strength is considered in relation to the number of and strength of motivation for competing alternatives.

The strength of achievement motivation depends upon the strength of achievement-related motives, and the knowledge, beliefs, and conceptions of the individual (e.g., P_s, competence, future orientation). The theory of achievement motivation (presented earlier) fits into the diagram as a specification of the determinants or components of the instigating and inhibitory forces for achievement-related and other activities. How the various tendencies to do and *not* to do are aroused and expressed in the stream of behavior is where the new dynamics of action fits into the broader scheme.

We have found it essential to include among the most relevant descriptive dimensions of personality: *abilities* (the longtime favorite of mental testers), *motives* (essentially the contribution of clinical psychology with its psychoanalytic emphasis on early socialization), and the cognitive structure of the individual which embraces the individual's *knowledge, beliefs,* and *conceptions.* This latter category has always been a favorite in social psychology. Here is where we would include not only Raynor's cognitive elaboration of the theory of achievement motivation but also, hopefully, the other cognitive variables now being identified by Heckhausen and Weiner (1972), Weiner (1972, 1974b), Kukla (1972), Heckhausen (1973), and their coworkers, who seek to enlarge our conception of the motivational significance of cognitive inferential and attributional processes, in terms of which people may differ.

All the dimensions of individual differences in personality are represented as having a developmental history involving an interaction of heredity and *formative* environment, $P = f(H \times E_f)$. This problem, not dealt with explicitly here where the focus has been the problem of *motivation,* $B = f(P \times E)$, has been a topic of major interest to others concerned mainly with *development* of *n* Achievement and/or anxiety (e.g., V. C. Crandall, 1969; V. J. Crandall, 1963; Heckhausen, 1967; Kagan & Moss, 1962; McClelland, 1951, 1961, 1965; McClelland & Winter, 1969; Rosen *et al.*, 1969; Sarason *et al.*, 1960; Smith, 1969a, b; Veroff, 1965, 1969; Weiner, 1974a; Winterbottom, 1953, 1958).

I have long argued that the problem of motivation is logically prior to the problem of development (Atkinson, 1969a; Atkinson & Raynor, 1974, p. 4). I simply mean that one must first identify the characteristics of personality that need to be taken into account in the interaction with environment to explain behavior in order to identify the theoretically relevant dependent variables for developmental psychology. The aim, in this diagram, is to acknowledge the importance of both the genetic or biological heritage and the social or cultural heritage as sources of individual differences in personality.

We can pull it all together, and illustrate the relation of basic psychology to applied psychology, by showing how principles evolved in experimental and conceptual analysis apply to the well-documented fact that the correlation between our best diagnostic tests of scholastic or academic aptitude (level of intellective performance on a test) and grade point average at college (cumulative achievement) typically fall between about .25 and .50 (Atkinson, 1974a).

A numerical illustration is given in Table 11 where the following assumptions are made.

1. Individual differences in ability and strength of motivation for academic work are uncorrelated.
2. Level of performance = Ability × Efficiency.
3. The relationship between strength of motivation and efficiency of performance is nonmonotonic (see Figure 9).
4. The relationship between strength of motivation and time spent in academic activity (in the long run) is monotonic and approximately linear (see Figure 14).
5. The strength of motivation is typically weaker under conditions of normal work than when taking a test.

Careful inspection of the table will help to identify so-called "overachievers." They turn out to be persons whose very strong motivation produces inefficiency, and therefore underestimates of true ability on tests, but which leads them to spend much more time than others in relevant academic activity (A5, B5, C5, etc).

The "underachievers" are persons who are only moderately (optimally) motivated on a test. They score the highest, but when even less motivated in normal everyday work, they are both less efficient and spend less time than others at work (e.g., A3, B3).

For this simple hypothetical example ($N = 20$), the linear correlation between test score and grade point average is .37. If we assumed that one-fourth of the students were ones in whom $M_F > M_S$ rather than $M_S > M_F$ and that they therefore had less resistance to overcome in normal work and so had motivation increase (+1) instead of decrease (−1) in normal work as for the others, the

TABLE 11

True Ability and Motivation as Determinants of the Level of Intellective Performance (on an Ability Test) and Cumulative Academic Achievement (Grade Average in College): A Hypothetical Numerical Illustration Emphasizing the Dual Role of Motivation Assumed in Figure 15[a]

	Ability test situation				Conditions of normal academic work					
Name of subject[b]	True ability	Motivation	Efficiency	Level of test performance	True ability	Motivation[c]	Efficiency	Level of performance	Time spent in work	Cumulative achievement
A3	100	3	1.00	100	100	2	.80	80	2	160
A4	100	4	.80	80	100	3	1.00	100	3	*300*
A2	100	2	.80	80	100	1	.50	50	1	50
B3	80	3	1.00	80	80	2	.80	64	2	128
B4	80	4	.80	64	80	3	1.00	80	3	*240*
				$-Q_1$						
B2	80	2	.80	64	80	1	.50	40	1	40
C3	60	3	1.00	60	60	2	.80	48	2	96
A5	100	5	.50	50	100	4	.80	80	4	*320*
C4	60	4	.80	48	60	3	1.00	60	3	180
C2	60	2	.80	48	60	1	.50	30	1	30
				–Md						
B5	80	5	.50	40	80	4	.80	64	4	*256*
D3	40	3	1.00	40	40	2	.80	32	2	64
D4	40	4	.80	32	40	3	1.00	40	3	120
D2	40	2	.80	32	40	1	.50	20	1	20
C5	60	5	.50	30	60	4	.80	48	4	*192*
				$-Q_3$						
D5	40	5	.50	20	40	4	.80	32	4	128
E3	20	3	1.00	20	20	2	.80	16	2	32
E4	20	4	.80	16	20	3	1.00	20	3	60
E2	20	2	.80	16	20	1	.50	10	1	10
E5	20	5	.50	10	20	4	.80	16	4	64

[a]From Atkinson (1974a).

[b]Subjects are named according to their true level of ability (A = 100, B = 80, C = 60, D = 40, E = 20) and their strength of motivation (T_a) in the ability test situation. See Figure 15 to identify determinants of T_a.

[c]It is assumed here that all subjects are less strongly motivated during normal work (–1) than in the test situation.

correlation (N = 80) falls between .33 and .48 depending upon how similar or different the hypothetical students are assumed to be in motivation for incompatible time-consuming activities (Sawusch, 1974).

This is enough to show that one may deduce one of the best documented empirical facts in the literature on mental testing from principles developed studying achievement motivation. Extensions of this type of analysis and discussion of the obvious implications regarding so-called intelligence tests and the interrelationship between ability and motivation are presented elsewhere (Atkinson, 1974a; Atkinson, Lens, & O'Malley, 1976).

One can also find in Table 11 a viable hypothesis concerning the repeatedly reported drop in scholastic aptitude scores between the 1950s and 1970s, a period in which grades in college were rising. Consider hypothetical Subjects B3 and B4 as analogous to the average student in the 1950s and 1970s respectively. The trend in test score, B3 to B4, is down, but the trend in cumulative achievement is, paradoxically, up. What is different about the two? One is more highly motivated, both at the time of the test and in normal acacemic work, than the other. Is there any reasonable basis for assuming an intensification of motivation among students between the 1950s and 1970s? The percentage of 18–22-year-olds attending college rose from about 20% to more than double that in the 20-year span. How might that social fact influence the perceived relationship between test score and admission to one of the better colleges in the country? How might that social fact influence the perceived instrumentality of good performance in college to selection for some postcollege opportunity for which GPA is one of the important selection criteria? What is the motivational effect of seeing a present activity as instrumental to more distant future goals in a population in which $M_S > M_F$ is the modal personality?

Motivation and Society

Can one take the method of content analysis of "thought samples" (McClelland *et al.*, 1953/1976, Chapter 10) that was experimentally validated on college students in the twentieth century, which has contributed to a substantial theoretical advance, and apply it to the literature of the past and present societies to learn something about motivation and society? David McClelland believed so two decades ago and initiated a program of research on societal motivation even before we had firmly established the construct validity of TAT *n* Achievement. He and his colleagues, careful to obtain representative samples of the literature of various societies, have provided a harbinger of what behavioral science is to become (McClelland, 1958c, 1961). Using the contemporary method of content analysis for *n* Achievement (and other social motives, *n* Affiliation, *n* Power) much as anthropologists and archeologists have been using the radium carbon-dating method derived from modern advances in nuclear physics, they have obtained quantitative measures of concern over achievement expressed in the literature of different societies.

Among the conclusions reached in this innovative venture is evidence that a decline in concern over achievement in the literature of a society precedes the decline of a society. It has been shown in reference to ancient Greece, medieval Spain, and ancient Crete (McClelland, 1958c, 1961, 1971b).

In a study of the relationship between *n* Achievement in the literature of England and an index of economic activity in the port of London from 1550 to 1800, Bradburn and Berlew (1961; also in McClelland, 1961) discovered the amazing correspondence shown in Figure 16. The trend for motivational imagery in literature anticipates a comparable trend in the economic activity of the society by about 50 years.

Shall we take this time lag seriously? What might it imply for us, if the whole line of argument concerning achievement motivation and society is correct including the data mentioned at the outset from deCharms and Moeller (1962) and now shown in Figure 17?

McClelland's comparison of *n* Achievement scores obtained from readers in 21 different societies in 1925 was found to be positively correlated with an index of economic development of those societies between 1925 and 1950. His further interest in this problem has lead him to consider ways of enhancing the achievement motivation of interested businessmen (McClelland & Winter, 1969), an activity also now being pursued with students having academic difficulties (e.g., Kolb, 1965; McClelland, 1965).

Fear of success in women is another motivational problem related to an important social change in this age of reappraisal and redefinition of the role of male and female (anticipated by Mead, 1949). The results of the very earliest comparative study of TAT *n* Achievement in males and females by Veroff, *et al.* (1953) found that high-school boys, like college men, expressed more achievement imagery imaginatively following experimental induction of achievement motivation. But high-school girls did not. They expressed as much concern about achievement in stories about men under relaxed conditions as did both they and the boys when achievement motivation had been experimentally aroused beforehand. And then, way back in 1950, they produced very little concern about achievement when writing about female characters. Sue Wilcox (in Veroff *et al.*, 1953) found the same to be true of Michigan college women when tested under the very relaxed conditions of their dorm, in the evening, and long before the era of the coed dormitory.

Lesser, Krawitz, and Packard (1963) helped to clarify the problem by plotting results obtained separately for talented Hunter College girls who were achieving academically up to their potentials (achievers) and those who definitely were not (underachievers) as shown in Table 12.

Notice that the achieving women showed the expected increase in achievement motivation in stories about women (but not men). In contrast, the under-

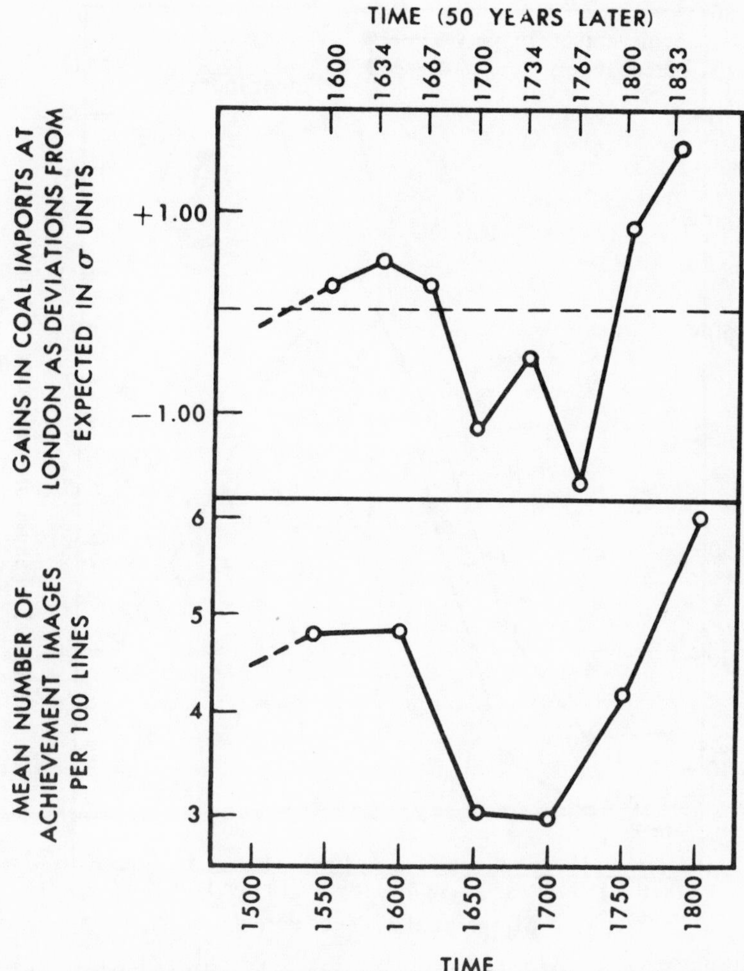

FIGURE 16 Average *n* Achievement levels in English literature (1550–1800) compared with rates of gain in coal imports in London 50 years later. (From McClelland, 1961, p. 139.)

achievers showed an increase when motivation had been induced before stories were written in response to pictures of males. Was this a displaced expression of interest in achieving among women who were conflicted about their social role as Mead (1949) had argued? Their academic difficulty could be taken as objective evidence of that conflict (see also Alper, 1974; Crandall, 1969; Hoffman, 1972; Lesser, 1973; Stein & Bailey, 1973).

The seminal study of Matina Souretis Horner (1968, 1970, 1974a) focused upon evidence of fear of success in women as a key to the problem. Her data,

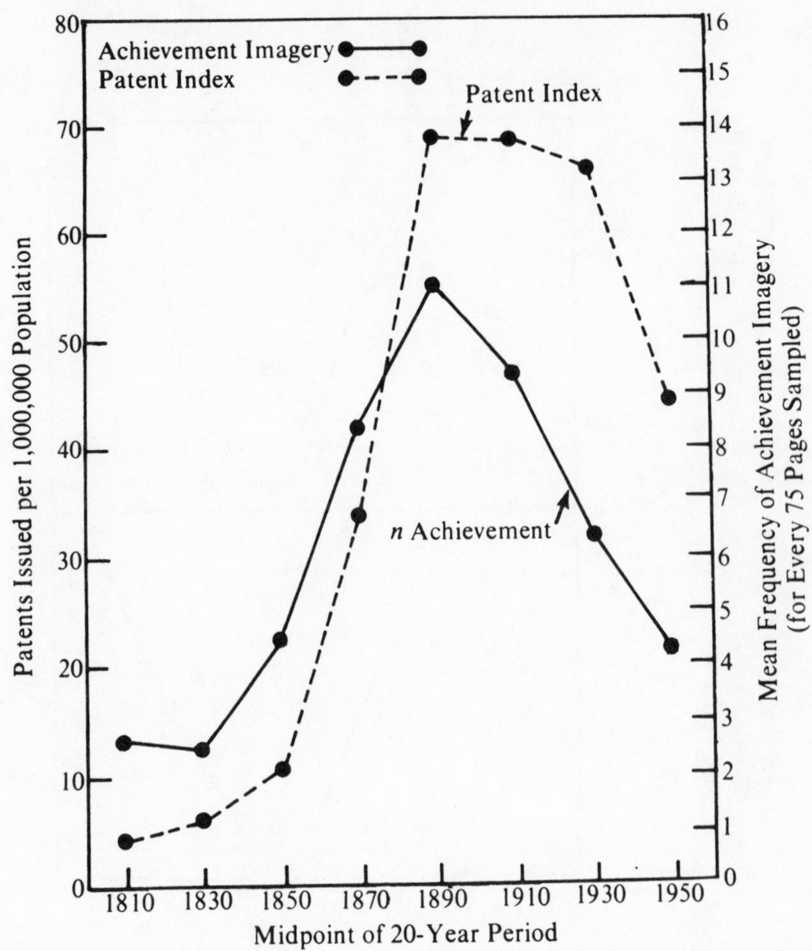

FIGURE 17 Mean frequency of achievement imagery in children's readers and patent index in the United States, 1800–1950. (From deCharms & Moeller in McClelland, 1961, p. 150).

collected among female Michigan college students in 1965, showed 62% of women displaying some evidence of a negative consequence (e.g., social rejection or worse) when a heroine succeeded in an imaginative story. Only 9% of the male heroes suffered that fate. In comparing women with men in general, 67% of whom would perform better under conditions of interpersonal conflict than when working alone, Horner found that 93% of the minority of women who were apparently *not* fearful of success showed the same pattern as that of most men. But 77% of the women who had expressed some indication of fear of

TABLE 12

Mean n Achievement Scores of Achieving and Underachieving Girls Under Neutral and Achievement-Oriented Experimental Conditions to Pictures Containing Female and Male Characters[a]

		Experimental conditions				
		Neutral		Achievement oriented		
		3 female pictures	3 male pictures	3 female pictures	3 male pictures	Total for all experimental conditions and pictures
Group	N	M	M	M	M	M
Achievers	(40)	4.80	5.43	6.03	4.78	5.26
Underachievers	(40)	2.93	4.18	2.25	6.20	3.89
Total for all subjects	(80)	3.86	4.80	4.14	5.49	

[a]From Lesser *et al.* (1963). Copyright 1963 by the American Psychological Association. Reproduced by permission.

success imaginatively performed better when working alone than in a competitive situation.

At this writing, the results of many follow-up studies are sharpening description of the problem. The literature abounds with new studies. It is of vital interest to both young women and young men as traditional assumptions about what is expected of them in life are being reexamined and as both appraise the potential gains and costs of new life styles.

Given the yield of 25 years of study of achievement motivation in men, with evidence made integratable by consistent use of the same experimentally validated thematic apperceptive measure of *n* Achievement, there is reason for confidence that a similar concentration of effort, an occasional creative insight, and consistent use of a heuristic method should yield a more coherent picture of motivational effects of both sex and race on motivation for achievement than I am prepared to attempt at this time. (But see Feld & Lewis, 1969; Katz, 1967; Veroff, 1969.)

PERSONALITY AND BEHAVIORAL PROCESSES

It is difficult to imporve on Kurt Lewin's (1946) statement of the interrelatedness of the study of individual differences and of lawful behavioral processes which is expressed in systematic study of achievement motivation.

> A law is expressed in an equation which relates certain variables. Individual differences have to be conceived of as various specific values which these variables have in a particular case. In other words, general laws and individual differences are merely two aspects of one problem; they are mutually dependent on each other and the study of the one cannot proceed without the study of the other [p. 794].

Personality is embedded in the two basic problems of psychology. In the study of *motivation*, $B = f(P, E)$, it is an independent variable. In the study of *development*, $P = f(H, E_f)$, where H refers to heredity and E_f, to the formative social environment, personality is the dependent variable.

Having identified *abilities, motives, knowledge, beliefs,* and *conceptions* as attributes of personality that are essential for a lawful account of human motivation and action, we have set a problem for those interested in developmental psychology. We have defined three attributes of personality, each having a developmental history. It will be a more complete, coherent and useful account when we have formulated principles accounting for change in personality, that is, the origin and growth of particular abilities, motives, knowledge, beliefs, and conceptions. This is what we need a developmental psychology of, not merely a descriptive account of conditions that produce a change in behavior between one and another occasion under similar conditions. This is what it means to say that the study of motivation is logically prior to the study of development.

A final word. This essay has emphasized the evolution of theory relating personality–motivation–action. Those who, like myself, are very skeptical of conjectural psychologizing from an armchair as a substitute for theory in science may find it somewhat reassuring to know that the trilogy of progress reports from Michigan: *Motives in Fantasy, Action, and Society* (1958), *A Theory of Achievement Motivation* (1966), and *Motivation and Achievement* (1974) were based, respectively, on 37 studies involving 40 different investigators and 4,655 subjects; 18 studies involving 12 different investigators (of whom 9 were new ones) and 4,939 subjects; 33 studies involving 17 different investigators (of whom 12 were new ones) and 4,554 subjects, by my hasty count. Among these studies were the primary results of 25 doctoral dissertations (23 from Michigan), each of which had a critical, standard-setting committee to satisfy. And that is really only part of the contemporary literature on achievement motivation given selective emphasis, for reasons already stated in this chapter.

REFERENCES

Allport, G. W. *Personality: A psychological interpretation.* New York: Holt, 1937.

Alper, T. G. Achievement motivation in college women: A now-you-see-it – now-you-don't phenomenon. *American Psychologist,* 1974, *29,* 194–203.

Alpert, R., & Haber, R. N. Anxiety in academic achievement situations. *Journal of Abnormal and Social Psychology,* 1960, *61,* 207–215.

Angelina, A. L. Un novo método par avaliar a motivacão numana. Unpublished doctoral dissertation, Universidade de São Paulo, Brazil, 1955.

Atkinson, J. W. Studies in projective measurement of achievement motivation. Unpublished doctoral dissertation, University of Michigan, 1950. Ann Arbor: Univ. Microfilms Publ. #1945. pp. 145.

Atkinson, J. W. The achievement motive and recall of interrupted and completed tasks. *Journal of Experimental Psychology,* 1953, *46,* 381–390. Also in D. C. McClelland (Ed.), *Studies in motivation.* New York: Appleton-Century-Crofts, 1955.

Atkinson, J. W. Explorations using imaginative thought to assess the strength of human motives. In M. R. Jones (Ed.), *Nebraska Symposium on Motivation* (Vol. 2). Lincoln: University of Nebraska Press, 1954. Pp. 56–112.

Atkinson, J. W. Motivational determinants of risk-taking behavior. *Psychological Review,* 1957, *64,* 359–372.

Atkinson, J. W. (Ed.). *Motives in fantasy, action, and society.* Princeton, N.J.: Van Nostrand, 1958. (a)

Atkinson, J. W. Thematic apperceptive measurement of motives within the context of a theory of motivation. In J. W. Atkinson (Ed.), *Motives in fantasy, action, and society.* Princeton, N.J.: Van Nostrand, 1958. (b)

Atkinson, J. W. Toward experimental analysis of human motivation in terms of motives, expectancies, and incentives. In J. W. Atkinson (Ed.), *Motives in fantasy, action, and society.* Princeton, N.J.: Van Nostrand, 1958. (c)

Atkinson, J. W. Personality dynamics. *Annual Review of Psychology,* 1960, *11,* 225–290.

Atkinson, J. W. *An introduction to motivation.* Princeton, N.J.: Van Nostrand, 1964.

Atkinson, J. W. The mainsprings of achievement-oriented activity. In J. Krumboltz (Ed.), *Learning and the educational process.* Chicago: Rand-McNally, 1965.

Atkinson, J. W. Comments on papers by Crandall and Veroff. In C. P. Smith (Ed.), *Achievement-related motives in children.* New York: Russell Sage Foundation, 1969. (a)

Atkinson, J. W. Measuring achievement-related motives. Unpublished final report, NSF Project GS-1399, University of Michigan, 1969. (b)

Atkinson, J. W. Motivational determinants of intellective performance and cumulative achievement. In J. W. Atkinson & J. O. Raynor (Eds.), *Motivation and achievement.* Washington, D.C.: Winston, 1974. (a)

Atkinson, J. W. Strength of motivation and efficiency of performance. In J. W. Atkinson & J. O. Raynor (Eds.), *Motivation and achievement.* Washington, D.C.: Winston, 1974. (b)

Atkinson, J. W., Bastian, J. R., Earl, R. W., & Litwin, G. H. The achievement motive, goal setting, and probability preferences. *Journal of Abnormal and Social Psychology,* 1960, *60,* 27–36.

Atkinson, J. W., & Birch, D. *The dynamics of action.* New York: Wiley, 1970.

Atkinson, J. W., & Birch, D. The dynamics of achievement-oriented activity. In J. W. Atkinson & J. W. Raynor (Eds.), *Motivation and achievement.* Washington, D.C.: Winston, 1974.

Atkinson, J. W., Bongort, K., & Price, L. H. Explorations using computer simulation to comprehend TAT measurement of motivation. *Motivation and Emotion,* 1977, *1,* 1–27.

Atkinson, J. W., & Cartwright, D. Some neglected variables in contemporary conceptions of decision and performance. *Psychological Reports,* 1964, *14,* 575–590.

Atkinson, J. W., & Feather, N. T. (Eds.). *A theory of achievement motivation.* New York: Wiley, 1966.

Atkinson, J. W., Heyns, R. W., & Veroff, J. The effect of experimental arousal of the affiliation motive on thematic apperception. *Journal of Abnormal and Social Psychology,* 1954, *49,* 405–410. Also in J. W. Atkinson (Ed.), *Motives in fantasy, action, and society.* Princeton; N.J.: Van Nostrand, 1958.

Atkinson, J. W., Lens, W., & O'Malley, P. M. Motivation and ability: Interactive psychological determinants of intellective performance, educational achievement, and each other. In W. H. Sewell, R. M. Hauser, & D. L. Featherman (Eds.), *Schooling and achievement in American society.* New York: Academic Press, 1976.

Atkinson, J. W., & Litwin, G. H. Achievement motive and test anxiety conceived as motive to approach success and to avoid failure. *Journal of Abnormal and Social Psychology,* 1960, *60,* 52–63. Also in J. W. Atkinson & N. T. Feather (Eds.), *A theory of achievement motivation.* New York: Wiley, 1966.

Atkinson, J. W., & McClelland, D. C. The projective expression of needs. II. The effect of different intensities of the hunger drive on thematic apperception. *Journal of Experimental Psychology,* 1948, *38,* 643–658.

Atkinson, J. W., & O'Connor, P. A. *Effects of ability grouping in schools related to individual differences in achievement-related motivation.* Project 1283 of Cooperative Research Program of the Office of Education, United States Department of Health, Education, and Welfare, 1963. (Microfilm or copies available from Photoduplication Center, Library of Congress, Washington, D.C.)

Atkinson, J. W., & O'Connor, P. A. Neglected factors in studies of achievement-oriented performance: Social approval as an incentive and performance decrement. In J. W. Atkinson & N. T. Feather (Eds.), *A theory of achievement motivation.* New York: Wiley, 1966.

Atkinson, J. W., & Raphelson, A. C. Individual differences in motivation and behavior in particular situations, *Journal of Personality,* 1956, *24,* 349–363.

Atkinson, J. W., & Raynor, J. O. (Eds.). *Motivation and achievement.* Washington, D.C.: Winston (Halsted Press/Wiley), 1974.

Atkinson, J. W., & Reitman, W. R. Performance as a function of motive strength and expectancy of goal attainment. *Journal of Abnormal and Social Psychology,* 1956, *53,* 361–366. Also in J. W. Atkinson (Ed.), *Motives in fantasy, action, and society.* Princeton, N.J.: Van Nostrand, 1958.

Atkinson, J. W., & Walker, E. L. The affiliative motive and perceptual sensitivity to faces. *Journal of Abnormal and Social Psychology,* 1956, *53,* 38–41.

Bachman, J. B., Kahn, R. L., Mednick, M. T., Davidson, T. N., & Johnston, L. D. *Youth in transition.* Vol. 1. *Blueprint for a longitudinal study of adolescent boys.* Ann Arbor: Survey Research Center, Institute for Social Research, 1967.

Benedict, R. *Patterns of culture.* Boston: Houghton-Mifflin, 1934.

Birch, D. Shift in activity and the concept of persisting tendency. In K. W. Spence & J. T. Spence (Eds.), *The psychology of learning and motivation: Advances in research and theory* (Vol. II). New York: Academic Press, 1968.

Birch, D. Measuring the stream of activity. *Michigan Mathematical Psychology Publication. MMPP 72-2.* Ann Arbor: University of Michigan, 1972.

Blankenship, V. Computer simulation of achievement risk preference assuming substitution. Unpublished manuscript, University of Michigan, March 10, 1976.

Bongort, K. Revision of program by Seltzer and Sawusch: Computer program written to simulate the dynamics of action. Unpublished program, University of Michigan, September 4, 1975.

Bradburn, N. M., & Berlew, D. E. Need for achievement and English economic growth. *Economic Development and Cultural Change,* 1961, *10,* 8–20.

Broadhurst, P. L. The interaction of task difficulty and motivation: The Yerkes–Dodson Law revived. *Acta Psychologica,* 1959, *16,* 321–338.

Cartwright, D., & Festinger, L. A quantitative theory of decision. *Psychological Review,* 1943, *50,* 595–621.

Clark, R. A. The projective measurement of experimentally induced levels of sexual motivation. *Journal of Experimental Psychology,* 1952, *44,* 391–399.

Conant, J. B. *Science and common sense.* New Haven, Conn.: Yale University Press, 1951.

Crandall, V. C. Sex differences in expectancy of intellectual and academic reinforcement. In C. P. Smith (Ed.), *Achievement-related motives in children.* New York: Russell Sage Foundation, 1969.

Crandall, V. J. Achievement. In H. W. Stevenson (Ed.), *Child psychology, the 62nd yearbook of the national society for the study of education* (Part 1). Chicago: University of Chicago Press, 1963.

Crockett, H. J., Jr. The achievement motive and differential occupational mobility in the United States. *American Sociological Review,* 1962, *27,* 191–204. Also in J. W. Atkinson & N. T. Feather (Eds.), *A theory of achievement motivation.* New York: Wiley, 1966.

Crockett, H. J., Jr. Social class, education, and motive to achieve in differential occupational mobility. *Sociological Quarterly,* 1964, *5,* 231–242.

Crockett, H. J., Jr., & Schulman, J. L. *Achievement among minority Americans: A conference report.* Cambridge, Mass.: Schenkman Publ., 1973.

Cronbach, L. J. Coefficient alpha and the internal structure of tests. *Psychometrika,* 1951, *16,* 297–334.

Cronbach, L. J. The two disciplines of scientific psychology. *American Psychologist,* 1957, *12,* 671–684.

deCharms, R., & Moeller, G. H. Values expressed in American children's readers: 1800–1950. *Journal of Abnormal and Social Psychology,* 1962, *64,* 136–142.

Descartes, R. Discourse on method (1637). In J. Veitch (translator), *Religion of Science Library No. 38.* Chicago: Open Court Publ., 1935.

Duncan, O. D., Featherman, D. L., & Duncan, B. *Socioeconomic background and achievement.* New York: Seminar Press, 1972.

Edwards, A. L. *Edwards personal preference schedule manual.* New York: Psychological Corporation, 1954.

Edwards, W. The theory of decision making. *Psychological Bulletin,* 1954, *51,* 380–417.

Entin, E. E. The relationship between the theory of achievement motivation and performance on a simple and a complex task. Unpublished doctoral dissertation, University of Michigan, 1968.

Entin, E. E. Effects of achievement-oriented and affiliative motives on private and public performance. In J. W. Atkinson & J. O. Raynor (Eds.), *Motivation and achievement.* Washington, D.C.: Winston (Halsted Press/Wiley), 1974.

Entwistle, D. R. To dispel fantasies about fantasy-based measures of achievement motivation. *Psychological Bulletin,* 1972, *77,* 377–391.

Eysenck, H. J. Personality and experimental psychology. *British Psychological Society Bulletin,* 1966, *19,* 62, 1–28.

Feather, N. T. Subjective probability and decision under uncertainty. *Psychological Review,* 1959, *66,* 150–164.

Feather, N. T. The relationship of persistence at a task to expectation of success and achievement related motives. *Journal of Abnormal and Social Psychology,* 1961, *63,* 552–561.

Feather, N. T. The study of persistence. *Psychological Bulletin,* 1962, *59,* 94–115. Also in J. W. Atkinson & N. T. Feather (Eds.), *A theory of achievement motivation.* New York: Wiley, 1966.

Feld, S. C., & Lewis, J. The assessment of achievement anxieties in children. In C. P. Smith (Ed.), *Achievement-related motives in children.* New York: Russell Sage Foundation, 1969.

Feld, S., & Smith, C. P. An evaluation of the objectivity of the method of content analysis. In J. W. Atkinson (Ed.), *Motives in fantasy, action, and society.* Princeton, N.J.: Van Nostrand, 1958.

Feshbach, S. The drive reducing function of fantasy behavior. *Journal of Abnormal and Social Psychology,* 1955, *50,* 3–11.

French, E. G. Some characteristics of achievement motivation. *Journal of Experimental Psychology,* 1955, *50,* 232–236. Also in J. W. Atkinson (Ed.), *Motives in fantasy, action, and society.* Princeton, N.J.: Van Nostrand, 1958.

French, E. G. Motivation as a variable in work partner selection. *Journal of Abnormal and Social Psychology,* 1956, *53,* 96–99.

French, E. G. Development of a measure of complex motivation. In J. W. Atkinson (Ed.), *Motives in fantasy, action, and society.* Princeton, N.J.: Van Nostrand, 1958.

French, E. G., & Thomas, F. H. The relation of achievement motivation to problem-solving effectiveness. *Journal of Abnormal and Social Psychology,* 1958, *56,* 46–48.

Haber, R. N., & Alpert, R. The role of situation and picture cues in projective measurement of the achievement motive. In J. W. Atkinson (Ed.), *Motives in fantasy, action, and society.* Princeton, N.J.: Van Nostrand, 1958.

Hamilton, J. O. Motivation and risk taking behavior: A test of Atkinson's theory. *Journal of Personality and Social Psychology,* 1974, *29,* 856–864.

Hayashi, T., & Habu, K. A research on achievement motive: An experimental test of the "thought sampling" method by using Japanese students. *Japanese Psychological Research,* 1962, *4,* 30–42.

Heckhausen, H. *Hoffnung und Furcht in der Leistungsmotivation.* Verlag Anton Hain: Meisenheimam Glan, 1963.

Heckhausen, H. *The anatomy of achievement motivation.* New York: Academic Press, 1967.

Heckhausen, H. Achievement motive research: Current problems and some contributions towards a general theory of motivation. In W. J. Arnold (Ed.), *Nebraska Symposium on Motivation* (Vol. 16). Lincoln: University of Nebraska Press, 1968.

Heckhausen, H. Intervening cognitions in motivation. In D. E. Berlyne & K. B. Madsen (Eds.), *Pleasure, reward, preference: Their nature, determinants, and role in behavior.* New York and London: Academic Press, 1973.

Heckhausen, H., & Weiner, B. The emergence of a cognitive psychology of motivation. In P. Dodwell (Ed.), *New horisons in psychology.* London: Penguin Books, 1972.

Hermans, H. J. M. A questionnaire measure of achievement motivation. *Journal of Applied Psychology,* 1970, *54,* 353–363.

Hoffman, L. Early childhood experiences and women's achievement motives. *Journal of Social Issues,* 1972, *28* (2), 129–155.

Horner, M. Sex differences in achievement motivation and performance in competitive and noncompetitive situations. Unpublished doctoral dissertation, University of Michigan, 1968.

Horner, M. S. Feminity and successful achievement. In J. Bardwick, E. M. Douvan, M. S. Horner, & D. Gutmann (Eds.), *Feminine personality and conflict.* Belmont, Calif.: Brooks/Cole, 1970.

Horner, M. S. The measurement and behavioral implications of fear of success in women. In J. W. Atkinson & J. O. Raynor (Eds.), *Motivation and achievement.* Washington, D.C.: Winston, 1974. (a)

Horner, M. S. Performance of men in noncompetitive and interpersonal competitive achievement-oriented situations. In J. W. Atkinson & J. O. Raynor (Eds.), *Motivation and achievement.* Washington, D.C.: Winston, 1974. (b)

Huber, R. M. *The American idea of success.* New York: McGraw-Hill, 1971.

Hull, C. L. *Principles of behavior.* New York: Appleton-Century-Crofts, 1943.

Inkeles, A., & Levinson, D. J. National character: The study of modal personality and sociocultural systems. In G. Lindzey & E. Aronson (Eds.), *The handbook of social psychology* (Vol. 4). Reading, Mass.: Addison-Wesley, 1969.

James. W. *The principles of psychology* (Vol. 2). New York: Holt, 1890.

Jones, E. E., Rock, L., Shaver, K. G., Goethals, G. R., & Ward, L. M. Pattern of performance and ability attributions: An unexpected primacy effect. *Journal of Personality and Social Psychology,* 1968, *10,* 317–340.

Kagan, J., & Moss, H. A. *Birth to maturity.* New York: Wiley, 1962.

Kardiner, A. *Psychological frontiers of society.* New York: Columbia University Press, 1945.

Katz, I. The socialization of academic motivation in minority group children. In D. Levine (Ed.), *Nebraska Symposium on Motivation* (Vol. 15). Lincoln: University of Nebraska Press, 1967.

Klinger, E. Fantasy *n* Achievement as a motivational construct. *Psychological Bulletin,* 1966, *66,* 291–308.

Kluckhohn, C. H., & Murray, H. A. (Eds.). *Personality in nature, society and culture.* New York: Knopf, 1948.

Kolb, D. A. Achievement motivation training for under-achieving high-school boys. *Journal of Personality and Social Psychology,* 1965, *2,* 783–792.

Kuhn, T. S. *The structure of scientific revolutions.* Chicago: University of Chicago Press, 1962.

Kukla, A. Foundations of an attributional theory of performance. *Psychological Review,* 1972, *79,* 454–470.

Lansing, J., & Heyns, R. Need affiliation and frequency of four types of communication. *Journal of Abnormal and Social Psychology,* 1959, *58,* 365–372.

Lehman, H. C. *Age and achievement.* Princeton: Princeton University Press, 1953.

Lesser, G. S. Achievement motivation in women. In D. C. McClelland & R. S. Steele (Eds.), *Human motivation: A book of readings.* Morristown, N.J.: General Learning Press, 1973.

Lesser, G. S., Krawitz, R. N., & Packard, R. Experimental arousal of achievement motivation in adolescent girls. *Journal of Abnormal and Social Psychology,* 1963, *66,* 59–66.

Lewin, K. *Conceptual representation and measurement of psychological forces.* Durham, N.C.: Duke University Press, 1938.

Lewin, K. Defining the "field at a given time." *Psychological Review,* 1943, *50,* 292–310.

Lewin, K. Behavior and development as a function of the total situation. In L. Carmichael (Ed.), *Manual of child psychology.* New York: Wiley, 1946.

Lewin, K., Dembo, T., Festinger, L., & Sears, P. S. Level of aspiration. In J. McV. Hunt (Ed.), *Personality and the behavior disorders* (Vol. 1). New York: Ronald Press, 1944.

Linton, R. *The cultural background of personality.* New York: Appleton-Century, 1945.

Lipset, S. M. *The first new nation.* New York: Basic Books, 1963.

Lipset, S. M. Anglo-American society. In D. Sills (Ed.), *International Encyclopedia of the Social Sciences* (Vol. 1). New York: Macmillan & The Free Press, 1968.

Lipset, S. M., & Bendix, R. *Social mobility in industrial society.* Berkeley: University of California Press, 1959.

Litwin, G. H. Motives and expectancies as determinants of preference for degrees of risk. Unpublished honors dissertation, University of Michigan, 1958.

Litwin, G. H. Achievement motivation, expectancy of success, and risk-taking behavior. In J. W. Atkinson & N. T. Feather (Eds.), *A theory of achievement motivation.* New York: Wiley, 1966.

Lowell, E. L. The effect of need for achievement on learning and speed of performance. *Journal of Psychology,* 1952, *33,* 31–40.

Mahone, C. H. Fear of failure and unrealistic vocational aspiration. *Journal of Abnormal and Social Psychology,* 1960, *60,* 253–261.

Mandler, G., & Cowen, J. E. Test anxiety questionnaires. *Journal of Consulting Psychology,* 1958, *22,* 228–229.

Mandler, G., & Sarason, S. B. A study of anxiety and learning. *Journal of Abnormal and Social Psychology,* 1952, *47,* 166–173.

Maslow, A. H. *Motivation and personality.* New York: Harper & Row, 1954.

McClelland, D. C. *Personality.* New York: William Sloane, 1951.

McClelland, D. C. Some social consequences of achievement motivation. In M. R. Jones (Ed.), *Nebraska Symposium on Motivation* (Vol. 3). Lincoln: University of Nebraska Press, 1955.

McClelland, D. C. Methods of measuring human motivation. In J. W. Atkinson (Ed.), *Motives in fantasy, action, and society.* Princeton, N.J.: Van Nostrand, 1958. (a)

McClelland, D. C. Risk-taking in children with high and low need for achievement. In J. W. Atkinson (Ed.), *Motives in fantasy, action, and society.* Princeton, N.J.: Van Nostrand, 1958. (b)

McClelland, D. C. The use of measures of human motivation in the study of society. In J. W. Atkinson (Ed.), *Motives in fantasy, action, and society.* Princeton, N.J.: Van Nostrand, 1958. (c)

McClelland, D. C. *The achieving society.* Princeton, N.J.: Van Nostrand, 1961. (Reissue, New York: Irvington, Publishers, Inc., 1976.)

McClelland, D. C. Toward a theory of motive acquisition. *American Psychologist,* 1965, *20,* 321–333.

McClelland, D. C. *Assessing human motivation.* Morristown, N.J.: General Learning Press, 1971. (a)

McClelland, D. C. *Motivational trends in society.* Morristown, N.J.: General Learning Press, 1971. (b)

McClelland, D. C., & Atkinson, J. W. The projective expression of needs. I. The effect of different intensities of the hunger drive on perception. *Journal of Psychology,* 1948, *25,* 205–232.

McClelland, D. C., Atkinson, J. W., Clark, R. A., & Lowell, E. L. *The achievement motive.* New York: Appleton-Century-Crofts, 1953. (Reissue. New York: Irvington Publishers, Inc., 1976.)

McClelland, D. C., Baldwin, A. L., Bronfenbrenner, U., & Strodtbeck, F. L. *Talent and society.* Princeton; N.J.: Van Nostrand, 1958.

McClelland, D. C., Clark, R. A., Roby, T. B., & Atkinson, J. W. The projective expression of needs. IV. The effect of need for achievement on thematic apperception. *Journal of Experimental Psychology,* 1949, *39,* 242–255.

McClelland, D. C., & Liberman, A. M. The effect of need for achievement on recognition of need-related words. *Journal of Personality,* 1949, *18,* 236–251.

McClelland, D. C., & Winter, D. G. *Motivating economic achievement.* New York: The Free Press, 1969.

McKeachie, W. J. Motivation, teaching methods and college learning. In M. R. Jones (Ed.), *Nebraska Symposium on Motivation* (Vol. 9). Lincoln: University of Nebraska Press, 1961.

Mead, M. *Sex and temperament in three primitive societies.* New York: Morrow, 1935.

Mead, M. *Male and female.* New York: Morrow, 1949.

Mehrabian, A. Male and female scales of tendency to achieve. *Educational and Psychological Measurement,* 1968, *28,* 493–502.

Mehrabian, A. Measures of achieving tendency. *Educational and Psychological Measurement,* 1969, *29,* 445–451.

Miller, N. E. Liberalization of basic S–R concepts: Extensions to conflict behavior, motivation, and social learning. In S. Koch (Ed.), *Psychology: A study of a science* (Vol. 2). New York: McGraw-Hill, 1959.

Morgan, C. D., & Murray, H. A. A method for investigating fantasy. The Thematic Apperception Test. *Archives of Neurology and Psychiatry,* 1935, *34,* 289–306.

Morris, J. Propensity for risk-taking as a determinant of vocational choice. *Journal of Personality and Social Psychology,* 1966, *3,* 328–335.

Moulton, R. W. Effects of success and failure on level of aspiration as related to achievement motives. *Journal of Personality and Social Psychology,* 1965, *1,* 399–406. Also in J. W. Atkinson & N. T. Feather (Eds.), *A theory of achievement motivation.* New York: Wiley, 1966.

Moulton, R. Motivational implications of individual differences in competence. In J. W. Atkinson & J. O. Raynor (Eds.), *Motivation and achievement.* Washington, D.C.: Winston, 1974.

Moulton, R. W., Raphelson, A. C., Kristofferson, A. B., & Atkinson, J. W. The achievement motive and perceptual sensitivity under two conditions of motive arousal. In J. W. Atkinson (Ed.), *Motives in fantasy, action, and society.* Princeton, N.J.: Van Nostrand, 1958.

Murray, H. A. The effect of fear upon estimates of the maliciousness of other personalities. *Journal of Social Psychology,* 1933, *4,* 310–329.

Murray, H. A. Techniques for a systematic investigation of fantasy. *Journal of Psychology,* 1937, *3,* 115–143.

Murray, H. A. *Explorations in personality.* New York: Oxford University Press, 1938.

Murray, H. A. *Thematic Apperception Test manual.* Cambridge, Mass.: Harvard University Press, 1943.

Mussen, P. H., & Scodel, A. The effects of sexual motivation under varying conditions of TAT sexual responsiveness. *Journal of Consulting Psychology,* 1955, *19,* 90.

O'Connor, P., Atkinson, J. W., & Horner, M. Motivational implications of ability grouping in schools. In J. W. Atkinson & N. T. Feather (Eds.), *A theory of achievement motivation.* New York: Wiley, 1966.

Peak, H. Attitude and motivation. In M. R. Jones (Ed.), *Nebraska Symposium on Motivation* (Vol. 3). Lincoln: University of Nebraska Press, 1955.

Raphelson, A. C. The relationship between imaginative, direct verbal, and physiological measures of anxiety in an achievement situation. *Journal of Abnormal and Social Psychology,* 1957, *54,* 13–18.

Raynor, J. O. Future orientation and motivation of immediate activity: An elaboration of the theory of achievement motivation. *Psychological Review,* 1969, *76,* 606–610.

Raynor, J. O. Relationships between achievement-related motives, future orientation, and academic performance. *Journal of Personality and Social Psychology,* 1970, *15,* 28–33.

Raynor, J. O. Future orientation in the study of achievement motivation. In J. W. Atkinson & J. O. Raynor (Eds.), *Motivation and achievement.* Washington, D.C.: Winston (Halsted Press/Wiley), 1974. (a)

Raynor, J. O. Motivation and career striving. In J. W. Atkinson & J. O. Raynor (Eds.), *Motivation and achievement.* Washington, D.C.: Winston (Halsted Press/Wiley), 1974. (b)

Raynor, J. O., Atkinson, J. W., & Brown, M. Subjective aspects of achievement motivation immediately before an examination. In J. W. Atkinson & J. O. Raynor (Eds.), *Motivation and achievement.* Washington, D.C.: Winston (Halsted Press/Wiley), 1974.

Raynor, J. O., & Rubin, I. S. Effects of achievement motivation and future orientation on level of performance. *Journal of Personality and Social Psychology,* 1971, *17,* 36–41.

Reitman, W. R. Motivation induction and behavioral correlates of the achievement and affiliation motives. Unpublished doctoral dissertation, University of Michigan, 1957.

Reitman, W. R. Motivation induction and the behavioral correlates of the achievement and affiliation motives. *Journal of Abnormal and Social Psychology,* 1960, *60,* 8–13.

Revelle, W., & Michaels, E. J. The theory of achievement motivation revisited: the implications of inertial tendencies. *Psychological Review,* 1976, *83,* 394–404.

Riccuiti, H. N., & Clark, R. A. *A comparison of need-achievement stories written by experimentally "relaxed" and "achievement-oriented" subjects: Effects obtained with new pictures and revised scoring categories.* Princeton, N.J.: Educational Testing Service, 1954.

Rosen, B. C., Crockett, H. J., Jr., & Nunn, C. Z. *Achievement in American society.* Cambridge, Mass.: Schenkman Publ., 1969.

Rotter, J. B. *Social learning and clinical psychology.* Englewood Cliffs, N.J.: Prentice-Hall, 1954.

Sales, S. M. Some effects of role overload and role underload. *Organizational Behavior and Human Performance,* 1970, *5,* 592–608.

Sanford, R. N. The effects of abstinence from food upon imaginal processes: A preliminary experiment. *Journal of Psychology,* 1936, *2,* 129–136.

Sarason, S. B., Davidson, K. S., Lighthall, F. F., Waite, R. R., & Ruebush, B. K. *Anxiety in elementary school children.* New York: Wiley, 1960.

Sawusch, J. R. Computer simulation of the influence of ability and motivation on test performance and cumulative achievement and the relation between them. In J. W. Atkinson & J. O. Raynor (Eds.), *Motivation and achievement.* Washington, D.C.: Winston, 1974.

Sears, R. R. Success and failure: A study of motility. In *Studies in Personality.* New York: McGraw-Hill, 1942.

Sears, R. R. A theoretical framework for personality and social behavior. *American Psychologist,* 1951, *9,* 476–483.

Seltzer, R. A. Simulation of the dynamics of action. *Psychological Reports,* 1973, *32,* 859–872.

Seltzer, R. A., & Sawusch, J. R. A program for computer simulation of the dynamics of action. In J. W. Atkinson & J. O. Raynor (Eds.), *Motivation and achievement.* Washington, D.C.: Winston, 1974.

Sewell, W. H. Inequality of opportunity for higher education. *American Sociological Review,* 1971, *36,* 793–809.

Sewell, W. H., Hauser, R. M., & Featherman, D. L. (Eds.). *Schooling and achievement in American society.* New York: Academic Press, 1976.

Shipley, T. E., and Veroff, J. A projective measure of need for affiliation. *Journal of Experimental Psychology,* 1952, *43,* 349–356.

Smith, C. P. Situational determinants of the expression of achievement motivation in thematic apperception. Unpublished doctoral dissertation, University of Michigan, 1961.

Smith, C. P. The influence of testing conditions and need for achievement scores and their relationship to performance scores. In J. W. Atkinson & N. T. Feather (Eds.), *A theory of achievement motivation.* New York: Wiley, 1966.

Smith, C. P. (Ed.). *Achievement-related motives in children.* New York: Russell Sage Foundation, 1969. (a)

Smith, C. P. The origin and expression of achievement-related motives in children. In C. P. Smith (Ed.), *Achievement-related motives in children.* New York: Russell Sage Foundation, 1969. (b)

Smith, C. P., & Feld, S. How to learn the method of content analysis for *n* Achievement, *n* Affiliation, and *n* Power. In J. W. Atkinson (Ed.), *Motives in fantasy, action, and society.* Princeton, N.J.: Van Nostrand, 1958.

Spence, K. W. *Behavior theory and conditioning.* New Haven: Yale University Press, 1956.

Spielberger, C. D. (Ed.). *Anxiety and behavior.* New York: Academic Press, 1966.

Stein, A. H., & Bailey, M. M. The socialization of achievement orientation in females. *Psychological Bulletin,* 1973, *80,* 345–366.

Taylor, J. A., & Spence, K. W. The relationship of anxiety level to performance in serial learning. *Journal of Experimental Psychology,* 1952, *44,* 61–64.

Thomas, E. J., & Zander, A. The relationship of goal structure to motivation under extreme conditions. *Journal of Individual Psychology,* 1959, *15,* 121–127.

Tolman, E. C. *Collected papers in psychology.* Berkeley: University of California Press, 1951.

Tolman, E. C. Principles of performance. *Psychological Review,* 1955, *62,* 315–326.

Veroff, J. Development and validation of a projective measure of power motivation. *Journal of Abnormal and Social Psychology,* 1957, *54,* 1–8.

Veroff, J. Thematic apperception in a nationwide sample survey. In J. Kagan & G. S. Lesser (Eds.), *Contemporary issues in thematic apperceptive methods.* Springfield, Ill.: Charles C. Thomas, 1961.

Veroff, J. Theoretical background for studying the origins of human motivational dispositions. *Merill-Palmer Quarterly,* 1965, *11,* 3–18.

Veroff, J. Social comparison and the development of achievement motivation. In C. P. Smith (Ed.), *Achievement-related motives in children.* New York: Russell Sage Foundation, 1969.

Veroff, J., Atkinson, J. W., Feld, S., & Gurin, G. The use of thematic apperception to assess motivation in a nationwide interview study. *Psychological Monographs,* 1960, *74* (12, Whole No. 499).

Veroff, J., & Feld, S. *Marriage and work in America.* New York: Van Nostrand-Reinhold, 1970.

Veroff, J., Feld, S., & Crockett, H. Explorations into the effects of picture cues on thematic apperceptive expression of achievement motivation. *Journal of Personality and Social Psychology,* 1966, *3,* 171–181.

Veroff, J., Feld, S., & Gurin, G. Achievement motivation and religious background. *American Sociological Review,* 1962, *27,* 205–217.

Veroff, J., & Veroff, J. B. Reconsideration of a measure of power motivation. *Psychological Bulletin,* 1972, *78,* 279–291.

Veroff, J., Wilcox, S., & Atkinson, J. W. The achievement motive in high school and college-age women. *Journal of Abnormal and Social Psychology,* 1953, *48,* 103–119.

Vitz, P. The relation of aspiration to need achievement, fear of failure, incentives, and expectancies. Unpublished honors thesis, University of Michigan, 1957.

Vroom, V. H. *Work and motivation.* New York: Wiley, 1964.

Walker, E. L., & Atkinson, J. W. The expression of fear-related motivation in thematic apperception as a function of proximity to an atomic explosion. In J. W. Atkinson (Ed.), *Motives in fantasy, action, and society.* Princeton, N.J.: Van Nostrand, 1958.

Weiner, B. New conceptions in the study of achievement motivation. In B. Maher (Ed.), *Progress in experimental personality research* (Vol. 5). New York: Academic Press, 1970.

Weiner, B. *Theories of motivation.* Chicago: Rand McNally, 1972.

Weiner, B. *Achievement motivation and attribution theory.* Morristown, N.J.: General Learning Press, 1974. (a)

Weiner, B. An attributional interpretation of expectancy-value theory. In B. Weiner (Ed.), *Cognitive views of human motivation.* New York: Academic Press, 1974. (b)

Weiner, B., & Kukla, A. An attributional analysis of achievement motivation. *Journal of Personality and Social Psychology,* 1970, *15,* 1–20.

Weinstein, M. S. Achievement motivation and risk preference. *Journal of Personality and Social Psychology,* 1969, *13,* 153–172.

Whalen, R. E. Sexual motivation. *Psychological Review,* 1966, *73,* 151–163.

Winter, D. *The power motive.* New York: Free Press, 1973.

Winterbottom, M. The relation of childhood training in independence to achievement motivation. Unpublished doctoral dissertation, University of Michigan, 1953. Also in J. W. Atkinson (Ed.), *Motives in fantasy, action, and society.* Princeton, N.J.: Van Nostrand, 1958.

Yerkes, R. M., & Dodson, J. D. The relation of strength of stimulus to rapidity of habit formation. *Journal of Comparative and Neurological Psychology,* 1908, *18,* 459–482.

3
Authoritarianism

Frances Cherry

Indiana University

Donn Byrne

Purdue University

In tracing the history of the study of the authoritarian personality, one is tracing concomitantly the history of the way in which the traditional study of personality has merged with the experimental analysis of social behavior. The original research published in *The Authoritarian Personality* (Adorno, Frenkel-Brunswik, Levinson, & Sanford, 1950) began as an effort to identify the "potentially fascistic" individual, that person who would be susceptible to anti-Semitic ideology and, more generally, to anti-democratic political appeals. The search for this designated personality type was founded on the assumption that psychologists could isolate a "more or less enduring organization of forces within the individual " and that consistency of behavior is attributable to the "persisting forces of personality (Adorno *et al.*, 1950, p. 5)." The assumption of stable dispositions which are reflected in cross-situationally consistent behaviors is basic to the development of personality typologies. Personality is conceived of as a predisposition to particular modes of behavior and its measurement potentially allows us to predict behavior.

Several major challenges to this conceptualization have been advanced both within personality psychology and psychology-at-large. First, personality researchers during the fifties became concerned with the reliability of their measuring instruments (Rotter, 1954). Concern with psychometric issues such as response sets and biases sidetracked the study of this personality dimension away from investigations of its potential influence on social behavior. It became of prime importance to know the extent to which one was measuring "authoritarianism" or some confound rather than to relate whatever it was the F scale measured to social behaviors.

The second major trend of importance in the historical development of the study of authoritarianism was an early criticism that the construct reflected solely the liberal biases of its originators. The picture presented of the authoritarian could be seen as an extreme caricature of a rigid personality, a hostile and repressed bigot concerned primarily with rejecting all that did not fit consistently into his negative worldview. Masling (1954) was one of the first to make note of the overemphasis on the authoritarian as a maladjusted individual, a proposition for which no empirical support could be found. Furthermore, Shils (1954) criticized exclusion of authoritarianism of the left and the assumption that equalitarians are the exact opposite to authoritarians. In a similar vein, Rokeach (1960) developed the construct of dogmatism to encompass both an authoritarianism of the right and of the left.

Finally, theoretical developments within the study of personality were also to leave their mark on the study of the authoritarian personality. Mischel (1973) likens the challenge of situationism for personality theory to a paradigm crisis. In his earlier writings Mischel (1968, 1971) emphasized the importance of the interaction of personality and situational variables. In a more recent paper (Mischel, 1973) he refrains from asserting that situations are always more powerful determinants of behavior than personality dispositions. Rather, he suggests: "The relative importance of individual differences will depend on the situation selected, the type of behavior assessed, the particular individual differences sampled, and the purpose of the assessment [p. 255]."

Considering these trends in social-personality psychology, we may want to use the study of authoritarianism as a model for the interplay between social behavior and personality traits. In this chapter, both theoretical and research contributions to the study of authoritarianism will be reviewed insofar as they lead toward a synthesis of personality and situational forces in determining behavioral outcomes. More detailed summaries of research findings can be found in works by Byrne (1974), Kirscht and Dillehay (1967), and Christie and Cook (1958). First, we will examine the study of authoritarianism as reflected in the search for a reliable measure free of acquiescent response tendencies. Secondly, the search for the antecedents and correlates of authoritarianism will be examined. Finally, we will trace the shift in emphasis from personality dispositions to the interactive approach in which personality and situational forces are considered as joint determinants of authoritarian behavior. Using three areas of social behavior relevant to the construct of authoritarianism, conformity and obedience, punitiveness, and the expression of sexuality, we will attempt to provide generalizations concerning the strength of the interactive approach. We will suggest that investigators must look to definitions of both the situation and the role requirements confronting the individual actor in order to predict accurately the behavior of both authoritarians and equalitarians. To the extent that the situation or role is poorly defined and ambiguous for the individual, one would expect to find personality differences emerging to fill in the gaps. Mischel

(1973) has expressed this notion in the following manner: "To the degree that the situation is 'unstructured,' the subject will expect that virtually *any* response from him is equally likely to be equally appropriate, and variance from individual differences will be greatest [p. 276]."

THE SEARCH FOR A RELIABLE MEASURE OF AUTHORITARIANISM

Theoretical Background

In the original volume, *The Authoritarian Personality,* one can find scales which were developed to assess anti-Semitic prejudice (A-S), ethnocentrism (E), and political and economic conservatism (PEC). The authors wanted, however, to develop a measure of an individual's susceptibility to antidemocratic ideology without specific mention of any racial or ethnic minority. This construct was to become known as authoritarianism and was measured by the Fascist scale (*F* scale). Included in the measuring instrument were items designed to tap the composite of beliefs thought to be associated with the authoritarian syndrome. This syndrome was conceptualized as indicative of individuals who would rigidly adhere to conventional values (*conventionalism*), obeying proponents of these values (*authoritarian submission*), and advocating punishment for violators (*authoritarian aggression*). Furthermore, the authoritarian would be likely to exhibit an overly negative view of mankind (*destructiveness* and *cynicism*), oppose any reliance on subjective feelings (*anti-intraception*), and readily accept supernatural determinants of behavior and categorical thinking (*superstition* and *stereotypy*). The authoritarian is preoccupied with power relationships and exhibits a *power* and *toughness* orientation. Overly concerned with issues regarding *sexuality,* the authoritarian projects his own sexual and aggressive motivations onto those around him (*Projectivity*). It was these nine components of the authoritarian syndrome that the California *F* scale was intended to tap. The scale, in its third and final revision, is presented in Table 1. Responses to the scale were measured by a 6-point Likert scale format requiring agreement or disagreement to each of the expressed opinions.

The theoretical underpinnings for the subcomponents were primarily psychoanalytic and were supported largely by interview and projective data. Very briefly, authoritarians were thought to be individuals with strict superegos controlling a weak ego. The superego was the chief structure underlying the adherence to externally imposed conventional standards and the authoritarian submission to individuals who impose these standards. The outgroup was the target of hostility resulting from this particular aberration of superego functioning. A weak ego, not completely in control of behavior and unaccepting of the responsibility for feelings and actions, was the structure assumed to underlie rigid categorical thinking, rejection of feelings as a basis for action, and the

TABLE 1

The California *F* Scale[a]

1. Sex crimes, such as rape and attacks on children, deserve more than mere imprisonment; such criminals ought to be publicly whipped, or worse.
2. What the youth needs most is strict discipline, rugged determination and the will to work and fight for family and country.
3. There is hardly anything lower than a person who does not feel a great love, gratitude, and respect for his parents.
4. Every person should have complete faith in some supernatural power whose decisions he obeys without question.
5. Young people sometimes get rebellious ideas, but as they grow up they ought to get over them and settle down.
6. Obedience and respect for authority are the most important virtues children should learn.
7. Homosexuals are hardly better than criminals and ought to be severely punished.
8. Nowadays when so many different kinds of people move around and mix together so much, a person has to protect himself especially carefully against catching an infection or disease from them.
9. People can be divided into two distinct classes: the weak and the strong.
10. No sane, normal, decent person could ever think of hurting a close friend or relative.
11. Some day it will probably be shown that astrology can explain a lot of things.
12. Nowadays more and more people are prying into matters that should remain personal and private.
13. If people would talk less and work more, everybody would be better off.
14. An insult to our honor should always be punished.
15. Most of our social problems would be solved if we could somehow get rid of the immoral, crooked, and feeble-minded people.
16. When a person has a problem or worry, it is best for him not to think about it, but to keep busy with more cheerful things.
17. Science has its place, but there are many important things that can never possibly be understood by the human mind.
18. The wild sex life of the old Greeks and Romans was tame compared to some of the goings-on in this country, even in places where people might least expect it.

19. Human nature being what it is, there will always be war and conflict.
20. The true American way of life is disappearing so fast that force may be necessary to preserve it.
21. What this country needs most, more than law and political programs, is a few courageous, tireless, devoted leaders in whom the people can put their faith.
22. No weakness or difficulty can hold us back if we have enough will power.
23. Familiarity breeds contempt.
24. Some people are born with an urge to jump from high places.
25. Most people don't realize how much our lives are controlled by plots hatched in secret places.
26. A person who has bad manners, habits, and breeding can hardly expect to get along with decent people.
27. Nobody ever learned anything really important except through suffering.
28. Wars and social troubles may someday be ended by an earthquake or flood that will destroy the whole world.
29. The business man and the manufacturer are much more important to society than the artist and the professor.

Scoring Key

On a six-point scale, all items are scored in the following way:

Strong support, agreement	=6
Moderate support, agreement	=5
Slight support, agreement	=4
Slight opposition, disagreement	=3
Moderate opposition, disagreement	=2
Strong opposition, disagreement	=1

(Omitted items receive a score of 4.)

NOTE. Instructions to subjects can be found in Table 2.

[a]Abridgement of "F-Scale Clusters: Forms 45 and 40" (pp. 255–257) in *The Authoritarian Personality* by T. W. Adorno *et al.* (1950). Copyright 1950 by The American Jewish Committee. (By permission of Harper & Row, Publishers, Inc.)

projection of sexual and aggressive motives onto others. Both the conventional superego and weak ego share the blame for the power and toughness espoused by the authoritarian and the cynical view he has of mankind. Finally, the authoritarian was thought to be plagued by unresolved Oedipal complexes ("My mother was a Saint." – Nixon, 1974). Id impulses could be expressed only indirectly as exemplified by the authoritarian's exaggerated concern with sexuality and with hostility toward those who violate the mores of the ingroup.

Measurement Problems

The concern over the reliability of the *F* scale as a measure of these various subcomponents was stimulated by an early methodological paper by Hyman and Sheatsley (1954). Their major criticism focused on the confounding of authoritarianism with acquiescent response biases. Empirical support for such a bias was provided in a study by Bass (1955) which attributed a larger proportion of the variance in *F* scale scores to acquiescence than to the authoritarian content of the scale. Despire errors in Bass' use of factor analytic techniques (Kerlinger, 1958; Messick & Jackson, 1957), the basic problem was the fact that authoritarianism is indicated by agreement with scale items and thus was potentially confounded with the tendency to acquiesce. This problem was attacked by a variety of investigators who attempted both to demonstrate the importance of the measurement bias and to overcome it.

Several issues have been raised in the literature regarding the confounding of acquiescence and authoritarianism. While most of those conducting research saw the problem as solvable by the development of scales which balanced positively and negatively worded items, this was not a unanimous conclusion. It was argued that this solution would never be wholly satisfactory in that the meaning of a response to a reversed item could still be equivocal (Gage & Chatterjee, 1960; Gage, Leavitt, & Stone, 1957). The individual who endorses a reversed item could be the equalitarian logically expressing nonauthoritarianism or the authoritarian psychologically submitting to any opinionated expression of social issues.

Despite this criticism, several attempts have been made to construct a scale which would allow for a separation of acquiescence and authoritarianism. This search was undoubtedly encouraged by Couch and Keniston's (1960) data indicating that response sets to agree and authoritarianism were orthogonal dimensions and that balanced *F* scales could be expected to eliminate the influences of response bias.

While it sounds as if the problem should be quite simple to solve, the reversal of a positively worded item turned out to be no easy task. Consider some examples. Bass (1955) attempted to reverse the items logically as in "Familiarity breeds contempt" being reworded to "Familiarity does not breed contempt." The use of the negative, however, does not rule out the possibility that both high- and low-scoring subjects will agree with the new statement, resulting in low discriminatory power of the item.

This particular problem was to lead some test constructors to emphasize more than a logical reversal of items. Jackson and Messick (1957) maintained that one has to retain the expressional style of the original item while the viewpoint expressed should be in the opposite direction of the positively worded item. So, for example, the item "Obedience and respect for authority are the most important virtues children should learn," was reversed to read "A love of freedom and complete independence are the most important virtues children should learn." Looking at other examples of attempts to reverse this item, it becomes clearer that not all items are both logical and psychological reversals which completely eliminate acquiescent bias:

> One of the most important things children should learn is when to disobey authorities [Christie, Havel, & Seidenberg, 1958].
>
> There are other virtues children should learn at least as important as obedience and respect for authority [Peabody, 1966].
>
> In teaching children there are much more important things to stress than obedience and respect for authority [Leavitt, Hax, & Roche, 1955].

The first example places emphasis on disobedience as a virtue while the latter examples stress only that there are other unnamed virtues "at least as important" or "much more important" than obedience to authority. While the authoritarian might logically endorse the last two items, thus contributing to the acquiescence problem, the first item is more in line with objections to the violation of externally imposed standards.

Consider another item, "Every person should have complete faith in some supernatural power whose decisions he obeys without question." Jackson and Messick (1957) provide the following reversal: "Every person should have complete faith in his own judgment, not in some supernatural power whose decision he obeys without question." Chapman and Campbell (1957) reversed this item to read, "It is unnecessary and undesirable for a person to have complete faith in some supernatural power whose decisions he obeys without question." Once again, differences in the reversal may well account for positive correlations between acquiescence and authoritarianism. An authoritarian, overly concerned with appearing desirable, might well agree with the latter statement while finding it quite a simple matter to reject the Jackson and Messick item.

Balanced *F* scale

While it has been maintained that an appropriately balanced scale was a blind research alley (Peabody, 1966) and that response biases were being unduly overemphasized in psychological research (Rorer, 1965), others argued that this was not the case. Those espousing the latter position established statistical criteria to be applied in the construction of reversed items. It was concluded that in reversing items one must take into account both the direction of the item and the extremeness relative to the original item (Christie, Havel, & Seidenberg, 1958; Samelson & Yates, 1967). Altemeyer (1969) established two criteria which he hoped would overcome the problem of double agreement. First, only items which correlate negatively with the original item and have test–retest reliability equivalent to the original should be used. Second, the mean of the reversed item should be approximately the same distance from the neutral point as that of the original and, of course, on the other side of the neutral point. After much item testing, he found 15 reversed items which met these criteria. For example. the best reversed item, "One should not react against every insult to his honor," had a high negative correlation with the original item and, in contrast to the mean endorsement of 2.7 for the original, had a mean of 5.3. The correlation of the balanced and unbalanced versions of the *F* scales was .89. In validating this scale, Fischer (1970) has subsequently found it uncorrelated with a measure of social desirability whereas the original *F* scale was significantly positively correlated.

Another recent version of a balanced *F* scale which includes items correlated with the original scale was devised by Byrne (1974). The scale is reprinted in full in Table 2 along with a scoring key and instructions to respondents. In this instrument, only items which afforded the appropriate logical and psychological reversal of response were retained in the final scale. The correlation of this scale with the original *F* scale is .84. In general, then, it appears to be possible to measure authoritarianism while eliminating the confounding influence of acquiescence.

THE SEARCH FOR THE CORRELATES AND THE ANTECEDENTS OF AUTHORITARIANISM

An extensive amount of research has attempted to provide us with the patterns of child-rearing techniques which result in the transmission of authoritarianism across generations and with a profile of the authoritarian personality. It has been widely assumed that the profile of the equalitarian and the patterns of rearing which result in this profile are the converse of the authoritarian. There is some support for this notion, although the earliest attempts to classify "low-scoring" types suggests that not all equalitarians are alike (Adorno *et al.*, 1950). Phrased in psychoanalytic terms, only one equalitarian type, the "genuine liberal," reflected a balance between superego, ego, and id functioning.

Parental Antecedents of Authoritarianism

One of the earliest concerns of those working in the area of authoritarianism focused on the transmission of the syndrome from parents to offspring. A distinction between rational and inhibitory authority conceptualized by Fromm (1941) was to provide the major rationale for analyzing child-rearing techniques which promoted authoritarianism. A rational authority restricts a child's behavior with a view to his or her welfare. Inhibitory authority is motivated by the parents' need to dominate and to assert their position of dominance relative to the child. Stemming from these two modes of authority is the general picture of the authoritarian parent as harsh and threatening in his use of punishment, demanding obedience and socially acceptable behavior from the child. Presumably the equalitarian parent is the direct opposite. More objective evidence for an autocratic–democratic distinction in child-rearing practices was provided by Levinson and Huffman (1955). They developed a Traditional Family Ideology Scale which measures several dimensions of child-rearing behavior; they found a strong relationship between autocratic family attitudes and authoritarianism (.70). Hart (1957) focused specifically on punishment techniques used by mothers and divided these into love-, or non-love-oriented patterns. He found a correlation of .63 between the mother's use of non-love-oriented techniques and her *F* scale score. Similarly, Block (1955) found restrictive attitudes towards child rearing on the part of fathers strongly correlated with their *F* scale scores.

A study by Byrne (1965) noted that little can be concluded about the transmission of ideologies across generations from intraindividual correlations. One must begin to look at the relationship between authoritarianism and family ideology of both parents and their children. Byrne conducted such a study with college students and their parents in order to assess the interindividual correlations necessary to the transmission of authoritarianism. He found that mother's and father's *F* scale scores were significantly related to that of the son, while only the mother's *F* score was related to her daughter's score. While the relationships are significant, Byrne commented that several additional factors need to be taken into account in order to predict the child's authoritarianism. Children are undoubtedly influenced by the authoritarian–democratic teaching styles which they encounter in school (Levitt, 1955) and by their position in their peer group. Both of these factors would account for some of the variance in the individual's resultant authoritarianism.

The foregoing research does suggest that authoritarian individuals transmit their patterns of influence to their children in a somewhat circular system. Yet, we know very little about the dynamic process of interaction between parent and child which accomplishes this goal. This becomes particularly crucial when we consider some recent data provided by Baumrind (1972). She notes that black families are characterized as being more authoritarian than white families, at least as reflected in the *F* scale scores of parents. However, compared with white families, the authoritarian black family produces more independent and assertive daughters of preschool age. Baumrind also points out that black parents in her sample discouraged dependency in their daughters, were more emotionally expressive in their interactions, and encouraged the spontaneous expression of emotion. Independence and expressiveness are not traditionally associated with authoritarian child-rearing techniques. Baumrind concludes that authoritarian ideology may not in all cases be accompanied by authoritarian child-rearing

TABLE 2
The Balanced *F* Scale[a]

Instructions to Subjects:
PUBLIC OPINION SCALE

The following sets of items are an attempt to assess the opinions of college students about a number of important personal, academic, and social issues. The best answer to each statement is your *personal opinion.* We have tried to cover many different and opposing points of view; you may find yourself agreeing strongly with some of the statements, disagreeing just as strongly with others, and perhaps uncertain about others; whether you agree or disagree with any statement, you can be sure that many people feel the same way you do.

Mark your opinion about each statement on the answer sheet (following the statements) according to how much you agree or disagree with it. Please mark every one.

(P) 1. There is hardly anything lower than a person who does not feel a great love, gratitude, and respect for his parents.
(P) 2. An insult to our honor should always be punished.
(P) 3. Books and movies ought not to deal so much with the unpleasant and seamy side of life; they ought to concentrate on themes that are entertaining or uplifting.
(P) 4. What the youth needs most is strict discipline, rugged determination and the will to work and fight for family and country.
(P) 5. No sane, normal, decent person could ever think of hurting a close friend or relative.
(P) 6. Young people sometimes get rebellious ideas, but as they grow up they ought to get over them and settle down.
(R) 7. The findings of science may some day show that many of our most cherished beliefs are wrong.
(R) 8. It is highly unlikely that astrology will ever be able to explain anything.
(R) 9. People ought to pay more attention to new ideas, even if they seem to go against the American way of life.
(P) 10. If people would talk less and work more, everybody would be better off.
(P) 11. A person who has bad manners, habits, and breeding can hardly expect to get along with decent people.

(R) 12. Insults to our honor are not always important enough to bother about.

(R) 13. It's all right for people to raise questions about even the most sacred matters.

(P) 14. Obedience and respect for authority are the most important virtues children should learn.

(R) 15. There is no reason to punish any crime with the death penalty.

(R) 16. Anyone who would interpret the Bible literally just doesn't know much about geology, biology, or history.

(P) 17. In this scientific age the need for a religious belief is more important than ever.

(R) 18. When they are little, kids sometimes think about doing harm to one or both of their parents.

(R) 19. It is possible that creatures on other planets have founded a better society than ours.

(R) 20. The prisoners in our corrective institutions, regardless of the nature of their crimes, should be humanely treated.

(P) 21. The sooner people realize that we must get rid of all the traitors in the government the better off we'll be.

(R) 22. Some of the greatest atrocities in man's history have been committed in the name of religion and morality.

Scoring Key

On a six-point scale, items are scored in the following way:

		(P)	(R)
Strong support, agreement	=	7	1
Moderate support, agreement	=	6	2
Slight support, agreement	=	5	3
Slight opposition, disagreement	=	3	5
Moderate opposition, disagreement	=	2	6
Strong opposition, disagreement	=	1	7

(Omitted items receive a score of 4.)

[a] From Byrne (1974). On the balance *F* scale, as well as on the California *F* scale (Table 1), a person's score is the sum of his or her scores on all the items in the scale. A relatively high score reflects an authoritarian orientation, while a relatively low score reflects a nonauthoritarian (equilitarian) orientation.

techniques, as exemplified in the differences between black and white middle-class homes. Her data encourage us to look at the dynamics of parental child-rearing techniques, emphasizing the interplay between personal ideology and social behavior.

An additional finding in Byrne's (1965) study of authoritarianism in parents and their offspring emphasizes this point. He observed that one low-authoritarian parent of either sex is sufficient for producing a low-authoritarian child. A thorough behavioral analysis of the teaching of authoritarian behavior, reflected in punishment techniques for example, could explicate this finding. We need to know how parents share authority and responsibility for disciplining their children which ultimately leads to the child's own use of authority. A relatively simple paradigm is proposed. Homogeneous and heterogeneous couples with respect to *F* scale scores could be drawn from diverse social class and ethnic backgrounds. These couples, along with their children of various ages could be observed and analyzed in a variety of situations which require the administration of punishments and rewards. The children might then be placed in similar situations with peers. One would be interested in comparing the child's use of discipline with the peer before and after parental influences. Using this type of methodology, the development of autocratic–democratic techniques of behavioral control could be assessed.

Profile of the Authoritarian

A monumental number of studies has been devoted to the correlation of the *F* scale with other attitudinal and personality measures. Extensive reviews of this material can be found elsewhere (Christie & Cook, 1958; Kirscht & Dillehay, 1967; Titus & Hollander, 1957). *The Authoritarian Personality* reported strong correlations of the *F* scale with measures of ethnocentrism (.73), negative attitudes towards Jews (.53), and conservative economic and political views (.52). In further correlational studies, authoritarianism has been highly related to measures of prejudice toward members of minority groups (Campbell & McCandless, 1951; Martin & Westie, 1959), although the correlations have often been of very low magnitude (Kelly, Ferson, & Holtzman, 1958; Klein, 1963). As for more specific evidence of conservative political and social beliefs, high authoritarians tend to endorse conservative political candidates (Leventhal, Jacobs, & Kudirka, 1964; Wrightsman, Radloff, Horton, & Mecherikoff, 1961), express negative attitudes towards socialized medicine (Mahler, 1953), and were more in favor of American involvement in Vietnam (Izzett, 1971) than equalitarians. In terms of religious participation, high authoritarians are more likely than equalitarians to attend church regularly (Jones, 1958) and frequently (Byrne, 1974); such individuals are also more often of Protestant or Catholic faith than either Jewish or unafilliated (Dustin & Young, 1974; Jones, 1958). The totality of these and other findings tend to provide a conservative and conventional profile of the authoritarian in terms of an overlapping political, religious, and ethnic ideology.

Yet another line of research has attempted to link authoritarianism with broader cognitive processes. The authoritarian syndrome implied rigidity in thinking about people and events and an intolerance for ambiguous input, both of a social and nonsocial nature (Berkowitz, 1960; Harvey, 1963; Steiner & Johnson, 1963a). In their review of the literature on the cognitive correlates of authoritarianism, Kirscht and Dillehay (1967) have concluded, "Cognitive rigidity and haste in resolving conceptual ambiguities seem to be characteristic of authoritarian persons. Before becoming apparent, such modes of functioning, however, may require novel material, situations involving real concern, and the absence of structural constraint [p. 46]." The emphasis these authors have placed on the moderating features of situational inputs is particularly supportive of our arguments concerning the interaction of situational and personality influences on behavior. The profile which emerges of the authoritarian both in attitudinal and cognitive terms is only valid to the extent that we begin to specify dimensions of the context in which behavior occurs. Specifically, we need to know the scale values of our situation in terms of its novelty, its ability to involve the subject, its alternatives and expectations for responding. Only when we have a multidimensional analysis of stimulus situations would we be able to interpret the meaning of positive, nonsignificant, or reversed findings. An example of the way in which unknown situational factors may affect the role of authoritarianism is provided by Titus and Hollander (1957). They note that reversals for the predicted behavior of authoritarians were frequently found in the areas of leadership and group behavior. They are able to conclude rather emphatically that ". . . the *F* scale correlates most systematically with other paper-and-pencil measures, and least systematically with interpersonal behaviors, particularly as situational conditions are varied [Titus & Hollander, 1957, p. 62]."

It may be seen, then, that work on the antecedents and correlates of authoritarianism has led us directly to a behavioral analysis of the syndrome. It is to the development of this analysis that we shall now turn our attention.

BACKGROUND: PERSONALITY AND SITUATIONAL DETERMINANTS OF AUTHORITARIAN BEHAVIOR

In *The Authoritarian Personality,* Adorno and his coworkers attempted to isolate individuals predisposed to antidemocratic behavior. These authors attributed the variance in behavioral outcomes to the "climate of opinion" at the time. More recently, one of the original researchers (Sanford, 1973) reiterated the view that personality is responsive to the social system in which the person is living. One would expect to find that individuals with antidemocratic ideologies would often not put them into action and that "overt action depends very largely upon the situation at the moment." By situation, however, this group was referring to socioeconomic and political conditions rather than the types of immediate situational features which experimental social psychologists have come to regard as potent determinants of social behavior; e.g., role requirements, presence of others, social influence attempts, persuasive communications by high status sources, experimenter influence. This does not of course imply that broader societal factors are unimportant. As the archival work of Sales (1973) has shown, authoritarian behaviors increased with environmental threats in the 1930s and late 1960s. Still, we would argue that within this larger framework it is still necessary to focus on specific interpersonal situational influences.

Largely drawing upon psychoanalytic theory, Adorno and his colleagues took the view that personality was highly responsive to the social environment, but they assumed that such effects were limited primarily to early life within the family (Adorno *et al.,* 1950, p. 6). Their notion was that personality develops as a structured entity which, although modifiable through experience, can become quite resistant to change. This resistance is what ultimately accounts for the cross-situational consistency in behavior assumed by the traditional model of personality. The authors suggested a weighting of "fixity" and "flexibility," an alliterative version of the suggested weighting of personality and situational factors in the determination of ideologically relevant behaviors. Unfortunately, these weightings were never really explored in the original investigations.

Not long after the publication of *The Authoritarian Personality,* Christie and Jahoda (1954) produced an edited volume of papers aimed at a critical review of research and theory in authoritarianism up to that point. With regard to the determination of the interactive effects of personality and situation, several contributors to that volume foreshadowed the emphasis developed in this chapter. Although Shils' (1954) main concern was with the neglect of authoritarianism of the left, he did assess the relationship of personality to social behavior in the original writings of Adorno *et al.* (1950).

> The authors tell us nothing of the actual roles of their subjects and for this reason, they encounter no obstacles to their view that political conduct follows from personality traits [Shils, 1954, p. 43].

More telling than his critique of Adorno *et al.* (1950) is his view on what one might expect in an actual test of the relationship between personality and conduct.

> Persons of quite different dispositions, as long as they have some reasonable measure of responsiveness to the expectations of others will behave in a more or less uniform manner, when expectations are relatively uniform [Shils, 1954, p. 43].

For Shils, the role requirements of an actor and the expectations of and approval of others are more potent determinants of at least public political behavior than the individual's personality disposition. It is important to note that Shils suggested personality traits would dominate public behavior when expectations are unknown to the actor, that is, when there is greater flexibility in the situation (Shils, 1954, p. 44).

In the same volume, Christie takes up the issue with greater explicitness. He stressed that the ultimate importance of any scale measure was its empirically derived relationship to other measures of behavior. He was able to provide evidence that individuals scoring high or low on the *F* scale were noticeably different with regard to behaviors predictable from the syndrome of authoritarianism. Christie's (1954) comments suggest the potential importance of being able to scale situations: "most social scientists agree that the interaction between persisting personality characteristics and the requirements of any given situation cannot be predicted unless the relevant dimensions of both sets of variables are known [p. 182]." While much energy has gone into defining the relevant dimensions of authoritarianism, considerably less energy has been devoted to dimensionalizing situations with respect to relevant characteristics for evoking authoritarian behavior. That this is a necessary task is supported by earlier findings of Christie (1952) and Levinson and Schermerhorn (1951) suggesting that situational factors far outweigh personality considerations in determining behavioral outcomes.

While investigators might have turned their attention to the situations they were studying, this was not the immediate concern. As discussed previously, Hyman and Sheatsley's (1954) methodological criticisms inspired many individuals to turn their attention over the next decade to issues of scale construction.

A review of the authoritarianism literature published in 1967 by Kirscht and Dillehay corroborates the view that methodological innovations were the major trend in research of the 1960s. The bulk of this volume deals with authoritarianism as a correlated set of personality, attitudinal, and cognitive belief systems. Only a small portion of the book is devoted to the relationship between authoritarianism and social behavior, despite these authors' assertion that "authoritarian deeds have more social consequence than authoritarian thoughts [Kirscht & Dillehay, 1967, p. 2]." Their review did, however, cover several areas which were considered important to the authoritarian syndrome and which would differentiate the behavior of authoritarians and equalitarians: attitude change in response to persuasive communications, choice of group membership, susceptibility to small group pressures, and leadership style.

Often, in reviewing the published literature, we found that authors have been hard pressed to explain nonsignificant findings or reversals of predicted findings. If any generalizations can be made, it is that authors generally resort to arguments which are quite reminiscent of those used to account for attitude-behavior inconsistencies. Argued for example, is that the measure of authoritarianism is more sophisticated than the one-shot unreliable measure of the chosen behavior, or that the behavior in question is multidetermined and complex.

THE INTERACTION OF PERSONALITY AND SITUATION: THREE EXAMPLES

To examine the interaction of personality and situation, it seems useful to establish empirically situations which are most likely to be relevant to the content of the personality measure. One empirical clue to areas where authoritarianism might have predictive utility can be derived from factor analytic studies[1] of the *F* scale.

Factor analyzing several related scales, O'Neil and Levinson (1954) found the *F* scale items to load on factors labeled Authoritarian Submission and Masculine Strength Façade. The former factor combined items which indicated unquestioning obedience to authority with a theme of punitiveness towards violators running through it. Masculine Strength Façade might reflect the power and toughness orientation of the authoritarian and the dimension of authoritarian aggression. Lee and Warr (1969) factor analyzed a balanced *F* scale and isolated a general factor of authoritarianism which included subcomponents of tough mindedness and personal morality. The *F* scale seems to emphasize sensitivity to social influence, the expression of aggression, and a concern with sexual morals. Thus, we have chosen to look at the interaction of personality and situational features with respect to the areas of conformity and obedience to authority, punitive and/or hostile behavior, and the expression of judgments regarding erotica.

Conformity and Obedience to Authority

Authoritarians have been conceptualized as individuals who are likely to be overly subservient to authority figures. Lacking internal standards, they are forced to use these figures as a source of influence in choosing appropriate behavior. In tasks involving perceptual stimuli, attitudes, and opinions, authoritarianism has been positively related to conformity to the judgments of others (Crutchfield, 1955; Nadler, 1959; Wells, Weinert, & Rubel, 1956). Not all studies confirm this relationship, however. Both the absence of a positive relationship (Endler, 1961) and a negative relationship between authoritarianism and conformity (Wagman, 1955) have been obtained.

How are we to account for this diversity of results? At this point, we require a shift in emphasis to the stimulus situation in which we are measuring conformity behavior. The situation, according to Mischel (1973) is powerful, "to the degree that [it] lead[s] all persons to construe the particular events the same way, induce uniform expectancies regarding the most appropriate response pattern,

[1] Factor analyses, to be sure, are sensitive to age, educational background, social class variables, etc. However, unanimity of structure is not necessary since we are looking only for commonalities which would suggest situations worthy of exploration.

provide adequate incentives for the performance of that response pattern, and instill the skills necessary for its satisfactory construction and execution [p. 276]." To the extent that our situations are dissimilar in these aspects of evocative power, we would expect to find varying authoritarian–equalitarian relationships to conformity. With respect to the measurement of conformity, for example, Back and Davis (1965) have found that correlations of three different measures of behavior (a perceptual judgment task, self-reports of acceptance of peer group norms, and self-reports of authority pressures) did not exceed .28. Similarly, Vaughan (1964) has reported that only 20% of his sample were consistent conformers across four conformity measures. It appears essential that we have some assessment of the extent to which our response measures have common characteristics. Jaccard (1974) has suggested that tasks be conceptualized like items on a personality inventory. Using criteria such as the behavior's ambiguity and its base rate we are more likely to come up with "good items" which can discriminate among personality types.

Once we have, for example, the base rate conformity responses of authoritarians and equalitarians for an array of conformity situations, then minor alterations in situational inputs would lead to statements regarding the interaction of situational and trait variables. For example, Hollander and Willis (1967) regard the status and competence of the influence source, the ambiguity of the the task stimuli, and the public or private nature of the response as some of the crucial situational determinants of conformity behavior. These aspects of the situation could be altered for a battery of conformity tasks and perhaps account for otherwise puzzling findings of minimal trait differences or reversals in which equalitarians conform to a greater extent than authoritarians.

Let us take the status of the authority as a specific example. Generally, it has been found that authoritarians are more conforming and less hostile to high status sources than are equalitarians (Roberts & Jessor, 1958; Steiner & Johnson, 1963b). In a recent judicial decision-making study by Mitchell (1973), however, those high on the *F* scale were less likely than those with low scores to obey the judge's instructions either to disregard or to pay special attention to information about the defendant's background. It might be that authoritarians do not perceive the role of the judge in society as a legitimate authority figure. In order to understand this unexpected reversal of response to an authority figure, we need information about authoritarians' and equalitarians' differential perceptions of judicial authority. Flacks (1969) suggests three features central to the attribution of an authority as legitimate. An attribution of legitimacy to an authority will be made to the extent that the authority is perceived as benefiting one's values, as trustworthy, and as having consensual support. If authoritarians and equalitarians differentially attribute legitimate authority, this would be reflected in the authority's capacity to influence conformity behavior.

Milgram's (1965) examination of obedience to authority provides us with another situation which discriminates high and low authoritarians but could conceivably be altered to minimize or reverse these differences. Elms and Milgram (1966) selected a subsample of subjects from the four-part "Proximity Series" of obedience studies. Twenty fully obedient subjects from the Proximity and Touch conditions and 20 fully defiant subjects from the Remote and Voice Feedback Conditions were assessed with respect to authoritarianism.

Without looking at personality factors, it is known that alterations in the distance between subject and victim influenced obedience. When individuals had contact with their victim, either by being in the same room or by having to place the victim's hand on the shock apparatus, obedience was greatly reduced. This suggests that any situational change which alters the subject–victim distance makes the subject's involvement in hurting another harder to minimize. What is important to know in terms of this discussion is whether such variations have equal effects for authoritarians and equalitarians or whether they interact with authoritarianism. Elms and Milgram (1966) did demonstrate in their follow-up that the obedient subjects scored higher on the *F* scale than defiant subjects. They praised the experimenter and derogated the victim more than the defiant subjects. Elms and Milgram did not sample authoritarians and equalitarians from all four situational conditions so the question remains open as to the nature of the interaction between authoritarianism and subject–victim distance, that is, between personality and situational factors.

Milgram (1974) argues in his book, *Obedience to Authority,* that his experiments were prototypic of situations which involve superordinate and subordinate roles. There is a social etiquette in the obedience situation which binds authority–subject–victim into a triadic interaction. The rules of interaction are changed by altering any one of these roles – for example, the possibility of retaliation from the victim or a shift of responsibility from experimenter to subject. Our basic question is how these alterations in the situation (and role definitions) differentially affect the behavior of authoritarians and equalitarians.

Aggression and Punitiveness

We have been suggesting that generalizations about authoritarianism cannot be meaningful without understanding its interaction with situational variations. This is particularly evident in the area of authoritarian aggression. Authoritarians have been conceptualized as having strong generalized hostility drives which are primarily directed at those who violate conventional standards. Given this characterization, our predictions would always be couched in terms of greater punitiveness and aggression of authoritarians than equalitarians.

Past research has provided evidence that authoritarians are likely to advocate punitive measures to control another's behavior (Dustin & Davis, 1967), but with no differences between authoritarians and equalitarians with respect to overall aggression (Epstein, 1965). Once again, we have little idea of the interrelatedness of our situations and their similarity in the capacity to evoke differences in high- and low-scoring subjects. Without a battery of situations we essentially have no conceptual basis on which to make comparisons.

Several studies suggest that the tendency for authoritarians to be more punitive than equalitarians will vary with alterations in the stimulus situation. Epstein (1965) manipulated the status of the victim in the typical Buss aggression paradigm. High and low status were indicated by the victim's dress, family income, parental employment, and future educational goals. It was found that authoritarians were punitive toward the low-status victim, while equalitarians behaved punitively toward the high-status victim. What is interesting here is that both subject groups were punitive, the differences in their behavior being attributable to characteristics of the victim. This study supports the notion that personality and situation are interactive rather than the notion that one type of determinant typically outweighs the other.

This general schema is supported by research in the area of judicial decision making. Several studies have found authoritarianism predictive of greater punitiveness towards violators of the law (Boehm, 1968; Jurow, 1971; Rokeach & McLellan, 1970; Vidmar & Crinklaw, 1973). A series of studies, however, challenge the pervasiveness of this main effect in favor, once again, of an interaction with situational variables.

Two studies by Mitchell and Byrne (1972, 1973) indicate that high authoritarians are more biased by character information concerning the defendant than are equalitarians. Punishment decisions reflect this authoritarian bias in that such individuals will be punitive towards a negatively described or attitudinally dissimilar defendant while equalitarians will not discriminate between irrelevantly positive and negative defendants. The process underlying this difference has been explained in two different ways. It has been suggested that authoritarians do not separate their affective state from the decision-making process (Mitchell & Byrne, 1973) and that authoritarians have greater recall of character information than do equalitarians (Berg & Vidmar, 1975). Whatever the process, character information interacts with authoritarianism to influence the outcome of punishment.

Going beyond this general finding, our interest in the interaction of situation and personality compels us to question how stable this particular pattern of results may be. Are there not instances where the finding would be minimized or even reversed? What deviations can be made in the stimulus context which would alter and reverse this pattern of results?

In a study by Mitchell (1973), a scenario was developed which was successful in reversing the typical pattern of findings. A rock concert gets out of hand and in the course of events a citizen is killed by a policeman or vice versa. When the defendant in the case is a positively or negatively described *citizen,* the usual interaction of character and authoritarianism is found: authoritarians being more punitive toward a negative defendant than a positive one; equalitarians tending to ignore the information about character. When the positive or negative defendant is a *policeman,* however, the interaction is reversed. Now we find that equalitarians are more punitive toward the negatively described policeman than toward the positive one, while authoritarians do not discriminate between police of different character descriptions. The results of this study are presented graphically in Figure 1. It is informative with respect to these findings that Larsen (1968) reports a positive correlation between authoritarianism and favorable attitudes toward the police. It would appear that such attitudes manifest themselves in behavior through the combined influences of the subject's personality and the defendant's characteristics.

As in the case of conformity, it is argued that we will understand the interaction of personality and situation to the extent that we can determine the crucial elements of the situational context to which subjects are exposed. What we are essentially doing when we discover mitigated or reversed effects is to reveal the extent to which authoritarians and equalitarians differentially construe the situation with which they are confronted. An equalitarian will behave "like an authoritarian" to the extent that we can create a situation which evokes the same construction of events, namely, that conformity, aggression, or whatever are justified and acceptable modes of behavior in that context.

Response to Erotic Stimuli

Whether motivated by a desire to punish those who violate conventional standards or by the need to project unwanted sexual impulses onto others, the authoritarian has fairly predictable attitudes towards sexually explicit stimulus materials. Compared to equalitarians, authoritarians judge sexual themes in paintings (Eliasberg & Stuart, 1961) and in books and photographs (Byrne, Cherry, Lamberth, & Mitchell, 1973) as more pornographic. Authoritarians also project negative emotional reactions to members of the opposite sex who are

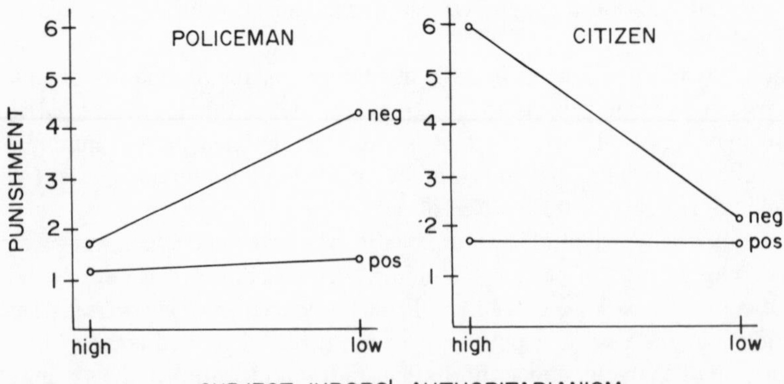

FIGURE 1 Punishment as a function of subject–jurors' authoritarianism, description of the defendant, and status of the defendant. (From Mitchell, 1973.)

exposed to erotic material (Griffitt, 1973) and tend to advocate that legal restrictions be placed on erotic materials (Byrne *et al.,* 1973).

While the image of the censorious authoritarian attempting to restrict others from enjoying access to erotica has some basis in reality, once again we are cautious about generalizing these tendencies independent of specifications of the situation. In a recent study by Schettino and Byrne (1974), themes of violence were presented to subjects, and it was found that equalitarians reacted more negatively than authoritarians. From these findings we might predict an interaction of theme content with the trait dimension of authoritarianism. While authoritarians might attempt to restrict the availability of erotic materials, equalitarians might be equally likely to censor the distribution of materials containing themes of violence. A sampling of situations that range from purely erotic to purely violent (plus some situations presenting sexual violence) might provide us with a clearer picture of the interplay between context and trait in censorship behavior.

SUMMARY

The study of authoritarianism has been traced through its development from a search for measuring devices, antecedents, and correlates to an emphasis on the interaction of trait and situation in authoritarian-relevant behaviors. In areas of behavior relevant to the syndrome of authoritarianism, we have attempted to suggest a particular approach to this interaction. A battery of situations are required which tap conformity, punitive, or censoring behavior. We need to know to what extent these behavioral situations are related and the essential characteristics that provide a consistent discrimination between authoritarians and equalitarians as measured by the *F* scale. Once we have achieved accurate knowledge of situational variables, we will be able to identify those features of the situation which accentuate, minimize, or reverse what have been thought to be basic personality differences in behavior.

ACKNOWLEDGMENTS

Work on this chapter was supported in part by Grant SOC 74-15254 from the National Science Foundation.

REFERENCES

Adorno, T. W., Frenkel-Brunswik, E., Levinson, D. J., & Sanford, R. N. *The authoritarian personality.* New York: Harper & Row, 1950.

Altemeyer, R. A. Balancing the F scale. *Proceedings of the 77th Annual Convention of the American Psychological Association,* 1969, *4,* 417–418.

Back, K., & Davis, K. Some personal and situational factors relevant to the consistency and prediction of conforming behavior. *Sociometry,* 1965, *28,* 227–240.

Bass, B. H. Authoritarianism or acquiescence? *Journal of Abnormal and Social Psychology,* 1955, *51,* 616–623.

Baumrind, D. An exploratory study of socialization effects on black children: Some black–white comparisons. *Child Development,* 1972, *43,* 261–267.

Berg, K. S., & Vidmar, N. Authoritarianism and recall of evidence about criminal behavior. *Journal of Research in Personality,* 1975, *9,* 147–157.

Berkowitz, L. Judgmental processes in personality functioning. *Psychological Review,* 1960, *67,* 130–142.

Block, J. Personality characteristics associated with fathers' attitudes toward child-rearing. *Child Development,* 1955, *26,* 41–48.

Boehm, V. R. Mr. Prejudice, Miss Sympathy, and the authoritarian personality: An application of psychological measuring techniques to the problem of jury bias. *Wisconsin Law Review,* 1968, 734–750.

Byrne, D. Parental antecedents of authoritarianism. *Journal of Personality and Social Psychology,* 1965, *1,* 369–373.

Byrne, D. *An introduction to personality.* Englewood Cliffs, N.J.: Prentice-Hall, 1974.

Byrne, D., Cherry, F., Lamberth, J., & Mitchell, H. E. Husband–wife similarity in response to erotic stimuli. *Journal of Personality,* 1973, *41,* 385–394.

Campbell, D., & McCandless, B. R. Ethnocentrism, xenophobia, and personality. *Human Relations,* 1951, *4,* 185–192.

Chapman, L. J., & Campbell, D. T. Response set in the F scale. *Journal of Abnormal and Social Psychology,* 1957, *54,* 129–132.

Christie, R. Changes in authoritarianism as related to situational factors. *American Psychologist,* 1952, *7,* 307–308. (Abstract)

Christie, R. Authoritarianism re-examined. In R. Christie & M. Jahoda (Eds.), *Studies in the scope and method of "The Authoritarian Personality."* Glencoe, Ill.: Free Press, 1954.

Christie, R., & Cook, P. A guide to published literature relating to the authoritarian personality through 1956. *Journal of Psychology,* 1958, *45,* 171–199.

Christie, R., Havel, J., & Seidenberg, B. Is the F Scale irreversible? *Journal of Abnormal and Social Psychology,* 1958, *56,* 143–159.

Christie, R., & Jahoda, M. (Eds.), *Studies in the scope and method of "The Authoritarian Personality."* Glencoe, Ill.: Free Press, 1954.

Couch, A., & Keniston, K. Yeasayers and naysayers: Agreeing response set as a personality variable. *Journal of Abnormal and Social Psychology,* 1960, *60,* 151–174.

Crutchfield, R. S. Conformity and character. *American Psychologist,* 1955, *10,* 191–198.

Dustin, D. S., & Davis, H. P. Authoritarianism and sanctioning behavior. *Journal of Personality and Social Psychology,* 1967, *6,* 222–224.

Dustin, D., & Young, R. K. Unpublished data reported in D. Byrne, *An introduction to personality.* Englewood Cliffs, N.J.: Prentice-Hall, 1974.

Eliasberg, W. G., & Stuart, I. R. Authoritarian personality and the obscenity threshold. *Journal of Social Psychology,* 1961, *55,* 143–151.

Elms, A. C., & Milgram, S. Personality characteristics associated with obedience and defiance toward authoritative command. *Journal of Experimental Research in Personality,* 1966, *1,* 282–289.

Endler, N. S. Conformity analyzed and related to personality. *Journal of Social Psychology,* 1961, *53,* 271–283.

Epstein, R. Authoritarianism, displaced aggression, and social status of the target. *Journal of Personality and Social Psychology,* 1965, *2,* 585–589.

Fischer, E. H. Authoritarianism and agreement response style in predicting altruistic attitudes: Tests of a newly balanced *F* scale. *Proceedings of the Annual Convention of the APA,* 1970, *5,* 327–328.

Flacks, R. Protest or conform: Some social psychological perspectives on legitimacy. *Journal of Applied Behavioral Science,* 1969, *5,* 127–160.

Fromm, E. *Escape from freedom.* New York: Holt, Rinehart & Winston, 1941.

Gage, N. L., & Chatterjee, B. B. The psychological meaning of acquiescence set: Further evidence. *Journal of Abnormal and Social Psychology,* 1960, *60,* 280–283.

Gage, N. L., Leavitt, G. S., & Stone, G. C. The psychological meaning of acquiescence set for authoritarianism. *Journal of Abnormal and Social Psychology,* 1957, *55,* 98–103.

Griffitt, W. Response to erotica and the projection of response to erotica in the opposite sex. *Journal of Experimental Research in Personality,* 1973, *6,* 330–338.

Hart, I. Maternal child-rearing practices and authoritarian ideology. *Journal of Abnormal and Social Psychology,* 1957, *55,* 232–237.

Harvey, O. J. Authoritarianism and conceptual functioning in varied conditions. *Journal of Personality,* 1963, *31,* 462–470.

Hollander, E. P., & Willis, R. H. Some current issues in the psychology of conformity and nonconformity. *Psychological Bulletin,* 1967, *68,* 62–76.

Hyman, H. H., Sheatsley, P. B. "The authoritarian personality" – A methodological critique. In R. Christie & M. Jahoda (Eds.), *Studies in the scope and method of "The Authoritarian Personality."* Glencoe, Ill.: Free Press, 1954.

Izzett, R. R. Authoritarianism and attitudes toward the Vietnam war as reflected in behavioral and self-report measures. *Journal of Personality and Social Psychology,* 1971, *17,* 145–148.

Jaccard, J. J. Predicting social behavior from personality traits. *Journal of Research in Personality,* 1974, *7,* 358–367.

Jackson, D. N., & Messick, S. J. A note on "ethnocentrism" and acquiescent response sets. *Journal of Abnormal and Social Psychology,* 1957, *54,* 132–134.

Jones, M. B. Religious values and authoritarian tendency. *Journal of Social Psychology,* 1958, *45,* 83–89.

Jurow, G. L. New data on the effect of a "death qualified" jury on the guilt determination process. *Harvard Law Review,* 1971, *84,* 567–611.

Kelly, J. G., Ferson, J. E., & Holtzman, W. H. The measurement of attitudes toward the Negro in the South. *Journal of Social Psychology,* 1958, *48,* 305–317.

Kerlinger, F. N. On authoritarianism and acquiescence: An added note to Bass and Messick and Jackson. *Journal of Abnormal and Social Psychology,* 1958, *56,* 141–142.

Kirscht, J. P., & Dillehay, R. C. *Dimensions of authoritarianism: A review of research and theory.* Lexington, Ky.: University of Kentucky Press, 1967.

Klein, E. B. Stylistic components of response as related to attitude change. *Journal of Personality,* 1963, *31,* 38–51.

Larsen, K. S. Authoritarianism and attitudes toward police. *Psychological Reports,* 1968, *23,* 349–350.

Leavitt, H. J., Hax, H., & Roche, J. H. "Authoritarianism" and agreement with things authoritative. *Journal of Psychology,* 1955, *40,* 215–221.

Lee, R. E., & Warr, P. B. The development and standardization of a balanced F scale. *Journal of General Psychology,* 1969, *81,* 109–129.

Leventhal, H., Jacobs, R. L., & Kudirka, J. Authoritarianism, ideology, and political candidate choice. *Journal of Abnormal and Social Psychology,* 1964, *69,* 539–549.

Levinson, D. J., & Huffman, P. E. Traditional family ideology and its relation to personality. *Journal of Personality,* 1955, *23,* 251–273.

Levinson, D. J., & Schermerhorn, R. A. Emotional–attitudinal effects of an intergroup relations workshop on its members. *Journal of Psychology,* 1951, *31,* 243–256.

Levitt, E. E. The effect of a 'causal' teacher training program on authoritarianism and responsibility in grade school children. *Psychological Reports,* 1955, *1,* 449–458.

Mahler, I. Attitudes toward socialized medicine. *Journal of Social Psychology,* 1953, *38,* 273–282.

Martin, J. G., & Westie, F. R. The tolerant personality. *American Sociological Review,* 1959, *24,* 521–528.

Masling, H. H. How neurotic is the authoritarian? *Journal of Abnormal and Social Psychology,* 1954, *33,* 21–42.

Messick, S., & Jackson, D. N. Authoritarianism or acquiescence in Bass' data. *Journal of Abnormal and Social Psychology,* 1957, *54,* 424–427.

Milgram, S. Some conditions of obedience and disobedience to authority. *Human Relations,* 1965, *18,* 57–76.

Milgram, S. *Obedience to authority.* New York: Harper & Row, 1974.

Mischel, W. *Personality and assessment.* New York: Wiley, 1968.

Mischel, W. *Introduction to personality.* New York: Holt, Rinehart & Winston, 1971.

Mischel, W. Toward a cognitive social learning reconceptualization of personality. *Psychological Review,* 1973, *80,* 252–283.

Mitchell, H. E. Authoritarian punitiveness in simulated juror decision-making: The good guys don't always wear white hats. Paper presented at the meeting of the Midwestern Psychological Association, Chicago, May 1973.

Mitchell, H. E., & Byrne, D. Minimizing the influence of irrelevant factors in the courtroom: The defendant's character, judge's instructions, and authoritarianism. Paper presented at the meeting of the Midwestern Psychological Association, Cleveland, May 1972.

Mitchell, H. E., & Byrne, D. The defendant's dilemma: Effects of jurors' attitudes and authoritarianism on judicial decisions. *Journal of Personality and Social Psychology,* 1973, *25,* 123–129.

Nadler, E. B. Yielding, authoritarianism, and authoritarian ideology regarding groups. *Journal of Abnormal and Social Psychology,* 1959, *58,* 408–410.

Nixon, R. M. Farewell speech. Washington, D.C., August, 1974.

O'Neil, W. M., & Levinson, D. J. A factorial exploration of authoritarianism and some of its ideological concomitants. *Journal of Personality,* 1954, *22,* 449–463.

Peabody, D. Authoritarianism scales and response bias. *Psychological Bulletin,* 1966, *65,* 11–23.

Roberts, A. H., & Jessor, R. Authoritarianism, punitiveness, and perceived social status. *Journal of Abnormal and Social Psychology,* 1958, *56,* 311–314.

Rokeach, M. *The open and closed mind: Investigations into the nature of belief systems and personality systems.* New York: Basic Books, 1960.

Rokeach, M., & McLellan, D. D. Comment: Dogmatism and the death penalty: A reinterpretation of the Duquesne poll data. *Duquesne Law Review,* 1970, *8,* 125–129.

Rorer, L. G. The great response-style myth. *Psychological Bulletin,* 1965, *63,* 129–156.

Rotter, J. B. *Social learning and clinical psychology.* Englewood Cliffs, N.J.: Prentice-Hall, 1954.

Sales, S. M. Threat as a factor in authoritarianism: An analysis of archival data. *Journal of Personality and Social Psychology,* 1973, *28,* 44–57.

Samelson, F., & Yates, J. F. Acquiescence and the *F* scale: Old assumptions and new data. *Psychological Bulletin,* 1967, *68,* 91–103.

Sanford, N. Authoritarian personality in contemporary perspective. In J. Knutson (Ed.), *Handbook of Political Psychology.* San Francisco: Jossey-Bass, 1973.

Schettino, A., & Byrne, D. Affective and evaluative response to violent stimuli. Unpublished manuscript, Purdue University, 1974.

Shils, E. Authoritarianism: "Right" and "left." In R. Christie & M. Jahoda (Eds.), *Studies in the scope and method of "The Authoritarian Personality."* Glencoe, Ill.: Free Press, 1954.

Steiner, I. D., & Johnson, H. H. Authoritarianism and "tolerance of trait inconsistency." *Journal of Abnormal and Social Psychology,* 1963, *67,* 388–391. (a)

Steiner, I. D., & Johnson, H. H. Authoritarianism and conformity. *Sociometry,* 1963, *26,* 21–34. (b)

Titus, H. E., & Hollander, E. P. The California F scale in psychological research. *Psychological Bulletin,* 1957, *54,* 47–64.

Vaughan, G. M. The trans-situational aspect of conforming behavior. *Journal of Personality,* 1964, *32,* 335–354.

Vidmar, N., & Crinklaw, L. D. Retribution and utility as motives in sanctioning behavior. Paper presented at the meeting of the Midwestern Psychological Association, Chicago, May 1973.

Wagman, M. Attitude change and authoritarian personality. *Journal of Psychology,* 1955, *40,* 3–24.

Wells, W. D., Weinert, G., & Rubel, M. Conformity pressure and authoritarian personality. *Journal of Psychology,* 1956, *42,* 133–136.

Wrightsman, L. S., Jr., Radloff, R. W., Horton, D. L., & Mecherikoff, M. Authoritarian attitudes and presidential voting preferences. *Psychological Reports,* 1961, *8,* 43–46.

4
Psychological Differentiation

Stephen A. Karp
George Washington University

For more than 25 years, H. A. Witkin and his colleagues, as well as numerous other investigators, have been carrying out research on a dimension of individual functioning called, at various stages in its history, perception of the upright, field dependence, analytic cognitive style, and psychological differentiation. The findings resulting from these studies have been summarized in two major reports, covering the work from its inception to 1962 (Witkin, Lewis, Hertzman, Machover, Meissner, & Wapner, 1954/1972; Witkin, Dyk, Faterson, Goodenough, & Karp, 1962/1974).

Since 1962, the growing body of literature on psychological differentiation has made necessary a more segmented approach, with separate reviews on such topics as psychopathology (Witkin, 1965b), personality (Goodenough, in press), body concept (Witkin, 1965a), evaluation and guidance (Witkin, 1973), learning and memory (Goodenough, 1975), and cross-cultural effects (Witkin & Berry, 1975).

It is the aim of this chapter to summarize, briefly, the history of the earlier studies and some of the major findings which helped to define the differentiation dimension as well as to describe the various measurement techniques associated with it. This will serve as background for the major focus of this report, a survey of the research exploring relationships between psychological differentiation and social, interpersonal styles and behaviors.

To carry out this task, and still remain within the space limitations of a chapter within a book, it has been necessary to make numerous decisions as to what to include as relevant and central. The impossibility of adequately summarizing all of the pertinent literature becomes apparent when one considers that there are over two thousand reports on studies bearing on the differentiation dimension, a substantial portion of which have some relevance for the issues to be considered here. A list of the pertinent references, in itself, could more than fill the present chapter.[1]

Such editorial decisions have been made with the aim of focusing on themes and studies which, to this author, can provide the reader with the most comprehensive picture of what differentiation means and does not mean.

HISTORY

Some of the earliest studies bearing on what was to become the psychological differentiation dimension were designed to clarify an issue in space perception raised by the repetition, by Gibson and Mowrer (1938), of a classic study (Wertheimer, 1912) on the perception of the upright. The issue had to do with the kinds of cues used to determine the verticality of objects, principally the relative importance of cues provided by the visual environment and cues provided by the body of the perceiver. Wertheimer ingeniously separated the two types of cues by having his subjects judge the position of a scene viewed through a tilted mirror (thus distorting the available visual cues while body cues were left intact). His findings led him to the view that visual cues were preeminent in such spatial perception, whereas Gibson and Mowrer's replication led them to the opposite view.

Collaborating with S. Asch (Asch & Witkin, 1948a, b; Witkin & Asch, 1948a, b), Witkin devised a situation in which external referents to the vertical (represented by a square frame) could be manipulated independently of body referents while subjects judged the position of a rod enclosed by the frame. The apparatus used, called the rod and frame test (RFT), is depicted in Figure 1. Another situation, devised by Witkin (1949), compared use of external and body referents in evaluation of the spatial position of the perceiver's own body. Seated in a specially constructed chair which could be tilted left or right, within a room which could also be tilted left or right, the subject was asked to judge his own position while chair and room were tilted and to direct the adjustment of the chair to the vertical while the room remained in its tilted position. This body adjustment test (BAT) provided a second situation in which environmental and body referents could be evaluated separately.

A third situation provided for manipulation of information furnished the subject by his own body, while information from his visual environment remained constant. This was accomplished by placing the tilting room apparatus on a "trolley track" and moving it in a circular path while the subject adjusted his tilted chair to the upright. Manipulation of body information about the

[1] Annotated bibliographies of studies of psychological differentiation have been compiled by Witkin, Oltman, Cox, Erlichman, Hamm, and Ringler (1973) and Witkin, Cox, Friedman, Hrishikesan, and Siegel (1974).

FIGURE 1 Rod and frame apparatus as seen by the subject in a darkroom.

location of the vertical was brought about by the effect of the centrifugal force, created by the moving room, upon the subject's perception of gravity.

Although studies of performance in these perceptual situations yielded information on the original issue of the relative use of external and internal referents in judging the upright, two types of findings peripheral to the original hypotheses proved to be of major importance. Individuals differed markedly in the extent to which they used body versus external information in their judgments and they tended to be self-consistent in their performance across the three different test situations. Thus, a person who relied heavily on the frame to determine the position of the rod was also likely to rely upon the position of the room in determining the position of his body.

These additional findings were of major importance in changing the direction of Witkin's work from an attempt to understand the effects of stimulus characteristics on spatial perception to an attempt to understand characteristics of individuals that contributed to their different ways of perceiving the upright.

This new thrust took the form of intensive studies of individual differences in perceptual and personality characteristics as these related to spatial orientation among groups of college students, psychiatric patients, and children.

To touch upon just a few of the major findings of these early studies, in the area of perception the embedded figures test or EFT (see Figure 2) was developed and found to correlate significantly and substantially with the RFT and BAT. Subjects who made greater use of external referents in judging the upright took more time to locate simple geometric figures embedded in more complex ones. Findings with the EFT contributed to a broadening of conceptualization about the perceptual dimension being studied. Whereas spatial orientation was at issue in the RFT, BAT, and rotating room test, the high correlations with EFT contributed to the view that what these four tests measured in common was the degree to which the perceiver was dependent upon information from the visual field which surrounded an object in making judg-

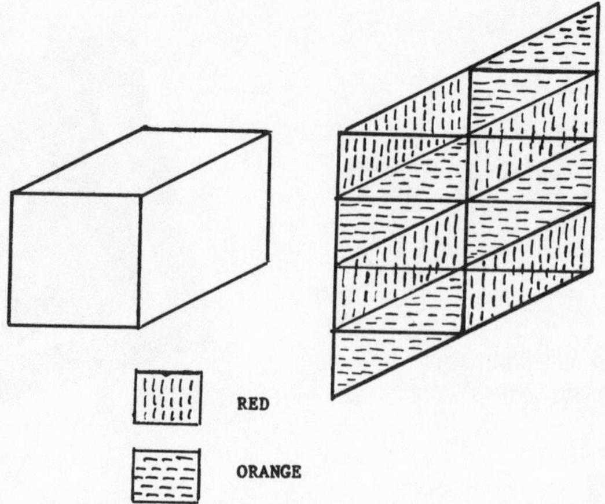

FIGURE 2 A simple (left) and a complex (right) figure, comprising a pair of EFT figures.

ments about that object. This led to the description of the perceptual dimension under study as involving "field-dependence–independent" (FD–I).[2]

In the area of perception–personality relationships, three kinds of findings emerged from studies comparing typical performance on a wide variety of personality measures (interview, Rorschach, TAT, Sentence Completion, MMPI, Human Figure Drawings) to FD–I scores. FD individuals were found to be more passive and to lack self-assurance in operating under a variety of environmental pressures; regarding impulse handling, they were found less aware of their own inner lives, more afraid of aggressive and sexual impulses, and able to maintain less control over these impulses; with regard to self-views, they were found to display relatively low self-esteem and less body- and self-acceptance.

Developmentally, children were found to change in the direction of increasing FI between 8 and 17 years. Starting during adolescence, sex differences were found in FD–I, with women slightly more FD than men.[3]

These early studies (reported in 1954) led to a further series by Witkin and his coworkers, as well as other investigators, directed toward refining and elaborating on earlier findings of manifestations of FD–I in cognitive functions and personality characteristics and further exploring the origins and development of FD–I.

[2] The FD–I dimension represents a scoring continuum on an interval scale. Convenience of usage, however, has led to describing individuals as field dependent (FD) or field independent (FI). As used here FD and FI mean relative positions on the FD–I continuum.

[3] A recent review of cross-cultural studies (Witkin & Berry, 1975) reports absence of such sex differences in certain societies, particularly those where social conformity is *not* stressed.

The new studies, reported by Witkin and his colleagues in 1962, involved the extensive and intensive study of a group of 68 10-year-old boys and their mothers, as well as more limited studies of many hundreds of children and adults. One focus of these studies was the further specification of the abilities involved in performance on tests of FD–I. Two hypotheses, of the many that were evaluated, suggested that FD–I was but a special case of ability to resist distraction or that it was simply a manifestation of general intelligence.

The distraction hypothesis was evaluated by a factor analytic study of 150 college men (Karp, 1963). Subjects were given the BAT, EFT, and RFT, as well as other tests of overcoming embeddedness and several tests involving ability to locate figures in distracting, but not embedding, fields. The tests of FD–I loaded different factors than the distraction tests, with no overlap and negligible correlations between factors. These results suggested that the embedding nature of surrounding stimuli was an essential element of tests of FD–I.

The general intelligence hypothesis, which persists in some quarters to this day (e.g., Vernon, 1972a), was based upon the finding of significant correlations between FD–I measures and IQ tests such as the WISC and Stanford–Binet. To evaluate it, several factor analytic studies of perceptual and intellectual tests were carried out, including the investigation referred to above of 150 college men, and studies of 10- and 12-year-old children (Goodenough & Karp, 1961). In each, a battery of tests including Wechsler subtests and the three measures of FD–I was factor analyzed. Each study yielded an FD–I factor which also loaded Wechsler block design and object assembly subtests. Of all of the Wechsler subtests, block design and object assembly are most like the tests of FD–I in that they require ability to overcome embeddedness. In the case of block design, where the subject is shown a design to be reproduced with either four or nine blocks, the structure of the total design serves to obscure the locations of the component blocks. To perform this task quickly, one must be able to ignore or "break up" this embedding structure. Object assembly contains a series of jigsawlike pieces which must be put together in the proper configuration to form a familiar object (e.g., an elephant). The pieces do not correspond to usual parts of the object to be assembled and tend to provide misleading sets. Only by breaking up the given structures of the parts can one develop effective hypotheses needed to reach a solution.

Based on these and related results, the relationships between total IQ and FD–I may be viewed as being "carried" by those IQ items which measure ability to overcome embeddedness (FD–I). Intellectual items requiring other kinds of abilities, such as verbal comprehension or short-term memory, showed only low correlations with FD–I measures.

The evidence cited above, along with that of many other studies, led to the need for a construct, broader than FD–I, to describe ability to overcome embeddedness in a wide variety of perceptual and intellectual situations. The concept of "Global versus Analytical Cognitive Style" was thus adopted.

A second major focus of studies conducted between 1954 and 1962 concerned manifestations of FD–I in personality. Based upon the broad findings of the earlier work, hypotheses were refined and a series of specific studies were designed to test these hypotheses. These later studies reflected methodological changes from the earlier studies in that a greater variety of approaches to personality assessment were used with greater emphasis on experimental manipulation and use of objective measures.

Findings from these studies contributed to the view that FI persons tend to hold relatively articulated concepts of their own bodies, experiencing more clearly body boundaries, body parts, and the relationship of parts and boundaries; that such individuals tend to have a better developed sense of separate identity, experiencing more clearly the self as structured and distinct from others; and such individuals are likely to make use of kinds of defenses against impulses which are relatively structured and specialized (e.g., isolation, intellectualization), rather than more global and nonspecific ones (like denial).

Evidence was also gathered on relationships between FD–I and psychopathology. Although FD people were found no more likely than FI ones to develop pathology or to be found in a mental hospital, the kinds of pathology they develop tend to differ markedly. FD patients most often displayed kinds of symptoms associated with the kinds of body and self views, identity problems, and defenses found among FD persons in the normal population (like alcoholism or hysterical neurosis); in contrast, FI patients usually displayed symptoms which reflected their needs for greater separation of self from others and impulse from intellect (like obsessive–compulsive neurosis).

Regarding the origins of FD–I, studies were carried out on the relationship between styles of mothering and development of FD–I, using interview and questionnaire data from mothers and FD–I test scores of their children. Mothers of FI children engaged in rearing practices which emphasized the development of autonomy and separation to a greater extent than mothers of FD children.

The kinds of self-consistency displayed by individuals across perceptual, intellectual, and personality domains, in experiencing themselves, others, and the physical world as more articulated and discrete or as more global and fused, and the evidence, now extended down to age five, that development proceeds from earlier FD toward increasing FI, led to the adoption of the concept of psychological differentiation, based in part upon the theories of Werner (1948) and Lewin (1935), as a potentially useful framework within which to view the diverse evidence gathered to that point and from which to develop new hypotheses.

As some of the terminology used in the works of Witkin and others may not be familiar to the reader, a brief recapitulation of the hierarchy of concepts used by this group of investigators may be in order.

At the highest level of generality is *psychological differentiation,* which represents a general style of functioning which may be manifested in cognitive functions, concepts of self and others, interpersonal activities, defenses, forms of pathology, or many other areas.

Within certain areas in which differentiation may be manifested, such as body concept, self concept, and kinds of defenses, the term *articulated* versus *global* has been used to describe extreme styles.

In the realm of cognitive functions, manifestations of psychological differentiation have been described as reflecting an *analytical* versus *global* style or approach.

Among various types of cognitive functions, manifestations of psychological differentiation in perception have been described as reflecting a dimension of *field dependence–independence* (FD–I).

MEASURES OF FIELD DEPENDENCE–INDEPENDENCE

With the rapid expansion of the number of investigators carrying out research on psychological differentiation has come a proliferation of measures described by such investigators as tapping the FD–I dimension. This is most dramatic in the case of embedded figures, with over 20 measures reported in the literature. For many of these measures, insufficient data on reliability or validity is available to evaluate their usefulness in testing hypotheses about FD–I. For others, reported or known validity may not be sufficient.

As an example, several studies have used a test called Hidden Pictures as a measure of FD–I. This has been based upon the loading of that test and a version of EFT on Thurstone's (1944) factor called Flexibility of Closure. Yet, when Hidden Pictures, EFT, and RFT were given to the same group of 10-year-old boys (Goodenough & Karp, 1961) and found to load the same FD–I factor, the loading of Hidden Pictures was minor (.27) as compared to that of EFT (.69) and RFT (.69). This would suggest that there may be relatively little overlap between Hidden Pictures and tests of FD–I.

Most of the impetus to develop new tests of FD–I has been prompted by practical reasons, such as the need for a group form of the EFT or for an RFT that does not require a dark room for testing. Several such new tests have shown high reliability and high validity when compared to the standard tests.

Oltman, Raskin, and Witkin, using original EFT figures, developed a group form of this test (GEFT) which correlates .63 for females and .82 for males with the standard EFT and has reliability of .82 (Witkin, Oltman, Raskin, & Karp, 1971). Jackson, Messick, and Myers (1964) developed several group versions, the most valid of which (HFT–V) correlates .75 for men and .84 for women with EFT. Reliability of this test is .83.

Other varieties of EFT (e.g., Gottschaldt Figures, developed by Thurstone, 1944, and CF–1, a variant of the Thurstone measure described by French,

Ekstrom, & Price, 1963) have shown somewhat lower validity when compared to the standard EFT.

The CEFT, a version of the EFT developed by Karp and Konstadt for use with children aged 5 to 12, has been found relatively reliable and valid (Witkin *et al.*, 1971).[4] Recent development of a preschool version of EFT by Coates (1972) may provide a means of evaluating FD–I in even younger children.

Among RFT-type measures, Oltman's (1968) Portable RFT (PRFT) shows high validity (.90) and reliability (.95) for males and females.

Witkin and his colleagues have also used measures, other than those of FD–I, to tap the psychological differentiation dimension. Of these, the block design subtest of the WAIS or WISC and a measure of articulation of body concept (ABC) derived from human figure drawings, have been most frequently employed. Although both measures have been shown to relate highly to measures of FD–I, often loading the same factors, validity tends to fall in the .4 to .7 range, suggesting the potential (as is the case for some of the variants of EFT) for slippage and an increase in ambiguity of results obtained with these measures, when compared to results obtained with standard EFT or RFT procedures.

To review, briefly, the status of various tests of FD–I, it would appear that studies using the standard EFT or RFT or variants of these which have demonstrated validity of .7 or greater (GEFT, HFT–V, CEFT, and PRFT) are most clearly tapping the FD–I dimension. Some further caution would appear warranted when tests in the middle range of validity, such as Gottschaldt Figures, CF–1, WISC or WAIS block design, or the ABC figure drawing scale, are used. Even greater caution, if not outright skepticism, might be in order for tests of lower or unknown validity which purport to reflect FD–I.

Finally, a word may be in order on the relationship between standard EFT and RFT measures. Although most of the factor analytic evidence (see, for example, the studies described above) suggests that EFT and RFT load (very highly) the same factor, individual studies have reported a wide range of correlations between the tests (0 to .9). Although some investigators might disagree (e.g., Vernon, 1972a), it would appear that a preponderance of evidence favors the view that EFT and RFT are highly related.

FIELD DEPENDENCE–INDEPENDENCE AND SOCIAL BEHAVIOR

Of the personality characteristics associated with psychological differentiation, one cluster, subsumed under the name "sense of separate identity," has particular relevance for social behavior. Witkin and his colleagues (1962/1974) viewed

[4] The development of CEFT to cover a different age range than EFT precluded validation of the children's version against the standard EFT. Thus, most of the evidence on validity of the CEFT comes from construct validation studies. Where CEFT and EFT overlap, at ages 11–12, these instruments correlated .83 for girls and .86 for boys.

sense of separate identity as reflecting experience of the self as distinct and separated from others, with clear recognition of certain needs, feelings, and characteristics as belonging to the self, and experience of the self as relatively structured, with well formed and articulated internal frames of reference.

Early evidence associating FI with greater sense of separate identity came, primarily, from studies using two broad categories of manifestation of separate identity, reliance upon others for guidance and support and susceptibility to influence from external sources. It was hypothesized that more differentiated individuals, who experienced themselves and the world around them in a more articulated manner, who were better able to analyze and structure aspects of their experience, might be expected to function relatively effectively on their own, with less need for information and guidance from others, with detailed inner standards against which to evaluate suggestions from others and, as a consequence, with less dependence upon external assessments for development and maintenance of self-views. Less differentiated persons, on the other hand, who experienced themselves and the environment in a less articulated fashion, who had poorer abilities to analyze and structure their own experiences or external stimuli, might be expected, as a consequence, to rely more heavily upon information, evaluation, and suggestions arising from sources other than themselves, such as parents, teachers, authorities, and even peers.

To date, substantial evidence has accumulated on manifestations of FD–I in various kinds of social behavior. Much of this evidence bears on the issues of need for guidance or information and susceptibility to influence. However, there is also a considerable body of evidence which may be seen as reflecting other kinds of manifestations of sense of separate identity and still further evidence associating FD–I with aspects of social behavior which reflect other attributes than sense of separate identity.

This chapter focuses on these three types of evidence, with the hope of arriving at some overview of the current status of the separate identity issue as well as some sense of direction as to the relevance of FD–I for other types of social behavior.

For convenience of presentation, the studies reviewed here have been organized into four broad categories: use of other persons as sources of information, perception of others, self-description, and communication with others.

Use of Other Persons as Sources of Information

Seeking Information from Others

Several studies have considered differences between FI and FD individuals in seeking information from authority figures as to how to behave. For example, Witkin *et al.* (1962/1974) recorded extratest comments of 10-year-old boys given the standard TAT. FD boys, significantly more often than FI boys, asked questions of the experimenter designed to elicit further definition and specification of the task (such as, "should the story have a happy ending?").

When the subjects were given four difficult tasks with instructions to ask the experimenters for help whenever it was needed – and subjects were of the same sex as experimenters – FD subjects asked for help significantly more often than the FI ones. This difference did not obtain when experimenter – subject pairs were of mixed sex, a situation in which sex role issues may have exerted a confounding effect (Johnson, 1973).

Studies of selection of FD and FI patients for different kinds of therapy bear upon this issue as well. Greene (1972) found therapists to choose supportive therapy for FD patients and modifying therapy for FI patients. Similarly, Karp, Kissin, and Hustmyer, Jr. (1970) found that alcoholic patients selected for insight psychotherapy were significantly more FI than patients selected for (more structured) pharmacologic therapies. Witkin, Lewis, and Weil (1968) found therapists to respond to FD patients with more active direction than they used with FI patients.

That this differential response by therapists is paralleled by different needs of patients finds support in the results of a study by Koff (1972). New patients of a free mental health clinic were questioned, prior to entering psychotherapy, as to their expectations about the role of the therapist who would be assigned to them. FD patients expected advice and guidance from their therapists to a significantly greater extent than did FI patients.

Taken together, the evidence from therapy studies would suggest that FD patients expect the therapist to provide them with information and guidance or structure to a greater extent than do FI patients. Therapists recognize this difference and respond by providing more information and assigning FD patients to more structured forms of therapy.

Thus, most of the evidence favors the view that FD individuals seek information, guidance, or structure from authority figures to a greater extent than do FI individuals.

Two studies considered differences in FD and FI individuals in seeking information from peers, rather than authority figures. In a study of communication during problem solving, Goldstone (1974) composed 20 groups of 4 persons each, from 40 subjects at each extreme of FD–I, with 10 groups containing all FD or all FI subjects and 10 groups containing 2 subjects of each extreme. The problem was to arrive at a group story for a TAT card. Each group discussion was recorded and a sample of the discussion rated on Bales' Interaction Process Analysis for statements reflecting positive acts, negative acts, questions, and answers. No differences were found in frequency of different kinds of statements, either in terms of homogeneity of groups or FD–I of individuals. Thus, FD subjects were no more likely than FI subjects to ask their peers for information.

Mausner and Graham (1970) had subjects make judgments of the rate of flicker of flashing lights, after hearing the judgment of a partner, under two conditions, one in which the subject had been led to believe that his judgments were quite accurate and his partner's inaccurate and another in which the reverse beliefs were fostered. The judgments of FI subjects were little influenced by those of the partner under either condition. FD persons, on the other hand, shifted their judgments toward those of the partner to a greater extent when they believed the partner to be a more accurate judge than themselves than when they believed the partner to be less accurate.

Thus, with regard to peers as sources of information, FD subjects would appear to use such sources to a greater extent than FI subjects, but only when they believe that such peers have information which can be useful.

Finally, Nevill (1974) studied effects upon FD–I of placing an individual in a dependency arousing situation. All subjects were given a difficult task to perform, for which they required and received information from the experimenters. For half the subjects, randomly selected, this help from the experimenters was removed halfway through the task, while the remaining subjects received continuous help. Upon completing the task, all subjects were tested with the RFT and EFT. The dependency-arousal group (help removed) was significantly more FD than the control group.

Taken together, the studies reported above provide some instances in which FD subjects seek information from outside sources to a greater extent than do FI subjects and other instances in which no differences are found. From this evidence it would appear that FD individuals do not, generally, take every opportunity they may find to solicit information from others. Rather, they do this selectively, on the basis of the potential usefulness of the information that might be obtained. Where information is needed and the potential source is believed to have such information, it appears that FD individuals will solicit and use information to a greater extent than FI individuals.

Response to Unsolicited Suggestion Or Pressure by Others

Two types of studies of suggestibility or response to group pressure in relation to FD–I have appeared in the literature, those offering suggestions through instructional sets and those assessing changes in judgments or attitudes in response to bogus statements or judgments by authorities or groups of peers.

Studies of suggestibility, using instructional sets, have varied widely in the strength of the suggestion used. Thus, in three studies that used the autokinetic situation, set for perceiving movement of a stationary pinpoint of light was relatively weak, in that subjects were told that they "may or may not see the light move." Under these conditions, neither EFT nor RFT performance was related to amount of movement reported (Brothers & Gaines, 1973; Cancro & Voth, 1969; Marino, Fitzgibbons, & Mirabile, Jr., 1970).

Under conditions of moderately strong suggestion, four investigations found FD subjects relatively suggestible, while a fifth did not. Linton and Graham (Linton, 1952, 1955; Linton & Graham, 1959) studied a group of 53 male undergraduates with the BAT, EFT, and an autokinetic movement situation. In the latter situation, subjects were tested in pairs, one member of each pair being the naive subject and the second member a planted confederate, whose estimates of amount of movement were, by design, at variance with those of the naive subject. A significant relationship was obtained between FD–I and a measure of influencibility, with FD subjects more influenced than FI subjects by the judgments of the confederate.

Using the autokinetic word technique, where subjects were told that they were being tested on their *ability* to perceive words being written by a pinpoint of light, Mednick and Schaffer (cited by Witkin *et al.,* 1962/1974) found a significant relationship between FD performance on the RFT and number of words reported, whereas Vaught and Hunter (1967) failed to replicate these results.

Segal and Barr (1969) studied phi movement under baseline conditions and after the suggestion that there will be movement. FD student nurses were most affected by the suggestion. Sanguiliano (1951) gave her subjects three tests of suggestibility. In one such test, for example, subjects were shown a series of bottles, each labeled with the name of a different odor. For the first few trials, bottles actually contained the odors corresponding to their labels. On later trials they contained odorless water, regardless of the label. Suggestibility was inferred from the number of odors attributed to odorless bottles. A combined suggestibility index related significantly to BAT, FD subjects being more suggestible.

Three studies used relatively strong instructional sets. Krippner and Brown (1973) attached subjects to a source of electrical current and suggested that the effects would include increased relaxation. Based upon self-reports of effects, FI subjects were found *more* suggestible than FD subjects. It may be noted, however, that the suggestion in this study ran counter to what the subject might have expected when appraising the situation. The anticipation of electric shock might lead most persons to a set for discomfort, rather than relaxation as was suggested by the experimenters. It is thus difficult to know whether subjects were responding to the stimulus, with increased tension, or to the instructions, with increased relaxation.

Brandsma (1971), in each of three sessions, gave subjects a different (placebo) pill and different instructions as to expected effects of the pill (greater sensitivity, less sensitivity, or neither) on their experiencing of tones or shock. GSR, heart rate, pulse volume, and subject's report of effects were monitored. CF–1 was found unrelated to responsivity to the instructional sets.

Using a driving simulator (an actual auto, on rollers, which felt and sounded real), with instructions to subjects as to what to do if they experienced motion sickness, Testa (1969) found more incidents of illness among extreme FD than extreme FI subjects. When placed in this situation with no suggestion of possible negative effects, FI subjects reported illness more frequently.

Finally, Murphy (1966) studied effects of sensory deprivation under strong, moderate, and weak suggestions as to expected effects. Under strong suggestion, both FD and FI subjects showed effects. Under weak suggestion, neither showed effects. Under moderate suggestion, FD subjects were affected in the direction of the suggestion, whereas FI subjects were not.

The Murphy results are quite consistent with those of the separate studies using instructional sets of varying strength. Whereas studies using very strong or very weak instructional sets rarely obtained differences between FD and FI performers in response to the set, studies using moderately strong suggestions were consistent in their findings, with FD subjects more responsive to the suggestions than FI subjects. Overall, it would appear that FD subjects are more readily affected by suggestion arising from instructional sets than are FI ones.

Another group of studies evaluated effects of bogus opinions of authorities on judgments made by subjects. Several of these studies measured attitudes on the same issue twice, before and after subjects were given an "authoritative" statement on the issue that was at variance with their own views.

Thus, the Linton and Graham (1959) investigation, described earlier, included measures of attitudes on three current issues (such as the practicality of an automic submarine) before and after subjects were shown "authoritative newspaper-type articles" at variance with their earlier opinions. FD subjects were influenced to a significantly greater extent than FI ones. Using HFT, rather than BAT and EFT, and more timely issues for judgment, Glass, Lavin, Henchy, Gordon, Mayhem, and Donohoe (1969) failed to replicate the Linton and Graham findings. Nor did Kumpf and Gotz-Marchand (1973) find FD subjects more influenced than FI subjects by opinions attributed to authorities.

However, Doktor and Hamilton (1973) found FD business administration students more likely to accept consultants' reports than FI subjects. McCarrey, Dayhaw, and Chagnon (1971) found FD graduate students to shift in their ratings of various important political figures and organizations (following endorsements by important authorities) to a greater extent than FI students.

Change in college women's opinions, on ten issues of moderate social importance, measured before and after the introduction of disagreeing opinions of friends and authorities, was unrelated to EFT performance (Goebel, 1966). When a self-report scale of acceptance of authority opinions was used, this was found unrelated to FD–I (Messick & Fritzky, 1963).

In two other studies, authority opinions took the form of statements, by the experimenters, about the personality of the subject. Simon and Wilde (1971) provided their 77 undergraduates with bogus personality evaluations. They found no relation of CF–1 performance to scores on a scale of subject's acceptance of these evaluations as accurate. Similarly, Soat (1974) gave subjects the Tennessee Self-Concept Scale and then a bogus personality evaluation. Acceptance of this evaluation as accurate was not related to FD–I.

A problem common to these last studies involves the believability of the personality evaluations. Although it might normally be expected that an evaluation of a personality test by a psychologist might be believed by a naive subject, providing such an evaluation and then asking the subject if he or she believes it to be accurate might serve to sow considerable doubt as to the legitimacy of the evaluation. Thus, suspiciousness or gullibility, rather than acceptance of authority opinion, may have been at issue in these studies.

The weight of the evidence on influence of authority opinions would favor the view that there is no relationship between FD–I and persuasibility. As has been noted above, however, studies which employ deception as a means of changing attitudes run the risk of obtaining results based upon the effectiveness of the deception. It is thus difficult, for example, to know whether Glass *et al.* (1969) failed to replicate the Linton and Graham findings for reasons relevant to the issue of FD–I and influencibility or because of differences in the effectiveness of the deception. It is not unreasonable to speculate that, in the ten years that elapsed between these studies, subjects have become more suspicious about being deceived by psychologists.

A number of studies looked into responsivity of FD and FI persons to group pressure, using modifications of the Asch (1956) group-pressure situation, in which a group of planted confederates, posing as subjects, announce judgments designed to be at variance with those of the naive subject. Subjects are classified as "yielders" if their stated judgments tend to conform with those of the group. It should be noted, in considering results of studies using this technique, that yielding to group pressure (or resisting it) may occur for any of a variety of reasons, with varied implications for the personality of the yielder. Thus, yielding because the group judgment has shaken one's certainty about one's own perceptions appears very different from yielding so as not to sound out of step, even though one remains certain that his perceptions are correct.

A study of 88 student nurses (Rosner, 1956, 1957) used the original Asch procedure to identify 20 high and 20 low yielders. Standard EFT scores, although in the expected direction (associating yielding with FD), did not significantly distinguish the groups.[5] Weinberg (1970) exposed 30 FI and 30 FD subjects to an Asch situation, in which stooges gave prescribed judgments of ambiguous visual stimuli. FD subjects were found to conform to stooges' judgments significantly more frequently than FI subjects.

Four studies used Crutchfield's (1955) modification of the Asch procedure, in which the person is seated, alone, in front of a panel of lights and told that there are other subjects, in other rooms, seated before similar light panels, who will make the same series of judgments. Judgments of each subject are represented by lights at different locations on the board. In actuality, there are no other subjects and the experimenter controls the lights so as to be able to manipulate "group pressure" through false information fed the naive subject.

In this situation, Crutchfield (1957) found yielding related to Gottschaldt Figures, but not to RFT; Elliot (1961) found no relation to EFT; Paeth (1973) found yielders more FD on HFT–V; and Shaffer (1970) found yielding related to EFT for both sexes, but to RFT only for men.

Several studies of other cultures (Eskimo, Canadian Indian, Hong Kong), using an Asch variant in which a "native" assistant announces bogus group norms,

[5] EFT was also scored in terms of total correct responses (usually highly correlated with standard time scores). These scores were significantly related to yielding.

found no relationship of yielding to FD–I (Berry, 1967; Berry & Annis, 1974; Dawson, Young, & Choi, 1974). Studies using other modifications of the Asch procedure (e.g., taped voices of other subjects making judgments) found no relation of yielding to FD–I (Balance, 1967; Busch & Deridder, 1973).

Considered together, the evidence appears mixed as to the relation of FD–I to yielding to group pressure, with the majority of studies suggesting no relation. There appears, however, to be some relationship between the kind of Asch variant used and the likelihood of finding FD subjects yielding more frequently than FI ones. In those situations that were the least immediate, realistic, and convincing in portraying the group that was applying the pressure (e.g., via announced norms), consistent findings were of no relationship of yielding to FD–I. Where the pressuring peers were more believably and immediately represented (e.g., via the Crutchfield response board), half the studies showed significant relations between FD and yielding while the other half did not.

Such a trend might lead to the hypothesis that FD persons are most likely to yield to group pressure when such pressure is perceived as emanating from real people with whom they are able to interact. The Rosner and Weinberg studies provide the best tests of this hypothesis; however, the varied results obtained by these investigators might warrant further research on this issue.

For anyone contemplating such a replication, a word of caution may be in order. Subjects of the 1970s are not as naive as they (apparently) were in the 1950s when Asch developed this technique, and many have come to associate deception with psychological research. It would therefore appear that a believable setting (clearly not a psychology laboratory) and a believable explanation of the purpose for which the subject is being asked to make judgments publicly, as well as the use of subjects who are relatively unsophisticated about psychological research, would be minimal requirements for such a study.

Taken together, the variety of evidence reported above does not provide a simple answer to the question of whether FD and FI individuals differ in susceptibility to pressure or suggestions from others. There are, however, some trends in the data to suggest that such differences may be more likely when the experimental situation is relatively realistic and believable and when the subject views it as important and meaningful. Under such circumstances, it would appear likely that FD persons would be affected more than FI ones by suggestions or pressures. Where instructional sets, rather than suggestions by authorities or peers, are used to influence opinions or behaviors, sets that provide moderately strong suggestion are most likely to distinguish FD and FI subjects in influencibility.

Conformity to Societal Standards

Of eight studies reported in the literature on social conformity in relation to FD–I, six used self-report scales of conformity.

McGilligan (1971) found FD performance on the RFT significantly related to the Achievement via Conformance scale of the California Psychological Inventory for 40 ninth graders. Messick and Fritzky (1963) found HFT unrelated to a measure of agreement with the majority for 88 male undergraduates. Morf, Kavanaugh, and McConville (1971) found conformity, from Jackson's Personality Inventory, unrelated to a variant of PRFT. Williams (1969) found Gottschaldt Figures only marginally related to seven Cattell UI 20 tests of social conformity. Scheibner (1969), studying 193 college students, found Gottschaldt Figures related to a self-report scale of compliance for females (with FD subjects more compliant), but not for males. Bissiri (1971) found expressed opposition to societal standards unrelated to EFT or RFT performance among 16- to 19-year-old males.

Thus, the evidence suggests that there is little if any relation between FD–I and self-description as conforming. Where actual nonconforming behavior was studied, however, results were quite different.

Larsen and White (1974) selected 60 undergraduates at the Idaho State University, 30 with deviant hair length (below the shoulders) and 30 with nondeviant hair length (at Idaho State only 3–4% of male undergraduates wore hair below the shoulders). Deviants were substantially and significantly more FI than nondeviants.

In a major cross-cultural study of social conformity, Witkin, Price-Williams, Bertini, Christiansen, Oltman, Ramirez, and van Meel (1974) sampled 25 children of each sex, at each of 2 age levels (9–11 and 13–15), in each of 2 villages, in each of 3 countries (Holland, Italy, and Mexico). The 2 villages in each country were selected for their differences in social emphasis on conformity, one village of each country emphasizing conformity to family, religious, and political authority substantially more than the other. Differentiation was measured with a battery of 4 tests, PRFT, either CEFT or EFT (depending upon the child's age), block design, and the ABC scale applied to figure drawings. For each test, for each age group, and in each country, children of conformity-stressing societies were significantly more FD (or less well differentiated) than children of villages which did not stress conformity.

It thus seems clear that when conformity is assessed by actual behaviors or life styles of a conforming or nonconforming nature, FD individuals are more conforming than FI individuals. In contrast – and this kind of split occurs in studies of other characteristics as well – when individuals are asked to describe their own conformity behavior, the majority of studies suggest no relationship of conformity to FD–I.

Seeking Support and Approval from Others

Studies of FD–I in relation to seeking of support and approval from others are relatively limited in number and in variety of approaches. Three studies used ratings by observers of children's interactions with other children and adults.

Bucky (1970) had clinical psychologists observe the interactions of preschool children with adult experimenters and rate the children for need for approval, direction, and structure. These ratings were found unrelated to performance on Banta's Early Childhood EFT (for which validity, as a measure of FD–I, is as yet not established).

Pedersen and Wender (1968), studying 30 2½-year-old boys in a research nursery school, had teachers rate the children on orality, attention seeking, physical contact seeking, and autonomous play. Four years later, the children were recalled for testing with the CEFT. FD–I was found unrelated to seeking attention (r = .16) or to seeking physical contact (r = .26). Since four years intervened between the teachers' ratings and CEFT testing and data is not available on stability of these ratings over so long a period of time, it is impossible to predict what these relationships would have been had they been obtained concurrently.

Crandall and Sinkeldam (1964) found teachers' ratings of dependency behaviors (help seeking, approval seeking, and affection seeking) unrelated to a form of EFT for 50 children (7–12½ years) in a day camp.

Two studies used patient dropout rates from therapy to make inferences about FD–I and need for support. Robinson (1972) studied FD and FI patients in 12-week growth groups, focused either on intrapersonal processes or on ingroup relations. In neither type of group did the patient receive "supportive" therapy. Of the 40 patients, the 15 who dropped out prior to the end of the group experience were significantly more FD than the remainers.

In a study by Karp, Kissin, and Hustmyer, Jr. (1970) dropouts from individual insight therapy were significantly more FD than remainers, whereas no differences were found among dropouts from (more supportive) pharmacologic therapies. In interpreting these studies there is, of course, considerable risk in assuming that the supportive or nonsupportive nature of the therapy mode is a principal factor in determining dropout behavior.

On the basis of the available evidence, it would appear reasonable to consider the issue whether FD individuals are more likely to seek support and approval from others than are FI individuals as still unresolved, with a clear need for further, more definitive study.

Striving for Autonomy

Several studies, using a wide variety of techniques of assessment, bear on this issue. In one such study, 20-year-old women (middle to upper middle class) who had left home or were about to do so (to go to school, for a job, etc.) were significantly more FI than those remaining at home with parents (Fliegel, 1955).

In a study of over 300 eighth-grade students, Vernon (1972b) found no relationship between teachers' ratings of independence and RFT performance. Gluck (1973), using teacher ratings of self-direction for 54 first-grade children, found this measure to load the same factor as ABC ratings of figure drawings (see discussion of measures of FD–I, above), but a different factor than CEFT. Teacher ratings of freedom from social distractibility for 48 fifth-grade boys were significantly related to CF–1 performance of the boys, FD subjects being more distracted by others (Beckerle, 1966).

Ratings of 84 preschool children by their teachers on autonomy in task and social situations correlated significantly with FI on the Early Childhood EFT (Banta, 1970). As has been noted, validity of this measure is unknown at this time. Nadeau (1968) studied 108 nursery-school boys with a variant of CEFT (the easier items) and teachers' ratings of several aspects of autonomous behavior. One such rating (plays alone) showed a low (−.21) but significant correlation with this version of CEFT, whereas the other ratings (works things out alone, −.15; ignores adults, −.17; a loner, −.18) were not significantly related. Tendency to play alone was associated with greater FI.

In the study by Crandall and Sinkeldam, cited above, teachers' ratings of achievement via independent efforts were significantly related to EFT performance, with FI children rated as more independent. Carrigan (1967) found FI subjects to rely more upon themselves than did FD subjects when faced with interpersonal criticism from an experimenter. Coates, Lord, and Jakabovics (1975) found FI nursery-school girls to prefer to work alone on individual projects to a significantly greater extent than FD girls.

In a study of 30 nursery-school boys, rated at age 2½ by two teachers on autonomous play and then recalled four years later for CEFT testing, the relationship between these measures (.26) was in the predicted direction, associating autonomy with FI, but not significant (Pedersen & Wender, 1968). As has been noted earlier, it is difficult to predict what the relationship might have been had the measures been obtained concurrently.

Bell (1955) developed a self-report scale of inner versus other directedness, based upon the Riesman (1950) concept, which she found significantly correlated with measures of FD–I among college males. FI subjects tended to be inner rather than other directed.

In a study of nursery school boys and girls, Beller (1962) obtained ratings on each child on each of four measures of striving for autonomous achievement. A composite of the four measures related significantly to the CHEF (an earlier version of CEFT), with FI subjects showing greater efforts toward autonomy than FD children.

Collectively, the above evidence provides considerable support for the view that FI individuals are more interested in and directed toward autonomous activities than are FD individuals.

Summary.

A wide variety of evidence has been reviewed on relationships between FD–I and use of other persons as sources of information, guidance, and direction or proneness to be influenced by others.

In general, the weight of the evidence favors the view that FI individuals strive for autonomy from others to a greater extent than do FD individuals. FD persons are more likely to seek or use information from others when the information is needed and when the source is deemed likely to possess such information. This may extend to such diverse sources as peers, teachers, therapists, and even society at large, toward which FD individuals would appear to be more conforming than FI individuals.

Regarding use of others for support and guidance in a general way, divorced from needs for information in specific situations, evidence is inconclusive as to whether FD and FI individuals differ.

Perception of Others

Forming Impressions of Others

Several studies have considered the relevance of FD–I to the kinds of impressions individuals form about others. The greatest number of these have been concerned with accuracy of prediction or perception of others' behaviors, motives, and feelings. A smaller number of studies have looked at various aspects of styles of perception of others.

Among studies of accuracy of perception, Braun (1971) evaluated 48 Veteran's Administration therapists and their psychoneurotic male patients, after 10–14 therapy sessions, for ability of the therapists to predict their patients' responses to a 60-item *Q* sort describing the therapist. For male therapists, FI was significantly related to accuracy of prediction, whereas among females FD therapists made the best predictions.

In a study of 30 college counselors, samples of their interviews with clients were rated by judges for accuracy of empathy. No relation was found with EFT performance of the counselors (Carlino, 1972). Loewenstein (1971) studied 30 students in a counseling program, with tapes of their interviews rated by their supervisors on empathy, based upon Truax' Accurate Empathy Scale. Though FI students showed a trend toward greater accuracy, no significant differences were obtained.

Conklin and Zingle (1969) showed each of 63 Canadian school counselors 6 different films from the Cline Interpersonal Perception Film series. Subjects were required to predict which of a list of 20 adjectives the interviewee had previously checked as self-descriptive, which 20 (out of 40) short statements had actually been voiced during the interview, and which 20 (of 40) items related to the physical and behavioral makeup of the interviewee were correctly descriptive. On each of the measures, FI counselors showed greater accuracy than FD counselors.

Richards (1970) studied 127 counselor education students with GEFT and a rating scale of cognitive accuracy. Trainees at FI or FD extremes were less accurate than those in the middle of the range.

Taft (1956) had subjects, participants in a weekend assessment program, judge each other with regard to conformity, sociability, carefulness, drive, assertiveness, and persuasiveness. Ratings were compared to those of staff members to obtain an accuracy measure. FI subjects (Gottschaldt Figures) were more accurate than FD subjects.

Smith and Kleine (1969) compared teachers' ratings of their students' peer popularity, psychomotor abilities, and arithmetic abilities, respectively, to peer ratings of popularity and psychomotor ability and to performance on an arithmetic test. FI teachers were significantly more accurate than FD teachers.

Colker (1972) had male college students observe a videotape of a group discussion and then fill out a questionnaire asking about interactions and behavioral styles of group members. A significant relationship was obtained between FD–I and social perception, with FI subjects more accurate. Danielian (1964) found no relationship between accuracy of judgment of 25 traits of persons portrayed on film and RFT performance.

Wolitzky (1973) presented college students with brief statements, of neutral content, read so as to convey a particular emotion. FI subjects (GEFT and PRFT) were significantly more accurate than FD subjects in identifying the intended emotion. In a similar study, Cooper (1967) failed to obtain significant results, although differences were in the same direction. When college students were shown films of counseling sessions and asked to record their reactions, there was no relation of sensitivity to affective interactions and FD–I (Olesker, 1971).

Chapman (1967) studied 12 college students from each extreme and 12 from the middle of the range of HFT performance. Subjects made up stories to structured and unstructured stimulus cards. These stories were transcribed, with every fifth word deleted, and then shown to decoders, a group of 104 other students who had received the HFT. Decoders were given the task of filling in the blank spaces in the stories, scores reflecting the verbatim accuracy of the fill-ins. FI decoders were more accurate than FD decoders (regardless of the FD–I of the story teller).

Martin and Toomey (1973) gave male undergraduates the EFT and the Hogan Empathy Scale, which taps such abilities as social perceptiveness, awareness of own impressions of others, and insightfulness into own and others' motives. FI individuals were significantly more empathic than FD subjects.

Welkowitz (cited by Witkin, Moore, Goodenough, & Cox, in press) had subjects rate the warmth of therapists from tape recordings of therapy sessions. These were compared to ratings made by the actual therapists and patients. FD subjects were more accurate than FI individuals in their global ratings of therapist warmth.

Shows (1967) studied 80 male undergraduates for ability to identify a series of pictures from lists of adjectives descriptive of these pictures. Two lists of adjectives were developed by judges, one seen as likely to be employed by FD individuals and the other by FI individuals. Subjects did better at matching descriptions to pictures when they were given the adjectives predicted as matching their own cognitive style than when they received mismatched adjectives.

Of the 16 studies of accuracy of perception of others, FI perceivers were found more accurate in 7 studies, FD perceivers more accurate in 1 study, and mixed results or no differences were found in 8 studies. Yet, within this mixture of results, there appear to be some trends which might support a hypothesis about accuracy of perception of others. In 2 studies which required a very high degree of specificity of prediction (what was said in an interview, what words were deleted from sentences), FI subjects were significantly more accurate than FD individuals. Where a single, overall, and relatively nonspecific rating (therapist warmth) was required, FD subjects were more accurate.

Putting this together, one might hypothesize that when accuracy of description of another person requires analytical ability, as in the case of filling in missing words of a story, FI persons, who have better developed analytical abilities, tend to be more accurate. Where accuracy of description of others requires global concepts or impressions, FD persons tend to be more accurate. This view is not inconsistent with the findings of the study by Shows, that FD and FI persons use different kinds of concepts to describe things.

Another group of studies of perception of others have implications for style of perceiving, rather than accuracy of perceiving.

Nightingale (1971) studied 64 male undergraduates with EFT and PRFT. They were also shown three silent movies about three different persons and then asked questions about the persons. FD subjects more frequently made statements describing the competence or social success of the character and more frequently referred to external or superficial qualities than did FI individuals. FD subjects also expressed more liking for and approval of the characters.

Bieri, Bradburn, and Galinsky (1958) had their college subjects each name seven persons they knew. They were then given combinations of three of those persons and asked to name a characteristic on which two of the three were alike and the third different. Characteristics used by the subjects were classified as *external* constructs if they referred to such qualities as interests, activities, physical qualities and as *internal* constructs if they referred to deeper and less obvious qualities, such as underlying motives or personality characteristics. FI women tended to use internal constructs to a significantly greater degree than did FD women. Though in the same direction, this difference was not significant for men. Using a similar measure with 10-year-old boys, Witkin *et al.* (1962/1974) found FI boys to use internal constructs significantly more often than did FD boys.

Kavanaugh and Weissenberg (1973) had 127 male undergraduates observe a videotape of the interaction of a supervisor and a subordinate. Subjects then filled out a questionnaire on leadership qualities of the supervisor. Factor analysis of this data yielded two distinct dimensions of leadership qualities, *consideration* and *initiating structure.* FI subjects tended to make relatively discrete ratings of each supervisor on the two dimensions, whereas the ratings of

FD subjects of each supervisor tended to be similar for the two dimensions. This would suggest that FD subjects were making their ratings upon the basis of global impressions.

Gardner, Lohrenz, and Schoen (1968) gave Concealed Figures to 28 husband–wife pairs. In addition, each subject rated each of nine known persons (e.g., subject's mother, Al Capone, Joseph Stalin) on a series of adjectives of a semantic differential scale. One's score was the standard deviation of nine ratings of different persons, the higher the score, the more diverse the ratings. Factor analysis showed Concealed Figures (.73) and variability of person ratings (.32) to load the same factor, FI individuals using more varied ratings than FD subjects.

Goldweber (1966) found FI subjects better able than their FD peers to recognize and organize inconsistent characteristics into their overall impressions of a person. Klau (1973), studying 52 male college freshmen with GEFT and *Q* sort ratings of their task partners, found FD subjects to form more extreme impressions than FI subjects.

O'Leary, Donovan, and Hague (1974) and Rhodes, Carr, and Jurji (1968) used the Interpersonal Discrimination Test (Carr, 1965), the main score of which is the number of different categories employed to describe seven persons (oneself and six others known to the subject). In each study, FI individuals used a significantly greater number of categories than FD persons.

The results of these studies are consistent in suggesting that FI persons tend to perceive and describe others in more discrete and analytical fashion and that FD persons tend to form more global and general impressions of others. This is quite consistent with the ways in which FI and FD persons have been found to perceive other aspects of the environment, their own bodies, and themselves.

Attention to Social Stimuli

A number of studies have investigated relationships between FD–I and attention to or interest in social stimuli, particularly other people. Many of these studies have been guided by the hypothesis that FD persons, having greater needs for information from external sources, would spend more time and energy in attending to such sources.

Studies of this type can be divided into four main subgroups, based upon the strategy by which attentiveness to others was assessed. One group focused on time spent in eye contact with or looking at others, another on memory for faces or names of others, a third on interest in physical proximity to others, and a fourth on vocational interests and choices which could be interpreted as reflecting interest in working in proximity to others.

Among eye contact studies, Beller (1958) found FD–I related to frequency of looking at others, particularly at the teacher, among nursery-school students. This occurred even in free-play situations in which the teacher had no role. FD children looked more often.

In another study, fourth-grade students were given a routine letter cancellation task on two occasions, one with an "approving" and one with a "disapproving" experimenter. Occasions were recorded when subjects looked away from the task and at another person (the experimenter or another student). FD students gazed significantly more often at others than did FI students in the disapproval condition, when this had followed earlier experience of approval (Konstadt & Forman, 1965).

Among college students interviewed about various kinds of earlier life experiences, FI subjects persisted longer than the FD ones in looking at the interviewer when questioned about long-term or negative emotional memories. No differences were obtained when recall of relatively neutral (and easily retrieved) factual material was involved (Meskin & Singer, 1974). Badarocco (1973) studied extreme FD and FI college women in a similar interview situation. A measure of total amount of eye contact with the interviewer, obtained from videotape recordings, was unrelated to FD–I. When the data was analyzed by interview content, FI subjects showed the most eye contact when talking about neutral topics and FD subjects when talking about what they liked about themselves.

In the study by Nevill (1974) on dependency arousal, referred to above, both EFT and RFT correlated significantly with length of time spent looking at the experimenter. FD subjects looked longer.

Kendon and Cook (1969) studied the locus of gaze of 15 subjects in pairs, instructed to introduce themselves and talk for about 30 min. EFT scores correlated significantly (−.44) with percentage of time spent in gazing at one's listener, with FI persons gazing more. No relation was found for RFT, nor for either test in amount of time spent by the listener in gazing at the speaker.

When 28 7- to 10-year-old children were given a series of problems, some of which could only be solved by observing social cues provided by the experimenter (e.g. who inclined her head toward the correct alternative), Ruble and Nakamura (1972) report a trend for FD subjects to be more aware of these social cues than FI subjects. However, FD subjects glanced significantly more often at the experimenter than did FI subjects.

From the series of studies described above, two main trends in the evidence may be abstracted. There appears to be no consistent trend for either FD or FI perceivers to look more at others as a general mode of approach to social, interpersonal situations. However, the type of situation or task given the subject may have a differential effect on looking behavior. Where the situation involves self-evaluation or where success at a task requires information which the subject does not have, FD individuals tend to look at an experimenter or teacher significantly longer or more often than do FI subjects.

Two studies considered FD–I in relation to recognition of others. Messick and Damarin (1964) studied 50 college students in a "photo-judging" situation. Shown photos of 79 people, subjects were asked to estimate the age of each. Two hours later they were asked, unexpectedly, to judge 40 additional photos

(20 of which were repeats from the first set) and, also, to identify those they remembered from the earlier task. Correct recall of faces correlated significantly (−.29) with HFT performance, FD students recalling more faces.

In a study of Air Force captains, who had just completed a busy stay at an assessment center, FD–I on the RFT was significantly related to memory for faces of other center assessees, with FD associated with better memory (Crutchfield, Woodworth, & Albrecht, 1958).

In both studies, learning of faces was incidental to the tasks the subjects were engaged in at the time the faces were encountered. When Baker (1967) instructed subjects to learn faces, FD subjects showed no advantage. This would imply that FD subjects recalled more faces not because they were better at remembering faces, but rather that they were more interested in the faces of others.

Four studies considered FD–I in relation to preference for physical proximity to others. Justice (1969) had subjects write out a summary of their thoughts and feelings about each of two topics and then walk into a room in which the experimenter was seated to present this summary orally to him. The distance from the experimenter at which each subject chose to make the presentation was subsequently measured. FD subjects were found to stand significantly closer to the experimenter than were FI subjects.

In another study, staff members of a psychiatric hospital were asked to place themselves at optimal, maximal, and minimal distances from the experimenter at which they felt comfortable in holding a conversation. FD staff members chose distances significantly closer to the experimenter than did FI staff members (Holley, 1972).

Trego (1971) had subjects approach the experimenter along a corridor until they reached the distance that they usually maintained in social interactions. This was done four times, in corridors varying in length (although the subject was always placed, initially, at the same distance from the experimenter). FI subjects were significantly more variable in the distance they maintained from the experimenter than were FD subjects. These results would suggest that the response of FD individuals was based, relatively exclusively, upon the location of the experimenter, whereas other factors, unrelated to the experimenter, influenced the positioning of FI subjects.

In another study, the subject's nonverbal behaviors, while being interviewed, were videotaped and classified as "distancing" (crossing arms or legs, leaning away, etc.) or "approaching" (like leaning toward), under two conditions of actual physical distance from the interviewer (2 and 5 ft.). At both distances, FI subjects engaged in distancing behavior significantly more often than did FD subjects (Greene, 1973).

Taken together, this group of studies suggests consistent differences between FD and FI persons in distancing behaviors. FD individuals appear to prefer greater proximity to others, or at least to experimenters and interviewers, than do FI persons.

A large number of studies have been carried out which bear on the relationship between vocational interests and choices and FD–I. Several of these investigations are of particular relevance to the present discussion in that they involve vocational activities which can, fairly clearly, be classified as centering around, on the one hand, work with people and, on the other, work with things or abstractions.

To cite just a few examples, samples of advanced students or professionals in science, mathematics, architecture, and engineering (relatively "thing oriented" fields) have been found significantly more FI than control groups, whereas samples of teachers and social workers (relatively "people oriented" fields) have been found significantly more FD (Barrett & Thornton, 1967; Braun, 1971; Distefano, 1969; Holtzman, Swartz, & Thorpe, 1971; MacKinnon, 1962; Peterson & Sweitzer, 1973).

Within professions that provide opportunities for both types of activities, FD people have been found to choose activities involving more interaction with people. Thus, psychiatric nurses were found more FD than surgical nurses (Quinlan & Blatt, 1972), clinical psychologists more FD than experimental psychologists (Nagle, 1967), and psychiatrists whose practice favored interpersonal relations with patients more FD than psychiatrists whose practice involved more impersonal therapy modes (Pollack & Kiev, 1963).

With scant exception, numerous other studies of vocational interests provide results consistent with those reported above (see Witkin, Moore, Goodenough, & Cox, in press, for a detailed review of this literature).

In all, the vast majority of the evidence would appear to support the view that FD persons, under a variety of circumstances, tend to be more interested in working with other people, remember their faces better, prefer physical proximity to others and, under conditions of stress or need for information, tend to look more often at others.

Sociometric Choice

Several studies have considered the relationship of psychological differentiation to sociometric choice, with regard to FD–I of the person making the choice, of the object of choice, or both.

Iscoe and Carden (1961) had sixth-grade boys and girls make same-sex choices of classmates they liked. Popular boys were FI and popular girls FD. Among 68 female undergraduates at the University of Saskatchewan, sociometric choices with regard to clothing (frequency of mention as a fashion leader, fashion follower, individual dresser, indifferent dresser, or conventional dresser) were found unrelated to EFT performance (Kernaleguen & Compton, 1968). Victor (1973) had 50 master's candidates nominate members of their group for various activities, including social interaction (who would you like to take to a party?). HFT scores were unrelated to being chosen as a party companion.

Dreyer, McIntire, and Dreyer (1973) studied 113 children who knew each other for at least 7 months. Shown pictures of each of the other children, each subject was asked to select three that she would like most to play with. Boys tended to choose FI boys and girls to choose FD girls. Among 387 eighth-grade students, Vernon (1972b) found no relationship between RFT performance and sociometric nominations. Dingman (1971) found student counselees to rate their FD counselors as better communicators than their FI counselors.

One study considered FD–I of the selector. Webb (1972) used a questionnaire as an indirect measure of subject's liking of the experimenter, after the latter presented the subject with bogus feedback (claimed to be based upon test results) regarding the likelihood that the subject would succeed in college. Under conditions of contrast in feedback (both positive and negative statements by the experimenter), FD subjects liked the experimenter the most when negative statements about their chances for success were followed by positive statements. This would imply that recency of positive contact is more important for FD than for FI subjects in determining their sociometric choices.

Several studies considered FD–I of both selector and selectee. Schaefer (1973) had males in a university executive training program choose others in the program on each of several bases (competence in certain areas, as task-group fellow members, as social companions). Subjects also rated their past frequency of communication with each of the other trainees. Individuals were found to communicate most frequently with others similar in FD–I. They also tended to select, as advice sources, persons similar to themselves. However, similarity was not a factor in choosing social companions. Welkowitz (cited by Oltman, Goodenough, Witkin, Freedman, & Friedman, 1975) found that students, at a small university which allowed them to select their roommates, chose other students similar to themselves in FD–I. Greene (1972), in a study of therapists referred to earlier, had patients make ratings, after five therapy sessions, of how their therapists viewed them (the patients). Ratings of therapists' views were more positive when patient and therapist were similar in FD–I than when they differed.

When teachers rated their students and students their teachers on various personal characteristics, including competence, ratings were most positive for dyads alike in FD or FI (Distefano, 1969). In a similar study, James (1973) found like teacher–student pairs to display more interpersonal attraction than unlike pairs.

In a study of conflict resolution, Oltman *et al.* (1975) found interpersonal attraction lower for FI dyads than for mixed or FD dyads. It may be noted, however, that dyads were selected on the basis of initial disagreement about the choice–dilemma problems they were asked to attempt to resolve.

Overall, the evidence strongly favors the view that people's social companions tend to be like themselves in FD–I. Sometimes such similarity may even affect choices regarding competence. There are, however, exceptions to this trend which suggest the importance of the specific situation to the selection process. Thus, for example, in the study by Oltman *et al.* (1975) pairs of FI subjects may have been too competitive to work out choice dilemma solutions to their mutual satisfaction. Similarly, the type of activity for which one is chosen may have an important effect. In the Schaefer (1973) study, one exception to the finding that peers similar to the selector in FD–I were seen as most competent involved choosing others for their financial expertise. Here, presumably, the basis of choice was the actual ability of the selectee. If, indeed, this was the case, one might postulate that competence, when easy to assess, might take precedence over similarity in FD–I as a basis for selection. Thus, in the Schaefer study, when trainees were asked to choose others as general task group members, the qualifications for which are vague and difficult to assess, they tended to choose people like themselves. When asked to choose financial experts, involving qualities more objectively ascertainable (as via grades in certain courses), they presumably made their choices on the basis of such qualities, rather than on other, irrelevant characteristics such as FD–I.

Apparent exceptions to this trend to choose like persons (although this can only be inferred as FD–I of the selectors was not reported) were the three studies done with children (sixth to eighth graders). In two of these, FI boys and FD girls were most popular, while the third study found no relationships. These findings raise the possibility that children make sociometric choices on a somewhat different basis than adults.

Self-Descriptions of Interpersonal Styles

Numerous studies have investigated relationships between the FD–I dimension and characteristics of interpersonal style such as dependence, autonomy, dominance, self-sufficiency, need for nurturance, and need for succorance as defined by self-report scales. Because the evidence from studies using such self-report scales is consistent within itself and often at variance with results of studies of similar characteristics which use methods other than self-report, it would appear useful to deal with this large body of evidence in one place in this chapter.

Twenty-eight studies, which used 21 different self-report scales or factors measuring, according to their titles or descriptions, aspects of social dependence or independence, were sampled from a considerably larger body of literature. The results of these studies are summarized in Table 1. Of the 48 correlations reported between measures (or factors) of FD–I and such self-report measures, 31 were not significant, 12 were significant in associating FD with dependence, and 5 were significant in the opposite direction, associating FI with dependence.

TABLE 1
Summary of Studies Relating Field Dependence Measures to Various Self-Report Measures of Dependence–Independence

Authors	Year	FD–I test(s)*	Barron Independence	Cattell Q IV	Edwards Personal Preference Schedule: Nurturance	Succorance	Intraception	Dominance	Autonomy	MMPI Dy	Other**
Adkins	1964	EFT									0[a]
Andrews & Brown	1974	RFT/EFT	0								
Arner	1972	CEFT									+[b]
Blackburn	1972	EFT									+[c]
Clar	1971	EFT			0	0		+	0		
Dana & Goocher	1959	EFT				0		0	0		
Dolson	1973	PRFT								0	
Elliot	1961	RFT/EFT	+								
Gardner, Jackson, & Messick	1960	RFT/EFT			0	0	0	0	0		
Goldstein *et al.*	1968	RFT			0			0			–[d,f] 0[e]
Gruenfeld & Weissenberg	1974	EFT/HFTV									+[g]
Hellcamp & Marr	1965	var. RFT									0[h]
Johnson, Neville, & Workman	1969	RFT		0,+							

Kogan & Wallach	1964	var. GEFT								0^i
McFarland	1966	EFT								$+^j$
Ogden	1965	RFT/EFT			+		0	0		
Ohnmacht	1968	CF1/HFT3		0						
Marlowe	1958	TGT			+	+	0	0		
Rhodes & Yorioka	1968	EFT							0	
Sherman	1974	RFT/GEFT			0,+					0^k
Shipman & Heath	1967	RFT			–				–	
Solar, Davenport, & Bruehl	1969	RFT	+							
Stein, Korchin, & Cooper	1972	RFT/EFT								$-^l$
Thomy	1972	PRFT		0						
Trainor	1972	EFT								0^l
Trego	1971	RFT								0^m

*Where a study used several FD–I measures, results for the most valid of these are reported; var. indicates that a variant of a standard measure of FD–I was used.

**Other measures are: (a) biographical inventory; (b) self-reliance scale; (c) Dynamic Personality Inventory; (d) GAMIN Ascendence; (e)–(f) Leary Dominance I, II; (g) Adjective Check List, Independence; (h) Dependence items on Rokeach Dogmatism Scale; (i) Saunders' Self-Sufficiency; (j) Survey of Interpersonal Values, Independence; (k) Kessler P-D; (l) California Psychological Inventory, Dominance; (m) Pensacola Dependency Scale.

+ refers to a significant r, or common factor loading, associating FI with dominance, independence, autonomy.

– refers to a significant r, or common factor loading, associating FI with dependence, need for succorance.

0 refers to an association found not significant.

The evidence appears substantial that dependence or independence, as measured by self-report scales, is unrelated to FD–I.

Further proliferation of studies of this type promises little clarification of the issues involved. Rather, it might be useful to design studies aimed at clarifying discrepancies between results which used self-report scales and those which used behavioral or other measures of apparently similar personality characteristics. This problem has remained unsolved since 1953, when Gordon found that FD patients rated themselves as more independent than their therapists rated them.

Communication with Others

Self-Disclosure

Studies of self-disclosure, in relation to FD–I, are few in number but quite consistent in their results. Sousa-Poza, Rohrberg, and Shulman (1973) selected 13 FI and 13 FD extremes from a pool of unmarried male undergraduates. They were given the GEFT, PRFT, and the 60-item Jourard Scale of Self-Disclosure. Total self-disclosure was significantly higher for FD than for FI subjects. These results did not vary with targets or topics of disclosure.

Berry (1972) studied three Canadian Indian groups, using Kohs Blocks as a measure of FD–I and a modification of Jourard's self-disclosure scale. For each society, a significant correlation was obtained between the measures, associating FI with greater reserve.

In a study of 60 nurses, all students or recent graduates, with WAIS block design and ABC ratings of figure drawings used to reflect differentiation, less differentiated subjects, when asked to speak on a topic, made significantly more self-referred affective statements than did the more differentiated subjects (Gates, 1971).

Thus, studies of five different groups of subjects from two different kinds of cultures tend to support the view that FD persons are more self-disclosing than FI persons.

Role Playing

Several studies focused on relations of FD–I to aspects or styles of role playing.

Arbuthnot (1974) assigned subjects, recruited from an introductory psychology course, to role-playing dyads in which they were given the role of one of a pair of antagonists. Measured before and after role playing on their attitudes toward issues upon which the antagonism was based, FD subjects tended to be more affected than FI subjects in their judgments, based upon which of the two roles they had played. This might suggest that FD subjects identified more with the characters they played than did FI subjects.

Coan (1964) had subjects act out a part, in any way they chose, in each of four situations (e.g. the subject had just been dismissed from the university for cheating). They were rated on eight measures of role playing. These measures, along with RFT scores and those of a large battery of other tests of perception and personality, were intercorrelated and factor analyzed. Factor 1, defined by RFT performance, loaded three role-playing measures (role rejection and two measures of hesitation in starting to play a role), with FD subjects more reluctant to role play than FI subjects. Unrelated role-playing measures involved amount and rate of movement in the role and length of time taken to complete the role-playing sessions.

Ekman and Friesen (1974) instructed 21 nurse trainees to present, on two successive trials, a true or a distorted account of their feelings to a social worker. Five subjects could not carry off the deception and "confessed" before completing the performance. They did not differ from the completers with regard to FD–I.

Futterer (1973) gave the HFT to 60 undergraduates of each sex along with Feffer's role-taking tasks, in which the subject tells a story in response to a TAT-like stimulus picture and then retells the story from the point of view of each of the characters. Factor analysis showed two role-taking tasks and HFT to load the same factor. FI subjects were higher in role-taking ability than FD subjects. Using the Feffer situation, Perkins (1973) similarly found CEFT significantly correlated with role-taking ability for 109 fourth to sixth grade students.

Though the studies of role playing are few in number and varied in focus, their results are not inconsistent with the hypothesis that FD and FI individuals carry their global or analytical styles into role-playing activities. Where the task in the role-playing situation is more analytical, as in the Feffer situation where subjects are evaluated for ability to describe distinct roles for different characters, FI subjects do this more successfully than FD subjects. Further, FI subjects appear to be able to maintain separation of self from role to a greater extent than do FD subjects, who tend to become personally involved in the roles they play.

Differences from Others

Several studies bear on the issue of differences between FD and FI persons in ways in which they respond to differences between themselves and other persons with whom they interact. These investigations have, so far, centered around two issues: congruence of speech of members of a dyad; and resolution of conflicts or development of group solutions to problems.

Results of three studies of speech patterns are too varied to permit general conclusions. In one such study, Marcus (1970) had pairs of subjects engage in 30-minute conversations which were recorded and scored for congruence (tendency of the conversation partners to match their length of pauses between statements). FD of one or both members of a pair was associated with greater speech congruence of the pair.

Welkowitz and Feldstein (1970), using a similar technique, scored conversations for length of pauses, switching pauses (latency in response to a statement by one's partner), and verbalizations. For a group of 40 subjects, randomly paired as to FD–I of each member of the pair, tendency of the pair to contain two FD members related significantly to congruence of length of pauses, but not to congruence of length of verbalizations or switching pauses (although an *r* of −.36 for the latter measure suggests a trend toward greater congruence among FI pairs). Rogalski (1968) found the same three measures of congruence unrelated to the FD–I of pairs or their individual members.

The available evidence appears fairly evenly divided on the question of whether FD persons tend to adapt their speech patterns to those of a conversational partner. This issue might profit from further study, with particular attention to the circumstances under which the conversation is carried on (topics, instructions, physical proximity of the dyad, etc.).

Results were also mixed among five studies of conflict resolution or group problem solving among similar and dissimilar dyads and small groups. Oltman *et al.* (1975) in an above mentioned experiment, studied 40 extreme FD or FI college women. Based upon subjects' individually expressed views on a choice dilemma problem, they were combined into disagreeing pairs. Groups were further composed so as to vary the similarity of members of a pair on FD–I. Instructed to meet and attempt to work out a mutually satisfactory solution to the choice dilemma problem, pairs were rated on their achievement of such a solution. Pairs of FI subjects most often failed to arrive at a solution.

Solar, Davenport, and Bruehl (1969) chose 10 subjects of each extreme of FD–I (from a pool of 100 undergraduate women) based upon their RFT performance. Combined into pairs of one FD and one FI member, each pair was placed in the RFT situation with instructions to work out a placement of the rod acceptable to both members. Solutions were significantly closer to the original (individual) rod placements of the FI members of pairs than to those of the FD members, suggesting greater influence of FI persons in dyadic problem solving.

In a study of 24 undergraduates, Hornstein (1974) paired subjects varying in FD–I and sex to discuss moral dilemmas and to reach agreement on a course of action. A further restriction on forming pairs was that the members of a pair had earlier expressed conflicting views on the issues to be discussed (e.g., integration, euthanasia). Discussions were scored for length of verbal statements, number of interruptions, and extent of modification of one's initial position, none of which related to FD–I of the participants or similarity of the pair in FD–I. These results may have been confounded by sex differences, with individuals, regardless of FD–I, behaving differently with same sex and opposite sex partners.

Davis (1970) studied wheel networks, five-person communication groups, with one central member, who could communicate with any of the others, and four members on the periphery, who could communicate only with adjacent members. The groups were given the task of working out symbol identification problems. Two types of groups were studied, those with an FI central member and FD peripheral members and those with the reverse arrangement. Groups with an FI central member took less time to solve the problems and reported more satisfaction with the experience than those with an FD central member.

In a study described above, Goldstone (1974) found no relation of FD–I of group members to types of statements made (positive, negative, questions, answers) in arriving at a group story for a TAT card.

Two of the studies described above called for the solution of problems of fact (identification of symbols or location of the vertical). Under those conditions, FD individuals tended to defer to their FI peers in reaching solutions. The remaining studies posed ethical or other judgmental problems for which no factual solutions were possible. Here, there is no evidence of greater deference on the part of FD than FI subjects (although Oltman and his colleagues report a trend in that direction). Nor, when verbal interactions were analyzed in detail, were FD and FI individuals different in the kinds of statements they made while discussing a solution.

There appears to be no consistent evidence that FD persons, in interacting with others, tend to behave in ways that reduce their differences with others. The evidence does suggest that the circumstances of dyadic or group interaction may have an effect on such behavior. When groups are faced with problems of fact – and FD members do not have the information necessary for solution – they appear more likely than FI subjects to solicit information and base their actions upon such information.

In this regard, it might be interesting to speculate what results Goldstone and Hornstein might have obtained had their problem-solving tasks involved factual problems.

Summary

With regard to communication with others, FD persons appear to be more willing to disclose information about themselves to others. They maintain less distance than FI persons from the roles they are asked to play. They may or may not, as a general approach, defer more to others in group conflict resolution or problem-solving tasks. However they appear to do so when problems to be solved are of a factual, rather than ethical or judgemental, nature.

OVERVIEW

Considering the body of evidence that has emerged on the relationship between psychological differentiation and various aspects of social behavior, this reviewer is inclined to draw four broad conclusions in addition to the inevitable one that there are numerous remaining problems which require further research.

First, it would appear that substantial support has come forth for that part of Witkin's formulation of psychological differentiation that links sense of separate identity with FD–I. What seems most clear from the varied evidence reported above is that FI individuals appear to think and to behave in ways which suggest a commitment to maintenance of autonomy from others. They appear to prefer to work out problems for themselves, rather than seek solutions from others, and prefer their own judgments or interpretations to those provided by other persons or suggested by situations. They conform less to societal standards, view others in a more analytical (and thus distant) fashion, maintain more physical space between themselves and others, choose careers oriented more toward work with things or abstractions than work with people, and show more reserve in disclosing information about themselves.

Relatively FD people appear more interested in work with and proximity to other people. They are more willing to solicit information from other people and to be guided by them. They are more conforming to society. They do not, however, slavishly follow the dictates of others. Rather, they would appear to assess situations in which they find themselves and, when it makes sense or appears useful, to solicit the views of others. Thus, the maintenance of autonomy, so important to FI people, appears considerably less important to FD individuals.

The research has also served to delineate, quite sharply, aspects of separate identity which are and are not relevant to FD–I. Most clearly, self-views as dependent or independent, conforming or nonconforming, affected by authority or unaffected, have no relation to FD–I. FD persons do not describe themselves as helpless and dependent or as subject to the needs or whims of others. Nor do they behave in such a manner in defending or maintaining their own social or moral judgments. The evidence would suggest that it is principally when information is lacking which is needed to solve a real problem or decide on a course of action that FD individuals tend to seek information and direction from others to a greater extent than FI individuals. This is, most likely, a realistic and adaptive mode of functioning for persons of less well-developed analytical abilities.

Further, the recent literature has also emphasized the potential contribution of the FD–I and psychological differentiation constructs to our understanding of a wide variety of social behaviors not directly related to sense of separate identity. Considerable useful information on patient–therapist and teacher–student interactions, on empathy and clinical judgment, and on role playing, self-disclosure, and sociometric choice, has emerged.

Finally, this research has served to highlight, once again, the risks which accompany research designs which require deception of subjects. A number of instances have been identified where results may have differed as a function of the believability of the situation in which a subject is placed. There would appear to be ample evidence that most subjects, whether FD or FI, are far less gullible than we researchers might wish them to be.

REFERENCES

Adkins, W. R. The relationship of three cognitive controls to reports of effective and ineffective life behavior (Doctoral dissertation, Columbia University, 1963). Ann Arbor, Mich.: University Microfilms, 1964, No. 64-1542.

Andrews, R., & Brown, E. Firstborns, only children, sex, and three dependency measures. *Perceptual and Motor Skills,* 1974, *39,* 773–774.

Arner, M. A study of cognitive style and its concomitant traits and characteristics in adolescent educable mental retardates. (Doctoral dissertation, New York University, 1972). Ann Arbor, Mich.: University Microfilms, 1972, No. 72-20,615.

Arbuthnot, J. Cognitive style and modification of moral judgment. *Psychological Reports,* 1974, *34,* 273–274.

Asch, S. E. Studies of independence and conformity: I. a minority of one against a unanimous majority. *Psychological Monographs,* 1956, *70*(1, Whole No. 416).

Asch, S. E., & Witkin, H. A. Studies in space orientation: I. Perception of the upright with displaced visual fields. *Journal of Experimental Psychology,* 1948, *38,* 325–337. (a)

Asch, S. E., & Witkin, H. A. Studies in space orientation: II. Perception of the upright with displaced visual fields and with body tilted. *Journal of Experimental Psychology,* 1948, *38,* 455–477. (b)

Badaracco, M. L. Eye contact in relation to perception-personality characteristics and verbal interaction content. Unpublished doctoral dissertation, Colorado State University, 1973.

Baker, E. Perceiver variables involved in the recognition of faces. Unpublished doctoral dissertation, University of London, 1967.

Balance, W. D. G. Acquiescence: Acquiescent response style, social conformity, authoritarianism, and visual field dependency (Doctoral dissertation, University of Alabama, 1967). Ann Arbor, Mich.: University Microfilms, 1967, No. 68-1027.

Banta, T. J. Tests for the evaluation of early childhood education: The Cincinnati Autonomy Test Battery (CATB). In J. Hellmuth (Ed.), *Cognitive studies.* New York: Brunner/Mazel, 1970.

Barrett, G. V., & Thornton, C. L. Cognitive style differences between engineers and college students. *Perceptual and Motor Skills,* 1967, *25,* 374–376.

Beckerle, G. P. Behavioral traits related to psychological differentiation in pre-adolescent boys (Doctoral dissertation, Michigan State University, 1966). Ann Arbor, Mich.: University Microfilms, 1966, No. 67-7519.

Bell, E. G. Inner-directed and other-directed attitudes. Unpublished doctoral dissertation, Yale University, 1955.

Beller, E. A study of dependency and perceptual orientation. Paper presented at the meeting of the American Psychological Association, Washington, September 1958.

Beller, E. K. Personality correlates of perceptual discrimination in children. In E. K. Beller & J. le B. Turner (Eds.), *A study of dependency and aggression in early childhood.* New York: Child Development Center Progress Report, 1962.

Berry, J. W. Independence and conformity in subsistence-level societies. *Journal of Personality and Social Psychology,* 1967, *7,* 415–418.

Berry, J. W. Differentiation across cultures: cognitive style and affective style. Paper presented at the meeting of the Association for Cross-Cultural Psychology, Hong Kong, August 1972.

Berry, J. W., & Annis, R. C. Acculturative stress: The role of ecology, culture, and differentiation. *Journal of Cross-Cultural Psychology,* 1974, *5,* 382–406.

Bieri, J., Bradburn, W. M., & Galinsky, M. D. Sex differences in perceptual behavior. *Journal of Personality,* 1958, *26,* 1–12.

Bissiri, G. R. Adolescent negativism, field-independence, and the development of integrated structures (Doctoral dissertation, Claremont Graduate School and University Center, 1971). Ann Arbor, Mich.: University Microfilms, 1971, No. 71-29,635.

Blackburn, R. Field dependence and personality structure in abnormal offenders. *British Journal of Social and Clinical Psychology,* 1972, *2,* 175–177.

Brandsma, J. M. The effects of personality and placebo-instructional sets on psychophysiological responding (Doctoral dissertation, Pennsylvania State University, 1971). Ann Arbor, Mich.: University Microfilms, 1971, No. 72-13,817.

Braun, J. A. The empathic ability of psychotherapists as related to therapist perceptual flexibility and professional experience, patient insight, and therapist–patient similarity (Doctoral dissertation, Fordham University, 1971). Ann Arbor, Mich.: University Microfilms, 1971, No. 71-26,956.

Brothers, R., & Gaines, R. Perceptual differences between hippies and college students. *Journal of Social Psychology,* 1973, *91,* 325–335.

Bucky, S. F. The interaction between Negro and white preschool children and Negro and white experimenters and its effect on tests of motor impulse control, reflectivity, creativity and curiosity (Doctoral dissertation, University of Cincinnati, 1970). Ann Arbor, Mich.: University Microfilms, 1970, No. 71-5452.

Busch, J. C., & Deridder, L. M. Conformity in preschool disadvantaged children as related to field-dependence, sex, and verbal reinforcement. *Psychological Reports,* 1973, *32,* 667–673.

Cancro, R., & Voth, H. M. Autokinesis and psychological differentiation. *Perceptual and Motor Skills,* 1969, *28,* 99–103.

Carlino, L. A. A study of college counselors: Their field orientation and its relationship with accurate empathy. (Doctoral dissertation, St. John's University, 1972). Ann Arbor, Mich.: University Microfilms, 1972, No. 72-31,011.

Carr, J. E. The role of conceptual organization in interpersonal discrimination. *Journal of Psychology,* 1965, *59,* 159–176.

Carrigan, W. C. Stress and psychological differentiation (Doctoral dissertation, State University of New York at Buffalo, 1967). Ann Arbor, Mich.: University Microfilms, 1967, No. 67-10,120.

Chapman, H. H. Field dependence and communication effectiveness (Doctoral dissertation, University of Oklahoma, 1967). Ann Arbor, Mich.: University Microfilms, 1967, No. 67-11,997.

Clar, P. N. The relationship of psychological differentiation to client behavior in vocational choice counseling (Doctoral dissertation, University of Michigan, 1971). Ann Arbor, Mich.: University Microfilms, 1971, No. 71-23,723.

Coan, R. W. Factors in movement perception. *Journal of Consulting Psychology,* 1964, *28,* 394–402.

Coates, S. *The Preschool Embedded Figures Test – PEFT.* Palo Alto, Calif.: Consulting Psychologists Press, 1972.

Coates, S., Lord, M., & Jakabovics, E. Field dependence–independence, social–non-social play, and sex differences in preschool children. *Perceptual and Motor Skills,* 1975, *40,* 195–202.

Colker, R. L. Social perception and influence as a function of field dependence–independence (Doctoral dissertation, University of Pittsburgh, 1972). Ann Arbor, Mich.: University Microfilms, 1972, No. 73-16,349.

Conklin, R. C., & Zingle, H. W. Counsellor sensitivity and cognitive style. *Western Psychologist,* 1969, *1,* 19–28.

Cooper, L. W. The relationship of empathy to aspects of cognitive control (Doctoral dissertation, Yale University, 1967). Ann Arbor, Mich.: University Microfilms, 1967, No. 67-7003.

Crandall, V. J., & Sinkeldam, C. Children's dependent and achievement behavior in social situations and their perceptual field dependence. *Journal of Personality,* 1964, *32,* 1–22.

Crutchfield, R. S. Conformity and character. *American Psychologist,* 1955, *10,* 191–198.

Crutchfield, R. S. Personal and situational factors in conformity to group pressure. Paper presented at the meeting of the International Congress of Psychology, Brussels, 1957.

Crutchfield, R. S., Woodworth, D. C., & Albrecht, R. E. *Perceptual performance and the effective person.* Lackland Air Force Base, Texas: Personnel Laboratory, Wright Air Development Center, 1958.

Dana, R. H., & Goocher, B. Embedded-figures and personality. *Perceptual and Motor Skills,* 1959, *9,* 99–102.

Danielian, J. Accuracy of person perception, physical perceptual style, and selected personality variables (Doctoral dissertation, Columbia University, 1964). Ann Arbor, Mich.: University Microfilms, 1964, No. 65-2014.

Davis, D. W. The effects of individual, structural, and positional variables on problem-solving groups (Doctoral dissertation, George Peabody College for Teachers, 1970). Ann Arbor, Mich.: University Microfilms, 1970, No. 70-23,348.

Dawson, J. L. M., Young, B. M., & Choi, P. P. C. Developmental influences in pictorial depth perception among Hong Kong Chinese children. *Journal of Cross-Cultural Psychology,* 1974, *5,* 3–22.

Dingman, R. L. A study of cognitive style differences as a factor of communications in school counseling (Doctoral dissertation, Wayne State University, 1971). Ann Arbor, Mich.: University Microfilms, 1971, No. 72-14, 544.

Distefano, J. J. Interpersonal perceptions of field-independent and field-dependent teachers and students. Unpublished doctoral dissertation, Cornell University, 1969.

Doktor, R. H., & Hamilton, W. F. Cognitive style and acceptance of management recommendations. *Management Science,* 1973, *19,* 884–894.

Dolson, M. A. Hospitalization, differentiation, and dependency (Doctoral dissertation, University of Pittsburgh, 1973). Ann Arbor, Mich.: University Microfilms, 1973, No. 73-27,149.

Dreyer, A. S., McIntire, W. G., & Dreyer, C. A. Sociometric status and cognitive style in kindergarten children. *Perceptual and Motor Skills,* 1973, *37,* 407–412.

Ekman, P., & Friesen, W. V. Detecting deception from the body or face. *Journal of Personality and Social Psychology,* 1974, *29,* 288–298.

Elliot, R. Interrelationships among measures of field dependence, ability, and personality traits. *Journal of Abnormal and Social Psychology,* 1961, *63,* 27–36.

Fliegel, Z. O. Stability and change in perceptual performance of a late adolescent group in relation to personality variables. Unpublished doctoral dissertation, New School for Social Research, 1955.

French, J. W., Ekstrom, R. B., & Price, L. A. *Kit of reference tests for cognitive factors.* Princeton: Educational Testing Service, 1963.

Futterer, J. W. Social intelligence, role-taking ability, and cognitive style: A factor analytic study (Doctoral dissertation, Loyola University of Chicago, 1973). Ann Arbor, Mich.: University Microfilms, 1973, No. 73-23,147.

Gardner, R. W., Jackson, D. N., & Messick, S. J. Personality organization in cognitive controls and intellectual abilities. *Psychological Issues,* 1960, *2,* 1–148.

Gardner, R. W., Lohrenz, L. J., & Schoen, R. A. Cognitive control of differentiation in the perception of persons and objects. *Perceptual and Motor Skills,* 1968, *26,* 311–330.

Gates, D. W. Verbal conditioning, transfer and operant level "speech style" as functions of cognitive style (Doctoral dissertation, City University of New York, 1971). Ann Arbor, Mich.: University Microfilms, 1971, No. 71-30,719.

Gibson, J. J., & Mowrer, O. H. Determinants of the perceived vertical and horizontal. *Psychological Review,* 1938, *45,* 300–323.

Glass, D. C., Lavin, D. E., Henchy, T., Gordon, A., Mayhem, P., & Donohoe, P. Obesity and persuasibility. *Journal of Personality,* 1969, *37,* 407–414.

Gluck, E. A. T. Psychological differentiation and reading achievement in first grade children (Doctoral dissertation, Boston University Graduate School, 1973). Ann Arbor, Mich.: University Microfilms, 1973, 73-14,140.

Goebel, M. C. P. Cognitive styles and opinion change (Doctoral dissertation, Catholic University of America, 1966). Ann Arbor, Mich.: University Microfilms, 1966, No. 67-6849.

Goldstein, G., Neuringer, C., Reiff, C., & Shelly, C. H. Generalizability of field dependency in alcoholics. *Journal of Consulting and Clinical Psychology,* 1968, *32,* 560–564.

Goldweber, A. M. Cognitive controls and individual differences in forming impressions of personality (Doctoral dissertation, New York University, 1966). Ann Arbor, Mich.: University Microfilms, 1966, No. 67-6020.

Goldstone, M. W. Verbal participation in small groups as a function of group composition. (Doctoral Dissertation, George Washington University, 1974). Ann Arbor, Mich.: University Microfilms, 1974, No. 74-22,255.

Goodenough, D. R. *The role of individual differences in field dependence as a factor in learning and memory* (ETS RB-75-8). Princeton, N.J.: Educational Testing Service, 1975.

Goodenough, D. R. Field dependence. In H. London & J. Exner (Eds.), *Dimensions of personality.* New York: Wiley, in press.

Goodenough, D. R., & Karp, S. A. Field dependence and intellectual functioning. *Journal of Abnormal and Social Psychology,* 1961, *63,* 241–246.

Gordon, B. An experimental study of dependence–independence in a social and laboratory setting. Unpublished doctoral dissertation, University of Southern California, 1953.

Greene, L. R. Effects of field independence, physical proximity, and evaluative feedback on affective reactions and compliance in a dyadic interaction (Doctoral dissertation, Yale University, 1973). Ann Arbor, Mich.: University Microfilms, 1973, No. 73-26,285.

Greene, M. A. Client perception of the relationship as a function of worker–client cognitive styles (Doctoral dissertation, Columbia University, 1972). Ann Arbor, Mich.: University Microfilms, 1972, 72-31,213.

Gruenfeld, L. W., & Weissenberg, P. Relationship between supervisory cognitive style and social orientation. *Journal of Applied Psychology,* 1974, *59,* 386–388.

Hellcamp, D. T., & Marr, J. N. Dogmatism and field dependency. *Perceptual and Motor Skills,* 1965, *20,* 1046–1048.

Holley, M. Field-dependence–independence, sophistication-of-body-concept, and social distance selection (Doctoral dissertation, New York University, 1972). Ann Arbor, Mich.: University Microfilms, 1972, No. 72-20,635.

Holtzman, W. H., Swartz, J. D., & Thorpe, J. S. Artists, architects, and engineers – Three contrasting modes of visual experience and their psychological correlates. *Journal of Personality,* 1971, *39,* 432–449.

Hornstein, G. A. A contextual and cognitive style analysis of conflict resolution in dyadic interactions. Unpublished master's thesis, Clark University, 1974.

Iscoe, I., & Carden, J. A. Field dependence, manifest anxiety, and sociometric status in children. *Journal of Consulting Psychology,* 1961, *25,* 184.

Jackson, D. N., Messick, S., & Myers, C. J. Evaluation of group and individual forms of embedded-figures measures of field-independence. *Educational and Psychological Measurement,* 1964, *24,* 177–192.

James, C. D. R. A cognitive style approach to teacher–pupil interaction and the academic performance of black children. Unpublished master's thesis, Rutgers University, 1973.

Johnson, C. P. Oral dependence and its relationship to field dependence and dependent behavior in same and mixed sex pairs (Doctoral dissertation, State University of New York at Buffalo, 1973). Ann Arbor, Mich.: University Microfilms, 1973, No. 74-4409.

Johnson, D. T., Neville, C. W., & Workman, S. N. Field independence and the Sixteen Personality Factor Questionnaire: A further note. *Perceptual and Motor Skills,* 1969, *28,* 670.

Justice, M. T. Field dependency, intimacy of topic, and interpersonal distance (Doctoral dissertation, University of Florida, 1969). Ann Arbor, Mich.: University Microfilms, 1969, No. 70-12,243.

Karp, S. A. Field dependence and overcoming embeddedness. *Journal of Consulting Psychology,* 1963, *27,* 294–302.

Karp, S. A., Kissin, B., & Hustmyer, F. E., Jr. Field dependence as a predictor of alcoholic therapy dropouts. *Journal of Nervous and Mental Disease,* 1970, *150,* 77–83.

Kavanagh, M. J., & Weissenberg, P. Relationship between psychological differentiation and perceptions of supervisory behavior. *Proceedings of the 81st Annual Convention of the American Psychological Association,* 1973, *8,* 571–572. (Summary)

Kendon, A., & Cook, M. The consistency of gaze patterns in social interaction. *British Journal of Psychology,* 1969, *60,* 481–494.

Kernalaguen, A. P., & Compton, N. H. Body-field perceptual differentiation related to peer perception of attitudes toward clothing. *Perceptual and Motor Skills,* 1968, *27,* 195–198.

Klau, L. G. The formation of first impressions in field-dependent and field-independent persons (Doctoral dissertation, City University of New York, 1973). Ann Arbor, Mich.: University Microfilms, 1973, No. 73-11,355.

Koff, J. H. W. Field dependence and psychotherapy expectancies, presenting symptoms, defensive style, and length of stay in psychotherapy (Doctoral dissertation, George Washington University, 1972). Ann Arbor, Mich.: University Microfilms, 1972, 72-18,590.

Kogan, N., & Wallach, M. *Risk taking.* New York: Holt, Rinehart and Winston, 1964.

Konstadt, N., & Forman, E. Field dependence and external directedness. *Journal of Personality and Social Psychology,* 1965, *1,* 490–493.

Krippner, S., & Brown, D. P. Field independence/dependence and electrosone 50 induced altered states of consciousness. *Journal of Clinical Psychology,* 1973, *29,* 316–319.

Kumpf, M., & Gotz-Marchand, B. Reduction of cognitive dissonance as a function of magnitude of dissonance, differentiation, and self-esteem. *European Journal of Social Psychology,* 1973, *3,* 255–270.

Larsen, J. P., & White, B. A. Comparison of selected perceptual and personality variables among college men, deviant and non-deviant in hair length. *Perceptual and Motor Skills,* 1974, *38,* 1315–1318.

Lewin, K. *A dynamic theory of personality.* New York: McGraw-Hill, 1935.

Linton, H. B. Relations between mode of perception and the tendency to conform (Doctoral dissertation, Yale University, 1952). Ann Arbor, Mich.: University Microfilms, 1952, No. 65-8142.

Linton, H. B. Dependence on external influence: Correlates in perception, attitudes, and judgment. *Journal of Abnormal and Social Psychology,* 1955, *51,* 502–507.

Linton, H., & Graham, E. Personality correlates of persuasibility. In C. I. Hovland & I. Janis (Eds.), *Personality and persuasibility.* New Haven: Yale University Press, 1959.

Loewenstein, A. P. Cognitive style and empathic behavior in counseling. Unpublished doctoral dissertation, University of Miami, 1971.

MacKinnon, D. W. The personality correlates of creativity: A study of American architects. In G. Nielson (Ed.), *Proceedings of the XIV International Congress of Applied Psychology* (Vol. 2). *Personality research.* Copenhagen: Munksgaard, 1962.

Marcus, E. S. The relationship of psychological differentiation to the congruence of temporal patterns of speech (Doctoral dissertation, New York University, 1970). Ann Arbor, Mich.: University Microfilms, 1970, No. 70-19,016.

Marlowe, D. Some psychological correlates of field independence. *Journal of Consulting Psychology,* 1958, *22,* 334.

Marino, D. R., Fitzgibbons, D. J., & Mirabile, C. S., Jr. Attention deployment in field dependence and autokinetic movement. *Perceptual and Motor Skills,* 1970, *31,* 155–158.

Martin, P. L., & Toomey, T. C. Perceptual orientation and empathy. *Journal of Consulting and Clinical Psychology,* 1973, *41,* 313.

Mausner, B., & Graham, J. Field dependence and prior reinforcement as determinants of social interaction in judgment. *Journal of Personality and Social Psychology,* 1970, *16,* 486–493.

McCarrey, M. W., Dayhaw, L. J., & Chagnon, G. P. Attitude shift, approval need, and extent of psychological differentiation. *Journal of Social Psychology,* 1971, *84,* 141–149.

McFarland, H. B. *Comparison of perceptual field independence and personality scale of independence* (Report No. 24). Coral Gables, Fla.: University of Miami, 1966.

McGilligan, R. P. Psychological differentiation, abilities, and personality (Doctoral dissertation, St. Louis University, 1971). Ann Arbor, Mich.: University Microfilms, 1971, No. 72-23,970.

Meskin, B. B., & Singer, J. L. Daydreaming, reflective thought, and laterality of eye movements. *Journal of Personality and Social Psychology,* 1974, *30,* 64–71.

Messick, S., & Damarin, F. Cognitive styles and memory for faces. *Journal of Abnormal and Social Psychology,* 1964, *69,* 313–318.

Messick, S., & Fritzky, F. J. Dimensions of analytic attitude in cognition and personality. *Journal of Personality,* 1963, *31,* 346–370.

Morf, M. E., Kavanaugh, R. D., & McConville, M. Intratest and set differences on a portable rod and frame test. *Perceptual and Motor Skills,* 1971, *32,* 727–733.

Murphy, D. F. Sensory deprivation, suggestion, field dependence, and perceptual regression. *Journal of Personality and Social Psychology,* 1966, *4,* 289–294.

Nadeau, G. H. Cognitive style in preschool children: A factor analytic study (Doctoral dissertation, University of Minnesota, 1968). Ann Arbor, Mich.: University Microfilms, 1968, No. 68-17,702.

Nagle, R. M. Personality differences between graduate students in clinical and experimental psychology at varying experience levels (Doctoral dissertation, Michigan State University, 1967). Ann Arbor, Mich.: University Microfilms, 1967, No. 68-1108.

Nevill, D. Experimental manipulation of dependency motivation and its effects on eye contact and measures of field dependency. *Journal of Personality and Social Psychology,* 1974, *29,* 72–79.

Nightingale, H. B. Field dependence and person perception (Doctoral dissertation, New York University, 1971). Ann Arbor, Mich.: University Microfilms, 1971, No. 72-3107.

Ogden, W. E. Field dependency in a sample of university counseling center clients (Doctoral dissertation, University of Kansas, 1965). Ann Arbor, Mich.: University Microfilms, 1965, No. 66-6043.

Ohnmacht, F. W. Note on the validity of the Sixteen Personality Factor Questionnaire measure of field independence. *Perceptual and Motor Skills,* 1968, *27,* 564.

O'Leary, M. R., Donovan, D. M., & Hague, W. H. Interperson differentiation, locus of control, and cognitive style among alcoholics. *Perceptual and Motor Skills,* 1974, *39,* 997–998.

Olesker, W. B. Physiognomic sensitivity, psychological differentiation, sexual similarity, and empathy (Doctoral dissertation, New York University, 1971). Ann Arbor, Mich.: University Microfilms, 1971, No. 71-28,551.

Oltman, P. K. A portable rod-and-frame apparatus. *Perceptual and Motor Skills,* 1968, *26,* 503–506.

Oltman, P. K., Goodenough, D. R., Witkin, H. A., Freedman, N., & Friedman, F. Psychological differentiation as a factor in conflict resolution. *Journal of Personality and Social Psychology,* 1975, *32,* 730–736.

Paeth, C. A. A Likert scaling of student value statements, field independence-field dependence, and experimentally induced change (Doctoral dissertation, Oregon State University, 1973). Ann Arbor, Mich.: University Microfilms, 1973, No. 73-25,368.

Pedersen, F. A., & Wender, P. H. Early social correlates of cognitive functioning in six-year-old boys. *Child Development,* 1968, *39,* 185–193.

Perkins, C. J. A study of perceptual correlates to role-taking ability with fourth through sixth grade children (Doctoral dissertation, Oregon State University, 1973). Ann Arbor, Mich.: University Microfilms, 1973, No. 73-21, 319.

Peterson, J. M., & Sweitzer, G. Field-independent architecture students. *Perceptual and Motor Skills,* 1973, *36,* 195–198.

Pollack, I. W., & Kiev, A. Spatial orientation and psychotherapy: An experimental study of perception. *Journal of Nervous and Mental Disease,* 1963, *137,* 93–97.

Quinlan, D. M., & Blatt, S. J. Field articulation and performance under stress: Differential predictions in surgical and psychiatric nursing training. *Journal of Consulting and Clinical Psychology,* 1972, *39,* 517.

Rhodes, R. J., Carr, J. E., & Jurji, E. D. Interpersonal differentiation and perceptual field differentiation. *Perceptual and Motor Skills,* 1968, *27,* 172–174.

Rhodes, R. J., & Yorioka, G. N. Dependency among alcoholics and non-alcoholic institutionalized patients. *Psychological Reports,* 1968, *22,* 1343–1344.

Richards, T. D. The effects of cognitive style sets of flexibility upon counselor perception: Field dependence and repression-sensitization in relation to empathic accuracy (Doctoral dissertation, New York University, 1970). Ann Arbor, Mich.: University Microfilms, 1970, No. 71-24,807.

Riesman, D. *The lonely crowd.* New Haven: Yale University Press, 1950.

Robinson, W. H. The differential effects of "relational immediacy" and "intrapersonal immediacy" workshops on field dependent and field independent participants. Unpublished doctoral dissertation, University of Waterloo (Canada), 1972.

Rogalski, C. J. Individual differences in verbal behavior: Their relationship to the field articulation principle (Doctoral dissertation, New York University, 1968). Ann Arbor, Mich.: University Microfilms, 1968, No. 69-11,840.

Rosner, S. Studies of group pressure. Unpublished doctoral dissertation, New School for Social Research, 1956.

Rosner, S. Consistency in response to group pressures. *Journal of Abnormal and Social Psychology,* 1957, *55,* 145–146.

Ruble, D. N., & Nakamura, C. Y. Task orientation versus social orientation in young children and their attention to relevant social cues. *Child Development,* 1972, *43,* 471–480.

Sangiuliano, I. A. An investigation of the relationship between the perception of the upright in space and several factors in personality organization. Unpublished doctoral dissertation, Fordham University, 1951.

Schaefer, S. D. Some cognitive factors influencing interpersonal choice in task situations

(Doctoral dissertation, Stanford University, 1973). Ann Arbor, Mich.: University Microfilms, 1973, No. 73-30,470.

Scheibner, R. M. Field dependence-independence as a basic variable in the measurement of interest and personality (Doctoral dissertation, Temple University, 1969). Ann Arbor, Mich.: University Microfilms, 1969, No. 69-16,291.

Segal, S. J., & Barr, H. L. Effect of instructions on phi phenomenon, criterion task of "tolerance for unrealistic experiences." *Perceptual and Motor Skills,* 1969, *29,* 483–486.

Shaffer, C. E. Field articulation and conformity. Paper presented at the meeting of the Southeastern Psychological Association, Louisville, Ky., April 1970.

Sherman, J. A. Field articulation, sex, spatial visualization, dependency, practice, laterality of the brain, and birth order. *Perceptual and Motor Skills,* 1974, *38,* 1223–1235.

Shipman, W. G., & Heath, H. A. What does the rod and frame measure? Paper presented at the meeting of the Midwestern Psychological Association, Chicago, May 1967.

Shows, W. D. Psychological differentiation and the A–B dimension: a dyadic interaction hypothesis. Unpublished doctoral dissertation, Duke University, 1967.

Simon, W. E., & Wilde, V. Ordinal position of birth, field dependency, and Forer's measure of gullibility. *Perceptual and Motor Skills,* 1971, *33,* 677–678.

Smith, L. M., & Kleine, P. F. Teacher awareness: Social cognition in the classroom. *School Review,* 1969, *77,* 245–256.

Soat, D. M. Cognitive style, self-concept, and expressed willingness to help others (Doctoral dissertation, Marquette University, 1974). Ann Arbor, Mich.: University Microfilms, 1974, No. 74-22,305.

Solar, D., Davenport, G., & Bruehl, D. Social compliance as a function of field dependence. *Perceptual and Motor Skills,* 1969, *29,* 299–306.

Sousa-Poza, J. F., Rohrberg, R., & Shulman, E. Field dependence and self-disclosure. *Perceptual and Motor Skills,* 1973, *36,* 735–738.

Stein, K. B., Korchin, S. J., & Cooper, L. Motoric, ideational, and sensory expressive styles: Further validation of the Stein and Lenrow types. *Psychological Reports,* 1972, *31,* 335–338.

Taft, R. Some characteristics of good judges of others. *British Journal of Psychology,* 1956, *47,* 19–29.

Testa, C. J. The prediction and evaluation of simulator illness symptomatology (Doctoral dissertation, University of California at Los Angeles, 1969). Ann Arbor, Mich.: University Microfilms, 1969, No. 69-16,932.

Thomy, V. A. Relationship among three factors reflecting independence: Witkin's field independence and R. B. Cattell's objective test and questionnaire independence factors (Doctoral dissertation, George Washington University, 1972). Ann Arbor, Mich.: University Microfilms, 1972, No. 72-18,598.

Thurstone, L. L. *A factorial study of perception.* Chicago: University of Chicago Press, 1944.

Trainor, J. J. The Embedded Figures Test as a predictive device (Doctoral dissertation, California School of Professional Psychology, 1972). Ann Arbor, Mich.: University Microfilms, 1972, No. 72-33,291.

Trego, R. E. An investigation of the Rod and Frame Test in relation to emotional dependence and social cue attentiveness (Doctoral dissertation, Texas Christian University, 1971). Ann Arbor, Mich.: University Microfilms, 1971, No. 72-7617.

Vaught, G. M., & Hunter, W. Autokinetic word writing and field-dependence. *Psychonomic Science,* 1967, *7,* 335–336.

Vernon, P. E. The distinctiveness of field independence. *Journal of Personality,* 1972, *40,* 366–391. (a)

Vernon, P. E. Sex differences in personality structure at age 14. *Canadian Journal of Behavioral Sciences,* 1972, *4,* 283–297. (b)

Victor, J. B. Peer judgments of teaching competence as a function of field-independence and dogmatism. Paper presented at the meeting of the Eastern Psychological Association, Washington, D.C., May 1973.

Webb, D. The effect of ordering and contrast of feedback and perceptual style on liking of an evaluative source (Doctoral dissertation, University of Cincinnati, 1972). Ann Arbor, Mich.: University Microfilms, 1972, No. 73-3825.

Weinberg, H. J. Changing perceptions on the RFT by conditioning subjects to relieve dissonance and/or escape from the anxiety in a new manner (Doctoral dissertation, University of Nebraska, 1970). Ann Arbor, Mich.: University Microfilms, 1970, No. 70-17,768.

Welkowitz, J., & Feldstein, S. Relation of experimentally manipulated interpersonal perception and psychological differentiation to the temporal patterning of conversation. *Proceedings of the 78th Annual Convention of the American Psychological Association,* 1970, *5,* 387–388. (Summary)

Werner, H. *Comparative psychology of mental development.* Chicago: Follett, 1948.

Wertheimer, M. Experimentelle Studien über das Sehen von Bewegung. *Zeitschrift für Psychologie,* 1912, *61,* 161–265.

Williams, M. L. Analytical ability, social conformity and *n* influence as a function of temporal and spatial disembedding skill (Doctoral dissertation, Ohio State University, 1969). Ann Arbor, Mich.: University Microfilms, 1969, No. 69-22,230.

Witkin, H. A. Perception of the body position and of the position of the visual field. *Psychological Monographs,* 1949, *63,* 1–46.

Witkin, H. A. Development of body concept and psychological differentiation. In S. Wapner & H. Werner (Eds.), *The body percept.* New York: Random House, 1965. (a)

Witkin, H. A. Psychological differentiation and forms of pathology. *Journal of Abnormal Psychology,* 1965, *70,* 317–336. (b)

Witkin, H. A. *The role of cognitive style in academic performance and in teacher–student relations* (RB 73-11). Princeton, N.J.: Educational Testing Service, 1973.

Witkin, H. A., & Asch, S. E. Studies in space orientation: III. Perception of the upright in the absence of a visual field. *Journal of Experimental Psychology,* 1948, *38,* 603–614. (a)

Witkin, H. A., & Asch, S. E. Studies in space orientation: IV. Further experiments on perception of the upright with displaced visual fields. *Journal of Experimental Psychology,* 1948, *38,* 762–782. (b)

Witkin, H. A., & Berry, J. W. Psychological differentiation in cross-cultural perspective. *Journal of Cross-Cultural Psychology,* 1975, *6,* 4–87.

Witkin, H. A., Cox, P. W., Friedman, F., Hrishikesan, A. G., & Siegel, K. N. *Supplement No. 1, field-dependence-independence and psychological differentiation: Bibliography with index* (RB 74-42). Princeton, N.J.: Educational Testing Service, 1974.

Witkin, H. A., Dyk, R. B., Faterson, H. F., Goodenough, D. R., & Karp, S. A. *Psychological differentiation: Studies of development.* Potomac, Md.: Lawrence Erlbaum Associates, 1974. (Originally published, New York: Wiley, 1962.)

Witkin, H. A., Lewis, H. B., Hertzman, M., Machover, K., Meissner, P. B., & Wapner, S. *Personality through perception: An experimental and clinical study.* Westport, Conn.: Greenwood Press, 1972. (Originally published, New York: Harper and Brothers, 1954.)

Witkin, H. A., Lewis, H. B., & Weil, E. Affective reactions and patient–therapist interactions among more differentiated and less differentiated patients early in therapy. *Journal of Nervous and Mental Disease,* 1968, *146,* 193–208.

Witkin, H. A., Moore, C. A., Goodenough, D. R., & Cox, P. W. Field-dependent and field-independent cognitive styles and their educational implications. *Review of Educational Research,* in press.

Witkin, H. A., Oltman, P. K., Cox, P. W., Erlichman, E., Hamm, R. M., & Ringler, R. W. *Field-dependence-independence and psychological differentiation: A bibliography through 1972 with index* (RB 73-62). Princeton, N.J.: Educational Testing Service, 1973.

Witkin, H. A., Oltman, P. K., Raskin, E., & Karp, S. A. *Manual for the embedded figures tests.* Palo Alto, Calif.: Consulting Psychologists Press, Inc., 1971.

Witkin, H. A., Price-Williams, D., Bertini, M., Christiansen, B., Oltman, P. K., Ramirez, M., & van Meel, J. Social conformity and psychological differentiation. *International Journal of Psychology,* 1974, *9,* 11–29.

Wolitzky, D. L. Cognitive controls and person perception. *Perceptual and Motor Skills,* 1973, *36,* 619–623.

5
Introversion/Extraversion

Glenn Wilson

Institute of Psychiatry (Maudsley Hospital).
University of London

In this chapter I will attempt to show the importance of introversion–extraversion as a concept which bridges the disciplines of biology and social psychology. An attempt will be made to demonstrate a causal chain of associations running all the way from genetics through anatomic and physiological structures in the brain to behavior observed in the laboratory setting, responses to questionnaires, and eventually to various forms of social behavior at both the interpersonal and societal levels such as suggestibility, affiliation, person perception, academic and occupational performance, sexual behavior, and criminality.

Like most of the studies reviewed, this account will start at the psychological level with the personality construct of extraversion itself: its historical development, description, measurement, structure, and usefulness as part of a dimensional system of psychodiagnostics. We then consider the evidence for its genetic origins, and two theories of its neurological basis along with the experimental evidence relating to them. Finally, we move in the antireductive direction and look at the kinds of social behavior which differentiate extraverts and introverts. Most of these relationships are empirical and would probably hold good whichever theory of the biological basis of extraversion turns out to be supported, if any. Nevertheless, it is instructive to have encountered the theories first, so that they can be kept in mind when considering the links with complex social phenomena.

HISTORICAL BACKGROUND TO THE CONCEPT

Although the terms introversion and extraversion are today often associated with the name of the Swiss psychiatrist C.G. Jung, they may be found in the earliest English dictionaries. Dr. Johnson's dictionary, published in 1755, used the terms in a physical sense, but by the late nineteenth century they were defined in ways very similar to current usage. Extraversion was described as a "turning outward of the mind" onto people and objects in the external world; introversion as "inner directedness," a preference for abstract ideas rather than concrete objects. Today, the scope of these terms is rather broader: extraversion also refers to impulsive, sociable tendencies, and introversion implies controlled and responsible behavior.

Interest in a related distinction goes back as far as the second century and the Greek physicians, Hippocrates and Galen. They identified four major temperamental types: the melancholic, the choleric, the sanguine, and the phlegmatic, and four "humors" (a bit like hormones) which were supposed to be responsible for them. Their physiological theory is now regarded as somewhat quaint, but the descriptive scheme still used. It was an over–simplification in that people cannot be neatly pigeon–holed into four categories. A solution to that problem was provided in the nineteenth century by Wilhelm Wundt. He pointed out that the four-way classification of the Greeks could be accommodated by two independent and continuous variables of emotional response: *strength* of emotions, and *speed of change.* Studies using factor analysis have since confirmed the broad descriptive usefulness of such a two-dimensional scheme, but different names are now used. What Wundt called speed of change is now usually labeled introversion–extraversion and his strength factor is now called emotional instability or neuroticism.

Figure 1 shows how these two major dimensions of personality relate to the Greek typology. The advantage of the dimensional system over the categorical system is that an individual can be described more flexibly by assigning him a point anywhere within the space formed by the two factors. Most people are in the middle range of these dimensions with relatively few falling toward the extremes.

MEASUREMENT OF EXTRAVERSION TODAY

Introversion–extraversion is most commonly assessed by questionnaire. Among the more famous self-report measures are the "social introversion" scale of the *Minnesota Multiphasic Personality Inventory* (MMPI), and the "extraversion" scale of the *Eysenck Personality Inventory* (EPI). Examples of the kinds of items used in the latter are given in Table 1. The picture of the extravert and introvert provided by the EPI is given by Eysenck and Eysenck (1964):

> The typical extravert is sociable, likes parties, has many friends, needs to have people to talk to, and does not like reading or studying by himself. He craves excitement, takes chances, often sticks his neck out, acts on the spur of the moment, and is generally an impulsive individual. He is fond of practical jokes, always has a ready answer, and generally likes change; he is carefree, easygoing, optimistic, and likes to "laugh and be

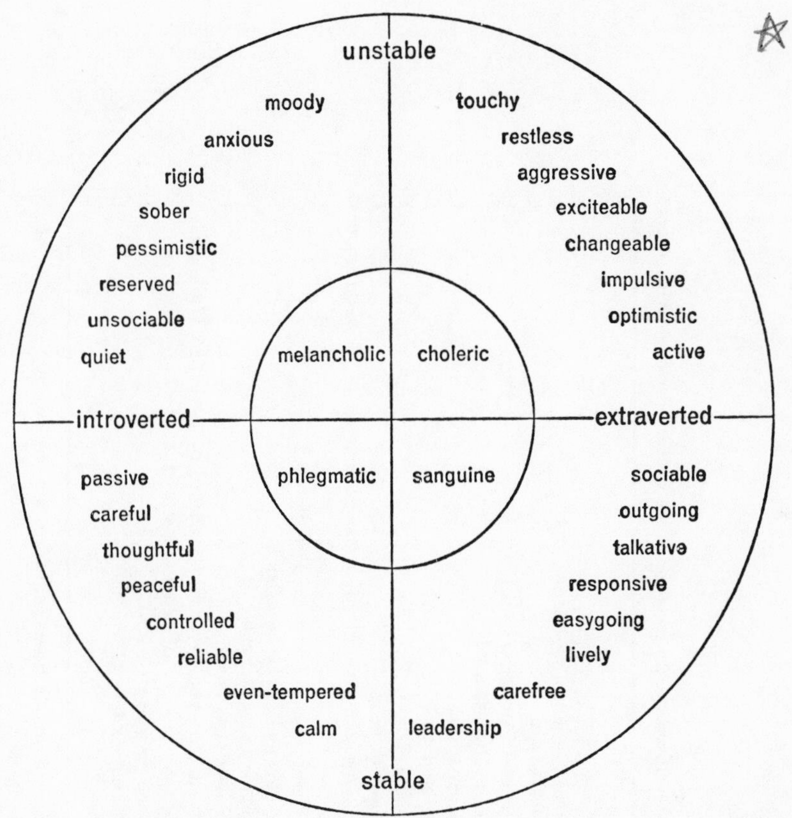

FIGURE 1 Two major dimensions of personality revealed by factor analysis compared with the four Greek categories. (From Eysenck, 1967.)

merry". He prefers to keep moving and doing things, tends to be aggressive and lose his temper quickly; altogether his feelings are not kept under tight control, and he is not always a reliable person.

The typical introvert is a quiet, retiring sort of person, introspective, fond of books rather than people; he is reserved and distant except to intimate friends. He tends to plan ahead, "looks before he leaps," and distrusts the impulse of the moment. He does not like excitement, takes matters of everyday life with proper seriousness, and likes a well-ordered mode of life. He keeps his feelings under close control, seldom behaves in an aggressive manner, and does not lose his temper easily. He is reliable, somewhat pessimistic and places great value on ethical standards [p. 8].

These descriptions of the characteristic introvert and extravert do not conform exactly to the traditional or Jungian definitions, but they are fairly close. Differences in detail may be due to the fact that the earlier descriptions were based on uncontrolled observation and intuitive theorizing, whereas Eysenck's dimensions are established empirically by means of factor analysis.

TABLE 1

Items of the Kind Used to Measure Introversion–Extraversion in the Eysenck Personality Inventory[a]

Item	Scoring
Do you often long for excitement?	E
Are you usually carefree?	E
Do you stop and think things over before doing anything?	I
Would you do almost anything for a dare?	E
Do you often do things on the spur of the moment?	E
Generally, do you prefer reading to meeting people?	I
Do you prefer to have few but special friends?	I
When people shout at you do you shout back?	E
Do other people think of you as very lively?	E
Are you mostly quiet when you are with people?	I
If there is something you want to know about would you rather look it up in a book than talk to someone about it?	I
Do you like the kind of work that you need to pay close attention to?	I
Do you hate being with a crowd who play jokes on one another?	I
Do you like doing things in which you have to act quickly?	E
Are you slow and unhurried in the way you move?	I
Do you like talking to people so much that you never miss a chance of talking to a stranger?	E
Would you be unhappy if you could not see lots of people most of the time?	E
Do you find it hard to enjoy yourself at a lively party?	I
Would you say that you were fairly self-confident?	E
Do you like playing pranks on others?	E

[a]Items for which "yes" is scored in the introvert direction are marked I; items for which "yes" is scored for extraversion are marked E.

Apart from questionnaires and other rating techniques, indirect or "objective" measures of extraversion–introversion are sometimes used. These depend upon knowing that there is a close correlation between the questionnaire measure and some other kind of behavior or physiological response. For example, there have been several reports that introversion is related to the amount of saliva that an individual will produce in his mouth when a standard amount of lemon juice is placed on his tongue. This finding is of considerable theoretical interest, but the relationship is also apparently so strong – correlations of up to .7 have been reported (Eysenck, 1970b) – that the "lemon-drop test" has been employed in other studies as an "objective" measure of introversion–extraversion. Another piece of behavior that has sometimes been used as an extraversion measure, even though the actual correlation is rather low, is the color/form ratio on tests such as the Rorschach. Apparently extraverts tend to respond more to the color of a visual display and introverts to the form, so that this test may also be used as a measure of extraversion. These are just two examples of the many perceptual, motor, physiological, and other kinds of behavior that correlate with questionnaire measures of extraversion, and may therefore be used as measures of that personality dimension in their own right.

THE EXTRAVERSION DIMENSION IN CONTEXT

Extraversion is one of three dimensions of temperament that Eysenck considers to be of prime importance. The other two are *neuroticism* (also called emotional instability) and *psychoticism* (now often called "toughmindedness"). These three personality dimensions, which are often referred to as *E, N,* and *P* respectively, are conceived as independent from one another (i.e. uncorrelated) and are thought to provide a good summary of the varieties of normal and abnormal personality. Two of them are shown in Figure 1. The placement of the various trait-descriptive adjectives in relation to them illustrates how individuals can fall at any position between the extremes on either dimension. With reference to the extraversion axis, most people are actually ambiverted rather than extreme extraverts or introverts, and they may be more or less stable or neurotic regardless of their position on E. The third dimension, psychoticism, refers to behavior that is bizarre, impersonal, hostile and antisocial; it may be thought of as coming straight out of the diagram from the cross in the center, and projecting back through the other side of the paper – since it is independent of the other two it matters not which end is labeled "tough" and which "tender." This complicates the situation geographically since an individual can be located anywhere in the three-dimensional space according to his coordinates on the three dimensions.

It is necessary to understand this model of personality in order to fully appreciate the modern concept of extraversion because it is partly defined in terms of its relationship to (and independence from) other major personality factors. (Readers who wish to know more about this system of personality classification, and to discover their own position within it, are referred to Eysenck and Wilson's (1976) book, *Know Your Own Personality*).

Factor analysis is often labeled a dubious technique because different workers using it tend to come up with different solutions. Cattell (1963), for example, is famous for having identified sixteen personality dimensions using factor analysis. How can this be reconciled with Eysenck's view that there are only three? Actually, the dispute between Cattell and Eysenck is more apparent than real; the only difference is that they are dealing at different levels of generality. Cattell's sixteen factors are not independent of each other, and being thus intercorrelated they can themselves be factor analyzed. When this is done, "second order" factors are obtained that are very similar to Eysenck's major dimensions. Naming factors is partly arbitrary, however, and Cattell prefers the label "exvia–invia" to extraversion–introversion.

Whether one deals at a primary factor level (as does Cattell) or the second order level (as Eysenck usually does) is a matter of preference and depends upon one's purpose. The primary factors give a more detailed picture of the personality; on the other hand, their reliability and separability are questionable (Eysenck, 1972b) and they may be of less theoretical interest, being more difficult to pin to biological substrates. Factor analysts are agreed, however, upon a hierarchical model of personality, such as that illustrated for extraversion in Figure 2.

TWO MAJOR COMPONENTS OF EXTRAVERSION

A large proportion of items in Table 1 can be classified into those that deal with aspects of *sociability* (e.g., Do you prefer reading to meeting people? Do you find it hard to enjoy yourself at a lively party?) and those that refer to forms of *impulsiveness* (Do you stop and think things over before doing anything? When people shout at you do you shout back?). The discriminability of these two main components of extraversion has been confirmed by factor analysis, the correlation between sociability and impulsiveness subfactors being typically around .5. As can be seen from Figure 1, impulsiveness tends to be an unstable (neurotic) form of extraversion, while sociability is associated with stability or "adjustment." Overall, extraversion is fairly independent of neuroticism.

Several other subfactors of extraversion can be identified at the primary factor level (activity, liveliness, excitability, etc., see Figure 2) but sociability and impulsiveness emerge as the clearest components, and have been studied most often. It sometimes turns out that correlations between extraversion and other kinds of behavior are attributable exclusively to the effect of one or other of the two subfactors. For example, on monotonous tasks such as keeping watch for

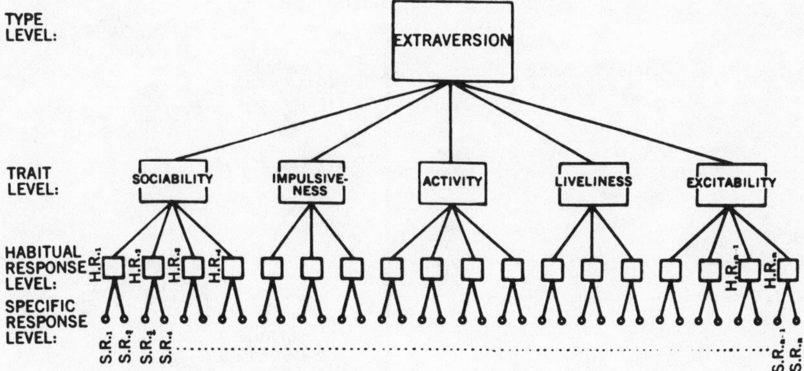

FIGURE 2 The hierarchical structure of extraversion. (From Eysenck, 1947.)

infrequent signals extraverts show marked deterioration over time; introverts maintain their initial level of performance much better and often show no decrement at all. A recent study by Thackray, Jones, and Touchstone (1974) revealed that increasing attention lapses of extraverts relative to introverts on a reaction-time task were a function of their impulsiveness, not their sociability. The importance of studying impulsiveness separately from sociability will also be seen when theories of the biological basis of personality are considered. Jeffrey Gray, of Oxford University, believes that impulsiveness is a personality "primary," rather than extraversion.

EXTRAVERSION AND ABNORMAL BEHAVIOR

Eysenck (1957; 1970a) has applied his three-dimensional system of personality description to the domain of psychiatric disorder. He first demonstrated that neurotics could be classified according to whether they are introvert or extravert – an hypothesis of C. G. Jung (1923). Anxious, phobic, obsessional, compulsive, and depressive neurotics were found to be generally introverted according to their performance on questionnaire and objective test measures; hysterics and psychopaths were found to be relatively extraverted (see Figure 3). It has become customary to call introverted neuroses "dysthymic" and the extraverted neurotics "hysterical," although a wide range of antisocial behaviors is characteristic of the latter group.

When the third dimension of personality, psychoticism, is considered, Eysenck's dimensional diagnostic system naturally becomes more elaborate. The addition of the third dimension to his system was partly necessitated by the discovery that neurotic and psychotic illnesses did not represent increasing degrees of the same disease process but were actually qualitatively different

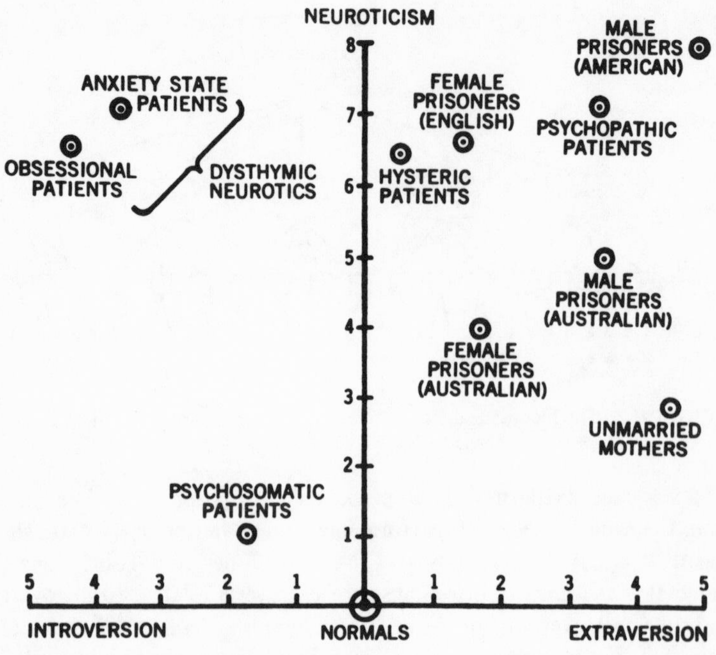

FIGURE 3 Positions of various groups in relation to questionnaire measures of neuroticism and extraversion. (From Eysenck, 1965.)

disorders. Such a conslusion was reached on the basis of factor analysis and discriminant function analysis of symptom patterns and objective test performance, and was verified by differential heritability studies (children of neurotic parents are predisposed to develop neuroses but not psychoses, and vice versa). Diagnostic groups which are high on the psychoticism factor are schizophrenia, manic-depression, psychotic or endogenous depression, paranoia, and psychopathy (hence, also criminality). In relation to the extraversion dimension, schizophrenia (particularly the "process" kind) and psychotic depression are usually found to be introverted, while mania, manic-depressive psychosis, paranoia, and psychopathy tend to be extraverted.

The notion that traditional psychiatric groups can be specified by locating them within Eysenck's three-dimensional (ENP) space, has been supported by factor analytic studies of the MMPI scales (e.g., Wakefield, Yom, Bradley, Doughtie, & Cox, 1974). Typically these show a factor of neuroticism loading on hypochondriasis, depression, and hysteria, a factor of psychoticism loading on paranoia, schizophrenia, and mania, and a factor of extraversion loading on social introversion (negatively), psychopathy, and mania. Furthermore, it is doubtful that the MMPI provides any more information than is obtainable from scores on the three factors.

This dimensional view of psychiatric disorder implies that abnormal behavior is continuous with normal behavior. Usually abnormality would be expected to represent an extreme position on one or more of the three dimensions, particularly neuroticism and psychoticism. This scheme seems appropriate for describing a great deal of abnormal behavior, but it has definite limitations. Some disorders such as epilepsy and homosexuality just do not fit the structure at all; either they are better conceived within the traditional medical model or they refer to deviant habits so specific that they are not well accommodated by Eysenck's primary dimensions. Other disorders, perhaps including schizophrenia, may be predisposed by a locus within the dimensional system but are also partly determined by a specific gene disorder, this being superimposed upon the polygenic basis of the dimensional system. For a detailed discussion of the problems of classification, diagnosis, and origins of psychiatric disorder see Eysenck (1970a). For the moment it is sufficient to note that different neuroses and psychoses may be partly differentiated by their positions in relation to the introversion–extraversion dimension.

The social relevance of the Eysenck diagnostic system may be illustrated by a rather interesting case study: an epidemic of overbreathing that occurred in a North of England school. As reported by Moss and McEvedy (1966), it began with one or two girls complaining of dizziness and fainting, and by late morning "they were going down like ninepins." Eighty-five of the most severely affected girls were taken to hospital by ambulance and the school was closed. Twice it was reopened and the same thing happened again. Attempts to find a physical cause proved negative, but since this behavior appeared classically "hysterical," Moss and McEvedy decided to compare the personalities of the girls who were affected with those of the girls who were immune. As expected, the girls who had been susceptible to the epidemic (about one-third of the school) were very much higher in both neuroticism and extraversion than those who were not affected. The investigators concluded that the epidemic was hysterical, and noted that the population had been rendered vulnerable by a recent outbreak of polio in the area.

THE GENETIC BASIS OF EXTRAVERSION

Shields (1976) has reviewed evidence for the partial inheritance of extraversion. Several studies have compared the similarity of identical (monozygotic) and fraternal (dizygotic) twins on questionnaire measures of extraversion. DZ twins show much less concordance than MZ twins; typically correlations of about .2 as compared with .5. The former correlation is about the same as that for normal siblings and for parent/child correlations; it is the MZ twins who show the unusually high similarity. Furthermore, it does not seem to matter whether, or at what age, the identical twins are separated from each other. In one study identical twins were actually *more* alike when they had been raised *apart* than when they had been raised together. This finding applied to both extraversion and neuroticism. It seems that identical twins often react against each other in such a way as to enhance any differences that there are between them (e.g., a tendency for one to take the lead) and this effect may be sufficient to cover over any environmental effects that would make for similarity of personalities.

Clearly, heredity plays a major part in determining extraversion scores. Quantitative estimates of the proportion of variance due to heredity and environment differ from study to study, but typically they indicate that about half of the variance is contributed by genetic factors. There is suggestive evidence that extraversion is slightly higher in heritability than other major personality dimensions, although this is by no means a consistent finding. Studies which have looked at extraversion subfactors such as sociability, impulsivity, and activity (e.g., Buss, Plamin, & Willerman, 1973; Eaves & Eysenck, 1975) have generally found these components to be roughly similar as regards the proportion of their variance that is due to heredity. Therefore, the hypothesis that sociability may be more open to environmental influences than impulsiveness (Eysenck & Eysenck, 1963) has not so far been substantiated.

Readers not familiar with the concept of heritability may be surprised to learn that an attribute such as extraversion can be strongly influenced by the genes without there being close similarity between parents and children. The actual correlations between parents and children on personality variables are very low (around .2) and the use of midparent scores (based on an average of the two parents) does not improve prediction of the child's characteristics very much. The main reason is that genes determine *differences* from our parents as well as similarities, just as they determine differences between siblings. Parents with more than one child often observe that their offspring display stable differences in temperamental characteristics that were discernable almost from the moment of birth. These parents will insist that they did not treat their children differently, and they are probably right – such differences are in large part innate. Heritability coefficients are based on the extent to which intra-family correlations covary with different degrees of genetic relationship, and parents are not as closely related to their children as identical twins are to each other.

If about half of the variance along the extraversion dimension is due to heredity, what is responsible for the remainder? Presumably there are various environmental influences which affect extraversion, but at present we are unable to say for sure which particular aspects of the environment are influential. Does a coeducational school make one more sociable than a single sex school? Do authoritarian parents and teachers make one less impulsive? Are there certain dietary deficiencies which make one less lively and active? With the exception of prefrontal lobotomy, which is known to lessen impulse control, no environmental factors capable of influencing extraversion have been clearly identified yet.

EYSENCK'S AROUSAL THEORY

The most highly developed theory of extraversion is that of Eysenck (1967). He believes the differences between extraverts and introverts are due to individual differences in the functioning of the reticular activation system. This structure in the brain stem is thought by neurophysiologists to be responsible for producing non-specific arousal in the cerebral cortex in response to external stimulation, and Eysenck hypothesizes that introverts are more highly aroused than extraverts given the same conditions of stimulation. Paradoxically, this results in the introverts showing more restrained or "inhibited" behavior because the cortex is exercising control over the more primitive, impulsive, lower brain centers. Neuroticism is postulated to reflect the general lability (Changeability) of the autonomic nervous system as controlled from the midbrain.

The arousal concept is thought to explain most of the differences between extraverts and introverts that have been observed in the laboratory and in real life. For example, introverts are supposed to acquire conditioned responses more rapidly than extraverts because their higher arousal facilitates the formation of connections. The difference in conditionability in turn accounts for the different types of abnormal behavior to which introverts and extraverts are prone. Emotional (high *N*) introverts develop dysthymic symptoms because of their overready conditioning to normally neutral stimuli. The hysterical and psychopathic behavior of the emotional extravert is said to result from a failure of the conditioning which constitutes the normal socialization process in childhood.

Let us consider some of the experimental evidence relevant to this theory. The most direct way of testing the notion that introverts are higher in arousal than extraverts would seem to be to examine the EEGs (brain waves) of the two personality types. The EEG consists of moment-to-moment fluctuations in voltage across two points on the scalp – low amplitude and high frequency is believed to reflect high arousal. In a review of more than a dozen studies which related extraversion to EEG arousal, Gale (1973) found a very confusing pattern of results. Some of the studies showed extraverts to be less aroused than introverts, some showed them to be more aroused, while still others indicated that they are equally aroused. Commenting on these discrepancies, Gale points out that the EEG is not a fixed and immutable characteristic of an individual like his eye color, so it is reasonable to suppose that there are certain conditions under which introverts will be more aroused and other conditions which would produce higher arousal in extraverts. In the typical EEG experiment subjects are instructed just to sit and relax and not think about anything; since this is impossible, what the subject *does* think about probably has an important influence on his EEG. In an attempt to explain the contradictory results, Gale observes that extraverts appear as more highly aroused when the experimental procedure is either very interesting or excruciatingly boring; otherwise introverts show higher arousal. Perhaps some tasks are so lonely and tedious that they become stressful and thus (paradoxically) arousing to the sensation-hungry extravert. Another possibility is that extraverts, when put into a situation that is boring to them, contrive to raise their level of arousal by imagination, fidgeting, or whatever means they can find, thus confounding any attempt to demonstrate in such a direct way that they are chronically less aroused than introverts. At present, then, it is necessary to conclude that there is no evidence that people at one end or other of the extraversion–introversion dimension show uniformly higher EEG arousal across various experimental situations.

The pharmacological evidence is rather more favorable to Eysenck's theory. If introverts are chronically more aroused than extraverts we would expect them to be more difficult to sedate with a depressant drug such as sodium amatyl, and indeed, this is the case. Sedation threshold, which may be measured by EEG changes, slurring of speech, or loss of facility on cognitive tasks such as adding digits, is significantly higher in dysthymic patients (introverted neurotics) than hysterics (extraverted neurotics) (e.g., Claridge & Herrington, 1963). There is also some evidence that depressant drugs have an extraverting effect upon behavior, while stimulants have an introverting effect. For example, Laverty (1958) found that injections of sodium amatyl resulted in a significant shift towards extraversion on a questionnaire measure, as well as consistent behavior changes (increased talkativeness, sociability, and excitability). Many other studies have shown that stimulant and depressant drugs affect performance on laboratory tests in a manner predictable from the differing performance of introverts and extraverts on them (e.g., Gupta, 1974b; McPeake & DiMascio, 1965).

Another fairly direct deduction from Eysenck's arousal theory is that introverts would be more sensitive to stimuli at all levels of intensity. Studies reprinted in Eysenck (1971a) indicate that, in general, introverts do have lower sensory thresholds (i.e., greater sensitivity to barely detectable stimuli) as well as lower pain thresholds (less tolerance of painful stimuli) than extraverts. This is consistent with the arousal theory of introversion, especially since amphetamine has independently been shown to reduce pain tolerance.

A closely related question is that of preferred levels of sensory stimulation. Eysenck has produced a model to predict the relationship between level of stimulation and pleasantness of affect. In Figure 4 the thick line shows that medium levels of stimulation are preferred by people in general; both very high levels of stimulation (pain) and very low levels (sensory deprivation) are aversive. The curve for introverts is displaced to the left and that for extraverts displaced

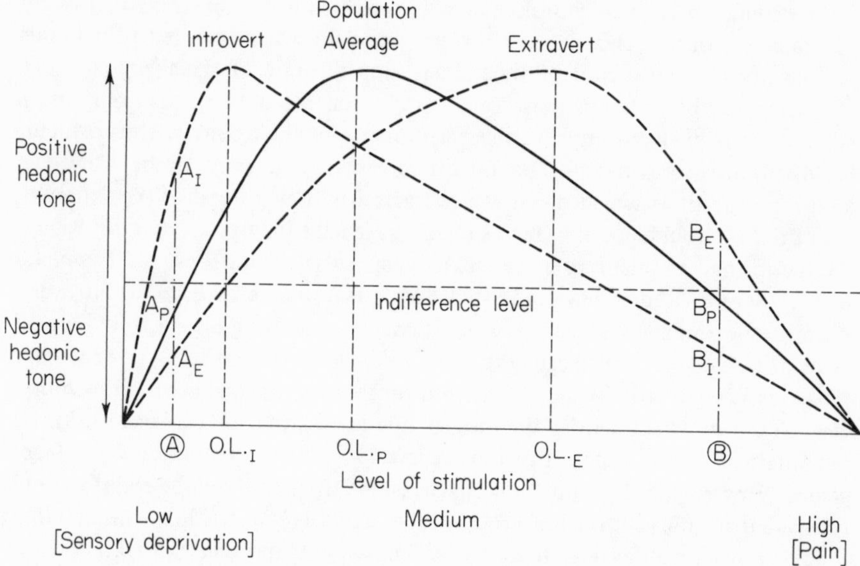

FIGURE 4 A model of the relationship between hedonic tone and level of stimulation for different personality types. The letters O.L. refer to optimal level; A and B are two points along the intensity axis at which marked differences between introverts and extraverts should appear (differences opposite in direction). (From Eysenck 1970b.)

to the right. This would mean that introverts should tolerate sensory deprivation better than extraverts and pain less well. Experimental results have generally been in accord with this model (e.g., Hill, 1975, Ludvigh & Happ, 1974).

An indirect yet clear demonstration of "stimulus hunger" in extraverts was provided by Weisen (1965). He showed that extraverts would work quite hard to obtain a "reward" of loud jazz music and bright lights; introverts, by contrast, would work to avoid these same stimuli. Another ingenious study of this kind is that of Holmes (1967), using the pupillary response. When a bright light was shone into the subjects' eyes, introverts showed faster pupillary contraction (as though trying to protect themselves from the strong stimulus). In a dark adaptation situation, however, the extraverts showed faster pupillary dilation (as though trying to enhance stimuli in this perceptual deprivation condition). This finding is particularly impressive since, if the speed of pupillary response was critical, one personality type or the other should be quicker at both constriction *and* dilation. As it is, the study suggests that the pupillary response assists in a process of stimulus intensity control where the optimal intensity is higher for extraverts than introverts.

On vigilance performance tasks (keeping watch for irregular signals) introverts generally perform better than extraverts, especially when required to maintain the vigil for a long period of time. Increasing the rate of signal presentation, increasing the background noise (e.g., turning on a radio), or providing social stimulation is likely to improve the performance of the extravert thus reducing his disadvantage relative to the introvert. Since these may all be viewed as arousing conditions which offset the characteristic low arousal of the extravert, such findings would also appear to support Eysenck's theory.

Experiments on memory have proved particularly supportive of Eysenck's theory. Several studies have indicated that extraverts are superior to introverts on verbal learning tasks such as paired associates and digit span, but they all involve fairly short-term recall tests, and we now know that long-term memory processes need to be distinguished from those involved in short-term memory. One of the most influential theories in this area is that of Walker (1958). He hypothesized that any perceptual event sets up a perseverative trace which fades gradually over time. If motivation or arousal is sufficient it will be transferred to permanent memory through a process called *consolidation.* While consolidation is taking place retrieval is temporarily inhibited to protect the trace against disruption; high arousal therefore faciliates consolidation but, at the same time, makes immediate recall more difficult. Such an interaction between arousal at the time of learning and the amount of time elapsing before recall is tested has been experimentally demonstrated on several occasions (e.g., Kleinsmith & Kaplan, 1963). When verbal learning takes place under conditions of high arousal immediate recall is poor but long-term recall is relatively good; learning under low arousal generally follows a reverse pattern, starting off well but deteriorating over time. Now, if extraverts are lower in arousal than introverts, they ought to be superior to introverts when memory is tested shortly after learning. Introverts, however, should be superior when it comes to long-term recall. Howarth and Eysenck (1968) confirmed this hypothesis using recall intervals varying from immediate testing to a 24-hr delay. The predicted cross-over occurred after about five minutes. Their results (see Figure 5) are strikingly similar to those of Kleinsmith and Kaplan and it seems likely that a single mechanism applies to both. Presumably the lower arousal in extraverts produces weaker consolidation which interferes with recall less at short-term intervals but does not favor long-term recall.

M. W. Eysenck (1974a) took this line of research a step further, studying interactions between extraversion–introversion (taken as a measure of trait arousal) and Thayer's Activation–Deactivation Adjective Checklist (assumed to be an indication of transient state-arousal) in determining fluency in a word association task. As found in previous studies, extraverts produced associates more fluently (despite equivalence in vocabularies) but there was a significant interaction between extraversion and activation; high activation was found to enhance performance for extraverts, but reduced it for introverts. This again

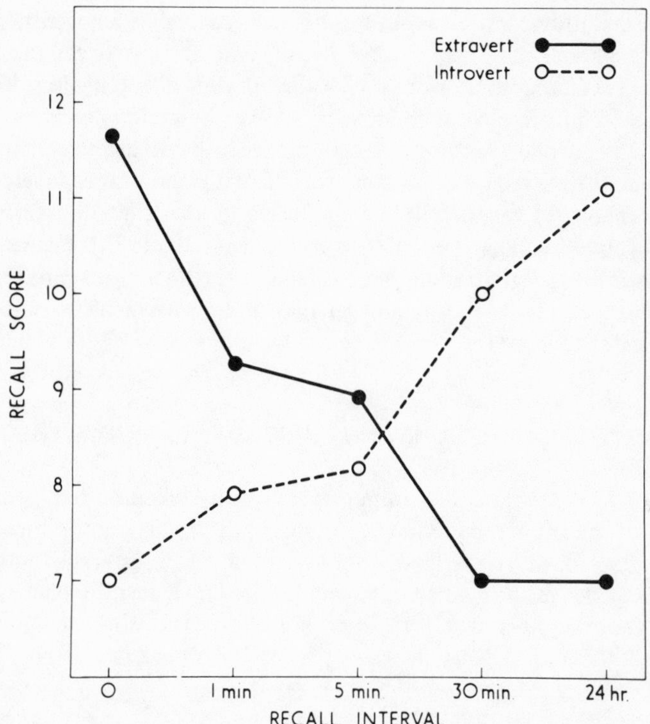

FIGURE 5 Recall scores of five groups of extraverts and five groups of introverts after different recall intervals. Introverts show reminiscence as recall interval increases; extraverts show forgetting. (From Howarth & Eysenck, 1968.)

supports the idea that introverts tend toward overarousal for the optimum performance of certain tasks, while extraverts are inclined to be underaroused. Presumably, extraverts are normally more fluent than introverts because they are less subject to cortical censorship processes.

Eysenck junior has since confirmed this finding under several other experimental conditions, including a paradigm which involved the use of controlled new learning, thus ensuring equivalent storage of learned material before the testing of retrieval (1974b). Again transient activation and trait extraversion produced a highly significant interaction effect on memory retrieval. Extraverts responded more quickly under high activation than low activation; the reverse was true for introverts. These experiments by M. W. Eysenck suggest that transient activation levels affect memory via the same mechanism as the personality characteristic of introversion – the unifying concept being probably best described as arousal.

One other experiment that supports Eysenck's arousal theory is concerned with the generalization of classically conditioned responses. When an emotional response is conditioned to a word, the CR may generalize along either of two dimensions: phonetically (e.g., cat–hat) or semantically (e.g., cat–animal). Usually the semantic dimension predominates, but the phonetic dimension assumes greater importance in children or adults whose alertness is impaired in some way (by alcohol or tiredness, etc.). If extraverts are lower in cortical arousal than introverts we would expect them to show a relatively greater amount of phonetic generalization, and this hypothesis was confirmed in a recent study by Schalling, Levander, and Wredenmark (1975). Figure 6 shows GSR scores in the generalization phase of their experiment; the extraverts show a striking preponderance of phonetic generalization, whereas there is hardly any difference for the introverts.

SENSITIVITY TO REWARD AND PUNISHMENT: GRAY'S THEORY

Gray (1972, 1973) starts out from physiological evidence that points to a separation of reward and punishment systems in the brain. Approach behavior is apparently controlled by the medial forebrain bundle and lateral hypothalamus, while mechanisms in the medial septal and hippocampal areas have an inhibitory function. Gray suggests that introverts and extraverts differ in their relative

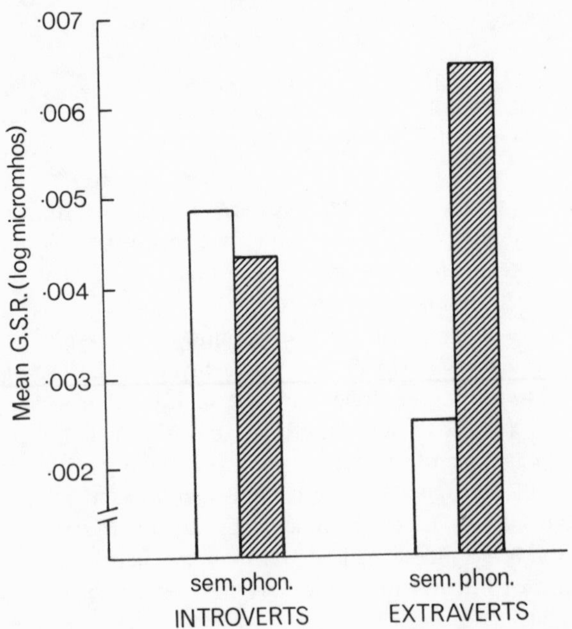

FIGURE 6 Generalization of conditioned GSRs along semantic and phonetic dimensions for introverts and extraverts. (From Schalling, Levander, & Wredenmark, 1975.)

sensitivities to threats of punishment and promises of reward. Introverts, he believes, are more sensitive to punishment; extraverts are oriented more toward the pursuit of rewards with relatively little heed of the consequences of their behavior. At the physiological level this means that introverts have a more reactive septohippocampal "stop system" and extraverts are more reactive in the medial forebrain bundle and lateral hypothalamic areas (the "go system"). Neuroticism, according to Gray, is an additive function of the reward and punishment systems, high *N* people being sensitive to both. Thus the neurological substrates in Gray's theory run diagonaly in relation to Eysenck's two major dimensions of personality, corresponding to the positions of the traits "anxiety" and "impulsivity."

Gray points out that the two major clusters of neuroses discussed by Eysenck (the dysthymic and the hysteric/antisocial groups) then fall directly on the personality dimensions corresponding to their postulated neural bases. He also claims that the effects of frontal leucotomy are consistent with his theory. This operation involves severing the orbital frontal cortex from the rest of the septohippocampal stop system, and is believed to be effective with typically

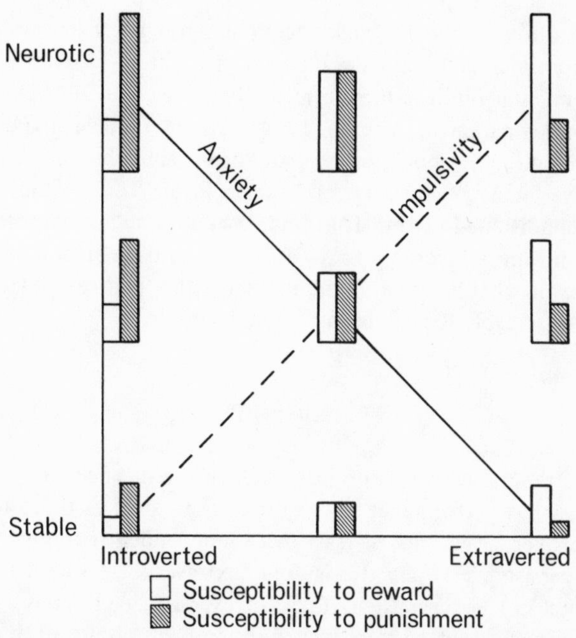

FIGURE 7 Proposed relationships of (a) susceptibility to signals of reward and susceptibility to signals of punishment to (b) the dimensions of introversion-extraversion and neuroticism. The dimensions of anxiety and impulsivity (diagonals) represent the steepest rate of increase in susceptibility to signals of punishment and reward, respectively. (From Gray, 1973.)

dysthymic symptoms such as obsessions, agoraphobia, anxiety, and depression. According to Gray, Eysenck's theory would need to suppose that the frontal cortex was a part of two separate mechanisms to account for this effect (interference with one reducing neuroticism and interference with the other causing a shift away from introversion towards extraversion), which is not very parsimonious. However, while there is evidence that leucotomy shifts people in the direction of extraversion (e.g., Petrie, 1952), it is still an open question whether there is any reduction in neuroticism following the operation.

The causal chains postulated by Eysenck and Gray are compared in Figure 8. The difficulty in choosing between them is that similar predictions emerge in many areas. In fact, much of Gray's theory could be derived from that of Eysenck. Eysenck would say that introverts are more sensitive to punishment because a stimulus of standard intensity has a greater effect upon them. Thus their pain threshold is lower and punishment of any kind is experienced as more severe. By corollary, extraverts are reward seekers because they require more intense reward before any impression is made. On the other hand, Gray's theory has the advantage that it does not assume a general factor of conditionability – a concept that is becoming increasing untenable in the face of recent experimental evidence.

Gray's modification of the Eysenck theory has not yet been systematically tested in an experimental program comparable to that of Eysenck's, but there are some experimental findings that seem to fit it very well. For example, in a verbal conditioning paradigm, Gupta (1974a) found that when positive reinforcement was used (e.g., "good" rather than "bad") and when the experimenter was an attractive female, extraverts conditioned faster. Under other conditions the introverts conditioned faster. This finding supports the idea of Gray that extraverts respond more favorably to rewards than punishments. It also provides a demonstration of what has been found in many other contexts, that extraverts respond better to sociable than to isolated conditions.

INTELLIGENCE

Overall, extraverts and introverts do not differ in intelligence. However, recent work has shown that performance on cognitive tasks such as those found in IQ tests may be broken down into at least three independent components: speed, accuracy, and persistence. When this is done, extraverts are found to be faster, but less accurate and less persistent than introverts (e.g., Brierley, 1961). The extraverts are also inclined to start well but slip back progressively relative to introverts. When these interactions are collapsed (i.e., across different types of subjects or different components of intelligence) the differences are usually obscured.

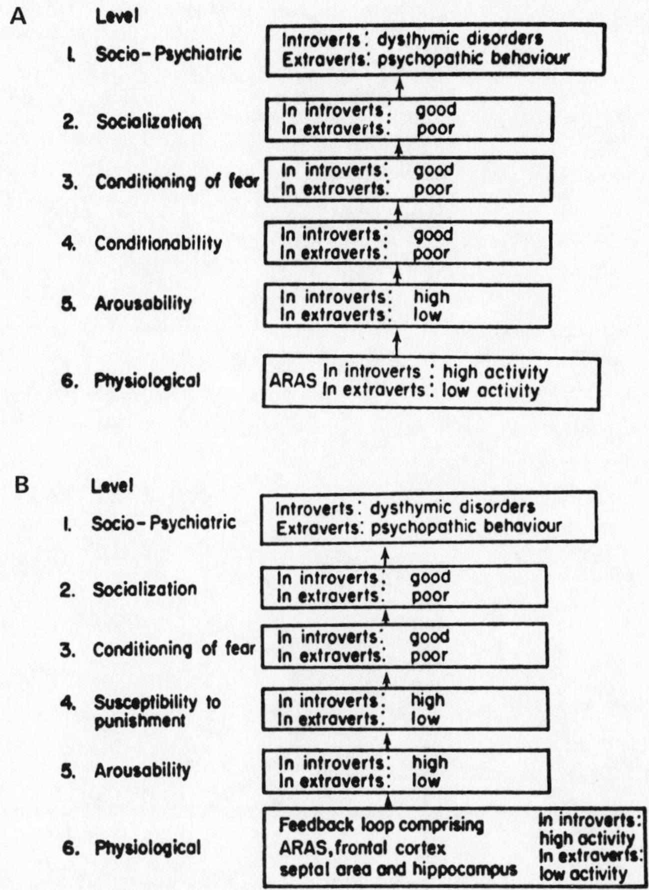

FIGURE 8 Eysenck's theory of introversion-extraversion (a) compared with Gray's modification (b). Alterations are made at levels 4 and 6. ARAS refers to the ascending reticular activating system. (From Gray, 1973.)

An illustrative study is that of Mohan and Kumar (1973) who conducted a detailed analysis of the performance of introverts and extraverts on the Standard Progressive Matrices IQ test. The performance of 100 students, balanced for sex, was examined in terms of items done correctly, wrongly, abandoned, and not attempted. These four outcomes were related to the difficulty level of the problems and time spent on the test. As expected, the extraverts began with an edge over the introverts but showed a greater deterioration in performance, thus allowing the introverts to draw ahead by the end of the test (see Figure 9). In terms of overall IQ scores the two personality types came out about equal.

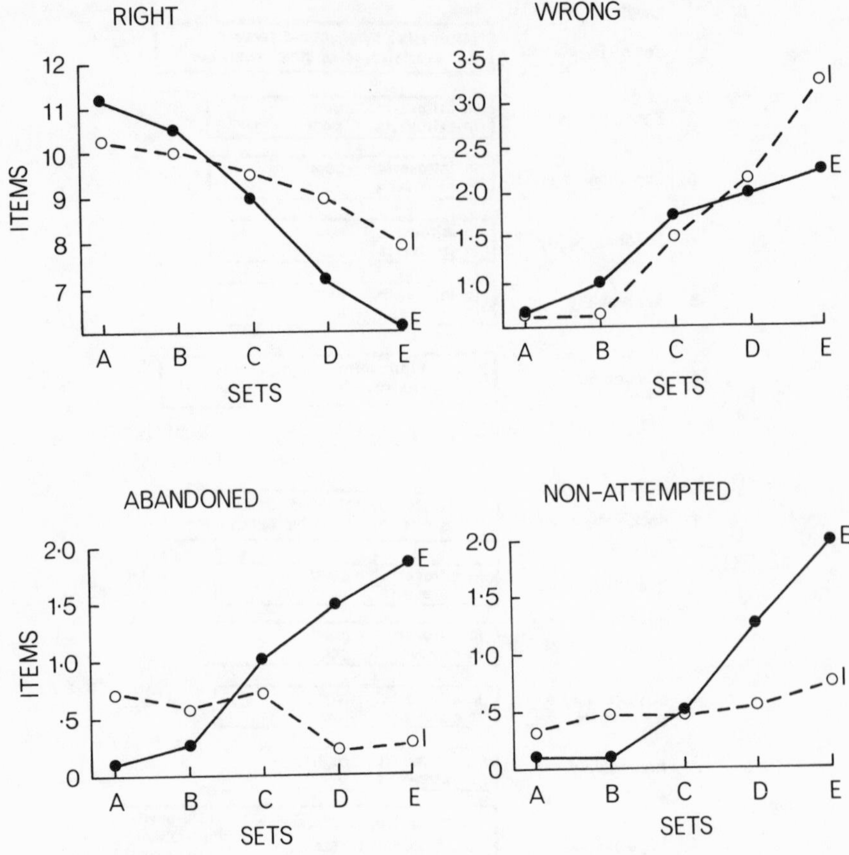

FIGURE 9 Analysis of performance of introverts and extraverts on the Standard Progressive Matrices. (From Mohan & Kumar, 1973.)

EDUCATION

If, as we have said, introverts are superior on long-term memory performance, persistence, and application, we might expect them to show higher educational attainment than extraverts. Generally speaking this is found to be so: introverts do better at school and obtain higher university grades (though extraverts are sometimes rated as better by their teachers at the primary school level). The advantage of introverts becomes progressively clear into the university years, perhaps because there is less variation in intelligence, and personality differences are enhanced in importance as a result (Eysenck, 1974).

In a large scale survey of factors relating to the academic performance of students at Birmingham University in England, Wankowski (1973) found that introverts had obtained better grades at secondary school and were more likely to obtain a good class of degree at university. Neuroticism, however, was also important, high *N* acting to inhibit academic achievement. Thus, stable introverts were most likely to obtain good honors degrees, neurotic extraverts least. Wankowski also found that personality was related to choice of subject; introverts preferred abstract, theoretical subjects, while extraverts chose practical and "people-oriented" areas of study. Personality was also linked with reasons for withdrawal from the university; students who withdrew for academic reasons, such as examination failure, tended to be neurotic extraverts while those who withdrew for medical and psychiatric reasons tended to be neurotic introverts.

Although introverts show better overall academic achievement, certain teaching methods and conditions of learning appear to be advantageous to extraverts. Leith (1974) studied the interactions between personality and methods of teaching in determining achievement on a genetics course. Over 200 students who had no previous knowledge of the material to be learned were involved in the study. Two teaching methods were compared: *discovery learning,* which stressed individuality, personal interaction, flexibility and spontaneity in teaching, tolerance of uncertainty and error making, and global effects rather than precise detail; and *reception learning,* which emphasized obedience, regularity, standardization, formality, and direct instruction. These two methods were equally effective overall, but there was a clear tendency for the extraverts to benefit more from the informal "discovery" learning, while introverts learned better with the formal "reception" approach. This interaction was observed when achievement was tested one week after the learning period and again when subjects were retested without warning a month later (see Figure 10).

In another experiment, using social psychology students, Leith considered the question of whether introverts and extraverts would learn better by themselves, paired with another person of the opposite personality type, or paired with someone of the same personality. Overall, introverts learned slightly better, but their advantage was only seen when they were working individually. In the two "social" conditions the extraverts were about equally good. There was some indication that the introverts were more debilitated when paired with an extravert than when working with an introvert partner. For both introverts and extraverts, working in homogeneous (like-personality) pairs produced the best learning performance.

The results of these studies by Leith may be accounted for within the terms of Eysenck's theory by assuming that extraverts are more easily bored by formal and isolated learning conditions. It seems they need a greater amount of

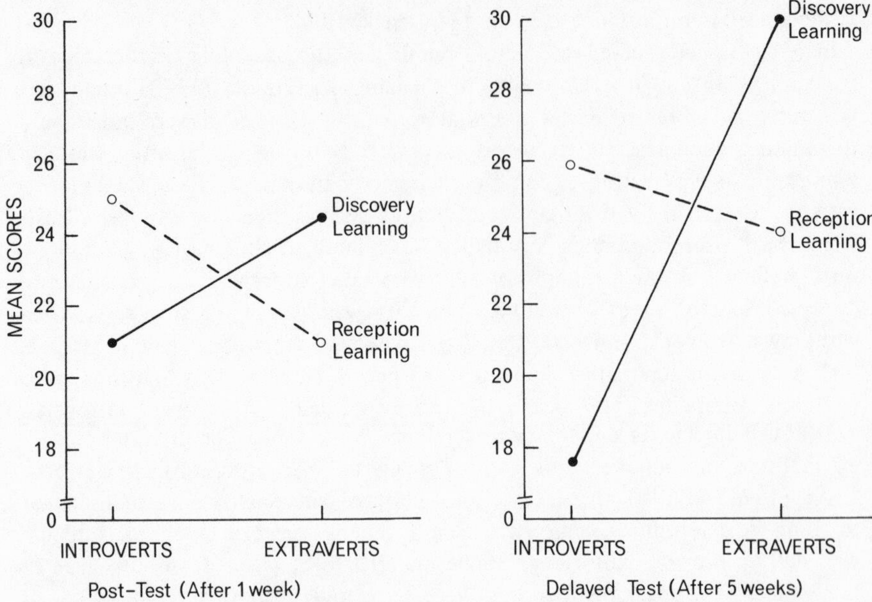

FIGURE 10 Interactions of strategies of instruction (direct vs discovery) with extraversion on two occasions of testing achievement and problem solving. (From Leith, 1974.)

stimulation in order to maintain their interest and attention (presumably because of their lower arousal) and this may be provided either by novelty and variety in the method of instruction or by social contact with fellow students. Given these conditions, extraverts may even perform better than introverts because the latter are likely to feel overwhelmed by excessive uncertainty and noisy companionship. Introverts, however, do better when conditions are structured and quiet. An important implication of this is that introverts are not necessarily intrinsically better students than extraverts; our current teaching methods may just happen to favor introverts.

Another important interacting variable is no doubt the degree of interest that the two personality types have in the task or material that is to be learned. For example, Hardy and Nias (1971) showed that introverts have more difficulty in learning to swim than extraverts. It is reasonable to suppose that the same would apply to many other outdoor, practical, and social skills that have greater intrinsic appeal to extraverts. Gray's theory would also draw attention to the likelihood that whether or not fear is generated in the learning situation would affect the relative performance of introverts and extraverts. Swimming offers physical and social rewards but there is also a high possibility of fear conditioning occurring, which would be more injurious to the introvert.

OCCUPATIONAL PSYCHOLOGY

Eysenck (1971b) discusses a number of papers that link extraversion with vocational preferences and various aspects of industrial performance. In general, extraverts show superior social skills: for example, ability to relate to other people, to take a personal interest in them and their problems, and to anticipate their reactions. Thus they tend to gravitate towards, and often excel, in jobs that involve dealing with other people (such as sales and personnel work, nursing, and teaching). The ability of the introvert to resist boredom and persist with a task for a long period of time, however, is also valuable in certain occupational contexts. Introverts are more reliable and conscientious, more punctual, absent less often, and stay longer at a job (having less need for novelty and excitement). While on the job, the extraverts probably waste more time talking to their work mates, smoking, drinking coffee, and generally seeking diversion from the routine.

As an example of the kind of study that has been done using the Eysenck Personality Inventory in the applied setting we may cite Jessup and Jessup (1971). A group of 205 Royal Airforce pilot cadets were tested early in their training program and the scores compared with their success or failure in passing the course. Failure rates for the 4 personality quadrants were: stable introverts 14%, stable extraverts 32%, neurotic extraverts 37%, and neurotic introverts 60%. In other words, the neurotic introverts were by far the worst group and stable introverts the best. Extraverts did not seem to be greatly affected by their level of emotionality as measured by the *N* scale. While the theoretical reasons for these differences were unclear, this represented a high degree of predictive validity for the personality measures which was independent of the current selection techniques. Therefore the Jessups suggested that it might have some usefulness in addition to them.

In similar fashion, extraversion has been shown to correlate with many other occupationally relevant abilities. Unfortunately, the usefulness of questionnaires such as the EPI for purposes of selection is limited by their ready fakeability. Although extraversion scores are little affected by instructions to "fake good," people can make themselves out to be highly extraverted or introverted at will and this could lead to faulty employment decisions. Perhaps some of the indirect measures of extraversion will prove more useful in the applied setting, such as perceptual and motor tests that correlate with questionnaire measured extraversion.

RISK TAKING AND ACCIDENT PRONENESS

There is evidence that extraverts take more risks than introverts. Figuratively and literally they are greater gamblers. This is in line with Eysenck's description of the extraverts as impulsive, and Gray's view of extraverts as reward seekers who are inclined to disregard the possible unpleasant consequences of their behavior. Both writers see introverts as more controlled, responsible, and fearful.

In one of the earliest studies of personality in relation to accident proneness, Fine (1963) investigated the driving records of 1000 freshmen at the University of Minnesota. Dividing them into extreme extraverts, introverts, and intermediaries, with the MMPI, he found that the extreme extraverts had significantly more accidents and more traffic offenses recorded against them than the other groups.

Craske (1968) administered the EPI to 70 male and 30 female outpatients appearing in a minor trauma clinic that dealt with accidents such as minor fractures, crash injuries, and torn ligaments. For the males, extraversion was significantly related to accident history; the neuroticism scale did not correlate for either men or women. When individual items which discriminated accident repeaters from people reporting only one accident were isolated, the four critical questions from the extraversion scale were seen to be concerned with impulsiveness rather than sociability. Three N scale items also discriminated repeaters from one-timers and these referred to feelings of guilt and depression. Personality scores did not relate to the type of accident that was had, whether classified according to cause or seriousness.

Shaw and Sichel (1971) compared the personalities of bus drivers with good and bad safety records. The positions of very safe and dangerous drivers within the two Eysenck dimensions are shown in Figure 11. There was total separation between them, the bad drivers being more extravert and neurotic. A large group of drivers with moderate safety records fell in between these two extreme groups.

Overall, it seems that neurotic extraverts are the most accident prone personality group measured by the EPI, that is, people high on Gray's impulsiveness dimension.

CRIMINALITY AND ANTISOCIAL BEHAVIOR

Similar considerations would lead us to expect a greater amount of antisocial behavior from extraverts than introverts. From Eysenck's theory such an association is predicted because extraverts are supposed to be less susceptible to the kinds of conditioning that constitute the socialization process, and Gray's theory would predict that extraverts would be more prone to crime and antisocial behavior because they are impulsive reward seekers. Whatever the reason, this has been found to be case: apart from their violations on the road, extraverts break institutional rules of all kinds and find their way to prison more often than introverts (Eysenck, 1971b). Extraverts are also more likely to become recidivists than introverts (Eysenck & Eysenck, 1974). In addition, unmarried

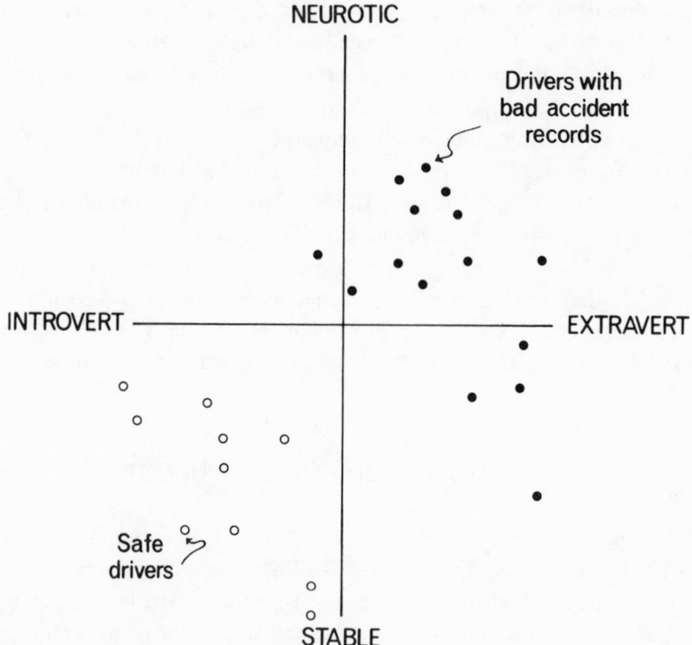

FIGURE 11 Positions of good and bad drivers in relation to neuroticism and extraversion. (Modified from Shaw & Sichel, 1971.)

mothers and VD patients are more extravert than comparable control subjects, and extraverts tend to smoke more (Coan, 1973).

Extraversion, however, is not the only temperamental predictor of delinquent and antisocial behavior. The above relationships are usually stronger when high levels of neuroticism are also involved, and the psychoticism factor is a better predictor than either extraversion or neuroticism. Most of the current research on the temperamental basis of criminality and antisocial behavior is now focusing primarily on the *P* dimension, although, as stated, neuroticism and extraversion are positively implicated.

SOCIAL AND POLITICAL ATTITUDES

Eysenck (1961) found that extraverts tended to be "toughminded" in their attitudes and introverts relatively "tenderminded." This dimension of toughmindedness versus tendermindedness had earlier (Eysenck, 1954) been identified in the domain of social and political attitudes as a second major factor, running orthogonal to (i.e. independent of) radicalism–conservatism. Toughminded attitudes are described as practical rather than idealistic, expedient rather than altruistic, dogmatic rather than flexible, and active rather than passive. For example, toughminded people tend to favor euthanasia, easy divorce, compulsory sterilization, and capital punishment, as against the religious and humanitarian values expressed by tenderminded people.

Eaves and Eysenck (1974) recently discovered that toughmindedness is partly heritable (a coefficient of .54 being found). This study, using identical/fraternal twin comparisons, also included personality measures, and it was possible to show that the correlation between extraversion and toughmindedness was genetic rather than environmental. In other words, although variance along the toughmindedness and extraversion dimensions individually is only about half determined by heredity, the connection between them is entirely due to heredity.

SEXUAL ATTITUDES AND BEHAVIOR

Focusing specifically on attitudes to sex, Eysenck (1976) has found that extraverts are more permissive. They confess to higher degrees of libido, and are less prone to nervousness and inhibition in their sexual escapades. As regards sexual behavior, they have intercourse more frequently, in more different positions, and with a greater variety of partners than introverts. Extraverts also enjoy sexual humor more than introverts, who prefer cognitive styles of humor such as puns and jokes based on incongruity (Eysenck & Wilson, 1976). All these relationships are consistent with the picture of the extravert as a sociable, outgoing, risky, and sensation-seeking individual and the introvert as cautious, reserved, reliable, and thoughtful.

SOCIAL INFLUENCE

Studies in the areas of suggestibility, conformity, and compliance have produced complex findings with respect to the differences between extraverts and introverts.

In some circumstances extraverts appear to be more open to social influence than introverts. They are more inclined to change their judgements under the influence of prestige suggestions (Sinha & Ojha, 1963) and to change their evaluation of paintings after discovering the name (and thus reputation) of the artist (Mohan & Mohan, 1965). They are more field dependent as measured by the Rod and Frame Test (Fine & Danforth, 1975), and extravert children are more responsive to peer influences regarding antisocial behavior (Rim & Seidenross, 1971).

On the other hand, introverts are more susceptible to the autokinetic effect, that is, seeing a stationary light in the dark as moving when there is some social pressure to do so (Panek, 1962). Also, their judgements of taste intensity are more likely to change in parallel with manipulations in the intensity of ambient light (Wilson & Gregson, 1967). Organ (1975) gave bonus points to business school students for performance on random quizzes which tested daily preparation. The introverts obtained more bonus points throughout the program and maintained a steadier performance record over a period of time. Extreme extraverts actually showed a significant downward trend over time, which suggests that they were progressively losing interest.

In several other situations, no differences between introverts and extraverts have been found. According to Claridge (1970) placebo reactors are neither consistently extraverted nor introverted, though they tend to be high on neuroticism. In a study of religious conversion, Roberts (1965) found virtually no difference between extraverts and introverts except for a slight tendency for the introverts to show more gradual (less sudden) changes in religious conviction.

When an introvert encounters an extravert with different views on a controversial topic, the introvert is more likely to be persuaded to modify his position (Carment, Miles, & Cervin, 1965). It is not clear whether this is because extraverts are more stubborn, more assertive, more plausible, or simply more talkative (they were observed to do most of the talking during the meeting).

Becker and Munz (1975) looked at personality in relation to reciprocation of interviewer disclosures. Disclosure was manipulated by having interviewers of the same sex as the subjects vary the extent to which they revealed things about themselves to the subjects. While reciprocation was observed in the sense that subjects were more prepared to talk about their own intimate secrets following a lead from the interviewer, there was no difference between introverts and extraverts in this respect.

Results in the area of hypnotic susceptibility have been particularly complex and contradictory. Lang and Lazovik (1962) found that extraverts were easier to hypnotize than introverts and Hilgard and Bentler (1963) found that subjects in the neurotic-extravert (hysteric) quadarant were most readily hypnotizable. However, in a series of studies by H. B. Gibson and his associates (Gibson & Corcoran, 1975; Gibson & Curran, 1974) there has emerged a consistent tendency for neurotic introverts and stable extraverts to be most suggestible. No adequate explanation of these inconsistencies has yet been suggested, though Gibson has put forward some interesting hypotheses for future research. One is that the type of hypnotic induction procedure might be critical; neurotic introverts might be more susceptible to an authoritarian procedure which emphasizes "task-motivating instructions," while stable extraverts might respond more to permissive procedures that maximize interpersonal reinforcement. A second suggestion is that an uncomplicated correlation between hypnotizability and extraversion might emerge if the effect of neuroticism was minimized by administration of a tranquilizer. When these experiments have been done, we might be closer to an understanding of the connection between personality and hypnotic susceptibility.

In summary, it seems that either extraverts or introverts may appear as more open or susceptible to social influence, depending upon the particular conditions of motivation. When social rewards and excitement are offered as incentives, the extraverts appear more likely to comply and cooperate. In conscience arousing situations, and those that are relatively impersonal, the introverts are often more motivated to comply.

AFFILIATION

Since sociability is an important component of extraversion we would expect extraverts to show a greater interest in being with other people in real-life situations. One of the simplest tests of this hypothesis is to examine personality correlates of preferred physical proximity. Leipold (1963) and Patterson and Holmes (1966) found that extraverts would approach an interviewer more closely and talk longer in response to questions than introverts. Williams (1963) found no difference in approach tendencies, but extraverts would allow others to approach them more closely. Sewell and Heisler (1973) found that subjects high on the Exhibition and Impulsivity scales of the Personality Research Form would position their chair closer to the experimenter when asked to "pull up a chair" for an interview. On the other hand, Porter, Argyle, and Salter (1970) found no relation between extraversion and proximity in a number of interview and conversational conditions. Inconclusive results have also been reported by Meisels and Canter (1970) and Williams (1971).

A study by Tolor (1975), using symbolic people arranged in representational space, also produced fairly inconclusive results. Female extraverts positioned themselves closer to a "boyfriend" figure, but further away from a "boss" figure, than female introverts. No such differences were found for males.

Shapiro and Alexander (1969) studied extraversion–introversion differences within the design of Schachter's (1959) classic study of anxiety and affiliation. The subjects' anxiety was raised by threats of electric shock of different degree, then they were given the choice of waiting alone or with other people. As the situational anxiety increased, affiliation tendencies increased for extraverts but decreased for introverts. This result suggests that if extraverts are made anxious they tend to gravitate towards other people, but if introverts are made anxious they prefer to be alone.

Studies of eye contact also suggest greater sociability in extraverts. Mobbs (1968) classified subjects on the basis of the Heron Sociability Scale and each had a short conversation with an experimenter who stared continuously at him. Extraverts engaged in more reciprocal eye contact than either introverts or ambiverts. Kendon and Cook (1969) correlated MPI extraversion scores with various measures of visual behavior and found a positive correlation between extraversion and the frequency of looking while talking. Rutter, Morley, and Graham (1972) divided subjects into extraverts and introverts on the basis of the EPI and had them take part in a 4-min conversation with the experimenter. Extraverts looked more frequently, engaged in more frequent periods of eye contact while speaking, and initiated more looks and speech bursts. Thus there does seem to be a positive relationship between extraversion and gaze, though the particular indices which emerge as significantly related vary from study to study.

Finally, at least two studies have indicated that extraverts talk more and sooner than introverts (Carment, Miles, & Cervin, 1965; Leipold, 1963), and Cook (1968) found that extraverts prefer to sit directly opposite another person in a variety of situations, whereas introverts would more often choose a right angle arrangement.

There is some evidence, then, that extraverts are more interested in making contact with other people. This can be interpreted several ways. It can be viewed as validation of the questionnaires, since sociability is a part of extraversion by definition. At a more theoretical level it could be interpreted in terms of Eysenck's theory, extraverts seeking social contact as a means of maintaining cortical arousal and introverts seeking solitude to keep their arousal down to a tolerable level. Zajonc (1965) has reviewed evidence that social contact is arousing. Another possibility is that the relationship is mediated by some other personality variable, such as confidence or assertiveness (which are higher in extraverts).

BIRTH ORDER

In the classic studies of Schachter (1959), birth order was found to be associated with affiliative behavior as well as anxiety. In particular, firstborn and only children were found to be more affiliative than later born children. This was observed most strikingly under anxiety-provoking situations, but held up even when the degree of induced anxiety was held constant. Though the reasons for this relationship are not entirely clear, it suggests that extraverts (being affiliative) might be overrepresented amongst firstborn children.

Research has, in general, not supported this hypothesis. Several studies have produced entirely negative results (e.g., Farley, 1975); others have produced complex and inconsistent results. McCormick and Baer (1975) obtained EPI scores from 120 college students from two-child families in which the age range between siblings was not more than six years. A significant interaction between sex and birth order was found in determining extraversion scores, firstborn males and secondborn females being more extraverted. No easy explanation of this result presents itself. Birth order may merit further study as a factor bearing on extraversion, but at the moment it appears that its influence is very weak at best.

ATTRACTION

There is a very slight tendency for extraverts to be more popular than introverts, the correlation averaging .10 according to a review of several studies by Mann (1959). The correlation of extraversion with leadership is slightly higher on average (.15), though it varies a great deal from one study to another. Presumably, extraverts tend to emerge as informal group leaders because they are relatively assertive, more interactive with others, and slightly more popular.

Hendrick and Brown (1971) split popularity into several different aspects and considered the question of whether introverts and extraverts prefer their own kind. The EPI was used to classify 205 students into introvert and extravert groups, and these subjects were required to evaluate bogus strangers who conformed to the stereotype of introvert and extravert respectively. On four out of six attributes the extravert stranger was preferred by both extravert and introvert subjects (especially the extraverts). These were: "liking," "interesting at party," "ideal personality," and "prefer as leader." On two other measures, however, ("reliable as friend," "honest and ethical") the introvert stranger was preferred by the introvert subjects, and there was no strong preference expressed by extravert subjects. These results suggest the interplay of three generalizations:

(1). Other things being equal, people like other people who are similar to themselves.

(2). Extraverts are generally more popular than introverts in that they are seen as more likeable, interesting, and influential.

(3). Introverts are perceived as having the qualities of honesty, stability, and reliability more than extraverts.

Stern and Grosz (1966) observed the behavior of patients in group therapy in relation to their personality scores. In line with the affiliation studies, extraverts interacted more with other patients. It was also found that patients tended to interact with others who were like themselves in terms of introversion–extraversion. That is, extraverts liked to talk with other extraverts, and introverts also preferred their own kind. This supports one of the generalizations implicit in the results of Hendrick and Brown (1971), that people prefer their own personality type. However, contrasting results were found for the internal–external control dimension; in this case patients tended to interact with *dissimilar* others. All we can say, then, is that in a group situation, interaction patterns are partly determined by the personalities of the individuals concerned, one of the important dimensions being extraversion.

Studies of partner choice indicate that people select mates and marry almost at random as far as extraversion–introversion is concerned. If anything there is a very slight tendency for people to mate with others similar to themselves on this dimension. As regards sexual preferences, extravert men tend to prefer large breasted women, and extravert women tend to prefer sporty, muscular men (Wilson & Nias, 1976).

PERSON PERCEPTION

There is a suggestion that introverts are more accurate at judging the personality characteristics of other people (Vingoe & Antonoff, 1968). Subjects in this study were 66 freshmen women living in the same dormitory. They were given the EPI and the California Personality Inventory, and rated their peers on dimensions from these same tests. "Good" judges were relatively introverted (*E* scores averaging 10.8 as against 14.8 for the "bad" judges) and less neurotic (mean scores 9.1 and 12.3, respectively). Good judges were also more tolerant of other people and tended to "fake good" according to their Lie Scale scores. Perhaps the peer ratings made by the "good" judges corresponded more to the peers' self-descriptions because they were relatively flattering. It is hard to know how to interpret the results of this study.

Brown and Hendrick (1971) found that extraverts were more "visible" than introverts in the sense that they were more accurately perceived by other people. This applied to the perceptions of both extraverts and introverts; both personality types perceived extraverts more accurately. An examination of discrepancies between the perceived selves and ideal selves of the two personality types revealed that while the extraverts were reasonably happy being extravert, the introverts would have liked to be less introverted than they were. In other words, both types saw extraversion as a more ideal type of personality. Introverts pretending to be more extravert than they actually were (because this is what they would prefer) might explain why they were less accurately perceived than extraverts. Brown and Hendrick also confirmed the finding that ideal leaders are perceived as extravert rather than introvert.

Duckworth (1975) divided 36 married couples into experimental and control groups and had them attend a session in which each partner tried to identify the feelings expressed by the other through vocal (but nonverbal communication). Emotions such as boredom, disgust, tenderness, etc. had to be conveyed through tone of voice and expression while reciting the standard phrase "What are you doing?". The experimental group underwent emotionally provocative disagreements before trying to identify the feelings of their partner, while the control group did not. The effect of these disagreements was to increase the ability of stable introvert males to identify the spouses' feelings, while this capacity was decreased in neurotic introvert males. This finding suggests that the differential susceptibility of various personality types to arousal and stress may be implicated in the ability to accurately perceive the emotional state of other people. In this area as in many others, an interaction between extraversion and neuroticism seems to be involved.

SOCIAL CLASS DIFFERENCES

If extraverts make better leaders we might expect them to be upwardly mobile in terms of social class. On the other hand, the superior academic performance of introverts, particularly at higher educational levels, might make for upward mobility. Child (1966) administered the Junior Maudsley Personality Inventory to a sample of children from various schools and related extraversion scores to the occupational status of their parents. Children of parents from Classes I and V (highest and lowest) were found to be significantly more introverted than those in Class III (Figure 12). Another finding was that children who obtained promotion to higher classes for good school work were significantly more introverted than an equivalent group of demoted children. This provided fairly direct evidence that introversion is upwardly mobile within the educational setting. It remains to be explained why children of lower-class parents are also more introverted than the middle-class children. Perhaps this introversion is of a slightly different kind, reflecting shyness, submissiveness, and "social phobia" rather than reliability, diligence, and other aspects of introversion that would make for upward mobility. (It has been noted above that persons may be unsociable either because they are afraid of other people or because they have a positive interest in abstract ideas.)

Unfortunately, the generality of Child's results with respect to the extraversion class relationship is questioned by the failure of the Eysencks to find any social-class trends for extraversion using a large sample of adult subjects reported in the latest (1975) manual for the EPI.

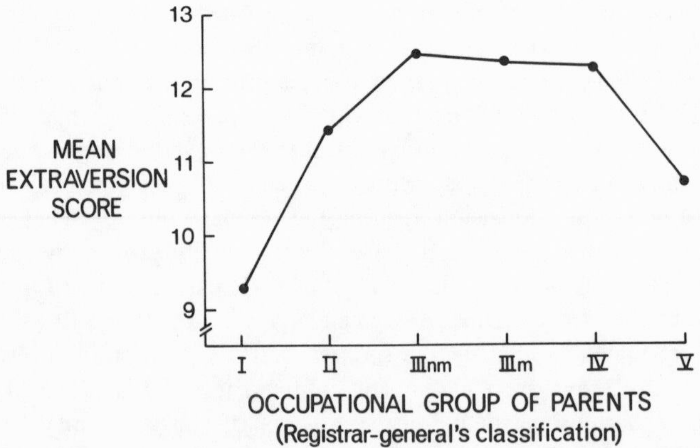

FIGURE 12 Extraversion scores of children in relation to the social class of their parents. Letters "m" and "nm" refer to *manual* and *nonmanual*, respectively. (Drawn from data of Child, 1966.)

CROSS-NATIONAL DIFFERENCES

Lynn and Hampson (1975) investigated cross-national differences in personality based on demographic and epidemiological data. The variables used were national rates of divorce, illegitimacy, accidents, crime, murder, suicide, alcoholism, chronic psychosis, and coronary heart disease, and the per capita consumption of calories, cigarettes, and caffeine. The theoretical and empirical relationship of these variables to extraversion and neuroticism was used to set up a model for their relationship among nations. For example, cigarette smoking and divorce were presumed to be indices of extraversion; suicide and alcoholism were expected to fall on an axis of neuroticism; and accidents, crime, murder, and illegitimacy were expected to load on both extraversion and neuroticism. This model was confirmed by principal components analysis of the relationships among these variables at the international level. Factor scores were then computed for the industrialized Western nations (see Figure 13). The United States appears to be the most extraverted nation, and Japan the most introverted.

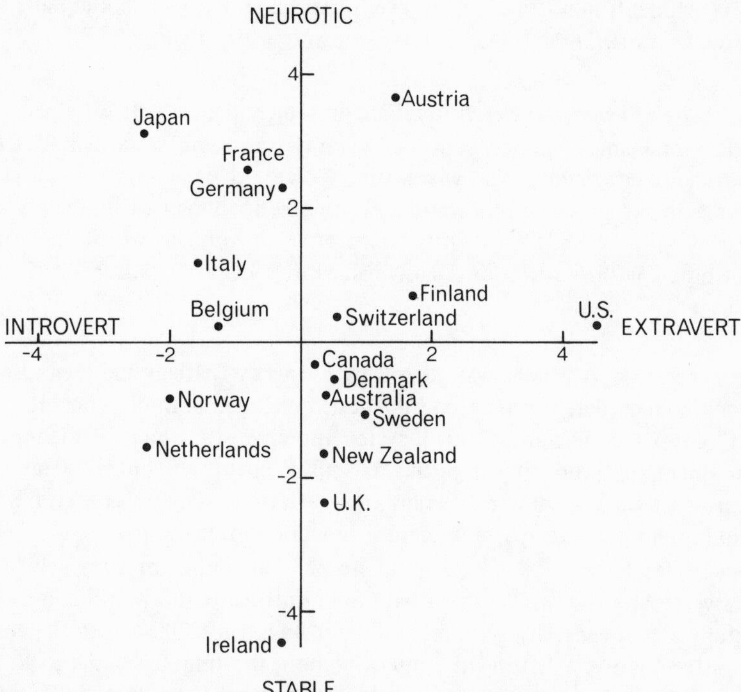

FIGURE 13 The positions of Western nations in relation to dimensions of neuroticism and introversion–extraversion determined by analysis of demographic and epidemiological data. (From Lynn & Hampson, 1975.)

These findings of Lynn and Hampson are supported by cross-national comparisons of norms on the EPI. Iwawaki, Eysenck, and Eysenck (1977) found that the Japanese were significantly more introverted and neurotic than a comparable English sample. There is also evidence that Americans are more extraverted than the English (Eysenck & Eysenck, 1971). Such data support Lynn and Hampson's methodology and findings, but do not throw any light on the origin of the observed differences. These might be due to genetic differences (perhaps arising from selective migration) or to cultural differences, or more likely, both.

PSYCHOTHERAPY

We have discussed the usefulness of the extraversion variable as part of a dimensional system of psychodiagnostics. Does the concept have any relevance to the therapeutic process?

A study of the relative effectiveness of different types of psychotherapy on extraverts and introverts was undertaken by Di Loreto (1971). He used a sample of 100 students admitting a high level of social and general anxiety and seeking treatment for it. Three types of treatment were compared:

(1) *Wolpe's systematic desensitization,* in which the patient is helped to relax while visualizing a graded series of anxiety-provoking situations; (2) *Rogers' client-centered therapy,* in which the patient is encouraged to disclose his feelings in the presence of a warm and empathetic therapist who merely clarifies what is said; and (3) *Ellis's rational-emotive therapy,* in which the patient is confronted with his irrational and maladaptive behavior patterns and urged to change.

The success of treatment was guaged by changes in patient and therapist ratings of anxiety and defensiveness, and the design included both placebo and "no-contact" control conditions. Overall, systematic desensitization was the most effective therapy, producing significant improvement in both extraverts and introverts. Client-centered therapy was effective only with extraverts, and rational–emotive therapy only seemed to work with introverts.

These results might be viewed as another illustration of Gray's theory that extraverts are responsive to reward and introverts to punishment. Rogers' therapy seems generally pleasant and rewarding, while Ellis's might be construed as fairly punitive. Whatever the interpretation, the time has come to go beyond the simple question of whether or not psychotherapy works, and ask what kind of treatment is most effective with what kind of patient. Introversion–extraversion is one patient variable that cannot be ignored in this connection.

CONCLUSION

Introversion–extraversion appears as a major dimension of individual differences relevant to many basic and social processes. Like intelligence, it is a truly psychological concept, slotting in between phenomena at the biological and social levels and providing an explanatory link between them. We have described a causal chain which runs all the way from genetics, through anatomical structures and physiological processes such as the reticular formation and cortical arousal to variations in extraversion measured by laboratory tests and questionnaires, thence to a wide range of behavioral domains such as neurosis, crime, accident proneness, sexual behavior, suggestibility, affiliation, person perception, humor preferences, and political attitudes. At each successive stage the genotypic level of introversion–extraversion is probably further modified by environmental influences, so that at the level of social behavior the link with heredity might seem tenuous. Nevertheless, there is evidence that biological factors are involved to such an extent that they cannot be ignored at any point in the chain – however much this goes against the current environmentalist zeitgeist.

The most highly developed and best supported theory of extraversion is that of Eysenck – a theory built upon the contributions of such unlikely coauthors as Hippocrates, Wundt, Jung, and Pavlov. Certain findings better fit Gray's modification of the Eysenck theory, but it remains to be seen whether his version will exhibit such wide-ranging explanatory power as Eysenck's original theory. Findings in the area of verbal learning and memory provide particularly striking support for Eysenck's arousal theory and it is difficult to see how Gray's theory could account for them. On the other hand, Gray's theory does very well with some of the verbal conditioning phenomena and it is a strength of his view that no general factor of conditionability is required. The concept of conditionability as a generalized attribute is increasingly being called into question. Whatever the outcome of future experiments, research on introversion–extraversion has reached a healthy state now that we have two and more theories to choose between that are formulated at the same scientific level.

Why is it important to link social behavior to biological predispositions via a personality concept such as extraversion–introversion? Only by doing so can we break out of the sterile circular exercise of "explaining" behavior as being caused by a trait when the existence of the trait is inferred from observing the behavior: For example, "Smith goes to parties because he is sociable." How do we know he is sociable? "Because he is frequently seen at parties." A truly causal theory requires that complex social behavior be linked back to independently observable events in another descriptive realm, and this is what the theories of Eysenck and Gray have achieved. Of course one's past experiences and present environmental conditions will have important influences on social behavior, but the need to postulate biological mechanisms that contribute strongly to extraversion–introversion differences is made clear from the heritability studies.

To the student of social behavior, theories and research in this area may also be of particular interest because they take us beyond common sense and the intuition of many an intelligent layman. Superceding these authorities has always been the difficult goal of the social scientist.

REFERENCES

Becker, J. F., & Munz, D. C. Extraversion and reciprocation of interviewers' disclosures. *Journal of Consulting and Clinical Psychology,* 1975, *43,* 593.

Brierley, H. The speed and accuracy characteristics of neurotics. *British Journal of Psychology,* 1961, *52,* 273–280.

Brown, S. R., & Hendrick, C. Introversion, extraversion, and social perception. *British Journal of Social and Clinical Psychology,* 1971, *10,* 313–319.

Buss, A. H., Plamin, R., & Willerman, L. The inheritance of temperaments. *Journal of Personality,* 1973, *41,* 513–524.

Carment, D. W., Miles, C. G., & Cervin, V. B. Persuasiveness and persuasibility as related to intelligence and extraversion. *British Journal of Social and Clinical Psychology,* 1965, *4,* 1–7.

Cattell, R. B. *The Sixteen Personality Factor Questionnaire (The 16PF).* Champaign, Illinois: Institute for Personality and Ability Testing, 1963.

Child, D. Personality and social status. *British Journal of Social and Clinical Psychology,* 1966, 5, 196–199.

Claridge, G. S. *Drugs and human behaviour.* London: Allen Lane, 1970.

Claridge, G. S., & Herrington, R. N. Excitation–inhibition and the theory of neurosis: A study of the sedation threshold. In H. J. Eysenck (Ed.), *Experiments with drugs.* New York: Pergamon, 1963.

Coan, R. W. Personality variables associated with cigarette smoking. *Journal of Personality and Social Psychology,* 1973, *26,* 86–104.

Cook, M. Studies of orientation and proximity. Unpublished paper, University of Oxford, 1968.

Craske, S. A study of the relationship between personality and accident history. *British Journal of Medical Psychology,* 1968, *41,* 325–326.

Di Loreto, A. O. *Comparative psychotherapy: An experimental analysis.* Chicago: Aldine, 1971.

Duckworth, D. H. Personality, emotional state and perception of non-verbal communications. *Perceptual and Motor Skills,* 1975, *40,* 325–326.

Eaves, L. J., & Eysenck, H. J. Genetics and the development of social attitudes. *Nature,* 1974, *249,* 288–289.

Eaves, L. J., & Eysenck, H. J. The nature of extraversion: A genetical analysis. *Journal of Personality and Social Psychology,* 1975, *32,* 102–112.

Eysenck, H. J. *Dimensions of personality.* London: Routledge and Kegan Paul, 1947.

Eysenck, H. J. *The psychology of politics.* London: Routledge & Kegan Paul, 1954.

Eysenck, H. J. *The dynamics of anxiety and hysteria.* London: Routledge & Kegan Paul, 1957.

Eysenck, H. J. Personality and social attitudes. *Journal of Social Psychology,* 1961, *53,* 243–248.

Eysenck, H. J. *Crime and personality.* New York: Houghton-Mifflin, 1965.

Eysenck, H. J. *The biological basis of personality.* Springfield, Illinois: Charles C. Thomas, 1967.

Eysenck, H. J. A dimensional system of psychodiagnostics. In A. H. Mahrer (Ed.), *New approaches to personality classification.* New York: Columbia University Press, 1970. (a)

Eysenck, H. J. *The structure of human personality.* London: Methuen, 1970. (b)

Eysenck, H. J. *Readings in extraversion–introversion I: Basic processes.* London: Staples, 1971. (a)

Eysenck, H. J. *Readings in extraversion-introversion II: Fields of application.* London: Staples, 1971. (b)

Eysenck, H. J. Human typology, higher nervous activity and factor analysis. In V. D. Nebylitsyn & J. A. Gray (Eds.), *Biological bases of individual behavior.* New York: Academic Press, 1972. (a)

Eysenck, H. J. Primaries or second-order factors: A critical consideration of Cattell's 16PF battery. *British Journal of Social and Clinical Psychology,* 1972, *11,* 265–269. (b)

Eysenck, H. J. Personality and learning: The experimental approach. *Association of Educational Psychologists 1974 Conference Proceedings, London, 1974.*

Eysenck, H. J. *Sex and personality.* London: Open Books, 1976.

Eysenck, H. J., & Eysenck, S. B. G. *Manual of the Eysenck Personality Inventory.* London: University of London Press, 1964.

Eysenck, H. J., & Eysenck, S. B. G. *Manual for the EPI* (French edition). Paris: Centre for Applied Psychology, 1971.

Eysenck, H. J., & Eysenck, S. B. G. *Manual of the Eysenck Personality Questionnaire.* London: Hodder and Stroughton, 1975.

Eysenck, H. J., & Wilson, G. D. *Know your own personality.* New York: Penguin, 1976.

Eysenck, M. W. Extraversion, arousal, and retrieval from semantic memory. *Journal of Personality,* 1974, *42,* 319–331. (a)

Eysenck, M. W. Individual differences in speed of retrieval from semantic memory. *Journal of Research in Personality,* 1974, *8,* 307–323. (b)

Eysenck, S. B. G., & Eysenck, H. J. On the dual nature of extraversion. *British Journal of Social and Clinical Psychology,* 1963, *2,* 46–55.

Eysenck, S. B. G., & Eysenck, H. J. Personality and recidivism in borstal boys. *British Journal of Criminology,* 1974, *14,* 385–387.

Farley, F. H. Birth order and a two-dimensional assessment of personality. *Journal of Personality Assessment,* 1975, *39,* 151–153.

Fine, B. J. Introversion–extraversion and motor vehicle driver behavior. *Perceptual and Motor Skills,* 1963, *12,* 95–100.

Fine, B. J., & Danforth, A. V. Field-dependence, extraversion and perception of the vertical: Empirical and theoretical perspectives of the Rod and Frame Test. *Perceptual and Motor Skills,* 1975, *40,* 683–693.

Gale, A. Individual differences: Studies of extraversion and the EEG. In P. Kline (Ed.), *New approaches in psychological measurement.* London: Wiley, 1973.

Gibson, H. B., & Corcoran, M. B. Personality and differential susceptibility to hypnosis: Further replication and sex differences. Unpublished paper, Hatfield Polytechnic, England 1975.

Gibson, H. B., & Curran, J. D. Hypnotic susceptibility and personality: A replication study. *British Journal of Psychology,* 1974, *65,* 283–291.

Gray, J. A. The psychophysiological nature of introversion–extraversion: A modification of Eysenck's theory. In V. D. Nebylitsyn & J. A. Gray (Eds.), *Biological bases of individual behavior.* New York: Academic Press, 1972.

Gray, J. A. Causal theories of personality and how to test them. In J. R. Royce (Ed.), *Multivariate analysis and psychological theory.* London: Academic Press, 1973.

Gupta, B. S. Extraversion and reinforcement in verbal operant conditioning. Unpublished study, Guru Nanak University, Amritsar, India, 1974. (a)

Gupta, B. S. Stimulant and depressant drugs and kinaesthetic figural after-effect. *Psychopharmacologia,* 1974, *36,* 275–280. (b)

Hardy, C. A., & Nias, D. K. B. An investigation of physical and personality factors in learning to swim. *Personality,* 1971, *2,* 1–7.

Hendrick, C., & Brown, S. R. Introversion, extraversion, and interpersonal attraction. *Journal of Personality and Social Psychology,* 1971, *20,* 31–36.

Hilgard, E. R., & Bentler, P. M. Predicting hypnotizability from the Maudsley Personality Inventory. *British Journal of Psychology,* 1963, *54,* 63–69.

Hill, A. B. Extraversion and variety seeking in a monotonous task. *British Journal of Psychology,* 1975, *66,* 9–13.

Holmes, D. S. Pupillary response, conditioning, and personality. *Journal of Personality and Social Psychology,* 1967, *5,* 98–103.

Howarth, E., & Eysenck, H. J. Extraversion, arousal, and paired associate recall. *Journal of Experimental Research in Personality,* 1968, *3,* 114–116.

Iwawaki, S., Eysenck, S. B. G., & Eysenck, H. J. Differences in personality between Japanese and English. *Journal of Social Psychology,* 1977, in press.

Jessup, G., & Jessup, H. Validity of the Eysenck Personality Inventory in pilot selection. *Occupational Psychology,* 1971, *45,* 111–123.

Jung, C. G. *Psychological types.* New York: Harcourt-Brace, 1923.

Kendon, A., & Cook, M. The consistency of gaze patterns in social interaction. *British Journal of Psychology,* 1969, *60,* 481–494.

Kleinsmith, L. J., & Kaplan, S. Paired associate learning as a function of arousal and interpolated interval. *Journal of Experimental Psychology,* 1963, *65,* 190–193.

Lang, P. J., & Lazovik, A. D. Personality and hypnotic susceptibility. *Journal of Consulting Psychology,* 1962, *26,* 317–322.

Laverty, S. G. Sodium amatyl and extraversion. *Journal of Neurology, Neurosurgery and Psychiatry,* 1958, *21,* 50–54.

Leipold, W. D. Psychological distance in a dyadic interview as a function of introversion–extraversion, anxiety, social desirability, and stress. Unpublished doctoral dissertation, University of North Dakota, 1963.

Leith, G. O. M. Individual differences in learning: Interactions of personality and teaching methods. *Association of Educational Psychologists 1974 Conference Proceedings,* London, 1974.

Ludvigh, E. J., & Happ, D. Extraversion and preferred level of sensory stimulation. *British Journal of Psychology,* 1974, *65,* 359–365.

Lynn, R., & Hampson, S. L. National differences in extraversion and neuroticism. *British Journal of Social and Clinical Psychology,* 1975, *14,* 223–240.

Mann, R. D. A review of the relationships between personality and performance in small groups. *Psychological Bulletin,* 1959, *56,* 241–270.

McCormick, K., & Baer, D. J. Birth order, sex of subject, and sex of sibling as factors in extraversion and neuroticism in two-child families. *Psychological Reports,* 1975, *37,* 259–261.

McPeake, J. D., & DiMascio, A. Drug-personality interaction in the learning of a nonsense syllable task. *Journal of Psychiatric Research,* 1965, *3,* 105–111.

Meisels, M., & Canter, F. M. Personal space and personality characteristics: A non-confirmation. *Psychological Reports, 1970,* 27, 287–290.

Mobbs, N. A. Eye contact in relation to social introversion/extraversion. *British Journal of Social and Clinical Psychology,* 1968, *7,* 305–306.

Mohan, J., & Mohan, V. Personality and variability in esthetic evaluation. *Psychological Studies,* 1965, *10,* 57–60.

Mohan, V., & Kumar, D. Qualitative analysis of the performance of introverts and extraverts on the Standard Progressive Matrices. Paper read at Diamond Jubilee Session of Indian Science Congress, Chandigarh, India, January 1973.

Moss, P. D., & McEvedy, C. P. An epidemic of overbreathing among schoolgirls. *British Medical Journal,* 1966, *26,* 1295–1300.

Organ, D. W. Extraversion, locus of control, and individual differences in conditionability in organizations. *Journal of Applied Psychology,* 1975, *60,* 401–404.

Panek, R. E. Relation between autokinesis and introversion–extraversion. *Journal of Consulting Psychology,* 1962, *26,* 477.

Patterson, M., & Holmes, D. S. Social interaction correlates of the MPI extraversion–introversion scale. *American Psychologist,* 1966, *21,* 724–725.

Petrie, A. *Personality and the frontal lobes.* London: Routledge and Kegan Paul, 1952.

Porter, E., Argyle, M., & Salter, V. What is signalled by proximity? *Perceptual and Motor Skills,* 1970, *30,* 39–42.

Rim, Y., & Seidenross, H. Personality and response to pressure from peers vs. adults. *Personality,* 1971, *2,* 35–43.

Roberts, F. J. Some psychological factors in religious conversion. *British Journal of Social and Clinical Psychology,* 1965, *4,* 185–187.

Rutter, D. R., Morley, I. E., & Graham, J. C. Visual interaction in a group of introverts and extraverts. *European Journal of Social Psychology,* 1972, *2,* 371–384.

Schachter, S. *The psychology of affiliation.* Stanford, Calif.: Stanford University Press, 1959.

Schalling, D., Levander, S. E., & Wredenmark, G. Semantic generalization as reflecting cortical functions in extravert and introvert subjects. Unpublished paper, University of Stockholm, 1975.

Sewell, A. F., & Heisler, J. T. Personality correlates of proximity preferences. *Journal of Psychology,* 1973, *85,* 151–155.

Shapiro, K. J., & Alexander, I. E. Extraversion–introversion, affiliation, and anxiety. *Journal of Personality,* 1969, *37,* 387–406.

Shaw, L., & Sichel, H. *Accident proneness.* New York: Pergamon, 1971.

Shields, J. Heredity and environment. In H. J. Eysenck & G. D. Wilson (Eds.), *A textbook of human psychology.* Baltimore: University Park Press, 1976.

Sinha, A. K. P., & Ojha, H. An experimental study of the operation of prestige suggestions in extraverts and introverts. *Journal of Social Psychology,* 1963, *61,* 29–34.

Stern, H., & Grosz, H. J. Verbal interactions in group psychotherapy between patients with similar and dissimilar personalities. *Psychological Reports* 1966, *7,* 1111–1114.

Thackray, R. I., Jones, K. N., & Touchstone, R. M. Personality and physiological correlates of performance decrement on a monotonous task requiring sustained attention. *British Journal of Psychology,* 1974, *65,* 351–358.

Tolor, A. Effects of procedural variations in measuring interpersonal distance by means of representational space. *Psychological Reports,* 1975, *36,* 475–491.

Vingoe, F. J., & Antonoff, S. R. Personality characteristics of good judges of others. *Journal of Counseling Psychology,* 1968, *15,* 91–93.

Wakefield, J. A., Yom, B. L., Bradley, P. E., Doughtie, E. B., & Cox, J. A. Eysenck's personality dimensions: A model for the MMPI. *British Journal of Social and Clinical Psychology,* 1974, *13,* 413–420.

Walker, E. L. Action decrement and its relation to learning. *Psychological Review,* 1958, *65,* 129–142.

Wankowski, J. A. *Temperament, motivation and academic achievement.* University of Birmingham Educational Survey and Counselling Unit, 1973.

Weisen, A. Differential reinforcing effects of onset and offset of stimulation on the operant behavior of normals, neurotics, and psychopaths. Unpublished doctoral dissertation, University of Florida, 1965.

Williams, J. L. Personal space and its relation to extraversion–introversion. Unpublished master's thesis, University of Alberta, 1963.

Williams, J. L. Personal space and its relation to extraversion–introversion. *Canadian Journal of Behavioral Science,* 1971, *3,* 156–160.

Wilson, G. D., & Gregson, R. A. M. Effects of illumination on the perceived intensity of acid tastes. *Australian Journal of Psychology,* 1967, *19,* 69–73.

Wilson, G. D., & Nias, D. K. B. *The mystery of love.* New York: Quadrangle, 1976.

Zajonc, R. B. Social facilitation. *Science,* 1965, *14,* 269–274.

6
Internal-External Control of Reinforcement

Bonnie R. Strickland[1]

University of Massachusetts–Amherst

Personality variables come and go but people continue to behave in their complex and unpredictable ways. The history of personality theory is filled with descriptions of personal characteristics thought to be predictive of human behavior. Early psychologists focused on instincts and later personologists devised elaborate conceptualizations of needs and motives. Many of the promising personality variables fell into disuse as investigators continually failed to predict behavior. Moreover, the sixties gave rise to an increasing debate between the "trait" psychologists and the "situationalists." The first group was composed of researchers who believed that certain, somewhat enduring, characteristics of persons could be identified and would provide explanation of how it is that people come to behave as they do. The latter group argued that personality variables were notoriously poor predictors because situational determinants override whatever fragile personality traits people carry with them. Throughout the debate, however, a number of investigators continued to look at individual belief systems, recognizing the importance of situational determinants, but still convinced that a person's expectancies about oneself in relation to one's world are important in influencing that individual's behavior. One expectancy variable that has had increasing impact on psychological experimentation has been the internal versus external control of reinforcement dimension (I–E). Simply stated, I–E refers to the degree to which an individual perceives that the events

[1] Any review of a topic as exhaustive as research on locus of control will almost of necessity fail to cover many important and significant experiments. In this chapter, I have tried to cite some of the early studies that set the framework for the major areas of research on I–E that followed as well as to choose representative later studies that extended the I–E implications. No doubt I have overlooked important work. As a good internal, I take responsibility for these omissions. As a good external, I attribute these to forces outside my control and hope I will be forgiven.

that happen to him or her are dependent on his or her own behavior or are the result of fate, luck, chance, or powers beyond one's personal control and understanding. Embedded firmly in a social learning theory (Rotter, 1954; Rotter, Chance, & Phares, 1972), which stresses the role of both expectancy and reinforcement value in behavior, beliefs about internal versus external control of reinforcement have been found to be predictive of, and related to, a wide range of behaviors across numerous situations with diverse groups of people. Extensive reviews attest to the impact of research on locus of control (Hill, Chapman, & Wuertzer, 1974; Joe, 1971; Lefcourt, 1966, 1972; MacDonald, 1973; Phares, 1973; Rotter, 1966; Strickland, 1973b; Throop & MacDonald, 1971) and literally hundreds of studies investigating this dimension are recorded in the psychological literature or are in progress. Books devoted entirely to research on locus of control are published (Phares, 1976) including one by Lefcourt (1976) who uses the internal/external expectancy dimension to address the questions concerning freedom and determinism raised by Skinner (1971). Lefcourt maintains that a person's belief that one can control one's own fate is necessary to resist tyranny and to survive and enjoy life. He argues that a belief in internal control, even if an illusion, leads people to live adaptively. Carlson, in the 1975 *Annual Review of Psychology,* remarks that locus of control is "Undoubtedly, . . . the single most popular topic in current personality research." She goes on to state, however, that "the internal–external control variable appears to be one of the fads which periodically captures the field [p. 396]." Whether the locus of control dimension serves as a rich base on which to build more precise predictions about behavior or whether it fades with the fads of yesteryear depends to a large extent on present and future research with this variable. The purpose of this chapter is to review the history of research on locus of control expectancies in relation to social behavior, to survey some of the most salient current studies, and to raise some problems and issues surrounding internal/external expectancies.

THEORETICAL BACKGROUND

Research on the internal/external dimension, also called locus of control, first began in the psychological laboratories of Ohio State University in the mid-1950s. Phares (1957) demonstrated that a subject's perception of locus of control was related to expectancies about success or failure in a judgement task. When subjects perceived success at the task to be dependent on skill, they responded to a past experience of success or failure by appropriately wagering on their next judgement. Subjects given chance instructions were more likely to adopt a "gambler's" stance since, apparently, their success was dependent on luck. Basically, Phares found that subjects predicted their potential success on a task according to whether or not they perceived task results as dependent on their performance or as being capricious and unpredictable because results were due to luck or chance. When subjects believed their performance to affect results, they made appropriate and realistic judgements which followed their past performance. In chance or luck conditions, subjects made judgements unrelated to and independent of their performance.

James and Rotter (1958) found that varying instructions as to whether a task was to be considered skill– or chance-based also influenced extinction trials after acquisition. Subjects under chance instructions showed the usual greater resistance to extinction in a partial (50%) reinforcement condition. Apparently, when told that performance depended on chance, the subject continued to keep trying during extinction as if the reinforcement might "magically" appear again. Under 100% reinforcement conditions subjects in the chance condition extinguished more quickly as if their luck had changed. When subjects were given skill instructions, a reversal of the reinforcement/extinction results occurred in that subjects in the partial reinforcement condition extinguished more quickly and in the 100% reinforcement condition, more slowly. These results suggest that individuals who are operating as if they are skilled in a certain task and who have been led to believe that they have successfully (with 100% success feedback) mastered the task may find it difficult to accept the fact that their performance is no longer proficient.

James (1957) reported differences between skill and chance groups in acquisition of expectancies and significantly greater generalization of expectancies from one task to another under skill rather than chance instructions. Several other investigators (Holden & Rotter, 1962; Rotter, Liverant, & Crowne, 1961) also found that the almost universally held assumption of the superiority of partial over 100% reinforcement during extinction appeared to be valid only in chance situations. The importance of all these studies has to do with the fact that human learning and/or performance appears not only to be a function of reinforcement but also is dependent on the individual's perception of locus of control of reinforcement.

Knowing that situational differences in relation to instructions or perceptions about skill and chance could so dramatically affect performance, a naturally occurring question had to do with the degree to which individuals hold more generalized expectancies about internal versus external locus of control. The IE concept was defined:

> When a reinforcement is perceived by the subject as following some action of his own but not being entirely contingent upon his action, then, in our culture, it is typically perceived as the result of luck, chance, fate, as under the control of powerful others, or as unpredictable because of the great complexity of the forces surrounding him. When the event is interpreted in this way by an individual, we have labeled this a belief in *external control.* If the person perceives that the event is contingent upon his own behavior or his relatively permanent characteristics, we have termed this a belief in *internal control* [Rotter, 1966, p.1].

Thus, the I–E dimension is considered an expectancy variable within a social learning model which basically describes behavior as a function of expectancies, reinforcement, and the impact of psychological situations (Rotter, 1954; Rotter, Chance, & Phares, 1972). The general formula is that the potential for a behavior to occur in any specific psychological situation is a function of the expectancy that the behavior will lead to a particular reinforcement in that situation and the value of that reinforcement. Expectancies in each situation are determined not only by specific experiences in that situation, but also, to some varying extent, by experiences in other situations which the individual perceives as similar. Generalized expectancies would be most predictive in novel or ambiguous situations and relatively less important when an individual finds himself in a situation similar to experiences he has had in the past, about which he has some understanding. *Specific* expectancies in certain situations similar to those encountered in the past lead to the greatest degree of prediction, while *generalized* expectancies may be predictive across more diverse situations although to a more moderate degree. It is also important to remember that within the social learning model, I–E is only one of the potential determinants of behavior. For the most precise prediction, reinforcement value and the situation must also be taken into account. Individuals are likely to respond differently depending on how important it is to them to receive the reinforcements that may be forthcoming in a particular situation. For some individuals, academic achievement is a particularly valued accomplishment while others prefer recognition through physical or athletic skills. These two groupings of people would be expected to respond quite differently when offered the opportunity to go to the library or to the gymnasium. Moreover, the structure of a given situation may override the individual's characteristic mode of responding. The scholar will quickly leave the library when a fire alarm sounds and the athlete will retire to the shower when hurt or defeated. The prediction of complex human behavior is not a simple matter but calls for attention to a number of dimensions. Rotter's social-learning theory has emphasized both cognition and behavior, expectancy and reinforcement, and individual characteristics plus situational influences. Possibly because of propitious blending, the theory is still viable and predictive after some 20 years of investigation and research.

Aside from the reasons inherent in the theoretical development of locus of control expectancies, the increased popularity of the I–E construct may also depend, to some large extent, on a shifting perception of the problems and difficulties that face contemporary Americans. In a time of considerable economic growth following World War II, personality researchers were particularly intrigued with investigations of individual achievement motivation. Additionally, a large number of psychologists turned their attention to the unbelievable cruelties of the Nazi extermination camps and wondered as to how they could have come into being. Much of this focus, again, was on the individual, as investigators considered the makeup of the "fascist" character. Generally, personality patterns of specific motives and needs were described and investigated. Individuals were pictured as being able to effect change and assume responsibility. Not only was a person accountable for his or her own behavior but could also design and participate in social structures which facilitate human productivity and happiness. Through the decade of the sixties, however, individual Americans appeared to become increasingly disillusioned with the possibilities of individual action. It was hard to believe that one person, working alone, like Lee Harvey Oswald or James Earl Ray, could change the course of this nation's history. It was even more difficult to believe that an individual could effect some positive social change through his or her lone voice or vote. The effects of large-scale social actions such as the Civil Rights movement and protests against the Vietnam War were a long time coming to fruition and were painfully slow and disheartening for those involved. No wonder then, people began to attend to the relationships between themselves and the world in which they found themselves. Feelings of powerlessness and concerns about control constitute a natural laboratory for the investigation of generalized expectancies about behavior and reinforcement. A large number of psychologists turned their attention to describing perceptions about locus of control and individual differences in these beliefs.

Development of I–E Assessment Instruments

Within the social learning framework, a number of early assessment instruments were devised and investigators began to identify the degree to which individuals appear to hold generalized expectancies about internal versus external control of reinforcement. The primary scale which grew out of the early research was one devised by Rotter (1966) based on the initial instruments of James and Phares. The scale uses a forced-choice format. The items were culled from a much larger pool of items which had been written to have face validity. Items were selected from the larger pool only if both alternative answers were feasible possibilities for a large number of subjects. Items were also selected on the basis of a moderate to high correlation with total score and a low correlation with the Marlowe–Crowne Social Desirability scale (Crowne & Marlowe, 1960). Internal consistency estimates on the scale are stable and test–retest reliabilities substantial. Moreover, each item related to at least one of two criterion behaviors, namely trials to extinction in a laboratory task (Rotter, Liverant, & Crowne, 1961) and the attempts of tubercular patients to actively understand their disorder and improve their life conditions (Seeman & Evans, 1962). These two-pronged criteria underscore and foreshadow the subsequent research with the locus of control dimension in that, from the beginning, I–E appeared to be predictive of both laboratory and field behaviors. The I–E variable has been investigated not only in the most precise of experimental laboratory situations but also in hospitals, schools, and even in the streets during the social-action movements of the sixties.

When the I–E scale was first developed, early researchers suggested that responses to the instrument reflected one general factor (Franklin, 1963; Rotter, 1966). Later factor analyses of the original scale and subsequent measures of I–E (Gurin, Gurin, Lao, & Beattie, 1969; Mirels, 1970; Nowicki, in press; Reid & Ware, 1973, 1974) suggest several separate factors although these vary from population to population and across sexes. This development gave rise to a continuing debate about the uni- versus multidimensionality of the I–E construct; that is, does I–E represent a general belief about internal versus external control of reinforcement or are I–E expectancies comprised of a number of different components?

While the Rotter scale continues to be used as a generalized measure for adults, several new instruments have been developed or designed to tap specific factors assumed to be embedded within locus of control expectancies. Collins (1974) converted Rotter's 23 forced-choice items to 46 Likert scale items and administered these to 300 college student subjects. Factor analyses of the responses revealed evidence of a common theme of internal–external control of reinforcement running through the items but superimposed on this were 4 distinct factors, belief in a difficult world, a just world, a predictable world, and a politically responsive world. In a similar vein, Levenson (1972, 1973c; Levenson & Miller, 1976) with a modified version of Rotter's items finds an internal factor and reports 2 components of the external dimension, a belief that events are controlled by powerful others and a belief that the world is unordered (chance) (see Table 1).

In using the various I–E scales the investigator is faced with the decision as to whether to consider the assumed generality of I–E or to focus on specific factors. To further complicate matters, an investigator also has the choice of designing an I–E measure specific to a certain situation or characteristic. For example, some investigators have developed instruments to tap I–E expectancies in relation to beliefs about health and physical well-being (Kirscht, 1974; Wallston, Maides, & Wallston, 1976; Wallston, Wallston, Kaplan, & Maides, in press).

The Wallstons and their colleagues find their specific IE/health scale to improve prediction of health-related behavior. For example, with their measure but not with the Rotter scale, they were able to identify internals, in contrast to individuals whom they call externals, who sought additonal health information when given the opportunity. Obviously, experimenters have wide options and their investigations are a function of their theoretical stance and their own bias and focus.

Investigators are also plagued with problems of definition of the I–E construct. Some investigators consider I–E to reflect beliefs about contingencies of reinforcement, both positive and negative. Others focus more on the "control" aspects of I–E, that is if an individual perceives reinforcement as dependent on his/her behavior then one will naturally engage in behaviors that lead to reinforcement. Internal individuals will be more controlling, will expect to succeed, and so on. Currently, the definition of I–E, in spite of the rather clear statements of Rotter and others, remains cloudy and subject to the interpretation of the individual investigator or theorist. Some experimenters, most notably Virginia Crandall (Crandall, 1973; Crandall, Katkovsky, & Crandall, 1965), have continually emphasized that prediction can be improved by specifying the valence of the subsequent reinforcement, that is, are the reinforcing events positive or negative? It is quite conceivable that some individuals expect positive events to occur in their lives due to their own effort and also believe negative events to be a result of luck, fate, etc. Others may believe the exact opposite in that they are responsible for the tragic things that happen to them but positive events result from a benevolent other or from fate, or "lucky breaks." The differing interpretations of I–E and the alleged shortcomings of the psychometric instruments have clearly been sources of considerable confusion in I–E research. In spite of these drawbacks, however, research has continued unabated and, as with any theoretical construct, a more definite understanding of I–E depends on further investigation.

Because of the widespread influence and importance of expectancies in relation to adult behavior, it was only natural that investigators would also turn their attention to the development of I–E expectancies in children and the relationship of these beliefs to children's performance. To this end, a number of measures more appropriate for children were developed (Adams-Webber, 1969; Battle & Rotter, 1963; Bialer, 1961; Crandall, Katkovsky, & Crandall, 1965; Dies, 1968; Gruen, 1971; Gruen, Korte, & Baum, 1974; Mischel, Zeiss, & Zeiss, 1974; Stephens & Delys, 1973).

Through the years, the Crandall Intellectual Achievement Responsibility (IAR) measure has been the most popular instrument for assessing I–E beliefs in children. This scale is composed of items specific to intellectual and academic pursuits and subjects must note responsibility for both negative and positive events. Because of the specificity of items within the IAR, Nowicki and Strickland (1973) developed another measure to assess generalized I–E in children (see Table 2). Items in this scale not only reflect beliefs about intellectual and school-related behaviors but also other general perceptions such as superstition and beliefs about behavior/reinforcement contingencies in relation to parents and friends. Test–retest reliabilities and internal consistency estimates are high. Comparable forms were also developed for other populations ranging from preschool and primary youngsters (Nowicki & Duke, 1974b) through college age and adult (Nowicki & Duke, 1974a) to geriatric samples (Duke, Shaheen, &

TABLE 1

Internal, Powerful Others, and Chance Locus of Control Scales[a]

Directions: On the back of this page is a series of attitude statements. Each represents a commonly held opinion and there are no right or wrong answers. You will probably disagree with some items and agree with others. We are interested in the extent to which you agree or disagree with such matters of opinion.

Read each statement carefully. Then indicate the extent to which you agree or disagree by circling the number in front of each statement.[b] The numbers and their meaning are indicated below:

If you agree strongly – circle +3
If you agree somewhat – circle +2
If you agree slightly – circle +1

If you disagree slightly – circle –1
If you disagree somewhat – circle –2
If you disagree strongly – circle –3

First impressions are usually best in such matters. Read each statement, decide if you agree or disagree and the strength of your opinion, and then circle the appropriate number in front of the statement. *Give your opinion on every statement.*

If you find that the numbers to be used in answering do not adequately indicate your own opinion, use the one which is *closest* to the way you feel. Your responses will be kept confidential.

Internal Scale

1. Whether or not I get to be a leader depends mostly on my ability.
4. Whether or not I get into a car accident depends mostly on how good a driver I am.
5. When I make plans, I am almost certain to make them work.
9. How many friends I have depends on how nice a person I am.
18. I can pretty much determine what will happen in my life.
19. I am usually able to protect my personal interests.
21. When I get what I want, it's usually because I worked hard for it.
23. My life is determined by my own actions.

Powerful Others Scale

3. I feel like what happens in my life is mostly determined by powerful people.
8. Although I might have good ability, I will not be given leadership responsibility without appealing to those in positions of power.
11. My life is chiefly controlled by powerful others.
13. People like myself have very little chance of protecting our personal interests when they conflict with those of strong pressure groups.
15. Getting what I want requires pleasing those people above me.
17. If important people were to decide they didn't like me, I probably wouldn't make many friends.
20. Whether or not I get into a car accident depends mostly on the other driver.
22. In order to have my plans work, I make sure that they fit in with the desires of people who have power over me.

Chance Scale

2. To a great extent my life is controlled by accidental happenings.
6. Often there is no chance of protecting my personal interest from bad luck happenings.
7. When I get what I want, it's usually because I'm lucky.
10. I have often found that what is going to happen will happen.
12. Whether or not I get into a car accident is mostly a matter of luck.
14. It's not always wise for me to plan too far ahead because many things turn out to be a matter of good or bad fortune.
16. Whether or not I get to be a leader depends on whether I'm lucky enough to be in the right place at the right time.
24. It's chiefly a matter of fate whether or not I have a few friends or many friends.

---

[a] From Levenson and Miller (1976). Copyright 1976 by the American Psychological Association. Reproduced by permission.

[b] All 24 locus of control items (8 for each scale) are administered. In the format used for subjects, each item is preceded by the following 6-point scale: +3 +2 +1 −1 −2 −3. Subject's score on each scale is the sum of his or her responses on the eight items in the scale. The higher the score the greater the subject's degree of expectancy for the particular locus of control tapped by the scale. The numbering represents the order in which items appear.

TABLE 2.

Nowicki–Strickland Locus of Control Scale for Children[a,b]

1. Do you believe that most problems will solve themselves if you just don't fool with them? (Yes)
2. Do you believe that you can stop yourself from catching a cold? (No)
3. Are some kids just born lucky? (Yes)
4. Most of the time do you feel that getting good grades means a great deal to you? (No)
5. Are you often blamed for things that just aren't your fault? (Yes)
6. Do you believe that if somebody studies hard enough he or she can pass any subject? (No)
7. Do you feel that most of the time it doesn't pay to try hard because things never turn out right anyway? (Yes)
8. Do you feel that if things start out well in the morning that it's going to be a good day no matter what you do? (Yes)
9. Do you feel that most of the time parents listen to what their children have to say? (No)
10. Do you believe that wishing can make good things happen? (Yes)
11. When you get punished does it usually seem it's for no good reason at all? (Yes)
12. Most of the time do you find it hard to change a friend's (mind) opinion? (Yes)
13. Do you think that cheering more than luck helps a team to win? (No)
14. Do you feel that it's nearly impossible to change your parent's mind about anything? (Yes)
15. Do you believe that your parents should allow you to make most of your own decisions? (No)
16. Do you feel that when you do something wrong there's very little you can do to make it right? (Yes)
17. Do you believe that most kids are just born good at sports? (Yes)
18. Are most of the other kids your age stronger than you are? (Yes)
19. Do you feel that one of the best ways to handle most problems is just not to think about them? (Yes)
20. Do you feel that you have a lot of choice in deciding who your friends are? (No)
21. If you find a four leaf clover do you believe that it might bring you good luck? (Yes)
22. Do you often feel that whether you do your homework has much to do with what kind of grades you get? (No)

23. Do you feel that when a kid your age decides to hit you, there's little you can do to stop him or her? (Yes)
24. Have you ever had a good luck charm? (Yes)
25. Do you believe that whether or not people like you depends on how you act? (No)
26. Will your parents usually help you if you ask them? (No)
27. Have you felt that when people were mean to you it was usually for no reason at all? (Yes)
28. Most of the time, do you feel that you can change what might happen tomorrow by what you do today? (No)
29. Do you believe that when bad things are going to happen they just are going to happen no matter what you try to do to stop them? (Yes)
30. Do you think that kids can get their own way if they just keep trying? (No)
31. Most of the time do you find it useless to try to get your own way at home? (Yes)
32. Do you feel that when good things happen they happen because of hard work? (No)
33. Do you feel that when somebody your age wants to be your enemy there's little you can do to change matters? (Yes)
34. Do you feel that it's easy to get friends to do what you want them to? (No)
35. Do you usually feel that you have little to say about what you get to eat at home? (Yes)
36. Do you feel that when someone doesn't like you there's little you can do about it? (Yes)
37. Do you usually feel that it's almost useless to try in school because most other children are just plain smarter than you are? (Yes)
38. Are you the kind of person who believes that planning ahead makes things turn out better? (No)
39. Most of the time, do you feel that you have little to say about what your family decides to do? (Yes)
40. Do you think it's better to be smart than to be lucky? (No)

---

[a] From Nowicki and Strickland (1973). Copyright 1973 by the American Psychological Association. Reproduced by permission.

[b] The test is usually administered by giving each subject a test form with yes-no alternatives. The experimenter then reads each question, usually twice, and has the subject mark the answer that is appropriate for that individual. The external answer is given in parentheses after each scale item. Subject's score is the total number of items answered in the external direction.

Nowicki, 1974). These additional forms offer obvious advantages in regard to longitudinal and developmental research.

MAJOR AREAS OF RESEARCH

Conformity and Resistance to Social Influence

Once the original I–E scale was available for researchers, a number of experimenters began to explore the network of behaviors associated with locus of control beliefs. One of the first behaviors investigated was conformity. Odell (1959) had found a .33 ($p < .05$) correlation between a prototype of the Rotter I–E scale and Barron's Independence of Judgement scale, with externals more likely to be identified as conforming. Crowne and Liverant (1963), using a typical Asch-type conformity paradigm, then investigated behavioral conformity. Following the responses of confederates, who gave judgements of stimuli at variance with actual presentations, subjects were asked to rate how certain they felt about their own judgements and were given $10.00 in quarters to bet on their responses. As expected, subjects assessed as external conformed more to inaccurate responses, which were confidently stated by the confederates, and bet more money on the judgement of their peers than on their own independent perceptions and judgements. Internals[2] were less likely than externals to yield to pressure from others and appeared more likely to trust their own responses.

Other investigators became immediately interested in the ways in which locus of control expectancies might be predictive of responses to other forms of social influence. In a verbal conditioning experiment, described as a word-association task, Strickland (1970), by head nod and subtle verbal cues, attempted to influence subjects by reinforcing a desired verbal response, namely verbs. During acquisition trials, internal subjects denied being influence and during extinction, when the experimenter was no longer reinforcing verbs, were more likely to give verb responses in an almost oppositional manner. In a similar experiment, Getter (1966) found evidence of what he called "latent conditioning" of verbal responses during extinction for internal subjects. Gore (1962) showed TAT cards to subjects and tried to influence them to produce longer stories by subtle and covert nonverbal cues. Internals shortened stories to the subtly reinforced cards with a seeming reluctance to allow themselves to be manipulated or controlled by the experimenter. Within an attitude change paradigm, Ritchie and Phares

[2] The terms "internal" and "external" are used here to refer to individuals who have been classified on the basis of responses to the Rotter scale, or other I–E measures, as falling below/above the mean or median in a particular sample or, in some instances, in the lower or upper grouping (such as lower/upper one third) of a distribution of I–E scores. On the Rotter scale, scoring is such that a high numerical score is "external" while a low score is "internal." The use of these terms is not meant to imply a typology since individuals fall along a continuum of I–E responding.

(1969) were able to demonstrate that both internals and externals were likely to shift opinions about national budget expenditures but differentially. Externals responded more in high prestige conditions, when arguments were attributed to a high government official, than to a low-prestige figure. Internals appeared less impressed by the source of information but did respond to the content of the information provided. Ryckman, Rodda, and Sherman (1972) subjected college students to influence from a high prestige source who was depicted as having either relevant or irrelevant expertise concerning student activism. Again, externals were more likely than internals to change opinions regardless of the relevance of expertise. Biondo and MacDonald (1971) found externals to be more compliant than internals when asked to rate grading procedures after high- and low-influence communication about course grades. As in the verbal conditioning studies, internals reacted negatively to the high influence message. Even in fantasy production, Johnson, Ackerman, Frank, and Fionda (1968) found internals to describe story "heroes" as resisting pressure. Doctor (1971) replicated the verbal conditioning studies and found externals who were aware of the reinforcement contingencies to give the highest rate of the desired responses. When internals were aware, they showed no clear disposition as to either respond to influence or oppose it. Ude and Vogler (1969) report internals to become aware of verbal conditioning cues to a greater extent than externals. Jolley and Spielberger (1973) report an interactive effect of I–E and trait anxiety on verbal conditioning among aware subjects but no significant main effect for either variable alone. Alegre and Murray (1974) found greater verbal conditioning and intent to cooperate with the experimenter among externals in contrast to internals. While the preponderance of research evidence suggests a relationship between responses to verbal conditioning demands and I–E expectancies, it should be noted that Baron (1969) and Lichtenstein and Crain (1969) have failed to find this expected relationship.

Generally, in regard to social influence the bulk of the I–E research does support the contention that externals are more compliant and internals appear to be less influenced by experimental demands when they perceive that they are being subtly manipulated. The findings are not so clear when internals are fully aware of the demands of the situation. When conditions are straightforward, internals may or may not cooperate with the experimenter's demands, possibly depending on the nuances of the experimenter's voice and behaviors, and the subject's perception of what is desired of him or her or what is desirable for him or her. Responses of internals also appear to be determined by the degree to which they can take responsibility for some of their own behavior and not react as pawns in the experiment. For example, Sherman (1973) had subjects either read persuasive messages about lowering the voting age or else write essays which opposed their original beliefs about the voting issue. When internals wrote essays, they were more likely to change their attitudes, suggesting that when they have committed themselves to an argument, they are more likely to follow through. Externals, on the other hand, responded more to reading the persuasive statements.

If internals, in contrast to externals, are more resistant to social influence, then one would expect I–E beliefs to be substantially related to reactance tendencies. Brehm (1966) has proposed that the elimination, or threatened elimination, of the freedom to engage in an available alternative behavior will result in a motivational arousal to recover that freedom, which he calls reactance. Although Jones (1970) found no relationship between I–E scores and a measure of reactance arousal, a case can still be made conceptually for the analogy between Brehm's distinction between personal and impersonal modes of elimination of freedom and internal versus external expectancies about locus of control. Cherulnik and Citrin (1974) hypothesized that internals would exhibit greater reactance, in the form of reporting an increase in the desirability of eliminated freedoms, when this occurred for personal reasons. They predicted that the relative magnitude of the effect would be reversed for externals, who, they believed, would be more reactive in the impersonal mode. The experimenters had all their subjects rate four contemporary posters as to attractiveness. Two groups of subjects were told that they would receive a poster two days later while a third group served as a control and simply rerated the posters following a two-day time span. When the experimental subjects arrived for their posters, one group was told that one poster, the one rated third highest originally, was unavailable, due to a loss in transit (impersonal mode). The other group was told that loss was due to some unspecified personal characteristic (personal mode). Subjects were then asked to rerate the posters. Control subjects did not change their ratings of the "lost" poster but, in the experimental groups, internals responded more strongly to the personal in contrast to the impersonal elimination of freedom and increased their favorability ratings for that poster. The results were reversed for externals.

Generally, then, I–E appears to be clearly related to conforming and compliant behavior. Internals are more likely to maintain their own individual judgement in the face of contrasting evidence from external sources that call their perceptions and/or behaviors into question. Externals, on the other hand, succumb to pressure from others particularly when the outside source is seen as prestigious or an "expert." Moreover, internals not only appear to resist influence but react more strongly than externals to the loss of personal freedom. Internals do this in some cases by engaging in behaviors which are oppositional to the responses desired by the experimental agent who is attempting to manipulate or change behavior. Internals appear to want to "keep the reins in their own hands," behaving in ways which facilitate independence and negate the other's influence.

Information Seeking and Task Performance

If externals respond to the demands of others more readily than internals and are more susceptible to various kinds of social influence, then an interesting question is raised as to just what cues and sources of information internals do rely on. Do internals and externals use different strategies to gather information, utilize cues, and engage in goal-directed behaviors? The original studies investigating locus of control beliefs and information seeking were conducted by Seeman (1963) and Seeman and Evans (1962). Within a prison population, Seeman matched young inmates on intellectual measures and then presented them with information about prison regulations and opportunities for parole. When retested, internal prisoners were significantly more likely than externals to recall salient information about the prison and their responsibilities for release. Seeman and Evans also assessed hospitalized tubercular patients as to I–E beliefs and found internal patients to know more about their disease and to ask more questions of the health staff than external patients. In a later study, Pines and Julian (1972) found internals in problem-solving situations to be particularly oriented toward gathering and processing information while externals seemed more concerned with social requirements and doing what was expected of them in the experimental situation. Additionally, Pines (1973) investigated those stimulus conditions which instigate task-relevant information processing to ascertain if internals and externals differ systematically in responding to physical and social reality as sources of information. In a free-recall memory task, Pines found internals to respond more to task opportunities to organize the to-be-remembered words than the externals. Additional time for recall of the verbal material was a more potent facilitator of the internals' memory performance than of the externals'. The presence of an observing audience facilitated the externals' retention but had no effect on the internals. Lefcourt, Hogg, and Sordoni found internals to appear more comfortable when working in isolation than when fully "observed" by a video camera behind a mirror (cited in Lefcourt, 1976). Opposite results were found for externals. Several other investigators (Baron, Cowan, Ganz, & McDonald, 1974; Baron & Ganz, 1972; Fitz, 1971) also report that internals appear distracted and impeded by social stimuli when they are called upon to perform certain tasks, while the performance of externals is enhanced.

In contrast to externals, internals take more time to deliberate about decisions in difficult, skill-demanding, or intellectual tasks (Gozali, Cleary, Walster, & Gozali, 1973; Julian & Katz, 1968; Lefcourt, Lewis, & Silverman, 1968; Rotter & Mulry, 1965) and appear to value success more in difficult tasks as well as to be more dissatisfied after failure in easy tasks (Karabenick, 1972). When involved in cognitive tasks, internals appear to outperform externals on both intentional and incidental learning (DuCette & Wolk, 1973; Wolk & DuCette, 1974). Ducette and Wolk (1972) also report internals to be better at finding cues which facilitate more accurate judgements, at recalling performance more adequately, and making better use of information for estimating subsequent performance than do externals. Lefcourt and his colleagues (Lefcourt, Gronnerud, & McDonald, 1973; Lefcourt & Wine, 1969), adding field dependence/independence as a mediating variable, report high field independent internals to be more cognitively alert than other I–E/field dependence groupings. Internals appear to be able to come to terms with experimental uncertainty (Lefcourt, Sordoni, & Sordoni, 1974) and even to engage in mirthful responses to dissonance and interpersonal role playing (Lefcourt, Antrobus, & Hogg, 1974).

All in all, then, internals appear to depend on their own abilities and interpretations of the task demands while the externals respond to social influence. Internals take time to deliberate about task performance, value success, and focus on the relevant stimulus cues of a task without leaning on others for explication or social reinforcement. In fact, internals may even be impeded in performance by social stimuli. They appear to wish to focus directly on task demands in an effort to facilitate performance without distraction by social pressure. This strategy appears to work for internals in that they do outperform externals on certain cognitive tasks.

Attribution Processes

The findings that internals and externals attend to, and rely on, different kinds of cues provided by the self and the environment suggest that they may differ in their causal attributions about their own and others' behavior. Logically, then, one would expect locus of control beliefs to play a role in the attribution process. For example, within deCharms' (1968) theory, internals should act like Origins, people who perceive their behavior to be determined by their own choosing, and externals like Pawns, people who perceive their behavior to be determined by outside forces. An assumption pervasive in the psychological literature is that a sense of control implies high perceived choice (Kelley, 1967; Lefcourt, 1976). Empirically, the locus of control dimension does appear to be related to freedom of choice. Jones, Worchel, Goethals, and Grumet (1971) found that the attributions of internals were more affected by perceived choice than those of externals in regard to a target person's freedom in taking attitudinally relevant actions. In a series of studies, Harvey and his colleagues also found beliefs about internal control related to perceived choice, specifically when options were positively valenced (Harvey, Barnes, Sperry, & Harris, 1974; Harvey & Harris, 1975; Harvey & Johnston, 1973). Steiner (1970) notes that I–E beliefs may parallel beliefs about perceived freedom but cautions that the valence of sources of control must be considered.

Locus of control beliefs also appear to hold implications for the attribution of responsibility for "real-life" accidents. Phares and Wilson (1972) had subjects read case descriptions, differing in situational ambiguity and outcome severity, of auto accidents and assign four different ratings of degree of reaponsibility to the individuals involved. Internals were found to attribute a higher level of responsibility for accidents than externals. In cases with severe outcomes, internals attributed more responsibility when cases were ambiguous although when descriptions were highly structured, no I–E differences appeared. When outcomes were not severe, internals and externals did not differ in responsibility attribution under ambiguous conditions but internals attributed greater responsibility under structured conditions. The experimenters suggest that internals and externals judge the degree of responsibility of others in a manner similar to the patterns they use in judging their own responsibility. Sosis (1974) divided high-school subjects into internal, moderate, and external groups on the basis of Rotter's scale and then had them read a detailed description of an automobile accident and the man driving the car. Again, internals assigned the most responsibility to the driver for the accident, moderates an intermediate amount, and the externals the least. Internals also judged the driver more harshly. Internals appeared to judge the accident as a case of negligent behavior for which the driver was responsible while externals saw the accident as a case of bad luck. While these findings give no clear picture of what an internal or external would actually do in a driving situation or following an accident, they do suggest that the individual is projecting his own beliefs onto the driver and implicitly suggest that internals might take more responsibility for an accident than externals. Schiavo (1973) completed a similar experiment in which female subjects rated the personal characteristics and responsibility of a stimulus person who experienced a chemical laboratory accident which varied in severity and type of consequence. Internals reported that they were less like the accident perpetrator than did externals; however, they did not hold the person more accountable. Hochreich (1972) had subjects respond to the court martial of Lieutenant Calley following the My Lai incidents. Among college males, although not for females, externals were significantly more likely to underplay the individual responsibility of Lieutenant Calley and his men, projecting most of the blame for what happened at My Lai onto the United States Government and military establishment.

Several investigators have considered the degree to which I–E may be predictive of attribution of causality of success and failure in task performance. Generally, internals are more likely to attribute success to their own abilities and externals attribute failure to luck or chance (Davis & Davis, 1972; Gilmore & Minton, 1974; Lefcourt, Hogg, Struthers, & Holmes, 1975; Sobel, 1974). Krovetz (1974) asked subjects to make judgements about word meanings and then reinforced them according to five different schedules ranging from little to extreme success. He found internals to stress skill components of the experimental situation to explain their outcomes in four of the five conditions. Externals indicated that chance was an important determinant of their performance outcome. In the extreme success condition, these results were reversed. Krovetz explained this diverse finding as possibly arising because internals felt that they had not really mastered the concepts needed to be successful on the task and externals may have believed that their success was too great to be attributed solely to chance. In a study examining attribution of blame for outcomes, Phares, Wilson, and Klyver (1971) failed subjects on a cognitive task in distracting and nondistracting conditions. Internals placed significantly less blame on external sources than did externals in the nondistracting condition.

Basically, I–E beliefs do appear related to attributions about locus of causality and responsibility. Internals stress skill aspects of task performance and attribute success to their own behavior. Externals perceive chance as a determinant of outcome, particularly failure. Internals are less blaming of external distractions when called upon to perform than are externals and more likely to attribute the consequences of accidents or violent actions to individual responsibility. None of these findings is particularly surprising in that the I–E model developed originally from experimental manipulations of skill–chance situations and has always been tied theoretically to the perception of contingencies between behavior and outcome.

In addition to the I–E model, a number of other comprehensive attribution theories about perceived determinants of outcomes are available within social psychology. Heider's (1958) *naive analysis of action* model presents outcomes as the joint effects of personal factors (can and try) and environmental factors. Weiner and his colleagues (Weiner, Frieze, Kukla, Reed, Rest, & Rosenbaum, 1971; Weiner & Kukla, 1970) extend this model by devising a classification scheme for four causal dimensions. Ability and effort describe qualities of the actor, whereas task difficulty and luck describe external, environmental factors. Further, ability and task difficulty may have enduring (dispositional) characteristics, while effort and luck are variable in magnitude. These models are similar to and yet different from I–E, and unfortunately, many times they have been confounded in the psychological literature. Obviously, further research investigating the implications of each of these theoretical models is necessary. Perhaps some of the confusion has arisen because a number of investigators working somewhat independently have begun to recognize the predictive value of attributions about causality. Beliefs about locus of control clearly fit within an attributional framework but should be differentiated from other similar models. To complicate matters even further, one might also note that I–E overlaps conceptually with at least two more value-laden attribution models, namely perceptions about a "just" versus an "unjust" (Lerner, 1974) and a malevolent versus a benevolent world (Steiner, 1975).

Achievement and Competence Behaviors

Research on information processing and task performance clearly suggests that internals may be more achievement striving than externals. They seem to be able to take advantage of situations to improve task performance and engage in goal-directed behavior. A long history of research with children has been conducted which has helped to clarify the relationships between beliefs in internality and school achievement. Much of this research was accomplished by the Crandalls and their colleagues using long-range data collected as part of a Fels Institute project. Using an early form of the IAR, Crandall, Katkovsky, and Preston (1962) examined free-play measures of achievement and found that for males, internal scores on the IAR were predictive of time spent in intellectual activities such as involvement in skill and quiz games and looking through books containing scientific information. Also, for young males, internal beliefs were significantly related to a measure of intelligence as well as reading and math achievement. Chance (1965) found the IAR predictive of intelligence and achievement for third graders, including females. The relationship between internality on the IAR and school achievement as reflected by good grades has been replicated for both elementary and high school students, with the strongest correlations for males (Crandall, Katkovsky, & Crandall, 1965; McGhee & Crandall, 1968).

Other measures of I–E have also been predictive of school achievement. With a generalized measure of locus of control beliefs in children, Nowicki and Strickland (1973) found internal beliefs related to school grades, particularly for males, among over 1,000 students in grades 3 through 12. When females (in a third-grade sample) were further identified as low on social desirability responding, internality was also related to school achievement (Nowicki & Walker, 1974). With a group-administered pictorial I–E measure, Gruen, Korte, and Baum (1974) found internality related to school grades for second graders, as did Bottinelli and Weizmann (1973). With almost half a million children across the country, Coleman, Campbell, Hobson, McPartland, Mood, Weinfeld, and York (1966) found a belief in one's destiny to be a more robust predictor of academic success for minority students than a large number of teacher and school factors that they noted. With black economically disadvantaged eighth graders, Buck and Austrin (1971) found internals to be more achieving and rated by their teachers as more positive and less deviant in classroom behavior than externals. Partialing out intelligence, Lessing (1969), using Strodtbeck's Personal Control scale, found a sense of personal control to be related to grade-point averages for eighth- and eleventh-grade students from the Chicago schools. Harrison (1968), controlling for socio-economic level, reports internal children, as assessed by his "View of the Environment Test" to do better in school than externals. Brown and Strickland (1972) found internality on the Rotter scale to be related to high grade-point averages for white college males. Lao (1970), with a sample of almost 1500 black males drawn from colleges in the deep South, found a belief in personal control to be related to grade-point averages as well as entrance test scores and performance on an anagram measure. Internal personal control students were also more academically self-confident than externals. Prociuk and Breen (1974), using the Levenson Internal, Powerful Others, and Chance scales, found internal beliefs to be related to study habits and attitudes as well as course grades among college students. The Powerful Others and Chance scales were negatively related to the same indices although not to the same degree. Students who believe in Chance control performed more poorly academically than persons who perceive their reinforcements as a function of Powerful Others. Further, Prociuk and Breen (1975), using the Levenson scales, divided subjects into internals, groupings they called congruent externals (individuals who had high scores on the Chance scale), and defensive externals (individuals with high scores on the Powerful Others scale). They found internals academically superior to both of the external groups with defensive externals also demonstrating higher grade point averages than congruent externals. Although some investigators report only weak, confounded, or insignificant relationships between internality and academic performance for college students (Eisenman & Platt, 1968; Hjelle, 1970; Massari & Rosenblum, 1972; Wareheim, 1972; Wolfe, 1972), generally, even with the use of widely different instruments, locus of control beliefs appear to be related to school performance, particularly for children, over and beyond some of the more traditional measures.

Aside from school achievement situations, internal as opposed to external children are also more likely to engage in related competence-type behaviors (Strickland, 1972b). Waters (1972) found fourth- and fifth-grade male internals to persist longer on a difficult and time-consuming task described as dependent on their own skill than external males who, in contrast, persisted longer under chance instructions. Ludwigsen and Rollins (1972) administered concept formation tasks to 11- and 12-year-olds under reinforcement, verbalization, and control conditions. Their results indicated that over all conditions with intelligence levels controlled, internals had a significantly higher rate of problem solution and, in line with research presented earlier, appeared to go about gathering information about task solution more efficiently than externals. Controlling for age and intelligence, Crandall and Lacey (1972) found internality related to improved performance on an embedded figure test, particularly for females. Although Stephens (1972) could not replicate this finding with a younger group of children and a different measure, DuCette, Wolk, and Friedman (1972) found internality to be predictive of creativity as measured by uniqueness of responses to ambiguous stimuli for both black and white 9- to 11-year-old, lower class males. Mischel, Zeiss, and Zeiss (1974) conducted a series of studies in which preschool children were offered the option of accepting smaller rewards early during a task or to continue to work in the hope of receiving larger rewards. They found that children who reported internal beliefs about success were significantly more likely to persist in effort than children who were external for success. Internality for failure was not related to children's choices except on a task in which they expected punishment for failure and were led to believe that they could escape punishment by their performance.

Several other experimenters have noted a theoretical link between internal expectancies and the willingness to defer gratification. Delay of gratification has been thought to be a correlate of maturity and ego strength and appears to be related to the process of being able to plan ahead. This definition suggests that the individual expects that reinforcements will follow certain efforts on his/her part. In 1961, Bialer found a relationship between internal expectancies and the choosing of delayed, more valuable rewards in a sample of 89 children, both normal and mentally retarded, who ranged in chronological age from 6 to 14 years. Several investigators attempted to replicate these findings, with mixed results. Walls and Smith (1970) found internal more than external children to choose to wait for a 7¢ as opposed to an immediate 5¢ prize. However, Walls and Miller (1970) found no relationship between internality and delay behavior in a small sample of welfare and vocational rehabilitation clients though both delay and internality were related to amount of education. Controlling for education and socioeconomic background, Zytkoskee, Strickland, and Watson (1971) tested both black and white ninth graders. They found the black children to be both more external and less likely to delay rewards than the white subjects but no relationship between locus of control scores and delay. In a subsequent study, Strickland (1972a) administered a newer measure of locus of control and controlled for the race of the experimenter by having both black and white adults offer immediate or delayed rewards. She found that delay behavior was dependent on the race of the experimenter and also, within the white sample, but not the black, a belief in internal control was significantly related to one's choice of a more valuable, delayed reward. She was also able to replicate the I–E/delay relationship with a group of elementary school children, all white, between eight and ten years old (Strickland, 1973a).

The studies just reported all used a typical delay paradigm in which subjects were asked to choose between small immediate rewards, such as candy or prizes, or increased amounts of these to be delivered at a later time. In one of the few studies investigating significant and important life-decision choices, Erikson and Roberts (1971) studied institutionalized adolescent delinquents who were offered the opportunity of attending a public school removed from the reformatory in which they were residing. Attending the public school, however, meant that the inmate's release from the reformatory would be delayed. Those inmates who chose to attend school and remain longer in the reformatory were compared with those who chose to leave the reformatory early. When other inmates were questioned about the "delayers" as opposed to the "nondelayers," responses about the delayers were overwhelmingly more likely to be classified as internal than those for the nondelayers. Basically, internal beliefs and behaviors, aside from the choice behavior, were significantly more likely to be attributed to the inmates who made the choice to attend school and delay release. Cross and Tracy (1971) studied 119 black and white young males who were either institutionalized or in active contact with the juvenile court. They found internality to be related to interpersonal maturity for the whole sample but I–E/future time perspective and guilt relationships were dependent on race. The interpersonally mature black males were more external with a shorter time perspective while interpersonally mature white males were more internal but no different in time perspective than immature males.

In regard to other time-related judgements, Walls and Smith (1970) found internals more accurate in judging the lapse of a minute than externals. Generally, internals report longer future-time perspective (Platt & Eisenman, 1968; Shybut, 1968) than externals and appear to be capable of more "delaying capacity" as assessed by Kagan's Matching Familiar Figures Test and the Porteus Mazes (Shipe, 1971).

Taken overall, internality is directly related to achievement behavior. Not only do internals appear to work harder at intellectual and performance tasks, but their efforts also appear to be rewarded in that they make better grades and receive more desirable reinforcements by delaying immediate gratification. These findings, of course, have important and significant implications for education. If intellectual performance is valued in this society, then ways of enhancing academic performance become particularly salient. If beliefs about contingencies between one's own behavior and subsequent outcomes are related to performance, as they appear to be, then one approach to improving performance is to have individuals give up an external orientation and move toward more internal perceptions. When an individual perceives that his or her behavior determines outcomes, that individual can be expected to engage in more individual efforts to increase subsequent reward. Moreover, different strategies of education and/or remediation are suggested for internals and externals. Apparently, internals prefer to rely on their own efforts while externals may need more initial structure and support from others.

Interpersonal Behaviors

While much research has accumulated suggesting that internality is related to academic achievement and task performance, much less is known about I–E and interpersonal behaviors. Nowicki and Roundtree (1971) did find internal school children to be more socially popular with their peers than externals. Further, Duke and Nowicki (1973) devised a measure for assessing preferred interpersonal distance and report I–E to be a mediating variable in regard to the distance at which people report themselves to be comfortable with others. I–E was not related to preferred distancing of people for whom there has been a specific experiencing base, such as mother, father, or best friend. However, when subjects were asked to report how comfortable they felt with persons for whom they would hold generalized expectancies such as strangers, older persons, or authority figures like policemen or politicians, internals were significantly more likely to place these persons closer in interpersonal space than externals. Duke and Nowicki interpret these findings as suggesting that internals may feel more competent and comfortable in dealing with persons whom they do not know than do externals who appear to prefer to keep strangers at a distance. Other support for this conceptualization arises from the work of Ferguson and Kennelly (1974). Using an Authorities Figure Perception test, they found internals more than externals to perceive figures in authority as more encouraging of constructive environmental manipulations, as more supportive when difficulty is encountered, as more positively reinforcing, as having more predictable standards, as acting more upon issue-oriented reasons, and in a generally more favorable light.

Duke and Nowicki also found internals to be less likely than externals to distance persons of other races. Again, internals, in contrast to externals, may feel more comfortable and less prejudiced toward people whom they perceive as different from themselves. Another study with relevance to racial preference has been reported by Nowicki and Tanner (in press). They replicated the classic study of the Clarks (1939) who had black children choose a black or white doll. The Clarks reported that 66% of the black children preferred the white doll. Nowicki and Tanner, some 35 years later, found only 28% of the black children in their sample of 6- to 8-year-olds choosing the white as opposed to the black doll. Moreover, the black children who did choose the black doll were significantly more internal than those choosing the white doll.

Several studies have been completed relating I–E to interpersonal attraction. Phares and Wilson (1971) had internal and external subjects read I–E scales which were allegedly completed by strangers whom they were asked to evaluate. Internal subjects were more attracted to the internal than the external stranger while external subjects did not appear to differentiate. Nowicki and Blumberg (1975) asked internal and external subjects to listen to a tape of an alleged stranger of the same age and sex of the subject. The tapes were prepared to reflect internal or external emphasis and subjects were then asked to indicate their degree of liking for the stranger. The investigators had hypothesized that similarity of locus of control orientation would lead to greater initial attraction than a complementary locus of control orientation. Contrary to prediction, results showed that both internal and external subjects reported themselves to be significantly more attracted to the internal than to the external stranger.

In a situation of interaction with a person who gave both rewarding and punishing feedback to subject responses, Holmes and Jackson (1975) found internals to report themselves as feeling less angry, perceiving the person as being more friendly, and feeling more attracted to the person than externals. In a situation of no evaluative feedback, the reverse was found with internals more angry, seeing the other as less friendly and less attractive than the externals.

When an individual is serving as an agent of change and power, I–E is also predictive of that person's attempt to influence others. Phares (1965) found internals more persuasive than externals when asked to attempt to change a recipient's expressed attitude on various issues. Goodstadt and Hjelle (1973) had subjects serve as supervisors to three fictitious workers, one of whom presented a supervisory problem. In dealing with the problem worker, external subjects used significantly more coercive power (threat of deduction of points, threat of firing, etc.) than did internals, who relied more on personal persuasive powers. The authors explained these results in terms of differential expectancy of successful influence on the part of internals and externals suggesting that the internals' positive expectations of successful influence led them to rely on personal persuasion. Conversely, the use of more coercive power by externals is consistent with minimal expectations of successful influence. A study by Ryckman and Sherman (1974) also investigated I–E and personal control. They had subjects select partners or opponents with superior, equal, or inferior abilities for cooperative ventures but only after they had become thoroughly convinced of their own lack of ability on the task. When they perceived themselves as having good ability, internals selected partners of equal ability for cooperative activities. Externals tended to select inferior-ability partners under the same conditions thus virtually ensuring defeat for their teams.

Overall, internals and externals appear to have differing styles of interpersonal interaction. Internals seem less threatened by persons who are different from them and report themselves to be more tolerant of others. Generally, internals appear to be better liked than externals. In dyadic interchange, internals are more persuasive with a preference for personal and positive influence in contrast to externals who rely more on coercive power. These rather strong findings are particularly intriguing in view of the fact that so little research seems to have been accomplished in this area. Apparently, the I–E dimension offers the possibility of enriched understanding of a number of interpersonal behaviors including prejudice, the assumption of power, and reactions to evaluation and control by others. This research might also be extended beyond individual interpersonal interactions to group phenomena. In view of society's great need to improve the quality of human interaction, the continued investigation of I–E and interpersonal behaviors seems particularly important.

Social Action and Political Beliefs

In regard to large-scale social interaction, internals again appear to respond differently from externals, particularly in relation to attempts to change aversive life situations. When research first began with the I–E dimension, an obvious area of interest had to do with social activism. In the early 1960s black students, particularly in the South, were moving to resist segregation and bring about equality of opportunity for black people. At a large black undergraduate university, Gore and Rotter (1963) asked students to commit themselves to varying degrees of social activism ranging from doing nothing, to signing petitions, to marching on the state capital, to taking a "freedom ride" across the Southeastern states. As expected, they found internal students more likely to commit themselves to the more dramatic types of social action. Strickland (1965) replicated this work using I–E responses of young black activists involved in voter registration in rural areas of the Southeast, who were living in situations of daily harrassment and threats to their well-being. She found these persons who were, at that time, in the forefront of Civil Rights activities in regard to community organization and voting rights, to be significantly more internal than matched nonactivists. These data were collected in the early sixties. As the decade progressed, the nature of the activist movement changed, especially as the general population and particularly as minority-group members came to identify more specifically the problems of discrimination. Moreover, the American populace was shaken by a series of assassinations of important political figures and became increasingly concerned about involvement in the war in Southeast Asia. Paralleling the swift flux of social change and the increasing complexity and differentiation of motives and allegiances characterizing social activism were attempts to design I–E measures to assess more specific expectancies about personal as opposed to system control. The Gurins and their colleagues (Gurin, Gurin, Lao, & Beattie, 1969), with a sample of black college students, factor analyzed the Rotter scale and identified two major components. One, consisting of items phrased in the first person, appeared to reflect feelings of personal control. The second, consisting mostly of items phrased in the third person, had to do with general or ideological beliefs about internal and external control. Gurin and Katz (1966) found that black students who focused on discrimination, or system blame, in explaining the disadvantaged position of blacks in this country held somewhat higher aspirations than those students who espoused personal control. They were more likely to aspire for pioneering jobs not ordinarily held by Negroes. Lao (1970), using the two factors with black college males, found beliefs in personal control to be related to academic competence but not related to innovative social action. She did find a higher degree of involvement in and commitment to Civil Rights activities, as well as preference for collective protest action, among students who blamed the system. In a similar vein, although using the original Rotter scale, Sank and Strickland (1973) found, in the later days of the Civil Rights protests, individuals who espoused a militant, as opposed to a more moderate revolutionary stance, to be significantly more external than internal. Ransford (1968), within the context of the Watts riot, found among 312 black males who were heads of household, that those scoring toward the external end of the Rotter scale viewed violence as necessary for racial justice. Of the 16 men who admitted participating in violent action, 15 were external. Ransford interprets these data in terms of feelings of powerlessness. In a more complicated fashion, the research of Forward and Williams (1970) as well as Caplan's (1970) review of the "new ghetto man" present the black militant as *both* high in personal internality and in system blame.

As many of these researchers note, participation in social action may not only reflect appropriate and reasonable attempts to change aversive conditions but may also be a furious outcry raised in frustration and anger against situations seen as fixed and unchangeable. Prediction of social action by the I–E dimension is complicated not only by the different meanings people hold about sources of oppression but also by the diverse goals which participation in the movement may fulfill for them.

In regard to other salient social and political issues of the late sixties and early seventies – although the results are sometimes inconsistent (Abramowicz, 1974) – several studies have been conducted which demonstrate a relationship between I–E and social activism. Pawlicki and Almquist (1973) found members of a women's liberation group to be more internal than college female nonmembers. When education and income of family were controlled, internality was still related to group membership although only marginally when age was controlled. Sanger and Alker (1972) factor analyzed the I–E scale and found members of a women's liberation group, in contrast to a control group of nonmembers, to be more internal in their sense of personal control and more external on beliefs about the Protestant Ethic and feminist ideology. Ryckman, Rodda, and Sherman (1972) found internals more unfavorable than externals toward student activism although Granberg and May (1972) could demonstrate no relationship between I–E and attitudes and action orientations toward the Vietnam War. Rosen and Salling (1971) report internality to be related to reported political activity but Abramowicz (1974) cautions that with any investigation of social activism in relation to I–E beliefs, one must consider the multifactor clusters within the I–E scale, some of which may relate to social–political activities and some of which may not.

In addition to the I–E/social action research, a number of experimenters have been interested in the degree to which I–E expectancies may predict political beliefs or affiliation. In the late fifties and early sixties, Rotter (1966) found no differences in the I–E scores among college students who identified themselves as Republican, Democrat, or independent. Similarly, Johnson (1961) reports no differences between supporters of Nixon and supporters of Kennedy in the 1960 presidential election. In regard to personal or political ideology, internals, particularly males, appear to more strongly endorse the Protestant Ethic than do externals (MacDonald, 1972; Mirels & Garrett, 1971). Fink and Hjelle (1973) administered several ideology belief scales to subjects and found internals to score higher than externals on a "traditional American" questionnaire which emphasized beliefs that getting ahead in life is largely based on a person's character and ability; lower on a conservative scale which stresses a preference for status quo and aversion toward change; and lower on a "New Left" scale which emphasizes control of individual behavior via institutions and impersonal bureaucracies. Thomas (1970) interviewed and administered a shortened version of the Rotter scale to 60 politically active families who lived in a Chicago suburb, half of whom were conservative and half liberal. Conservative parents were more internal than liberal parents and right-wing students more internal than the left-wing group. Similarly for males, but not for females, Silvern and Nakamura (1971) found externality related to left-wing views and protest activity. In one of the few studies actually using a multidimensional approach to I–E in relation to social activism, Levenson and Miller (1976) differentiated college students according to responses on the Levenson measure of I–E and according to political ideology and activism. They found that for liberal students beliefs in Control by Powerful Others are positively related to increased activism while these results are reversed for more conservative students. For example, using two feminist groups, they found militant lesbians to report higher expectancies of Control from Powerful Others and less personal control in their lives than did members of a relatively inactive chapter of a national women's liberation group. Students who attended a regional conference of Students for a Democratic Society also reported significantly higher Control by Powerful Others than did political science majors who belonged to a nonactivist liberal group.

Generally, internals endorse a traditional "Horatio Alger" orientation emphasizing individual responsibility, while externals may be more concerned with the control on individuals exerted by institutional pressures. This interpretation is complicated, however, by the possible multifactor aspects of the Rotter scale, particularly in terms of factors such as personal control and system blame, or a self–other distinction (Gurin *et al.,* 1969; Mirels, 1970), as well as differential components of externality such as Chance or Control by Powerful Others (Levenson & Miller, 1976). Generally, the research, even with its limitations, suggests that internals do attempt to take responsibility for their lives and to change uncomfortable and aversive situations. They appear to support political structures that emphasize individual responsibility although it is difficult to link internal beliefs to any specific current political ideology. In many instances, I–E beliefs appear to be related to participation in social action movements although a direct one-to-one relationship is complicated by the myriad of motives and opportunities inherent in large group, large-scale activities.

Defensive Externality

While much of the I–E research has focused on the positive attributes of internals, who are seen as achieving and engaging in active mastery behaviors, less attention has been paid to a description of persons who are assessed as external. Exceptions to this focus are the work of Phares, Rotter, and their colleagues and some relatively recent consideration of externality and maladjustment. Phares (1974) and Rotter (1975) both discuss two possible interpretations of a high externality score. In some cases, an external belief may represent an accurate portrayal of a person's reality. Some cultures espouse external, fatalistic attitudes and an individual assimilated into this culture would be assumed to hold these beliefs. External expectancies on the part of persons who are members of societies or groups which, indeed, have little control over the economic and social forces surrounding them likely reflect a realistic appraisal that their behavior is not likely to influence successfully the environment in which they live. Aside from this grouping of externals whose beliefs may be veridical representations of their culture, some external individuals may use their beliefs to shield or protect themselves from anxiety or distress which occurs as a result of personal inadequacies. The espousal of an external locus of control orientation may be a defensive maneuver which functions to reduce stress and the accepting of responsibility for one's own behavior. The hypothesis of "defensive externality" is based on a long series of studies which demonstrate that externals appear to be more willing to admit threatening stimuli to awareness and have less need to deny unfavorable personal information since they may have already decided that events beyond their control are responsible for their failures or shortcomings (Efran, 1963; Hochreich, 1975; Lipp, Kolstoe, James, & Randall, 1968; Phares, 1971; Phares & Lamiell, 1974a, 1974b; Phares, Ritchie, & Davis, 1968; Snyder & Larson, 1972).

Generally, defensive externals are identified on the basis of their I–E scores plus other variables. Hamsher, Geller, and Rotter (1968) found that male externals were significantly more likely than internals to report that they do not trust that the verbal promises of others can be relied on. Hochreich (1974) then used trust as a moderator variable and found that defensive external (or low-trust) males, in contrast to congruent (or high-trust) external males and internals, would attribute less responsibility to story heroes in failure conditions, particularly achievement situations. Hochreich could not replicate these findings for females and suggests that the concept of defensive externality may not be appropriate for females in that women appear to have experienced different cultural expectations for success in our society and may not need to resort to externality or blame projection as a defense. Females may also be using other defensive maneuvers. Midgley and Abrams (1974) found external more likely than internal college women to express a high level of motivation to avoid success.

Externals may also choose to place themselves in situations in which little opportunity is available for veridical feedback about their performance. Although some investigators report no relationship between externality and risk taking (Butterfield, 1964; Gold, 1966; Minton & Miller, 1970) or even a reverse relationship between externality and risk taking (Strickland, Lewicki, & Katz, 1966), a number of studies in this area find externals, in contrast to internals, to be characterized as engaging in more extreme behavior in regard to risk taking, shifts in level of aspiration, and estimation of success (Battle & Rotter, 1963; DuCette & Wolk, 1972; Feather, 1967a, b; 1968, Julian & Katz, 1968; Lefcourt, 1967; Liverant & Scodel, 1960). The preference of externals for either extremely easy or extremely difficult goals suggests that they may not have developed the ability or motivation to make critical judgements about their own behavior. They may also be setting goals defensively thus putting themselves in a situation of receiving sparse feedback about their skills in conditions where they are reputedly being tested on their own abilities. The failure to shift estimates appropriately may be an indication that the external is not using immediate past performance to predict one's behavior and continual success or failure tells this individual little about personal skills.

To summarize, in contrast to internals, externals, when given a choice, are likely to put themselves in situations of low risk so that they easily attain their goals or in conditions of extremely high risk so that failure does not reflect their own ineptitude. They seem to be hesitant about taking risks that might lead to failure, thus giving themselves few opportunities to critically test their abilities. The reasons for this are not entirely clear in that scores on the external end of the I–E scale have usually appeared more heterogenous than those on the internal end (Hersch and Scheibe, 1967) and possibly reflect several kinds of externality. Moreover, some individuals, who usually act in an internal fashion, may answer in the external direction. These individuals, called defensive externals, are assumed to be presenting an external stance to relieve themselves of responsibility for their own actions.

Health-Related Behaviors

Whether external expectancies serve as a defensive maneuver or not, research on I–E clearly suggests that externals are more likely than internals to report undesirable and unfavorable personal characteristics about themselves. Among normally functioning individuals, investigators have found externality related to debilitating, although not facilitating, anxiety (Butterfield, 1964; Feather, 1967a; Platt & Eisenman, 1968; Shybut, 1970; Strassberg, 1973; Watson, 1967) as well as to the holding of irrational values (MacDonald & Games, 1972) and indices of maladjustment on paper and pencil questionnaires (Duke & Nowicki, 1973; Hersch & Scheibe, 1967; Powell & Vega, 1972). With hospitalized patients, a number of researchers report a relationship between externality and severity of psychiatric diagnosis, particularly schizophrenia (Cash & Stack, 1973; Cromwell, Rosenthal, Shakow, & Zahn, 1968; Duke & Mullins, 1973; Lefcourt, 1976; Levenson, 1973a; Lottman & DeWolfe, 1972; Palmer, 1971; Shybut, 1968; Smith, Pryer, & Distephane, 1971).

Of considerable theoretical interest is the degree to which depression may be related to locus of control expectancies. Initially, it might appear that persons who hold a strong belief that they are responsible for the results of their behavior would be more likely to become depressed when life events do not go well for them. Phares (1972) has hypothesized that "depressions tend to be associated with people who possess a strong generalized expectancy that outcomes are their own responsibility [p. 466]." On the other hand, a feeling of powerlessness and inability to influence and control one's life often appears to be a salient concomitant of depressive symptomatology. This feeling of loss of control and power sounds strikingly like a belief in external control. Strickland (1974) and Lefcourt (1976) have both hypothesized a relationship between depression and externality. Much of the empirical literature supports this contention (Abramowicz, 1969; Calhoun, Cheney, & Dawes, 1974; Dinardo, 1972; Goss & Morosko, 1970; Hale, 1975; Naditch, Gargan, & Michael, 1975; Wareheim & Foulds, 1971). Particularly relevant to work on "learned helplessness" (Seligman, 1974) is experimental evidence suggesting that externals, in contrast to internals, are less likely to be able to take steps to avoid aversive situations. Hiroto (1974) manipulated escape/avoidance conditions and found in subsequent testing that externals, as opposed to internals, were slower to escape or avoid an aversive tone, required more trials to reach avoidance criterion, and made fewer avoidance responses. Dweck and Repucci (1973) had children persist in tasks after prolonged noncontingent failure and found externals, who took less personal responsibility for outcomes, to exhibit a worsening of performance in contrast to internal children. Dweck (1975) subsequently trained children who were judged "helpless," in the sense of being passive in response to challenges which they were actually capable of meeting, to assume responsibility for failures with attributions made to effort. She found improved performance following failure experiences in contrast to a second group who received only success experiences. These experimental manipulations suggest that "learned helplessness" and external expectancies may be parallel beliefs and, further, may be modified by reattribution training. However, contrary to expectation, Roth and Bootzin (1974) found "helpless" college students initiating more controlling behavior over an aversive event following a learned helplessness manipulation and experimentally induced expectancies of external control. Obviously, all of these studies must be interpreted with caution, not only because they raise questions about I–E but because of the problems inherent in diagnosing depression, particularly chronic versus reactive depression. It would not be surprising to find that persons who report long-term depressive symptomotology also report external expectancies while internals may be more likely to become immediately depressed in failure situations. If internals do perceive events as contingent on their own behavior and do move to attempt to improve their life conditions in a more adaptive way than externals, then their depression may lift more quickly.

Often the treatment of depressives is fraught with difficulties surrounding suicide threats, attempts, and the possibility of actual self-destruction. Several investigators have considered the relationship between suicidal thought and behavior and locus of control beliefs in an attempt to better understand and describe life-threatening behaviors. Lambley and Silbowitz (1973) could not predict the contemplation of suicide via Rotter's scale but Williams and Nickels (1969), in a study of 235 college students, found externality related to suicide potentiality as measured by the MMPI. Crepeau (1975) also asked students how often they had contemplated suicide. Generally, he found frequency of suicide ideation to be linearly related to I–E with persons reporting high suicide ideation also being more external than students who had never considered suicide. However, he found a small group of students, 3 within a sample of 89, to report that at some previous time they had contemplated suicide daily. These students had more internal scores than the other groupings. These results are likely artifactual in view of the small number. On the other hand, daily ideation may represent a determined effort to end one's life and an active move to change one's life situation quite drastically. If this is the case, the internal scores would not be surprising. Also, since these students were obviously not successful suicides in spite of their ideation, they may have instead worked out their life problems in a more adaptive way. Melges and Weisz (1971) talked with 15 patients who had recently made serious suicide attempts. They asked them to recall as vividly as possible the feelings and thoughts they were experiencing immediately before the attempt. Using pre- and posttest measures, they found increased externality following the specific suicide ideation. Additionally, patients reported more negative evaluations of the future and less extension of a span of awareness toward the future. Both of these variables were also related to changes toward externality. Thus, the immediate suicide impulse may reflect a feeling of loss of control and inability to foresee a pleasant future.

Although, as indicated so far, the bulk of the evidence points to a relationship between externality and maladjustment or psychopathology, paradoxically as with the daily suicide ideation in Crepeau's study, locus of control scores in some selected samples of maladaptively functioning persons appear to be more internal than external. In contrast to Palmer (1971), Naditch (1975), and Nowicki and Hopper (1974) who report alcoholics to be more external, Goss and Morosco (1970) and Oziel, Obitz, and Keyson (1972) found alcoholics to be more internal than normal controls. Other investigators (Berzins & Ross, 1973; Calicchia, 1974; Smithyman, Plant, & Southern, 1974) also report drug abusers to be more internal than nondrug abusers. Finally, Harrow and Ferrante (1969) reported 5 upper-middle-class manic patients in a psychiatric hospital as having a mean score of 4 on the I–E scale which is significantly more internal than reported means for other diagnostic groups and most normal samples. These findings obviously do not fit into an overall schema of externality and psychopathology. However, it should be noted that both of these conduct disorders and the manic symptomotology are characteristically active forms of behavior in contrast to schizophrenia or depression, disorders which are often marked by passivity and withdrawal. Also, as always, the particular testing situation must be considered. As Rotter (1975) notes, drug and alcohol abusers may "have been told so many times and by so many people that their cure is 'up to them' that they have fully recognized that this is the attitude that they are supposed to present to the staff when they are trying to appear cooperative in the treatment program, either in an institution or as an outpatient [p. 8]. Moreover, the findings of a significant relationship between need for approval and internality often reported with the Rotter scale (Rotter, 1966) pose an assessment problem in that approval-motivated individuals may deny psychopathological symptoms. If this is the case, then the reported correlations between externality and psychopathology may be the result of an approval-motivated response set rather than, or in addition to, locus of control beliefs.

Nonetheless, the overwhelming evidence suggests that there is indeed a relationship between the holding of external beliefs and general indices of maladjustment. If this is the case, then intriguing questions are raised about the degree to which I–E beliefs may also be predictive of response to psychotherapy. One would expect that internals might begin therapy less defensively and possibly at a less disturbed level than externals. Additionally, the data which suggest that internals attempt to understand and change aversive life situations would point toward the internal's likelihood of responding to and benefiting from psychotherapeutic attempts to a greater extent than externals. This assumption, of course, depends on the type of therapy used, since internals would be expected to be resistant to approaches that might limit their control or freedom. Moreover, Nowicki, Bonner, and Feather (1972) report that the relationship of I–E to patient perceptions of therapists depends on the type of therapeutic techniques used by the therapist.

Friedman and Dies (1974) matched extreme internal and external college students on two anxiety measures and then divided them into three comparable groups each of which received one of three forms of therapy over a five-week period, namely, counseling, systematic desensitization, and automated desensitization. At the end of treatment, subjects were asked about their degree of satisfaction with therapy. Externals provided with counseling and systematic desensitization reported that they felt they had retained too much control of therapy while internals generally indicated an optimal amount of control in counseling. Regardless of treatment conditions, internals reported that if given a choice, they would have significantly more often chosen "more client control" than externals. Results also indicated that internals were more likely to attempt to individualize therapy and appeared more resistant to the control implied in the two behavior therapies.

Abramowicz, Abramowicz, Roback, and Jackson (1974) randomly assigned 26 mildly distressed college students to a nondirective or one of 3 directive groups all led by the same therapist. Internals appeared to be more responsive to the nondirective than to the directive approach, whereas the reverse was true for externals. In a 23-hr marathon group situation for hospitalized female drug abusers, Kilmann and Howell (1974) found internal patients, in contrast to externals, to evidence greater efforts to be successful and involved in therapy, to understand themselves, and to become more reflective, and serious. Within therapy groups, internals consistently showed greater pre- to post therapy gains. Kilmann (1974) also reports that internal patients who participated in the highly structured 23-hr group marathon, during which they were severely limited in participant freedoms, shifted significantly toward externality following the group experience, their I–E scores being similar to those of a control group with no treatment. With an encounter-group procedure, Diamond and Shapiro (1973) found significant changes in locus of control beliefs with participants reporting themselves to be more internal following the group experience. Gillis and Jessor (1970) have shown a relationship between the client's internal beliefs and therapist-rated favorable outcome in psychotherapy and a number of studies have demonstrated that internality can be taught effectively to clients in individual psychotherapy (Dua, 1970; Pierce, Schauble, & Farkas, 1970; Smith, 1970) as well as to academic underachievers through counseling, group psychotherapy, or structured group experiences (Felton & Biggs, 1972, 1973; Felton & Davidson, 1973; Felton & Thomas, 1972; Nowicki & Barnes, 1973; Reimanis, 1974).

A question related to how clients respond to counseling or psychotherapy as a function of I–E is how does the functioning of mental health personnel relate to their I–E beliefs. Several studies in the recent psychological literature suggest that locus of control beliefs may be important in determining the efficacy of mental health care delivery. Beckman (1972) found that volunteers at a state mental hospital, in contrast to undergraduate controls, were significantly more internal and less likely to feel that patients should be restricted in their social functioning. Felton (1973) found mental-health workers to become more internal following enrollment in a process-oriented training program. Likewise, Martin and Shepel (1974) trained 21 senior female nurses from urban hospitals in counseling, emphasizing developing a helping relationship, identifying and exploring problem areas, and devising plans of action. Through pre- and posttesting, they found both an increase in counseling perceptiveness and a shift toward internality. A correlation of .56 was found between internality and counseling skills at the posttesting and the investigators suggest that I–E assessment may be a useful selection device to optimize training effectiveness with lay counselors.

Aside from research on I–E and emotional well-being, a considerable amount of investigation has been focused on I–E and physical health. As early as 1962 in one of the criterion studies for the original Rotter scale, Seeman and Evans found evidence that internal hospitalized patients with tuberculosis were more likely to have an understanding of their disease than their external counterparts. The medical staff also rated internal patients as being higher in objective knowledge about tuberculosis. In wards where information was difficult to obtain, internals were significantly less satisfied with the flow of information than externals. With the great concern in the sixties about a link between cigarette smoking and cancer, several studies appeared suggesting that internals were less likely to be smokers than externals (Coan, 1973; Straits & Sechrest, 1963; Williams, 1973) and more likely to be able to change smoking behavior (Foss, 1973; James, Woodruff, & Werner, 1965; Platt, 1969).

The studies on locus of control and smoking suggest that internals take precautions to guard against danger and to protect their health. In a study of inoculations against influenza, Dabbs and Kirscht (1971) report that college students who were assessed as internal, according to eight selected "motivational" variables, were more likely than externals to have been inoculated although internals on eight selected "expectancy" items were likely not to have taken the shots. These results are somewhat confusing in regard to the relationship between motivation to exert control and expectancy of control but do suggest that the locus of control variable is operating as one takes precautions against influenza. Williams (1972a), in a large-scale study with high-school students, found that subjects assessed as internal reported greater use of seat belts when riding in automobiles than did externals. Additionally, internal students were significantly more likely than externals to engage in preventive dental care, that is, to go to the dentist for check-ups and maintenance even when teeth or gums were not sore or hurting (Williams, 1972b). Sonstroem and Walker (1973), with college males, report an internal orientation to be related to positive attitudes about physical exercise, to participation in voluntary exercise, and to cardiovascular fitness. MacDonald (1970) found for a sample of middle-class married college females that internals were more likely to practice contraception. Segal and DuCette (1973) report middle-class white high-school females who became pregnant more likely to be external. In interesting contrast, black high-school pregnant females were more internal.

When people are subjected to extensive or stressful life changes, their susceptibility to disease appears to be greater (Holmes & Masuda, 1973). Are persons who hold internal beliefs better able to adapt to stressful life changes than externals? MacDonald and Hall (1971) asked healthy college students how they thought various physical handicaps would affect their social relationships and feelings about themselves. Internals anticipated less severe consequences of handicaps than did externals, perhaps reflecting the internal's belief that one can adapt to aversive life situations.

Are locus of control beliefs related to physical health and well-being? Naditch, Gargan, and Michael (1975) collected data on 547 males in Army basic training. They found internal expectancy to be positively related to life contentment. Additionally, external beliefs were positively related to self-reported depression and anxiety, and negatively related to an index of denial. Additional findings on the relationship between life satisfaction and locus of control emerge from another large-scale study of 502 white males, aged 45 to 69, conducted by Palmore and Luikart (1972). They considered a battery of physical and psychological tests completed by subjects in relation to Cantril's measure of life satisfaction. They found that self-rated health had the most influence on life satisfaction while amount of organizational activity and belief in internal control were the second and third most important variables. Organizational activity was mainly related to intelligence and internal control orientation among males and to lack of employment and physical performance status among females. Several variables thought to be related to life satisfaction had little or no relationship including age, sex, total social contacts, career anchorage, marital status, and intelligence. With a group of elderly subjects, Wolk and Kurtz (1975) investigated I–E in relation to activity, adjustment, and life satisfaction. With 92 noninstitutionalized males and females between the ages of 60 and 85, they found internality to be significantly related to a paper-and-pencil assessment of involvement in social, community, and political affairs, adaptive levels of developmental task accomplishments, and more emotional balance and satisfaction with life. They suggest that the relationship between expectancy for internal control and a belief in and exertion of effectance appears to be prevalent throughout the life span. However, Wolk and Kurtz did investigate noninstitutional elderly. If the elderly are in institutions where their own personal control is minimal then a belief in external control might be more conducive to long-range adaptation. Thus, Felton and Kahana (1974) studied an institutionalized elderly population using an assessment of locus of control in relation to the institution. They found external control beliefs to be related positively to ratings of satisfaction and morale. The fact that I–E expectancies emerge as such salient variables in studies of life satisfaction suggests that either internals are able to influence their life situation in such a way as to be contended, or contentment leads to a belief that one does control the events that happen to oneself. Although correlative data leave unanswered questions about the direction of causality, locus of control beliefs and life satisfaction are quite clearly related.

Some research is available linking locus of control and specific physical disorders. Naditch (1974) considered data on over 400 black men and women who were diagnosed as having essential hypertension. Among highly discontented externals, the rate of hypertension was 46.2%, more than double the 21.3% rate for the total sample, and considerably higher than among more contented externals or internals. Only a 7.1% rate of hypertension was found among the low discontent group. Darrow (1973) found that among several hundred men who presented themselves to a Community Health Clinic for diagnosis and treatment of venereal disease, internal men were significantly less likely than externals to be infected with gonorrhea. Venereal disease in females did not seem to be related to I–E. However, internal females were significantly more likely to return for follow-up treatment with the appearance of new symptoms than were external females. Darrow interprets this latter finding as being likely due to the tendencies of these women to notice physiological changes and to seek an explanation for the reappearance of symptoms after treatment. Eggland (1973) found first- and fourth-grade male and female children who were diagnosed as having cerebral palsy to be more external than matched nonhandicapped children. Strickland and Hill (1974) also found that elementary-school males who were identified as having severe problems in reading (dyslexic) were more external than a control group of males who were achieving normally in school. Bruhn, Hampton, and Chandler (1971) compared a group of 36 male hemophiliacs, aged 12 and older, with a control group of normals. Overall, the hemophilic group was more internal than normals but, within the hemophilic group, a marginally severe group was significantly more external than either a mild or severe group. The authors suggest that the marginally severe hemophilic views his clinical state as somewhat unpredictable and is more dependent on external cues as determining his well-being.

Locus of control beliefs may also be influential in a patient's attempts to affect health care. Johnson, Leventhal, and Dabbs (1971) report that among 62 women patients who had received abdominal surgery, internality was related to ability to influence post-operative care and, if they were firstborns, internals had longer hospital stays than externals. Weaver (1972) found that internal patients with severe kidney disorders who were using dialysis machines to stay alive were significantly more likely to comply with diet restrictions and keep scheduled appointments more regularly than external patients. Kilpatrick, Miller, and William (1972) examined dialysis patients in several different cities. They found that patients in Atlanta were more internal on the Rotter scale than Charleston and New York dialysis patients who were more internal than control patients. Moreover, they found a correlation of −.49 between months of dialysis treatment and externality in Charleston patients. Patients in different treatment centers appear to hold varying beliefs about locus of control and their beliefs may change as a function of length of treatment. I–E expectancies may also vary as a function of chronicity of disability. Wendland (1973) assessed 80 males, ages 18 to 35, who were institutionalized as a result of severe muscular skeletal impairment. Individuals who were disabled for less than a year and a half were more external than persons who had been disabled for more than three years. Wendland suggests that disabled patients show a tendency to expect increased direction from external forces during the critical period following disability onset.

Ireland (1973) used several measures of I–E to test 25 male veterans who had emphysema. Even with intelligence partialed out, he found a relationship of .42 ($p < .05$) between internality and knowledge of emphysema. Ratings of participation in treatment were difficult to obtain, however, and no clear I–E prediction emerged. Dinardo (1972) investigated responses of 53 hospitalized patients to spinal cord injury. The patients completed the Rotter I–E scale, the Repression–Sensitization measure and indices of self-concept and depression. Dinardo also obtained patient adjustment ratings from the hospital staff. Internals had a more positive self-concept, and reported themselves less depressed than externals. When the two personality inventories were combined, internal repressors showed the best adjustment and external sensitizers the poorest adjustment to spinal cord injury.

Stokols (1974) has suggested that social learning theory offers a variety of behavioral approaches to the problem of cardiovascular risk and several experimenters have considered the relationship of I–E beliefs to voluntary control of heart rate. Ray (1974) found that internal subjects were better able to decrease heart rate than a comparison group. In addition, internals and externals reported different strategies for controlling heart rate. DeGood (1972) put 2 groups of 60 male subjects through a 30-min stress task. The "control" group could rest for 1 min during the task whenever they chose. The "no-control" group received rest periods assigned by the experimenter. Blood pressure arousal in the "no-control" group was significantly higher than in the "control" group. He found no unequivoval evidence that I–E beliefs as assessed by the Rotter scale were related to the degree of situational blood pressure arousal but he reports that this failure to predict might be due to the unpredictability of the external subject's blood pressure reaction. Fotopoulos (1971) also found I–E differences among subjects asked to control heart rate under biofeedback conditions. Internals were significantly more capable of increasing their heart rate with neither external feedback nor reinforcement. External subjects were incapable of increasing heart rate without reinforcement but could do so under a reinforcement paradigm. After first myocardial infraction in 58 male patients, Garrity (1973) found that subject's perception of health status, social class, and belief in internal control predicted return to work. In a study of brain-wave activity, Johnson and Meyer (1974) trained 12 females on EEG alpha feedback and found internals significantly better able to increase their alpha activity than externals.

The above studies, although not completely clear and consistent, do suggest that I–E beliefs are related to a number of aspects of emotional and physical well-being, ranging from preventive to remedial health care. Internals report themselves to be more psychologically adjusted than externals and they respond to psychotherapy differentially. In relation to physical disorders, internals appear to take precautions against accidents and disease and they also seem to be somewhat more likely to be able to control physiological functioning through biofeedback mechanisms. I–E may be related to susceptibility to disease or disorder since internals are more likely to report themselves as experiencing less life stress and as being generally more healthy than externals.

Antecedents of I–E Beliefs

Despite the wealth of research findings relating I–E beliefs to a myriad of behaviors across a wide range of subject populations, including children, surprisingly little attention has been focused on the antecedent conditions for the development of generalized expectancies. As locus of control emerges as a salient and significant variable for a number of achievement, interpersonal, and health phenomena, an important area of continued investigation is, logically, the ways in which internal or external beliefs develop, stabilize, and remain constant over time.

Stephens and his colleagues (Stephens, 1971, 1972b, 1973; Stephens & Delys, 1973) have considered the development of I–E expectancies in children as young as three years of age. Using interview techniques and simple questions which the child can understand ("What sort of things do you do that make your mother smile?"), they have assessed I–E beliefs in children and related them to two major areas of interest, namely intelligence and parent–child relationships. Stephens suggests that internal beliefs are correlates of intellectual and cognitive alertness. Moreover, while he had difficulty describing discrete parental acts associated with I–E expectancy development, he was able to show, at a more general level, that maternal variables such as warmth, attentiveness, and what he describes as "good quality of parent–child relationship" are all related to internality. These data are very similar to the results reported by other experimenters who have investigated I–E beliefs in children in relation to observed parent–child interactions (DeWitte, 1970; Katkovsky, Crandall, & Good, 1967; Solomon, Houlihan, Busse, & Parelius, 1971). Generally they find internal beliefs facilitated by, or at least related to, parental warmth, support, and approval as well as a lack of criticism and high parental dominance or control. These findings are also quite similar to the data generated by retrospective investigations in which adults are asked to report on their own rearing. Internal, in contrast to external, adults report a positive, consistent upbringing with approval for independence striving and few hostile, controlling, or overprotective behaviors on the part of their parents (Berzins, 1973; Chance, 1972; Cromwell, 1963; Davis & Phares, 1969; Epstein & Komorita, 1970; MacDonald, 1971; Nowicki & Segal, 1974; Patsula, 1969; Shores, 1968; Tolor, 1967; Tolor & Jalowiec, 1968; Wichern & Nowicki, in press). The consistency of these results is quite impressive especially considering that several different measures of I–E were used across the various studies and the time span covered was over ten years.

However, on a second glance, the data may not be as strong and the findings as straightforward as one might hope. As mentioned earlier, few of the studies actually used observation of parental–child interactions and some recent research by Crandall (1973) suggests that the association between I–E and parental–child relationships may be more complex than has previously been assumed. Moreover, peer interactions may also be contributing significantly to I–E expectancies.

Crandall (1973) recovered data from the longitudinal files of the Fels Research Institute for maternal–child interactions across several ages (0–3, 3–6, and 6–10 years) for subjects who were assessed as to I–E beliefs as young adults. As the subjects were growing up, trained observers had visited the home, observed maternal–child interactions and recorded detailed narrative reports. The observers had also recorded the behavior of the subjects in relation to peers and authority in nursery school and day camp. Crandall found, as expected, that mothers had pushed their offspring toward early independence; however, unexpectedly, she found almost the reverse of the earlier reported warmth and support in child-rearing patterns. In contrast to the recollective data, she found the mothers of internal females to be lacking in affection, somewhat rejecting, and punitive and critical toward their daughters. Involvement and contact was low and the general home adjustment appeared to be poor. These behaviors were likewise observed for the mothers of internal males although to a less noticeable extent than for the mother–daughter interactions. Unfortunately, little or no data were available for paternal–child behaviors. Crandall found adult internals, as children, to have been relatively unlikely to imitate or solicit help from adults, however, male internals were highly active and involved with peers. Female internals were likely to engage in tasks involving mechanical manipulations, and both male and female internals were observed to be more aggressive as children, particularly toward peers. Crandall suggests that a lessening of the attachment–dependency bonds between mothers and children with accompanying noxious maternal treatment may have forced the adult internal, as a child, to experience increased contact with peers and other environmental stimuli thus learning to become more reliant and observant of one's own behavior–reinforcement contingencies. Crandall also cautions that I–E beliefs may remain in a state of flux from childhood through adolescence so recollective data must be examined with a concern for stability. Levenson (1973b) also found sex differences in reported relationships between parents and children leading to adult internality. She had college students complete her multifactor locus of control scale and also respond to a perceived parenting questionnaire. For males, internality was related positively to perceived maternal instrumental behavior, while for females internality was related negatively to maternal protectiveness. As one would hypothesize from a multidimensional perspective, subjects who reported their parents to have used more punishing and controlling-type behaviors were found to have greater expectations of Control by Powerful Others. Subjects who viewed their parents as using unpredictable standards had stronger Chance control orientations.

Thus, the results of investigations of antecedent conditions for the development of internal and external expectancies appear somewhat confusing and even contradictory. Generally, in using recollective data from adult internals, investigators, except Levenson, find childhood to be characterized by warm, accepting, nurturing behaviors on the part of parents with some push toward independence. However, when actual mother–child interactions are observed and subjects are assessed as to I–E beliefs as adults, Crandall reports that, particularly for females, mothers may actually be critical and lacking in affection toward their children. Reconciliation of these data will depend on further investigation. One should not be surprised to learn that developmental antecedents for locus of control beliefs are substantially related to the sex of the individual. Since achievement and internal behaviors may be attained at some cost to femininity as defined by cultural stereotypes, young females who become internal may have early on acquired independent and "masculine" behaviors in rebellion against an overly critical mother who models the traditional female role. Additionally, more research on parental–child and peer interactions is also necessary.

Changes in I–E Beliefs

How stable are I–E beliefs across the life span? Several investigators (Gruen, Korte, & Baum, 1974; Nowicki & Strickland, 1973; Penk, 1969) report increasing internality with age among children. However, Crandall *et al.* (1965) found increasing internality only into the eighth through tenth grades and then a reverse trend, particularly for males, through the twelfth grade. These findings suggest that at certain times in one's life, such as the approaching uncertainty of life events following high-school graduation, an individual may feel more external. Supporting this hypothesis is the work of Kiehlbauch (1967), who studied young men in a reformatory. He found inmates' locus of control scores at both the beginning and end of their sentences to be relatively more external than at the midpoint of their sentences. Anxiety scores showed a similar relationship to length of imprisonment. When entering an institution about which one knows little and facing the uncertainties of institutional living, an individual might reasonably feel helpless and anxious. As a person comes to understand the environmental contingencies, he or she might become more internal in orientation although with impending release, the old uncertainties and external expectancies may return. Kielbauch also tested a group of inmates who were returned slowly to the community through a "work release" program in which they worked outside of the institution during the day for several weeks. In contrast to the others, this group did not show a rise in externality before their release. These data suggest that when faced with situations which are unknown, or unpredictable, persons may shift locus of control expectancies accordingly. These findings are also similar to the above mentioned research of Wendland (1973) who found physically disabled male subjects to report themselves to be external in the year and a half following onset of disability while patients handicapped for over three years were more internal. Gorman (1968) studied supporters of Eugene McCarthy immediately following the events of the 1968 Democratic National Convention when their candidate lost the nomination as presidential candidate. Their I–E scores were significantly more external than would be expected on the basis of I–E norms. In a sample of Yale undergraduates, following the draft lottery, MacArthur (1970) found students who became less susceptible to being drafted as a result of the drawing of numbers, to become more external than students whose draft status was not affected. However, Kaplan and Moore (1972) were not able to replicate these findings although they did find I–E changes among males subjected to the draft after the lottery. Contrary to MacArthur, they suggest that it is loss of freedom rather than a "lucky" experience that leads to greater externality. Eisenman (1972) had subjects participate in a verbal-conditioning experiment in which they were either told that their performance was dependent on "clinical sensitivity" which leads to excellent guesses or that success on the task was really a function of random guesses. Subjects who received instructions about random guesses became more external following the experiment. Subjects who were led to believe that their performance was a function of clinical sensitivity became more internal. Smith (1970) also found that crisis patients, having experienced a six-week crisis-resolution period, also experienced a significant change in locus of control expectancies toward internality. Thus, it appears that within both laboratory and real-life situations, locus of control beliefs are likely to shift as a function of situations. A shift toward externality occurs under conditions of chance or life difficulty and a shift toward internality is a function of feelings of personal efficacy.

Interestingly, when older adults are tested on I–E beliefs, their mean scores on the traditional measures appear to be lower (more internal) than those of younger adults assessed at the same time (Driver, 1974; Duke, Shaheen, & Nowicki, 1974; Wolk & Kurtz, 1975). At first, this might be surprising in that the populations studied have included, in some cases, elderly persons who were confined to nursing homes. However, if one considers the fact that I–E beliefs of these persons developed during an earlier period when mastery and competence behaviors were assumed to be important determinants of life satisfaction and, indeed, that one is responsible for one's destiny, then these data are quite sensible. Some additional support for this hypothesis, that I–E beliefs have changed (become more external) for the general populace over a number of years, is reported by Rotter (1975), who has tested college students with his scale over a span of some 15 years. He found that in the late fifties, mean scores were about 8 (with a standard deviation of about 4). By the early seventies, mean scores were 12 (standard deviation about 4) and appeared to be leveling off. Rotter suggests that the events of the late sixties in which numbers of young people, both black and white, attempted to change governmental policy on racial discrimination and the war in Southeast Asia and the ensuing disillusionment about economic and social justice led to an increase in feelings of alienation and to the belief that individuals had little control over their own destinies.

In summary, I–E beliefs do appear to change over the years in which a child matures, with increasing internality with increasing age. Change or stability of beliefs during adulthood have been more difficult to assess but I–E beliefs do appear to be flexible in response to specific events in one's life. In times of great adversity, when an individual perceives oneself as powerless and unable to influence events, one's beliefs may become more external. When things appear to be going well and this positive state of events is perceived as contingent on one's own effort, internality increases. Locus of control expectancies also appear to reflect general perceptions about the nature of one's social, cultural, and economic world. Elderly populations are often internal apparently since their I–E beliefs developed at a time of emphasis on mastery and responsibility. Young college adults' I–E scores, as a group, have become more external over the last 15 years.

Socio-economic and Cultural Differences in I–E

The bulk of the research reported here and in other reviews has involved North Americans and predominantly white middle-class groups. One must be especially cautious in generalizing these results to other populations, particularly since a number of researchers report more external scores among lower socioeconomic groupings (Battle & Rotter, 1963; Gruen, Korte, & Baum, 1974; Nowicki & Strickland, 1973; as well as the reviews of Joe, 1971; Lefcourt, 1972).

Clearly, membership in different socio-economic classes or cultures may lead to noticeable differences in the complex web of relationships between I–E expectancies and social behaviors. One might expect persons living in countries where the social and economic order is tightly controlled by the government to be more external. External beliefs might also be expected to prevail in countries or within religious groupings where destiny and fatalism are emphasized. Some cross-cultural I–E data are available, particularly since several of the traditional I–E measures have been translated into other languages. In 1969, Hsieh, Shybut, and Lotsof administered an I–E measure to three groups of high-school students with roughly similar socioeconomic backgrounds: a group of Hong Kong Chinese, a group of American-born Chinese, and a group of native Anglo-Americans. They found the Hong Kong Chinese to be the most external and the Anglo-Americans to be the most internal. The scores of the American-born Chinese fell between the mean scores of the other two groups. Reitz and Groff (1972) studied nonsupervisory laborers in the United States, Mexico, and Thailand. They found the Thai workers to be the most external, the American workers the most internal, and the Mexican workers to have intermediate scores. Parsons, Schneider, and Hansen (1970) compared the I–E beliefs of North American and Danish college undergraduates. They found the Danish males to be more external than the American males but no significant differences between the female samples. In a wide-ranging study across five different cultures, McGinnies, Nordholm, Ward, and Bhanthumnavin (1974) administered an I–E scale to over 1500 university students in Australia, New Zealand, Japan, Sweden, and the United States. They found the Swedish students to be the most external followed by the Japanese. Both of these groups were different from the other 3, which were not significantly different from each other. Moreover, they found the females in all countries to have higher external scores than the males.

McGinnies and Ward (1974) attempted to replicate the resistance-to-influence findings, reported by other investigators for North American students (summarized above), across the same 5 countries investigated by McGinnies *et al.* (1974). They used high- and low-credibility conditions to study subjects' reactions to a persuasive communication arguing for the extension of international maritime boundaries. Subjects in all countries were more persuaded by the high as opposed to the low credible communicator. Japanese were most persuaded followed by subjects from Sweden, New Zealand, Australia, and the United States, in that order. Internals and externals were differentially reactive to source credibility depending upon their countries of origin. Among American and Japanese subjects, the high-credibility source was more influential with the externals and the low-credibility source affected both internals and externals to an approximatlely equal (and lesser) extent. However, different trends appeared for subjects in the other three countries in that internals appeared to be more affected by the high credibility source than externals. These findings clearly indicate that it is important to consider the possible moderating effects of cultural differences when one is attempting to predict social behaviors from I–E beliefs.

And finally, several additional studies demonstrate the complexities of cross-cultural differences on I–E. Carment (1974), using male subjects, found Indian workers and university students (all Hindu) to be more internal on the basis of total scores from Rotter's scale than Canadian workers and university students. However, when the scale was subdivided into several components, he found that Canadian students were more internal than the Indian students in terms of personal control and both Canadian students and workers more external than their Indian counterparts in terms of control ideology and systems control. No significant differences were found between worker and student groups within countries. Finally, although one would hypothesize a relationship between externality and membership in a culture that espouses fatalism, Garza and Ames (1974), controlling for socioeconomic class, found Mexican-American students to be more internal on Rotter's scale than Anglo-American students. Mexican-Americans were also more internal on two components of the full scale, the luck and fate dimension, and a respect dimension. They argue that the cultural stereotype of the fatalism of Mexican-Americans may be incorrect or that, at least, Mexican-American college students appear to be more internally oriented than their Anglo-American counterparts. The generalizability of this study, however, is limited due to the utilization of only college students as subjects. Some investigators have considered locus of control beliefs among children of different cultures (Gruen, Korte, & Baum, 1974; Stephens, 1971, 1972a). Generally, they find Mexican and American-Indian children to be more external than Anglo-American children.

Obviously, socio-economic and cultural placement is related to I–E beliefs. This is in no way surprising in view of the fact that generalized beliefs about contingencies of reinforcement reflect learned expectancies both in relation to one's own pattern of behavior reinforcement and the more general attitudes and teachings of the larger society. Continued research in this area might be particularly fruitful not only in regard to contemporary societies but also in relation to the folklore, myths, and achievement indices of older cultures or the earlier history of present-day groupings. For example, it would be intriguing to know if generalized internal beliefs among large numbers of individuals within a culture were related to a flowering of economic trade, the waging of war, or a concern with educational and artistic creations. In contrast, investigators might determine the degree to which externality might be related to unrest within a populace or the decline of an empire. Clues about the beliefs of persons living at a time of historical upheaval and change as well as at times of tranquility and comfort may shed light not only on theoretical descriptions of personality but on an understanding of cultural and social structures as well.

PROBLEMS AND ISSUES

As mentioned above, I–E expectancies are likely to be enmeshed in the political and cultural net within which an individual finds oneself. Additionally, it may well be that the holding of I–E beliefs is also related to sex-role stereotypes and the degree to which one perceives or presents oneself as masculine or feminine. Although I–E scores are not usually different for males and females, Nowicki (1973) had college students complete the Rotter scale as if they were "super male" or "super female." When asked to assume a highly masculinized role, the mean I–E scores for both sexes was 1.78. Super females had a mean score of 22.65. Hochreich (1975b) replicated this finding with essentially the same results. The fact that subjects can dissimulate and bias assessment instruments in the direction that they wish is not surprising, but does, of course, raise the time-worn questions concerning the accuracy and meaning of scores on any personality instruments that purport to measure individual differences. Purists may wish to argue that the locus of control dimension, as it has been assessed, is tapping only a Horatio Alger-like, ideological orientation that has little to do with consistent beliefs about contingencies of reinforcement. Perhaps this is so. Certainly, clarifying the definition and meaning of locus of control beliefs has been and remains a major problem in I–E research. Confusion about I–E arises both from difficulties of definition and problems as to the assumptions about the uni- versus multidimensionality of the various assessment instruments. It is crucially important to delineate further the complex interactive effects of differing I–E expectancies on behavior. More over, there are obvious interactive effects of I–E with other personality variables which should be explored and explained.

Aside from the multifactor aspects of the I–E instruments, one other specific problem of assessing I–E is the degree to which responding in the internal direction may be reflecting a social desirability bias. In the early development of the Rotter I–E scale, Rotter attempted to lessen social desirability pull by using a forced-choice format and eliminating items with high social desirability. Nonetheless, examination of studies correlating I–E and the Marlowe–Crowne

Social Desirability scale reveal an average correlation of −.23 (Rotter, 1966). Several recent studies have also generated findings of moderately high correlations between internal locus of control scores and social desirability measures (Cone, 1971; Hjelle, 1971; Vuchinich & Bass, 1974). Hjelle found internal alternatives for each item to be significantly more socially desirable than the corresponding external item. In one of the few noncorrelative studies investigating I–E and social desirability, Harris (1975) had well over 200 subjects complete the Rotter scale under conventional testing situations. Subjects then retook the Rotter scale under one of three conditions: a conventional condition similar to the first test administration; a validation condition, in which subjects were asked to answer the I–E scale in the more socially desirable fashion; and a "bogus pipeline" condition, which consisted of monitoring the responses of subjects to the I–E scale. Subjects were led to believe that the polygraph which was allegedly recording their physiological responses, was capable of determining their "true" beliefs. Subjects in the conventional condition did not change their I–E responding. In the validation condition, subjects chose more internal items as representing socially desirable responses. The most intriguing results had to do with the bogus pipeline condition. Individuals who had previously chosen internal items now presented themselves as more external, believing their responses to be monitored by a machine which could supposedly determine their degree of honesty. Thus, a number of subjects had evidently initially answered the Rotter scale in a socially desirable fashion suggesting that their I–E scores are not a veridical representation of locus of control expectancies. These data are particularly interesting in view of the more commonly held conceptualization of externals, particularly the defensive externals, as the subjects who may dissimulate on the I–E scale.

Even beyond the assessment difficulties, perhaps the most disturbing problem that one encounters within the locus of control literature is the extent to which I–E research has been divorced from the theory which spawned it. In spite of psychometric limitations, the traditional measures of I–E have been predictive, and they are often included in studies when there is no logical or theoretical reason for them to be there. Sometimes within these studies, I–E continues to predict, resulting in conflicting and confusing explanations as to why this might be the case. The banner of I–E expectancies has been raised without the supporting theoretical pillars of reinforcement value and situational contingencies, leading to very shaky conceptualizations indeed. Some investigatiors also attack the social learning theory from which the notion of a generalized expectancy about locus of control arose. They argue that Rotter's theory is sterile and tied to a static rather than dynamic view of behavior. In fact, I–E has often been mistakenly interpreted as a "trait" variable. No doubt the theory does have drawbacks, but in many ways it has offered a rich and yet practical conceptualization of behavior. When some behavior theorists were emphasizing overt behavior and attacking mediation concepts, Rotter's theory continued to include both reinforcement and expectancies as well as situational influences. This formulation appears particularly impressive now that behaviorists are increasingly considering cognitive mediating variables and covert behavior.

In line with a failure to be appreciative of the theoretical net from which I–E developed, is the simplistic approach used by many researchers to see internals as the "good guys" and externals as the "baddies." While much of the I–E research does suggest that internality is related to adaptive and competence-type behaviors, one must be more than cautious in suggesting that conversely, externals are universally maladaptive and incompetent. Indeed whatever evaluative adjectives one wished to use with either "side," equally abusive or complimentary ones can be found for the other. Internals might be called arrogant, manipulative, or passive–aggressive at the same time that they are described as achieving and independent. The defensive external might just as well be called realistic and able to adjust to conflicting demands. Evaluative judgments without supporting data as well as misinterpretations of attributes or characteristics have no place in scientific inquiry.

Perhaps the problem of definition that has plagued the I–E construct has also been a reason why this variable has caught the interest of innumerable researchers and a large number of laymen. Whatever the refined definition of I–E that further work may yield, its meaning ordinarily has to do with attitudes about determinism and freedom. Obviously, the I–E dimension has tapped beliefs that people feel are significant and important in regard to the ways they live. Expectancies about internal versus external locus of control, even if illusory, appear to be related to a wide range and a large number of significant social behaviors.

ACKNOWLEDGMENTS

I would particularly like to thank Bobbi Fibel for her invaluable help in the literature search. I am also grateful to Shelly Chaiken, W. Daniel Hale, and Carol Reinhardt for their careful reading of and suggestions about the manuscript.

The writing of this chapter was also partially supported by funds available through the National Institute of Child Health and Development Grant HD08952.

REFERENCES

Abramowicz, C. V., Abramowicz, S. I., Roback, H. B., & Jackson, C. Differential effectiveness of directive and nondirective group therapies as a function of client internal–external control. *Journal of Consulting and Clinical Psychology,* 1974, *42,* 849–853.

Abramowicz, S. I. Locus of control and self-reported depression among college students. *Psychological Reports,* 1969, *25,* 149–150.

Abramowicz, S. I. Research on internal-external control and social political activism. *Psychological Reports,* 1974, *34,* 619–621.

Adams-Webber, J. Generalized expectancies concerning the locus of control of reinforcements and the perception of moral sanctions. *British Journal of Social and Clinical Psychology,* 1969, *8,* 340–343.

Alegre, C., & Murray, E. J. Locus of control, behavioral intention, and verbal conditioning. *Journal of Personality,* 1974, *42,* 668–681.

Baron, R. A. The effects of intertrial activity and locus of control orientation on verbal operant conditioning. *Psychonomic Science,* 1969, *15,* 69–71.

Baron, R. M., Cowan, G., Ganz, R. L., & McDonald, M. Interaction of locus of control and type of performance feedback: Correlations of external validity. *Journal of Personality and Social Psychology,* 1974, *30,* 285–292.

Baron, R. M., & Ganz, R. L. Effects of locus of control and type of feedback on the task performance of lower-class black children. *Journal of Personality and Social Psychology,* 1972, *21,* 124–130.

Battle, E. S., & Rotter, J. B. Children's feelings of personal control as related to social class and ethnic group. *Journal of Personality,* 1963, *31,* 482–490.

Beckman, L. Locus of control and attitudes toward mental illness among mental health volunteers. *Journal of Consulting and Clinical Psychology,* 1972, *38,* 84–89.

Berzins, J. I. Locus of control in dimensional versus typological perspectives. Paper presented at the meeting of the American Psychological Association, Montreal, August 1973.

Berzins, J. I., & Ross, W. F. Locus of control among opiate addicts. *Journal of Consulting and Clinical Psychology,* 1973, *40,* 84–91.

Bialer, I. Conceptualization of success and failure in mentally retarded and normal children. *Journal of Personality,* 1961, *29,* 303–320.

Biondo, J., & MacDonald, A. P. Internal–external locus of control and response to influence attempts. *Journal of Personality,* 1971, *39,* 407–419.

Bottinelli, S. B., & Weizmann, F. Task independence and locus of control orientation in children. *Journal of Personality Assessment,* 1973, *37,* 375–381.

Brehm, J. W. *A theory of psychological reactance.* New York: Academic Press, 1966.

Brown, J. C., & Strickland, B. R. Belief in internal–external control of reinforcement and participation in college activities. *Journal of Consulting and Clinical Psychology,* 1972, *38,* 148.

Bruhn, J. G., Hampton, J. W., & Chandler, B. C. Clinical marginality and psychological adjustment in hemophilia. *Journal of Psychosomatic Research,* 1971, *15,* 207–213.

Buck, M. R., & Austrin, H. R. Factors related to school achievement in an economically disadvantaged group. *Child Development,* 1971, *42,* 1813–1826.

Butterfield, E. C. Locus of control, test anxiety, reactions to frustration, and achievement attitudes. *Journal of Personality,* 1964, *32,* 298–311.

Calhoun, L. G., Cheney, T., & Dawes, A. S. Locus of control, self-reported depression, and perceived causes of depression. *Journal of Consulting and Clinical Psychology,* 1974, *42,* 736.

Calicchia, J. P. Narcotic addiction and perceived locus of control. *Journal of Social Issues,* 1974, *26*(1), 59–74.

Caplan, N. The new ghetto man: A review of recent empirical studies. *Journal of Social Issues,* 1970, *26,* 59–74.

Carlson, R. Personality. *Annual Review of Psychology,* 1975, *26,* 393–414.

Carment, D. W. Internal versus external control in India and Canada. *International Journal of Psychology,* 1974, *9,* 45–50.

Cash, T. F., & Stack, J. J. Locus of control among schizophrenics and other hospitalized psychiatric patients. *Genetic Psychology Monographs,* 1973, *87,* 105–122.

Chance, J. E. Internal control of reinforcements and the school learning process. Paper presented at the meeting of the Society for Research in Child Development, Minneapolis, March 1965.

Chance, J. E. Academic correlates and maternal antecendents of children's belief in external or internal control of reinforcements. In J. B. Rotter, J. E. Chance, & E. J. Phares (Eds.),

Applications of a social learning theory of personality. New York: Holt, Rinehart and Winston, 1972.

Cherulnik, P. D., & Citrin, M. M. Individual difference in psychological reactance: The interaction between locus of control and mode of elimination of freedom. *Journal of Personality and Social Psychology,* 1974, *29,* 398–404.

Clark, K. B., & Clark, M. P. Development of consciousness of self and emergence of racial identification. *Journal of Social Psychology,* 1939, *10,* 591.

Coan, R. W. Personality variables associated with cigarette smoking. *Journal of Personality and Social Psychology,* 1973, *26,* 86–104.

Coleman, J. S., Campbell, E. Q., Hobson, C. J., McPartland, J., Mood, A. M., Weinfeld, F. D., & York, R. L. *Equality of educational opportunity* (Superintendent of Documents Catalog No. FS 5.238:38001). Washington, D.C.: U.S. Government Printing Office, 1966.

Cone, J. D. Social desirability scale values and ease of responding to personality statements. *Proceedings of the Annual Convention of the American Psychological Association,* 1971, *6,* 119–120.

Collins, B. E. Four components of the Rotter Internal–External scale: Belief in a difficult world, a just world, a predictable world, and a politically responsive world. *Journal of Personality and Social Psychology,* 1974, *29,* 381–391.

Crandall, V. C. Differences in parental antecedents of internal–external control in children and young adulthood. Paper presented at the meeting of the American Psychological Association, Montreal, August 1973.

Crandall, V. C., Katkovsky, W., & Crandall, V. J. Children's belief in their own control of reinforcements in intellectual–academic achievement situations. *Child Development,* 1965, *36,* 91–109.

Crandall, V. J., Katkovsky, W., & Preston, A. Motivational and ability determinants of children's intellectual achievement behaviors. *Child Development,* 1962, *33,* 643–661.

Crandall, V. C., & Lacey, B. W. Children's perceptions of IE control in intellectual–academic situations and their Embedded Figures Test performance. *Child Development,* 1972, *43,* 1123–1134.

Crepeau, J. J. The effects of stressful live events and locus of control on suicidal ideation. Unpublished research, University of Massachusetts, 1975.

Cromwell, R. L. A social learning approach to mental retardation. In N. R. Ellis (Ed.), *Handbook of mental deficiency.* New York: McGraw-Hill, 1963.

Cromwell, R. L., Rosenthal, D., Shakow, D., & Zahn, T. P. Reaction time, locus of control, choice behavior, and description of parental behavior in schizophrenic and normal subjects. *Journal of Personality,* 1968, *29,* 363–380.

Cross, H. J., & Tracey, J. J. Personality factors in deliquent boys: Differences between blacks and whites. *Journal for Research in Crime and Deliquency,* 1971, *8,* 10–22.

Crowne, D. P., & Liverant, S. Conformity under varying conditions of personal commitment. *Journal of Abnormal and Social Psychology,* 1963, *66,* 545–547.

Crowne, D. P., & Marlowe, D. A new scale of social desirability independent of psychopathology. *Journal of Consulting Psychology,* 1960, *24,* 349–354.

Dabbs, J. M., & Kirscht, J. P. "Internal Control" and the taking of influenza shots. *Psychological Reports,* 1971, *28,* 959–962.

Darrow, W. W. Innovative health behavior: A study of the use, acceptance and use-effectiveness of the condom as a venereal disease prophylactic. Unpublished doctoral dissertation, Emory University, 1973.

Davis, W. L., & Davis, D. E. Internal–external control and attribution of responsibility for success and failure. *Journal of Personality,* 1972, *40,* 123–135.

Davis, W. L., & Phares, E. J. Parental antecedents of internal-external control of reinforcement. *Psychological Reports,* 1969, *24,* 427–436.

deCharms, R. *Personal causation: The internal affective determinants of behavior.* New York: Academic Press, 1968.

DeGood, D. E. Vascular effects of locus of control during shock avoidance performance in humans. *Dissertation Abstracts International,* 1972, *32,* 6641–6642.

DeWitte, L. L. Parental antecedents of adolescent beliefs in internal–external control of reinforcement. Unpublished master's thesis, University of Cincinnati, 1970.

Diamond, M. J., & Shapiro, J. L. Changes in locus of control as a function of encounter group experience. *Journal of Abnormal Psychology,* 1973, 514–518.

Dies, R. R. Electroconvulsive therapy: A social learning theory interpretation. *Journal of Nervous and Mental Disease,* 1968, *146,* 334–342.

Dinardo, Q. E. Psychological adjustment to spinal cord injury. *Dissertation Abstracts International,* 1972, *32,* 4206–4207.

Doctor, R. M. Locus of control of reinforcement and responsiveness to social influence. *Journal of Personality,* 1971, *39,* 542–551.

Driver, J. Personality differences in the elderly as a function of type and length of residence. Unpublished doctoral dissertation, University of Maryland, 1974.

Dua, P. S. Comparison of the effects of behaviorally oriented action and psychotherapy re-education in intraversion–extraversion, emotionality, and internal–external control. *Journal of Counseling Psychology,* 1970, *17,* 567–572.

DuCette, J., & Wolk, S. Locus of control and extreme behavior. *Journal of Consulting and Clinical Psychology,* 1972, *39,* 253–258.

DuCette, J., & Wolk, S. Cognitive and motivational correlates of general expectancy of control. *Journal of Personality and Social Psychology,* 1973, *26,* 420–426.

DuCette, J., Wolk, S., & Friedman, S. Locus of control and creativity in black and white children. *Journal of Social Psychology,* 1972, *88,* 297–298.

Duke, M. P., & Mullins, C. Interpersonal distance as a function of locus of control in hospitalized schizophrenics and non-schizophrenics. *Journal of Consulting and Clinical Psychology,* 1973, *41,* 230–234.

Duke, M. P., & Nowicki, S. Personality correlates of the Nowicki–Strickland locus of control scale for adults. *Psychological Reports,* 1973, *33,* 267–270.

Duke, M. P., Shaheen, J., & Nowicki, S. The determination of locus of control in a geriatric population and a subsequent test of the social learning model for interpersonal distance. *Journal of Psychology,* 1974, *86,* 277–285.

Dweck, C. S. The role of expectations and attributions in the alleviation of learned helplessness. *Journal of Personality and Social Psychology,* 1975, *31,* 674–685.

Dweck, C. S., & Repucci, N. D. Learned helplessness and reinforcement responsibility in children. *Journal of Personality and Social Psychology,* 1973, *25,* 109–116.

Efran, J. S. Some personality determinants of memory for success and failure. Unpublished doctoral dissertation, Ohio State University, 1963.

Eggland, E. T. Locus of control and children with cerebral palsy. *Nursing Research,* 1973, *22,* 329–333.

Eisenman, R. Experience in experiments and change in internal–external control scores. *Journal of Consulting and Clinical Psychology,* 1972, *39,* 434–435.

Eisenman, R., & Platt, J. Birth order and sex differences in academic achievement and internal–external control. *Journal of General Psychology,* 1968, *78,* 278–285.

Epstein, R., & Komorita, S. S. Self-esteem, success-failure, and locus of control in Negro children. *Developmental Psychology,* 1970, *4,* 2–8.

Erikson, R. V., & Roberts, A. H. Some ego functions associated with delay of gratification in male deliquents. *Journal of Consulting and Clinical Psychology,* 1971, *36,* 378–382.

Feather, N. T. Some personality correlates of external control. *Australian Journal of Psychology,* 1967, *19,* 252–260. (a)

Feather, N. T. Valence of outcome and expectation of success in relation to task difficulty and perceived locus of control. *Journal of Personality and Social Psychology,* 1967, *7,* 372–387. (b)

Feather, N. T. Valence of success and failure in relation to task difficulty: Past research and recent progress. *Australian Journal of Psychology,* 1968, *20,* 111–122.

Felton, B., & Kahana, E. Adjustment and situationally-bound locus of control among the institutionally aged. *Journal of Gerontology,* 1974, *29,* 295–301.

Felton, G. S. Teaching internalization to middle-level mental health workers in training. *Psychological Reports,* 1973, *32,* 1279–1282.

Felton, G. S., & Biggs, B. E. Teaching internalization to collegiate low achievers in group psychotherapy. *Psychotherapy: Theory, Research, and Practice,* 1972, *9,* 281–283.

Felton, G. S., & Biggs, B. E. Psychotherapy and responsibility: Teaching internalization to black low achievers through group therapy. *Small Group Behavior,* 1973, *4,* 147–155.

Felton, G. S., & Davidson, H. R. Group counseling can work in the classroom. *Academic Therapy,* 1973, *8,* 461–468.

Felton, G. S., & Thomas, L. J. How to beat the failure syndrome: A process-oriented learning program for collegiate low achievers. *College Student Journal Monograph,* 1972, *6,* 1–13.

Ferguson, B., & Kennelly, K. Internal–external locus of control and perception of authority figures. *Psychological Reports,* 1974, *34,* 1119–1123.

Fink, H. C., & Hjelle, L. A. Internal–external control and ideology. *Psychological Reports,* 1973, *33,* 967–974.

Fitz, R. J. The differential effects of praise and censure on serial learning as dependent on locus of control and field dependency. *Dissertation Abstracts International,* 1971, *31,* 4310.

Forward, J. R., & Williams, J. R. Internal–external control and black militancy. *Journal of Social Issues,* 1970, *26*(1), 75–92.

Foss, R. Personality, social influence, and cigarette smoking. *Journal of Health and Social Behavior,* 1973, *14,* 279–286.

Fotopoulos, S. Internal versus external control: Increase of heart rate by thinking under feedback and no-feedback conditions. *Dissertation Abstracts International,* 1971, *31,* 3703–3704.

Franklin, R. D. Youth's expectancies about internal versus external control of reinforcement related to N variables. Unpublished doctoral dissertation, Purdue University, 1963.

Friedman, M. L., & Dies, R. R. Reactions of internal and external test anxious students to counseling and behavior therapies. *Journal of Consulting and Clinical Psychology,* 1974, *42,* 921.

Garrity, T. F. Vocational adjustment after first myocardial infarction: Comparative assessment of several variables suggested in literature. *Social Science and Medicine,* 1973, 7(9), 705–717.

Garza, R. T., & Ames, R. E., Jr. A comparison of Anglo- and Mexican-American college students on locus of control. *Journal of Consulting and Clinical Psychology,* 1974, *42,* 919.

Getter, H. A. A personality determinant of verbal conditioning. *Journal of Personality,* 1966, *34,* 397–405.

Gillis, J. S., & Jessor, R. Effects of brief psychotherapy on belief in internal control: An exploratory study. *Psychotherapy: Theory, Research, and Practice,* 1970, *7,* 135–136.

Gilmore, T. M., & Minton, H. L. Internal versus external attribution of task performance as a function of locus of control, initial confidence and success-failure outcome. *Journal of Personality,* 1974, *42,* 159–174.

Gold, D. Preference for skill or chance tasks and I–E scores. *Psychological Reports,* 1966, *19,* 1279–1281.

Goodstadt, B. E., & Hjelle, L. A. Power to the powerless: Locus of control and the use of power. *Journal of Personality and Social Psychology,* 1973, *27,* 190–196.

Gore, P. M. Individual differences in the prediction of subject compliance to experimenter bias. Unpublished doctoral dissertation, Ohio State University, 1962.

Gore, P. M., & Rotter, J. B. A personality correlate of social action. *Journal of Personality,* 1963, *31,* 58–64.

Gorman, B. S. An observation of altered locus of control following political disappointment. *Psychological Reports,* 1968, *23,* 1094.

Goss, A., & Morosko, T. E. Relation between a dimension of internal–external control and the MMPI with an alcoholic population. *Journal of Consulting and Clinical Psychology,* 1970, *34,* 189–192.

Gozali, H., Cleary, T. A., Walster, G. W., & Gozali, J. Relationship between the internal-external control construct and achievement. *Journal of Educational Psychology,* 1973, *64,* 9–14.

Granberg, D., & May, W. I–E and orientations toward the Vietnam war. *Journal of Social Psychology,* 1972, *88,* 157–158.

Gruen, G. E. The development of an internal–external control scale. In J. W. Asher, J. F. Feldhausen, G. E. Gruen, R. G. Kane, E. McDaniel, M. I. Stephens, J. Towler, & G. H. Wheatley (Eds.), *The development of new measures of cognitive variables in elementary school children (Phase II).* Washington, D.C.: U.S. Office of Education, 1971.

Gruen, G. E., Korte, J. R., & Baum, J. F. Group measure of locus of control. *Developmental Psychology,* 1974, *10,* 683–686.

Gurin, P., Gurin, G., Lao, R., & Beattie, M. Internal–external control in the motivational dynamics of Negro youth. *Journal of Social Issues,* 1969, *25*(3), 29–53.

Gurin, P., & Katz, D. *Motivation and aspiration in the Negro college* (Final Report, Office of Education, Department of Health, Education, and Welfare). Washington, D.C.: United States Government Printing Office, 1966.

Hale, W. D. Dimensions of locus of control and self-reported depression. Paper presented at the meeting of the Eastern Psychological Association, New York, April 1975.

Hamsher, J. H., Geller, J. D., & Rotter, J. B. Interpersonal trust, internal–external control, and the Warren Commission Report. *Journal of Personality and Social Psychology,* 1968, *9,* 210–215.

Harris, W. G. An investigation of the IE scale's predictability using the bogus pipeline. Unpublished master's thesis, University of Massachusetts, 1975.

Harrison, F. I. Relationship between home background, school success, and adolescent attitudes. *Merrill–Palmer Quarterly,* 1968, *14,* 331–344.

Harrow, M., & Ferrante, A. Locus of control in psychiatric patients. *Journal of Consulting and Clinical Psychology,* 1969, *33,* 582–589.

Harvey, J. H., Barnes, R. D., Sperry, D. L., & Harris, B. Perceived choice as a function of internal–external locus of control. *Journal of Personality,* 1974, 437–452.

Harvey, J. H., & Harris, B. Determinants of perceived choice and the relationship between perceived choice and expectancy about feelings of internal control. *Journal of Personality and Social Psychology,* 1975, *31,* 101–106.

Harvey, J. H., & Johnston, S. Determinants of the perception of choice. *Journal of Experimental Social Psychology,* 1973, *9,* 164–179.

Heider, F. *The psychology of interpersonal relations.* New York: Wiley, 1958.

Hersch, P. D., & Scheibe, K. E. On the reliability and validity of internal–external control as a personality dimension. *Journal of Consulting Psychology,* 1967, *31,* 609–613.

Hill, R. A., Chapman, M. L., & Wuertzer, V. J. *Achievement competence training: A report, Part X: Locus of control: A study of the correlates.* Philadelphia: Research for Better Schools, 1974.

Hiroto, D. S. Learned helplessness and locus of control. *Journal of Experimental Psychology,* 1974, *102*(2), 187–193.

Hjelle, L. A. Internal–external control as determinant of academic achievement. *Psychological Reports,* 1970, *26,* 326.

Hjelle, L. A. Social desirability as a variable in the locus of control scale. *Psychological Reports,* 1971, *28,* 807–816.

Hochreich, D. J. Internal–external control and reaction to the My Lai court martials. *Journal of Applied Social Psychology,* 1972, *2,* 319–325.

Hochreich, D. J. Defensive externality and attribution of responsibility. *Journal of Personality,* 1974, *42,* 543–557.

Hochreich, D. J. Defensive externality and blame projection following failure. *Journal of Personality and Social Psychology,* 1975, *32,* 540–546. (a)

Hochreich, D. J. Sex-role stereotypes for internal–external control and interpersonal trust. *Journal of Consulting and Clinical Psychology,* 1975, *43,* 273. (b)

Holden, K. B., & Rotter, J. B. A nonverbal measure of extinction in skill and chance situations. *Journal of Experimental Psychology,* 1962, *63,* 519–520.

Holmes, D. S., & Jackson, T. H. Influence of locus of control in interpersonal attraction and affective reactions in situations involving reward and punishment. *Journal of Personality and Social Psychology,* 1975, *31,* 132–136.

Holmes, T. H., & Masuda, M. Life change and illness susceptibility. In J. P. Scott & E. C. Senay (Eds.), *Separation and depression: Clinical and research aspects.* Washington, D.C.: Publication No. 94 of the American Association for the Advancement of Science, 1973.

Hsieh, T. T., Shybut, J., & Lotsof, E. J. Internal versus external control and ethnic group membership: A cross-cultural comparison. *Journal of Consulting and Clinical Psychology,* 1969, *33,* 122–124.

Ireland, R. E. Locus of control among hospitalized pulmonary emphysema patients. *Dissertation Abstracts International,* 1973, *33,* 6091.

James, W. H. Internal versus external control of reinforcement as a basic variable in learning theory. Unpublished doctoral dissertation, Ohio State University, 1957.

James, W. H., Woodruff, A. B., & Werner, W. Effect on internal and external control upon changes in smoking behavior. *Journal of Consulting Psychology,* 1965, *29,* 184–186.

James, W. H., & Rotter, J. B. Partial and 100 percent reinforcement under chance and skill conditions. *Journal of Experimental Psychology,* 1958, *55,* 397–403.

Joe, V. C. Review of the internal–external control construct as a personality variable. *Psychological Reports,* 1971, *28,* 619–640.

Johnson, F. Y. Political attitudes as related to internal and external control. Unpublished master's thesis, Ohio State University, 1961.

Johnson, J. E., Leventhal, H., & Dabbs, J. M. Contribution of emotional and instrumental response processes in adaptation to surgery. *Journal of Personality and Social Psychology,* 1971, *20,* 65–70.

Johnson, R. C., Ackerman, J. M., Frank, H., & Fionda, A. J. Resistance to temptation and guilt following yielding and psychotherapy. *Journal of Consulting and Clinical Psychology,* 1968, *32,* 169–175.

Johnson, R. K., & Meyer, R. G. The locus of control construct in EEG alpha rhythm feedback. *Journal of Consulting and Clinical Psychology,* 1974, *42,* 913.

Jolley, M. T., & Spielberger, C. D. The effects of locus of control and anxiety on verbal conditioning. *Journal of Personality,* 1973, *41,* 443–456.

Jones, E. E., Worchel, S., Goethals, G. R., & Grumet, J. Prior expectancy and behavioral extremity as determinants of attitude attribution. *Journal of Experimental Social Psychology,* 1971, *7,* 59–80.

Jones, R. A. Volunteering to help: The effects of choice, dependence, and anticipated dependence. *Journal of Personality and Social Psychology,* 1970, *14,* 121–129.

Julian, J. W., & Katz, S. B. Internal versus external control and the value of reinforcement. *Journal of Personality and Social Psychology,* 1968, *8,* 89–94.

Kaplan, K. J., & Moore, M. Loss of freedom versus luck as determinants of externality: Failure to replicate the MacArthur draft lottery findings. *Representative Research in Social Psychology,* 1972, *3,* 39–45.

Karabenick, S. A. Valence of success and failure as a function of achievement motives and locus of control. *Journal of Personality and Social Psychology,* 1972, *21,* 101–110.

Katkovsky, W., Crandall, V. C., & Good, S. Parental antecedents of children's belief in internal–external control of reinforcement in intellectual achievement situations. *Child Development,* 1967, *38,* 765–776.

Kelley, H. H. Attribution theory in social psychology. In D. Levine (Ed.), *Nebraska Symposium on Motivation* (Vol. 15). Lincoln: University of Nebraska Press, 1967.

Kiehlbauch, J. B. Selected changes over time in internal–external control of expectancies in a reformatory population. Unpublished doctoral dissertation, Kansas State University, 1967.

Kilmann, P. R. Direct and non-direct marathon group therapy and internal–external control. *Journal of Counseling Psychology,* 1974, *21,* 380–384.

Kilmann, P. R., & Howell, R. J. Effects of structure of marathon group therapy and locus of control on therapeutic outcome. *Journal of Consulting and Clinical Psychology,* 1974, *42,* 912.

Kilpatrick, D. G., Miller, W. C., & William, A. R. Locus of control and adjustment to long term hemodialysis. Paper presented at the meeting of the American Psychological Association, Honolulu, September 1972.

Kirscht, J. P. Perceptions of control and health beliefs. *Canadian Journal of Behavioral Science,* 1974, *4,* 225–237.

Krovetz, M. L. Explaining success or failure as a function of one's locus of control. *Journal of Personality,* 1974, *42,* 175–189.

Lambley, P., & Silbowitz, M. Rotter's internal–external scale and prediction of suicide contemplators among students. *Psychological Reports,* 1973, *33,* 585–586.

Lao, R. C. Internal–external control and competent and innovative behavior among Negro college students. *Journal of Personality and Social Psychology,* 1970, *14,* 263–270.

Lefcourt, H. M. Internal versus external control of reinforcement: A review. *Psychological Bulletin,* 1966, *65,* 206–220.

Lefcourt, H. M. Effects of cue explication upon persons maintaining external control expectancies. *Journal of Personality and Social Psychology,* 1967, *5,* 372–378.

Lefcourt, H. M. Recent developments in the study of locus of control. In B. A. Maher (Ed.), *Progress in experimental personality research* (Vol. 6). New York: Academic Press, 1972.

Lefcourt, H. M. *Locus of control: Current trends in theory and research.* Hillsdale, N.J.: Lawrence Erlbaum Assoc., 1976.

Lefcourt, H. M., Antrobus, P., & Hogg, E. Humor response and humor production as a function of locus of control, field dependence, and type of reinforcement. *Journal of Personality,* 1974, *42,* 632–651.

Lefcourt, H. M., Gronnerud, P., & McDonald, P. Cognitive activity and hypothesis formation during a double entendre word association test as a function of locus of control and field dependence. *Canadian Journal of Behavioral Science,* 1973, *5,* 161–173.

Lefcourt, H. M., Hogg, E., Struthers, S., & Holmes, C. Causal attributions as a function of locus of control, initial confidence, and performance outcomes. *Journal of Personality and Social Psychology,* 1975, *32,* 391–397.

Lefcourt, H. M., Lewis, L., & Silverman, I. W. Internal versus external control of reinforcement and alteration in a decision making task. *Journal of Personality,* 1968, *36,* 663–682.

Lefcourt, H. M., Sordoni, C., & Sordoni, C. Locus of control and the expression of humor. *Journal of Personality,* 1974, *42,* 130–143.

Lefcourt, H. M., & Wine, J. Internal versus external control of reinforcement and the development of attention in experimental situationsl. *Canadian Journal of Behavioral Science,* 1969, *1,* 167–181.

Lerner, M. J. Social psychology of justice and interpersonal attraction. In T. L. Huston (Ed.), *Foundations of interpersonal attraction.* New York: Academic Press, 1974.

Lessing, E. E. Racial differences in indices of ego functioning relevant to academic achievement. *Journal of Genetic Psychology,* 1969, *115,* 153–167.

Levenson, H. Distinctions within the concept of internal–external control: Development of a new scale. Paper presented at the meeting of the American Psychological Association, Honolulu, September 1972.

Levenson, H. Multidimensional locus of control in psychiatric patients. *Journal of Consulting and Clinical Psychology,* 1973, *41,* 397–404. (a)

Levenson, H. Perceived parental antecedents of Internal, Powerful Others, and Chance locus of control orientations. *Developmental Psychology,* 1973, *9,* 260–265. (b)

Levenson, H. Reliability and validity of the I, P, and C scales: A multidimensional view of locus of control. Paper presented at the meeting of the American Psychological Association, Montreal, September 1973. (c)

Levenson, H., & Miller, J. Multidimensional locus of control in sociopolitical activists of conservative and liberal ideologies. *Journal of Personality and Social Psychology,* 1976, *33,* 199–208.

Lichtenstein, E., & Crain, W. The importance of subjective evaluation of reinforcement in verbal conditioning. *Journal of Experimental Research in Personality,* 1969, *3,* 214–220.

Lipp, L., Kolstoe, R., James, W., & Randall, H. Denial of disability and internal control of reinforcement: A study using a perceptual defense paradigm. *Journal of Consulting and Clinical Psychology,* 1968, *32,* 72–75.

Liverant, S., & Scodel, A. Internal and external control as determinants of decision making under conditions of risk. *Psychological Reports,* 1960, *7,* 59–67.

Lottman, T. J., & DeWolfe, A. S. Internal versus external control in reactive and process schizophrenia. *Journal of Consulting and Clinical Psychology,* 1972, *39,* 344.

Ludwigsen, K., & Rollins, H. Recognition of random forms as a function of source of cue, perceived locus of control, and socioeconomic level. Paper presented at the meeting of the Southern Psychological Association, Atlanta, April 1972.

MacArthur, L. A. Luck is alive and well in New Haven. *Journal of Personality and Social Psychology,* 1970, *16,* 316–318.

MacDonald, A. P. Internal–external locus of control and the practice of birth control. *Psychological Reports,* 1970, *27,* 206.

MacDonald, A. P. Internal–external locus of control: Parental antecedents. *Journal of Consulting and Clinical Psychology,* 1971, *37,* 141–147.

MacDonald, A. P. More on the Protestant Ethic. *Journal of Consulting and Clinical Psychology,* 1972, *39,* 116–122.

MacDonald, A. P. Internal–external locus of control. In J. P. Robinson & P. R. Shaver (Eds.), *Measures of social psychological attitudes.* Ann Arbor, Mich.: Institute for Social Research, University of Michigan, 1973.

MacDonald, A. P., & Games, R. G. Ellis' irrational values. *Rational Living,* 1972, *7,* 25–28.

MacDonald, A. P., & Hall, J. Internal–external locus of control and perception of disability. *Journal of Consulting and Clinical Psychology,* 1971, *36,* 338–343.

Martin, R. D., & Shepel, L. F. Locus of control and discrimination ability with lay counselors. *Journal of Consulting and Clinical Psychology,* 1974, *42,* 741.

Massari, D. J., & Rosenblum, D. C. Locus of control, interpersonal trust, and academic achievement. *Psychological Reports,* 1972, *31,* 355–360.

McGhee, P. E., & Crandall, V. C. Beliefs in internal–external control of reinforcements and academic performance. *Child Development,* 1968, *39,* 91–102.

McGinnies, E., Nordholm, L. A., Ward, C. D., & Bhanthumnavin, D. L. Sex and cultural differences in perceived locus of control among students in five countries. *Journal of Consulting and Clinical Psychology,* 1974, *42,* 451–455.

McGinnies, E., & Ward, C. D. Persuasibility as a function of source credibility and locus of control: Five cross cultural experiments. *Journal of Personality,* 1974, *42,* 360–371.

Melges, F. T., & Weisz, A. E. The personal future and suicidal ideation. *Journal of Nervous and Mental Disease,* 1971, *153,* 244–250.

Midgley, N., & Abrams, M. S. Fear of success and locus of control in young women. *Journal of Consulting and Clinical Psychology,* 1974, *42,* 737.

Minton, H. L., & Miller, A. G. Group risk-taking and internal–external control of group members. *Psychological Reports,* 1970, *26,* 431–436.

Mirels, H. L. Dimensions of internal versus external control. *Journal of Consulting and Clinical Psychology,* 1970, *34,* 226–228.

Mirels, H. L., & Garrett, J. B. The Protestant Ethic as a personality variable. *Journal of Consulting and Clinical Psychology,* 1971, *36,* 40–44.

Mischel, W., Zeiss, R., & Zeiss, A. Internal–external control and persistence: Validation and implications of the Stanford pre-school internal–external scale. *Journal of Personality and Social Psychology,* 1974, *29,* 265–278.

Naditch, M. P. Locus of control, relative discontent, and hypertension. *Social Psychiatry,* 1974, *9,* 111–117.

Naditch, M. P. Locus of control and drinking behavior in a sample of men in army basic training. *Journal of Consulting and Clinical Psychology,* 1975, *43,* 96.

Naditch, M. P., Gargan, M., & Michael, L. B. Denial, anxiety, locus of control, and the discrepancy between aspirations and achievements as components of depression. *Journal of Abnormal Psychology,* 1975, *84,* 1–9.

Nowicki, S. Predicting academic achievement of females from a locus of control orientation: Some problems and some solutions. Paper presented at the meeting of the American Psychological Association, Montreal, September 1973.

Nowicki, S. Factor structure of locus of control in children. *Journal of Genetic Psychology,* in press.

Nowicki, S., & Barnes, J. Effects of a structured camp experience on locus of control in children. *Journal of Genetic Psychology,* 1973, *122,* 247–252.

Nowicki, S., & Blumberg, N. The role of locus of control of reinforcement in interpersonal attraction. *Journal of Research in Personality,* 1975, *9,* 48–56.

Nowicki, S., Bonner, J., & Feather, B. Effects of locus of control and differential analogue interview procedures on the perceived therapeutic relationship. *Journal of Consulting and Clinical Psychology,* 1972, *38,* 434–438.

Nowicki, S., & Duke, M. P. A locus of control scale for college as well as noncollege adults. *Journal of Personality Assessment,* 1974, *38,* 136–137. , (a)

Nowicki, S., & Duke, M. P. A pre-school and primary locus of control scale. *Developmental Psychology,* 1974, *10,* 874–880. (b)

Nowicki, S., & Hopper, A. Locus of control correlates in an alcoholic population. *Journal of Consulting and Clinical Psychology,* 1974, *42,* 735.

Nowicki, S., & Roundtree, J. Correlates of locus of control in secondary age students. *Developmental Psychology,* 1971, *4,* 479.

Nowicki, S., & Segal, W. Perceived parental characteristics, locus of control orientation, and behavioral correlates of locus of control. *Developmental Psychology,* 1974, *10,* 33–37.

Nowicki, S., & Strickland, B. R. A locus of control scale for children. *Journal of Consulting and Clinical Psychology,* 1973, *40,* 148–155.

Nowicki, S., & Tanner, E. Racial preference behavior in black children as mediated by locus of control of reinforcement. *Journal of Social Psychology,* in press.

Nowicki, S., & Walker, C. The role of generalized and specific expectancies in determining academic achievement. *Journal of Social Psychology,* 1974, *94,* 275–280.

Odell, M. Personality correlates of independence and conformity. Unpublished master's thesis, Ohio State University, 1959.

Oziel, J. L., Obitz, F. W., & Keyson, M. General and specific perceived locus of control in alcoholics. *Psychological Reports,* 1972, *3,* 957–958.

Palmer, R. D. Parental perception and perceived locus of control in psychopathology. *Journal of Personality,* 1971, *3,* 420–431.

Palmore, E., & Luikart, C. Health and social factors relating to life satisfaction. *Journal of Health and Social Behavior,* 1972, *13,* 68–80.

Parsons, O. A., Schneider, J. M., & Hansen, A. S. Internal–external locus of control and national stereotypes in Denmark and the United States. *Journal of Consulting and Clinical Psychology,* 1970, *35,* 30–37.

Patsula, P. J. Felt powerlessness as related to perceived parental behavior. Unpublished doctoral dissertation, University of Alberta, 1969.

Pawlicki, R. E., & Almquist, C. Authoritarianism, locus of control, and tolerance of ambiguity as reflected in membership and nonmembership in a women's liberation group. *Psychological Reports,* 1973, *32,* 1331–1337.

Penk, W. Age changes and correlates of internal–external locus of control scale. *Psychological Reports,* 1969, *25,* 856.

Phares, E. J. Expectancy changes in skill and chance situations. *Journal of Abnormal and Social Psychology,* 1957, *54,* 339–342.

Phares, E. J. Internal–external control as a determinant of amount of social influence exerted. *Journal of Personality and Social Psychology,* 1965, *2,* 642–647.

Phares, E. J. Internal–external control and the reduction of reinforcement value after failure. *Journal of Consulting and Clinical Psychology,* 1971, *37,* 386–390.

Phares, E. J. A social learning approach to psychotherapy. In J. B. Rotter, J. E. Chance, & E. J. Phares (Eds.), *Applications of a social learning theory of personality.* New York: Holt, Rinehart, and Winston, 1972.

Phares, E. J. *Locus of control: A personality determinant of behavior.* Morristown, N.J.: General Learning Press, 1973.

Phares, E. J. Social learning theory, locus of control, and defensiveness. Paper presented at the XV Inter-American Congress of Psychology, Bogota, Colombia, December 1974.

Phares, E. J. *Locus of control in personality.* Morristown, N.J.: General Learning Press, 1976.

Phares, E. J., & Lamiell, J. T. Locus of control, probability of success, and defensiveness. Unpublished manuscript, Kansas State University, 1974. (a)

Phares, E. J., & Lamiel, J. T. Relationship of internal–external control to defensive preferences. *Journal of Consulting and Clinical Psychology,* 1974, *42,* 23–38. (b)

Phares, E. J., Ritchie, D. E., & Davis, W. L. Internal–external control and reactions to threat. *Journal of Personality and Social Psychology,* 1968, *10,* 402–405.

Phares, E. J., & Wilson, K. G. Internal–external control, interpersonal attraction, and empathy. *Psychological Reports,* 1971, *28,* 543–549.

Phares, E. J., & Wilson, K. G. Responsibility attribution: Role of outcome severity, situational ambiguity, and internal–external control. *Journal of Personality,* 1972, *40,* 392–406.

Phares, E. J., Wilson, K. G., & Klyver, N. W. Internal–external control and the attribution of blame under neutral and distractive conditions. *Journal of Personality and Social Psychology,* 1971, *18,* 285–288.

Pierce, R. M. Schauble, P. G., & Farkas, A. Teaching internalization behavior to clients. *Psychotherapy: Theory, Research, and Practice,* 1970, *7,* 217–220.

Pines, H. A. An attributional analysis of locus of control orientation and source of informational dependence. *Journal of Personality and Social Psychology,* 1973, *26,* 262–272.

Pines, H. A., & Julian, J. W. Effects of task and social demands on locus of control differences in information processing. *Journal of Personality,* 1972, *40,* 407–416.

Platt, E. S. Internal–external control and changes in expected utility as predictions of the change in cigarette smoking following role playing. Paper presented at the meeting of the Eastern Psychological Association, Philadelphia, April 1969.

Platt, J. J., & Eisenman, R. Internal–external control of reinforcement, time perspective, adjustment, and anxiety. *Journal of General Psychology,* 1968, *79,* 121–128.

Powell, A., & Vega, M. Correlates of adult locus of control. *Psychological Reports,* 1972, *30,* 455–460.

Prociuk, T. J., & Breen, L. J. Locus of control, study habits and attitudes, and college academic performance. *Journal of Personality,* 1974, *88,* 91–95.

Prociuk, T. J., & Breen, L. J. Defensive externality and its relation to academic performance. *Journal of Personality and Social Psychology,* 1975, *31,* 549–556.

Ransford, H. E. Isolation, powerlessness, and violence: A study of attitudes and participation in the Watts riot. *American Journal of Sociology,* 1968, *73,* 581–591.

Ray, W. J. The relationship of locus of control, self-report measures, and feedback to the voluntary control of heart rate. *Psychophysiology,* 1974, *11,* 527–534.

Reid, D. W., & Ware, E. E. Multidimensionality of internal–external control: Implications for past and future research. *Canadian Journal of Behavioral Science,* 1973, *5,* 264–271.

Reid, D., & Ware, E. E. Multidimensionality of internal versus external control: Addition of a third dimension and non-distinction of self versus others. *Canadian Journal of Behavioral Science,* 1974, *6,* 131–142.

Reimanis, G. Effects of locus of reinforcement control modification procedures in early graders and college students. *Journal of Educational Research,* 1974, *68,* 124–127.

Reitz, H. J., & Groff, G. K. Comparisons of locus of control categories among American, Mexican, and Thai workers. Paper presented at the meeting of the American Psychological Association, Honolulu, September 1972.

Ritchie, E., & Phares, E. J. Attitude change as a function of internal–external control and communicator status. *Journal of Personality,* 1969, *37,* 429–443.

Rosen, B., & Salling, R. Political participation as a function of internal–external locus of control. *Psychological Reports,* 1971, *29,* 880–882.

Roth, S., & Bootzin, R. B. The effects of experimentally induced expectancies of external control: An investigation of learning helplessness. *Journal of Personality and Social Psychology,* 1974, *29,* 253–264.

Rotter, J. B. *Social learning and clinical psychology.* Englewood Cliffs, N. J.: Prentice-Hall, 1954.

Rotter, J. B. Generalized expectancies for internal versus external control of reinforcement. *Psychological Monographs,* 1966, *80* (1, Whole No. 609).

Rotter, J. B. Some problems and misconceptions related to the construct of internal versus external control of reinforcement. *Journal of Consulting and Clinical Psychology,* 1975, *43,* 56–67.

Rotter, J. B., Chance, J. E., & Phares, E. J. *Applications of a social learning theory of personality.* New York: Holt, Rinehart, and Winston, 1972.

Rotter, J. B., Liverant, S., & Crowne, D. P. The growth and extinction of expectancies in chance controlled and skill tasks. *Journal of Psychology,* 1961, *52,* 161–177.

Rotter, J. B., & Mulry, R. C. Internal versus external control of reinforcement and decision time. *Journal of Personality and Social Psychology,* 1965, *2,* 598–604.

Ryckman, R. M., Rodda, W. C., & Sherman, M. F. Locus of control and expertise relevance as determinants of changes in opinion about student activism. *Journal of Social Psychology,* 1972, *88,* 107–114.

Ryckman, R. M., & Sherman, M. F. Locus of control and perceived ability level as determinants of partner and opponent choice. *Journal of Social Psychology,* 1974, *94,* 103–110.

Sanger, S. P., & Alker, H. A. Dimensions of internal–external locus of control and the women's liberation movement. *Journal of Social Issues,* 1972, *28*(4), 115–129.

Sank, Z. B., & Strickland, B. R. Some attitudes and behavioral correlates of a belief in militant or moderate social action. *Journal of Social Psychology,* 1973, *90,* 337–338.

Schiavo, R. S. Locus of control and judgements about another's accident. *Psychological Reports,* 1973, *32,* 483–488.

Seeman, M. Alienation and social learning in a reformatory. *American Journal of Sociology,* 1963, *69,* 270–284.

Seeman, M. & Evans, J. W. Alienation and learning in a hospital setting. *American Sociological Review,* 1962, *27,* 772–783.

Segal, S. M. & DuCette, J. Locus of control and pre-marital high school pregnancy. *Psychological Reports,* 1973, *33,* 887–890.

Seligman, M. E. P. Depression and learned helplessness. In R. J. Friedman & M. M. Katz (Eds.), *The psychology of depression: Contemporary theory and research.* Washington, D.C.: V. H. Winston, & Sons, 1974.

Sherman, S. J. Internal–external control and its relationship to attitude change under different social influence techniques. *Journal of Personality and Social Psychology,* 1973, *23,* 23–29.

Shipe, D. Impulsivity and locus of control as predictors of achievement and adjustment in mildly retarded and borderline youth. *American Journal of Mental Deficiency,* 1971, *1,* 12–22.

Shores, R. E. Motivated determinants and performance of learning disabled and normal children from differing social classes. *Dissertation Abstracts,* 1968, *28,* 4494.

Shybut, J. Time perspective, internal versus external control and severity of psychological disturance. *Journal of Clinical Psychology,* 1968, *24,* 312–315.

Shybut, J. Internal versus external control, time perspective and delay of gratification of high and low ego strength groups. *Journal of Clinical Psychology,* 1970, *26,* 430–431.

Silvern, I. E., & Nakamura, C. Y. Powerlessness, social-political action, social-political views: Their interrelation among college students. *Journal of Social Issues,* 1971, *27*(4), 137–157.

Skinner, B. F. *Beyond freedom and dignity.* New York: Knopf, 1971.

Smith, C. E., Pryer, M. W., & Distefano, M. K., Jr. Internal–external control and severity of emotional impairment among psychiatric patients. *Journal of Clinical Psychology,* 1971, 27, 449–450.

Smith, R. E. Changes in locus of control as a function of life crisis resolution. *Journal of Abnormal Psychology,* 1970, *75,* 328–332.

Smithyman, S. D., Plant, W. T., & Southern, M. L. Locus of control in two samples of chronic drug abusers. *Psychological Reports,* 1974, *34,* 1293–1294.

Snyder, C. R., & Larson, G. R. A further look at student acceptance of general personality interpretations. *Journal of Consulting and Clinical Psychology,* 1972, *38,* 384–388.

Sobel, R. S. The effects of success, failure, and locus of control of postperformance attribution of causality. *Journal of General Psychology,* 1974, *91,* 29–34.

Solomon, D., Houlihan, K. A., Busse, T. V., & Parelius, R. J. Parent behavior and child academic achievement, achievement striving and related personality characteristics. *Genetic Psychology Monographs,* 1971, *83,* 173–273.

Sonstroem, R. J., & Walker, M. I. Relationship of attitudes and locus of control to exercise and physical fitness. *Perceptual and Motor Skills,* 1973, *36,* 1031–1034.

Sosis, R. H. Internal–external control and the perception of responsibility of another for an accident. *Journal of personality and Social Psychology,* 1974, *30,* 393–399.

Steiner, I. D. Perceived freedom. In L. Berkowitz (Ed.), *Advances in experimental social psychology* (Vol. 5). New York: Academic Press, 1970.

Steiner, I. D. Benevolent versus malevolent views of the world. Unpublished manuscript, University of Massachusetts, 1975.

Stephens, M. W. Cognitive and cultural determinants of early IE development. Paper presented at the meeting of the American Psychological Association, Washington, September 1971.

Stephens, M. W. Cultural differences in early socialization of internal–external control expectancies. Paper presented at the meeting of the XXth International Congress of Psychology, Tokyo, August 1972. (a)

Stephens, M. W. Locus of control as mediator of cognitive development. Paper presented at the meeting of the American Psychological Association, Honolulu, September 1972. (b)

Stephens, M. W. Dimensions of locus of control: Impact of early educational experiences. Paper presented at the meeting of the American Psychological Association, Montreal, August 1973.

Stephens, M. W., & Delys, P. A. A locus of control measure for preschool children. *Developmental Psychology,* 1973, *9,* 55–65.

Stokols, D. The reduction of cardiovascular risk: An application of social learning perspectives. Paper presented at the American Heart Association Behavioral Science Conference on Cardiovascular Risk, Seattle, Washington, 1974.

Straits, B., & Sechrest, L. Further support of some findings about the characteristics of smokers and non-smokers. *Journal of Consulting Psychology,* 1963, *27,* 282.

Strassberg, D. S. Relationships among locus of control, anxiety and valued goal expectations. *Journal of Consulting and Clinical Psychology,* 1973, *2,* 319.

Strickland, B. R. The prediction of social action from a dimension of internal–external control. *Journal of Social Psychology,* 1965, *66,* 353–358.

Strickland, B. R. Individual differences in verbal conditioning, extinction, and awareness. *Journal of Personality,* 1970, *38,* 364–378.

Strickland, B. R. Delay of gratification as a function of race of the experimenter. *Journal of Personality and Social Psychology,* 1972, *22,* 108–112. (a)

Strickland, B. R. Locus of control and competence in children. Paper presented at the meeting of the American Psychological Association, Honolulu, September 1972. (b)

Strickland, B. R. Delay of gratification and internal locus of control in children. *Journal of Consulting and Clinical Psychology,* 1973, *40,* 338. (a)

Strickland, B. R. Locus of control: Where have we been and where are we going? Paper presented at the meeting of the American Psychological Association, Montreal, August 1973. (b)

Strickland, B. R. Locus of control and health-related behaviors. Paper presented at the meeting of the Inter-American Congress of Psychology, Bogota, Colombia, December 1974.

Strickland, B. R., & Hill, J. N. An investigation of some personality variables in male children with severe reading problems. Unpublished manuscript, University of Massachusetts, 1974.

Strickland, L. H., Lewicki, R. J., & Katz, A. M. Temporal orientation and perceived control as determinants of risk-taking. *Journal of Experimental Social Psychology,* 1966, *2,* 143–151.

Thomas, L. E. The I–E scale, ideological bias, and political participation. *Journal of Personality,* 1970, *38,* 273–286.

Throop, W. F., & MacDonald, A. P. Internal–external locus of control: A bibliography. *Psychological Reports,* 1971, *28,* 175–190.

Tolor, A. An evaluation of the Maryland Parent Attitude Survey. *Journal of Psychology,* 1967, *67,* 69–74.

Tolor, A., & Jalowiec, J. E. Body boundary, parental attitudes, and internal–external expectancy. *Journal of Consulting and Clinical Psychology,* 1968, *32,* 206–209.

Ude, L. K., & Vogler, R. E. Internal versus external control of reinforcement and awareness in a conditioning task. *Journal of Psychology,* 1969, *73,* 63–67.

Vuchinich, R. E., & Bass, B. A. Social desirability in Rotter's locus of control scale. *Psychological Reports,* 1974, *34,* 1124–1126.

Walls, R. T., & Miller, J. J. Perception of disability by welfare and rehabilitation clients. *Perceptual and Motor Skills,* 1970, *31,* 793–794.

Walls, R. T., & Smith, T. S. Development of preference for delayed reinforcement in disadvantaged children. *Journal of Educational Psychology,* 1970, *61,* 118–123.

Wallston, K., Maides, S., & Wallston, B. Health related information seeking as a function of health related locus of control and health value. *Journal of Research in Personality,* 1976, *10,* 215–222.

Wallston, B. S., Wallston, K. A., Kaplan, G. D., & Maides, S. A. Development and validation of the health locus of control scale. *Journal of Consulting and Clinical Psychology,* in press.

Wareheim, R. G. Generalized expectancies for locus of control and academic performance. *Psychological Reports,* 1972, *30,* 314.

Wareheim, R. G., & Foulds, M. L. Perceived locus of control and personal adjustment. *Journal of Consulting and Clinical Psychology,* 1971, *37,* 250–252.

Waters, D. Differential effects of skill and chance instructions on persistance times and attention breaks as a function of locus of control in elementary school children. Unpublished doctoral dissertation, Emory University, 1972.

Watson, D. Relationship between locus of control and anxiety. *Journal of Personality and Social Psychology,* 1967, *6,* 91–92.

Weaver, R. Internality, externality, and compliance as related to chronic home dialysis patients. Unpublished master's thesis, Emory University, 1972.

Weiner, B., Frieze, I., Kukla, A., Reed, L., Rest, S., & Rosenbaum, R. M. Perceiving the causes of success and failure. In E. E. Jones, D. Kanouse, H. H. Kelley, R. E. Nisbett, S. Valins, & B. Weiner (Eds.), *Attribution: Perceiving the causes of behavior.* Morristown, N.J.: General Learning Press, 1971.

Weiner, B., & Kukla, A. An attributional analysis of achievement motivation. *Journal of Personality and Social Psychology,* 1970, *15,* 1–20.

Wendland, C. J. Internal-external control expectancies of institutionally physically disabled. *Rehabilitation Psychology,* 1973, *20,* 180–186.

Wichern, F., & Nowicki, S. Independence training practices and locus of control orientation in children and adolescents. *Developmental Psychology,* in press.

Williams, A. F. Personality and other characteristics associated with cigarette smoking among young teenagers. *Journal of Health and Social Behaviors,* 1973, *14,* 374–380.

Williams, A. F. Factors associated with seat belt use in families. *Journal of Safety Research,* 1972, *4(3),* 133–138. (a)

Williams, A. F. Personality characteristics associated with preventive dental health practices. *Journal of American College of Dentists,* 1972, *39,* 225–234. (b)

Williams, C. G., & Nickles, J. B. Internal–external control dimension as related to accident and suicide proneness. *Journal of Consulting and Clinical Psychology,* 1969, *33,* 485–494.

Wolfe, R. N. Perceived locus of control and prediction of own academic performance. *Journal of Consulting and Clinical Psychology,* 1972, *38,* 80–83.

Wolk, S., & DuCette, J. Intentional performance and incidental learning as a function of personality and task dimensions. *Journal of Personality and Social Psychology,* 1974, *29,* 90–101.

Wolk, S., & Kurtz, J. Positive adjustment and involvement during aging and expectancy for internal control. *Journal of Consulting and Clinical Psychology,* 1975, *43,* 173–178.

Zytkoskee, A., Strickland, B. R., & Watson, J. Delay of gratification and internal versus external control among adolescents of low socioeconomic status. *Developmental Psychology,* 1971, *4,* 93–98.

7
Dogmatism

Ralph B. Vacchiano[1]
Fairleigh Dickinson University

Dogmatism was put forth by Rokeach (1954, 1960) as a generalized theory of authoritarianism (i.e., free of specific political, religious, and ideological beliefs) as opposed to a rightist form of authoritarianism hypothesized by Adorno, Frenkel-Brunswik, Levinson, and Sanford (1950). Rokeach (1960) conceived of dogmatism as being basically an organization of belief–disbelief systems designed to "serve two powerful and conflicting sets of motives at the same time: the need for a cognitive framework to know and to understand and the need to ward off threatening aspects of reality [p. 67]."

For most people both needs will operate independently to varying degrees. The belief system is open when the need to know predominates and reality is nonthreatening, thus permitting the individual to evaluate and react to objective reality. Conversely, when reality becomes threatening, the system becomes closed, the need to know lessens, with the result that the individual cannot separate information from source, and identifies with an absolute authority or a cause. This identification permits the individual to defend himself against feelings of isolation and self-depreciation or more specifically from anxiety.

The belief–disbelief system is considered to be organized along a central, intermediate, and peripheral dimension. Within the central region lie the person's primitive beliefs consisting of his knowledge about the physical world, himself, and others. The intermediate region contains beliefs pertaining to the nature of authority while the peripheral region contains beliefs derived from authority. The belief–disbelief system is further characterized by the isolation and differentiation of beliefs. Isolation occurs when the person fails to see the relationship among beliefs that are intrinsically related. Differentiation refers to the degree of articulation of beliefs within the system. Finally, belief–disbelief systems are organized along a time-perspective dimension ranging from a realistic integration of the past, present, and future for the open-minded, to an over-

[1] Ralph B. Vacchiano died on August 15, 1976.

emphasis of one time dimension, the future, for the closed-minded. As seen by Rokeach, the closed-minded or high dogmatic (HD) individual will hold primitive beliefs that the world is a threatening place (central region), that authority is absolute and others are to be accepted or rejected based on their agreement or disagreement with authority (intermediate region), and hold these beliefs in isolation from each other (peripheral region) along a time dimension which is narrow and oriented toward the future. The low dogmatic (LD), in contrast, holds primitive beliefs that the world is a nonthreatening place; he does not rely on absolute authority nor does he accept or reject people based on agreement or disagreement with any authority. The LD's beliefs are not held in isolation and there is greater communication (and less discrepancy) within and between belief–disbelief systems.

Since Rokeach's original work and the last major reviews of dogmatism (Ehrlich & Lee, 1969; Vacchiano, Strauss, & Hochman, 1969) a number of research investigators have continued to reevaluate and extend the concept of dogmatism resulting in a large number of research studies. This chapter attempts to review and synthesize these findings, especially as they pertain to social behavior, and includes discussions of the relationship of dogmatism to authoritarianism, religious and political attitudes and beliefs, prejudice, personality and maladjustment, interpersonal behavior, cognitive inconsistency, and situational threat.

DOGMATISM, AUTHORITARIANISM, AND THE DOGMATISM SCALE

Traditionally, investigators interested in the relationship between dogmatism and authoritarianism have centered their research around two main theoretical issues. In the first case, they have been concerned with the Dogmatism scale (DS) as a measure of general authoritarianism as opposed to an authoritarianism of the left or right (as in the case of the *F* scale). Secondly, a number of investigations have been concerned with the high and low dogmatics' reactions to authority figures.

Dogmatism Scale as a Measure of General Authoritarianism

A considerable amount of criticism had been leveled at the California *F* scale (Adorno *et al.,* 1950) shortly after its publication because it tapped a right authoritarianism only. Rokeach (1960), therefore, put forth the concept of dogmatism as a generalized theory of authoritarianism and the DS as a measure of this authoritarianism (Fruchter, Rokeach, & Novak, 1958; Rokeach, 1956, 1960; Rokeach & Fruchter, 1956). Most studies of dogmatism have used Form E, the fifth edition of Rokeach's Dogmatism scale (1956, 1960), which can be found in Table 1. In general, research tends to support Rokeach's concept. Kerlinger and Rokeach (1966) factor analyzed the items of the *F* and *D* scales

TABLE 1

Dogmatism Scale Form E[a]

INSTRUCTIONS

The following is a study of what the general public thinks and feels about a number of important social and personal questions. The best answer to each statement below is your *personal opinion.* We have tried to cover many different and opposing points of view; you may find yourself agreeing strongly with some of the statements, disagreeing just as strongly with others, and perhaps uncertain about others; whether you agree or disagree with any statement, you can be sure that many people feel the same as you do.

Mark each statement in the left margin according to how much you agree or disagree with it. Please mark every one. Write +1, +2, +3, or –1, –2, –3, depending on how you feel in each case.

+1: I AGREE A LITTLE	–1: I DISAGREE A LITTLE
+2: I AGREE ON THE WHOLE	–2: I DISAGREE ON THE WHOLE
+3: I AGREE VERY MUCH	–3: I DISAGREE VERY MUCH

1. The United States and Russia have just about nothing in common.
2. The highest form of government is a democracy and the highest form of democracy is a government run by those who are most intelligent.
3. Even though freedom of speech for all groups is a worthwhile goal, it is unfortunately necessary to restrict the freedom of certain political groups.
4. It is only natural that a person should have a much better acquaintance with ideas he believes in than with ideas he opposes.
5. Man on his own is a helpless and miserable creature.
6. Fundamentally, the world we live in is a pretty lonesome place.
7. Most people just don't give a "damn" for others.
8. I'd like it if I could find someone who would tell me how to solve my personal problems.

continued

TABLE 1 (*contd.*)

9. It is only natural for a person to be rather fearful of the future.
10. There is so much to be done and so little time to do it in.
11. Once I get wound up in a heated discussion I just can't stop.
12. In a discussion I often find it necessary to repeat myself several times to make sure I am being understood.
13. In a heated discussion I generally become so absorbed in what I am going to say that I forget to listen to what the others are saying.
14. It is better to be a dead hero than to be a live coward.
15. While I don't like to admit this even to myself, my secret ambition is to become a great man, like Einstein, or Beethoven, or Shakespeare.
16. The main thing in life is for a person to want to do something important.
17. If given the chance I would do something of great benefit to the world.
18. In the history of mankind there have probably been just a handful of really great thinkers.
19. There are a number of persons I have come to hate because of the things they stand for.
20. A man who does not believe in some great cause has not really lived.
21. It is only when a person devotes himself to an ideal or cause that life becomes meaningful.
22. Of all the different philosophies which exist in this world there is probably only one which is correct.
23. A person who gets enthusiastic about too many causes is likely to be a pretty "wishy-washy" sort of person.
24. To compromise with our political opponents is dangerous because it usually leads to the betrayal of our own side.
25. When it comes to differences of opinion in religion we must be careful not to compromise with those who believe differently from the way we do.

ness.

27. The worst crime a person could commit is to attack publicly the people who believe in the same thing he does.

28. In times like these it is often necessary to be more on guard against ideas put out by people or groups in one's own camp than by those in the opposing camp.

29. A group which tolerates too much differences of opinion among its own members cannot exist for too long.

30. There are two kinds of people in the world: those who are for truth and those who are against truth.

31. My blood boils whenever a person stubbornly refuses to admit he is wrong.

32. A person who thinks primarily of his own happiness is beneath contempt.

33. Most of the ideas which get printed nowadays aren't worth the paper they are printed on.

34. In this complicated world of ours the only way we can know what is going on is to rely on leaders or experts who can be trusted.

35. It is often desirable to reserve judgment about what's going on until one has had a chance to hear the opinions of those one respects.

36. In the long run the best way to live is to pick friends and associates whose tastes and beliefs are the same as one's own.

37. The present is all too often full of unhappiness. It is only the future that counts.

38. If a man is to accomplish his mission in life it is sometimes necessary to gamble "all or nothing at all."

39. Unfortunately, a good many people with whom I have discussed important social and moral problems don't really understand what's going on.

40. Most people just don't know what's good for them.

---

[a]From Rokeach (1956). Copyright 1956 by the American Psychological Association. Reproduced with permission. A person's score on the Dogmatism scale is the sum of his or her scores on all 40 items. A high dogmatic (HD) individual is defined as one who obtains a relatively high score on the scale, while a low dogmatic (LD) is one who obtained a relatively low score.

and found a "common core" of authoritarianism underlying both scales. However, a second-order factor analysis revealed that the two scales were factorially discriminable (a finding also noted by Warr, Lee, & Joreskog, 1969), with the DS representing a generalized authoritarianism independent of a particular ideological content. Although Peabody (1966) suggested that the DS may only measure "cognitive simplicity," Rokeach (1967) cited considerable evidence to support his contention that the DS measured general authoritarianism. Plant (1960) and Hanson (1968, 1970) both found that the DS taps a general authoritarianism as opposed to a rightist or leftist authoritarianism. Barker (1963) also demonstrated that dogmatism was independent of political ideology, but did find that it was related to a sense of commitment to a particular position on the political spectrum. Costin's (1968) findings led him to conclude that the DS measures general authoritarianism rather than simple-mindedness and its consequent acquiescence as suggested by Peabody (1966). In a cross-cultural study of Germans and Americans, Shaver, Hoffman, and Richards (1971) found that Germans scored significantly higher on both the *F* scale and the DS. The authors suggest that if one accepts the common view that the German subculture is conservatively authoritarian, then their findings support the contention that the *F* scale measures conservative authoritarianism while the DS is a measure of general authoritarianism.

Bailes and Guller (1970), Karabenick and Wilson (1969), and Larsen (1969) have reported significant correlations between the DS and pro-Vietnam (or pro-war) attitudes suggesting that the DS is not entirely independent of ideological orientation. However, Granberg and Corrigan (1972) found that, although the DS was ideologically correlated to a slight extent with pro-Vietnam attitudes, it was significantly less so than a modified version of the *F* scale. Granberg and Corrigan concluded that although Rokeach did not succeed completely in developing an ideologically free measure of authoritarianism, his scale was significantly less ideologically correlated than the modified *F* scale used in their study.

Measures of reliability for the DS are generally high for adult (Ehrlich, 1961a, b; Lichtenstein, Quinn, & Hover, 1961; Zagona & Zurcher, 1965a) and adolescent populations (Kemp & Kohler, 1965). High reliability has also been obtained for shortened versions of the DS (Schulze, 1962; Troldahl & Powell, 1965).

Dogmatism and Reactions to Authority

According to Rokeach's theory, we would expect HDs to show a greater dependency on absolute authority, to be more easily influenced by authority, and to confuse the veracity of the authority with the status of the authority. The great majority of research supports these hypotheses.

Powell (1962) had subjects evaluate statements dealing with domestic policy, foreign policy, and racial integration made by two of the leading 1960 presidential candidates and found that LDs were significantly more capable than HDs of distinguishing between the content of a message and its source. They were also able to evaluate the content and source on the basis of individual merits. Somewhat similar to Powell's finding is that of Bettinghaus, Miller, and Steinfatt (1970) who found that HDs, because of their dependency on authority, more frequently than LDs judged syllogistic arguments made by credible sources as valid and judged syllogistic arguments made by less credible sources as invalid.

Employing an autokinetic task, Vidulich and Kaiman (1961) exposed subjects to the judgments of high- and low-status confederates prior to the subjects making their own judgments about the direction of the light's movement. High dogmatics were significantly more conforming in their judgments to the high-status source than were LDs. Restle, Andrews, and Rokeach (1964) theorized that the HD's superior performance for reversal learning-set problems was due to his passive dependence on the experimenter, who was acting as a capricious authority, while the LD would look for a solution through a principle that was not contained in the problem. Conversely, in oddity problems, where principles could be deduced, LDs performed better than HDs, who relied on the experimenter's (authority's) reinforcements rather than looking for a principle. Kemp (1962) observed that HD counselor trainees in actual training situations "adjust their thinking and responses to the degree that they feel is acceptable and in accordance with the perceived demands of the instructor and the environment [p. 157]."

Larsen and Minton (1971) found a significant correlation between dogmatism and a scale designed to measure attributed social power to authority–non-authority relationships (e.g., policeman–citizen, professor–student, general–private, foreman–worker, king–subject). McCarthy and Johnson (1962) presented subjects with an official police (high authority) interpretation of the cause of a civil disturbance and the interpretation given by a student group (low authority) of the same disturbance. The HDs' dependence on authority was seen in their significantly greater acceptance of the police interpretation while LDs were found to more often select the low-authority explanation.

Within the context of Rosenthal's work on the experimenter expectancy effect, Lazlo and Rosenthal (1970) found that HDs were significantly more susceptible to the influence of high-status experimenters than were LDs. High-dogmatic subjects also agree more with a communication coming from a high-authority source than from a low-authority one. Low-dogmatic subjects do not seem to be differentially influenced by the authority of the communicator (Harvey & Hays, 1972). High dogmatics also seem to be more susceptible to hypnotic trance than LDs when the hypnotic induction is communicated by a high-authority figure (Vacchiano & Strauss, 1975). Low-dogmatic subjects perceive authority more realistically than HDs, recognizing both their positive as well as negative characteristics (Kemp, 1963). Feather (1967) found a relationship between dogmatism and membership in religious groups that are dependent on authority and tolerate little argument in adherence to religious beliefs. High dogmatics also seem to prefer authoritarian leadership (Mouw,

1969) as opposed to LDs, who prefer a democratic leadership style (Tosi, Quaranta, & Frumkin, 1968).

In his book, Rokeach (1960) directed his attention to problem solving by HD and LD subjects confirming his hypothesis that the more closed the individual's belief system, the more difficult it would be for him to find new solutions. Problem solving requires two processes, analysis and synthesis. In analysis the individual must overcome established beliefs; in synthesis new beliefs are organized and integrated into a substitute system. Rokeach suggested that HDs can be significantly influenced in the problem solving process by the presence of the experimenter because he is perceived to be an authority figure who holds the solution to the problem.

Schultz and DiVesta (1972) found that HDs achieved a large number of new beliefs in a problem-solving task when they received endorsement from an authority figure. Low dogmatics turned to new-belief alternatives more readily and rejected authority, particularly when it was irrelevant to the solution of the problem. Schultz and DiVesta note that LDs postpone judgment of the adequacy of a solution based mainly on authority endorsement, even though the information may be correct, and seek further information. The HDs' uncritical acceptance of authority endorsement facilitated their problem solving when new solutions received authority endorsement and hindered problem solving when old beliefs were endorsed. In problem solving, then, HDs are quite limited in evaluating information independent of its source because of their absolute and uncritical acceptance of authority. Conversely, LDs evaluate information on the basis of its objective validity as well as the reliability of the source. Thus they are not as influenced by authority (Ehrlich & Lee, 1969; Restle, Andrews, & Rokeach, 1964; Vacchiano, Strauss, & Hochman, 1969).

The only contradictory finding (that LDs are significantly influenced by authority) comes from Long (1971). Long drew subjects from varying ranks (superior, subordinate, peer) within the Florida Forest Service and had them make judgments of the length of a line with a confederate who was either a superior, subordinate, or peer. Low dogmatics were more influenced by authority (a superior) in their judgmental modifications than were high dogmatics. High dogmatics were more likely to be influenced when the confederate was a peer. These contradictory findings may be due to the nature of the hierarchial job structure from which the subjects were drawn. It is unclear, too, particularly for the peer group, whether subjects had on-the-job contact prior to the experiment. The possibility does exist, as Long suggests, that for this sample, the peer group may have served as an authority source.

Summary

Research clearly demonstrates that the DS, as opposed to the *F* scale, measures a more generalized form of authoritarianism. The studies reviewed here have employed both factor analytic techniques and comparisons of groups with known characteristics. Thus, research continues to support the construct and predictive validity of the DS.

The construct validity of the DS is further supported by the verification of a major hypothesis of dogmatism theory, namely the HD's dependency on authority. This review certainly supports the theory that HDs are dependent on and influenced by authority and demonstrate difficulty separating the merit of the communication from its source. This dependency on authority has been shown in many diverse settings. However, a majority of these studies tend to establish the authority source through written communications presented to subjects rather than actual interaction with the authority. Further, greater attention might be directed toward the characteristics of the authority source to determine the specific traits to which the HD might be reacting.

DOGMATISM, ATTITUDES, AND BELIEFS

Prejudice

In his major work, Rokeach (1960) found that HDs were more prejudiced toward other racial and religious groups. Hoge and Carroll (1973) and Rule and Hewitt (1970) support this finding in general. Kirtley (1968) noted that HDs were more susceptible to pressures for prejudice increase than prejudice decrease. Hood (1973) extended Rokeach's thesis to other than ethnic groups and demonstrated that HDs hold more stereotyped attitudes of homosexuals, suicidal persons, and the mentally ill than do LDs. In a subsequent study, Hood (1974) also found that the HDs' stereotyped attitudes toward the mentally ill could be reduced through classroom instruction but affective rejection of the mentally ill, as measured by semantic differential, increased significantly.

Perhaps one of the most fruitful lines of research stemming from Rokeach's work was the development of concepts pertaining to prejudice. Rokeach, Smith, and Evans (1960) suggested that differences in beliefs were more important than racial or ethnic factors in determining prejudice. Racial or ethnic prejudice was considered to be a special case of prejudice toward others based on assumed differences in beliefs. Employing a nine-point scale of potential for friendship (ranging from 1, meaning "I can't see myself being friends with such a person," to a 9, indicating "I can very easily see myself being friends with such a person") the researchers had subjects rate stimulus persons whose beliefs were similar or dissimilar to the subject's and who were of the same or different race or religion. Rokeach *et al.* (1960) found that "most of the time they [the subjects] discriminate on the basis of belief and not on the basis of racial or ethnic group when they are given the opportunity to react to social stimuli differing simultaneously on both characteristics [p. 153]." Subjects thus preferred as friends those people who held similar beliefs to their own, regardless of race or ethnicity.

A controversy ensued over the Rokeach *et al.* (1960) findings when Triandis (1961) objected to their interpreting "friendship" as a general measure of prejudice, pointing out that friendships involve relatively small social distances. Triandis utilized a 100-point equal-interval scale measuring a broad range of social distances ranging from willingness to marry a person (0 social distance) to willingness to participate in a lynching of a person (97 points in social distance) with such intermediate items as accepting a person as an intimate friend, a roommate, club member, and so on. Triandis (1961) found that "race was as frequently a factor in social distance as differences in belief systems of two persons [p. 186]." Rokeach (1961), however, objected to Triandis' belief statements as well as his definition of stimulus persons as being too vague and complicated. Byrne and Wong (1962) supported Rokeach's hypothesis when they employed a measure of "personal feelings of friendliness" and "willingness to work together" as their dependent variables. Subjects rated a hypothetical stranger with similar attitudes more positively than a stranger with dissimilar attitudes.

In an attempt to reconcile these differences, Stein, Hardyck, and Smith (1965) had subjects complete a teenage value scale containing items such as trying to please parents, having school spirit, living up to strict moral standards, etc., and then indicate how they felt toward white and black stimulus persons who held similar or dissimilar values. Similarity of values had a greater effect than race on both a social distance and a friendship measure. Stein *et al.* (1965) concluded that the discrepancy between Rokeach's and Triandis' findings could be explained by noting that

> when subjects are forced to evaluate stimulus individuals in terms of their beliefs, then belief congruence is more important than race. But when the belief component is not provided, spelled out in considerable detail, subjects will react in racial terms on the basis of assumptions concerning the belief systems of others, and of emotional or institutionalized factors [p. 289].

Triandis and Davis (1965) did not accept these studies as answering Triandis' (1961) earlier criticism, basically because the Stein *et al.* social distance scale was limited to positive items. Triandis and Davis contended that prejudice involves overt negative behaviors as well as the lack of positive behaviors. Utilizing semantic and behavioral differential scales, a factor analysis revealed two types of prejudice. One factor was identified as "conventional" prejudice in which sensitivity to the race factor was of primary concern while the second was "belief" prejudice where the concern was with the belief structure of the stimulus person. Triandis and Davis (1965) note that the "relative importance of the race and belief components varied systematically with the degree of intimacy implied by clusters of behaviors which the subjects indicated they were willing to undertake with the stimulus persons [p. 715]." For intimate behavior, race was a more important determinant of prejudice while belief was more important for nonintimate behavior. Although Triandis and Davis' findings received some support in the work of Willis and Balatao (1967) and Smith, Williams, and Willis (1967), the great majority of research supports Rokeach's hypothesis that belief congruence is more important than race or ethnic differences in determining prejudice (Anderson & Côté, 1966; Byrne & McGraw, 1964; Hendrick, Bixenstine, & Hawkins, 1971; Hendrick & Hawkins, 1969; Insko & Robinson, 1967; Robinson & Insko, 1969; Rokeach, 1968; Rokeach & Mezei, 1966; Rokeach & Rothman, 1965; Silverman & Cochrane, 1972; Stein, 1966).

Silverman (1974) has pointed out, however, that all the studies in belief congruence and prejudice, with the exception of the Rokeach and Mezei (1966) study, have required subjects to respond to "imagined" situations (such as imagine working with, marrying, living next to hypothetical white and Negro strangers) and to subsequently indicate to what degree they might be attracted to these individuals. Silverman suggests there is a serious question whether a subject will in fact do what he states he would do in these imagined situations. In addition, subjects in these "hypothetical stranger" experiments may give the most socially acceptable responses since they know their responses will have no real-life consequences in future relationships. In order to take into account the "consequences of choice factor," Silverman explored the relationship between behavioral consequences and racial discrimination as demonstrated in verbal expressions of intended behavior. Subjects in the consequences condition believed that their choice from among persons who varied in race, attitude, and value similarity would result in their future college roommate while subjects in a control group were aware that their choices would have no effect on their future roommate selection. Subjects responded to the Rokeach Value Survey, a scale requiring the individuals to rank in importance (as guiding principles in their lives) 2 sets of eighteen values, and an attitude survey in which they expressed their views on 4 controversial issues: special college admissions programs for blacks, student protest demonstrations, determination of course content by students, and abolishing the draft. Silverman found that belief congruence was more important than race in the selection of a roommate for both the consequential and inconsequential groups.

Political Beliefs

Rokeach (1956, 1960) suggested that high dogmatism characterized people at either extreme of the political spectrum regardless of the specific content of the political position. However, Bailes and Guller (1970), Karabenick and Wilson (1969), and Hanson (1970) all support Barker's (1963) earlier finding that there is no relationship between dogmatism and political extremity. Although Rokeach (1960) found the DS to be a more generalized measure of authoritarianism free of political content, he did find slight but positive correlations between dogmatism and the Politico-Economic Conservatism Scale (Adorno *et al.*, 1950) and suggested that "the chances are somewhat better than even that a closed-minded person will be conservative rather than liberal in his politics [p.

122]." Research would certainly support the conclusion that the close-minded person does take a more conservative position along the political spectrum, although as Rokeach suggested, this conservatism is a far cry from an extreme fascist conservatism (Baker & Schulberg, 1969; Bohr, 1968; Costin, 1971; DiRenzo, 1974; Hanson, 1973; Kirtley & Harkless, 1969; Rosen & Kenny, 1972; Steininger, Durso, & Pasquariello, 1972; Stewart & Webster, 1970). This conservatism would also seem to extend into areas involving broad political and social issues such as contraception (Lundy, 1972), sexual attitudes (Kilpatrick, Cauthen, Sandman, & Quattlebaum, 1968; Lundy, 1972), adoption (Dembroski & Johnson, 1969), and marijuana use (Lorentz, 1972). DiRenzo (1968, 1971) and Jones (1973) have found that dogmatism is also significantly associated with presidential preferences, with HDs favoring politically conservative candidates. Bailes and Guller's (1970) conclusion aptly sums up the research in this area. They note that dogmatism is related to the content of political beliefs (e.g., conservatism) and that the contents of the belief system "may be selectively incorporated on the basis of complex and subtle emotional appeals which differ from the high to low dogmatic individual. This again can be modified by the external pressure of group membership as well as by other factors including the context in which information is presented [p. 146]."

The interactive effect of dogmatism and issue salience (the degree of importance to the subject of various political issues) on political activity has been studied by Levy, Russell, Kimmel, Carrick, and Burnaska (1973). Earlier, Clouser and Hjelle (1970) found a significant relationship between Rotter's Internal–External scale (I–E) and dogmatism, the HDs being more external. Levy *et al.*, however, found I–E and dogmatism to be statistically independent and issue salience more important than both I–E and dogmatism in determining political activity. In general, HDs were less politically active than were LDs. In comparisons on the basis of both I–E and dogmatism, political activity was found to be lowest among HD externals. Internal HDs were as active politically as were LDs who were either high or low on I–E.

Religious Beliefs

Early research relating dogmatism and religion dealt mainly with differences in level of dogmatism for different religious groups. Rokeach (1960) had found with a Michigan State University sample that Catholics were more dogmatic than both Protestants and nonbelievers, while from a sample of New York college students he found Catholics and nonbelievers to be equally dogmatic and more so than Jews and Protestants. Subsequent research has continued to yield inconsistent findings. Glass (1971) noted that Episcopalians were significantly lower in dogmatism than Baptists, Presbyterians, Methodists, and Catholics. Koepp (1963) found Catholics more dogmatic than Jews, and DiRenzo (1967) found Catholics more dogmatic than nonbelievers. However, LoSciuto and Hartley (1963) found no significant difference in dogmatism for Catholics, Jews,

Protestants, and nonbelievers. Subsequently, Kilpatrick, Sutker, and Sutker (1970) found Catholics and nonbelievers less dogmatic than Jews and Protestants. Many of the contradictory results concerning dogmatism and religious beliefs can be attributed to differences in geographic norms and subcultural patterns. Webster (1967) reported that Northern subjects were more dogmatic than Southern subjects and Vacchiano *et al.* (1969) have pointed out the need for geographical norms for the DS. Kilpatrick *et al.* (1970) summarize their contradictory findings by concluding that the "culture or mores of a particular region may function differentially to produce intradenominational differences in dogmatism [p. 21]." Intradenominational differences in dogmatism have been substantiated by Bohr (1968), Gilmore (1970), and Stewart and Webster (1970).

Raschke (1973) broke from the more traditional comparison of religious groups to study dogmatism and the nature of religious beliefs in terms of "committed" versus "consensual" religiousity. In a factor analysis of Spilka's Religious Viewpoint Scale, LDs scored significantly higher on consensual religiousity. Thus they were seen as having their religious beliefs more integrated with other aspects of their life, their beliefs were more abstract and interrelated, and they were more open to examine beliefs different from their own. According to Raschke (1973), "the open-minded person can be expected to be discerning concerning the meaning and implications of his religious beliefs as well as willing to examine sympathetically beliefs different from his own [p. 341]." In contrast, Raschke found the closed-minded individual to hold his beliefs in more literal and concrete terms, ignoring contradictions, making value judgments in absolute terms of right or wrong with no concern for degrees. Raschke's study thus suggests that dogmatism should be related to the religious beliefs of the individual rather than to specific characteristics of various religious groups. DiGiuseppe (1971) also pointed out that religious group membership is not the only variable to consider in the analysis of dogmatism when he found that the more meaningful and important religion is to a person the higher will be his dogmatism score.

Attitude Change

Three studies seem to suggest that HDs are more likely to change their attitudes in response to social influence than LDs. Gold, Ryckman, and Rodda (1973) found that HDs exposed to counter-attitudinal information in a group discussion changed their attitude toward the group position. Both Norris (1965) and Cronkhite and Goetz (1971) have suggested that the HD is more persuasible. In the latter study (Cronkhite & Goetz, 1971), the authors found a significant correlation between scores on the DS and the Janis and Field Test of General Persuasibility and concluded that "dogmatism and general attitude instability are two symptoms which tend to accompany the syndrome of 'general persuasibility'[p. 348]."

Nature of Belief–Disbelief Systems

The belief system, according to Rokeach, is thought to be characterized by varying degrees of isolation, differentiation, and comprehensiveness of beliefs. Isolation occurs when logically contradictory beliefs exist together in the belief system, when there is an accentuation of differences and minimization of similarities between belief and disbelief systems (which serves to defend the validity of the belief system), when relevant facts are judged as irrelevant, and when there is a denial of obvious contradictions. Differentiation refers to the degree of "articulation or richness" of the belief system and is evidenced by the amount of information possessed by the individual about a belief or disbelief and by the extent to which any two disbelief subsystems are perceived as the same or different. The comprehensiveness of the system refers to the total number of disbeliefs contained within the disbelief system.

Several studies have investigated the relationship of cognitive isolation and differentiation to dogmatism, yielding inconsistent results. These studies have been extensively reviewed by Feather (1973). Feather (1969a) tested the hypothesis that HDs would demonstrate a greater discrepancy in the degree of differentiation between their belief and disbelief systems and would show less differentiation within their disbelief systems. Feather had subjects develop a set of pro and con arguments concerning specific issues of concern to them and subsequently had them respond to an attitudinal scale which measured the direction and strength of their attitude toward each issue. The total number of different pro and con arguments a subject reported was taken as a measure of cognitive differentiation. Thus when a positive attitude toward an issue was given, pro arguments were considered a representation of a subject's belief system while con arguments were taken as part of the disbelief system. For a negative attitude, the reverse interpretation for pro and con arguments was assumed. A measure of consistency was attained by noting the direction of the arguments relative to the attitude; that is, a pro argument was consistent with a positive attitude and a con argument was consistent with a negative attitude. The difference between the number of consistent and inconsistent arguments was expected to be greater for HDs than LDs, and HDs were expected to give fewer inconsistent arguments than LDs. Feather failed to find support for his hypothesis. He pointed out that his hypothesis that HDs would give fewer inconsistent arguments than LDs was not in contradiction to Rokeach's theory of cognitive isolation, as Franklin and Carr (1971) had suggested, since he saw:

> the closedminded person as one with a lower tolerance for inconsistency, and hence one whose cognitive structures would be relatively simple and consistent in comparison to those of the openminded person. . . . Cognitive isolation itself would be a mechanism by which a person could avoid cognitive confrontation with inconsistency, since cognitive elements not fitting together could be walled off into separate non-communicating compartments [Feather, 1973, p. 223].

In evaluating the results of his study, Feather suggested that his procedure might be at fault and suggested that future investigators obtain pro and con arguments as well as learning whether a subject agreed or disagreed with the pro and con argument.

Franklin and Carr (1971) adopted Feather's procedure with the suggested modification in experimental design and found support for their hypothesis that HDs will have a greater discrepancy in the degree of differentiation between belief and disbelief systems, will show less differentiation within disbelief systems, and will manifest greater isolation within the belief system, disbelief system, and between the belief and disbelief systems.

However, in a series of subsequent studies, Feather (1969b, c, 1970) has failed to support Rokeach's assumptions about dogmatism and cognitive differentiation and isolation. In his review of these studies, Feather (1973) notes that each of his experiments was designed to introduce new variables while also allowing for the replication of previous results, so that many variables have been manipulated including sex difference, timed versus untimed conditions in obtaining pro/con and agree/disagree arguments, variations in the nature of issues with which the arguments are concerned, variations in attitude measures (Likert-type scales and semantic differential), and variations in order of presentation of tests. Even with these experimental variations Feather notes that his studies are not an exact replication of Franklin and Carr's study and suggests that such a replication is in order. Feather also points out that an adequate test of Rokeach's hypothesis of belief differentiation and isolation is "beset by conceptual and methodological problems" that future research must consider. These include using populations other than university students (which all of the investigators have employed in this area) in order to obtain more extreme scores, developing more precise measures of cognitive differentiation and isolation, particularly since pro and con arguments are crude measures in that they assume equal weight of arguments and do not take into account interrelationships between arguments or information contained within arguments.

Summary

Research in the general area of the nature of belief systems has yielded mixed findings. Although not directly related to dogmatism, Rokeach's concept of belief congruence as the basis of ethnic or racial prejudice seems to have certainly stood up under extensive experimental research. Research in belief congruence, whether employing a hypothetical-stranger design or consequences of choice design as introduced by Silverman (1974), certainly suggests that belief congruence is a significant basis for racial and ethnic prejudice (or acceptance or intolerance of others).

Concepts more directly related to the HD's belief structure have not fared so well. Rokeach's original hypothesis that dogmatism would be independent of political or ideological content and that high dogmatism scores would characterize individuals at either extreme of political ideology has not been borne out. Research has indicated that the HD is more likely to adhere to a conservative position or one supported by authority (e.g., official government position). Part of the difficulty associated with research in this area, which has been suggested by Bailes and Guller (1970), is that there are many extraneous confounding factors involved in the study of political ideology. These factors, which may overshadow the basic relationship between dogmatism and political extremity, include emotional factors (which may have been involved in studies utilizing pro- or anti-Vietnam-withdrawal attitudes), peer expectations, and environmental settings (which have usually been within a university). Until further research can more adequately control such factors though, we must accept the weight of the evidence and conclude that HDs are more conservative in their political and broad social beliefs and attitudes (e.g., sexual attitudes, attitudes toward marijuana use) and more accepting of beliefs supported by authority.

Research in the area of religion has basically concentrated on measuring different levels of dogmatism between and within religious denominations (which are known to vary regarding belief in absolute authority) yielding inconsistent results. These inconsistencies, however, do not seem to be so much a weakness in dogmatism theory as an artifact of the varied populations and geographic areas sampled. Several investigators have suggested that HDs are more persuasible, being more likely to change attitudes, particularly under group pressure. These studies, however, have not indicated whether this attitude change is temporary or more long lasting, and there has not as yet been any systematized attempt to manipulate the belief structure of HDs within the theoretical framework of the central–peripheral dimension of belief systems. Finally, the conflicting results found between Franklin and Carr's (1971) and Feather's work in the study of cognitive isolation and differentiation leaves a very important area about the nature of belief systems open for further study and clarification. As Feather (1973) suggests, alternate measures of isolation and differentiation with more varied populations are needed.

PERSONALITY, DEFENSIVENESS, AND MALADJUSTMENT

Personality Structure

Rokeach (1960) has suggested that the concept of an open-and-closed belief system can be viewed as the "cornerstone of our attempts to understand whatever relationships may exist among personality, ideology, and cognitive functioning [p. 396]." As described above, the central region of the belief–disbelief system is assumed to contain primitive beliefs about the self. Since the closed-minded individual's beliefs about the self are those of inadequacy and self-hate, he compensates with egocentrism and an excessive concern with power (the latter being part of the intermediate and peripheral regions): Because of this egocentrism and condemnation of others, the HD experiences guilt which results in the use of various defenses which ultimately distort his world. Closed mindedness serves the function of protecting and preserving the beliefs about the self contained in the central region (particularly through beliefs held about authority), resulting in a cognitive system which protects the person against anxiety. From this, one would expect to find significant differences between high and low dogmatics in the self-concept (as well as related personality constructs), levels of anxiety, and types of personality dysfunction. Research has borne this out.

Plant, Telford, and Thomas (1965), utilizing the California Psychological Inventory, found HDs more psychologically immature and characterized as being impulsive, highly defensive, and stereotypic in their thinking, while LDs were described as being outgoing and enterprising, calm, mature, and forceful, efficient and clear thinking, responsible and likely to succeed in an academic setting (which, according to DiRenzo, 1974, would be in the liberal arts as opposed to the natural and physical sciences, which attract HDs because of their high degree of structure).

Hjelle and Lomastro (1971) found LDs scoring significantly lower on three scales of the Omnibus Personality Inventory: Autonomy, Religious Orientation, and Personal Integration; indicating that LDs were less accepting of traditional religious beliefs, more tolerant of ambiguities in their environment, and that they displayed fewer signs indicative of emotional disturbance. Mehrabian (1969) found achievement-oriented males (but not females) less dogmatic. Korn and Giddan (1964), utilizing three different scales from the California Personality Inventory, concluded that the more dogmatic an individual is, the less tolerant, secure, and flexible he is. This lack of flexibility was also noted by Hamilton (1971) and Parrott (1971). Although Rokeach (1960) makes a distinction between rigidity and dogmatism as separate entities, other investigators have drawn a parallel between dogmatism and rigidity or inflexibility (DiRenzo, 1967; Kamenske, 1966; Riley & Armlin, 1965; White & Alter, 1965).

A low but significant correlation between Machiavellianism and DS has suggested that there is a tendency for the HD to be detached and manipulative of others (Primavera & Higgins, 1973).

Rokeach (1960, 1968) has made beliefs about the self and the generalized other a major category within the central region of the central–peripheral dimension. Utilizing a specially constructed check-off scale of trait names, Lee and Ehrlich (1971) found that the close-minded person held more negative and contradictory beliefs about the self, had more negative attitudes toward others, and manifested a strong need for martyrdom. Lee and Ehrlich (1971) noted, "As a defense against negative self-beliefs, the more close-minded person was postulated to be self-proselytizing, as manifested by the compulsive repetition of beliefs, and to engage in self-aggrandizing behavior, as indicated by a need for status and power and a sense of moral self-righteousness [p. 919] ."

Vacchiano, Strauss, and Schiffman (1968), utilizing several diverse personality tests (the Edwards Personal Preference Schedule, the Tennessee Self-Concept Scale, and the 16-PF), identified personality traits which "logically" related to the dogmatic person. High dogmatics demonstrated a need to receive support, encouragement, and understanding from others; an intolerance for understanding the feelings and motives of others; and an avoidance of changing their environment. High dogmatics were low in ego strength, frustrated by changeable conditions, submissive and conforming, restrained, tense, impatient, and conservative and respectful of established ideas. The authors note that the HD person is confident in what he has been taught to believe, accepts the tried and true despite inconsistencies, and is cautious about accepting new ideas.

Dogmatism as a Defensive Network

Rokeach's contention that dogmatism "is nothing more than a total network of psychoanalytic defense mechanisms" was suggested by his initial finding that dogmatism was related to anxiety (Fruchter, Rokeach, & Novak, 1958; Rokeach & Fruchter, 1956). Although some inconsistencies appear, the general trend seems to indicate a positive relationship between dogmatism and anxiety (Byrne, Blaylock, & Goldberg, 1966; Castle, 1971; Hanson & Bush, 1971; Hanson & Clune, 1973; Norman, 1966; Rebhun, 1966; Rokeach & Restle, 1960; Smithers, 1970; Sticht & Fox, 1966). There are at least two sources of difficulty associated with research on the dogmatism–anxiety relationship. One derives from the fact that in some studies anxiety is created via an experimental manipulation while in others the focus is on the chronic anxiety level of the individual. A second has to do with the question of whether the dogmatic defense (or any defense) adequately controls "intense" anxiety. This latter point suggests that dogmatism, as any defense mechanism, may successfully control moderate levels of anxiety and thus low correlations between dogmatism and anxiety would be obtained. However with intense or acute anxiety the dogmatic defense may be less successful in controlling the anxiety being experienced by the person and a relationship between higher levels of anxiety and dogmatism would be obtained.

Further evidence for the relationship between dogmatism and defensiveness comes from studies on decision making. Both Long and Ziller (1965) and Taylor (1972) found that HDs are more rapid in their decisions and more confident in the decisions reached. Taylor (1972) equated decision making with a defensive reaction which "predisposes an individual to avoid prolonged information seeking when it could place a strain upon his capability of integrating contradictory information or cause him to change his decision [p. 444] ."

Because the future is so unpredictable (and thus capable of arousing considerable anxiety), Rokeach suggests that the HD, as a defense against this anxiety, will deemphasize the past and present and overemphasize or be preoccupied with the future, perhaps in order to create a feeling of control of the course of events. The HD's future-time orientation has been substantiated in various studies (Castle, 1971; Jay, 1969; Rokeach, 1954, 1956; Rokeach & Bonier, 1960; Zurcher, Willis, Ikard, & Dohme, 1967).

Kaplan and Singer (1963) found that HDs manifest significantly lower sensory acuity resulting in reduced self-awareness and concluded that "openness to sense impressions apparently runs parallel to openness of ideas, willingness to examine them critically, and careful analysis of thought [p. 490]." (But see also Houston, 1970.) In a similar vein, LoSciuto and Hartley (1963) found in a binocular-resolution task that LDs were more alert to religious symbols from other religions than HDs. The work of other investigators all seem to support the thesis that dogmatism is indeed a form of defense mechanism (Bernhardson, 1967; Byrne, Blaylock, & Goldberg, 1966; Cohen, 1961; Hallenbeck, 1965; Hallenbeck & Lundstedt, 1966; Lee & Ehrlich, 1971).

Maladjustment

Several investigators have noted that dogmatism is related to various manifestations of emotional maladjustment or poor self-concept (e.g., Kemp, 1961; Vacchiano, Strauss, & Schiffman, 1968; Webster, 1967). Ehrlich and Bauer (1966) found "that the high dogmatic patient is more likely than the low dogmatic patient to be diagnosed as functionally psychotic, as having a thinking disorder, and as having greater social and occupational impairment [p. 258]." Prognosis was poorer, hospitalization was longer, and drug therapy was more frequently given for the HD. High dogmatic females have been noted by both Norman (1966) (who employed only females in his study) and Richek, Mayo, and Piryean (1970) to differ significantly from low dogmatic females in scores on several of the MMPI scales. Norman's high and log dogmatics differed significantly on Scales F, K, D, Pt, Si, manifest anxiety (Taylor), and ego strength (Barron) which led him to conclude that HD females are anxious, depressed, socially introverted, lacking in ego strength, self-esteem, and overall personality adjustment. Richek, Mayo, and Piryean (1970) found no significant differences for their male group on the MMPI but did find that the more dogmatic the females, the more depressed, psychasthenic, and anxious they were.

A considerable amount of attention has been directed toward studying dogmatism in relation to psychotherapeutic improvement and change. In particular, some investigators have noted a relationship between dogmatism and potential for change in psychotherapy or improvement as a result of hospitalization. The expectation of a link between dogmatism and potential for change and improvement is based on investigations which have found an inverse relationship between dogmatism and learning and belief acquisition (Adams & Vidulich, 1962;

Christensen, 1963; Costin, 1965, 1968; Ehrlich & Lee, 1969; Frumkin, 1961; Restle, Andrews, & Rokeach, 1964). Thus, when utilizing subjective rating scales employed by hospital staffs, Ehrlich and Bauer (1966), Gelso (1970), and Lefcourt (1962) have found a positive relationship between low dogmatism and low degree of psychological disturbance and suitability for therapy in psychiatric hospital populations. However, Scheid and Gelso (1971) found that dogmatism was not a factor in level of adjustment of patients following hospitalization when more objective criteria were employed such as number of days out of the hospital and number of days employed.

Summary

A number of investigations have attempted to extend the concept of dogmatism into broader patterns of personality structure utilizing varied personality inventories. For the most part these studies substantiate specific predictions made by Rokeach about HDs (negative self-image, intolerance for others, and so on) while in other instances the studies broaden the description of the dogmatic individual and fit logically with what one would expect of an individual with a closed belief system.

Although these studies have employed different personality scales, they have yielded quite similar personality descriptions of the HD that can be grouped into three broad areas. These include low frustration tolerance (as manifested in impulsivity, immaturity, tenseness, impatience, low ego strength); negative images of self and others (as manifested in holding more negative and contradictory beliefs about the self and others, intolerance for the feelings of others, manipulation of others, self-aggrandizement); and conformity (as manifested in stereotyped thinking, inflexibility, being restrained and conservative, accepting established beliefs despite inconsistencies).

Less emphasis seems to have been placed on describing the LD, but the behavioral descriptions given see the open-minded individual as more mature, extroverted, tolerant of ambiguities, and less accepting of traditional beliefs.

Rokeach's thesis that dogmatism represents a "network" of various defense mechanisms appears to be well substantiated. From the nature of the personality patterns found for the HD, as well as his defensiveness, the finding that the HD experiences a greater degree of psychopathology, longer hospitalization, and poorer response to psychotherapy is not surprising and becomes a logical extension of Rokeach's theory. Perhaps the most significant factor in the research on personality and dogmatism rests in the fact that the concept provides a basis for unifying and integrating many related variables of personality. Future studies might be directed toward studying the origins of belief development in childhood, how open and closed belief systems affect the dynamics of a total family unit, and modification of closed mindedness in attempts at improving mental health such as in psychotherapy.

INTERPERSONAL AND GROUP BEHAVIOR

Interpersonal Attraction

Research on dogmatism in the area of interpersonal attraction has derived from the assumption that the HD is intolerant of opposing views and rejects persons holding such views. As Rokeach (1960) has stated

> the more closed our belief systems, the more we will reject others who disagree with us, and the more we will accept others *because* they agree with us [p. 80].

More specifically,

> . . . the more closed a person's belief system, the more he should evaluate others according to their agreement or disagreement with his own system; also the more difficult should it be to discriminate between and separately evaluate a belief and the person holding the belief. Conversely, the more open the belief system, the less should beliefs held in common be a criterion for evaluating others, and the more should others be positively valued, regardless of their beliefs [p. 63].

Most of the research reviewed in the section on prejudice, as well as Byrne's (1969) research program based on a reinforcement model of attraction, and balance theory (Heider, 1958) all point to a positive relationship between attitude similarity and attraction. In light of Rokeach's hypothesized relationship between dogmatism and agreement as a basis for evaluating others, one would expect the attitude similarity–attraction relationship to hold primarily or more strongly for HDs but less so or not at all for LDs. The experimental evidence does not provide support for this expectation.

Two experiments, utilizing the "hypothetical-stranger" design, have reported negative results. Gormly and Clore (1969) investigated the effects of dogmatism and exposure to similar or dissimilar attitudes of a hypothetical stimulus person, hypothesizing that HDs would increase attraction toward similar others and decrease attraction toward dissimilar others. Although there was a trend in the predicted direction ($p < .07$), the authors concluded that the DS was not a reliable predictor of differences in attraction ratings as a function of attitude similarity–dissimilarity. Similar results were found by Franklin (1971) who failed to find dogmatism having an effect on interpersonal attraction. Nor did dogmatism seem to interact with attitude similarity–dissimilarity in influencing interpersonal attraction. The evidence, then, in general, fails to support dogmatism theory. Whether this is due to the weakness of the theory or the experimental design cannot be answered. In both studies the hypothetical-stranger design was used and as Franklin (1971) suggests:

> this is a pre-interaction design which makes attitude similarity–dissimilarity salient for the subjects in their attraction ratings. Perhaps dogmatism operates to make attitude similarity–dissimilarity differentially salient when subjects are confronted with additional information about the other or when the attraction rating of the other is post-interaction [p. 9].

Is a person's level of dogmatism related to his likability? Hodges and Byrne (1972) found that attraction is more positive toward an open-minded "dissimilar" than toward a dogmatic "dissimilar." Rosenfeld and Nauman (1969) studied the effect of dogmatism upon the development of informal social relationships over a five-week period in a women's residential hall at a large university. Based on peer evaluations of interpersonal interactions (e.g., frequency of contact, amount of verbal contact), HDs became increasingly negatively evaluated by their peers and were insensitive to the negative receptions they received.

Interpersonal Perception

Although Tagiuri (1969) has pointed to the difficulty in establishing a consistent relationship between person perception and personality characteristics, several investigators have continued to seek such a relationship. Of interest here are those studies employing dogmatism as the major personality trait. Burke (1966), employing a procedure similar to that of some earlier studies on authoritarianism and person perception, had HD and LD college students judge what the "average" student's response to the Dogmatism scale would be and found LDs to be more accurate interpersonal perceivers (of the level of dogmatism of others) than HDs.

Jacoby (1971) has suggested that Burke's findings, as well as those of earlier studies on the effects of the perceiver's authoritarianism on the perception of others, may be the artifactual result of the pervasive tendency for subjects to estimate others' scores as higher than their own. Jacoby points to two major criticisms of prior research in this area that his study attempted to overcome. First, prior research presented the subject with a limited amount of data concerning the stimulus person; and second, accuracy was operationally defined as the difference between the stimulus person's true total score and the subject's estimate of that score. This could result in gross over- or underestimation. Jacoby suggests that given a Likert-type scale, greater accuracy may be obtained with estimates made on an item-by-item basis. In an attempt to overcome these limitations, Jacoby extended the subject–stimulus person interaction over a much longer duration, making it substantially more meaningful, and adjusted the scoring by having subjects estimate the stimulus person's responses to each of the 40 items of the *D* scale. His major hypothesis that open-minded subjects more accurately perceive the degree of dogmatism in others than closed-minded subjects was confirmed. Although not significant, the results were in the predicted direction for interaction time: increase in interaction time did not influence the accuracy of the HD's interpersonal perception but was positively related to the LD's increased accuracy. As was found in previous studies with authoritarianism, the higher the subject's dogmatism score, the higher was his estimate of the stimulus person's score. The subject's estimate was more strongly related to his own level of dogmatism than to the stimulus person's true level of dogmatism. High and low dogmatic stimulus persons were equally discernible.

Interpersonal Interaction

A number of investigators have directed their attention toward evaluating the effects of dogmatism on interpersonal interaction in groups. Altman and Haythorn (1967) examined the individual and group performance of dyadic groups, both homogeneous (two HDs or two LDs) and heterogeneous (one HD and one LD), under conditions of normal daily interaction patterns (control condition) or social isolation (experimental condition). Although there was no significant effect on individual task performance (which had been anticipated), there was a significant effect on performance for dyadic groups. Under control conditions, the heterogeneous dyads outperformed the homogeneous dyads; but under experimental conditions homogeneous dyads outperformed the heterogeneous groups. The authors suggest that the heterogeneous dyad produces mild stress which improves group performance under normal conditions, but when added to the stress of isolation contrasting dogmatism levels of group members lessen the effectiveness of group performance.

Druckman (1967), employing a dyadic bargaining situation, found that HDs were more resistant to change than LDs and less willing to compromise from a given position since they viewed compromise as defeat. Within an unstructured classroom situation, Zagona and Zurcher (1964, 1965a) observed differences between HDs and LDs in interpersonal interactions and found HDs to be concerned with the problem of leader selection and group structure. When challenged by authority, HDs became insecure, wavered in their convictions, and evidenced signs of reduced group cohesion. "Intellectual lethargy characterized the atmosphere of the HD classroom. An unwillingness to relate . . . to the subject matter, to the instructor, to other students [seemed to prevail] [Zagona & Zurcher, 1965b, p. 216]." Talley and Vamos (1972) explored the feelings and concerns expressed by HDs and LDs in a potentially threatening and ambiguous (i.e., a nondirective approach) situation created within a course in group dynamics. As Talley and Vamos (1972) hypothesized, HDs were concerned about "the physical setting, the organization and structure of the sessions, the topics discussed, the goals of the group, the evaluative technique of the group and its leader, and the level of satisfaction with the experience [p. 280]." Thus, as suggested by Rokeach (1960), HDs were threatened by the lack of structure and the leader's (or authority's) role in such situations.

From these findings one would expect to find differential reactions between HDs and LDs in group therapy, training groups, or individual therapy. Research has borne this out. In a study of the differential T-group behavior of HDs and LDs, Frye, Vidulich, Meierhoefer, and Joure (1972) found, as hypothesized, that the LDs made fewer statements rejecting the experimental situation and more statements which were self-revealing, central (as opposed to peripheral), relevant to the group interaction, and positive. The LD group also exhibited fewer behavioral manifestations of anxiety, annoyance, or boredom Ultimately the HD group matched or surpassed the LD group's frequency of statements on some of the coding dimensions, but it took longer:

> This is in keeping with the expected difficulty of establishing psychological safety in the high dogmatic group. However, it is possible that the same level of behavior in the high dogmatic group is a function of the HDs' behaviorally conforming to the trainer's expectations of what their behavior should be. The HDs may give the appearance of accepting "honesty" and "openness" without actually changing their values, which Rokeach described as "party line change" typical of the HD. The trainer in a T-group, even though non-directive, is an authority figure. While in his presence, the HD may behave the way he thinks the trainer wants him to, exhibiting his deference to authority figures while not actually integrating into his belief system the values he thinks the trainer wishes him to adopt [Frye *et al.,* 1972, p. 307].

In general, Frye *et al.* found the HDs to be rejecting of the unstructured T-group, to be more threatened by the lack of structure, and to manifest more anxiety by it. In another T-group evaluation, Joure, Frye, Meierhoefer, and Vidulich (1972) also found LDs to make a significantly greater number of changes after T-group exposure, usually in the direction of more honest self-appraisal.

Since it has been established that the dogmatic person is less open to change, more defensive, insecure, and threatened (Vacchiano, Strauss, & Hochman, 1969), one would expect dogmatism to have a significant role in counselor–client interactions. Research has suggested that the HD counselor is less effective (Kemp, 1962; Russo, Kelz, & Hudson, 1964). Allen (1967) notes that the dogmatic counselor can distort therapeutic interactions because of the HD's difficulty in understanding his own feelings and his low cognizance of the client's feelings. Other investigators, however, have found no relationship between dogmatism and counselor effectiveness (Ehrlich & Bauer, 1966; Milliken & Paterson, 1967; Rosen, 1967). Foulds (1971) correlated the dogmatism scores of graduate students in a practicum situation with ratings (made by trained judges) for the degree to which the student provided the patient with empathetic understanding, positive regard, and facilitative genuineness, and found no significant relationship. Foulds (1971) suggests, though, as have Kemp (1962) and Frye *et al.* (1972), that the HDs may have learned to make empathetic, understanding, and respectful responses because it was the "expected" thing to do.

Tosi (1970) has pointed out that prior investigations of counselor–client interaction have concentrated on counselor personality traits rather than investigating counselor–client variables jointly. Tosi therefore examined the effects of different levels of counselor and client dogmatism on the client's perception of the relationship after the initial encounter (i.e., degree of empathy, unconditional positive regard, level of regard, and congruence). Varying levels of counselor–client dogmatism combined additively to significantly effect the relationship measures. As more openness occurred in the counselor–client dyad the higher were the ratings of the relationship. Low and medium level dogmatics gave the highest ratings to relationships with counselors who were low or medium in dogmatism.

Cognitive Inconsistency and Situational Threat

Since dogmatism represents a closed cognitive organization of beliefs as well as a form of defense mechanism, one would expect the HD to be threatened by or avoid belief-discrepant information or situations which threaten his cognitive structure. For the most part, research has substantiated this hypothesis (Miller & Rokeach, 1968). Pyron's (1966) factor analysis of several attitudinal scales revealed a dogmatism factor involving the rejection of stimuli potentially threatening to the individual's perceptual and attitudinal organization. When faced with a group personality testing situation, HDs perceive the testing situation as more threatening than LDs (Tosi, Fagan, & Frumkin, 1968a, b). Rosenman (1967) reports that HDs are less accepting than LDs of a film which flaunts traditional beliefs of society. Hunt and Miller (1968) found that HDs show less tolerance for inconsistency when required to prepare belief-discrepant communications for public review. High dogmatics reveal less recall of inconsistent information and evaluate consistent information more positively (Kleck & Wheaton, 1967). A study on selective exposure to reading materials (Donohew, Parker, & McDermott, 1972) found tentative evidence that high dogmatics avoid discrepant materials and seek supportive or balanced materials while LDs expose themselves to discrepant information. Durand and Lambert (1975) found HDs less willing to attend speeches of presidential-primary candidates whose views were discrepant with their own. When using impression formation problems to measure tolerance of trait inconsistency, Foulkes and Foulkes (1965) found that HDs, when faced with discrepant information, tend to avoid compromise solutions by either changing greatly or adhering very closely to their original impression. White, Alter, and Rardin (1965) suggest, though, that the HD does not make such black or white decisions in all conceptual tasks but only when judging syndrome-relevant stimuli (e.g., undesirable social acts).

Summary

In the majority of studies reviewed it is evident that dogmatism does have a significant effect on interpersonal and group behavior. Although the evidence is weak for the effects of dogmatism on the link between attitude similarity and interpersonal attraction (due, perhaps, to the use of preinteraction designs)

Rosenfeld and Nauman's (1969) finding that HDs become increasingly negatively evaluated during informal social interactions indicates that dogmatism does have some effect on interpersonal attraction in actual group situations.

High dogmatics are also less accurate perceivers of dogmatism in others. When involved in group interaction, HDs have greater difficulty in matching the level of positive performance found in LDs and manifest a need for considerable structure, have difficulty in relating to other members of the group, and do not profit as much as the LDs from individual or group therapy or training group experiences. There is some suggestion, too, that HD counselors are less effective than LDs. High dogmatics are less tolerant when presented with information that is contradictory to their beliefs.

Research in the area of interpersonal and group behavior has become increasingly more applied in recent years, particularly in the clinical area. Future emphasis might well be extended to other applied areas such as industrial organizations and educational systems where the effectiveness of training and educational programs may be increased through a better understanding of the impact of dogmatism on such factors as motivation, job satisfaction, organizational role fulfillment, and responsiveness to new educational materials.

SUMMARY

Since Rokeach's publication of *The Open and Closed Mind,* research has substantiated many of the major hypotheses about dogmatism. Certainly the DS is a more generalized measure of authoritarianism than the *F* scale and the HD's dependency on authority is well documented. Although not directly related to dogmatism, Rokeach's theory of prejudice, based on belief congruence rather than racial or ethnic differences, has held up under extensive investigation. Research would also suggest that dogmatism or a closed-minded belief system can be viewed as a "cornerstone" for personality functioning and serve as a network of defense mechanisms which affects the individual's emotional adjustment and interpersonal and group interaction.

Several areas of Rokeach's theory, however, have not been substantiated. Although Rokeach felt that dogmatism would be independent of political ideology, research in both political beliefs as well as personality structure suggests that the HD takes a conservative position. The nature of beliefs in terms of cognitive isolation and differentiation has yet to be adequately substantiated. Studies on differences in levels of dogmatism among various religious faiths and denominations have not yet yielded consistent findings. In some instances the failure to support dogmatism theory may be due to difficulties in experimental design, while at other times inconsistencies appear because of definition of terms (such as "anxiety"), populations sampled (usually college students), and geographical areas sampled.

Dogmatism still continues to be a viable concept and receives considerable attention from researchers, probably because the concept of an open and closed belief system is so very basic in much of our behavior.

REFERENCES

Adams, H. E., & Vidulich, R. N. Dogmatism and belief congruence in paired-associate learning. *Psychological Reports,* 1962, *10,* 91–94.

Adorno, T. W., Frenkel-Brunswik, E., Levinson, D. J., & Sanford, R. N. *The authoritarian personality.* New York: Harper, 1950.

Allen, T. W. Effectiveness of counselor trainees as a function of psychological openness. *Journal of Counseling Psychology,* 1967, *14,* 35–41.

Altman, K., & Haythorn, W. W. The effects of social isolation and group composition on performance. *Human Relations,* 1967, *29,* 313–340.

Anderson, C. C., & Côté, A. D. J. Belief dissonance as a source of disaffection between ethnic groups. *Journal of Personality and Social Psychology,* 1966, *4,* 447–453.

Bailes, D. W., & Guller, I. B. Dogmatism and attitudes toward the Vietnam War. *Sociometry,* 1970, *33,* 140–146.

Baker, F., & Schulberg, H. C. Community mental health ideology, dogmatism, and political-economic conservatism. *Community Mental Health Journal,* 1969, *5,* 433–436.

Barker, E. N. Authoritarianism of the political right, center, and left. *Journal of Social Issues,* 1963, *19*(2), 63–74.

Bernhardson, C. S. Dogmatism, defense mechanisms, and social desirability responding. *Psychological Reports,* 1967, *20,* 511–513.

Bettinghaus, E., Miller, G., & Steinfatt, T. Source evaluation, syllogistic content, and judgments of logical validity by high- and low-dogmatic persons. *Journal of Personality and Social Psychology,* 1970, *16,* 238–244.

Bohr, R. H. Dogmatism and age of vocational choice in two religious orders. *Journal for the Scientific Study of Religion,* 1968, *7,* 282.

Burke, W. W. Social perception as a function of dogmatism. *Perceptual and Motor Skills,* 1966, *23,* 863–868.

Byrne, D. Attitudes and attraction. In L. Berkowitz (Ed.), *Advances in experimental social psychology* (Vol. 4). New York: Academic Press, 1969.

Byrne, D., Blaylock, B., & Goldberg, J. Dogmatism and defense mechanisms. *Psychological Reports,* 1966, *18,* 739–742.

Byrne, D., & McGraw, C. Interpersonal attraction toward Negroes. *Human Relations,* 1964, *17,* 201–213.

Byrne, D., & Wong, T. J. Racial prejudice, interpersonal attraction, and assumed dissimilarity of attitudes. *Journal of Abnormal and Social Psychology,* 1962, *65,* 246–253.

Castle, T. J. Temporal correlates of dogmatism. *Journal of Consulting and Clinical Psychology,* 1971, *36,* 70–81.

Christensen, C. M. A note on "Dogmatism and Learning." *Journal of Abnormal and Social Psychology,* 1963, *66,* 75–76.

Clouser, R. A., & Hjelle, L. A. Relationship between locus of control and dogmatism. *Psychological Reports,* 1970, *26,* 1006.

Cohen, I. H. Adaptive regression, dogmatism, and creativity. *Dissertation Abstracts,* 1961, *21,* 3522–3523.

Costin, F. Dogmatism and learning: A follow-up of contradictory findings. *Journal of Educational Research,* 1965, *59,* 186–188.

Costin, F. Dogmatism and the retention of psychological misconceptions. *Educational and Psychological Measurement,* 1968, *28,* 529–534.

Costin, F. Dogmatism and conservatism: An empirical follow-up of Rokeach's findings. *Educational and Psychological Measurement,* 1971, *31,* 1007–1010.

Cronkhite, G., & Goetz, E. Dogmatism, persuasibility, and attitude instability. *Journal of Communication,* 1971, *21,* 342–352.

Dembroski, B. G., & Johnson, D. L. Dogmatism and attitudes toward adoption. *Journal of Marriage and the Family,* 1969, *31,* 788–792.

DiGiuseppe, R. A. Dogmatism correlation with strength of religious conviction. *Psychological Reports,* 1971, *28,* 64.

DiRenzo, G. J. Dogmatism and orientations toward liturgical change. *Journal for the Scientific Study of Religion,* 1967, *6,* 278.

DiRenzo, G. J. Dogmatism and presidential preferences in the 1964 elections. *Psychological Reports,* 1968, *22,* 1197–1202.

DiRenzo, G. J. Dogmatism and presidential preferences: A 1968 replication. *Psychological Reports,* 1971, *29,* 109–110.

DiRenzo, G. J. Congruences in personality structure and academic curricula as determinants of occupational careers. *Psychological Reports,* 1974, *34,* 1295–1298.

Donohew, L., Parker, J. M., & McDermott, V. Psychophysiological measurement of information selection: Two studies. *Journal of Communication,* 1972, *22,* 54–63.

Druckman, D. Dogmatism, prenegotiation experience, and simulated group representation as determinants of dyadic behavior in a bargaining situation. *Journal of Personality and Social Psychology,* 1967, *6,* 279–290.

Durand, R. M., & Lambert, Z. V. Dogmatism and exposure to political candidates. *Psychological Reports,* 1975, *36,* 423–429.

Ehrlich, H. J. Dogmatism and learning. *Journal of Abnormal and Social Psychology,* 1961, *62,* 148–149. (a)

Ehrlich, H. J. Dogmatism and learning: A five-year follow-up. *Psychological Reports,* 1961, *9,* 283–286. (b)

Ehrlich, H. J., & Bauer, M. L. The correlates of dogmatism and flexibility in psychiatric hospitalization. *Journal of Consulting Psychology,* 1966, *30,* 253–259.

Ehrlich, H. J., & Lee, D. Dogmatism, learning, and resistance to change: A review and a new paradigm. *Psychological Bulletin,* 1969, *71,* 249–259.

Feather, N. T. Evaluation of religious and neutral arguments in religious and atheist student groups. *Australian Journal of Psychology,* 1967, *19,* 3–12.

Feather, N. T. Cognitive differentiation, attitude strength, and dogmatism. *Journal of Personality,* 1969, *37,* 111–126. (a)

Feather, N. T. Attitude and selective recall. *Journal of Personality and Social Psychology,* 1969, *12,* 310–319. (b)

Feather, N. T. Differentiation of arguments in relation to attitude, dogmatism, and intolerance of ambiguity. *Australian Journal of Psychology,* 1969, *21,* 21–29. (c)

Feather, N. T. Balancing and positivity effects in social recall. *Journal of Personality,* 1970, *38,* 602–628.

Feather, N. T. Cognitive differentiation, cognitive isolation, and dogmatism: Rejoinder and further analysis. *Sociometry,* 1973, *36,* 221–236.

Foulds, M. L. Dogmatism and ability to communicate facilitative conditions during counseling. *Counselor Education and Supervision,* 1971, *11,* 110–114.

Foulkes, D., & Foulkes, S. H. Self-concept, dogmatism, and tolerance of trait inconsistency. *Journal of Personality and Social Psychology,* 1965, *2,* 104–111.

Franklin, B. J. Attitude similarity, dogmatism, and interpersonal attraction. *Psychology,* 1971, *8,* 4–11.

Franklin, B. J., & Carr, R. A. Cognitive differentiation, cognitive isolation, and dogmatism. *Sociometry,* 1971, *34,* 230–237.

Fruchter, B., Rokeach, M., & Novak, E. G. A factorial study of dogmatism, opinionation, and related scales. *Psychological Reports,* 1958, *4,* 19–22.

Frumkin, R. M. Dogmatism, social class, values, and academic achievement in sociology. *Journal of Educational Sociology,* 1961, *34,* 398–403.

Frye, R. L., Vidulich, R. N., Meierhoefer, B., & Joure, S. Differential T-group behaviors of high and low dogmatic participants. *Journal of Psychology,* 1972, *81,* 301–309.

Gelso, C. Dogmatism and the prognosis of mental patients as judged by various staff members. *Journal of Clinical Psychology,* 1970, *26,* 98.

Gilmore, S. K. Personality differences between high and low dogmatic groups of Pentecostal believers. *Journal for the Scientific Study of Religion,* 1970, *9,* 235–238.

Glass, K. D. Denominational differences in religious belief, practice, anxiety and dogmatism. *Religious Education,* 1971, *66,* 204–206.

Gold, J. A., Ryckman, R. M., & Rodda, W. C. Differential responsiveness of dissonance manipulations by open- and closed-minded subjects in a forced compliance situation. *Journal of Social Psychology,* 1973, *90,* 73–83.

Gormly, A. W., & Clore, G. L. Attraction, dogmatism and attitude similarity–dissimilarity. *Journal of Experimental Research in Personality,* 1969, *4,* 9–13.

Granberg, D., & Corrigan, G. Authoritarianism, dogmatism, and orientations toward the Vietnam War. *Sociometry,* 1972, *35,* 468–476.

Hallenbeck, P. A study of the effects of dogmatism on certain aspects of adjustment to severe disability. *Dissertation Abstracts,* 1965, *25,* 6759–6760.

Hallenbeck, P. N., & Lundstedt, S. Some relations between dogmatism, denial and depression. *Journal of Social Psychology,* 1966, *70,* 53–58.

Hamilton, D. L. A comparative study of five methods of assessing self-esteem, dominance, and dogmatism. *Educational and Psychological Measurement,* 1971, *31,* 441–452.

Hanson, D. J. Dogmatism and authoritarianism. *Journal of Social Psychology,* 1968, *76,* 89–95.

Hanson, D. J. Validity test of the Dogmatism Scale. *Psychological Reports,* 1970, *26,* 585–586.

Hanson, D. J. Dogmatism and attitude extremity. *Journal of Social Psychology,* 1973, *89,* 155–156.

Hanson, D. J., & Bush, A. M. Anxiety and dogmatism. *Psychological Reports,* 1971, *29,* 366.

Hanson, D. J., & Clune, M. Dogmatism and anxiety in relation to childhood experience. *Journal of Social Psychology,* 1973, *91,* 157–158.

Harvey, J., & Hays, D. G. Effect of dogmatism and authority of the source of communication upon persuasion. *Psychological Reports,* 1972, *30,* 119–122.

Heider, F. *The psvchology of interpersonal relations.* New York: Wiley, 1958.

Hendrick, C., Bixenstine, V. E., & Hawkins, G. Race versus belief similarity as determinants of attraction: A search for a fair test. *Journal of Personality and Social Psychology,* 1971, *17,* 250–258.

Hendrick, C., & Hawkins, G. Race and belief similarity as determinants of attraction. *Perceptual and Motor Skills,* 1969, *29,* 710.

Hjelle, L. A., & Lomastro, J. Personality differences between high and low dogmatic groups of Catholic seminarians and religious sisters. *Journal for the Scientific Study of Religion,* 1971, *10,* 49–50.

Hodges, L. A., & Byrne, D. Verbal dogmatism as a potentiator of intolerance. *Journal of Personality and Social Psychology,* 1972, *21,* 312–317.

Hoge, D. R., & Carroll, J. W. Religiousity and prejudice in northern and southern churches. *Journal for the Scientific Study of Religion,* 1973, *12,* 181–197.

Hood, R. W., Jr. Dogmatism and opinions of mental illness. *Psychological Reports,* 1973, *32,* 1283–1290.

Hood, R. W., Jr. Cognitive and affective rejection of mentally ill persons as a function of dogmatism. *Psychological Reports,* 1974, *35,* 543–549.

Houston, B. K. Dogmatism and intolerance for sensory discrepancy. *Journal of Social Psychology,* 1970, *80,* 245–246.

Hunt, M. F., & Miller, G. R. Open- and closed-mindedness, belief-discrepant communication behavior, and tolerance for cognitive inconsistency. *Journal of Personality and Social Psychology,* 1968, *8,* 35–37.

Insko, C. A., & Robinson, J. E. Belief similarity versus race as determinants of reactions to Negroes by southern white adolescents: A further test of Rokeach's theory. *Journal of Personality and Social Psychology,* 1967, *7,* 216–221.

Jacoby, J. Interpersonal perceptual accuracy as a function of dogmatism. *Journal of Experimental Social Psychology,* 1971, *7,* 221–236.

Jay, R. L. Q technique factor analysis of the Rokeach Dogmatism Scale. *Educational and Psychological Measurement,* 1969, *29,* 453–459.

Jones, J. M. Dogmatism and political preferences. *Psychological Reports,* 1973, *33,* 640.

Joure, S., Frye, R., Meierhoefer, B., & Vidulich, R. Differential change among sensitivity training participants as a function of dogmatism. *Journal of Psychology,* 1972, *80,* 151–156.

Kamenske, G. Some personality factors in attitude toward technological change in a medium sized insurance company. *Dissertation Abstracts,* 1966, *26,* 4797–4798.

Kaplan, M. F., & Singer, E. Dogmatism and sensory alienation: An empirical investigation. *Journal of Consulting Psychology,* 1963, *27,* 486–491.

Karabenick, S., & Wilson, R. Dogmatism among war hawks and peace doves. *Psychological Reports,* 1969, *25,* 419–422.

Kemp, C. G. Influence of dogmatism on counseling. *Personnel and Guidance Journal,* 1961, *39,* 662–665.

Kemp, C. G. Influence of dogmatism on the training of counselors. *Journal of Counseling Psychology,* 1962, *9,* 155–157.

Kemp, C. G. Perception of authority in relation to open and closed belief systems. *Science Education,* 1963, *47,* 482–484.

Kemp, C. G., & Kohler, E. W. Suitability of the Rokeach Dogmatism Scale for high school use. *Journal of Experimental Education,* 1965, *33,* 383–385.

Kerlinger, F., & Rokeach, M. The factorial nature of the F and D Scales. *Journal of Personality and Social Psychology,* 1966, *4,* 391–399.

Kilpatrick, D. G., Cauthen, N. R., Sandman, C. A., & Quattlebaum, L. F. Dogmatism and personal sexual attitudes. *Psychological Reports,* 1968, *23,* 1105–1106.

Kilpatrick, D. G., Sutker, L. W., & Sutker, P. B. Dogmatism, religion, and religiosity, a review and re-evaluation. *Psychological Reports,* 1970, *26,* 15–22.

Kirtley, D. Conformity and prejudice in authoritarians of opposing political ideologies. *Journal of Psychology,* 1968, *70,* 199–204.

Kirtley, D., & Harkless, R. Some personality and attitudinal correlates of dogmatism. *Psychological Reports,* 1969, *24,* 851–854.

Kleck, R. E., & Wheaton, J. Dogmatism and responses to opinion-consistent and opinion-inconsistent information. *Journal of Personality and Social Psychology,* 1967, *5,* 249–252.

Koepp, E. F. Authoritarianism and social workers: The psychological study. *Social Work,* 1963, *8,* 37–43.

Korn, H. A., & Giddan, N. S. Scoring methods and construct validity of the Dogmatism Scale. *Educational and Psychological Measurement,* 1964, *24,* 867–874.

Larsen, K. S. Authoritarianism, hawkishness and attitude change as related to high and low status communications. *Perceptual and Motor Skills,* 1969, *28,* 114.

Larsen, K. S., & Minton, H. Attributed social power: A scale and some validity. *Journal of Social Psychology,* 1971, *85,* 37–39.

Lazlo, J. P., & Rosenthal, R. Subject dogmatism, experimenter status, and experimenter expectancy effects. *Personality: An International Journal,* 1970, *1,* 11–23.

Lee, D., & Ehrlich, H. J. Beliefs about self and others: A test of the dogmatism theory. *Psychological Reports,* 1971, *28,* 919–922.

Lefcourt, H. M. Clinical correlates of dogmatism. *Journal of Clinical Psychology,* 1962, *18,* 327–328.

Levy, S. G., Russell, J. C., Kimmel, M. J., Carrick, K., & Burnaska, R. F. Dogmatism, locus of control of reinforcement, importance of issues, and relationships to political activity. *Journal of Applied Social Science,* 1973, *3,* 119–131.

Lichtenstein, E., Quinn, R., & Hover, G. Dogmatism and acquiescent response set. *Journal of Abnormal and Social Psychology,* 1961, *63,* 636–638.

Long, B. H., & Ziller, R. C. Dogmatism and predecisional information search. *Journal of Applied Psychology,* 1965, *49,* 376–378.

Long, H. B. Information sources, dogmatism and judgment modifications. *Adult Education Journal,* 1971, *21,* 37–45.

Lorentz, R. J. Levels of dogmatism and attitudes toward marijuana. *Psychological Reports,* 1972, *30,* 75–78.

LoSciuto, L. A., & Hartley, E. L. Religious affiliation and open-mindedness in binocular resolution. *Perceptual and Motor Skills,* 1963, *17,* 427–430.

Lundy, J. R. Some personal correlates of contraceptive use among unmarried college students. *Journal of Psychology,* 1972, *80,* 9–14.

McCarthy, J., & Johnson, R. C. Interpretation of the "City Hall Riots" as a function of general dogmatism. *Psychological Reports,* 1962, *11,* 243–245.

Mehrabian, A. Measures of achieving tendency. *Educational and Psychological Measurement,* 1969, *29,* 445–451.

Miller, G. R., & Rokeach, M. Individual differences and tolerance for inconsistency. In R. P. Abelson, E. Aronson, W. J. McGuire, T. N. Newcomb, M. J. Rosenberg, & P. H. Tannenbaum (Eds.), *Theories of cognitive consistency: A sourcebook.* Chicago: Rand McNally, 1968.

Milliken, R. L., & Paterson, J. Relationship of dogmatism and prejudice to counseling effectiveness. *Counselor Education and Supervision,* 1967, *6,* 125–129.

Mouw, J. T. Effect of dogmatism on levels of cognitive processes. *Journal of Educational Psychology,* 1969, *60,* 365–369.

Norman, R. P. Dogmatism and psychoneurosis in college women. *Journal of Consulting Psychology,* 1966, *30,* 278.

Norris, E. L. Attitude change as a function of open- or closedmindedness. *Journalism Quarterly,* 1965, *42,* 571–575.

Parrott, G. Dogmatism and rigidity: A factor analysis. *Psychological Reports,* 1971, *29,* 135–140.

Peabody, D. Authoritarianism scales and response bias. *Psychological Bulletin,* 1966, *65,* 11–23.

Plant, W. T. Rokeach's Dogmatism Scale as a measure of general authoritarianism. *Psychological Reports,* 1960, *6,* 164.

Plant, W. T., Telford, C. W., & Thomas, J. A. Some personality differences between dogmatic and non-dogmatic groups. *Journal of Social Psychology,* 1965, *67,* 67–75.

Powell, F. A. Open- and closed-mindedness and the ability to differentiate source and message. *Journal of Abnormal and Social Psychology,* 1962, *65,* 61–64.

Primavera, L. H., & Higgins, M. Non-verbal rigidity and its relationship to dogmatism and Machiavellianism. *Perceptual and Motor Skills,* 1973, *36,* 356–358.

Pyron, B. A factor analytic study of simplicity–complexity of social ordering. *Perceptual and Motor Skills,* 1966, *22,* 259–272.

Raschke, V. Dogmatism and committed and consensual religiousity. *Journal for the Scientific Study of Religion,* 1973, *12,* 339–344.

Rebhun, M. T. Dogmatism and test anxiety. *Journal of Psychology,* 1966, *62,* 39–40.

Restle, F., Andrews, M., & Rokeach, M. Differences between open- and closed-minded subjects on learning-set and oddity problems. *Journal of Abnormal and Social Psychology,* 1964, *68,* 648–654.

Richek, H. G., Mayo, C. D., & Piryean, H. B. Dogmatism, religiosity, and mental health in college students. *Mental Hygiene,* 1970, *54,* 572–574.

Riley, J., & Armlin, N. J. The dogmatism scale and flexibility in maze performance. *Perceptual and Motor Skills,* 1965, *21,* 914.

Robinson, J. E., & Insko, C. A. Attributed belief similarity–dissimilarity versus race as determinants of prejudice: A further test of Rokeach's theory. *Journal of Experimental Research in Personality,* 1969, *4,* 72–77.

Rokeach, M. The nature and meaning of dogmatism. *Psychological Review,* 1954, *61,* 194–204.

Rokeach, M. Political and religious dogmatism: An alternative to the authoritarian personality. *Psychological Monographs,* 1956, *70* (18, Whole No. 425).

Rokeach, M. *The open and closed mind.* New York: Basic Books, 1960.

Rokeach, M. Comment on Triandis' paper. *Journal of Abnormal and Social Psychology,* 1961, *62,* 187–188.

Rokeach, M. Authoritarianism scales and response bias: Comment on Peabody's paper. *Psychological Bulletin,* 1967, *67,* 349–355.

Rokeach, M. *Beliefs, attitudes, and values.* San Francisco: Jossey-Bass, 1968.

Rokeach, M., & Bonier, R. Time perspective, dogmatism, and anxiety. In M. Rokeach, *The open and closed mind.* New York: Basic Books, 1960.

Rokeach, M., & Fruchter, B. A factorial study of dogmatism and related concepts. *Journal of Abnormal and Social Psychology,* 1956, *53,* 356–360.

Rokeach, M., & Mezei, L. Race and shared belief as factors in social choice. *Science,* 1966, *151,* 167–172.

Rokeach, M., & Restle, F. A fundamental distinction between open and closed systems. In M. Rokeach, *The open and closed mind.* New York: Basic Books, 1960.

Rokeach, M., & Rothman, G. The principle of belief congruence and the congruity principle as models of cognitive interaction. *Psychological Review,* 1965, *72,* 128–142.

Rokeach, M., Smith, P. W., & Evans, R. I. Two kinds of prejudice or one? In M. Rokeach, *The open and closed mind.* New York: Basic Books, 1960.

Rosen, J. Multiple-regression analysis of counselor characteristics and competencies. *Psychological Reports,* 1967, *20,* 1003–1008.

Rosen, C. V., & Kenny, C. T. Dogmatism and preference in 1970 Tennessee Senate campaign. *Journal of Psychology,* 1972, *82,* 171–174.

Rosenfeld, H., & Nauman, D. Effects of dogmatism on the development of informal relationships among women. *Journal of Personality,* 1969, *37,* 497–511.

Rosenman, M. F. Dogmatism and the movie "Dr. Strangelove." *Psychological Reports,* 1967, *20,* 942.

Rule, B. G., & Hewitt, D. Factor structure of anti-Semitism, self-concept and cognitive structure. *Personality: An International Journal,* 1970, *1,* 319–332.

Russo, J. R., Kelz, J. W., & Hudson, G. P. Are good counselors open-minded? *Counselor Education and Supervision,* 1964, *3,* 74–77.

Scheid, A. B., & Gelso, C. J. Dogmatism, hospital behavior, and post-hospitalization adjustment. *Journal of Consulting and Clinical Psychology,* 1971, *37,* 164.

Schultz, C. B., & DiVesta, F. J. Effects of expert endorsement of beliefs on problem-solving behavior of high and low dogmatics. *Journal of Educational Psychology,* 1972, *63,* 194–201.

Schulze, R. H. K. A shortened version of the Rokeach Dogmatism Scale. *Journal of Psychological Studies,* 1962, *13,* 93–97.

Shaver, J. P., Hofmann, H. P., & Richards, H. E. The Authoritarians of American and German teacher education students. *Journal of Social Psychology,* 1971, *84,* 303–304.

Silverman, B. Consequences, racial discrimination, and the principle of belief congruence. *Journal of Personality and Social Psychology,* 1974, *29,* 497–508.

Silverman, B., & Cochrane, R. Effect of the social context on the principle of belief congruence. *Journal of Personality and Social Psychology,* 1972, *22,* 259–268.

Smith, C. R., Williams, L., & Willis, R. H. Race, sex, and belief as determinants of friendship acceptance. *Journal of Personality and Social Psychology,* 1967, *5,* 127–137.

Smithers, A. Personality patterns and levels of dogmatism. *British Journal of Social and Clinical Psychology,* 1970, *9,* 183–184.

Stein, D. D. The influence of belief systems on interpersonal preference. *Psychological Monographs,* 1966, *80*(8, Whole No. 616).

Stein, D. D., Hardyck, J. A., & Smith, M. B. Race and belief: An open and shut case. *Journal of Personality and Social Psychology,* 1965, *1,* 281–289.

Steininger, M. P., Durso, B. E., & Pasquariello, C. Dogmatism and attitudes. *Psychological Reports,* 1972, *30,* 151–157.

Stewart, R., & Webster, A. Scale for theological conservatism and its personality correlates. *Perceptual and Motor Skills,* 1970, *30,* 867–870.

Sticht, T. G., & Fox, W. Geographical mobility and dogmatism, anxiety, and age. *Journal of Social Psychology,* 1966, *68,* 171–174.

Tagiuri, R. Person perception. In G. Lindzey & E. Aronson (Eds.), *The handbook of social psychology* (Vol. 3, 2nd ed.). Reading, Mass.: Addison-Wesley, 1969.

Talley, W. M., & Vamos, P. An exploratory study of dogmatism and its relation to group response. *Canadian Counsellor,* 1972, *6,* 278–282.

Taylor, R. N. Risk taking, dogmatism, and demographic characteristics of managers as correlates of information-processing and decision making behaviors. *Proceedings of the Annual Convention of the American Psychological Association,* 1972, 7(Pt. 1), 443–444.

Tosi, D. J. Dogmatism within the counselor-client dyad. *Journal of Counseling Psychology,* 1970, *17,* 284–288.

Tosi, D. J., Fagan, T. K., & Frumkin, R. M. Relation of levels of dogmatism and perceived threat under conditions of group personality testing. *Perceptual and Motor Skills,* 1968, *26,* 481–482. (a)

Tosi, D. J., Fagan, T. K., & Frumkin, R. M. Extreme levels of dogmatism and perceived threat under conditions of group personality testing. *Psychological Reports,* 1968, *22,* 638. (b)

Tosi, D. J., Quaranta, J. J., & Frumkin, R. M. Dogmatism and student teacher perceptions of ideal classroom leadership. *Perceptual and Motor Skills,* 1968, *27,* 750.

Triandis, H. C. A note on Rokeach's theory of prejudice. *Journal of Abnormal and Social Psychology,* 1961, *62,* 184–186.

Triandis, H. C., & Davis, E. Race and belief as determinants of behavioral intentions. *Journal of Personality and Social Psychology,* 1965, *2,* 715–725.

Troldahl, V., & Powell, F. A short-form dogmatism scale for use in field studies. *Social Forces,* 1965, *44,* 211–215.

Vacchiano, R. B., & Strauss, P. S. Dogmatism, authority, and hypnotic susceptibility. *The American Journal of Clinical Hypnosis,* 1975, *17,* 185–189.

Vacchiano, R. B., Strauss, P. S., & Hochman, L. The open and closed mind: A review of dogmatism. *Psychological Bulletin,* 1969, *71,* 261–273.

Vacchiano, R. B., Strauss, P. S., & Schiffman, D. C. Personality correlates of dogmatism. *Journal of Consulting Psychology,* 1968, *32,* 83–85.

Vidulich, R. N., & Kaiman, I. P. The effects of information source status and dogmatism upon conformity behavior. *Journal of Abnormal and Social Psychology,* 1961, *63,* 639–642.

Warr, P. B., Lee, R. E., & Joreskog, K. G. A note on the factorial nature of the F and D Scales. *British Journal of Psychology,* 1969, *60,* 119–123.

Webster, A. Patterns and relations of dogmatism, mental health and psychological health in selected religious groups. *Dissertation Abstracts,* 1967, *27,* 4142.

Willis, R. H., & Bulatao, R. A. Belief and ethnicity as determinants of friendship and marriage acceptance in the Philippines. *American Psychologist,* 1967, *22,* 539. (Abstract)

White, B. J., & Alter, R. D. Dogmatism, authoritarianism, and contrast effects in judgment. *Perceptual and Motor Skills,* 1965, *20,* 99–101.

White, B. J., Alter, R. D., & Rardin, M. Authoritarianism, dogmatism, and usage of conceptual categories. *Journal of Personality and Social Psychology,* 1965, *2,* 293–295.

Zagona, S. V., & Zurcher, L. A. Participation, interaction, and role behavior in groups selected from the extremes of the open-closed cognitive continuum. *Journal of Psychology,* 1964, *58,* 255–264.

Zagona, S. V., & Zurcher, L. A. Notes on the reliability and validity of the dogmatism scale. *Psychological Reports,* 1965, *16,* 1234–1236. (a)

Zagona, S. V., & Zurcher, L. A. The relationship of verbal ability and other cognitive variables to the open-closed cognitive dimension. *Journal of Psychology,* 1965, *60,* 213–219. (b)

Zurcher, L. A., Willis, J. E., Ikard, F., & Dohme, J. A. Dogmatism, future orientation, and perception of time. *Journal of Social Psychology,* 1967, *63,* 205–209.

8
Approval Motivation

Bonnie R. Strickland
University of Massachusetts—Amherst

One of the most vexing problems facing the personality theorist is the degree to which assessment and evaluation instruments accurately reflect the personal characteristics that the theorist is attempting to describe. When psychologists cannot predict behavior, the fault may lie not in the theoretical constructs which they have developed, but in the methods they have used to assess the network of individual characteristics in which they are interested. When a person is called upon to answer questions about oneself, the answers given may be highly dependent on the impression the individual is trying to convey, the attitudes and behaviors of the person asking the questions, the purpose of the assessments, the type of situation in which the questions are enmeshed, and all those other complex demand characteristics which permeate any interpersonal relationship. Even in the early years of psychological testing, psychologists were aware that many individuals may attempt to present themselves in a favorable light, perhaps by "faking good" or, in contrast, for one's own particular reasons, present oneself negatively by "faking bad." Early investigators saw response dissimulation as a source of variance which they hoped could be controlled or eliminated so that a more accurate picture of the individual in whom they were interested could emerge. Several of the well-known assessment instruments, including the MMPI, were designed with "lie" scales and sets of items to reflect positive and negative response bias.

The work of Edwards, especially, provided convincing evidence that many people in evaluative situations, as in responding to personality instruments, would present themselves in a socially desirable fashion. Edwards (1953, 1957) contended that any test item or personality statement could be described in terms of its position on a social desirability continuum. Indeed, he found a correlation of .87 between the social desirability of an item and its likelihood of endorsement under standard test-taking instructions, a finding replicated by

Wright (1957), who reports a correlation of .88. Edwards interpreted these results to mean that responses to test items may predominantly reflect social desirability bias rather than be a veridical endorsement of content. Using items from the MMPI, Edwards devised a scale consisting of items with clear social desirability value in an effort to identify those individuals who might be most likely to respond to items in a socially desirable manner, regardless of content. Knowing that an individual answers with high social desirability bias on the Edwards scale leads one to predict that this individual's self-description in other situations is also positively biased. However, the items on the Edwards scale, having been drawn from a clinical measure, were heavily loaded with pathological content. When a subject answers, for example, that his or her sleep is not fitful and disturbed, the test examiner cannot be certain whether this response reflects only socially desirable responding or, if indeed, the subject is considering content and is actually free of such symptoms. To overcome this drawback, Crowne and Marlowe (1960) designed a new scale of social desirability independent of psychopathology. Items were selected and included in the scale when they met a criterion of cultural approval, were highly improbable of occurrence, and had little or no pathological content. Following large-scale testing with a large number of items and subsequent item analysis, 33 true–false questions comprise the final version of the Marlowe–Crowne Social Desirability (M–C SD) scale (see Table 1). Crowne and Marlowe (1960) report internal consistency and test–retest coefficients to be high (.88) and other researchers also find substantial internal consistency and test–retest reliabilities (Bernhardson, 1967; Fisher, 1963; Miklich, 1966). Similar instruments to assess social desirability responding have been designed since (Ford, 1964), including shortened versions of the M–C SD (Greenwald & Satow, 1970). However, the M–C SD has been the measure of choice for most ongoing research on approval motivation with adults. The scale does not appear to be confounded with intelligence although some investigators (Klassen, Hornstra, & Anderson, 1975) report differential scores as a function of socioeconomic placement.

Because of the obvious implications of social desirability responding or approval motivation for children's behaviors, a number of instruments to tap this variable among younger populations have been developed (Cruse, 1963, 1966; Ford & Rubin, 1970; Walsh, Tomlinson-Keasey, & Klieger, 1974). The instrument for children with perhaps the most extensive use has been the Children's Social Desirability (CSD) Questionnaire (see Table 2) developed by Crandall, Crandall, and Katkovsky (1965). With a large sample of children (N=956) in grades 3 through 12, they found high split-half and test–retest reliabilities and report the scale to be unconfounded with social class, size of family, and ordinal position. Generally, they found socially desirable responses to be given more often by younger than older children, by dull rather than by bright subjects, by girls rather than boys, and by black children rather than white children. Similar findings with over one thousand 7–14 year old children who were administered the CSD are reported by Klein, Gould, and Corey (1969).

THEORETICAL BACKGROUND

Initially, the M–C SD was developed to serve the same purpose as the early Edwards scale; that is, to identify persons high on social desirability responding. Social desirability was still considered to rest within the test instrument and to be a source of bias for evaluative situations. Basically, an individual who answered the Edwards scale or the M–C SD in a socially desirable fashion would also be expected to be responsive to the social desirability aspects of any and all personality test items. However, Crowne and Marlowe (1964) also became particularly intrigued with why an individual found it important to try to appear in a favorable light. They began to focus on the individual meanings of positive test-taking dissimulation in an attempt to understand what led the subject to this kind of responding and what needs or purposes were served by this kind of test-taking behavior. Original social desirability conceptualizations were reformulated in terms of a motivational construct. Crowne and Marlowe couched their descriptions of approval-seeking responses within Rotter's social learning theory of personality (1954). They perceived approval-motivated responses to occur as a function of the expectancy that certain reinforcing events will result from those behaviors and because these reinforcements are valued. The approval-motivated individual responds to his need to gain acceptance, to obtain dependency gratification, and achieve recognition and/or status by engaging in approval-seeking behaviors in particular situations through positive self-presentation and denial of inadequacies. Individual differences in need for approval (Napp) imply behavioral differences in a number of diverse situations, and research with the approval motive has demonstrated the predictive value of this construct across a wide range of subject samples and situations.

MAJOR AREAS OF RESEARCH

In one of the earliest studies with the Napp variable, Marlowe and Crowne (1961) administered the M–C SD scale, the Edwards scale, and Barron's Independence of Judgement scale (a conformity measure) to college males. They then had these subjects participate in an experiment in which they were shown 12 ordinary empty sewing-thread spools and a box. Subjects were told to place the spools in the box one at a time, then to empty the box and refill it one spool at a time. Subjects then packed and unpacked the spools for 25 min during which time the experimenter held a stopwatch and pretended to be busily

TABLE 1

The Marlowe–Crowne Social Desirability Scale[a,b]

Listed below are a number of statements concerning personal attitudes and traits. Read each item and decide whether the statement is *true* or *false* as it pertains to you personally.

1. Before voting I thoroughly investigate the qualifications of all the candidates. (T)
2. I never hesitate to go out of my way to help someone in trouble. (T)
3. It is sometimes hard for me to go on with my work if I am not encouraged. (F)
4. I have never intensely disliked anyone. (T)
5. On occasion I have had doubts about my ability to succeed in life. (F)
6. I sometimes feel resentful when I don't get my way. (F)
7. I am always careful about my manner of dress. (T)
8. My table manners at home are as good as when I eat out in a restaurant. (T)
9. If I could get into a movie without paying and be sure I was not seen I would probably do it. (F)
10. On a few occasions, I have given up doing something because I thought too little of my ability. (F)
11. I like to gossip at times. (F)
12. There have been times when I felt like rebelling against people in authority even though I knew they were right. (F)
13. No matter who I'm talking to, I'm always a good listener. (T)
14. I can remember "playing sick" to get out of something. (F)
15. There have been occasions when I took advantage of someone. (F)

16. I'm always willing to admit it when I make a mistake. (T)
17. I always try to practice what I preach. (T)
18. I don't find it particularly difficult to get along with loud mouthed, obnoxious people. (T)
19. I sometimes try to get even rather than forgive and forget. (F)
20. When I don't know something I don't at all mind admitting it. (T)
21. I am always courteous, even to people who are disagreeable. (T)
22. At times I have really insisted on having things my own way. (F)
23. There have been occasions when I felt like smashing things. (F)
24. I would never think of letting someone be punished for my wrongdoings. (T)
25. I never resent being asked to return a favor. (T)
26. I have never been irked when people expressed ideas very different from my own. (T)
27. I never make a long trip without checking the safety of my car. (T)
28. There have been times when I was quite jealous of the good fortune of others. (F)
29. I have almost never felt the urge to tell someone off. (T)
30. I am sometimes irritated by people who ask favors of me. (F)
31. I have never felt that I was punished without cause. (T)
32. I sometimes think when people have a misfortune they only got what they deserved. (F)
33. I have never deliberately said something that hurt someone's feelings. (T)

---

[a]From Crowne and Marlowe (1960). Copyright 1960 by the American Psychological Association. Reproduced by permission.

[b]The socially desirable response alternative is given in the parentheses after each scale item. The subject's score is the total number of items answered in the socially desirable direction.

TABLE 2a

The Children's Social Desirability Scale[a,b]

This questionnaire lists a number of experiences that most children have at one time or another. Read each of these carefully. After you have read one, decide whether it does or does not fit you. If it *does,* put a T (for true) in front of the statement; if it *doesn't,* put an F (for false) in front of the statement.

If you have any questions at any time raise your hand, and one of the persons who passed out these questionnaires will come and explain it to you.

1. I always enjoy myself at a party. (T)
2. I tell a little lie sometimes. (F)
3. I never get angry if I have to stop in the middle of something I'm doing to eat dinner, or go to school. (T)
4. Sometimes I don't like to share my things with my friends. (F)
5. I am always respectful of older people. (T)
6. I would never hit a boy or girl who was smaller than me. (T)
7. Sometimes I do not feel like doing what my teachers want me to do. (F)
8. I never act "fresh" or "talk back" to my mother or father. (T)
9. When I make a mistake, I always admit I am wrong. (T)
10. I feel my parents do not always show good judgement. (F)
11. I have never felt like saying unkind things to a person. (T)
12. I always finish all of my homework on time. (T)
13. Sometimes I have felt like throwing or breaking things. (F)
14. I never let someone else get blamed for what I did wrong. (T)
15. Sometimes I say something just to impress my friends. (F)

16. I am always careful about keeping my clothing neat, and my room picked up. (T)
17. I never shout when I feel angry. (T)
18. Sometimes I feel like staying home from school even if I am not sick. (F)
19. Sometimes I wish that my parents didn't check up on me so closely. (F)
20. I always help people who need help. (T)
21. Sometimes I argue with my mother to do something she doesn't want me to. (F)
22. I never say anything that would make a person feel bad. (T)
23. My teachers always know more about everything than I do. (T)
24. I am always polite, even to people who are not very nice. (T)
25. Sometimes I do things I've been told not to do. (F)
26. I never get angry. (T)
27. I sometimes want to own things just because my friends have them. (F)
28. I always listen to my parents. (T)
29. I never forget to say "please" and "thank you." (T)
30. Sometimes I wish I could just "mess around" instead of having to go to school. (F)
31. I always wash my hands before every meal. (T)
32. Sometimes I dislike helping my parents even though I know they need my help around the house. (F)
33. I never find it hard to make friends. (T)
34. I have never been tempted to break a rule or a law. (T)
35. Sometimes I try to get even when someone does something to me I don't like. (F)

---

continued

TABLE 2a (*contd.*)

36. I sometimes feel angry when I don't get my way. (F)
37. I always help an injured animal. (T)
38. Sometimes I want to do things my parents think I am too young to do. (F)
39. I sometimes feel like making fun of other people. (F)
40. I have never borrowed anything without asking permission first. (T)
41. Sometimes I get annoyed when someone disturbs something I've been working on. (F)
42. I am always glad to cooperate with others. (T)
43. I never get annoyed when my best friend wants to do something I don't want to do. (T)
44. Sometimes I wish that the other kids would pay more attention to what I say. (F)
45. I always do the right things. (T)
46. Sometimes I don't like to obey my parents. (F)
47. Sometimes I don't like it when another person asks me to do things for him. (F)
48. Sometimes I get mad when people don't do what I want. (F)

[a]From Crandall, Crandall, and Katkovsky (1965). Copyright 1965 by the American Psychological Association. Reproduced by permission.

[b]Table 2a contains items in a True-False format suitable for children in grades six through twelve. The socially desirable response alternative is given in the parentheses after each scale item. Subject's score is the total number of items answered in the socially desirable direction.

TABLE 2b

The Children's Social Desirability Scale: Question Form[a]

Here are some questions about things that happen to all children your age. All the questions have been put on the record (experimenter points). When the person on the record asks you a question, you tell me your answer. If you can't hear a question or if you don't understand any of them, be sure to tell me and I'll have the record say it again.

1. Do you ever get angry if you have to stop in the middle of something you're doing to eat dinner or go to school? (N)
2. Does it sometimes bother you to share your things with your friends? (N)
3. Do you always enjoy yourself at a party? (Y)
4. Are you always polite to older people? (Y)
5. Do you sometimes tell a little lie? (N)
6. Do you ever hit a boy or girl who is smaller than you? (N)
7. Sometimes do you feel like doing other things instead of what your teacher wants you to do? (N)
8. Do you ever act "fresh" or "talk back" to your mother or father? (N)
9. When you make a mistake, do you always admit you are wrong? (Y)
10. Do you feel that your parents always show good judgement; that is, do they always make good choices? (Y)
11. Have you ever felt like saying unkind things to a person? (N)
12. Have you sometimes felt like throwing or breaking things? (N)
13. Do you ever let someone else get blamed for what you do wrong? (N)
14. Are you always careful about keeping your clothing neat and your room picked up? (Y)
15. Do you ever shout when you feel angry? (N)

continued

TABLE 2b (*contd.*)

16. Do you sometimes feel like staying home from school even if you are not sick? (N)
17. Sometimes, do you wish your parents didn't check up on you so closely? (N)
18. Do you always help people who need help? (Y)
19. Do you sometimes argue with your mother to let you do something she doesn't want you to do? (N)
20. Do you ever say anything that makes somebody else feel bad? (N)
21. Do you think your teachers know more about everything than you do? (Y)
22. Are you always polite, even to people who are not very nice? (Y)
23. Sometimes, do you do things you've been told not to do? (N)
24. Do you ever get angry? (N)
25. Do you sometimes want to own things just because your friends have them? (N)
26. Do you always listen to your parents? (Y)
27. Do you ever forget to say "please" and "thank you?" (N)
28. Do you sometimes wish you could just play around instead of having to go to school? (N)
29. Do you always wash your hands before every meal? (Y)
30. Do you sometimes dislike helping your parents even though you know they need your help around the house? (N)
31. Do you ever find it hard to make friends? (N)
32. Have you ever broken a rule? (N)
33. Sometimes, do you try to get even when someone does something to you that you don't like? (N)

34. Do you sometimes feel angry when you don't get your way? (N)
35. Do you always help a hurt animal? (Y)
36. Do you sometimes want to do things your parents think you are too young to do? (N)
37. Do you sometimes feel like making fun of other people? (N)
38. Have you ever borrowed anything without asking permission first? (N)
39. Do you sometimes get mad when someone disturbs something you've been working on? (N)
40. Are you always glad to cooperate with others? (Y)
41. Do you ever get angry when your best friend wants to do something you don't want to do? (N)
42. Do you sometimes wish that the other kids would pay more attention to what you say? (N)
43. Do you always do the right things? (Y)
44. Are there some times when you don't like to do what your parents tell you? (Mind your parents?) (N)
45. Are there times that you don't like it if somebody asks you to do something for him? (N)
46. Do you sometimes get mad when people don't do what you want them to do? (N)

---

[a]Table 2b is the question form of the children's social desirability scale and is suitable for children in grades three through five. The scale is administered orally and individually, usually via a recording. The socially desirable response alternative is given in the parentheses after each scale item. Subject's score is the total number of items answered in the socially desirable direction.

engaged in timing and recording notes on the subject's performance. Following this task, the subjects answered the questions below by means of a rating scale:

1. Was the task interesting and enjoyable?
2. Did the experiment give you an opportunity to learn about your abilities and skills?
3. From what you know about the experiment and the task involved in it, would you say the experiment was measuring anything important?
4. Would you have any desire to participate in other similar experiments? [Marlowe & Crowne, 1961, p. 111]

High Napp subjects[1] were significantly more likely than low Napp subjects to answer each of the questions in a positive fashion. They rated the task as enjoyable and interesting, felt they learned a great deal, believed the task to be of scientific value and importance, and said they would like to participate in similar experiments. The Independence of Judgment scale predicted only Question 2 and there were no significant correlations between scores on the Edwards scale and ratings on any of the four questions. Marlowe and Crowne interpreted these findings as providing construct validation for the M–C SD since high Napp subjects expressed highly favorable attitudes toward a repetitive and boring task performed to please the experimenters. They also noted a significant correlation between the M–C SD and Barron's Independence of Judgment scale (.54, $p < .05$). An immediate next research question had to do with the degree to which approval-motivated subjects might respond to influence in conformity tasks.

Conformity and Compliance Behavior

The original studies investigating approval motivation and conformity used typical Asch-type paradigms in which subjects find their judgments about perceptual stimuli in direct conflict with the responses given by others who are confederates of the experimenter. Strickland and Crowne (1962) had female undergraduate subjects listen to a series of taped "knocks" presented at a rate which could be readily and accurately perceived. Subjects heard the responses of three alleged subjects before their own response was recorded. On 12 of the 18 trials, the accomplices' judgements were inaccurate. High Napp subjects, as assessed by the M–C SD, conformed significantly more often than low Napp subjects to the inaccurate responses of the confederates. Again, the Edwards Social Desirability scale was not predictive of conforming behavior in this situation although Barron's Independence of Judgment scale was. A correlation of .42 ($p < .01$) was also found between the Barron scale and the M–C SD. Thus, the Napp variable, as measured by the M–C SD scale, was related to both

[1] Subjects are grouped as to high or low in approval motivation (Napp) depending on their scores on the M–C SD. Most of these high and low groupings are based on median splits although some may represent more extreme scores such as upper or lower third.

behavioral conformity and a paper-and-pencil measure of conformity. However, a weakness of this first study had to do with the fact that subjects were listening to tapes and were not actually engaged in face-to-face contact with other people. Marlowe and Crowne (1961) then replicated this study with a visual perceptual discrimination task and actual, interacting confederates. Again, high, as opposed to low, Napp subjects were significantly more likely to yield to pressure and conform to the inaccurate responses of the confederates.

Miller, Doob, Butler, and Marlowe (1965) investigated the degree to which high and low Napp subjects would change initial responses to personality statements to "conform" to the judgements of experts. Subjects completed a battery of personality tests and five months later were told that four psychology professors from Harvard had looked over their performance in a number of experiments and predicted their responses to the personality statements. Subjects were shown the judgements of the professors, some of which disagreed with the subjects' actual responses, and were asked whether they agreed or disagreed with the psychologists' ratings. All subjects conformed to the psychologists' judgements to a significant degree and no differences were found between high and low Napp subjects. The experimenters then replicated this study with high-school subjects and manipulated the expertise of the judges and the importance of the task results. One group of subjects was told that the judgments were made by psychology students taking a course in personality and a second group was told that the judgments were made by engineering students who had not taken such a course. Further, some subjects were told that the "experts' " predictions on the personality tests would determine grades and the possibility of majoring in psychology. Other subjects, in a low-importance condition, were told that the accuracy of prediction would lead to no specific outcomes. High Napp subjects conformed more to the responses of the judges when either expertise of the judges or the value of the test results were high. Low Napp subjects did not conform regardless of conditions. While the results of the Napp conformity studies appear fairly strong, it should be noted that some experimenters have failed to demonstrate the expected relationship (Breger, 1966; Hollander, Julian, & Haaland, 1965; Wiesenthal, 1974).

The findings that Napp is related to conformity and social influence suggest that Napp might also be influential in regard to persuasibility or attitude change. Salman (cited in Crowne & Marlowe, 1964) hypothesized that attitude change among high Napp subjects would be enhanced if they were compelled to make a public avowal of a newly acquired position. After assessing subjects on the M–C SD and their attitudes about disclosure of private and personal feelings, Salman ran a number of groups of subjects in which one person served as communicator, one as receiver, and one as observer. The communicator was asked to improvise a persuasive appeal and attempt to influence the receiver about the "importance and benefits of free expression of emotional feelings." As expected, high Napp subjects who served as communicators changed their attitudes in the advocated direction to a significantly greater degree than did test–retest controls. Low Napp communicators did not differ from control-group subjects. High Napp observers also significantly changed attitudes but no differences were found between high and low Napp subjects serving as receivers. Results were also highly dependent on the subjects' original attitudes. High Napp subjects who had been originally opposed to the issue were most likely to change while subjects who were originally in favor of the issue changed little. Salman suggests that the high Napp subjects who had originally opposed the issue and who were then asked to publicly endorse it, as well as to attempt to influence another, found themselves in a state of inconsistency which could only be resolved by a change in attitude.

In another attitude change study, Buckhout (1965) selected female undergraduate subjects who expressed positive attitudes toward television. In an experimental situation, he asked them to choose and verbalize one of a pair of forced-choice statements, one of which was pro television and one of which was anti television. He further told one group that he would say "good" if he agreed and say nothing if he disagreed. A second experimental group was told nothing. Subjects in both experimental groups received reinforcement for each antitelevision statement that they verbalized. A control group completed the forced-choice survey without feedback from the experimenter. In both the experimental groups, high Napp subjects were significantly more likely to express antitelevision statements while no such changes occurred for the low Napp subjects, nor for those in the control group. Moreover, in posttesting, following the conditioning sessions, high Napp subjects continued to be more negative in their attitudes toward television while no such findings emerged for low Napp and control subjects.

Skolnick and Heslin (1971) designed a study to investigate source credibility and quality of communication in an attitude change paradigm. College-student subjects were assessed as to Napp and one week later were presented arguments dealing with an alleged murder. For some subjects, the quality of the communication about the murder was high, for others it was low. The communication was also attributed to either a high- or low-credibility source. High Napp subjects failed to discriminate between different aspects of the communication and were more easily persuaded by the argument. Low Napp persons made a distinction between the high- and low-credibility sources and were persuaded by the former but not the latter. They also were more persuaded by the "high-quality" in contrast to the "low-quality" argument.

Some investigators (Rozelle, Evans, Lasater, Dembroski, & Allen, 1973) have found Napp to be related to intention-to-behave in an attitude change paradigm although not to actual behavior change following persuasive communication. Thus, behavioral predictions must be approached with caution. However, it does appear that, at least with the more typical attitude-change measures, approval-dependent persons are more likely to respond to persuasive messages than low Napp individuals.

In light of the presentations so far on the relationship between Napp and receptivity to various kinds of social influence, one might logically expect approval-motivated persons to be sensitive to the subtle cues presented by experimenters in "experimenter-bias" situations. Rosenthal (1966) has demonstrated repeatedly that experimenters tend to obtain data in experimental situations which are consistent with their expectations about the outcome of the experiment. But, Rosenthal does not find a difference in response to experimenter expectancies as a function of Napp. However, Smith and Flenning (1971) replicated a Rosenthal experiment and added a motivational-arousal condition designed to engage the subject in aiding the experimenter. Six male experimenters were asked to run subjects under one of two conditions. In one, the experimenters were given a set of photographs which they were to present to subjects for ratings as to "success or failure in living" and were told that ratings should be relatively high since the photographs were of highly successful business tycoons. In the second, the experimenters, given the identical photographs, were told that the ratings they could expect from the subjects that they ran would be relatively low since the pictures were of mental defectives in a state hospital. All experimenters told the subjects, "This is for my doctoral dissertation, and I'll really appreciate it if you'll make the very best ratings you can." High Napp subjects differed significantly in their mean ratings in the direction of the experimenter's expectancy while low Napp subjects showed no significant differences in mean ratings. Thus, it appears that approval motivation may be predictive of responses to subtle and unintended social influence on the part of experimenters who are not actually aware of their impact on the subject.

A number of experiments investigating the degree to which high Napp subjects may be compliant in verbal conditioning studies have also been conducted. Using a typical Greenspoon paradigm, Crowne and Strickland (1961) had 145 male and female college students serve as subjects. A male experimenter ran the males, and a female experimenter, the females. After a brief interview, subjects were asked to simply say words without using sentences or phrases and without counting. In a positive reinforcement group, after giving plural nouns as a response, the subject was reinforced by the experimenter's head nod and "Mm-hmm." In a negative reinforcement condition, subjects' plural nouns elicited an "Uh-uh" and a negative head shake. Subjects in a control group gave words with no reinforcement or cues from the experimenters. All subjects said words for 25 min during which the experimenter, as unobtrusively as possible, kept a frequency count of the responses, noting them as plural or nonplural. On the basis of the M–C SD, subjects were divided into high and low Napp groups, and frequencies of plural-noun responses were computed for five 5-min sections of the experimental task. Subjects were also grouped according to awareness level, and only subjects who denied being aware of the reinforcement contingencies were used in the final analysis of the data. As expected, high Napp subjects in the positive reinforcement condition were significantly more likely to emit plural words and in the negative reinforcement condition were significantly less likely to give plural responses. The low Napp groups failed to demonstrate any consistent changes in responses as a function of reinforcement and their responses were similar to the responses of control subjects.

Marlowe (1962) conducted individual interviews with 76 undergraduate students who had been assessed as to Napp on the M–C SD. Half of the subjects were reinforced with "Mm-hmm" every time they emitted a positive self-referent. The other half of the subjects participated in a control condition during which no reinforcement from the experimenter was forthcoming. Subjects were questioned as to the degree to which they were aware of the reinforcement cues and none admitted to being aware of the response–reinforcement contingencies. Within the experimental group, high Napp subjects gave significantly more positive self-referents than low Napp subjects. High and low Napp subjects were not significantly different from each other in the control condition. Since high Napp subjects may already have a high operant level for statements of positive self-reference, Dixon (1970) investigated the degree to which the conditioning of negative self-referents would be related to Napp. He found high Napp females to be significantly more likely to emit negative self-referents under reinforcement conditions while low Napp females were not influenced. Marlowe, Beecher, Cook, and Doob (1964) were further able to demonstrate that high Napp were significantly more likely than low Napp subjects to emit the desired responses in a Taffel-type procedure when subjects received vicarious reinforcement.

All in all, the early research on verbal conditioning was highly consistent in demonstrating that approval-motivated subjects were significantly more likely to respond to the subtle reinforcement cues of the experimenter and give a greater frequency of the desired verbal response than were low Napp subjects. However, a serious question was raised about this series of studies in that other experimenters were suggesting that verbal conditioning does not occur without awareness and implying that subjects had not been carefully interviewed as to their understanding of the experimental situation. Spielberger, Berger, and Howard (1963) were not able to replicate the Napp verbal-conditioning findings and, indeed, make the point that there cannot be verbal conditioning without awareness. Thus, they suggest that the Crowne, Strickland, and Marlowe studies were not demonstrating a verbal-conditioning effect although they might be showing conforming or compliant behavior among aware subjects. Likewise, Bryan and Lichtenstein (1966) found no relationship between Napp and verbal conditioning in a Taffel-type paradigm, across three levels of induced attitudes between experimenter and subject (likeability, desirability, and neutral). These discrepancies in findings might, of course, be due to a weakness in the approval motivation construct or to the methods for assessing awareness. In fact, high Napp subjects may not want to disappoint the experimenter if they perceive that the experimenter wishes to disguise the purpose of the experiment. Indeed, Golding and Lichtenstein (1970) found the M–C SD to have a significant negative correlation with level of confessed awareness in a deception experiment. One should also note, however, a major difference between the methodologies of the early and later studies in that the former utilized experimenters who were in most cases faculty members or, at the least, advanced graduate students. Ordinarily, experimenters initially spent some time in informal discussions with the subjects, attempting to enhance their reinforcement value as experimenters. The Spielberger *et al.* and Bryan and Lichtenstein studies each used an undergraduate experimenter who may not have had as much influence on the subject as a more senior experimenter. Finally, Strickland (1970) divided over 160 female subjects into awareness groupings on the basis of extensive postexperimental interviews. She found approval motivation to be related to greater verbal conditioning in a Taffel-type (word association) experiment across all awareness conditions, including a condition in which subjects denied awareness.

The findings that high, as opposed to low, Napp subjects are more likely to respond to the social cues and demands in an experimental situation also raise an interesting question as to the degree to which approval motivation may be related to reliance on more general environmental cues. Rosenfeld (1967) had male college students complete two measures of field dependence and a delayed auditory feedback task. Using the rod-and-frame test, he found high, as opposed to low, Napp subjects to be more field dependent, although he found no difference between them on Thurstone's embedded figures test. The delayed auditory feedback task required a subject to rely on his own internal cues and avoid being disrupted by external noise. This was accomplished by having each subject read aloud a 250-word textbook passage while his reading was relayed back to him through earphones .05 sec later. On this task, high Napp subjects appeared to be significantly more likely to be disrupted by the external cues than the low Napp subjects, in that they took longer to read the material under the delayed feedback condition than under a no-feedback condition.

In a different but related study of field dependence, Rotter and Tinkleman (1970) had high and low Napp subjects rate behaviors as either adjusted or maladjusted. These behavior-description items were mixed with others which were either clearly adjusted or maladjusted. The high Napp subjects were significantly affected by the field in which the items were placed in that they rated neutral items more in the direction of the external context than did low Napp subjects who appeared uninfluenced by context placement. Results of the Napp field dependence–independence research must be interpreted with caution, however, since some experimenters fail to find the expected relationships (Farley, 1974).

Generally, high, as opposed to low, Napp individuals are significantly more likely to engage in compliant behavior and attitude change. High Napp subjects appear to respond not only to social influence within an experimental situation by conforming to the demands of the experimenter and/or confederates but also rely more heavily on environmental cues than do low Napp persons. The low

Napp person appears to be able to abide by his own judgments, even in the face of conflicting testimony, using internal cues, and resisting influence to a greater degree than high Napp individuals.

Facilitation of Performance

One would hypothesize that on general performance tasks, high Napp persons would attempt to enhance their performance since favorable evaluation would depend on their doing well and pleasing others. In a series of experiments using simple motor-performance tasks, this indeed appeared to be the case. Strickland and Jenkins (1964) had male college subjects complete the M–C SD and then engage in a pursuit rotor task, in which they were asked to keep a stylus touching a small metal disc that rotated in front of them. Prior to the pursuit rotor task, subjects had completed a motor-steadiness test on which they received either positive or negative feedback. High Napp subjects performed better on the pursuit rotor than did low Napp subjects regardless of prior reinforcement conditions. Strickland (1965) then investigated the degree to which positive and negative feedback given during an actual task performance, might influence performance in relation to approval motivation. She had male subjects perform a motor-steadiness task during which they received either positive or negative feedback about their performance. High Napp subjects under positive conditions showed greater improvement over trials than did any other group. Under negative feedback conditions, high Napp subjects at first improved but then became significantly worse. Low Napp subjects appeared to be unaffected by reinforcement feedback and their performance did not change over trials.

In a third study, Willingham and Strickland (1965) had male subjects engage in six performance tasks: visual reaction time, finger tapping, the Minnesota Rate of Manipulation test, discrimination reaction time, pursuit behavior, and inverted alphabet printing. An interesting difference appeared between the three performance tasks behavioral in nature and the three paper-and-pencil measures. In each of the behavioral tasks, high Napp subjects performed significantly better than low Napp subjects. In the paper-and-pencil measures, however, Napp was not predictive.

Milburn, Bell, and Koeske (1970) had subjects perform in a free-learning situation in which they were seated facing a memory drum and asked to learn a list of words. In one experiment, subjects performed under approval and censure conditions, and the experimenters found increased performance across trials on the part of the high Napp subjects in both conditions. In a second experiment, experimenter–subject interaction was minimized by having the instructions automated and no praise or censure was given. In this experiment, no differences were found in learning performance as a function of Napp. Terris and Milburn (1972) essentially replicated these experiments using three levels of praise which differed in the obviousness of the evaluation (obvious, subtle, or no praise) and with three different experimenters. They found high Napp males to show a facilitation effect during the subtle praise condition but these findings were reversed for females; that is, low Napp females performed better under subtle praise. Further, Terris and Milburn report that performance on the task was also highly dependent on the particular experimenter who administered the subtle or obvious praise. Basically, they find partial support for the high Napp facilitation of performance hypothesis but also suggest that the complexity of interpersonal relationships between the experimenters and subjects influences performance.

Petzel (1972) found high Napp subjects to be more accurate in estimating their final examination scores in a general experimental psychology class. High Napp students were also significantly lower in their estimates than low Napp students, but all students overestimated how well they thought they would do. In terms of the high Napp facilitation hypothesis, it does appear that high Napp subjects have been sensitive to their past performance and are somewhat more "grade conscious" than low Napp subjects. Other academic-type learning responses will be reported in the section on children and approval motivation.

Overall, high Napp individuals appear to attempt to enhance their performance and do well in classic perceptual–motor and free-learning tasks, especially under conditions of feedback from the experimenter. These data lend additional construct validity to the approval motive concept in that high Napp subjects would be naturally expected to present themselves in as favorable a light as possible and to respond to the perceived demands of the experimenter that they perform as well as they can. Low Napp persons seem less concerned with facilitation of performance since they simply do not reach the increased performance levels of their high Napp counterparts.

Defensiveness

Once the early conformity and verbal conditioning studies offered strong validation for the Napp construct, a concerted effort began to identify more precisely the personal make up of the high Napp individual. Theoretically, the approval-motivated person would be assumed to be sensitive to cultural norms and eager to abide by those norms even at the expense of individuality. Questions were still raised as to why these particular persons found it so important to be approved of and accepted by others. Was there a defensive component to their behavior or were they simply good citizens who were adjusting to the demands of society by presenting themselves as personally likable and socially competent? To what lengths would high Napp individuals go to present themselves in a positive fashion?

Several investigators have studied the differential responses of high and low Napp persons when placed in conflict situations. One methodology used in these studies involves the recognition and verbal expression of sexual words. Barthel and Crowne (1962) exposed female subjects to a list of four neutral and six "taboo" words via tachistoscopic presentation and asked the subjects to identify the words as quickly as possible. On the basis of a postexperimental interview, subjects were divided into a group that believed perceptual speed or keenness to be the focus of the experiment or a group that referred to the social disapproval associated with the taboo words. Low Napp subjects did not display any effects of task categorization. High Napp subjects in the "perceptual speed" group were significantly quicker at recognizing the taboo words than high Napp subjects in the "social disapproval" group, who appeared to prolong recognition. Apparently high Napp subjects were in some conflict about the purpose of the experiment and resolved this by focusing on a perceived purpose and responding in an approval-motivated fashion. Schill (1972) has also found high, as opposed to low, Napp subjects to demonstrate lower sexual responsivity on a double-entendre word-association task. Schill and Pederson (1973) replicated this finding and added a condition in which subjects were given sensitizing instructions; that is, they were told that many of the words had sexual as well as neutral meanings. Under this condition, high Napp subjects increased their sexual responding although they never reached the levels of responding of the low Napp subjects. Schill and Pederson suggest that their findings support an inhibition interpretation of the high Napp person. The high Napp subject could clearly identify the sexual words but failed to do so until implicitly given permission by the experimenter.

Other experimenters have approached the investigation of self-presentation and defensiveness by considering Napp in relation to risk taking. In our culture, when one is expected to perform in a certain fashion, several alternatives may be open. For example, in goal setting, individuals may set their goals very low and thus ensure themselves success or may set them extremely high, implying that they are capable of substantial performance. Either extreme choice opens the possibility for negative evaluations in that an easy goal implies low confidence and high goals are less likely to be achieved. In a dart-throwing task, in which subjects could choose the distance they would stand from the goal, Barthel (cited in Crowne & Marlowe, 1964) found that high Napp subjects were significantly more likely than low Napp subjects to be restrictive in their goal setting. Low Napp individuals were more varied in their responses, appearing to be less tied to cultural norms that suggest a person should neither make a task too easy nor "show off" by making it more difficult. High Napp subjects were also more likely to be rigid and less likely to change their generalized expectancies for success in the dart-throwing task.

Thaw and Efran (1967) replicated the dart-throwing experiment and further reported high Napp subjects to choose to stand closer to the goal, thereby avoiding risk and attempting to ensure success. When a person does choose an extreme position in a task like dart throwing, one puts oneself in a situation of actually receiving little feedback about his optimal performance. Thus, it may well be that the risk-avoidant behavior of high Napp individuals provides them little opportunity for critical analysis of their behavior. Efran and Boylin (1967) investigated subjects' willingness to involve themselves in a group discussion in which they could learn something about the ways they interact with others. Subjects could either choose to be in the group as a participant or outside the group as an observer. High Napp subjects were significantly more likely to choose to observe, again avoiding the opportunity to learn something about their own behavior with its accompanying risk of negative evaluation. Kanfer and Marston (1964), in a psychotherapy analogue, had subjects express their opinions on a topic and were then asked to request comments from one of two experimenters. Experimenter One limited his feedback to reflective rephrasing of whatever the subject had said. Experimenter Two was directive and speculative about the subject's comments and his early experiences. Subjects who preferred the low-risk comments of Experimenter One had significantly higher M–C SD scores than subjects who preferred Experimenter Two.

The Kanfer and Marston study clearly suggests that high and low Napp individuals may respond differently to different techniques in psychotherapy. Moreover, approval-motivated persons may be unlikely to wish to disclose to their therapist information about negative aspects of themselves. Although some investigators have found no strong and consistent relationships between approval motivation and verbal self-relevation (Doster & Slaymaker, 1972; Doster & Strickland, 1971), Burhenne and Mirels (1970) found that high, as opposed to low, Napp college student subjects were significantly less disclosing in self-descriptive essays. Strickland and Crowne (1963) studied 85 outpatients, diagnosed predominantly as neurotic, who were being seen for individual therapy in a clinical setting. M–C SD scores were collected from each of the patients as were therapist evaluations of the patient's progress in therapy. Length of stay in therapy was also noted. Results suggested that high Napp patients were significantly more likely to terminate therapy after a shorter number of hours than were low Napp patients. One could argue that this occurred because high Napp patients may have been psychologically more healthy to begin with. However, when therapist ratings were calculated, high Napp patients were significantly more likely to be perceived by their therapists as defensive versus personally integrated. While impossible to know the reasons high Napp patients actually did leave therapy, one could hypothesize that the approval-dependent person finds it difficult to continue to discuss personal attributes of a negative nature thus leading to the termination of a therapeutic relationship in which critical analysis is necessary. This hypothesis is enhanced by the strong therapist evaluation of defensiveness.

The high Napp person's inhibition or defensiveness is also readily apparent in a number of test-taking situations. As would be hypothesized, relationships between M–C SD scores and the validity scales of the MMPI (the *K*, *L*, and *F* scales) are all substantial and in the expected direction (Crowne & Marlowe,

1964; Fisher & Parsons, 1962; Katkin, 1964; Stone, 1965). High Napp subjects appear to "fake good," to answer the "lie" items in the socially desirable direction, and to avoid "faking bad." These same experimenters, as well as Hoffman (1970), also examined relationships between M–C SD scores and the clinical scales of the MMPI. Generally, high Napp subjects present themselves as free of the clinical symptoms tapped by the scale, particularly for the extreme and severe clinical syndromes such as schizophrenia and psychopathic deviate. High Napp subjects are also more likely to report themselves as repressed on Byrne's Repression–Sensitization scale (Altrocci, Palmer, Hellman, & Davis, 1968; Bernhardson, 1967; Byrne, 1964; Feder, 1967; Kahn & Schill, 1971; Palmer & Altrocci, 1967; Silber & Grebstein, 1964) and less anxious on the Welsh and Taylor measure (Crowne & Marlowe, 1964; Katkin, 1964; Stone, 1965; Tedeschi, Berrill, & Gahagan, 1969). On measures like the California Psychological Inventory, high Napp subjects present themselves as socially responsible, self-controlled, and so on, with little general anxiety or hostility (Lefcourt, 1969; Lichtenstein & Bryan, 1966). On the semantic differential, high Napp subjects appear to be responding most strongly to the evaluative dimension, that is, presenting themselves on the basis of positive versus negative (good/bad) judgements of personality characteristics (Pervin & Lilly, 1967). Some investigators also report M–C SD scores to be related to internal locus of control scale scores (Harris, 1975; Hjelle, 1971; Rotter, 1966; Vuchinich & Bass, 1974).

Self-Esteem

Since an evaluative presentation of oneself, as represented by the M–C SD scale, appears so intimately tied to self-concept, one would naturally expect relationships between Napp and self-esteem variables. The relationships are likely complicated, however, by the defensive elements that seem to characterize high Napp individuals, and questions arise as to whether one is really "adjusted" simply because one tends to make a generally favorable self-presentation. McCarthy and Rafferty (1971) tested several groupings of college students and found low to moderate linear relationships between Napp, self-concept, and level of adjustment. They did not find the self-concept measures to be highly saturated with social desirability responding and they are somewhat reluctant to accept Napp as a major component in adjustment. Other investigators also report the relationship between Napp and the reporting of positive psychological health to be a complex one with little definitive information as yet available (Banikiotes, Russell, & Linden, 1971).

As with the self-concept research, the relationship between Napp and the reporting of positive mood states appears to be a complicated one. Several investigators report moderately positive and significant relationships between the M–C SD and mood level scores (Gorman & Wessman, 1974; Wareheim & Jones, 1972; Wessman & Ricks, 1966). Some have interpreted this as a problem of dissimulation, although Gorman, Wessman, and Ricks (1975) believe that under conditions of confidentiality and good rapport, repeated self-reports of mood appeared to share more variance with other important personality characteristics and situational influences than with social desirability or Napp per se. Klassen, Hornstra, and Anderson (1975) completed a large-scale survey study with almost a thousand persons, 18 years or older, who were asked to complete a shortened version of the M–C SD and also a number of mental health measures, particularly having to do with mood. They found small but consistent inverse relationships between Napp and symptom reporting.

One other study has some bearing on adjustment in relation to Napp. Scherer, Ettinger, and Murdick (1972) studied college students who reported on their use of a number of different kinds of drugs ranging from "soft" drugs such as marijuana to "hard" drugs which included amphetamines, LSD, etc. They found that hard-drug users in contrast to soft-drug users and nonusers were significantly more likely to be characterized as high in Napp. The authors interpret these results in terms of the social pressures operating on individuals and suggest that the hard-drug-oriented peer groups offer some opportunity for gaining approval simply by adherence to hard-drug use. Low Napp persons may feel less inclined to become dependent on drug use as a strategy for gaining approval. In view of the possible avoidant aspects of the high Napp individual, it may also be that a turning to hard drugs represents an escape and a feeling of well-being offering immediate release from feelings of personal inadequacy. Certainly, these results are in contradiction to suggestions that the overriding concern of the high Napp person is to appear favorably, in that hard-drug use does not fit easily into conventional standards of social acceptance and desirability.

Findings with objective personality testing instruments generally validate the approval-seeking presentation of high Napp persons as well as their defensiveness about personal inadequacy. It is also interesting to note the degree to which the approval-motivated individual's desire to appear in a favorable light will influence responses to more open, unstructured projective tests. With stimulus material which pulls no clearly defined responses, one would hypothesize on the basis of a defensiveness interpretation that the high Napp individual might be more guarded and constricted in his responding. Tutko (cited in Crowne & Marlowe, 1964) administered several typically-used projective techniques (the Rorschach, the Rotter Incomplete Sentences Blank, and selected cards from the Thematic Apperception Test (TAT)) in counterbalanced order under standard clinical procedure to 60 psychotic or borderline psychotic VA hospital patients. He created two experimental conditions by interviewing one group of patients under stressful conditions, saying "results . . . are often used to find out if people are mentally sick," and one under supportive conditions, reassuring the patients that testing was focused on the tests only and would have no bearing on their further hospitalization. Following the testing, 24 judges rated the protocols. Generally, as expected, patients gave more guarded responses in the stress conditions. Moreover, judges rated the responses of the high, in contrast to the low, Napp subjects as more defensive and less productive and revealing. High Napp patients were likely to reject the Rorschach and TAT cards, to give fewer responses, and to respond to all of the testing with simple, normative, innocuous responses. These latter findings are similar to those reported by Horton, Marlowe, and Crowne (cited in Crowne & Marlowe, 1964) who found high Napp subjects in a word-association test, more likely than low Napp subjects to give common responses and to restrict their verbal associations to conventional and popular words.

Lefcourt (1969) also looked at projective responses as a function of situational cues in testing (creative versus threat conditions) and Napp. He found high Napp subjects, particularly in the threat condition, to give significantly fewer Movement responses to the Baron inkblot test and to give them later in the test administration than low Napp subjects. In the same study, Lefcourt also added Repression–Sensitization as a predictive variable and found in the threat condition that the low Napp-repressor subjects produced more Movement responses than all the other groups while the high Napp-repressor group produced the least. When the groups were compared across creative versus threat conditions, the low Napp repressors increased their Movement responding in the threat condition and the high Napp repressors decreased their Movement responses in the creative condition. Lefcourt considers Movement responses to reflect greater participation, effort, and expressiveness in a testing situation so the fewer Movement responses of the high Napp subjects suggest a constrictive and defensive response to the projective stimuli, particularly under threat conditions.

The findings of both objective and projective testing suggest that high Napp subjects take pains to present themselves as psychologically healthy and that they guard against self-disclosure and self-revelation by giving conventional and popular responses. The inhibition or defensiveness aspect of approval motivation is further validated by a number of behavioral studies in which investigators find high as opposed to low Napp individuals to fail to give sexually taboo responses, to set either extremely high or low goals in performance tasks and thus guard against failure, and to avoid opportunities to learn more about themselves if this information might be negative. High Napp individuals appear to prefer different styles of therapist interaction and may find it particularly difficult to remain in situations (such as intensive psychotherapy) which encourage critical analysis of one's behavior.

Aggressive and Antisocial Behaviors

If the high Napp person is eager to please and maintain the good favor of others, then he or she must take pains to refrain from interpersonal behavior that may be fractious or harmful. In spite of frustration from others, which may often occur because the high Napp person finds that in spite of "good" behavior, one simply cannot always please others, the high Napp individual must avoid aggression and any retaliatory hostility. What happens when the high Napp individual is aroused to anger? How do approval-dependent persons handle aggressive impulses?

Conn and Crowne (1964) designed an experimental situation in which subjects were given clear provocation to anger by an accomplice. Male subjects were brought into a room and given instructions about playing a two-person nonzero sum game. The experimenter was then unexpectedly called away. Although the subject and the experimenter's accomplice had been given instructions not to discuss the game while the experimenter was absent, the accomplice described to the naive subject how they might both "beat" the game and win the greatest amount of money. When the experimenter returned, and the game conmenced, however, the accomplice proceeded to change his tactics, violating his secret agreement with the subject, and winning a large amount of money while the subject collected nothing. Control subjects completed a neutral task. At the conclusion of the game, the experimenter led the accomplice and subject to another room to await the final part of the experiment. The experimenter walked well ahead of the accomplice and subject so that the subject could comment on the game (and the double cross). Any verbal expression on the part of the subject was noted.

The small room in which the pair waited had a sign designating it as a "child therapy room" and was filled with toys. Raters were stationed beyond a one-way mirror to observe the interaction of the confederate and the subject. The accomplice maintained invariable good humor and attempted to have the subject interact with him in a playful and carefree way. He told jokes, crumpled up paper balls, and threw them toward the waste basket asking the subject to "guard" him, flew paper airplanes, and so on. The judges on the other side of the mirror noted all responses of the subject. The experimenter then returned for the subject, asked him to complete some questionnaires and give his reactions to the experiment and the accomplice, and then informed the subject of the deception.

High, as opposed to low, Napp subjects were significantly more euphoric in the play room situation as judged by the raters, blind to the subjects' M–C SD scores. High Napp subjects were significantly more likely to engage mirthfully with the accomplice. No such differences emerged for the control group. Further, approval-motivated subjects were significantly more favorable than low Napp subjects in their characterization of the accomplice and less likely to criticize him. Conn and Crowne interpret these findings as providing evidence that the conforming, submissive, and influencible behavior of approval-dependent individuals is associated with defense against hostility.

The Conn and Crowne experiment was focused on behavior following an anger-arousing situation. They found no differences between high and low Napp subjects in their evaluation of the accomplice following a control task. Likewise,

Fishman (1965) reported no differences between high and low Napp subjects in the degree of negative evaluation of an experimenter who asked them to engage in what might be a slightly frustrating task, counting backward from one hundred by threes. Fishman also found no difference in blood-pressure arousal following the task as a function of Napp. However, when Fishman confronted the subjects with failure and frustration during the "counting backwards" task, high Napp subjects were significantly less likely than low Napp subjects to evaluate the experimenter negatively. Among those subjects who demonstrated some verbal aggression against the experimenters following the frustration/failure task, there was a significant decrease in systolic pressure for low Napp but not for high Napp individuals. The expression of aggression might well be anxiety producing for high Napp individuals and they receive no emotional release from their aggressive behavior, even when legitimate. The converse seems true for the low Napp persons who show a decrease in emotional arousal, as assessed by systolic blood pressure, following the expression of legitimate aggression.

Altrocci and his colleagues (Altrocci, Palmer, Hellman, & Davis, 1968; Palmer & Altrocci, 1967) showed a film with highly aggressive verbal content (the deliberations of a jury in "Twelve Angry Men") and then had high and low Napp subjects rate the degree of hostility evidenced by the participants. Generally, M–C SD scores were not related to judgements about the hostile intent of the jurors until subjects were asked to make ratings based on their own "gut" reactions. Under these conditions, the high Napp males were significantly less likely to attribute hostile intent to the jurors than the low Napp males.

Taylor (1970) engaged high and low Napp subjects in an experimental task where they were asked to shock a "partner" who did not perform well on a reaction-time measure (in actuality there was no real partner). He found no difference in the amount of shock administered to the "partner" as a function of M–C SD scores. However, when subjects received shocks from the "partner," low Napp subjects quickly retaliated with more intense shocks. High Napp subjects did not increase their shocks when they received only minimum shock and only slowly increased their shock delivery as the shocks from the "partner" became more extreme.

Hetherington and Wray (1964) also suggest that high Napp may be an inhibiting factor in the expression of aggression. They assessed subjects as to need for aggression and Napp and then had them rank nonsense and aggressive cartoons as to humor. High aggressive subjects rated aggressive cartoons as funnier than did subjects low in aggression. Nonsense cartoons were rated higher by high, as opposed to low, Napp subjects. When subjects were given a drink of alcohol, high aggressive-high Napp subjects rated the aggressive cartoons as more humorous than did high aggressive-low Napp subjects and all of the low need-for-aggression subjects. Basically, Hetherington and Wray interpret these findings to mean that high Napp may be serving to defend against aggressive preferences until these inhibitions are lowered by alcohol.

Overall, it appears that Napp is not related to the expression of hostility or aggression until individuals are provoked, frustrated, or aggressed against. After anger-arousing situations, high Napp subjects appear to be less likely to take an aggressive stance toward the instigator while low Napp subjects respond with negative evaluations and aggressive expression.

One other aspect of antisocial behavior in relation to Napp has been investigated in some detail: cheating behavior. Cheating is of interest not only in its own right but also because the resolution of conflict inherent in a cheating situation, somewhat like sexual taboo responses, may give some clues regarding the defensive nature of the approval-motivated individual. One would expect the high Napp person to refrain from any open displays of behavior which are considered socially undesirable. On the other hand, the censure that the high Napp person might expect in a performance situation when not doing well may force that person to engage in behaviors which will ensure success, particularly if the behavior is not open to public scrutiny. In short, the use of a cheating paradigm may give clues as to whether the high Napp person is most desirous of engaging in proper behavior or more concerned with failure. When given the opportunity to cheat, individuals may refrain from cheating, showing most concern with positive (approach) behaviors, or cheat, and attempt to avoid failure.

The first study on Napp and cheating was conducted by Jacobson, Berger, and Millham (1970). Subjects were given the Digit Symbol test of the Wechsler Adult Intelligence Scale and were told that it was a measure of intelligence. Subjects were also asked to estimate the score that they expected to make and the score they would like to receive. Subjects then completed the task and all were told that they failed to meet norms of the test. In an experimental group, subjects were able to improve their scores by improperly completing additional items after the time limit. The control group had no such opportunity. High, as opposed to low, Napp females were significantly more likely to cheat. Also, high Napp subjects who gave congruent estimates of their aspiration levels and expectancy of success were more likely to engage in cheating behavior. Thus, Napp and self-satisfaction in expectancies interacted to produce the most cheating, suggesting a defensive, avoidant stance.

Berger (1971) attempted to replicate these findings and further added several conditions varying the degree to which the results of the task performance would be known to others. Subjects were told their scores would be made known in a public group session; were told they would only be made known in a private session with the experimenter; or would only be known to the subjects themselves. High Napp subjects cheated in all three conditions. However, low Napp subjects also cheated in the experimenter–subject condition, thus lending some confusion to the overall results.

Millham (1974) investigated cheating behavior as a function of Napp in a particularly complex design. He identified individual cheaters, measured the amount of cheating, investigated cheating following both success and failure, controlled the degree of success/failure, and analyzed results separately with respect to two aspects of the M–C SD: attribution of desirability and denial of undesirability. Subjects completed a simulated "intelligence test" in which they were given bogus feedback of success or failure. Immediately following the task, there was a period when subjects could modify their scores and believe their modification to go unchecked. Subjects were more likely to cheat after failure than after success and these subjects also had higher scores on the total M–C SD, as well as on both the attribution of desirability and denial components of Napp. Analysis of a sex by cheating interaction further demonstrated that with respect to the two components of Napp, women who cheated had significantly higher scores on both the attribution and denial components than women who did not cheat. They also had higher attribution component scores than men who cheated. However, men who cheated had significantly higher scores than non-cheating men only for the denial component of Napp. In considering the amount of cheating, Millham found that the attribution component of Napp was unrelated to amount of cheating but that high scorers on the denial component cheated less than low scorers. No relationships were found between total Napp scores and amount of cheating for men; however, females with high total scores cheated less than females with low total scores. Millham interprets these results as supporting an "avoidance" interpretation of Napp. He perceives the approval-motivated individual to be socially conforming only to the extent that such conformity avoids censure. When detection of cheating behavior, for example, is not viewed as likely, the high Napp person will violate social norms if such behavior aids in avoiding negative evaluation. Millham considers approval motivation as primarily defensive and avoidant; the aim is to avoid censure and not to obtain approval.

Generally, then, as expected, high Napp subjects are less likely to engage in aggressive and hostile actions toward others even under conditions of frustration and instigation to anger. However, when afforded an opportunity to engage in another type of antisocial behavior such as cheating, high Napp persons will change responses in an effort to appear to have performed well. In considering the cheating data, Millham suggests that the avoidance of censure or disapproval rather than an active seeking of approval is the primary motivation of high Napp persons. The validity of this interpretation is enhanced by findings noted in other sections of this chapter which also point to the defensive qualities of the high Napp individual.

Interpersonal Behaviors

If the high Napp person is sensitive to and dependent upon the approbation of others, then it is logical to expect differences in interpersonal relationships to occur as a function of approval motivation. For example, the high Napp individual may take greater pains to be liked by others, and interesting questions arise as to the degree to which Napp mediates attraction, if at all. Moreover, in social interchanges, high and low approval-dependent individuals might react quite differently to positive and negative evaluation from others.

Several investigators have manipulated degree of similarity of attitudes between persons assessed as to Napp and a stranger. Generally, they find high, more likely than low, Napp subjects to express greater attraction to strangers who are perceived as similar in attitudes (Ettinger, Nowicki, & Nelson, 1970; Nowicki, 1971; Posavac, 1971). Additionally, a number of investigators have examined the responses of high and low Napp individuals to strangers in situations of actual social interchange. Holstein, Goldstein, and Bem (1971) had male and female subjects interview and then rate one of two male confederates who either did or did not display positive expressive behaviors, such as smiling and eye contact. All subjects preferred interviewees who displayed positive cues over those who omitted such cues. High Napp males reported liking the interviewees better than did the low Napp males, regardless of expressive condition. High Napp females, however, expressed less liking of the male interviewee in the expressive condition. The investigators suggest that these reversed findings occur because the high Napp females found the expressive behavior of the opposite-sex interviewee, such as prolonged gazes and direct body orientation, to be too "close for comfort" and imply sexual intent.

Dies (1970) had 40 same-sex dyads work on a cooperative task. Both dyad members were exposed to an induced-failure experience and then made subsequent ratings as to whether blame could be ascribed to features of the experiment, transient personal states, and/or one's partner. High, in contrast to low, Napp subjects were significantly more likely to rationalize or excuse the failure by blaming various experimental factors and/or their partners. However, this was always done within the limits of a generalized tendency to seek social acceptance by expressing attitudes complimentary of the other person or the situation. Again, within the interpersonal situation, the high Napp partner is characterized as avoidant or defensive and attempting to protect a vulnerable self-image.

Jones and his colleagues have completed several studies investigating Napp in relation to evaluation from another who is giving agreeing or disagreeing feedback in a situation of social exchange. In one study (Jones & Schneider, 1968), low self-appraisals were induced for subjects and certainty about the self-appraisals was manipulated. Subjects then received positive and negative evaluations purportedly from a peer in reaction to their responses to a series of questions. Subjects for whom there was a high degree of certainty about low self-evaluations responded more favorably to the negative evaluator relative to the positive evaluator than those who were uncertain of their low self-appraisals. Napp was positively correlated with social reciprocity in the uncertain condition but not in the certain condition. In a similar experimental paradigm, Shrauger and Jones (1968) found a significant relationship between Napp scores and a more favorable description of the positive evaluator than the negative evaluator.

Jones and Tager (1972) ran subjects in groups of four in which they indicated their agreement or disagreement with one another's opinions on a personality inventory. These agreements or disagreements were actually controlled by the experimenter. Napp was not related to the evaluations of others' opinions but was related to subjects' response latencies in expressing their own opinions. High Napp subjects had longer response latencies in the agreement in contrast to the disagreement condition. The reverse was true for low Napp subjects. Jones and Tager interpret these findings to suggest that the high Napp subject defends against social disapproval by working hard to maintain a positive evaluation from another and spending less time when disagreed with, possibly denying the importance of the situation.

Finally, Natale (1975) examined the degree to which subjects in conversation would match vocal intensity and the degree to which this was related to Napp. Same-sex subjects met in dyads, although not in direct view of each other, and were asked to converse naturally. The dyads met for an hour a week over a three-week period. Indeed, vocal intensity convergence was related to Napp. The raising or lowering of one subject's voice was accompanied by a corresponding convergence on the part of the other subject and was related to Napp as assessed by the M–C SD. High Napp subjects contributed more to the convergence of vocal intensity than did low Napp subjects, although all subjects reported that they were unaware of any self-regulation of vocal intensity.

Generally, then, as one might expect, Napp is related to interpersonal interchange among adults. High Napp individuals appear to be more favorable in their evaluations of others who are perceived to be similar to them than are low Napp persons. Napp also appears to mediate social exchange or reciprocity with high Napp subjects responding more than low Napp subjects to positive or agreeing statements on the part of an interviewer or evaluator.

Approval Motivation in Children

With the findings that Napp is related to a number of social behaviors for adults, a naturally occurring question has to do with how approval motivation develops. What are the antecedent conditions that influence an individual toward high or low approval-dependency behaviors? How stable is Napp across time and across different age groups? Do parents play a large part in either inducing or reducing excessive approval motivation on the part of their children?

Since ordinal position appears to be related to some of the behavioral correlates of Napp in that firstborns have been found to be more conforming (Dittes, 1961; Schachter, 1964) and to have higher affiliative needs (Schachter, 1959) than later-borns, several investigators have considered family structure as an antecedent condition for the development of approval motivation. Moran (1967) and Nowicki (1971) both report firstborn females to be higher in Napp than later-borns. Johnson (1973) also found firstborn children, both male and female, to have higher Napp scores than later-borns. However, Walker and Tahmisian (1967) found no relationship between Napp and ordinal position. Masterson (1971) carefully controlled for family structure and found that subjects in larger families showed higher Napp scores, and, as in many other studies, females to have higher Napp scores than males. Family size and sex interacted with ordinal position in accounting for differences in approval motivation. Results of all of these studies, taken together, suggest that family structure and ordinal position are both influential antecedent conditions in the development of approval motivation although the specifics of these interactions are not at all clear.

The work of Allaman, Joyce, and Crandall (1972) is the most comprehensive investigation to date of antecedent conditions of Napp tendencies in children and young adults. These experimenters had access to data collected as part of a longitudinal study supported by Fels Institute which focused on both children's and parents' behavior over a span of some years. The Children's Social Desirability (CSD) scale (Crandall, Crandall, & Katkovsky, 1965) was individually administered to white, predominantly middle-class, children at three different times separated by 3-year intervals. Younger children had significantly higher Napp scores than older children. Younger females had higher scores than younger males but no significant sex differences appeared for older children. A group of 25 children who received the CSD twice showed rather low test–retest reliabilities over a 3-year span. Since a 1-month test–restest reliability coefficient for the CSD is .90 for children this age, the authors conclude that Napp responses are not very stable for children in the elementary-school years.

When the investigators considered the relationships of the children's Napp responses to Parent Behavior Ratings, they found that generally, "harsh" parental practices predicted subsequent high Napp responding, particularly for young males. Maternal hostility, criticism, restrictiveness, punitiveness, coerciveness, and lack of encouragement of skill development were all related to high Napp scores. Maternal hostility and criticism were most influential when they occured during infancy, while the remaining antecedents had a stronger effect when they occurred during the preschool years. Few predictive variables emerged for the young females.

Allaman *et al.* (1972) then considered a second group of young children ($N =$ 65) who completed the M–C SD scale. These subjects had also been studied when they were children in the Fels project. Twelve subjects had taken the CSD as adolescents and a correlation of .78 was found between the adult measure (M–C SD) and the children's scale, suggesting both that the different forms are comparable and also that Napp tendencies may be approaching stability by adolescence. Again, for the total young-adult sample, "harsh" parental practices predicted Napp responses but, in this case, the results were most striking for the females and not for the males. Lack of maternal warmth, criticism, restriction, and so on militated toward higher Napp responding in young adult females.

Perceived paternal rejection predicted high Napp responding for the young men. Other significant subject antecedents or correlates included imitation, conformity to parents, negative self-perceptions, traditional sex-role values, and poorer intellectual functioning. Noncompliance and dominance in infancy were unexpectedly related, to high Napp responding in adulthood, but a decrease in maternal involvement over the childhood years appeared to provide an explanation for these findings. Generally, it appears that parental child-rearing practices which communicate overt disapproval, threat or rejection, or a sharp drop in parental attention sensitize the child to the tenuousness of positive regard from the parents. In response, the child may develop generalized concerns about evaluation from others with an expectancy that these evaluations will be disapproving. Thus, the child is forced into culturally approved behaviors and attitudes (or at least reports them) in an attempt to gain approval from significant others.

Some findings do not necessarily support Allaman *et al.* in regard to the development of excessive approval dependency in relation to "harsh" parental practices. For example, Calhoun and Mikesell (1972), using recollective data, found in a sample of over 700 male college freshmen, that high Napp subjects reported their parents to be less controlling than low Napp subjects. One should, perhaps, be particularly careful in interpreting this data, in that the recollective responses may also be reflecting social desirability responding which is, of course, inherent in the Napp measures. Moreover, Kasl (1972) found that while Napp was not related to distortion of self-reported extracurricular activities and grades for high-school students, whose reports could be easily checked, high Napp students who had graduated the year earlier were significantly more likely than low Napp graduates to report having engaged in extracurricular activities and having received higher grades than were actually represented in their records. Thus, response bias may be particularly influential in recollective responses about early events.

Aside from studying the antecedent conditions for the development of Napp responding, a number of investigators have been interested in behavioral correlates of Napp in children. Walsh, Tomlinson-Keasey, and Klieger (1974), for example, found first graders who were low Napp responders on their Children's Social Desirability Measure also to be those children for whom special notation in the school records indicated psychological, speech, or disciplinary problems. There were significantly fewer notations for high Napp children. Crandall (1966) observed a "striking similarity" between the behaviors of high Napp adults and the personality attributes of high Napp secondary-school students as revealed in their scores on the California Psychological Inventory. Specifically, high Napp adolescents reported the same kind of concern about others' evaluations, the same low self-esteem and lack of self-confidence, and the same conventional, inhibited, controlled behaviors and beliefs as high Napp adults. High Napp females in contrast to the low-scoring females in Crandall's study expressed less physical and verbal aggression and withdrew from aggressive attack. High Napp males were less achieving and less persistent than their low Napp counterparts. Crandall also found females to be higher in Napp responding than males. Staub and Sherk (1970) found high Napp children to engage in less sharing behavior with other children. They also ate less candy in the presence of others. Staub and Sherk suggest that this behavior represents an inhibiting or inactive stance, particularly in novel situations, for the high Napp children. Tulkin, Muller, and Conn (1969) studied Napp and popularity among elementary school students. Using sociogram responses for fifth and sixth grade students, they found high Napp females to be the most popular among their peers while high Napp males were the least popular. They interpret these results within a sex-role theory which hypothesizes that high Napp behaviors are consistent with a female sex-role model but contrary to the male model.

Because of the obvious relationships between approval motivation and responses to praise or punishment for performance, considerable interest has been focused on Napp and academic achievement. One might hypothesize that the high Napp child would be particularly socialized to teacher and school demands with a view toward performing in ways that bring reward or acceptance. On the other hand, the defensive characterization of the high Napp individual might lead one to see the high Napp child so overly sensitive to the evaluations of others that the youngster restricts intellectual adventure and performs carefully and cautiously, avoiding academic risk.

Looking at intelligence and developmental test scores gathered on children from birth to adolescence, Allaman, Joyce, and Crandall (1972) found a lower level of intellectual functioning among children with high Napp scores than among the low scorers. This relationship appeared as early as one year of age for females, remained low to moderate in degree until age 12 where the relationship attained significance again. For males, a significant relationship between low intelligence scores and high Napp appeared at adolescence, emerging even more strongly than for the females. Allaman *et al.* suggest that the individual who receives rewards for intellectual competence may develop less dependency on the approval of others than the individual whose gratifications in the intellectual achievement area are minimized by a lack of skills and abilities.

Other investigators have also noted that high Napp children, in contrast to low Napp children, withdraw from classroom situations and have lower school grades (Lahaderne & Jackson, 1970). Crandall (1966) found high-scoring males to spend less time working alone on achievement tasks, making less effort to achieve, in general, and being less task persistent. Harter (1975) investigated persistence on discrimination tasks as a function of Napp, level of challenge, and whether or not the experimenter was present or absent. With fifth and sixth grade males and females as subjects, she found low Napp children to spend more time in the challenging (unsolvable) task than high Napp children, with negligible condition differences. High, in contrast to low, Napp subjects spent more time in the experimenter-present than in the experimenter-absent condition, with negligible task differences. On the solvable task, high Napp subjects required more trials to solve the problem than low Napp subjects, thus demonstrating poorer learning. Harter also found the sex differences reported by others, with greater mastery motivation on the part of the young males and greater Napp among the young females. Crowne, Holland, and Conn (1968) compared the performance of high and low Napp fifth- and sixth-grade subjects on a two-choice discrimination learning task. They found the high Napp children to show a performance deficit on both the initial discrimination task and a subsequent task involving an extradimensional shift. Further, high Napp subjects evidenced more signs of anxiety, such as impulsivity and accelerated heart rate. However, when Brannigan, Duchnowski, and Nyce (1974) attempted to replicate these findings with third- and fourth-grade children, they found high Napp subjects to make *fewer* errors than either a moderate or low Napp group. Monetary-social versus monetary-no-social reinforcement conditions produced no differences. They suggest that their failure to replicate Crowne *et al.* may reflect age-related factors in that approval motivation may be differentially operating for younger and older children, enhancing the performance of the younger student, who still may be quite dependent on the teacher or external cues and having a debilitating effect on older approval-motivated children, who have not achieved independence and a lesser reliance on authority.

Overall, the findings on the development of Napp in children are not altogether clear. "Harsh" parenting appears to lead to higher approval motivation, especially for young males when parent–child interactions are actually observed. Recollective data are characterized by more positive evaluations of the parents from high Napp adults. Possibly, the response biasing inherent in the Napp construct is influencing these results. The bulk of the research on Napp and learning for children, except with a young sample, supports a defensive interpretation of Napp. High Napp children appear to perform less well than low Napp children both in general academic and intellectual pursuits and on specific discrimination learning tasks. Additionally, they may be somewhat more socially withdrawn and/or conventional than their low Napp counterparts. It should be noted, however, that the age of the children must be carefully considered. Napp scores appear to become lower as children grow older and approval motivation may serve different functions for different age groups. Moreover, the use of different testing instruments, diverse populations, and experimental/administration conditions all contribute to a lessening of generalizability (Shriberg, 1974).

PROBLEMS AND ISSUES

Any motivational variable that is couched in terms of needs, such as *need* for approval, is at once subject to a number of criticisms. Motivational properties are particularly difficult to define. Also, assumptions are made about enduring personal characteristics which, a number of theorists argue, offer little prediction in the face of overriding situational influences. Most contemporary theorists would maintain that more accurate prediction occurs when behavior is considered as a function of both personality dispositions and the situation. Actually, Crowne and Marlowe anchored Napp within Rotter's social learning theory in which situations are important determinants of behavior. Unfortunately, investigators who have conducted research with the Napp variable have often divorced it from theory and treat Napp as a typical trait or motive. When this happens, of course, the research is limited by all of the problems of trait psychology. Another major criticism which can be leveled at Napp research, as well as most other research with individual difference characteristics, is that human behavior is enormously complex and experimenters would do well to take a systems approach to the study of individuals rather than looking piecemeal at single properties. Even within a systems approach, however, it is likely that Napp would emerge as one of the salient and important components of personality functioning.

A criticism that has been leveled more specifically at the Napp variable is that it is conceived as comprising two factors and yet is represented by only one assessment score. Crowne and Marlowe define Napp as approval-seeking behaviors in particular situations through both positive self-presentation and denial of inadequacies. As early as 1966, Jackson and Ford raised questions about this combination of characteristics of both approach and avoidance motivation. They argue that each of these two components should be identified separately and that they cannot be theoretically subsumed within a single framework. Possibly some individuals characteristically behave in a way to defend themselves against negative evaluation and do not necessarily take steps to present themselves actively in a positive fashion. Others may be approval-seeking by engaging in certain acts that will bring them approbation with little concern as to negative consequences. Some individuals may be both approval seeking and avoidant of negative evaluation. These two factors may or may not be related to each other and may operate differentially for different people. This lack of theoretical clarity about the makeup of the Napp dimension has led to considerable confusion.

The approach–avoidance aspects of Napp, particularly as they are not clearly defined, lead to further difficulties in terms of assessment. A single Napp score can hardly represent both of these factors adequately. Several investigators have tried to tease out the various contributions of the positively keyed versus the negatively keyed items of the M–C SD scale in an attempt to discover the degree to which these sets of items are related to each other and to the total score. If endorsing socially desirable items and denying undesirable items are equivalent, then the magnitude of correlations between these two sets of items should be quite high. Actual correlations between positively and negatively keyed items range from .45 to .57 (Ford, 1964; Greenwald & Clausen, 1970), suggesting that these two sets of items are moderately but not clearly equivalent and raising continued questions about the dual characteristics of Napp. Rump and Court (1971) found differential correlations between positively and negatively keyed items and Eysenck's Neuroticism scale, again suggesting that positive and negative components are different and may even lead to prediction differences. It should be noted that this shortcoming is not as pronounced in the Children's Social Desirability Scale. Brannigan (1974) found relatively high correlations between positively and negatively keyed items (.65–.72), suggesting that responses to either of the kinds of items are quite similar.

At the time that Crowne and Marlowe developed the Napp construct and an instrument to assess it, a number of researchers welcomed the opportunity to pursue an understanding of social behavior in relation to an individual difference variable that appeared to have wide applicability to conformity and social behavior. The American people were reading *The Organization Man* (Whyte, 1956) and were concerned with being directed according to inner versus outer forces, so poignantly described by Riesman (1950) in *The Lonely Crowd.* Individuals were frightened of losing themselves within the large corporations and were searching for identity and values beyond the early self-assurance of our forebears (Wheelis, 1958) whose entrepreneurial efforts appeared slightly outdated in an age of "think tanks" and organizational bureaucracy. Napp appeared an apt descriptive dimension for the button-down conformity of Madison Avenue and the quiet compliance of college students. Research on the Napp variable appeared to peak in the mid sixties and it is probably no accident of history that interest in this variable began to wane with the advent of assassinations and the unleashing of powerful dissention and potent disagreement with the government. Large masses of American people were not content with an easy acceptance of the politics of the cold war or the rhetoric of a destructive engagement in Southeast Asia. Psychologists found their interests turning from conformity and status quo to a concern with social action.

The Napp variable, even with its shortcomings, served many investigators well. It continues to be of considerable importance although experimenters tend to focus on Napp more as a secondary or mediating variable now than as an all encompassing individual difference variable (Hewitt & Goldman, 1974; Schneider & Turkat, 1975; Smith & Campbell, 1973). Napp is still alive and well but more likely to be aligned with other important personality dimensions for an increased and more accurate description of social behavior.

ACKNOWLEDGMENTS

I am particularly grateful to Carol Reinhardt for her help in preparing this chapter and to Bobbi Fibel for her invaluable literature search.

REFERENCES

Allaman, J. D., Joyce, C. S., & Crandall, V. C. The antecedents of social desirability response tendencies of children and young adults. *Child Development,* 1972, *43,* 1135–1160.

Altrocci, J., Palmer, J. Hellman, R., & Davis, H. The Marlow–Crowne, Repression–Sensitizer, and Internal–External Scales, and attribution of unconscious hostile intent. *Psychological Reports,* 1968, *23,* 1229–1230.

Banikiotes, P. G., Russell, J. M., & Linden, J. D. Social desirability, adjustment, and effectiveness. *Psychological Reports,* 1971, *29,* 581–582.

Barthel, C. E., & Crowne, D. P. The need for approval, task categorization, and perceptual defense. *Journal of Consulting Psychology,* 1962, *26,* 547–555.

Berger, S. E. The self-deceptive personality. Unpublished doctoral dissertation, University of Miami, 1971.

Bernhardson, C. S. The relationship between Facilitation–Inhibition and Repression–Sensitization. *Journal of Clinical Psychology,* 1967, *23,* 448–449.

Brannigan, G. G. Comparison of Yes–No and True–False forms of the children's social desirability scale. *Psychological Reports,* 1974, *34,* 898.

Brannigan, G. G., Duchnowski, A. J., & Nyce, P. A. Roles of approval motivation and social reinforcement in children's discrimination learning. *Developmental Psychology,* 1974, *10,* 843–846.

Breger, L. Further studies of the social desirability scale. *Journal of Consulting Psychology,* 1966, *30,* 281.

Bryan, J. H., & Lichtenstein, E. Effects of subject attitudes in verbal conditioning. *Journal of Personality and Social Psychology,* 1966, *3,* 188–189.

Buckhout, R. Need for social approval and attitude change. *Journal of Psychology,* 1965, *60,* 123–128.

Burhenne, D., & Mirels, H. Self-disclosure in self-descriptive essays. *Journal of Consulting and Clinical Psychology,* 1970, *35,* 409–412.

Byrne, D. Repression–sensitization as a dimension of personality. In B. A. Maher (Ed.), *Progress in experimental research* (Vol. 1). New York: Academic Press, 1964.

Calhoun, L. G., & Mikesell, R. H. Biodata antecedents of the need for approval in male college freshmen. *Developmental Psychology,* 1972, *7,* 226.

Conn, L. K., & Crowne, D. P. Instigation to aggression, emotional arousal, and defensive emulation. *Journal of Personality,* 1964, *32,* 163–179.

Crandall, V. Personality characteristics and social achievement behaviors associated with children's social desirability response tendencies. *Journal of Personality and Social Psychology,* 1966, *4,* 477–486.

Crandall, V., Crandall, V. J., & Katkovsky, W. A children's social desirability questionnaire. *Journal of Consulting Psychology,* 1965, *29,* 27–36.

Crowne, D. P., Holland, C. H., & Conn, L. K. Personality factors in discrimination learning in children. *Journal of Personality and Social Psychology,* 1968, *10,* 420–430.

Crowne, D. P., & Marlowe, D. A new scale of social desirability independent of psychopathology. *Journal of Consulting Psychology,* 1960, *24,* 349–354.

Crowne, D. P., & Marlow, D. *The approval motive: Studies in evaluative dependence.* New York: Wiley, 1964.

Crowne, D. P., & Strickland, B. R. The conditioning of verbal behavior as a function of the need for social approval. *Journal of Abnormal and Social Psychology,* 1961, *63,* 395–401.

Cruse, D. B. Socially desirable responses in relation to grade level. *Child Development,* 1963, *34,* 777–789.

Cruse, D. B. Socially desirable resonses at ages 3 through 6. *Child Development,* 1966, *37,* 909–916.

Dies, R. Need for social approval and blame assignment. *Journal of Consulting and Clinical Psychology,* 1970, *35,* 311–316.

Dittes, J. Birth order and vulnerability to differences in acceptance. *American Psychologist,* 1961, *16,* 358. (Abstract)

Dixon, T. Experimenter approval, social desirability, and statements of self-reference. *Journal of Consulting and Clinical Psychology,* 1970, *35,* 400–405.

Doster, J. A., & Slaymaker, J. Need approval, uncertainty anxiety, and expectancies of interview behavior. *Journal of Counseling Psychology,* 1972, *19,* 522–528.

Doster, J. A., & Strickland, B. R. Disclosing of verbal material as a function of information requested, information about the interviewer, and interviewee differences. *Journal of Consulting and Clinical Psychology,* 1971, *37,* 187–194.

Edwards, A. L. The relationship between judged desirability of a trait and the probability that the trait will be endorsed. *Journal of Applied Psychology,* 1953, *37,* 90–93.

Edwards, A. L. *The social desirability variable in personality assessment and research.* New York: Dryden, 1957.

Efran, J. S., & Boylin, E. R. Social desirability and willingness to participate in a group discussion. *Psychological Reports,* 1967, *20,* 402.

Ettinger, R. F., Nowicki, S., & Nelson, D. A. Interpersonal attraction and the approval motive. *Journal of Experimental Research in Personality,* 1970, *4,* 95–99.

Farley, F. H. Field dependence and approval motivation. *Journal of General Psychology,* 1974, *91,* 153–154.

Feder, C. A. Relationship of repression–sensitization to adjustment status, social desirability, and acquiescence response set. *Journal of Consulting Psychology,* 1967, *31,* 401–406.

Fisher, G. Normative and reliability data for the standard and the cross-validated Marlowe–Crowne Social Desirability Scale. *Psychological Reports,* 1963, *20,* 174.

Fisher, G., & Parsons, T. H. The performance of male prisoners on the Marlowe-Crowne Social Desirability Scale. *Journal of Clinical Psychology,* 1962, *18,* 140–141.

Fishman, C. G. Need for approval and the expression of agression under varying conditions of frustration. *Journal of Personality and Social Psychology,* 1965, *2,* 809–816.

Ford, L. H. A forced-choice, acquiescence-free, social desirability (defensiveness) scale. *Journal of Consulting Psychology,* 1964, *28,* 475.

Ford, L. H., & Rubin, B. A social desirability questionnaire for young children. *Journal of Consulting and Clinical Psychology,* 1970, *35,* 195–204.

Golding, S. L., & Lichtenstein, E. Confession of awareness and prior knowledge of deception as a function of interview set and approval motivation. *Journal of Personality and Social Psychology,* 1970, *14,* 213–223.

Gorman, B. S., & Wessman, A. E. The relationship of cognitive styles and moods. *Journal of Clinical Psychology,* 1974, *30,* 18–25.

Gorman, B. S., Wessman, A. E., & Ricks, D. F. Social desirability and self-reports of mood: A rejoinder. *Perceptual and Motor Skills,* 1975, *40,* 272–274.

Greenwald, H. J., & Clausen, J. D. Test of relationship between yea-saying and social desirability. *Psychological Reports,* 1970, *27,* 139–141.

Greenwald, H. J., & Satow, Y. A short social desirability scale. *Psychological Reports,* 1970, *27,* 131–135.

Harris, W. G. An investigation of the IE scale's predictability using the bogus pipeline. Unpublished master's thesis, University of Massachusetts, 1975.

Harter, S. Mastery motivation and need for approval in older children and their relationship to social desirability response tendencies. *Developmental Psychology,* 1975, *11,* 186–196.

Hetherington, W. M., & Wray, M. P. Aggression, need for social approval, and humor preferences. *Journal of Abnormal and Social Psychology,* 1964, *68,* 685–689.

Hewitt, J., & Goldman, M. Self-esteem, need for approval, and reactions to personal evaluations. *Journal of Experimental Social Psychology,* 1974, *10,* 201–210.

Hjelle, L. A. Social desirability as a variable in the locus of control scale. *Psychological Reports,* 1971, *28,* 807–816.

Hoffmann, H. Depression and defensiveness in self-descriptive moods of alcoholics. *Psychological Reports,* 1970, *26,* 23–26.

Hollander, E. P., Julian, J. W., & Haaland, G. A. Conformity process and prior group support. *Journal of Personality and Social Psychology,* 1965, *2,* 852–858.

Holstein, C. M., Goldstein, J. W., & Bem, D. J. The importance of expressive behavior, involvement, sex, and need-approval in inducing liking. *Journal of Experimental Social Psychology,* 1971, *7,* 534–544.

Jacobson, L. I., Berger, S. E., & Millham, J. Individual differences in cheating during a temptation period when confronting failure. *Journal of Personality and Social Psychology,* 1970, *15,* 48–56.

Jacobson, L. I., & Ford, L. H. Need for approval, defensive denial, and sensitivity to cultural stereotypes. *Journal of Personality,* 1966, *34,* 596–609.

Johnson, P. B. Birth order and Crowne–Marlowe social desirability scores. *Psychological Reports,* 1973, *32,* 536.

Jones, S. C., & Schneider, D. J. Certainty of self-appraisal and reactions to evaluation from others. *Sociometry,* 1968, *31,* 395–403.

Jones, S. C., & Tager, R. Exposure to others, need for social approval, and reactions to agreement and disagreement from others. *Journal of Social Psychology,* 1972, *86,* 111–120.

Kahn, M., and Schill, T. Anxiety report in defensive and nondefensive repressors. *Journal of Consulting and Clinical Psychology,* 1971, *36,* 300.

Kanfer, F. H., & Marston, A. R. Characteristics of interactional behavior in a psychotherapy analogue. *Journal of Consulting Psychology,* 1964, *28,* 456–467.

Kasl, S. V. Relationship of distortion in self-reports of grades and extracurricular activities to the Crowne–Marlowe measure of approval motive. *Psychological Reports,* 1972, *30,* 252–254.

Katkin, E. S. The Marlowe–Crowne Social Desirability Scale: Independent of psychopathology? *Psychological Reports,* 1964, *15,* 703–706.

Klassen, D., Hornstra, R. K., & Anderson, P. B. Influence of social desirability on symptom and mood reporting in a community survey. *Journal of Consulting and Clinical Psychology,* 1975, *43,* 448–452.

Klein, E. B., Gould, L. J., & Corey, M. Social desirability in children: An extension and replication. *Journal of Consulting and Clinical Psychology,* 1969, *33,* 128.

Lahaderne, H. M., & Jackson, P. W. Withdrawal in the classroom: A note on some educational correlates of social desirability among school children. *Journal of Educational Psychology,* 1970, *61,* 97–101.

Lefcourt, H. Need for approval and threatened negative evaluation as determinants of expressiveness in a projective test. *Journal of Consulting and Clinical Psychology,* 1969, *33,* 96–102.

Lichtenstein, E., & Bryan, J. H. CPI correlates of the need for approval. *Journal of Clinical Psychology,* 1966, *22,* 453–455.

Marlowe, D. Need for social approval and the operant conditioning of meaningful verbal behavior. *Journal of Consulting Psychology,* 1962, *26,* 79–83.

Marlowe, D., Beecher, R. S., Cook, J. B., & Doob, A. N. The approval motive, vicarious reinforcement, and verbal conditioning. *Perceptual and Motor Skills,* 1964, *19,* 523–530.

Marlowe, D., & Crowne, D. P. Social desirability and response to perceived situational demands. *Journal of Consulting Psychology,* 1961, *25,* 109–115.

Masterson, M. L. Family structure variables and need approval. *Journal of Consulting and Clinical Psychology,* 1971, *36,* 12–13.

McCarthy, B. W., & Rafferty, J. E. Effect of social desirability and self-concept scores on the measurement of adjustment. *Journal of Personality,* 1971, *35,* 576–583.

Miklich, D. R. Social desirability and "acquiescence response set." *Psychological Reports,* 1966, *19,* 887–890.

Milburn, T. W., Bell, N., & Koeske, G. F. Effect of censure or praise and evaluative dependence on performance in a free-learning task. *Journal of Personality and Social Psychology,* 1970, *15,* 43–47.

Millham, J. Two components of need for approval score and their relationship to cheating following success and failure. *Journal of Research in Personality,* 1974, *8,* 378–392.

Miller, N., Doob, A. N., Butler, D. C., & Marlowe, D. The tendency to agree: Situational determinants and social desirability. *Journal of Experimental Research in Personality,* 1965, *1,* 78–83.

Moran, G. Ordinal position and approval motivation. *Journal of Consulting Psychology,* 1967, *31,* 319–320.

Natale, M. Convergence of mean vocal intensity in dyadic communication as a function of social desirability. *Journal of Personality and Social Psychology,* 1975, *32,* 790–804.

Nowicki, S. Ordinal position, approval motivation, and interpersonal attraction. *Journal of Consulting and Clinical Psychology,* 1971, *36,* 265–267.

Palmer, J., & Altrocci, J. Attribution of hostile intent as unconscious. *Journal of Personality,* 1967, *35,* 164–177.

Pervin, L. A., & Lilly, R. S. Social desirability and self-ideal self ratings on the semantic differential. *Educational and Psychological Measurement,* 1967, *27,* 845–853.

Petzel, T. P. Approval motivation and self-estimates of academic performance. *Journal of Consulting and Clinical Psychology,* 1972, *39,* 199–201.

Posavac, E. J. Need for approval as a moderator of interpersonal attraction based on attitude similarity. *Journal of Social Psychology,* 1971, *85,* 141–142.

Riesman, D. *The lonely crowd.* New Haven: Yale University Press, 1950.

Rosenfeld, J. M. Some perceptual and cognitive correlates of strong approval motivation. *Journal of Consulting Psychology,* 1967, *31,* 507–512.

Rosenthal, R. *Experimenter effects in behavioral research.* New York: Appleton-Century-Crofts, 1966.

Rotter, J. B. *Social learning and clinical psychology.* Englewood Cliffs, N. J.: Prentice-Hall, 1954.

Rotter, J. B. Generalized expectancies for internal versus external control of reinforcement. *Psychological Monographs,* 1966, *80* (1, Whole No. 609).

Rotter, G., & Tinkleman, V. Anchor effects in development of behavior rating scales. *Educational and Psychological Measurement,* 1970, *30,* 311–318.

Rozelle, R. M., Evans, R. I., Lasater, T. M., Dembroski, T. M., & Allen, B. P. Need for approval as related to the effects of persuasive communications on actual, reported and intended behavior change – A viable predictor? *Psychological Reports,* 1973, *33,* 719–725.

Rump, E. E., & Court, J. The Eysenck Personality Inventory and social desirability response set with student and clinical groups. *British Journal of Social and Clinical Psychology,* 1971, *10,* 42–54.

Schachter, S. Birth order and sociometric choice. *Journal of Abnormal and Social Psychology,* 1964, *68,* 453–456.

Schachter, S. *The psychology of affiliation.* Stanford, Calif.: Stanford University Press, 1959.

Scherer, S. E., Ettinger, R. F., & Murdick, N. J. Need for social approval and drug use. *Journal of Consulting and Clinical Psychology,* 1972, *38,* 118–121.

Schill, T. Need for approval, guilt, and sexual stimulation and their relationship to sexual responsivity. *Journal of Consulting and Clinical Psychology,* 1972, *38,* 31–35.

Schill, T., & Pederson, V. Effects of instructions on free associative sexual responses of subjects varying in need for approval. *Journal of Consulting and Clinical Psychology,* 1973, *40,* 490.

Schneider, D. J., & Turkat, D. Self-presentation following success or failure: Defensive self-esteem models. *Journal of Personality,* 1975, *9,* 85–95.

Shrauger, J. S., & Jones, S. C. Social validation and interpersonal evaluations. *Journal of Experimental Social Psychology,* 1968, *4,* 315–323.

Shriberg, L. D. Descriptive statistics for two children's social desirability scales, general and test anxiety, and locus of control in elementary school children. *Psychological Reports,* 1974, *34,* 863–870.

Silber, L. D., & Grebstein, L. C. Repression–sensitization and social desirability responding. *Journal of Consulting Psychology,* 1964, *28,* 559.

Skolnick, P., & Heslin, R. Approval dependence and reactions to bad arguments and low credibility sources. *Journal of Experimental Research in Personality,* 1971, *5,* 199–207.

Smith, R. E., & Campbell, A. L. Social anxiety and strain toward symmetry in dyadic attraction. *Journal of Personality and Social Psychology,* 1973, *28,* 101–107.

Smith, R. E., & Flenning, F. Need for approval and susceptibility to unintended social influence. *Journal of Consulting and Clinical Psychology,* 1971, *36,* 383–385.

Spielberger, C. D., Berger, A., & Howard, K. Conditioning of verbal behavior as a function of awareness, need for social approval, and motivation to receive reinforcement. *Journal of Abnormal and Social Psychology,* 1963, *67,* 241–246.

Staub, E., & Sherk, L. Need for approval, children's sharing behavior and reciprocity in sharing. *Child Development,* 1970, *41,* 243–252.

Stone, L. A. Relationships between response to Marlowe–Crowne social desirability scale and MMPI scales. *Psychological Reports,* 1965, *17,* 179–182.

Strickland, B. R. Need approval and motor steadiness under positive and negative conditions. *Perceptual and Motor Skills,* 1965, *20,* 667–668.

Strickland, B. R. Individual differences in verbal conditioning, extinction, and awareness. *Journal of Personality,* 1970, *38,* 364–378.

Strickland, B. R., & Crowne, D. P. Conformity under conditions of simulated group pressure as a function of the need for social approval. *Journal of Social Psychology,* 1962, *58,* 171–181.

Strickland, B. R., & Crowne, D. P. Need for approval and the premature termination of psychotherapy. *Journal of Consulting Psychology,* 1963, *27,* 95–101.

Strickland, B. R., & Jenkins, O. Simple motor performance under positive and negative approval motivation. *Perceptual and Motor Skills,* 1964, *19,* 599–605.

Taylor, S. Aggressive behavior as a function of approval motivation and physical attack. *Psychonomic Science,* 1970, *18,* 195–196.

Tedeschi, J., Berrill, D., & Gahagan, J. Social desirability, manifest anxiety, and social power. *Journal of Social Psychology,* 1969, *77,* 231–239.

Terris, W., & Milburn, T. W. Praise, evaluative dependence, and the experimenter as factors in a free-learning task. *Journal of Psychology,* 1972, *81,* 183–194.

Thaw, J., & Efran, J. S. The relationship of need for approval to defensiveness and goal setting behavior: A partial replication. *Journal of Psychology,* 1967, *65,* 41.

Tulkin, S., Muller, J., & Conn, L. Need for approval and popularity: Sex differences in elementary school students. *Journal of Consulting and Clinical Psychology,* 1969, *33,* 35–39.

Vuchinich, R. E., & Bass, B. A. Social desirability in Rotter's locus of control scale. *Psychological Reports,* 1974, *34,* 1124–1126.

Walker, C. E., & Tahmisian, J. Birth order and student characteristics: A replication. *Journal of Consulting Psychology,* 1967, *31,* 219.

Walsh, J. A., Tomlinson-Keasey, C., & Klieger, D. M. Acquisition of the social desirability response. *Genetic Psychology Monographs,* 1974, *89,* 241–272.

Wareheim, R. G., & Jones, D. Social desirability responding and self-report of immediate mood affect states. *Perceptual and Motor Skills,* 1972, *35,* 190.

Wessman, A., and Ricks, D. F. *Mood and personality.* New York: Holt, Rinehart, and Winston, 1966.

Wheelis, A. *The quest for identity.* New York: Norton, 1958.

Whyte, W. H., Jr. *The organization man.* New York: Simon and Schuster, 1956.

Willingham, A., & Strickland, B. R. Need for approval and simple motor performance. *Perceptual and Motor Skills,* 1965, *21,* 879–884.

Wiesenthal, D. L. Some effects of the confirmation and disconfirmation of an expected monetary reward on compliance. *Journal of Social Psychology,* 1974, *92,* 39–52.

Wright, C. E. Relations between normative and ipsative measures of personality. Unpublished doctoral dissertation. University of Washington, 1957.

9
Sex Differences

Kay Deaux

Purdue University

Sex as a variable in social behavior has come out of the closet in the 1970s. Although developmental psychologists have maintained an important wedge (e.g., Maccoby, 1966; Maccoby & Jacklin, 1974), personality and social psychologists have tended to keep the door to sex differences closed, regarding sex as something between a nuisance and an irrelevance. Yet despite persistent tendencies to use only one sex in a study or, when using both, to omit analysis of possible differences (Carlson, 1971; Dan & Beekman, 1972; Holmes & Jorgensen, 1971), personality and social psychologists have uncovered considerable evidence for the existence of sex differences in social behavior.

Given the recent emergence of sex as a scientifically respectable pursuit, it becomes particularly important to consider these past findings. Integration is necessary now to prevent mere accumulation in the future. It is the intent of this chapter to analyze the past findings of sex differences by means of specified organizing principles; and further, by this analysis, to point out directions where future research might be pursued.

THE STATUS OF SEX AS A PERSONALITY VARIABLE

Before considering the evidence for similarities and differences between the sexes, it is necessary to give some consideration to the status of sex as an individual difference variable. Unlike standard personality variables, sex is (1) descriptive rather than conceptual; (2) dichotomous rather than continuous; and (3) readily identifiable to most observers. Together, these features have important consequences for the subsequent analysis.

Sex as a Descriptive Characteristic

All the other individual difference variables which are considered in this volume are psychological constructs. Investigators have developed a particular concept and have devised measures by which individuals can be categorized as relatively high or low on the dimension in question. Involved in this concept formulation is generally some minitheory that relates the conceptual individual difference variable to a defined range of behaviors which are theoretically meaningful.

In contrast, sex is simply a descriptive label by which the population can be categorized, in a manner similar to birth order, race, or social class. The categorization is physical rather than psychological, though investigators often make implicit and occasionally explicit assumptions about psychological differences between the groups.[1] While one may observe behavioral differences among each of these groups, the conceptual and theoretical links must subsequently be established. We need to move from a statement in the form of "People with big toes act one way and people with small toes act another way" to an understanding of the psychological principles operative in the behavior.

By attending to sex differences, we may find clues to the psychological dimensions which predict behavior. Ultimately, we shall probably find that the variance accounted for by these psychological dimensions is far greater than the variance accounted for by the descriptive characteristics of sex. As such, an analysis of sex differences serves as a directional marker rather than a final destination.

Sex as a Dichotomous Variable

A related issue in undertaking an analysis of sex differences is the fact that sex is dichotomous. People are identified by one of two labels, and a comparison of the two groups is made. While investigators of more standard personality variables may choose this tactic of analysis (such as comparing a group of high achievers to a group of low achievers, with groups defined by a mean or median split), a basic analysis of sex differences has no other alternative. Unless the underlying conceptual variables have a perfect correlation with this dichotomous descriptive variable (an unlikely outcome), we find that our categories are not homogeneous. Indeed, most studies of sex differences find considerable overlap between the two sexes on all response measures of interest. In the subsequent discussion, comparisons of males and females will often be made. However, in each case it is important to remember that we are concerned with relative

[1] Attempts to "psychologize" the sex variable have traditionally relied on some form of masculinity–femininity scale, though both the concept and its measurement have been subject to considerable criticism (Bem, 1974; Constantinople, 1973). Further attention will be given to this issue below.

tendencies rather than nonoverlapping distributions. Once again, the ultimate goal must be the identification of conceptual dimensions rather than an assumption that psychological differences correlate with the dichotomous physical characteristic.

Sex as an Identifiable Feature

A third aspect of sex becomes important when we consider the genesis of sex differences in behavior. Unlike birth order and social class, and unlike more standard personality characteristics, one's sex is an immediately obvious feature (with a statistically small number of exceptions). Not only is sex identifiable to social scientists as a means of categorization, but it is identifiable to everyone in their daily encounters. Because this identification process is quite simple, the development of stereotypes is facilitated. Stereotypes are most pronounced when, as in the case of race and ethnic group, members of the particular group can be readily identified.

There can be little doubt that stereotypes about women and men are rampant (Broverman, Vogel, Broverman, Clarkson, & Rosenkrantz, 1972). Certain characteristics are believed to be typical of men and others typical of women; coincidentally certain tasks and activities are believed to be in the province of one or the other sex.

Furthermore, the identifiability of sex allows a person to establish a set of expectations about a particular individual who is representative of the stereotyped group. Consequently, interactions with a specific individual may be influenced by the stereotypes which are held. Essentially, we are talking about a self-fulfilling prophecy: differences which are believed to exist may be developed and/or perpetuated via the specific interactions which take place. For example, an assumption that a woman is overemotional while a man has tight rein over his feelings can lead to the appointment of only the man to leadership positions thought to require the latter attribute. Given this appointment, an observer sees "proof" that men are naturally dominant while women are content to fill a subservient role.

Because of this identifiability and the related development of stereotypes, it is imperative to consider sex in a social context. An analysis of the differences between women and men must recognize the importance of process and interaction as sources of behavioral differences.

A Framework for the Analysis of Sex Differences

In line with the points made above, the analysis of sex differences in social behavior offered here will attempt to provide a conceptual framework for observed sex differences. Two major principles are suggested, both of which rely on an interplay between person and situation factors.

The first principle is concerned with self-presentation styles of women and men. Basically, it is assumed that men are more likely to adopt a style in which assertion of self and establishment of status are important. In contrast, women adopt a status-neutralizing style from which more affiliative and equalitative behaviors result. Situations become important to the extent that they allow and/or facilitate the emergence of one or both of these presentation strategies.

A second principle is equally important and again underlines the importance of considering both person and situation in any analysis of social behavior. Conceptually, this second factor can be defined as task familiarity. Specifically, we will consider how norms and experience define a range of tasks which are believed to be appropriate for each sex, and how the predictability of behavior increases when the sex of the individual and the particular sex linkage of the task are taken into account.

SELF-PRESENTATION STRATEGIES

The working assumption in the discussion which follows is that many of the differences between women and men can be viewed in terms of self-presentation strategies: divergent choices which are made in presenting oneself and in interacting with others. Basically, the male choice can be characterized as a status assertive mode. In individual behavior, this choice takes the form of asserting high expectancies, presenting a powerful image, and minimizing any show of deficiency. In interaction, the strategy is to assert status and establish some distance between oneself and another. The female choice, in contrast, is proposed to be one with affiliative intent. Rather than assert status, the woman attempts to neutralize status, decrease distance, and establish links with others which are of a more equalitative nature.

This distinction is similar to the agency–communion distinction proposed by Bakan (1966) and elaborated upon by Carlson (1972), though this discussion assumes a conscious development of strategies (Goffman, 1959, 1967) rather than an underlying philosophical difference between the sexes. In appearance the distinction between instrumental and expressive behaviors is also similar, although I personally find fault with the latter terms. "Instrumental" and "expressive" seem to imply a difference in goal orientation: instrumental suggests a concern with goal attainment, while expressive most often connotes a focus on means and a correspondent lack of goal concern. I do not believe that distinction accurately reflects the differences between women and men. While the two strategies may be quite different, it does not follow that goals are less important in one case or even that goals are different (though they may be). Both strategies may, in fact, allow one to gain control but the method of this gain can differ.

These two strategies are not conceptualized as opposite ends of a single dimension. Rather they represent two separate modes of interaction, which both men and women theoretically can choose with greater or lesser frequency. Situations may also be structured so that only one of the strategies is appropriate.

Yet despite the theoretically equal probability of men and women adopting each mode, men and women in Western society are characterized by relatively greater use of the assertive and affiliative strategies respectively. The development of these selective patterns is multidetermined. In this development, the greater average physical size and strength of the male of the species is not unimportant. The belief that greater size means greater status and power has been well documented, and these beliefs generalize to the perceptions of women and men (Osgood, Suci, & Tannenbaum, 1957). Furthermore, we will assume that the strategies are reinforced in socialization as well. While the direct evidence for such socialization differences between women and men is not overwhelmingly strong (Maccoby & Jacklin, 1974), there is considerable evidence that sterotyped presentations of men and women depict clear differences in the assertive–affiliative distinction (McArthur & Resko, 1975; Weitzman, Eifler, Hokada, & Ross, 1972; Women on Words and Images, 1972).

Furthermore, I would argue that the divergent choices of presentation strategies do not become apparent until early adolescence (an area in which research has been more sparse). There are a number of reasons for this delayed development. First, size and appearance differences between males and females begin to diverge sharply at this age. With the advent of puberty, sex roles become more important. As the adolescent attempts to define an identity (Erikson, 1959), the consequences of various strategies are more clearly defined, through the approval of peers as well as parental agents. While developmental investigators have frequently chosen younger age groups in an attempt to ferret out the relative contributions of socialization and heredity, my own hunch is that the adoption of presentation strategies can be studied more profitably from the preteen years on. However, a full discussion of origins must be postponed until the differences themselves have been adequately conceptualized.

While the distinction is somewhat artificial, the self-presentation strategies of men and women can be considered in two forms: individual and interactional. Clearly the presence of an observing experimenter generally precludes a truly individual situation. In this, as in most other instances, the individual (subject) is aware of presenting an impression which will be interpreted by someone else. However, because this situation does not involve extensive interaction, there is some value in considering individual presentation behaviors separately from more active interpersonal encounters.

Individual Presentation Strategies

As a general rule, men present an image of themselves as accomplished, powerful, and competent, in keeping with a strategy of self-assertiveness. Women, in contrast, are less likely to adopt this assertive strategy, choosing instead to present themselves as more typical in performance, less competent, and less likely to excel relative to men. When possible, women will instead emphasize affiliative and equalitative concerns.

Performance expectancy and evaluation. Studies concerned with the prediction and evaluation of performance are heavily loaded toward an assertive strategy. In these areas we find a consistent tendency for men to predict a better performance for themselves than do women (Crandall, 1969; Deaux & Farris, 1977; Montanelli & Hill, 1969). Furthermore, available evidence suggests that both sexes err in their estimates: men overestimate their performance and women underestimate theirs (Crandall, 1969; Deaux & Farris, 1977). Specific task characteristics may modify these expectancies, though in the main the higher male expectancy persists.

When women and men are asked to evaluate a performance upon its completion, similar biases are in evidence. Men consistently judge their performance more favorably than do women (Deaux & Farris, 1977; Deaux, White, & Farris, 1975). Furthermore, when men and women are asked to attribute the reasons for their success or failure, similar differences in self-enhancement are found. Consistent with initial expectancies men will attribute their success to ability, while denying responsibility for their failure. Women are more prone to accept lack of ability as a valid reason for their failure, while choosing less self-enhancing reasons (such as luck) for their success (Deaux, 1976b).

Self esteem. Measures of general self-esteem show no substantial differences between women and men (Maccoby & Jacklin, 1974). At first glance, this lack of a difference may seem somewhat surprising, in that men tend to be more self-enhancing in their performance predictions and subsequent evaluations. However, most measures of self-concept contain a variety of items, only some of which tap an assertiveness dimension. Other items reflect a general acceptance of oneself. One possibility which remains to be tested is that subanalyses of self-esteem scales may reveal sex differences: men should show higher scores on those items that tap the assertive dimension; while women should score higher on items reflecting acceptance (Deaux, 1976a).

Evidence for two different patterns of self-presentation being reflected in the self-concept is reported by Maccoby and Jacklin (1974). Measures of self-concept which stress potency and power show males to be consistently higher than females. In contrast, measures of self which reflect a social–personal orientation indicate that women view themselves more positively on this dimension. These differences underline the point made earlier. To the extent that the situation (or the particular instrument) limits responses along one of the two specified dimensions, sex differences will be apparent. In contrast, a situation (or instrument) which allows both strategies to be expressed may reveal similar outcomes which have developed from different strategies.

Interaction Strategies

While the differences between women and men are evidenced in individual presentation strategies, interaction settings show the differences much more strongly. In these instances, strategies of self-presentation are actively developed and used. As a general rule, interaction situations find men attempting to assert status and establish dominance, essentially creating a distance between themselves and an other. Women, on the other hand, show a preference for more affiliative relationships in which status is minimized and equality is sought. Phrased in another way, we can look at the male pattern as a vertical one, in which a pecking order is established, while the female pattern is horizontal in nature, creating links rather than ladders. These two quite different strategies are apparent across a wide variety of social behaviors.

Nonverbal behavior. Investigators who have analyzed filmed and live sequences of human interaction in terms of nonverbal communication patterns have found three distinct factors which appear across a variety of nonverbal modalities (Mehrabian, 1971, 1972). Two of these factors also show sharp differences between the sexes: specifically, the status-dominance factor and the affiliation–evaluation factor. (A third factor of activity has not shown any consistent sex differences.)

Nonverbal behavior is a fascinating but difficult area of observation, in part because a similar gesture may be serving two quite different purposes. For example, eye contact may be used to affiliate and to intensify a mutual attraction; on other occasions, eye contact by means of a stare or sudden fixation may serve to establish distance and dominance. Touching can be viewed in the same terms. A touch may serve to establish dominance (Henley, 1973a, b) or it may indicate an affiliative approach. Thus our distinctions between men and women cannot be phrased wholly in terms of quantitative differences in the use of a particular nonverbal form; qualitative differences within modalities must be considered as well. As a general statement, we can say that men tend to use those forms of nonverbal behavior which maintain distance or assert status between themselves and another. Women, in contrast, tend to minimize distance and increase affiliation in their use of nonverbal language.

Let us briefly consider the evidence which supports these distinctions. In distancing behavior, men show a preference for greater space between themselves and another person than do women (Argyle & Dean, 1965; Evans & Howard, 1973; Exline, 1971). Women also report being more uncomfortable in the absence of eye contact, while men show some preference for nonvisual interaction (Argyle, Lalljee, & Cook, 1968). In these discussion situations, eye contact is primarily being used as an affiliative tool. However, eye contact also can indicate anger (Ekman, 1971) or a signal for flight (Ellsworth, Carlsmith, & Henson, 1972). Indeed, subjects will reliably interpret an extended gaze as a sign of dominance (Thayer, 1969). Although no solid research evidence is available, I would expect that this particular form of eye contact would be used more frequently by males than females.

Touching is a third form of nonverbal communication in which extensive sex differences are found. In general, men touch more often but women are touched more often. As Henley (1973a, b) has pointed out, patterns of touching behavior frequently parallel dominance patterns. Thus the male's more frequent initiation of touch towards a woman can be interpreted as an exertion of status or dominance. While insufficient research has been done on the use of touch in same-sex dyads, these contacts may well reflect similar differences in the perception of the meaning of touch. Women appear to be allowed more intimate physical exchange in society in the United States, for example in hugging goodbye, whereas males tend to confine themselves to a handshake. Interestingly, the instances in which we observe close male contact, as in organized sports, are also cases where status needs may be exerted in competition with an opposing team, thus allowing more intimacy with one's own teammates.

In this, as in many other areas of research, the cross-cultural generality of the findings needs to be explored. However, the differences seem to be less pronounced in many other cultures, pointing to the importance of socialization in any analysis of differences between women and men.

In summary, there is considerable evidence in the nonverbal literature that men and women are opting for different modes of interaction. Men use touch, eye contact, and distancing to assert and maintain status and ascendence; women use these modes in a different manner, to connect and to affiliate.

Verbal interchange. Other areas of research also show different patterns of male and female behavior which are consistent with an assertive–affiliative distinction. Self-disclosure research, for example, generally shows that women are more willing to reveal information about themselves than are men (Cozby, 1973; Jourard, 1964; Jourard & Lasakow, 1958). These differences are apparent in both quantitative and qualitative measures, and in both initiation and response. Women initiate more intimate questions with a partner and respond with more personal information about themselves, though men in some instances believe that they have been more personal (Sermat & Smyth, 1973). In further support of the affiliative differences, women report feeling more similar to their partner following a self-disclosure session while men perceive less compatibility. It is possible that these perceptions of similarity reflect the differing intents of men and women, with women seeking a smaller distance between themselves and others than do men.

Most analysis of self-disclosure has been based on a single scale of intimacy, wherein topics are prescaled according to group ratings. It would be interesting to conduct finer analyses on the content of disclosures, considering both an assertive dimension and an affiliative dimension. We might predict that the content of men's disclosures would tend to reflect a greater concern with asserting status, while women would be more prone to gear their disclosure toward affiliative themes, despite possibly equivalent levels of intimacy.

In normal conversation, differences between women and men are also apparent. For example, consistent with a status-assertiveness premise, men are more likely to initiate topics and to interrupt when someone else is speaking (Thorne & Henley, 1973). Qualitative analyses of group discussions show a similar divergence between the sexes. Men are more likely to offer opinions, give suggestions, give information, and disagree (Piliavin & Martin, 1974; Strodtbeck & Mann, 1956). Each of these behaviors can be interpreted as an exertion of status. Women, in contrast, show more behaviors which can be interpreted as attempts at bridging distance and creating a greater bond (a mode which has in other contexts been termed "expressive"). Such behaviors include agreeing, seeming friendly, and asking for information and opinions. Once again, we find an apparent difference in strategy and intent as women and men interact with others.

Coalition formation and bargaining. If self-presentation strategies differ for women and men, then differences would be expected in situations which stress bargaining and competition tactics. Unfortunately, the vast majority of studies in this area have relied on the Prisoner's Dilemma paradigm, and separation of motives in this paradigm is difficult under the best of circumstances (Nemeth, 1973). Furthermore, since subjects are frequently unclear about the consequence of various choices, strategies cannot be actively executed. Some evidence within this paradigm does suggest, however, that women are responding more to the interpersonal aspects of these games, while men are more concerned with winning. Women will, for example, show more alteration in their play as a function of partner characteristics (Kahn, Hottes, & Davis, 1971), and will utilize breaks in the playing periods to discuss interpersonal rather than game-oriented topics (Hottes & Kahn, 1974).

More direct evidence of differing strategies can be found in studies of coalition formation (Bond & Vinacke, 1961; Vinacke, 1959). In the typical Vinacke situation, three players have the opportunity to form various alliances which will facilitate their winning the game more easily. Men show a fairly consistent pattern of allying with another member in order to triumph over a third, and consequently, weaker member. Women, in contrast, generally attempt to form coalitions which involve all members. It is important to note that this more inclusive strategy by women is not less effective in terms of monetary payoff (Bond & Vinacke, 1961). Women in fact win as much or more on the average than do men who choose the more competitive strategy, underlining the earlier point that different strategies may be equally instrumental in goal attainment.

In a related vein, studies of larger group behavior have often focused on the emergence of group leaders. As leadership is clearly an assertion of status, it should come as no surprise that emergent leaders are typically male (Megargee, 1969; Strodtbeck & Mann, 1956).

Still another form of bargaining behavior where sex differences are apparent is reward allocation. In the main, studies of reward allocation derive from an equity model (Adams, 1965), which suggests that rewards or outcomes should be proportional to input. Consistent with an interpretation of sex differences as selected strategies, men and women do not differ in their adherence to the equity norm when judging hypothetical situations (Wicker & Bushweiler, 1970). However, when the male or female is engaged in actual interaction with another person, evidence of differences in presentation strategies emerges. In general, men take a greater share of the reward for themselves than do women, in accord with their greater concern with asserting status (Lane & Messé, 1971; Leventhal & Anderson, 1970; Leventhal & Lane, 1970). In contrast, women show a reluctance to claim advantage over a partner, even though that partner has previously claimed a greater-than-deserved share of the reward (Kahn, 1972). It seems quite probable that reward allocation studies present opportunities for both assertive and affiliative strategies, and future research in this area could be directed at the various goals which specific responses may be serving.

Aggression. At least a brief mention should be given to aggression. Of all social behaviors, aggression shows the most pronounced and consistent sex differences (Maccoby & Jacklin, 1974). There seems to be little doubt that aggression can be viewed as a means of asserting status, both in animal and human contexts, and thus this evidence is quite consistent with the previous analysis. While studies of initiated aggression point quite clearly to male predominance, two points should be made which stress the choice of aggression as a presentation strategy rather than an automatic response. First of all, there is evidence suggesting that women may easily learn aggressive behavior in a modeling situation, but simply choose not to enact the learned behavior (Bandura, 1965). Secondly, studies which have included conditions in which another person directly aggresses against the subject frequently find the woman equally willing to retaliate (Harris, 1973, 1974; Taylor & Epstein, 1967). These lines of evidence support the assumption that men and women typically choose different strategies despite an ability to pursue either one; and further that situational pressures, such as direct attack, may minimize the differences in the choices of women and men.

SEX-LINKED TASK CHARACTERISTICS

The assertive–affiliative distinction can account for a wide variety of sex differences in social behavior, particularly when the person dimension is considered in conjunction with situational allowances. However, not all of the observed sex differences can be explained within this framework. It is also necessary to consider a second type of person–situation interaction: the sex linkage of tasks.

The relationship between sex linkage of tasks and the behavior of women and men is a simple familiarity proposition. In areas or tasks which are masculine in association, males should make stronger, more frequent, and more confident behavior choices than women. Conversely, in areas associated with women, women should excel over men. Such an assumption requires some basis for defining the masculinity or femininity of a task. The casual approach is simply to make assumptions about areas of greater familiarity to men and women. A more systematic approach is to prescale situations on their perceived masculinity or femininity by the population which is to be sampled. A third method is for the experimenter to arbitrarily label a task as masculine or feminine, with the assumption that experimental subjects will assume greater familiarity with one or the other task. Unfortunately, possible sex linkage of tasks has been an infrequent concern in research, and this analysis must rely primarily on assumption. One should note that the generalizability of these labels may be limited to the particular population in question. There is no reason to assume, for example, that a task considered masculine in our society will be perceived in the same light in another society. Such variations across cultures point to the necessity of prescaling situations with each population of interest in order to make valid predictions of outcome.

While the concept of sex-linked task familiarity is a simple one, the quantity of evidence is persuasive in attributing it considerable importance. Evidence for sex-linked task properties can be found in many areas of social behavior: conformity, altruism, performance expectancies, and achievement behavior (in particular, fear of success tendencies). Let us consider each of these areas in turn.

Conformity. Conformity is a classic instance of a behavior which was originally considered to be a standard personality difference between the sexes, but which in recent light appears to be much more situationally dependent. Although the historic attitude change program of the Yale school is often cited as evidence that women are more persuasible than men are (Janis & Field, 1959), more careful analysis of the total body of literature shows no consistent main effects (Eagly, 1976). Similarly, despite the pervasive assumption that women conform more than men, the evidence to date suggests a much more limited conclusion (Eagly, 1976).

In large part, sex differences in conformity can be related to the task, as shown by Sistrunk and McDavid (1971). To demonstrate this situational link, Sistrunk and McDavid prescaled a large number of issues on a dimension of masculinity–femininity. In the actual conformity test, the authors selected an equal number of items which were judged to be more familiar to men, more familiar to women, or equally familiar to both sexes. The results clearly showed that conformity was directly related to task familiarity. Men conformed more on feminine items than did women or than did men on either masculine or neutral items, and women conformed more on masculine items than they did on either feminine or neutral items. Such evidence is clear testimony to the importance of task characteristics in conclusions about sex differences.

Presumably, we could scale all possible tasks which have been used in conformity and opinion change studies and be able to predict sex differences in conformity as a function of the polarization of the task. In this light, it has been suggested (Sistrunk & McDavid, 1971) that the many earlier studies may have used spatial tasks which are more familiar to men, a suggestion which would be in line with the findings that men generally excel on tasks requiring visual–spatial skill (Maccoby & Jacklin, 1974). Finding that conformity relates to task familiarity does not require us to say that, on an absolute basis, there will be no differences between men and women in conformity. If men are familiar with a greater number of issues than women, then we could still anticipate more overall conformity by women. Yet it is important to stress that the interaction between person and situation, rather than the person per se, is the source of the difference.

Altruism. The influence of sex-linked task characteristics can also be seen in studies of altruism. In this instance, a conclusion that one or the other sex is more prone to lend help has been less pronounced (Deaux, 1976a; Maccoby & Jacklin, 1974). Yet in the midst of this seeming equality, there is considerable evidence that sex-linked task characteristics strongly influence the proportion of men and women willing to help.

Several years ago (Deaux, 1972), I suggested that helping studies could be classified into one of two types: intervention, in which the potential helper must take the initiative to offer help; and respondent, in which the helper is replying to a direct request for help. At that time I concluded that intervention situations were likely to elicit greater male help, while respondent situations would be influenced by sex-linked task characteristics. However, additional consideration has suggested that both types of help are substantially determined by task characteristics. While studies of intervention have more often shown greater male helping (e.g., Piliavin, Rodin, & Piliavin, 1969), these same studies generally focus on situations with which men might be more familiar or capable, such as changing tires on the highway (e.g., Bryan & Test, 1967; Pomazal & Clore, 1973). Other intervention situations which are more neutral in character, such as picking up a lost letter (Gross, 1972) or reporting a shoplifting (Latané & Darley, 1970) typically find no sex differences. Studies of respondent help show the same patterns of influence by task characteristics.

While in these earlier studies one can only infer that the task is masculine in its linkage, a more recent study has directly tested the assumption that characteristics of the task will affect relative proportions of helping behavior. Primmer,

Jaccard, Cohen, Wasserman, and Hoffing (1974) arranged for strangers to approach shoppers waiting in the checkout line of a drug store and to request that the shopper purchase either a depilatory (feminine item) or chewing tobacco (masculine item) with money the stranger provided. The results of this study clearly support the argument that characteristics of the task interact with the sex of the potential helper in determining frequency of altruistic behavior. A request to purchase a depilatory resulted in 80% agreement from female shoppers, and only 65% from male shoppers; conversely, the chewing tobacco request resulted in help from 90% of the male shoppers and 60% of the female shoppers. The sex of the individual making the request had little effect on altruistic responses.

In summary, to the extent that we can classify a task as either masculine or feminine in its orientation, we have a basis for predicting greater help by that sex which is more familiar with the task. On neutral tasks, in contrast, we should expect to find no difference.

Performance expectancy. In an earlier section, evidence was presented to show the tendency for males to estimate higher levels of performance for themselves than do females, consistent with men's greater use of assertive strategies. Within this general trend, however, there is some evidence that the specific labeling of a task as masculine or feminine can alter these expectancies (Deaux & Farris, 1977; Stein, Pohly, & Mueller, 1971). Tasks labeled or believed to be feminine will elicit higher expectancies from women than tasks labeled masculine; the converse is true for men.

Achievement and fear of success. A final area in which the influence of task-linked characteristics can be seen is the recent literature on fear of success. Within the earlier literature on standard achievement behavior, sex differences were also apparent, and while this area is too extensive to be fully covered here (cf. Atkinson & Feather, 1966; Atkinson & Raynor, 1974; McClelland, Atkinson, Clark, & Lowell, 1953; and the chapter by Atkinson in this volume) a few brief comments are appropriate. The early finding that women do not react to achievement-arousing instructions in the same degree that men do has been explained in two ways. One explanation relies on two different motives, achievement for men and affiliation for women, which is similar to our distinction between assertive and affiliative strategies. Alternatively, it has been suggested that men and women do not differ in their achievement needs per se, but rather only in the areas in which achievement behavior is displayed. Such a proposition is clearly consistent with the present analysis of sex-linked task characteristics and their influence on male and female performance. While the evidence on these points is not conclusive (cf. Stein & Bailey, 1973, for a fuller discussion of the issues), task characteristics must remain a strong contender.

More direct evidence for the importance of task characteristics is seen in the recent investigations of fear of success. By this time, most readers are undoubtedly familiar with the concept of fear of success posited by Horner (1968, 1972). According to Horner, fear of success is a motive thought to be more prevalent in women than in men, and one which impedes progress toward a goal as suggested by the original achievement formulation. Later writers have, however, questioned several aspects of fear of success, including its status as a motive (Alper, 1974; Feather & Raphelson, 1974; Monahan, Kuhn & Shaver, 1974).

The most direct evidence that expressions of fear of success are highly dependent on task characteristics is found in a recent study by Cherry and Deaux (1975). These authors used both the familiar leads of John and Anne in medical school, and in addition, leads concerning a hypothetical John or Anne in nursing school. The results clearly supported the interpretation that fear of success represents a fear of the consequences of success, and that for both men and women such consequences are perceived as highly negative when the success occurs in an out-of-role situation, as when John succeeds in nursing school or when Anne succeeds in medical school. Percentages of fear of success stories in this study were 40% for males responding to John in medical school and 63% to John in nursing school. For women the percentages were 50% for Anne in medical school and 13% for Anne in nursing school. This study clearly demonstrates that a hypothesized motive, postulated to differentiate between men and women, is in fact directly influenced by sex-linked characteristics in the particular situation.

Summarizing the above, there is evidence in a number of areas of social behavior – conformity, altruism, performance expectancies, and fear of success and achievement – that the specific patterns of men and women are not all-pervasive. Instead, characteristics of the task should be carefully analyzed for possible sex-linked connotations which may modify the responses of the subject.

SEX DIFFERENCES: WHEN, WHERE, AND WHY?

In the preceding pages, the literature on sex differences has been considered in terms of two general principles. With these classification tools, a vast proportion of the literature appears to fall into line. In this concluding section, I would like to underline the general issues which have emerged, as well as to comment on some of the unresolved issues in the study of sex differences.

1. *Analyses of person factors and situation factors are interdependent processes.* Historically, discussions of sex differences have attempted to delineate a set of characteristics which will consistently differentiate men and women. Thus, in summary articles (Garai & Scheinfeld, 1968; Terman & Tyler, 1954) we find essentially a categorization of differences between the sexes. Such a pattern of analysis has been evident with more standard personality variables as well. This earlier belief that personality and individual difference variables could provide a

full explanation of human behavior has been submerged by the situational perspective on human behavior (e.g., Mischel, 1968). While the controversy between traitism and situationism continues to flurry (Bowers, 1973), it would appear that our study of human behavior is now ready to accede to the value of each of these approaches as necessary complements. As pointed out many years ago (Sherif & Sherif, 1956), the relative influence of personality and situation variables will depend on the clarity of the situation. In a highly amorphous situation, we may expect personality differences, or variations in choices of strategies, to emerge more clearly. In contrast, the heavily structured situation typically used by the social psychologist is less conducive to the emergence of individual differences.

The validity of this proposition is seen clearly in an analysis of sex difference research. In both of the organizing principles used here, situation and personality interact. In the one instance, we find that situations may differ in the extent to which assertive and affiliative strategies are possible. In situations where only one or the other strategy is feasible, we may find men and women differing on a quantitative basis. In contrast, situations which provide both possible actions will show qualitative differences in behavior.

The second organizing principle relies equally heavily on both person and situation factors. By assessing the familiarity of the person with the particular task, far greater variance is explained than either of the simple main effects could handle. In sex differences, as in many other personality variables, the interaction term becomes primary in importance.

2. *Sex differences will be minimal when self-presentation is not at issue and when differential familiarity with the task cannot be established.* Because this analysis of sex differences in social behavior has relied on self-presentational strategies, a number of assumptions can be derived as to when sex differences will not be found. One general rule of thumb is that the less "social" the situation, the less likely sex differences are to emerge (assuming neutrality of the task). Thus in investigations of impression formation, cognitive balance and consistency, and many types of problem solving, we find little evidence of sex differences. These situations are essentially abstract: the individual is focused not on the presentation of self but on completion of a task. Sex differences may well emerge if the subject is asked either to predict or evaluate the performance; but the performance itself should not show consistent differences.

Another possible derivation is that sex differences should be most apparent in the initial stages of an encounter, and may diminish over time. In a sense I am suggesting that once the initial image is established, other alternatives can be tried. Studies of marriage relationships would offer an interesting test of this assumption. Nguyen, Nguyen, and Heslin (1974), for example, found that married women perceived touch as a means of asserting status whereas unmarried women reacted only on an affiliative dimension. Similarly, we might suspect that in a relationship of some duration, women would develop more assertive behaviors, would be willing to claim more competence, and the like. Men, in contrast, could be expected to be more willing to self-disclose and to relax their assertions of status.

A third conclusion is that to the extent the stereotypes are altered and sex-role-appropriate behavior is less stringently defined, sex differences will also subside. While task familiarity will continue to be a predictor variable, covariation with sex may not continue.

3. *The relationship between sex as a descriptive variable and masculinity–femininity as a personality variable is tenuous.* Classically, investigators who recognized the nonpsychological nature of sex as a variable attempted to make a translation through formulation of various masculinity–femininity scales. However, such scales have recently come under fire on a number of counts (Bem, 1974; Constantinople, 1973). Predominant among the criticisms are the assumptions that masculinity and femininity are bipolar opposites and that they can be represented on a single dimension. Various conceptions are now being proposed which separate the two dimensions, viewing masculinity and femininity as two distinct patterns of behavior (Bem, 1974, 1975; Spence, Helmreich, & Stapp, 1975).

Although the recognition that masculinity and femininity are separate dimensions is a promising advance, there may be a continuing error in assuming that either of these two concepts is unitary in its meaning. As has been argued, both choices of strategy and task familiarity can account for considerable variation in the behavior of the sexes. However, these two dimensions do not necessarily covary. An individual may be assertive, yet be more familiar with traditionally "feminine" tasks, and vice versa. Personality scales or experimental designs which assume equivalence of these two factors may be less productive than an approach which considers the two factors as separate predictors of behavior. As an example, to the extent that a masculinity scale measures assertive strategies, one should be able to use this scale to predict an individual's behavior in a situation such as group discussion which allows assertive behavior. I suspect, however, that forecasting ability would be much less accurate if the same scale were used to predict interest in fixing cars or playing football.

Beyond this need for reconceptualization, it may also be reasonable to consider dropping the terms masculinity and femininity altogether. If the major personality dimension involved in masculinity is a status assertiveness, and the major factor in femininity is affiliation, then why not use the latter terms? Masculinity and femininity have been overburdened with meaning in the past, and semantics as well as scientific understanding might be advanced by using the more parsimonious terms.

4. *The issue of cross-cultural generality.* The above point regarding the separation of personality and task conceptions of masculinity and femininity has implications for cross-cultural issues as well. Our knowledge of the generality of

sex differences across societies is rather rudimentary. While some evidence has suggested that traits such as dominance and aggression have a wide degree of generality, other evidence points equally persuasively to the influence of situational demands on the development of sex differences (Barry, Bacon, & Child, 1957; Whiting & Edwards, 1973). It was suggested earlier that differences in status assertiveness stem in part from the simple physical differences between women and men. If this is true, then studies across cultures should show high generality in this domain.

In contrast, the portion of variance which can be attributed to task familiarity might be expected to vary widely, depending on the particular customs and socialization patterns of the society in question. We cannot expect any great generality in this regard: each society must be studied individually in order to determine sex-linked task assignments.

It is worth noting that the relative value of males and females in a society may be free to vary, despite some constancy in self-presentation strategies. Thus that society which places a premium on horizontal relationships may show a relatively higher status for women than the more vertically inclined society. These issues are complex ones, and work is only beginning to pursue the questions involved.

In many respects, our understanding of sex differences is embryonic. The recognition of sex as an important variable, and the attention of investigators to potential differences, is indeed a breakthrough. The next moves must be in the direction of firmly establishing the basis of divergences, and delving into the factors which determine those varying behaviors. Such a program of research cannot be limited to a single society. Though much of our present data is rather parochial, one would hope to see a broader cross-cultural investigation of the relative influences of sex and situation in patterns of human behavior.

ACKNOWLEDGMENTS

I am grateful to Frances Cherry, Elizabeth Farris, and Brenda Major for their ideas and conversations which contributed to this chapter.

REFERENCES

Adams, J. S. Inequity in social exchange. In L. Berkowitz (Ed.), *Advances in experimental social psychology* (Vol. 2). New York: Academic Press, 1965.

Alper, T. G. Achievement motivation in college women: A now-you-see-it-now-you-don't phenomenon. *American Psychologist,* 1974, *29,* 194–203.

Argyle, M., & Dean, J. Eye contact, distance and affiliation. *Sociometry,* 1965, *28,* 289–304.

Argyle, M., Lalljee, M., & Cook, M. The effects of visibility on interaction in a dyad. *Human Relations,* 1968, *21,* 3–17.

Atkinson, J. W., & Feather, N. T. (Eds.). *A theory of achievement motivation.* New York: Wiley, 1966.

Atkinson, J. W., & Raynor, J. O. (Eds.). *Motivation and achievement.* Washington, D.C.: Winston, 1974.

Bakan, D. *The duality of human existence.* Chicago: Rand McNally, 1966.

Bandura, A. Influence of model's reinforcement contingencies on the acquisition of imitative responses. *Journal of Personality and Social Psychology,* 1965, *1,* 589–595.

Barry, H. III, Bacon, M. K., & Child, I. L. A cross-cultural survey of some differences in socialization. *Journal of Abnormal and Social Psychology,* 1957, *55,* 327–332.

Bem, S. L. The measurement of psychological androgyny. *Journal of Consulting and Clinical Psychology,* 1974, *42,* 155–162.

Bem, S. L. Sex-role adaptability: One consequence of psychological androgyny. *Journal of Personality and Social Psychology,* 1975, *31,* 634–643.

Bond, J. R., & Vinacke, W. E. Coalitions in mixed-sex triads. *Sociometry,* 1961, *24,* 61–75.

Bowers, K. S. Situationism in psychology: An analysis and a critique. *Psychological Review,* 1973, *80,* 307–336.

Broverman, I. K., Vogel, S. R., Broverman, D. M., Clarkson, F. E., & Rosenkrantz, P. S. Sex-role stereotypes: A current appraisal. *Journal of Social Issues,* 1972, *28,*(2), 59–78.

Bryan, J. H., & Test, M. A. Models and helping: Naturalistic studies in aiding behavior. *Journal of Personality and Social Psychology,* 1967, *6,* 400–407.

Carlson, R. Where is the person in personality research? *Psychological Bulletin,* 1971, *75,* 203–219.

Carlson, R. Understanding women: Implications for personality theory and research. *Journal of Social Issues,* 1972, *28*(2), 17–32.

Cherry, F., & Deaux, K. Fear of success vs. fear of gender-inconsistent behavior. A sex similarity. Paper presented at the meeting of the Midwestern Psychological Association. Chicago, May 1975.

Constantinople, A. Masculinity–femininity: An exception to a famous dictum? *Psychological Bulletin,* 1973, *80,* 389–407.

Cozby, P. C. Self-disclosure: A literature review. *Psychological Bulletin, 1973, 79,* 73–91.

Crandall, V. C. Sex differences in expectancy of intellectual and academic reinforcement. In C. P. Smith (Ed.), *Achievement-related motives in children.* New York: Russell Sage, 1969.

Dan, A. J., & Beekman, S. Male versus female representation in psychological research. *American Psychologist,* 1972, *27,* 1078.

Deaux, K. Sex and helping: Expectations and attributions. Paper presented at the meeting of the American Psychological Association, Honolulu, September 1972.

Deaux, K. *The behavior of women and men.* Monterey, Cal.: Brooks/Cole, 1976 (a)

Deaux, K. Sex: A perspective on the attribution process. In J. H. Harvey, W. J. Ickes, & R. F. Kidd (Eds.). *New directions in attribution research.* Hillsdale, N.J.: Erlbaum, 1976. (b)

Deaux, K., and Farris E. Attributing causes for one's performance: The effects of sex, norms, and outcome. *Journal of Research in Personality,* 1977, in press.

Deaux, K., White, L., & Farris, E. Skill versus luck: Field and laboratory studies of male and female preferences. *Journal of Personality and Social Psychology,* 1975, *32,* 629–636.

Eagly, A. H. Sex differences in influenceability. Unpublished manuscript, University of Massachusetts. 1976.

Ekman, P. Universals and cultural differences in facial expressions of emotion. In J. K. Cole

(Ed.), *Nebraska Symposium on Motivation* (Vol. 19). Lincoln: University of Nebraska Press, 1971.

Ellsworth, P. C., Carlsmith, J. M., & Henson, A. The stare as a stimulus to flight in human subjects: A series of field experiments. *Journal of Personality and Social Psychology,* 1972, *21,* 302–311.

Erikson, E. Identity and the life cycle. *Psychological Issues,* 1959, *1,* 1–71.

Evans, G. W., & Howard, R. B. Personal space. *Psychological Bulletin,* 1973, *80,* 334–344.

Exline, R. Visual interaction: The glances of power and preference. In J. K. Cole (Ed.), *Nebraska Symposium on Motivation* (Vol. 19). Lincoln: University of Nebraska Press, 1971.

Feather, N. T., & Raphelson, A. C. Fear of success in Australian and American student groups: Motive or sex-role stereotype? *Journal of Personality,* 1974, *42,* 190–201.

Garai, J. E., & Scheinfeld, A. Sex differences in mental and behavioral traits. *Genetic Psychology Monographs,* 1968, *77,* 169–299.

Goffman, E. *The presentation of self in everyday life.* Garden City, N.Y.: Doubleday Anchor, 1959.

Goffman, E. *Interaction ritual.* Garden City, N.Y.: Doubleday Anchor, 1967.

Gross, A. E. Sex and helping: Intrinsic glow and extrinsic show. Paper presented at the meeting of the American Psychological Association, Honolulu, September 1972.

Harris, M. B. Field studies of modeled aggression. *Journal of Social Psychology,* 1973, *89,* 131–139.

Harris, M. B. Mediators between frustration and aggression in a field experiment. *Journal of Experimental Social Psychology,* 1974, *10,* 561–571.

Henley, N. M. The politics of touch. In P. Brown (Ed.), *Radical psychology.* New York: Harper & Row, 1973. (a)

Henley, N. M. Status and sex: Some touching observations. *Bulletin of the Psychonomic Society,* 1973, *2,* 91–93. (b)

Holmes, D. S., & Jorgensen, B. W. Do personality and social psychologists study men more than women? *Representative Research in Social Psychology,* 1971, *2,* 71–76.

Horner, M. Sex differences in achievement motivation and performance in competitive and noncompetitive situations. Unpublished doctoral dissertation, University of Michigan, 1968.

Horner, M. S. Toward an understanding of achievement-related conflicts in women. *Journal of Social Issues,* 1972, *28*(2), 157–176.

Hottes, J. H., & Kahn, A. Sex differences in a mixed-motive conflict situation. *Journal of Personality,* 1974, *42,* 260–275.

Janis, I. L., & Field, P. B. Sex differences and personality factors related to persuasibility. In I. L. Janis & C. I. Hovland (Eds.), *Personality and persuasibility.* New Haven: Yale University Press, 1959.

Jourard, S. M. *The transparent self.* Princeton, N.J.: Van Nostrand, 1964.

Jourard, S. M., & Lasakow, P. Some factors in self-disclosure. *Journal of Abnormal and Social Psychology,* 1958, *56,* 91–98.

Kahn, A. Reactions to generosity or stinginess from an intelligent or stupid work partner: A test of equity in a direct exchange relationship. *Journal of Personality and Social Psychology,* 1972, *21,* 117–123.

Kahn, A., Hottes, J., & Davis, W. L. Cooperation and optimal responding in the Prisoner's Dilemma game: Effects of sex and physical attractiveness. *Journal of Personality and Social Psychology,* 1971, *17,* 267–279.

Lane, I. M., & Messé, L. Equity and distribution of rewards. *Journal of Personality and Social Psychology,* 1971, *20,* 1–17.

Latané B., & Darley, J. M. *The unresponsive bystander: Why doesn't he help?* New York: Appleton-Century-Crofts, 1970.

Leventhal, G. S., & Anderson, D. Self-interest and maintenance of equity. *Journal of Personality and Social Psychology,* 1970, *15,* 57–62.

Leventhal, G. S., & Lane, D. W. Sex, age, and equity behavior. *Journal of Personality and Social Psychology,* 1970, *15,* 312–316.

Maccoby, E. E. (Ed.). *The development of sex differences.* Stanford, Cal.: Stanford University Press, 1966.

Maccoby, E. E., & Jacklin, C. N. *The psychology of sex differences.* Stanford, Cal.: Stanford University Press, 1974.

McArthur, L. Z., & Resko, B. G. The portrayal of men and women in American television commercials. *Journal of Social Psychology,* 1975, *97,* 209–220.

McClelland, D. C., Atkinson, J. W., Clark, R. A., & Lowell, E. L. *The achievement motive.* New York: Appleton-Century-Crofts, 1953.

Megargee, E. Influence of sex roles on the manifestation of leadership. *Journal of Applied Psychology,* 1969, *53,* 377–382.

Mehrabian, A. Nonverbal communication. In J. K. Cole (Ed.), *Nebraska Symposium on motivation* (Vol. 19) Lincoln: University of Nebraska Press, 1971.

Mehrabian, A. *Nonverbal communication.* Chicago: Aldine-Atherton, 1972.

Mischel, W. *Personality and assessment.* New York: Wiley, 1968.

Monahan, L., Kuhn, D., & Shaver, P. Intrapsychic versus cultural explanations of the "Fear of Success" motive. *Journal of Personality and Social Psychology,* 1974, *29,* 60–64.

Montanelli, D. S., & Hill, K. T. Children's achievement expectations and performance as a function of two consecutive reinforcement experiences, sex of subject, and sex of experimenter. *Journal of Personality and Social Psychology,* 1969, *13,* 115–128.

Nemeth, C. A critical analysis of research utilizing the Prisoner's Dilemma paradigm for the study of bargaining. In L. Berkowitz (Ed.), *Advances in experimental social psychology* (Vol. 6). New York: Academic Press, 1973.

Nguyen, M. L., Nguyen, T. D., & Heslin, R. The meaning of touch as a function of sex and marital status. Unpublished manuscript, Purdue University, 1974.

Osgood, C. E., Suci, G. J., & Tannenbaum, P. H. *The measurement of meaning.* Urbana: University of Illinois Press, 1957.

Piliavin, J. A., & Martin, R. R. The effects of the sex composition of groups on style of social interaction. Unpublished manuscript, University of Wisconsin, 1974.

Piliavin, I. M., Rodin, J., & Piliavin, J. A. Good Samaritanism: An underground phenomenon? *Journal of Personality and Social Psychology,* 1969, *13,* 289–299.

Pomazal, R. J., & Clore, G. L. Helping on the highway: The effects of dependency and sex. *Journal of Applied Social Psychology,* 1973, *3,* 150–164.

Primmer, C., Jaccard, J., Cohen, J. L., Wasserman, J., & Hoffing, A. The influence of the sex-appropriateness of a task on helping behavior in the laboratory and the field. Unpublished manuscript, University of Illinois, 1974.

Sermat, V., & Smyth, M. Content analysis of verbal communication in the development of a relationship: Conditions influencing self-disclosure. *Journal of Personality and Social Psychology,* 1973, *26,* 332–346.

Sherif, M., & Sherif, C. W. *Social psychology.* New York: Harper & Row, 1956.

Sistrunk, F., & McDavid, J. W. Sex variable in conforming behavior. *Journal of Personality and Social Psychology,* 1971, *17,* 200–207.

Spence, J. T., Helmreich, R., & Stapp, J. Ratings of self and peers on sex-role attributes and their relation to self-esteem and conceptions of masculinity and femininity. *Journal of Personality and Social Psychology,* 1975, *32,* 29–39.

Stein, A. H., & Bailey, M. M. The socialization of achievement orientation in females. *Psychological Bulletin,* 1973, *80,* 345–366.

Stein, A. H., Pohly, S. R., & Mueller, E. The influence of masculine, feminine, and neutral tasks on children's achievement behavior, expectancies of success and attainment values. *Child Development,* 1971, *42,* 195–207.

Strodtbeck, F. L., & Mann, R. D. Sex role differences in jury deliberations. *Sociometry,* 1956, *19,* 3–11.

Taylor, S. P., & Epstein, S. Aggression as a function of the interaction of the sex of the aggressor and the sex of the victim. *Journal of Personality,* 1967, *35,* 474–486.

Terman, L. M., & Tyler, L. E. Psychological sex differences. In L. Carmichael (Ed.), *A manual of child psychology.* New York: Wiley, 1954.

Thayer, S. The effect of interpersonal looking duration on dominance judgements. *Journal of Social Psychology,* 1969, *79,* 285–286.

Thorne, B., & Henley, N. Sex differences in language, speech, and nonverbal communication. Unpublished manuscript, November 1973.

Vinacke, W. E. Sex-roles in a three-person game. *Sociometry,* 1959, *22,* 343–360.

Weitzman, L. J., Eifler, D., Hokada, E., & Ross, C. Sex-role socialization in picture books for pre-school children. *American Journal of Sociology,* 1972, *77,* 1125–1150.

Whiting, B., & Edwards, C. P. A cross-cultural analysis of sex differences in the behavior of children aged three through eleven. *Journal of Social Psychology,* 1973, *91,* 171–188.

Wicker, A. W., & Bushweiler, G. Perceived fairness and pleasantness of social exchange situations: Two factorial studies of inequity. *Journal of Personality and Social Psychology,* 1970, *15,* 63–75.

Women on Words and Images, *Dick and Jane as victims: Sex stereotyping in children's readers.* Princeton, N.J.: Women on Words and Images, 1972.

Author Index

Numbers in *italics* refer to pages on which the complete references are listed.

N

O

P

Q

R

S

W

Subject Index

R

S

T